Perspectives on Literacy

Edited by

Eugene R. Kintgen
Barry M. Kroll
Mike Rose

SOUTHERN ILLINOIS UNIVERSITY PRESS
Carbondale and Edwardsville

Library of Congress Cataloging-in-Publication Data

Perspectives on literacy.

  Bibliography: p.
  Includes index.
  1. Literacy. I. Kintgen, Eugene R. II. Kroll,
Barry M., 1946–   . III. Rose, Mike.
LC149.P47 1988   428.4   87-23575
ISBN 0-8093-1457-6
ISBN 0-8094-1458-4 (pbk.)

Permission to quote from copyright sources is acknowledged on the first page of
    each essay.

The paper used in this publication meets the minimum requirements of American
    National Standard for Information Sciences—Permanence of Paper for
    Printed Library Materials, ANSI Z39.48-1984. ∞™

Contents

Part Three
Educational Perspectives

Part Four
Community Perspectives

Preface

In preparing this collection, we have benefited from both happy coincidence and our colleagues' direct assistance. In the fall of 1986, two of us independently prepared and taught introductory graduate courses in literacy at different institutions—Mike Rose as a visiting professor at Carnegie-Mellon University, and Gene Kintgen, whose course was the inaugural offering in the Ph.D. program in Language, Literature, and Literacy at Indiana University. This collection derives from a consolidation of the reading lists used for those courses, a consolidation very much in its etymological sense of "making solid": although both courses treated the theoretical backgrounds of literacy, Kintgen's emphasized the historical and linguistic aspects, while Rose's stressed the contemporary and psychological. Each realized that important aspects of the large topic of literacy were being slighted—Kintgen consulted with Barry Kroll at the time about ways to achieve a better balance—but neither saw an easy way to include everything he wanted in one course. Only when we later compared notes and experiences did we realize that consolidation was not only desirable and necessary, but actually possible. The collection we present here, then, is composed of articles that we have tested in the classroom. Having used them ourselves, we feel confident in saying that they provide a balanced introduction suitable for use at the advanced undergraduate or graduate level, though of course they can be supplemented by one of the general introductions to the subject or by more specialized collections of readings on particular aspects of literacy. The extensive bibliography is provided as a research guide to those who would like to pursue any of the topics raised in the articles in greater detail.

Our colleagues have been a constant support: the faculty and students of the Rhetoric Program at Carnegie-Mellon University were a rich source of critical commentary, and the members of the Literacy Program at Indiana University have provided a continuing forum for discussion of matters related to literacy. The Office of Research and Graduate Development at Indiana University assisted financially. We would especially like to thank Richard L. Enos, of Carnegie-Mellon University, for his advice, Don Gray of Indiana for his continued guidance and support, and Kenney Withers, the director of Southern Illinois University Press, who brought together independent workers in the field of literacy and thereby strengthened all of their research.

Introduction

Eugene R. Kintgen
Barry M. Kroll
Mike Rose

*W*hy Johnny Can't Read. The title is instantly familiar to thousands, perhaps millions, of people who have never read Rudolf Flesch's 1955 book about reading pedagogy. Most of those people don't know that the book is an extended argument for the "phonics first" method of reading instruction and against the "look and say" method. Instead, the title has become a rallying cry for those who are interested in, or worried about, the supposed decline in the ability to read during the past two or three decades: a title like "What If Johnny Still Can't Read?" (from a Canadian business journal) illustrates the genre. And it seems that as more people become worried about a "crisis" in literacy, the solutions proposed become simpler and simpler: witness the "back to basics" movement, which assumes, quite incorrectly, that the "basics" required and expected today are the same as those taught a generation or two ago. This collection of essays is partially a response to the current interest in the question of literacy and illiteracy in the Western world; its aim is to provide the requisite background for informed and intelligent discussion of the many issues surrounding the question of literacy today.

Since people first began to read and write, literacy has been a problematic concept. Plato has Socrates oppose literacy on the grounds that written language could not respond differently to different readers, could not answer their particular questions, and so could not help them think. Furthermore, instead of improving memory, writing induced forgetfulness (*Phaedrus* 274–77). In the Middle Ages, "a group of Goths allegedly told Queen Amalasuntha, 'letters are removed from manliness and the teaching of old men results for the most part in a cowardly and submissive spirit' " (Cipolla 41). And, as the Middle Ages advanced, most rulers (Charlemagne and Alfred among the few exceptions) left reading and writing to specialists, much as modern businesses hire trained accountants to handle the "books" without denigrating other executives who lack this particular skill. After the Civil War in England, when the political consequences of widespread literacy had become more obvious, there were arguments that education should be curtailed among the working classes, since "ignorance was 'the appointed lot of all born to poverty and the drudgeries of life, . . . the only opiate capable of infusing that sensibility, which can enable them to endure the miseries of the one and the fatigues of the other . . . a cordial, administered by the gracious hand of providence, of which they ought never to be deprived by an ill-judged and improper education' " (Altick 32). Today, in the West, the problem of literacy has become the familiar one of achieving the universal ability to read and write. And yet, among nations nominally literate, there are reports that as much as 25 percent of the population is unable to read and write well enough to function effectively in society; a 1975 study in the United States concluded that fifty-seven million people were in this category (for further discussion, see the selection by Hunter and Harmon in this volume).

Much of the concern about literacy, both now and in the past, stems from what people have assumed its consequences to be. We can isolate at least three types of consequences: cognitive, economic, and social. Many researchers (Goody and Watt in this volume offer a classic example) propose a "Great Divide" theory, which suggests that literacy affects the ways the members of a society think: literate thought is conceptual, nonliterate thought, concrete. As opposed to their nonliterate counterparts, literates engage in abstraction, generalization, systematic thinking, defining, logos rather than mythos, puzzlement over words as words, and speculation on the features of language. These changes in cognitive capacity lead to history, logic, astronomy, taxonomic science in the modern sense, and even to democracy. The assumption here is that literacy itself confers certain general and wide-ranging cognitive skills that can be applied in different areas. Other researchers, however, have argued that the consequences of literacy, far from invariable or automatic, depend on its social context. Kathleen Gough, in an article in this collection, demonstrates how literacy will be adapted to the society that uses it; it becomes what Scribner and Cole call a *practice:* "a recurrent, goal-directed sequence of activities using a particular technology and particular systems of knowledge . . . [a set of] socially developed and patterned ways of using technology and knowledge to accomplish tasks." Literacy is then

> a set of socially organized practices which make use of a symbol system and a technology for producing and disseminating it. Literacy is not simply knowing how to read and write a particular script but applying this knowledge for specific purposes in specific contexts of use. The nature of these practices, including, of course, their technological aspects, will determine the kinds of skills ("consequences") associated with literacy. (*The Psychology of Literacy* 236)

As Scribner and Cole demonstrate in detail in *The Psychology of Literacy,* and more briefly in the article we have included here, the cognitive consequences of literacy are real but limited, and they do not constitute a revolution in thinking.

The economic consequences of literacy often seem the most important. Today there is a widespread, commonsensical belief that it is necessary to be literate in order to be economically successful, and indeed, the large percentage of illiterates whose earnings are below the poverty level seems to support this. UNESCO linked literacy and economic development strongly, assuming that a "takeoff" percentage of the population—usually 40 percent—had to be literate before a country could develop a stable, Western-style economy. And it therefore seems logical to project this viewpoint back into the past, and to relate literacy and wealth historically, at least once literacy had become widespread enough to cease being a special skill, like accounting (though unlike accountants, scribes never made very much). But careful research has revealed that literacy and economic success were not always linked, and that in any case, where they do seem to be related, the question of causality is still an open one. This is most obvious in societies where literacy was introduced for religious reasons, as for instance in Sweden, where Charles XI's Church Law of 1686 required every person to be able to read before being confirmed, which was itself a prerequisite for marriage. Great social and religious pressure for everybody to "learn to read and see with their own eyes what God bids and commands in His Holy Word" led to a widespread ability to read (writing was not emphasized) without having much effect on the economic structure of the society (Johansson).

More recently, Harvey Graff has demonstrated that in three nineteenth-century Canadian towns, literacy was much less important for economic success than were other factors: "Class, ethnicity, and sex were the major barriers of social inequality. The majority of Irish Catholic adults, for example, were literate . . . but they stood lowest in wealth and occupation, as did laborers and servants. Women and blacks fared little better, regardless of literacy. . . . social realities contradicted the promoted promises of literacy" (*Literacy Myth* 320–21). And the current situation in the United States is summed up by Carman St. John Hunter and David Harmon as follows:

> [P]overty and the power structures of society are more responsible for low levels of literacy than the reverse. . . . For most persons who lack literacy skills, illiteracy is simply one factor interacting with many others—class, race and sex discrimination, welfare dependency, unemployment, poor housing, and a general sense of powerlessness. The acquisition of reading and writing skills would eliminate conventional illiteracy among many but would have no appreciable effect on the other factors that perpetuate the poverty of their lives. (9–12)

The relation between literacy and economic success, straightforward as it may seem, is thus extremely complex, depending more on the social structure than on the acquisition of a particular skill that confers universal economic benefit.

The social consequences of literacy concern the ways that literates function as members of their societies. "The skills of reading, writing, and counting," according to a 1947 UNESCO report, "are not, however, an end in themselves. Rather they are the essential means to the achievement of a fuller and more creative life" (Levine 27). This fuller and more creative life includes an increased receptivity to new ideas and thus to various kinds of social change: "The rise of literacy and its dissemination to the popular classes," Graff observes, is often "associated with the triumph of light over darkness, of liberalism, democracy, and of universal unbridled progress" (*The Literacy Myth* xv). Non-literates tend to preserve their culture as it is; literates are more open to experimentation and change. But even this is not always true: Kenneth Lock-ridge, after a detailed study of literacy in colonial New England, concluded that "there is no evidence that literacy ever entailed new attitudes among men, even in the decades when male literacy was spreading rapidly towards universality, and there is positive evidence that the world view of literate New Englanders remained as traditional as that of their illiterate neighbors" (14). And John Oxenham reminds us that

> we have always to bear in mind that there have been literate social groups, who so far from being inventive and trusting, have been content merely to copy their ancient scriptures and pass them on virtually unaltered. It may be, then, that literate people can respond more readily to leadership for change in culture, technology, social mores, but that literacy by itself does not induce appetites for change, improvement, or exploration. (52)

Indeed, everyday observation of those around us indicates that literacy affects different people in quite diverse ways, making some more receptive to change and others less so.

Those who wonder why Johnny can't read are more concerned with the consequences of literacy than with its definition, but the history of the term reveals that its meaning is as problematic as its effects. As Daniel and Lauren Resnick make clear in "The Nature of Literacy: A Historical Explanation" (included in this volume), we can speak of at least four distinct stages in the development of the current meaning of literacy. First is the *signature stage*, in which the ability to sign one's name on documents is taken as proof of literacy. The second stage is often called the *recitation stage*. Demonstration of literacy at this stage requires the ability to read from a familiar text or recite portions of it from memory without any necessary understanding of what is "read." In the West the Bible was usually the text chosen; in Islamic countries, the Koran. The third stage is the *comprehension stage*, in which literates are expected to be able to read and comprehend unfamiliar material in a fairly literal way. The final stage is the one we are in now, the *analysis stage*, in which literacy entails reading unfamiliar material with comprehension, analyzing it, and drawing inferences from it.

Complicating any attempt to define "literacy" is the fact that the word always had two distinct meanings. One, which we may call descriptive, referred to the abilities whose succession has just been traced. The second, the evaluative, assesses the possession of a body of knowledge, usually of literature or the "rules" of accepted usage. This meaning apparently derives from classical Latin *litteratus*, "which meant 'literate' in something like the modern [descriptive] sense and also (in the most classical usage of Cicero) described a person with *scientia litteratum*, meaning a 'knowledge of letters' in the sense of 'literature' " (Clanchy 1979: 177). This sense is apparent when a person who perpetrates a grammatical error or misquotes an author in a letter to the editor of a newspaper is described as "illiterate" by those who wish to stigmatize the writer's intelligence or viewpoint.

A further complication is the recent introduction of the term *functional literacy* to identify the abilities necessary for survival in a given society. This term has almost as many definitions as *literacy* itself, but what they share is a sense that literacy must be defined in relation to a particular society or culture. Kenneth Levine, for example, has suggested that "functional literacy can be defined as the possession of, or access to, the competences and information required to accomplish transactions entailing reading and writing [in] which an individual wishes—or is compelled—to engage" (43). This definition attempts to strike a balance between personal initiative—what the individual "wishes" to engage in—and social pressure of various kinds—what the individual is "compelled" to do. At the same time, the stipulation that the individual may have "access to" the necessary competences and information, rather than "possession of" them, allows for community involvement of the kind to be discussed below (see pp. xvi–xvii).

Any discussion of literacy or illiteracy, then, must begin with some basic settling of terms. When we ask why Johnny can't read, what do we expect him to read? Is he to read familiar materials, or texts he has never seen before? What do we expect him to get out of his reading? Is it enough if he merely reads the words aloud, or must he be able to answer questions based on the text? Must he be able to analyze the material, and perhaps criticize it? Must he be able to justify his own views about the matter covered? Literacy as a cover term is so broad that it must almost be defined for each occasion on which it is used.

Just as a single definition of literacy is insufficient, so is scrutiny from within the confines of a single academic discipline. A second goal of this collection, then, is to bring together mutually illuminating work from different areas. It now seems clearer than ever before that the reading and writing students do in classrooms, at whatever educational level, cannot and should not be sharply distinguished from the reading and writing they do in other, non-academic, contexts. If Johnny can't read in school, we must inquire not merely what method was used to teach him to read, but what functions reading serves in his life outside school. When Jane has trouble writing school assignments, we must wonder what purposes writing serves in her life and in the lives of those around her. In short, it has become clear that literacy is, as Scribner and Cole say, a practice, and to understand it we must inquire not only into its technology but also into its "specific purposes in specific contexts of use."

Thinking about literacy in this way leads us to investigate the relation between oral and written language and the relation between reading and writing. As Walter J. Ong explains:

> The word in its natural, oral habitat is part of a real, existential present. Spoken utterance is addressed by a real, living person to another real, living person or real, living persons, at a specific time in a real setting which includes always much more than mere words. Spoken words are always modifications of a total situation which is more than verbal. They never occur alone, in a context simply of words. (1982: 101)

Written words, on the other hand, "are isolated from the fuller context in which spoken words come into being" (101). Although writing is always read in some situation, it neither originates nor interacts in that situation as a speaker would; Socrates complained that "you might think [writings] spoke as if they had intelligence, but if you put a question with a wish for information on a point in what is said, there is one, one only, invariable reply" (*Phaedrus* 275). It is small wonder that people accustomed to language embedded in a larger social context should at first be suspicious of writing. Michael Clanchy documents the understandable suspicion with which writing was greeted in the Middle Ages: "The principle that 'oral witness deserves more credence than written evidence' was a legal commonplace. . . . Behind this principle lay the correct assumption that numerous documents used in legal claims, from the Donation of Constantine downwards, were forgeries. . . . The technology of written record was insufficiently advanced to be efficient or reliable" (1979: 210–11). Oral witnesses could be suborned, but they could also be interrogated in a way writing could not.

In our own time, we see continually that speaking and writing have different uses, as Michael Stubbs reminds us:

> Speech and writing are not in free variation. That is, it is not usually possible to choose one or the other. There are occasions where I may consider whether to send someone a note rather than ringing them up or going to talk to them face to face, but the choice of a particular medium is likely to have particular implications. Further, the choice of medium is normally determined by the social function of the communication. (108)

Anybody who has dealt with a bureaucracy will appreciate this distinction: although questions may be answered and misunderstandings clarified orally, the final agreement must be "in writing." But these differences should not blind us to the remarkably complex interaction between speech and writing, as in Shirley Brice Heath's description of reading in Trackton, one of the two towns in the Carolinas whose literacy patterns she studied:

> On all of these occasions for reading and writing, individuals saw literacy as an occasion for social activities: women shopped together, discussed local credit opportunities and products, and sales; men negotiated the meaning of tax forms, brochures on new cars, and political flyers. The evening newspaper was read on the front porch, and talk about the news drifted from porch to porch. . . . The only occasions for solitary reading by individuals were those in which elderly men and women read their Bible or Sunday School materials alone, or school-age children sat alone to read a library book or a school assignment. (1982: 99)

When studying literacy in a modern setting, then, we must always be aware that its relations with orality are likely to be intricate and significant.

The relation between reading and writing is equally complex. First, we must note an asymmetry between the two: most people read a good deal more than they write. Historically this tendency was more pronounced, basically for technological reasons: in contrast with the pencils and ball-point pens in use today, which permit relatively effortless writing, the styli and pens of hundreds of years ago were temperamental instruments, difficult to use and control. "Writing was certainly seen as an act of endurance in which 'the whole body labors' " (Clanchy 1979: 90), and this reminder of the physical effort involved explains why many authors, Chaucer among them, composed but left it to scribes to "write down" their works, much as contemporary authors "write" works but leave their reproduction and dissemination to the experts of the publishing world.

Complementing this technological difficulty was a great difference in the utility of reading and writing. Medieval sheriffs, for instance, had to read to announce royal proclamations, but didn't have to write anything themselves (Clanchy 1979: 219). The literacy campaign in Sweden in the seventeenth and eighteenth centuries emphasized the importance of reading the Bible and religious works, not writing about them, so nearly everybody learned to read but very few learned to write (Johansson 180). And even today, as Diehl and Mikulecky show, most jobs require a great deal more reading than writing.

Finally, until quite recently, the organization of education emphasized reading rather than writing: children were typically taught to read first, and only later taught to write, so that many children who were forced by financial conditions to drop out of school could read but not write (Spufford 1979: 128–29). Education interacts with technology and utility, of course: before the advent of cheap paper, children simply did not have the materials for doodling, drawing, and so forth, and so did not have the opportunity—as many children do today—to "write" something on a piece of paper and then go to their parents asking what it means. And when writing was seen as a specialized skill, comparable perhaps to computer programming today, there was naturally less urgency in imparting it to all students. The close connection between reading and writing that many researchers recognize today (see, for instance, Harste, Woodward, and Burke, or Tierney and Pearson in this volume) is thus a very recent phenomenon.

To some extent, the contemporary asymmetry between reading and writing can be related to use in a particular socioeconomic context. The ability to read is obviously more important for economic survival than the ability to write, simply because most jobs require more reading than writing. On the other hand, jobs with more responsibility, and consequently higher pay, require more writing than lower-level ones. Jay L. Robinson (this volume) argues that attention to the problems associated with the inability to read among the poor has been deflected by the more recent discovery of the inability of the middle class to write very well. "The present emphasis upon writing over reading doubtless reflects a bias in favor of the upper of our social classes," he writes, and goes on to quote Richard Hendrix' trenchant comment that "the emphasis on writing clarifies the gap between the commitment in principle to universal opportunity and the fact of unequal opportunity. Writing ability is unevenly distributed in our society along class lines. Indeed, writing and access to writing improvement is as good an indicator of the difference between, say, white collar and blue collar career tracks as we are likely to find." Literacy in a socioeconomic context, then, is highly likely to be oriented along class lines, with the better-paying white-collar jobs requiring more reading and writing than the lower-paying blue-collar ones.

But many contexts and purposes of literacy are more local and personal. In her seminal study of the uses of literacy in two towns in the Carolinas, Heath discovered purposes for literacy that were quite different from the critical, aesthetic, organizational, and recreational uses usually emphasized in school. These purposes included uses that were instrumental, such as "information about practical problems of daily life" (e.g., price tags and street signs); social-interactional, as "information pertinent to social relationships" (greeting cards or posters); news-related; memory-supportive; substitutes for oral messages (notes to school); provision of permanent record (tax forms); and confirmation, "support for attitudes or ideas already held, as in settling disagreements or for one's own reassurance, such as directions for assembling things or the Bible" (1980: 128–29). These functions of literacy are so typical and so familiar that we are likely to overlook them entirely when we think about literacy, primarily because we tend to associate literacy with what David Olson calls "the essayist technique": "not an ordinary language, not a mother tongue, but rather a form of language specialized to serve the requirements of autonomous, written, formalized text" (1977a: 270).

The essayist technique is taught in the classroom, and learning this "specific purpose" of school language is a formidable challenge, as David Bartholomae (this volume) points out:

> Every time a student sits down to write for us, he has to invent the university for the occasion. . . . The student has to learn to speak our language, to speak as we do, to try on the peculiar ways of knowing, selecting, evaluating, reporting, concluding, and arguing that define the discourse of our community. . . . he has to invent the university by assembling and mimicking its language while finding some compromise between idiosyncrasy, a personal history, on the one hand, and requirements of convention, the history of a discipline, on the other.

When the purposes of language in the classroom differ too radically from other purposes of language in students' lives—when the academic community and the outside community are too far apart, the compromise between the personal and the conventional too difficult—resistance and failure are the likely results. And these differences, as Frederick Erickson reminds us, may derive not from the individual personalities of student and teacher but from the institutional organization of education, for instance the power relations between student and teacher, dialect differences between them, or even the demands placed on both by standardized examinations and lesson plans.

On the other hand, when the purposes of literacy in the classroom can be related to students' other interests, education is much more successful. Paolo Freire has argued repeatedly that literacy instruction cannot exist in a vacuum, that it must be accompanied by "conscientization," a growing awareness of the literate person as a member of a particular social and political group. National literacy campaigns, such as the one in Nicaragua discussed by Robert Arnove, are most successful when they can depend on the enthusiasm generated by political or religious commitment. Kyle Fiore and Nan Elsasser demonstrate that the identification of personal and social concerns can lead to the desire to communicate about them, and that desire in turn provides the enthusiasm to master the requirements of literacy.

The ways in which college students invent the context for their reading and writing represent only one specialized example of a "specific purpose in a specific context of use," different in detail but not in kind from the ways in which people must appropriate the various contexts of literacy in their lives every day. To understand literacy, we must investigate its manifestations both inside and outside the classroom. And that investigation requires the interaction of researchers from many different disciplines. Anthropologists and historians provide the broad general perspective of how literacy functions in different cultures and different times and thereby reveal the arbitrary nature of our own (apparently natural) practices. Psychologists and sociologists show us how children achieve literacy, how they and adults use it, and what consequences it has for individuals and communities. Linguists and psycholinguists supply information about the different varieties of spoken and written language and the functional relations between them. Ethnologists investigate the social setting of literacy, its interaction with other aspects of the lives of those who have achieved it. Educators at all levels use this information to understand the practice of literacy and to try to improve instruction in it. It turns out that the answer to why Johnny can't read is a great deal more complicated than it originally appeared.

This collection of essays provides essential background reading in various aspects of literacy. "Aspects" is the key word in the preceding sentence, since we see literacy as an area of inquiry in which all its aspects implicate each other: one cannot study its consequences, its definition, or even its history without looking at its practice, and that means looking at the development of oral and written language, the connections between writing and reading, and so forth. Any organization imposed upon the field is thus bound to suggest false boundaries. We hope to avoid this as much as possible by our use of the word "perspectives," which implies different ways of looking at a complex subject rather than different subjects. Our first section, "Theoretical Perspectives," contains readings dealing with the various consequences, psychological and economic, of literacy. The second, "Historical Perspectives," provides an introduction to the development of literacy in different eras in the West, from the coming of literacy to the Greeks to the teaching of it in North America during the past century. "Educational Perspectives," the third section, contains essays treating the teaching of literacy in educational institutions, primarily at the secondary and postsecondary levels. The final section, "Community Perspectives," deals, from a number of different angles, with literacy outside the traditional classroom: the development of literacy among children and adults, the functions and uses of literacy in the workplace and elsewhere, the identity and problems of those who have not mastered literacy.

"Perspective" is derived from a Latin word meaning "to look into," and we think that describes the function of the readings we have gathered. Literacy is too often discussed as though it were a unitary, easily measured phenomenon that could be completely comprehended in one "correct" view. We feel that there is no such privileged perspective, but rather various ways of investigating a complicated and multidimensional topic. The articles in this collection, with their rich filiations, illustrate how complex the relations among the various dimensions of literacy are. We leave to our readers the pleasure of looking into them.

Part One

Theoretical Perspectives

1.
The Consequences of Literacy

Jack Goody
Ian Watt

The accepted tripartite divisions of the formal study of mankind's past and of his present are to a considerable extent based on man's development first of language and later of writing. Looked at in the perspective of time, man's biological evolution shades into prehistory when he becomes a language-using animal; add writing, and history proper begins. Looked at in a temporal perspective, man as animal is studied primarily by the zoologist, man as talking animal primarily by the anthropologist, and man as talking and writing animal primarily by the sociologist.

That the differentiation between these categories should be founded on different modes of communication is clearly appropriate; it was language that enabled man to achieve a form of social organization whose range and complexity were different in kind from that of animals; whereas the social organization of animals was mainly instinctive and genetically transmitted, that of man was largely learned and transmitted verbally through the cultural heritage. The basis for the last two distinctions, those based on the development of writing, is equally clear: to the extent that a significant quantity of written records are available, the prehistorian yields to the historian; and to the extent that alphabetical writing and popular literacy imply new modes of social organization and transmission, the anthropologist tends to yield to the sociologist.

But why? And how? There is no agreement about this question, nor even about what the actual boundary lines between non-literate and literate cultures are. At what point in the formalization of pictographs or other graphic signs can we talk of "letters," of literacy? And what proportion of the society has to write and read before the culture as a whole can be described as literate?

These are some of the many reasons why the extent to which there is any distinction between the areas and methods peculiar to anthropology and sociology must be regarded as problematic; and the difficulty affects not only the boundaries of the two disciplines but also the nature of the intrinsic differences in their subject matter.[1] The recent trend has been for anthropologists to spread their net more widely and engage in the study of industrial societies side by side with their sociological colleagues. We can no longer accept the view that anthropologists have as their objective the study of primitive man, who is characterized by a "primitive mind," while sociologists, on the other hand, concern themselves with civilized man, whose activities are guided by "rational thought" and tested by "logico-empirical procedures." The reaction against such ethnocentric views, however, has now gone to the point of denying that the distinction between non-literate and literate societies has any significant validity. This position seems contrary to our personal observation; and so it has seemed worthwhile to enquire whether there may not be, even from the most empirical and relativist standpoint, genuine illumination to be derived from a further consideration of some of the historical and analytic problems connected with the traditional dichotomy between non-literate and literate societies.

The Cultural Tradition in Non-Literate Societies

For reasons which will become clear it seems best to begin with a generalized description of the ways in which the cultural heritage is transmitted in non-literate societies, and then to see how these ways are changed by the widespread adoption of any easy and effective means of written communication.

When one generation hands on its cultural heritage to the next, three fairly separate items are involved. First, the society passes on its material plant, including the natural resources available to its members. Secondly, it transmits standardized ways of acting. These customary ways of behaving are only partly communicated by verbal means; ways of cooking food, of growing crops, of handling children may be transmitted by direct imitation. But the most significant elements of any human culture are undoubtedly channelled through words, and reside in the particular range of meanings and attitudes which members of any society attach to their verbal symbols. These elements include not only what we habitually think of as customary behaviour but also such items as ideas of space and time, generalized goals and aspirations, in short the *Weltanschauung* of every social group. In Durkheim's words, these categories of the understanding are "priceless instruments of thought which the human groups have laboriously forged through the centuries and where they have accumulated the best of their intellectual capital" (Durkheim 1915: 19). The relative continuity of these categories of understanding from one generation to another is primarily ensured by language, which is the most direct and comprehensive expression of the social experience of the group.

The transmission of the verbal elements of culture by oral means can be visualized as a long chain of interlocking conversations between members of the group. Thus all beliefs and values, all forms of knowledge, are communicated between individuals in face-to-face contact; and, as distinct from the material content of the cultural tradition, whether it be cave-paintings or hand-axes, they are stored only in human memory.

The intrinsic nature of oral communication has a considerable effect upon both the content and the transmission of the cultural repertoire. In the first place, it makes for a directness of relationship between symbol and referent. There can be no reference to "dictionary definitions," nor can words accumulate the successive layers of historically validated meanings which they acquire in a literate culture. Instead, the meaning of each word is ratified in a succession of concrete situations, accompanied by vocal inflections and physical gestures, all of which combine to particularize both its specific denotation and its accepted connotative usages. This process of direct semantic ratification, of course, operates cumulatively; and as a result the totality of symbol–referent relationships is more immediately experienced by the individual in an exclusively oral culture, and is thus more deeply socialized.

One way of illustrating this is to consider how the range of vocabulary in a non-literate society reflects this mode of semantic ratification. It has often been observed how the elaboration of the vocabulary of such a society reflects the particular interests of the people concerned. The inhabitants of the Pacific island of Lesu have not one, but a dozen or so, words for pigs (Powdermaker 1933: 292; Henle 1958: 5–18), according to sex, colour, and where they come from—a prolixity which mirrors the importance of pigs in a domestic economy that otherwise includes few sources of protein. The corollary of this prolixity is that where common emphases and interests, whether material or otherwise, are not specifically involved, there is little verbal development. Malinowski reported that in the Trobriands the outer world was only named in so far as it yielded useful things, useful, that is, in the very broadest sense;[2] and there is much other testimony to support the view that there is an intimate functional adaptation of language in non-literate societies, which obtains not only for the relatively simple and concrete symbol-referents involved above, but also for the more generalized "categories of understanding" and for the cultural tradition as a whole.

In an essay he wrote in collaboration with Mauss, "De quelques formes primitives de classification,"[3] Durkheim traces the interconnections between the ideas of space and the territorial distribution of the Australian aborigines, the Zuni of the Pueblo area and the Sioux of the Great Plains. This intermeshing of what he called the collective representations with the social morphology of a particular society is clearly another aspect of the same directness of relationship between symbol and referent. Just as the more concrete part of a vocabulary reflects the dominant interests of the society, so the more abstract categories are often closely linked to the accepted terminology for pragmatic pursuits. Among the LoDagaa of northern Ghana, days are reckoned according to the incidence of neighbouring markets; the very word for day and market is the same, and the "weekly" cycle is a six-day revolution of the most important markets in the vicinity, a cycle which also defines the spatial range of everyday activities.[4]

The way in which these various institutions in an oral culture are kept in relatively close accommodation one to another surely bears directly on the question of the central difference between literate and non-literate societies. As we have remarked, the whole content of the social tradition, apart from the material inheritances, is held in memory. The social aspects of remembering have been emphasized by sociologists and psychologists, particularly by Maurice

Halbwachs.[5] What the individual remembers tends to be what is of critical importance in his experience of the main social relationships. In each generation, therefore, the individual memory will mediate the cultural heritage in such a way that its new constituents will adjust to the old by the process of interpretation that Bartlett calls "rationalizing" or the "effort after meaning"; and whatever parts of it have ceased to be of contemporary relevance are likely to be eliminated by the process of forgetting.

The social function of memory—and of forgetting—can thus be seen as the final stage of what may be called the homeostatic organization of the cultural tradition in non-literate society. The language is developed in intimate association with the experience of the community, and it is learned by the individual in face-to-face contact with the other members. What continues to be of social relevance is stored in the memory while the rest is usually forgotten: and language—primarily vocabulary—is the effective medium of this crucial process of social digestion and elimination which may be regarded as analogous to the homeostatic organization of the human body by means of which it attempts to maintain its present condition of life.

In drawing attention to the importance of these assimilating mechanisms in non-literate societies, we are denying neither the occurrence of social change nor yet the "survivals" which it leaves in its wake. Nor do we overlook the existence of mnemonic devices in oral cultures which offer some resistance to the interpretative process. Formalized patterns of speech, recital under ritual conditions, the use of drums and other musical instruments, the employment of professional remembrancers—all such factors may shield at least part of the content of memory from the transmuting influence of the immediate pressures of the present. The Homeric epics, for instance, seem to have been written down during the first century of Greek literature between 750 and 650 B.C., but "they look to a departed era, and their substance is unmistakably old" (Finley 1954: 26).

Kinds of Writing and Their Social Effects

The pastness of the past, then, depends upon a historical sensibility which can hardly begin to operate without permanent written records; and writing introduces similar changes in the transmission of other items of the cultural repertoire. But the extent of these changes varies with the nature and social distribution of the writing system; varies, that is, according to the system's intrinsic efficacy as a means of communication, and according to the social constraints placed upon it, that is, the degree to which use of the system is diffused through the society.

Early in prehistory, man began to express himself in graphic form; and his cave paintings, rock engravings and wood carvings are morphologically, and presumably sequentially, the forerunners of writing. By some process of simplification and stylization they appear to have led to the various kinds of pictographs found in simple societies (Gelb 1952: 24). While pictographs themselves are almost universal, their development into a self-sufficient system capable of extended discourse occurs only among the Plains Indians (Voegelin 1961: 84, 91).

Pictographs have obvious disadvantages as means of communication. For one thing a vast number of signs are needed to represent all the important objects in the culture. For another, since the signs are concrete, the simplest sentence requires an extremely elaborate series of signs: many stylized representations of wigwams, footprints, totemic animals and so on are required just to convey the information that a particular man left there a few days ago. Finally, however elaborately the system is developed, only a limited number of things can be said.

The end of the fourth millennium saw the early stages of the development of more complex forms of writing, which seem to be an essential factor in the rise of the urban cultures of the Orient. The majority of signs in these systems were simply pictures of the outside world, standardized representations of the objects signified by particular words; to these were added other devices for creating word signs or logograms, which permitted the expression of wider ranges of meaning. Thus, in Egyptian hieroglyphics the picture of a beetle was a code sign not only for that insect but also for a discontinuous and more abstract referent "became" (Voegelin 1961: 75–6).

The basic invention used to supplement the logograms was the phonetic principle, which for the first time permitted the written expression of all the words of a language. For example, by the device of phonetic transfer the Sumerians could use the sign for *ti*, an arrow, to stand for *ti*, life, a concept not easy to express in pictographic form. In particular, the need to record personal names and foreign words encouraged the development of phonetic elements in writing.

But while these true writing systems all used phonetic devices for the construction of logograms (and have consequently been spoken of as word-syllabic systems of writing), they failed to carry through the application of the phonetic principle exclusively and systematically.[6] The achievement of a system completely based upon the representation of phonemes (the basic units of meaningful sound) was left to the Near Eastern syllabaries, which developed between 1500–1000 B.C., and finally to the introduction of the alphabet proper in Greece. Meanwhile these incompletely phonetic systems were too clumsy and complicated to foster widespread literacy, if only because the number of signs was very large; at least six hundred would have to be learned even for the simplified cuneiform developed in Assyria, and about the same for Egyptian hieroglyphs (Gelb 1952: 115; Diringer 1948: 48, 196). All these ancient civilizations, the Sumerian, Egyptian, Hittite and Chinese, were literate in one sense and their great advances in administration and technology were undoubtedly connected with the invention of a writing system; but when we think of the limitations of their systems of communication as compared with ours, the term "protoliterate," or even "oligoliterate," might be more descriptive in suggesting the restriction of literacy to a relatively small proportion of the total population.[7]

Any system of writing which makes the sign stand directly for the object must be extremely complex. It can extend its vocabulary by generalization or association of ideas, that is, by making the sign stand either for a more general class of objects or for other referents connected with the original picture by an association of meanings which may be related to one another either in a continuous or in a discontinuous manner. Either process of semantic extension is to some extent arbitrary or esoteric; and as a result the interpretation of these signs is neither easy nor explicit. One might perhaps guess that the Chinese sign for a man carries the general meaning of maleness; it would be more difficult to see that a conventionalized picture of a man and a broom is the sign for a woman; it's a pleasing fancy, no doubt, but not one which communicates very readily until it has been learned as a new character, as a separate sign for a separate word, as a logogram. In Chinese writing a minimum of three thousand such characters have to be learned before one can be reasonably literate (Moorhouse 1953: 90, 163) and with a repertoire of some fifty thousand characters to be mastered, it normally takes about twenty years to reach full literate proficiency. China, therefore, stands as an extreme example of how, when a virtually non-phonetic system of writing becomes sufficiently developed to express a large number of meanings explicitly, only a small and specially trained professional group in the total society can master it, and partake of the literate culture.

Although systems of word signs are certainly easier to learn, many difficulties remain, even when these signs are supplemented by phonemic devices of a syllabic sort. Other features of the social system are no doubt responsible for the way that the writing systems developed as they did; but it is a striking fact that—for whatever ultimate causes—in Egypt and Mesopotamia, as in China, a literate élite of religious, administrative and commercial experts emerged and maintained itself as a centralized governing bureaucracy on rather similar lines. Their various social and intellectual achievements were, of course, enormous; but as regards the participation of the society as a whole in the written culture, a wide gap existed between the esoteric literate culture and the exoteric oral one, a gap which the literate were interested in maintaining. Among the Sumerians and Akkadians writing was the pursuit of scribes and preserved as a "mystery," a "secret treasure." Royalty were themselves illiterate; Ashurbanipal (668–626 B.C.) records that he was the first Babylonian king to master the "clerkly skill" (Driver 1954: 62, 72). "Put writing in your heart that you may protect yourself from hard labour of any kind," writes an Egyptian of the New Kingdom: "The scribe is released from manual tasks; it is he who commands" (Childe 1941: 187–8; 1942: 105, 118). Significantly, the classical age of Babylonian culture, beginning under Hammurabi in the late eighteenth century B.C., appears to have coincided with a period when the reading and writing of Akkadian cuneiform was not confined to a small group, or to one nation; it was then that nearly all the extant literature was written down, and that the active state of commerce and administration produced a vast quantity of public and private correspondence, of which much has survived.

These imperfectly phonetic methods of writing continued with little change for many centuries;[8] so too did the cultures of which they were part.[9] The existence of an élite group, which followed from the difficulty of the writing system, and whose continued influence depended on the maintenance of the present social order, must have been a powerfully conservative force, especially when it consisted of ritual specialists;[10] and so, it may be surmised, was the nature of the writing system itself. For pictographic and logographic systems are alike in their tendency to reify the objects of the natural and social order; by so doing they register, record, make permanent the existing social and ideological picture. Such, for example, was the tendency of the most highly developed and longest-lived ancient writing system, that of Egypt, whose society has been described with picturesque exaggeration as "a nation of fellahin ruled with a rod of iron by a Society of Antiquaries."

This conservative or antiquarian bias can perhaps be best appreciated by contrasting it with fully phonetic writing; for phonetic writing, by imitating human discourse, is in fact symbolizing, not the objects of the social and natural order, but the very process of human interaction in speech: the verb is as easy to express as the noun; and the written vocabulary can be easily and unambiguously expanded. Phonetic systems are therefore adapted to expressing every nuance of individual thought, to recording personal reactions as well as items of major social importance. Non-phonetic writing, on the other hand, tends rather to record and reify only those items in the cultural repertoire which the literate specialists have selected for written expression; and it tends to express the collective attitude towards them.

The notion of representing a sound by a graphic symbol is itself so stupefying a leap of the imagination that what is remarkable is not so much that it happened relatively late in human history, but rather that it ever happened at all. For a long time, however, these phonetic inventions had a limited effect because they were only partially exploited: not only were logograms and pictograms retained, but a variety of phonograms were used to express the same sound. The full explicitness and economy of a phonetic writing system "as easy as A B C" were therefore likely to arise only in less advanced societies on the fringes of Egypt or Mesopotamia, societies which were starting their writing system more or less from scratch, and which took over the idea of phonetic signs from adjoining countries, and used them exclusively to fit their own language.[11] These phonetic signs could, of course, be used to stand for any unit of speech, and thus be developed either into syllabaries or into alphabets. In a few cases, such as Japanese, the particular nature of the language made it possible to construct a relatively simple and efficient syllabary; but as regards the great majority of languages the alphabet, with its signs for individual consonants and vowels, proved a much more economical and convenient instrument for representing sounds. For the syllabaries, while making writing easier, were still far from simple;[12] they were often combined with logograms and pictographs.[13] And whether by necessity or tradition or both, pre-alphabetic writing was still mainly restricted to élite groups. The Mycenaean script disappeared completely after the twelfth century B.C., a fact which was possible because of the very restricted uses of literacy and the close connection between writing and palace administration (Chadwick 1958: 130; 1959: 7–18). It is doubtful whether any such loss could have occurred in Greece after the introduction of a complete alphabetic script, probably in the eighth century B.C.

The alphabet is almost certainly the supreme example of cultural diffusion (Diringer 1948): all existing or recorded alphabets derive from Semitic syllabaries developed during the second millennium. Eventually there arose the enormous simplification of the Semitic writing system, with its mere twenty-two letters; and then only one further step remained: the Greek script, which is, of course, much closer than the Semitic to the Roman alphabet, took certain of the Semitic signs for consonants which the Greek language didn't need, and used them for vowels, which the Semitic syllabary did not represent.[14] The directness of our inheritance from these two sources is suggested by the fact that our word "alphabet" is the latinized form of the first two letters of the Greek alphabet, "alpha," derived from the Semitic "aleph," and "beta," from the Semitic "beth."

The reason for the success of the alphabet, which David Diringer calls a "democratic" script as opposed to the "theocratic" scripts of Egypt, is related to the fact that, uniquely among writing systems, its graphic signs are representations of the most extreme and most universal example of cultural selection—the basic phonemic system. The number of sounds which the human breath stream can produce is vast; but nearly all languages are based on the formal recognition by the society of only forty or so of these sounds. The success of the alphabet (as well as some of its incidental difficulties) comes from the fact that its system of graphic representation takes advantage of this socially conventionalized pattern of sound in all language systems; by symbolizing in letters these selected phonemic units the alphabet makes it possible to write easily and read unambiguously about anything which the society can talk about.

The historical picture of the cultural impact of the new alphabetic writing is not altogether clear. As regards the Semitic system, which was widely adopted elsewhere, the evidence suggests that the social diffusion of writing was slow. This was caused partly by the intrinsic difficulties of the system but mainly by the established cultural features of the societies which adopted it. There was, for one thing, a strong tendency for writing to be used as a help to memory rather than as an autonomous and independent mode of communication; and under such conditions its influence tended towards the consolidation of the existing cultural tradition. This certainly appears to be true of India and Palestine.[15] Gandz notes, for example, that Hebrew culture continued to be transmitted orally long after the Old Testament had begun to be written down. As he puts it, the introduction of writing

> did not at once change the habits of the people and displace the old method of oral tradition. We must always distinguish between the *first introduction* of writing and its *general diffusion*. It often takes several centuries, and sometimes even a millennium or more, until this invention becomes the common property of the people at large. In the beginning, the written book is not intended for practical use at all. It is a divine instrument, placed in the temple "by the side of the ark of the covenant that it may be there for a witness" (Deuteronomy xxxi. 26), and remains there as a holy relic. For the people at large, oral instruction still remained the only way of learning, and the memory—the only means of preservation. Writing was practised, if at all, only as an additional support for the memory . . .

It was not, in fact, until some six centuries after the original Hebrew adoption of the Semitic writing system that, at the time of Ezra (*c.* 444 B.C.), an official "generally recognized text" of the Torah was published, and the body of the religious tradition ceased to be "practically . . . a sealed book" and became accessible to anyone who chose to study it (Gandz 1935: 253–4).

Even so, of course, as the frequent diatribes against the scribes in the Gospels remind us,[16] there remained a considerable gap between the literati and the laymen; the professionals who plied their trade in the market-place belonged to "families of scribes," perhaps organized as guilds, within which the mystery was handed down from father to son.[17]

Anything like popular literacy, or the use of writing as an autonomous mode of communication by the majority of the members of society, is not found in the earliest societies which used the Semitic writing system; it was, rather, in the sixth and fifth centuries B.C. in the city states of Greece and Ionia that there first arose a society which as a whole could justly be characterized as literate. Many of the reasons why literacy became widespread in Greece, but not in other societies which had Semitic or, indeed, any other simple and explicit writing systems, necessarily lie outside the scope of this essay; yet considerable importance must surely be attributed to the intrinsic advantages of the Greek adaptation of the Semitic alphabet, an adaptation which made it the first comprehensively and exclusively phonetic system for transcribing human speech.[18] The system was easy, explicit and unambiguous—more so than the Semitic, where the lack of vowels is responsible for many of the cruces in the Bible: for instance, since the consonant in the Hebrew words is the same, Elijah may have been fed by "ravens" or "Arabs."[19] Its great advantage over the syllabaries lay in the reduction of the number of signs and in the ability to specify consonant and vowel clusters. The system was easy to learn: Plato sets aside three years for the process in the *Laws*,[20] about the time taken in our schools today; and the much greater speed with which alphabetic writing can be learned is shown, not only by such reports as those of the International Institute of Intellectual Cooperation in 1934,[21] but also by the increasing adoption of the Roman script, and even more widely of alphabetic systems of writing, throughout the world.

The extensive diffusion of the alphabet in Greece was also materially assisted by various social, economic and technological factors. In the first place, the eighth century saw a great burst of economic activity following the revival of the eastern trade which had declined after the Mycenaean collapse in the twelfth century (Starr 1961: 189–190, 349). Secondly, while the Greek society of the period had, of course, its various social strata, the political system was not strongly centralized; especially in the Ionic settlements there appears to have been a good deal of flexibility and in them we discern the beginnings of the Greek city state. Thirdly, the increased contact with the East brought material prosperity and technological advance. The wider use of iron, the advent of the true Iron Age, was perhaps one of the results (Starr 1961: 87–8, 357). More closely connected with literacy was the fact that trade with Egypt led to the importation of papyrus; and this made writing itself easier and less expensive, both for the individual writer and for the reader who wanted to buy books; papyrus was obviously much cheaper than parchment made from skins, more permanent than wax tablets, easier to handle than the stone or clay of Mesopotamia and Mycenae.

The chronology and extent of the diffusion of literacy in Greece remain a matter of debate. With the Mycenaean collapse in the twelfth century, writing disappeared; the earliest Greek inscriptions in the modified Semitic alphabet occur in the last two decades of the eighth century (Starr 1961: 169). Recent authorities suggest the new script was adopted and transformed about the middle of the eighth century in northern Syria.[22] The extensive use of writing probably came only slowly in the seventh century, but when it finally came it seems to have been applied in a very wide range of activities, intellectual as well as economic, and by a wide range of people.[23]

It must be remembered, of course, that Greek writing throughout the classical period was still relatively difficult to decipher, as words were not regularly separated (Kenyon 1951: 67); that the copying of manuscripts was a long and laborious process; and that silent reading as we know it was very rare until the advent of printing—in the ancient world books were used mainly for reading aloud, often by a slave. Nevertheless, from the sixth century onwards literacy seems to be increasingly presumed in the public life of Greece and Ionia. In Athens, for example, the first laws for the general public to read were set up by Solon in 594–3 B.C.; the institution of ostracism early in the fifth century assumes a literate citizen body—six thousand citizens had to write the name of the person on their potsherds before he could be banished (Carcopino 1935: 72–110); there is abundant evidence in the fifth century of a system of schools teaching reading and writing (*Protagoras*, 325 d) and of a book-reading public—satirized already by Aristophanes in *The Frogs*;[24] while the final form of the Greek alphabet, which was established fairly late in the fifth century, was finally adopted for use in the official records of Athens by decree of the Archon Eucleides in 403 B.C.

Alphabetic Culture and Greek Thought

The rise of Greek civilization, then, is the prime historical example of the transition to a really literate society. In all subsequent cases where the widespread introduction of an alphabetic script occurred, as in Rome for example, other cultural features were inevitably imported from the loan country along with the writing system; Greece thus offers not only the first instance of this change, but also the essential one for any attempt to isolate the cultural consequences of alphabetic literacy.

The fragmentary and ambiguous nature of our direct evidence about this historical transformation in Greek civilization means that any generalizations must be extremely tentative and hypothetical; but the fact that the essential basis both of the writing systems and of many characteristic cultural institutions of the Western tradition as a whole are derived from Greece, and that they both arose there simultaneously, would seem to justify the present attempt to outline the possible relationships between the writing system and those cultural innovations of early Greece which are common to all alphabetically literate societies.

The early development of the distinctive features of Western thought is usually traced back to the radical innovations of the pre-Socratic philosophers of the sixth century B.C. The essence of their intellectual revolution is seen as a change from mythical to logico-empirical modes of thought. Such, broadly speaking, is Werner Jaeger's view; and Ernst Cassirer writes that "the history of philosophy as a scientific discipline may be regarded as a single continuous struggle to effect a separation and liberation from myth."[25]

To this general picture there are two kinds of theoretical objection. First, that the crucial intellectual innovations—in Cassirer as in Werner Jaeger—are in the last analysis attributed to the special mental endowments of the Greek people; and in so far as such terms as "the Greek mind" and "genius" are not simply descriptive, they are logically dependent upon extremely questionable theories of man's nature and culture. Secondly, such a version of the transformation from "unphilosophical" to "philosophical" thought assumes an absolute—and untenable—dichotomy between the "mythical" thought of primitives and the "logico-empirical" thought of civilized man.

The dichotomy, of course, is itself very similar to Lévy-Bruhl's earlier theory of the "prelogical" mentality of primitive peoples, which has been widely criticized. Malinowski and many others have demonstrated the empirical elements in non-literate cultures,[26] and Evans-Pritchard (1937) has carefully analysed the "logical" nature of the belief systems of the Azande of the Sudan,[27] while on the other hand the illogical and mythical nature of much Western thought and behaviour is evident to anyone contemplating either our past or our present.

Nevertheless, although we must reject any dichotomy based upon the assumption of radical differences between the mental attributes of literate and non-literate peoples, and accept the view that previous formulations of the distinction were based on faulty premises and inadequate evidence, there may still exist general differences between literate and non-literate societies somewhat along the lines suggested by Lévy-Bruhl. One reason for their existence, for instance, may be what has been described above: the fact that writing establishes a different kind of relationship between the word and its referent, a relationship that is more general and more abstract, and less closely connected with the particularities of person, place and time, than obtains in oral communication. There is certainly a good deal to substantiate this distinction in what we know of early Greek thought. To take, for instance, the categories of Cassirer and Werner Jaeger, it is surely significant that it was only in the days of the first widespread alphabetic culture that the idea of "logic"—of an immutable and impersonal mode of discourse—appears to have arisen; and it was also only then that the sense of the human past as an objective reality was formally developed, a process in which the distinction between "myth" and "history" took on decisive importance.

Myth and history

Non-literate peoples, of course, often make a distinction between the lighter folk-tale, the graver myth, and the quasi-historical legend (e.g. the Trobriands; Malinowski 1926: 33). But not so insistently, and for an obvious reason. As long as the legendary and doctrinal aspects of the cultural tradition are mediated orally, they are kept in relative harmony with each other and with the present needs of society in two ways: through the unconscious operations of memory, and through the adjustment of the reciter's terms and attitudes to those of the audience before him. There is evidence, for example, that such adaptations and omissions occurred in the oral transmission of the Greek cultural tradition. But once the poems of Homer and Hesiod, which contained much of the earlier history, religion and cosmology of the Greeks, had been written down, succeeding generations were faced with old distinctions in sharply aggravated form: how far was the information about their gods and heroes literally true? How could its patent inconsistencies be explained? And how could the beliefs and attitudes implied be brought into line with those of the present?

The disappearance of so many early Greek writings, and the difficulties of dating and composition in many that survive, make anything like a clear reconstruction impossible. Greek had of course been written, in a very limited way, during Mycenaean times. At about 1200 B.C. writing disappeared, and the alphabet was not developed until some four hundred years later. Most scholars agree that in the middle or late eighth century the Greeks adapted the purely consonantal system of Phoenicia, possibly at the trading port of al Mina (Poseidon?). Much of the early writing consisted of "explanatory inscriptions on existing objects—dedications on offerings, personal names on property, epitaphs on tombs, names of figures in drawings" (Jeffery 1961: 46). The Homeric poems were written down between 750 and 650 B.C., and the seventh century saw first the recording of lyric verse and then (at the end) the emergence of the great Ionian school of scientist philosophers.[28] Thus within a century or two of the writing down of the Homeric poems, many groups of writers and teachers appeared, first in Ionia and later in Greece, who took as their point of departure the belief that much of what Homer had apparently said was inconsistent and unsatisfactory in many respects. The logographers, who set themselves to record the genealogies, chronologies and cosmologies which had been handed down orally from the past, soon found that the task led them to use their critical and rational powers to create a new individual synthesis. In non-literate society, of course, there are usually some individuals whose interests lead them to collect, analyse and interpret the cultural tradition in a personal way; and the written records suggest that this process went considerably further among the literate élites of Egypt, Babylon and China, for example. But, perhaps because in Greece reading and writing were less restricted to any particular priestly or administrative groups, there seems to have been a more thoroughgoing individual challenge to the orthodox cultural tradition in sixth-century Greece than occurred elsewhere. Hecataeus, for example, proclaimed at about the turn of the century, "What I write is the account I believe to be true. For the stories the Greeks tell are many and in my opinion ridiculous" (Jacoby 1931), and offered his own rationalizations of the data on family traditions and lineages which he had collected. Already the mythological mode of using the past, the mode which, in Sorel's words, makes it "a means of acting on the present" (Hulme 1941: 136; Redfield 1953: 125), has begun to disappear.

That this trend of thought had much larger implications can be seen from the fact that the beginnings of religious and natural philosophy are connected with similar critical departures from the inherited traditions of the past; as W. B. Yeats wrote, with another tradition in mind: "Science is the critique of myths, there would be no Darwin had there been no *Book* of Genesis" (Hone 1942: 405, our italics). Among the early pre-Socratics there is much evidence of the close connection between new ideas and the criticism of the old. Thus Xenophanes of Colophon (*fl. c.* 540 B.C.) rejected the "fables of men of old," and replaced the anthropomorphic gods of Homer and Hesiod who did "everything that is disgraceful and blameworthy among men" with a supreme god, "not at all like mortals in body and mind,"[29] while Heraclitus of Ephesus (*fl. c.* 500 B.C.), the first great philosopher of the problems of knowledge, whose system is based on the unity of opposites expressed in the *Logos* or structural plan of things, also ridiculed the anthropomorphism and idolatry of the Olympian religion.[30]

The critical and sceptical process continued, and, according to Cornford, "a great part of the supreme god's biography had to be frankly rejected as false, or reinterpreted as allegory, or contemplated with reserve as mysterious myth too dark for human understanding" (Cornford 1923: xv–xvi; Burnet 1908: 1). On the one hand the poets continued to use the traditional legends for their poems and plays; on the other the prose writers attempted to wrestle with the problems with which the changes in the cultural tradition had faced them. Even the poets, however, had a different attitude to their material. Pindar, for example, used *mythoi* in the sense of traditional stories, with the implication that they were not literally true; but claimed that his own poems had nothing in common with the fables of the past (1st Olympian Ode). As for the prose writers, and indeed some of the poets, they had set out to replace myth with something else more consistent, with their sense of the *logos,* of the common and all-encompassing truth which reconciles apparent contradictions.

From the point of view of the transmission of the cultural tradition, the categories of understanding connected with the dimensions of time and space have a particular importance. As regards an objective description of space, Anaximander (b. 610 B.C.) and Hecataeus (*fl. c.* 510–490), making use of Babylonian and Egyptian techniques, drew the first maps of the world (Warmington 1934: xiv, xxxviii). Then their crude beginnings were subjected to a long process of criticism and correction—by Herodotus (*History:* iv, 36–40) and others; and from this emerged the more scientific cartography of Aristotle, Eratosthenes and their successors (Warmington 1934: xvii, xli).

The development of history appears to have followed a rather similar course, although the actual details of the process are subject to much controversy. The traditional view gave priority to local histories, which were followed by the more universal accounts of Herodotus and Thucydides. Dionysius of Halicarnasus writes of the predecessors of these historians who, "instead of co-ordinating their accounts with each other, . . . treated of individual peoples and cities separately. . . . They all had the one same object, to bring to the general knowledge of the public the written records that they found preserved in temples or in secular buildings in the form in which they found them, neither adding nor taking away anything; among these records were to be found legends hallowed by the passage of time . . ." (Pearson 1939: 3).

Jacoby, however, has insisted "the whole idea is wrong that Greek historiography began with local history" (1949: 354). As far as Athens is concerned, history begins with the foreigner Herodotus, who, not long after the middle of the fifth century, incorporated parts of the story of the town in his work because he wanted to explain the role it played in the great conflict between East and West, between Europe and Asia. The aim of Herodotus' *History* was to discover what the Greeks and Persians "fought each other for" (*History:* I, 1; Finley 1959: 4); and his method was *historia,* personal inquiry or research into the most probable versions of events as they were to be found in various sources. His work rested on oral tradition and consequently his writings retained many mythological elements. So too did the work of the logographer, Hellanicus of Lesbos, who at the end of the fifth century wrote the first history of Attica from 683 to the end of the Peloponnesian war in 404. Hellanicus also tried to reconstruct the genealogies of the Homeric heroes, both backwards to the gods and forwards to the Greece of his own time; and this inevitably involved chronology, the objective measurement of time. All he could do, however, was to rationalize and systematize largely legendary materials (Pearson 1939: 193, 232). The development of history as a documented and analytic account of the past and present of the society in permanent written form took an important step forward with Thucydides, who made a decisive distinction between myth and history, a distinction to which little attention is paid in non-literate society (Malinowski 1922: 290–333). Thucydides wanted to give a wholly reliable account of the wars between Athens and Sparta; and this meant that unverified assumptions about the past had to be excluded. So Thucydides rejected, for example, the chronology that Hellanicus had worked out for the prehistory of Athens, and confined himself very largely to his own notes of the events and speeches he related, or to the information he sought out from eyewitnesses and other reliable sources (Thucydides: I, 20–2, 97).[31]

And so, not long after the widespread diffusion of writing throughout the Greek world, and the recording of the previously oral cultural tradition, there arose an attitude to the past very different from that common in non-literate societies. Instead of the unobtrusive adaptation of past tradition to present needs, a great many individuals found in the written records, where much of their traditional cultural repertoire had been given permanent form, so many inconsistencies in the beliefs and categories of understanding handed down to them that they were impelled to a much more conscious, comparative and critical attitude to the accepted world picture, and notably to the notions of God, the universe and the past. Many individual solutions to these problems were themselves written down, and these versions formed the basis for further investigations.[32]

In non-literate society, it was suggested, the cultural tradition functions as a series of interlocking face-to-face conversations in which the very conditions of transmission operate to favour consistency between past and present, and to make criticism—the articulation of inconsistency—less likely to occur; and if it does, the inconsistency makes a less permanent impact, and is more easily adjusted or forgotten. While scepticism may be present in such societies, it takes a personal, non-cumulative form; it does not lead to a deliberate rejection and reinterpretation of social dogma so much as to a semi-automatic readjustment of belief.[33]

In literate society, these interlocking conversations go on; but they are no longer man's only dialogue; and in so far as writing provides an alternative source for the transmission of cultural orientations it favours awareness of inconsistency. One aspect of this is a sense of change and of cultural lag; another is the notion that the cultural inheritance as a whole is composed of two very different kinds of material; fiction, error and superstition on the one hand; and, on the other, elements of truth which can provide the basis for some more reliable and coherent explanation of the gods, the human past and the physical world.

Logic and the Categories of Understanding

The importance of Plato in the later history of philosophy, of course, lies primarily in that aspect of his work which looks forward, and which did much to define the methods of Western thought; the present argument therefore requires a brief consideration of how far these are intrinsically connected with writing. Obviously the great majority of Greek ideas have their roots in the specific historical and social circumstances, for many of which one can find earlier sources and analogues in the great civilizations of the Near East and elsewhere. Yet it does not seem to be merely a matter of ethnocentric prejudice to say that in two areas at least the Greeks developed intellectual techniques that were historically unique, and that possessed intrinsic empirical advantages which led to their widespread adoption by most subsequent literate cultures: the first area is epistemological, where the Greeks developed a new kind of logical method; and the second area is that of taxonomy, where the Greeks established our accepted categories in the fields of knowledge—theology, physics, biology and so forth.

In the former, Plato is essentially an heir of the long Greek enterprise of trying to sort out truth, *episteme*, from current opinion, *doxa*. This epistemological awareness seems to coincide with the widespread adoption of writing, probably because the written word suggests an ideal of definable truths which have an inherent autonomy and permanence quite different from the phenomena of the temporal flux and of contradictory verbal usages. In oral cultures, words—and especially words like "God," "Justice," "Soul," "Good"—may hardly be conceived of as separate entities, divorced from both the rest of the sentence and its social context. But once given the physical reality of writing, they take on a life of their own; and much Greek thought was concerned with attempting to explain their meanings satisfactorily, and to relate these meanings to some ultimate principle of rational order in the universe, to the *logos*.

It was, of course, Plato and Aristotle who conceived that there might be a special intellectual procedure for this process; who imagined the possibility of a system of rules for thinking itself, rules which were quite distinct from the particular problem being thought about and which offered a more reliable access to truth than current opinion. In the *Phaedrus*, for example, Socrates is made to speak of the proper method for arriving at the truth in general; and this method consists in disregarding the body of popular assumptions and, instead, analysing each idea by an initial definition of terms, followed by the development of a unified argument with "a middle and extremities so composed as to suit each other and the whole work." This is to be achieved by "divisions and collections," by analysis of a problem into its constituent elements, and by subsequent rational synthesis (*Phaedrus:* 264 c; 265 d–266 b; 277 b–c).

This logical procedure seems essentially literate. On general grounds, because, as Oswald Spengler puts it, "writing . . . implies a complete change in the relations of man's waking consciousness, in that it *liberates it from the tyr-*

anny of the present; . . . the activity of writing and reading is infinitely more abstract than that of speaking and hearing" (1934: II, 149). On more practical grounds too, because it is difficult to believe that such a large and complex series of arguments as are presented in the *Republic,* for instance, or in Aristotle's *Analytics,* could possibly be created, or delivered, much less completely understood, in oral form.

There is also some fairly convincing evidence to suggest a more directly causal connection between writing and logic. The Greek word for an "element" was the same word as for a "letter of the alphabet"; and in the *Statesman* Plato compares the basic principles of his philosophy with the child's first contact with the alphabet,[34] on the grounds that each principle or letter is the key to an infinitely greater number of words or ideas than the particular ones through which it is learned. Plato develops this idea in the *Theaetetus* when Socrates compares the process of reasoning to the combination of irreducible elements or letters of the alphabet into syllables which, unlike their constituent letters, have meaning: "the elements or letters are only objects of perception, and cannot be defined or known; but the syllables or combinations of them are known and . . . apprehended."[35] From this it is not far to the way the letters of the alphabet are used to symbolize the manipulation of general terms in Aristotelian logic; the set sequence of the premises, arguments and conclusions of a syllogism has been represented by letters of the alphabet ever since Aristotle so used them in the *Analytics.* It is further significant that Aristotle felt that he had made his greatest philosophical contribution in the field of logic; for, as he says in *De Sophisticis Elenchis,* "on the subject of reasoning we had nothing else of an earlier date to speak of at all."[36]

The same process of dissection into abstract categories, when applied not to a particular argument but to the ordering of all the elements of experience into separate areas of intellectual activity, leads to the Greek division of knowledge into autonomous cognitive disciplines which has since become universal in Western culture and which is of cardinal importance in differentiating literate and non-literate cultures. Plato made one important step in this direction, for he developed both the word and the notion of theology to designate a separate field of knowledge (Jaeger 1947: 4–5). This kind of strict separation of divine attributes from the natural world, and from human life, is virtually unknown among non-literate peoples (Goody 1961: 142–64). Neglect of this fact has led to much misunderstanding of the non-empirical and magico-religious aspects of their culture; but the neglect is itself a tribute to the depth of the literate tradition's acceptance of the categories of understanding which it has inherited from Greece.

Plato, however, was too much the disciple of Socrates to take the compartmentalization of knowledge very far. This was left to his pupil, Aristotle, and to his school (Taylor 1943: 24–39); by the time of the death of Aristotle in 322 B.C. most of the categories in the field of philosophy, natural science, language and literature had been delineated, and the systematic collection and classification of data in all of them had begun.

With Aristotle the key methods and distinctions in the world of knowledge were fully, and for the most part permanently, established; and so, of course, were its institutions. It was Aristotle, according to Strabo,[37] who was the first man to collect books, and who taught the kings of Egypt to set up libraries; and although there had actually been earlier private collectors of books, Aristotle's library is the first of which much is known; it is from his collections that our word "museum" derives; and if "academy" commemorates the school of Plato, *lycée* carries us back to Aristotle's *Lyceum*.

Literate Culture: Some General Considerations

It is hardly possible, in this brief survey, to determine what importance must be attributed to the alphabet as the cause or as the necessary condition of the seminal intellectual innovations that occurred in the Greek world during the centuries that followed the diffusion of writing; nor, indeed, does the nature of the evidence give much ground for believing that the problem can ever be fully resolved. The present argument must, therefore, confine itself to suggesting that some crucial features of Western culture came into being in Greece soon after the existence, for the first time, of a rich urban society in which a substantial portion of the population was able to read and write; and that, consequently, the overwhelming debt of the whole of contemporary civilization to classical Greece must be regarded as in some measure the result, not so much of the Greek genius, as of the intrinsic differences between non-literate (or protoliterate) and literate societies — the latter being mainly represented by those societies using the Greek alphabet and its derivatives. If this is so, it may help us to take our contrast between the transmission of the cultural heritage in non-literate and alphabetically literate societies a little further.

To begin with, the ease of alphabetic reading and writing was probably an important consideration in the development of political democracy in Greece; in the fifth century a majority of the free citizens could apparently read the laws, and take an active part in elections and legislation. Democracy as we know it, then, is from the beginning associated with widespread literacy; and so to a large extent is the notion of the world of knowledge as transcending political units; in the Hellenic world diverse people and countries were given a common administrative system and a unifying cultural heritage through the written word. Greece is therefore considerably closer to being a model for the world-wide intellectual tradition of the contemporary literate world than those earlier civilizations of the Orient which each had its own localized traditions of knowledge: as Oswald Spengler put it, "*Writing is the grand symbol of the Far*" (1934: II, 150).

Yet although the idea of intellectual, and to some extent political, universalism is historically and substantively linked with literate culture, we too easily forget that this brings with it other features which have quite different implications, and which go some way to explain why the long-cherished and theoretically feasible dream of an "educated democracy" and a truly egalitarian society has never been realized in practice. One of the basic premises of liberal reform over the last century and a half has been that of James Mill, as it is described in the *Autobiography* of his son, John Stuart Mill:

> So complete was my father's reliance on the influence of reason over the minds of mankind, whenever it is allowed to reach them, that he felt as if all would be gained if the whole population were taught to read, if all sorts of opinions were allowed to be addressed to them by word and in writing, and if, by means of the suffrage, they could nominate a legislature to give effect to the opinions they adopted [p. 74].

All these things have been accomplished since the days of the Mills, but nevertheless "all" has not been "gained"; and some causes of this shortfall may be found in the intrinsic effects of literacy on the transmission of the cultural heritage, effects which can be seen most clearly by contrasting them with their analogues in non-literate society.

The writing down of some of the main elements in the cultural tradition in Greece, we say, brought about an awareness of two things: of the past as different from the present; and of the inherent inconsistencies in the picture of life as it was inherited by the individual from the cultural tradition in its recorded form. These two effects of widespread alphabetic writing, it may be surmised, have continued and multiplied themselves ever since, and at an increasing pace since the development of printing. "The printers," Jefferson remarked, "can never leave us in a state of perfect rest and union of opinion,"[38] and as book follows book and newspaper newspaper, the notion of rational agreement and democratic coherence among men has receded further and further away, while Plato's attacks on the venal purveyors of knowledge in the market-place have gained increased relevance.

But the inconsistency of the totality of written expression is perhaps less striking than its enormous bulk and its vast historical depth. Both of these have always seemed insuperable obstacles to those seeking to reconstruct society on a more unified and disciplined model: we find the objection in the book-burners of all periods; and it appears in many more respectable thinkers. In Jonathan Swift, for example, whose perfectly rational Houyhnhnms "have no letters," and whose knowledge "consequently . . . is all traditional."[39] These oral traditions were of a scale, Swift tells us, that enabled "the historical part" to be "easily preserved without burthening their memories." Not so with the literate tradition, for, lacking the resources of unconscious adaptation and omission which exist in the oral transmission, the cultural repertoire can only grow; there are more words than anybody knows the meaning of—some 142,000 vocabulary entries in a college dictionary like the *Webster's New World*. This unlimited proliferation also characterizes the written tradition in general: the mere size of the literate repertoire means that the proportion of the whole which any one individual knows must be infinitesimal in comparison with what obtains in oral culture. Literate society, merely by having no system of elimination, no "structural amnesia," prevents the individual from participating fully in the total cultural tradition to anything like the extent possible in non-literate society.

One way of looking at this lack of any literate equivalent to the homeostatic organization of the culturale tradition in non-literate society is to see literate society as inevitably committed to an ever-increasing series of culture lags. The content of the cultural tradition grows continually, and in so far as it affects any particular individual he becomes a palimpsest composed of layers of beliefs and attitudes belonging to different stages in historical time. So too, eventually, does society at large, since there is a tendency for each social group to be particularly influenced by systems of ideas belonging to different periods in the nation's development; both to the individual, and to the groups constituting society, the past may mean very different things.

From the standpoint of the individual intellectual, of the literate specialist, the vista of endless choices and discoveries offered by so extensive a past can be a source of great stimulation and interest; but when we consider the social effects of such an orientation, it becomes apparent that the situation fosters the alienation that has characterized so many writers and philosophers of the West since the last century. It was surely, for example, this lack of social amnesia in alphabetic cultures which led Nietzsche to describe "we moderns" as "wandering encyclopaedias," unable to live and act in the present and obsessed by a " 'historical sense' that injures and finally destroys the living thing, be it a man or a people or a system of culture" (1909: 9, 33). Even if we dismiss Nietzsche's views as extreme, it is still evident that the literate individual has in practice so large a field of personal selection from the total cultural repertoire that the odds are strongly against his experiencing the cultural tradition as any sort of patterned whole.

From the point of view of society at large, the enormous complexity and variety of the cultural repertoire obviously creates problems of an unprecedented order of magnitude. It means, for example, that since Western literate societies are characterized by these always increasing layers of cultural tradition, they are incessantly exposed to a more complex version of the kind of culture conflict that has been held to produce *anomie* in oral societies when they come into contact with European civilization, changes which, for example, have been illustrated with a wealth of absorbing detail by Robert Redfield in his studies of Central America.[40]

Another important consequence of alphabetic culture relates to social stratification. In the protoliterate cultures, with their relatively difficult nonalphabetic systems of writing, there existed a strong barrier between the writers and the non-writers; but although the "democratic" scripts made it possible to break down this particular barrier, they led eventually to a vast proliferation of more or less tangible distinctions based on what people had read. Achievement in handling the tools of reading and writing is obviously one of the most important axes of social differentiation in modern societies; and this differentiation extends on to more minute differences between professional specializations so that even members of the same socio-economic groups of literate specialists may hold little intellectual ground in common.

Nor, of course, are these variations in the degree of participation in the literate tradition, together with their effects on social structure, the only causes of tension. For, even within a literate culture, the oral tradition—the transmission of values and attitudes in face-to-face contact—nevertheless remains the primary mode of cultural orientation, and, to varying degrees, it is out of step with the various literate traditions. In some respects, perhaps, this is fortunate. The tendency of the modern mass-communications industries, for example, to promote ideals of conspicuous consumption which cannot be realized by more than a limited proportion of society might well have much more radical consequences but for the fact that each individual exposed to such pressures is also a member of one or more primary groups whose oral converse is probably much more realistic and conservative in its ideological tendency; the mass media are not the only, and they are probably not even the main, social influences on the contemporary cultural tradition as a whole.

Primary group values are probably even further removed from those of the "high" literate culture, except in the case of the literate specialists. This introduces another kind of culture conflict, and one which is of cardinal significance for Western civilization. If, for example, we return to the reasons for the relative failure of universal compulsory education to bring about the intellectual, social and political results that James Mill expected, we may well lay a major part of the blame on the gap between the public literate tradition of the school and the very different and indeed often directly contradictory private oral traditions of the pupil's family and peer group. The high degree of differentiation in exposure to the literate tradition sets up a basic division which cannot exist in non-literate society: the division between the various shades of literacy and illiteracy. This conflict, of course, is most dramatically focused in the school, the key institution of society. As Margaret Mead (1943: 637) has pointed out: "Primitive education was a process by which continuity was maintained between parents and children. . . . Modern education includes a heavy emphasis upon the function of education to create discontinuities—to turn the child . . . of the illiterate into the literate." A similar and probably even more acute stress develops in many cases between the school and the peer group; and, quite apart from the difficulties arising from the substantive differences between the two orientations, there seem to be factors in the very nature of literate methods which make them ill suited to bridge the gap between the street-corner society and the blackboard jungle.

First, because although the alphabet, printing, and universal free education have combined to make the literate culture freely available to all on a scale never previously approached, the literate mode of communication is such that it does not impose itself as forcefully or as uniformly as is the case with the oral transmission of the cultural tradition. In non-literate society every social situation cannot but bring the individual into contact with the group's patterns of thought, feeling and action: the choice is between the cultural tradition—or solitude. In a literate society, however, and quite apart from the difficulties arising from the scale and complexity of the "high" literate tradition, the mere fact that reading and writing are normally solitary activities means that in so far as the dominant cultural tradition is a literate one, it is very easy to avoid; as Bertha Phillpotts (1931: 162–3) wrote in her study of Icelandic literature:

> Printing so obviously makes knowledge accessible to all that we are inclined to forget that it also makes knowledge very easy to avoid. . . . A shepherd in an Icelandic homestead, on the other hand, could not avoid spending his evenings in listening to the kind of literature which interested the farmer. The result was a degree of really national culture such as no nation of today has been able to achieve.

The literate culture, then, is much more easily avoided than the oral one; and even when it is not avoided its actual effects may be relatively shallow. Not only because, as Plato argued, the effects of reading are intrinsically less deep and permanent than those of oral converse; but also because the abstractness of the syllogism and of the Aristotelian categorizations of knowledge do not correspond very directly with common experience. The abstractness of the syllogism, for example, of its very nature disregards the individual's social experience and immediate personal context; and the compartmentalization of knowledge similarly restricts the kind of connections which the individual can establish and ratify with the natural and social world. The essential way of thinking of the specialist in literate culture is fundamentally at odds with that of daily life and common experience; and the conflict is embodied in the long tradition of jokes about absent-minded professors.

It is, of course, true that contemporary education does not present problems exactly in the forms of Aristotelian logic and taxonomy; but all our literate modes of thought have been profoundly influenced by them. In this, perhaps, we can see a major difference, not only from the transmission of the cultural heritage of oral societies, but from those of protoliterate ones. Thus Marcel Granet relates the nature of the Chinese writing system to the "concreteness" of Chinese thought, and his picture of its primary concentration on social action and traditional norms suggests that the cultural effect of the writing system was in the direction of intensifying the sort of homeostatic conservation found in non-literate cultures; it was indeed conceptualized in the Confucian *tao-'tung*, or "orthodox transmission of the way." In this connection it may be noted that the Chinese attitude to formal logic, and to the categorization of knowledge in general, is an articulate expression of what happens in an oral culture (Granet 1934: vii–xi, 8–55; Hu Shih 1922). Mencius, for example, speaks for the non-literate approach in general when he comments: "Why I dislike holding to one point is that it injures the *tao*. It takes up one point and disregards a hundred others" (Richards 1932: 35).

The social tension between the oral and literate orientations in Western society is, of course, complemented by an intellectual one. In recent times the Enlightenment's attack on myth as irrational superstition has often been replaced by a regressive yearning for some modern equivalent of the unifying function of myth: "Have not," W. B. Yeats asked, "all races had their first unity from a mythology that marries them to rock and hill?" (1955: 194).

In this nostalgia for the world of myths Plato has had a long line of successors. The Rousseauist cult of the Noble Savage, for instance, paid unwitting tribute to the strength of the homogeneity of oral culture, to the yearning admiration of the educated for the peasant's simple but cohesive view of life, the timelessness of his living in the present, the unanalytic spontaneity that comes with an attitude to the world that is one of absorbed and uncritical participation, a participation in which the contradictions between history and legend, for example, or between experience and imagination, are not felt as problems. Such, for example, is the literary tradition of the European peasant from Cervantes' Sancho Panza to Tolstoy's Platon Karataev. Both are illiterate; both are rich in proverbial lore; both are untroubled by intellectual consistency; and both represent many of the values which, it was suggested above, are characteristic of oral culture. In these two works, *Don Quixote* and *War and Peace,* which might well be considered two of the supreme achievements of modern Western literature, an explicit contrast is made between the oral and literate elements of the cultural tradition. Don Quixote himself goes mad by reading books; while, opposed to the peasant Karataev, stands the figure of Pierre, an urban cosmopolitan, and a great reader. Tolstoy writes of Karataev that—in this like Mencius or like Malinowski's Trobrianders—he

> did not, and could not, understand the meaning of words apart from their context. Every word and every action of his was the manifestation of an activity unknown to him, which was his life. But his life, as he regarded it, had no meaning as a separate thing. It had a meaning only as part of a whole of which he was always conscious [*War and Peace*].

Tolstoy, of course, idealizes; but, conversely, even in his idealization he suggests one major emphasis of literate culture and one which we immediately associate with the Greeks—the stress upon the individual; Karataev does not regard "his life . . . as a separate thing." There are, of course, marked differences in the life histories of individual members of non-literate societies: the story of Crashing Thunder differs from that of other Winnebago (Radin 1926, 1927); that of Baba of Karo from other Hausa women (Smith 1954); and these differences are often given public recognition by ascribing to individuals a personal tutelary or guardian spirit. But on the whole there is less individualization of personal experience in oral cultures, which tend, in Durkheim's phrase, to be characterized by "mechanical solidarity"[41]—by the ties between like persons, rather than by a more complicated set of complementary relationships between individuals in a variety of roles. Like Durkheim, many sociologists would relate this greater individualization of personal experience in literate societies to the effects of a more extensive division of labour. There is no single explanation; but the techniques of reading and writing are undoubtedly of very great importance. There is, first of all, the formal distinction which alphabetic culture has emphasized between the divine, the natural, and the human orders; secondly, there is the social differentiation to which the institutions of literate culture give rise; third, there is the effect of professional intellectual specialization on an unprecedented scale; lastly, there is the immense variety of choice offered by the whole corpus of recorded literature; and from these four factors there ensues, in any individual case, the highly complex totality deriving from the selection of these literate orientations and from the series of primary groups in which the individual has also been involved.

As for personal awareness of this individualization, other factors doubtless contributed, but writing itself (especially in its simpler, more cursive forms) was of great importance. For writing, by objectifying words, and by making them and their meaning available for much more prolonged and intensive scrutiny than is possible orally, encourages private thought; the diary or the confession enables the individual to objectify his own experience, and gives him some check upon the transmutations of memory under the influences of subsequent events. And then, if the diary is later published, a wider audience can have concrete experience of the differences that exist in the histories of their fellow men from a record of a life which has been partially insulated from the assimilative process of oral transmission.

The diary is, of course, an extreme case; but Plato's dialogues themselves are evidence of the general tendency of writing to increase the awareness of individual differences in behaviour, and in the personality which lies behind them,[42] while the novel, which participates in the autobiographical and confessional direction of such writers as St. Augustine, Pepys and Rousseau, and purports to portray the inner as well as the outer life of individuals in the real world, has replaced the collective representations of myth and epic.

From the point of view of the general contrast between oral and alphabetically literate culture, then, there is a certain identity between the spirit of the Platonic dialogues and of the novel,[43] both kinds of writing express what is a characteristic intellectual effort of literate culture, and present the process whereby the individual makes his own more or less conscious, more or less personal selection, rejection and accommodation among the conflicting ideas and attitudes in his culture. This general kinship between Plato and the characteristic art form of literate culture, the novel, suggests a further contrast between oral and literate societies: in contrast to the homeostatic transmission of the cultural tradition among non-literate peoples, literate society leaves more to its members; less homogeneous in its cultural tradition, it gives more free play to the individual, and particularly to the intellectual, the literate specialist himself; it does so by sacrificing a single, ready-made orientation to life. And, in so far as an individual participates in the literate, as distinct from the oral, culture, such coherence as a person achieves is very largely the result of his personal selection, adjustment and elimination of items from a highly differentiated cultural repertoire; he is, of course, influenced by all the various social pressures, but they are so numerous that the pattern finally comes out as an individual one.

Much could be added by way of development and qualification on this point, as on much else that has been said above. The contrast could be extended, for example, by bringing it up to date and considering later developments in communication, from the invention of printing and of the power press to that of radio, cinema and television. All these latter, it may be surmised, derive much of their effectiveness as agencies of social orientation from the fact that their media do not have the abstract and solitary quality of reading and writing, but on the contrary share something of the nature and impact of the direct personal interaction which obtains in oral cultures. It may even be that these new modes of communicating sight and sound without any limit of time or place will lead to a new kind of culture: less inward and individualistic than literate culture, probably, and sharing some of the relative homogeneity, though not the mutuality, of oral society.

Summary

Recent anthropology has rightly rejected the categorical distinctions between the thinking of "primitive" and "civilized" peoples, between "mythopoeic" and "logico-empirical" modes of thought. But the reaction has been pushed too far: diffuse relativism and sentimental egalitarianism combine to turn a blind eye on some of the most basic problems of human history. Where the intellectual differences in the cultural traditions of complex and simple societies are given adequate recognition, the explanations offered are unsatisfactory. In the case of Western civilization, for example, the origins are sought in the nature of the Greek genius, in the grammatical structure of the Indo-European languages, or, somewhat more plausibly, in the technological advances of the Bronze Age and the associated developments in the division of labour.

In our view, however, insufficient attention has been paid to the fact that the urban revolution of the Ancient Near East produced one invention, the invention of writing, which changed the whole structure of the cultural tradition. Potentially, human intercourse was now no longer restricted to the impermanency of oral converse. But since the first methods of writing employed were difficult to master, their effects were relatively limited, and it was only when the simplicity and flexibility of later alphabetic writing made widespread literacy possible that for the first time there began to take concrete shape in the Greek world of the seventh century B.C. a society that was essentially literate and that soon established many of the institutions that became characteristic of all later literate societies.

The development of an easy system of writing (easy both in terms of the materials employed and the signs used) was more than a mere precondition of the Greek achievement: it influenced its whole nature and development in fundamental ways. In oral societies the cultural tradition is transmitted almost entirely by face-to-face communication; and changes in its content are accompanied by the homeostatic process of forgetting or transforming those parts of the tradition that cease to be either necessary or relevant. Literate societies, on the other hand, cannot discard, absorb, or transmute the past in the same way. Instead, their members are faced with permanently recorded versions of the past and its beliefs; and because the past is thus set apart from the present, historical enquiry becomes possible. This in turn encourages scepticism; and scepticism, not only about the legendary past, but about received ideas about the universe as a whole. From here the next step is to see how to build up and to test alternative explanations; and out of this there arose the kind of logical, specialized, and cumulative intellectual tradition of sixth-century Ionia. The kinds of analysis involved in the syllogism, and in the other forms of logical procedure, are clearly dependent upon writing, indeed upon a form of writing sufficiently simple and cursive to make possible widespread and habitual recourse both to the recording of verbal statements and then to the dissecting of them. It is probable that it is only the analytic process that writing itself entails, the written formalization of sounds and syntax, which make possible the habitual separating out into formally distinct units of the various cultural elements whose indivisible wholeness is the essential basis of the "mystical participation" which Lévy-Bruhl regards as characteristic of the thinking of non-literate peoples.

One of the problems which neither Lévy-Bruhl nor any other advocate of a radical dichotomy between "primitive" and "civilized" thought has been able to resolve is the persistence of "non-logical thinking" in modern literate societies. But, of course, we must reckon with the fact that in our civilization writing is clearly an addition, not an alternative, to oral transmission. Even in our *buch und lesen* culture, child rearing and a multitude of other forms of activity both within and outside the family depend upon speech; and in Western cultures the relation between the written and the oral traditions must be regarded as a major problem.

A consideration of the consequences of literacy in these terms, then, throws some light not only upon the nature of the Greek achievement but also upon the intellectual differences between simple and complex societies. There are, of course, many other consequences we have not discussed—for instance, the role of writing in the running of centralized states and other bureaucratic organizations; our aim has only been to discuss in very general terms some of the more significant historical and functional consequences of literacy.[44]

2.
Some Psychodynamics of Orality

Walter J. Ong

Sounded Word as Power and Action

As a result of the work just reviewed, and of other work which will be cited, it is possible to generalize somewhat about the psychodynamics of primary oral cultures, that is, of oral cultures untouched by writing. For brevity, when the context keeps the meaning clear, I shall refer to primary oral cultures simply as oral cultures.

Fully literate persons can only with great difficulty imagine what a primary oral culture is like, that is, a culture with no knowledge whatsoever of writing or even of the possibility of writing. Try to imagine a culture where no one has ever "looked up" anything. In a primary oral culture, the expression "to look up something" is an empty phrase: it would have no conceivable meaning. Without writing, words as such have no visual presence, even when the objects they represent are visual. They are sounds. You might "call" them back—"recall" them. But there is nowhere to "look" for them. They have no focus and no trace (a visual metaphor, showing dependency on writing), not even a trajectory. They are occurrences, events.

To learn what a primary oral culture is and what the nature of our problem is regarding such a culture, it helps first to reflect on the nature of sound itself as sound (Ong 1967, pp. 111–38). All sensation takes place in time, but sound has a special relationship to time unlike that of the other fields that register in human sensation. Sound exists only when it is going out of existence. It is not simply perishable but essentially evanescent, and it is sensed as evanescent. When I pronounce the word "permanence," by the time I get the "-nence," the "perma-" is gone, and has to be gone.

There is no way to stop sound and have sound. I can stop a moving picture camera and hold one frame fixed on the screen. If I stop the movement of sound, I have nothing—only silence, no sound at all. All sensation takes place in time, but no other sensory field totally resists a holding action, stabilization, in quite this way. Vision can register motion, but it can also register immobility. Indeed, it favors immobility, for to examine something closely by vision, we prefer to have it quiet. We often reduce motion to a series of still shots the better to see what motion is. There is no equivalent of a still shot for sound. An oscillogram is silent. It lies outside the sound world.

For anyone who has a sense of what words are in a primary oral culture, or a culture not far removed from primary orality, it is not surprising that the Hebrew term *dabar* means "word" and "event." Malinowski (1923, pp. 451, 470–81) has made the point that among "primitive" (oral) peoples generally language is a mode of action and not simply a countersign of thought, though he had trouble explaining what he was getting at (Sampson 1980, pp. 223–6), since understanding of the psychodynamics of orality was virtually nonexistent in 1923. Neither is it surprising that oral peoples commonly, and probably universally, consider words to have great power. Sound cannot be sounding without the use of power. A hunter can see a buffalo, smell, taste, and touch a buffalo when the buffalo is completely inert, even dead, but if he hears a buffalo, he had better watch out: something is going on. In this sense, all sound, and especially oral utterance, which comes from inside living organisms, is "dynamic."

The fact that oral peoples commonly and in all likelihood universally consider words to have magical potency is clearly tied in, at least unconsciously, with their sense of the word as necessarily spoken, sounded, and hence power-driven. Deeply typographic folk forget to think of words as primarily oral, as events, and hence as necessarily powered: for them, words tend rather to be assimilated to things, "out there" on a flat surface. Such "things" are not so readily associated with magic, for they are not actions, but are in a radical sense dead, though subject to dynamic resurrection (Ong 1977, pp. 230–71).

Oral peoples commonly think of names (one kind of words) as conveying power over things. Explanations of Adam's naming of the animals in Genesis 2:20 usually call condescending attention to this presumably quaint archaic belief. Such a belief is in fact far less quaint than it seems to unreflective chirographic and typographic folk. First of all, names do give human beings power over what they name: without learning a vast store of names, one is simply powerless to understand, for example, chemistry and to practice chemical engineering. And so with all other intellectual knowledge. Secondly, chirographic and typographic folk tend to think of names as labels, written or printed tags imaginatively affixed to an object named. Oral folk have no sense of a name as a tag, for they have no idea of a name as something that can be seen. Written or printed representations of words can be labels; real, spoken words cannot be.

You Know What You Can Recall: Mnemonics and Formulas

In an oral culture, restriction of words to sound determines not only modes of expression but also thought processes.

You know what you can recall. When we say we know Euclidean

geometry, we mean not that we have in mind at the moment every one of its propositions and proofs but rather that we can bring them to mind readily. We can recall them. The theorem "You know what you can recall" applies also to an oral culture. But how do persons in an oral culture recall? The organized knowledge that literates today study so that they "know" it, that is, can recall it, has, with very few if any exceptions, been assembled and made available to them in writing. This is the case not only with Euclidean geometry but also with American Revolutionary history, or even baseball batting averages or traffic regulations.

An oral culture has no texts. How does it get together organized material for recall? This is the same as asking, "What does it or can it know in an organized fashion?"

Suppose a person in an oral culture would undertake to think through a particular complex problem and would finally manage to articulate a solution which itself is relatively complex, consisting, let us say, of a few hundred words. How does he or she retain for later recall the verbalization so painstakingly elaborated? In the total absence of any writing, there is nothing outside the thinker, no text, to enable him or her to produce the same line of thought again or even to verify whether he or she has done so or not. *Aides-mémoire* such as notched sticks or a series of carefully arranged objects will not of themselves retrieve a complicated series of assertions. How, in fact, could a lengthy, analytic solution ever be assembled in the first place? An interlocutor is virtually essential: it is hard to talk to yourself for hours on end. Sustained thought in an oral culture is tied to communication.

But even with a listener to stimulate and ground your thought, the bits and pieces of your thought cannot be preserved in jotted notes. How could you ever call back to mind what you had so laboriously worked out? The only answer is: Think memorable thoughts. In a primary oral culture, to solve effectively the problem of retaining and retrieving carefully articulated thought, you have to do your thinking in mnemonic patterns, shaped for ready oral recurrence. Your thought must come into being in heavily rhythmic, balanced patterns, in repetitions or antitheses, in alliterations and assonances, in epithetic and other formulary expressions, in standard thematic settings (the assembly, the meal, the duel, the hero's "helper," and so on), in proverbs which are constantly heard by everyone so that they come to mind readily and which themselves are patterned for retention and ready recall, or in other mnemonic form. Serious thought is intertwined with memory systems. Mnemonic needs determine even syntax (Havelock 1963, pp. 87–96, 131–2, 294–6).

Protracted orally based thought, even when not in formal verse, tends to be highly rhythmic, for rhythm aids recall, even physiologically. Jousse (1978) has shown the intimate linkage between rhythmic oral patterns, the breathing process, gesture, and the bilateral symmetry of the human body in ancient Aramaic and Hellenic targums, and thus also in ancient Hebrew. Among the ancient Greeks, Hesiod, who was intermediate between oral Homeric Greece and fully developed Greek literacy, delivered quasi-philosophic material in the formulaic verse forms that structured it into the oral culture from which he had emerged (Havelock 1963, pp. 97–8, 294–301).

Formulas help implement rhythmic discourse and also act as mnemonic aids in their own right, as set expressions circulating through the mouths and ears of all. "Red in the morning, the sailor's warning; red in the night, the sailor's delight." "Divide and conquer." "To err is human, to forgive is divine." "Sorrow is better than laughter, because when the face is sad the heart grows wiser" (Ecclesiastes 7:3). "The clinging vine." "The sturdy oak." "Chase off nature and she returns at a gallop." Fixed, often rhythmically balanced, expressions of this sort and of other sorts can be found occasionally in print, indeed can be "looked up" in books of sayings, but in oral cultures they are not occasional. They are incessant. They form the substance of thought itself. Thought in any extended form is impossible without them, for it consists in them.

The more sophisticated orally patterned thought is, the more it is likely to be marked by set expressions skillfully used. This is true of oral cultures generally from those of Homeric Greece to those of the present day across the globe. Havelock's *Preface to Plato* (1963) and fictional works such as Chinua Achebe's novel *No Longer at Ease* (1961), which draws directly on Ibo oral tradition in West Africa, alike provide abundant instances of thought patterns of orally educated characters who move in these oral, mnemonically tooled grooves, as the speakers reflect, with high intelligence and sophistication, on the situations in which they find themselves involved. The law itself in oral cultures is enshrined in formulaic sayings, proverbs, which are not mere jurisprudential decorations, but themselves constitute the law. A judge in an oral culture is often called on to articulate sets of relevant proverbs out of which he can produce equitable decisions in the cases under formal litigation before him (Ong 1978, p. 5).

In an oral culture, to think through something in non-formulaic, non-patterned, non-mnemonic terms, even if it were possible, would be a waste of time, for such thought, once worked through, could never be recovered with any effectiveness, as it could be with the aid of writing. It would not be abiding knowledge but simply a passing thought, however complex. Heavy patterning and communal fixed formulas in oral cultures serve some of the purposes of writing in chirographic cultures, but in doing so they of course determine the kind of thinking that can be done, the way experience is intellectually organized. In an oral culture, experience is intellectualized mnemonically. This is one reason why, for a St. Augustine of Hippo (A.D. 354–430), as for other savants living in a culture that knew some literacy but still carried an overwhelmingly massive oral residue, memory bulks so large when he treats of the powers of the mind.

Of course, all expression and all thought is to a degree formulaic in the sense that every word and every concept conveyed in a word is a kind of formula, a fixed way of processing the data of experience, determining the way experience and reflection are intellectually organized, and acting as a mnemonic device of sorts. Putting experience into any words (which means transforming it at least a little bit—not the same as falsifying it) can implement its recall. The formulas characterizing orality are more elaborate, however, than are individual words, though some may be relatively simple: the *Beowulf*-poet's "whale-road" is a formula (metaphorical) for the sea in a sense in which the term "sea" is not.

Further Characteristics of Orally Based Thought and Expression

Awareness of the mnemonic base of the thought and expression in primary oral cultures opens the way to understanding some further characteristics of orally based thought and expression in addition to its formulaic styling. The characteristics treated here are some of those which set off orally based thought and expression from chirographically and typographically based thought and expression, the characteristics, that is, which are most likely to strike those reared in writing and print cultures as surprising. This inventory of characteristics is not presented as exclusive or conclusive but as suggestive, for much more work and reflection is needed to deepen understanding of orally based thought (and thereby understanding of chirographically based, typographically based, and electronically based thought).

In a primary oral culture, thought and expression tend to be of the following sorts.

(i) Additive Rather Than Subordinative

A familiar instance of additive oral style is the creation narrative in Genesis 1:1–5, which is indeed a text but one preserving recognizable oral patterning. The Douay version (1610), produced in a culture with a still massive oral residue, keeps close in many ways to the additive Hebrew original (as mediated through the Greek from which the Douay version was made):

> In the beginning God created heaven and earth. And the earth was void and empty, and darkness was upon the face of the deep; and the spirit of God moved over the waters. And God said: Be light made. And light was made. And God saw the light that it was good; and he divided the light from the darkness. And he called the light Day, and the darkness Night; and there was evening and morning one day.

Nine introductory "ands." Adjusted to sensibilities shaped more by writing and print, the *New American Bible* (1970) translates:

> In the beginning, when God created the heavens and the earth, the earth was a formless wasteland, and darkness covered the abyss, while a mighty wind swept over the waters. Then God said, "Let there be light," and there was light. God saw how good the light was. God then separated the light from the darkness. God called the light "day" and the darkness he called "night." Thus evening came, and morning followed—the first day.

Two introductory "ands," each submerged in a compound sentence. The Douay renders the Hebrew *we* or *wa* ("and") simply as "and." The New American renders it "and," "when," "then," "thus," or "while," to provide a flow of narrations with the analytic, reasoned subordination that characterizes writing (Chafe 1982) and that appears more natural in twentieth-century texts. Oral structures often look to pragmatics (the convenience of the speaker—Sherzer, 1974, reports lengthy public oral performances among the Cuna incomprehensible to their hearers). Chirographic structures look more to syntactics (organization of the discourse itself), as Givón has suggested (1979). Written discourse develops more elaborate and fixed grammar than oral discourse does because to provide meaning it is more dependent simply upon linguistic structure, since it lacks the normal full existential contexts which surround oral discourse and help determine meaning in oral discourse somewhat independently of grammar.

It would be a mistake to think that the Douay is simply "closer" to the original today than the New American is. It is closer in that it renders *we* or *wa* always by the same word, but it strikes the present-day sensibility as remote, archaic, and even quaint. Peoples in oral cultures or cultures with high oral residue, including the culture that produced the Bible, do not savor this sort of expression as so archaic or quaint. It feels natural and normal to them somewhat as the New American version feels natural and normal to us.

Other instances of additive structure can be found across the world in primary oral narrative, of which we now have a massive supply on tape (see Foley, 1980, for listing of some tapes).

(ii) Aggregative Rather Than Analytic

This characteristic is closely tied to reliance on formulas to implement memory. The elements of orally based thought and expression tend to be not so much simple integers as clusters of integers, such as parallel terms or phrases or clauses, antithetical terms or phrases or clauses, epithets. Oral folk prefer, especially in formal discourse, not the soldier, but the brave soldier; not the princess, but the beautiful princess; not the oak, but the sturdy oak. Oral expression thus carries a load of epithets and other formulary baggage which high literacy rejects as cumbersome and tiresomely redundant because of its aggregative weight (Ong 1977, pp. 188–212).

The clichés in political denunciations in many low-technology, developing cultures—enemy of the people, capitalist war-mongers—that strike high literates as mindless are residual formulary essentials of oral thought processes. One of the many indications of a high, if subsiding, oral residue in the culture of the Soviet Union is (or was a few years ago, when I encountered it) the insistence on speaking there always of "the Glorious Revolution of October 26"—the epithetic formula here is obligatory stabilization, as were Homeric epithetic formulas "wise Nestor" or "clever Odysseus," or as "the glorious Fourth of July" used to be in the pockets of oral residue common even in the early twentieth-century United States. The Soviet Union still announces each year the official epithets for various *loci classici* in Soviet history.

An oral culture may well ask in a riddle why oaks are sturdy, but it does so to assure you that they are, to keep the aggregate intact, not really to question or cast doubt on the attribution. (For examples directly from the oral culture of the Luba in Zaire, see Faik-Nzuji 1970.) Traditional expressions in oral cultures must not be dismantled: it has been hard work getting them together over the generations, and there is nowhere outside the mind to store them. So soldiers are brave and princesses beautiful and oaks sturdy forever. This is not to say that there may not be other epithets for soldiers or princesses or oaks, even contrary epithets, but these are standard, too: the braggart soldier, the unhappy princess, can also be part of the equipment. What obtains for epithets obtains for other formulas. Once a formulary expression has crystallized, it had best be kept intact. Without a writing system, breaking up thought—that is, analysis—is a high-risk procedure. As Lévi-Strauss has well put it in a summary statement "the savage [i.e. oral] mind totalizes" (1966, p. 245).

(iii) Redundant or "Copious"

Thought requires some sort of continuity. Writing establishes in the text a "line" of continuity outside the mind. If distraction confuses or obliterates from the mind the context out of which emerges the material I am now reading, the context can be retrieved by glancing back over the text selectively. Backlooping can be entirely occasional, purely *ad hoc*. The mind concentrates its own energies on moving ahead because what it backloops into lies quiescent outside itself, always available piecemeal on the inscribed page. In oral discourse, the situation is different. There is nothing to backloop into outside the mind, for the oral utterance has vanished as soon as it is uttered. Hence the mind must move ahead more slowly, keeping close to the focus of attention much of what it has already dealt with. Redundancy, repetition of the just-said, keeps both speaker and hearer surely on the track.

Since redundancy characterizes oral thought and speech, it is in a profound sense more natural to thought and speech than is sparse linearity. Sparsely linear or analytic thought and speech is an artificial creation, structured by the technology of writing. Eliminating redundancy on a significant scale demands a time-obviating technology, writing, which imposes some kind of strain on the psyche in preventing expression from falling into its more natural patterns. The psyche can manage the strain in part because handwriting is physically such a slow process—typically about one-tenth of the speed of oral speech (Chafe 1982). With writing, the mind is forced into a slowed-down pattern that affords it the opportunity to interfere with and reorganize its more normal, redundant processes.

Redundancy is also favored by the physical conditions of oral expression before a large audience, where redundancy is in fact more marked than in most face-to-face conversation. Not everyone in a large audience understands every word a speaker utters, if only because of acoustical problems. It is advantageous for the speaker to say the same thing, or equivalently the same thing, two or three times. If you miss the "not only . . . ." you can supply it by inference from the "but also . . . ." Until electronic amplification reduced acoustical problems to a minimum, public speakers as late as, for example, William Jennings Bryan (1860–1925) continued the old redundancy in their public addresses and by force of habit let them spill over into their writing. In some kinds of acoustic surrogates for oral verbal communication, redundancy reaches fantastic dimensions, as in African drum talk. It takes on the average around eight times as many words to say something on the drums as in the spoken language (Ong 1977, p. 101).

The public speaker's need to keep going while he is running through his mind what to say next also encourages redundancy. In oral delivery, though a pause may be effective, hesitation is always disabling. Hence it is better to repeat something, artfully if possible, rather than simply to stop speaking while fishing for the next idea. Oral cultures encourage fluency, fulsomeness, volubility. Rhetoricians were to call this *copia*. They continued to encourage it, by a kind of oversight, when they had modulated rhetoric from an art of public speaking to an art of writing. Early written texts, through the Middle Ages and the Renaissance, are often bloated with "amplification," annoyingly redundant by modern standards. Concern with *copia* remains intense in western culture so long as the culture sustains massive oral residue—which is roughly until the age of Romanticism or even beyond. Thomas Babington Macaulay (1800–59) is one of the many fulsome early Victorians whose pleonastic written compositions still read much as an exuberant, orally composed oration would sound, as do also, very often, the writings of Winston Churchill (1874–1965).

(iv) Conservative or Traditionalist

Since in a primary oral culture conceptualized knowledge that is not repeated aloud soon vanishes, oral societies must invest great energy in saying over and over again what has been learned arduously over the ages. This need establishes a highly traditionalist or conservative set of mind that with good reason inhibits intellectual experimentation. Knowledge is hard to come by and precious, and society regards highly those wise old men and women who specialize in conserving it, who know and can tell the stories of the days of old. By storing knowledge outside the mind, writing and, even more, print downgrade the figures of the wise old man and the wise old woman, repeaters of the past, in favor of younger discoverers of something new.

Writing is of course conservative in its own ways. Shortly after it first appeared, it served to freeze legal codes in early Sumeria (Oppenheim 1964, p. 232). But by taking conservative functions on itself, the text frees the mind of conservative tasks, that is, of its memory work, and thus enables the mind to turn itself to new speculation (Havelock 1963, pp. 254–305). Indeed, the residual orality of a given chirographic culture can be calculated to a degree from the mnemonic load it leaves on the mind, that is, from the amount of memorization the culture's educational procedures require (Goody 1968, pp. 13–14).

Of course oral cultures do not lack originality of their own kind. Narrative originality lodges not in making up new stories but in managing a particular interaction with this audience at this time—at every telling the story has to be introduced uniquely into a unique situation, for in oral cultures an audience must be brought to respond, often vigorously. But narrators also introduce new elements into old stories (Goody 1977, pp. 29–30). In oral tradition, there will be as many minor variants of a myth as there are repetitions of it, and the number of repetitions can be increased indefinitely. Praise poems of chiefs invite entrepreneurship, as the old formulas and themes have to be made to interact with new and often complicated political situations. But the formulas and themes are reshuffled rather than supplanted with new materials.

Religious practices, and with them cosmologies and deep-seated beliefs, also change in oral cultures. Disappointed with the practical results of the cult at a given shrine when cures there are infrequent, vigorous leaders— the "intellectuals" in oral society, Goody styles them (1977, p. 30)—invent new shrines and with these new conceptual universes. Yet these new universes and the other changes that show a certain originality come into being in an essentially formulaic and thematic noetic economy. They are seldom if ever explicitly touted for their novelty but are presented as fitting the traditions of the ancestors.

(v) Close to the Human Lifeworld

In the absence of elaborate analytic categories that depend on writing to structure knowledge at a distance from lived experience, oral cultures must conceptualize and verbalize all their knowledge with more or less close reference to the human lifeworld, assimilating the alien, objective world to the more immediate, familiar interaction of human beings. A chirographic (writing) culture and even more a typographic (print) culture can distance and in a way denature even the human, itemizing such things as the names of leaders and political divisions in an abstract, neutral list entirely devoid of a human action context. An oral culture has no vehicle so neutral as a list. In the latter half of the second book, the *Iliad* presents the famous catalogue of the ships—over four hundred lines—which compiles the names of Grecian leaders and the regions they ruled, but in a total context of human action: the names of persons and places occur as involved in doings (Havelock 1963, pp. 176–80). The normal and very likely the only place in Homeric Greece where this sort of political information could be found in verbalized form was in a narrative or a genealogy, which is not a neutral list but an account describing personal relations (cf. Goody and Watt 1968, p. 32). Oral cultures know few statistics or facts divorced from human or quasi-human activity.

An oral culture likewise has nothing corresponding to how-to-do-it manuals for the trades (such manuals in fact are extremely rare and always crude even in chirographic cultures, coming into effective existence only after print has been considerably interiorized—Ong 1967, pp. 28–9, 234, 258). Trades were learned by apprenticeship (as they still largely are even in high-technology cultures), which means from observation and practice with only minimal verbalized explanation. The maximum verbal articulation of such things as navigation procedures, which were crucial to Homeric culture, would have been encountered not in any abstract manual-style description at all but in such things as the following passage from the *Iliad* i. 141–4, where the abstract description is embedded in a narrative presenting specific commands for human action or accounts of specific acts:

> As for now a black ship let us draw to the great salt sea
> And therein oarsmen let us advisedly gather and thereupon a hecatomb
> Let us set and upon the deck Chryseis of fair cheeks
> Let us embark. And one man as captain, a man of counsel, there must be.

(quoted in Havelock 1963, p. 81; see also ibid., pp. 174–5). Primary oral culture is little concerned with preserving knowledge of skills as an abstract, self-subsistent corpus.

(vi) Agonistically Toned

Many, if not all, oral or residually oral cultures strike literates as extraordinarily agonistic in their verbal performance and indeed in their lifestyle. Writing fosters abstractions that disengage knowledge from the arena where human beings struggle with one another. It separates the knower from the known. By keeping knowledge embedded in the human lifeworld, orality situates knowledge within a context of struggle. Proverbs and riddles are not used simply to store knowledge but to engage others in verbal and intellectual combat: utterance of one proverb or riddle challenges hearers to top it with a more apposite or a contradictory one (Abrahams 1968; 1972). Bragging about one's own prowess and/or verbal tongue-lashings of an opponent figure regularly in encounters between characters in narrative: in the *Iliad*, in *Beowulf,* throughout medieval European romance, in *The Mwindo Epic* and countless other African stories (Okpewho 1979; Obiechina 1975), in the Bible, as between David and Goliath (1 Samuel 17:43–7). Standard in oral societies across the world, reciprocal name-calling has been fitted with a specific name in linguistics: flyting (or fliting). Growing up in a still dominantly oral culture, certain young black males in the United States, the Caribbean, and elsewhere, engage in what is known variously as the "dozens" or "joning" or "sounding" or by other names, in which one opponent tries to outdo the other in vilifying the other's mother. The dozens is not a real fight but an art form, as are the other stylized verbal tongue lashings in other cultures.

Not only in the use to which knowledge is put, but also in the celebration of physical behavior, oral cultures reveal themselves as agonistically programmed. Enthusiastic description of physical violence often marks oral narrative. In the *Iliad,* for example, Books viii and x would at least rival the most sensational television and cinema shows today in outright violence and far surpass them in exquisitely gory detail, which can be less revulsive when described verbally than when presented visually. Portrayal of gross physical violence, central to much oral epic and other oral genres and residual through much early literacy, gradually wanes or becomes peripheral in later literary narrative. It survives in medieval ballads but is already being spoofed by Thomas Nashe in *The Unfortunate Traveler* (1594). As literary narrative moves toward the serious novel, it eventually pulls the focus of action more and more to interior crises and away from purely exterior crises.

The common and persistent physical hardships of life in many early societies of course explain in part the high evidence of violence in early verbal art forms. Ignorance of physical causes of disease and disaster can also foster personal tensions. Since the disease or disaster is caused by something, in lieu of physical causes the personal malevolence of another human being—a magician, a witch—can be assumed and personal hostilities thereby increased. But violence in oral art forms is also connected with the structure of orality itself. When all verbal communication must be by direct word of mouth, involved in the give-and-take dynamics of sound, interpersonal relations are kept high—both attractions and, even more, antagonisms.

The other side of agonistic name-calling or vituperation in oral or residually oral cultures is the fulsome expression of praise which is found everywhere in connection with orality. It is well known in the much-studied present-day African oral praise poems (Finnegan 1970; Opland 1975) as all through the residually oral western rhetorical tradition stretching from classical antiquity through the eighteenth century. "I come to bury Caesar, not to praise him," Marcus Antonius cries in his funeral oration in Shakespeare's *Julius Caesar* (v. ii. 79), and then proceeds to praise Caesar in rhetorical patterns of encomium which were drilled into the heads of all Renaissance schoolboys and which Erasmus used so wittily in his *Praise of Folly*. The fulsome praise in the old, residually oral, rhetoric tradition strikes persons from a high-literacy culture as insincere, flatulent, and comically pretentious. But praise goes with the highly polarized, agonistic, oral world of good and evil, virtue and vice, villains and heroes.

The agonistic dynamics of oral thought processes and expression have been central to the development of western culture, where they were institutionalized by the "art" of rhetoric, and by the related dialectic of Socrates and Plato, which furnished agonistic oral verbalization with a scientific base worked out with the help of writing. More will be said about this later.

(vii) Empathetic and Participatory Rather Than Objectively Distanced

For an oral culture learning or knowing means achieving close, empathetic, communal identification with the known (Havelock 1963, pp. 145–6), "getting with it." Writing separates the knower from the known and thus sets up conditions for "objectivity," in the sense of personal disengagement or distancing. The "objectivity" which Homer and other oral performers do have is that enforced by formulaic expression: the individual's reaction is not expressed as simply individual or "subjective" but rather as encased in the communal reaction, the communal "soul." Under the influence of writing, despite his protest against it, Plato had rejected the poets from his Republic, for studying them was essentially learning to react with "soul," to feel oneself identified with Achilles or Odysseus (Havelock 1963, pp. 197–233). Treating another primary oral setting over two thousand years later, the editors of *The Mwindo Epic* (1971, p. 37) call attention to a similar strong identification of Candi Rureke, the performer of the epic, and through him of his listeners, with the hero Mwindo, an identification which actually affects the grammar of the narration, so that on occasion the narrator slips into the first person when describing the actions of the hero. So bound together are narrator, audience, and character that Rureke has the epic character Mwindo himself address the scribes taking down Rureke's performance: "Scribe, march!" or "O scribe you, you see that I am already going." In the sensibility of the narrator and his audience the hero of the oral performance assimilates into the oral world even the transcribers who are de-oralizing it into text.

(viii) Homeostatic

By contrast with literate societies, oral societies can be characterized as homeostatic (Goody and Watt 1968, pp. 31–4). That is to say, oral societies live very much in a present which keeps itself in equilibrium or homeostasis by sloughing off memories which no longer have present relevance.

The forces governing homeostasis can be sensed by reflection on the condition of words in a primary oral setting. Print cultures have invented dictionaries in which the various meanings of a word as it occurs in datable texts can be recorded in formal definitions. Words thus are known to have layers of meaning, many of them quite irrelevant to ordinary present meanings. Dictionaries advertise semantic discrepancies.

Oral cultures of course have no dictionaries and few semantic discrepancies. The meaning of each word is controlled by what Goody and Watt (1968, p. 29) call "direct semantic ratification," that is, by the real-life situations in which the word is used here and now. The oral mind is uninterested in definitions (Luria 1976, pp. 48–99). Words acquire their meanings only from their always insistent actual habitat, which is not, as in a dictionary, simply other words, but includes also gestures, vocal inflections, facial expression, and the entire human, existential setting in which the real, spoken word always occurs. Word meanings come continuously out of the present, though past meanings of course have shaped the present meaning in many and varied ways, no longer recognized.

It is true that oral art forms, such as epic, retain some words in archaic forms and senses. But they retain such words, too, through current use—not the current use of ordinary village discourse but the current use of ordinary epic poets, who preserve archaic forms in their special vocabulary. These performances are part of ordinary social life and so the archaic forms are current, though limited to poetic activity. Memory of the old meaning of old terms thus has some durability, but not unlimited durability.

When generations pass and the object or institution referred to by the archaic word is no longer part of present, lived experience, though the word has been retained, its meaning is commonly altered or simply vanishes. African talking drums, as used for example among the Lokele in eastern Zaire, speak in elaborate formulas that preserve certain archaic words which the Lokele drummers can vocalize but whose meaning they no longer know (Carrington 1974, pp. 41–2; Ong 1977, pp. 94–5). Whatever these words referred to has dropped out of Lokele daily experience, and the term that remains has become empty. Rhymes and games transmitted orally from one generation of small children to the next even in high-technology culture have similar words which have lost their original referential meanings and are in effect nonsense syllables. Many instances of such survival of empty terms can be found in Opie and Opie (1952), who, as literates, of course manage to recover and report the original meanings of the terms lost to their present oral users.

Goody and Watt (1968, pp. 31–3) cite Laura Bohannan, Emrys Peters, and Godfrey and Monica Wilson for striking instances of the homeostasis of oral cultures in the handing on of genealogies. In recent years among the Tiv people of Nigeria the genealogies actually used orally in settling court disputes have been found to diverge considerably from the genealogies carefully recorded in writing by the British forty years earlier (because of their importance then, too, in court disputes). The later Tiv have maintained that they were using the same genealogies as forty years earlier and that the earlier written record was wrong. What had happened was that the later genealogies had been adjusted to the changed social relations among the Tiv: they were the same in that they functioned in the same way to regulate the real world. The integrity of the past was subordinate to the integrity of the present.

Goody and Watt (1968, p. 33) report an even more strikingly detailed case of "structural amnesia" among the Gonja in Ghana. Written records made by the British at the turn of the twentieth century show that Gonja oral tradition then presented Ndewura Jakpa, the founder of the state of Gonja, as having had seven sons, each of whom was ruler of one of the seven territorial divisions of the state. By the time sixty years later when the myths of state were again recorded, two of the seven divisions had disappeared, one by assimilation to another division and the other by reason of a boundary shift. In these later myths, Ndewura Jakpa had five sons, and no mention was made of the two extinct divisions. The Gonja were still in contact with their past, tenacious about this contact in their myths, but the part of the past with no immediately discernible relevance to the present had simply fallen away. The present imposed its own economy on past remembrances. Packard (1980, p. 157) has noted that Claude Lévi-Strauss, T. O. Beidelman, Edmund Leach and others have suggested that oral traditions reflect a society's present cultural values rather than idle curiosity about the past. He finds this is true of the Bashu, as Harms (1980, p. 178) finds it also true of the Bobangi.

The implications here for oral genealogies need to be noted. A West African griot or other oral genealogist will recite those genealogies which his hearers listen to. If he knows genealogies which are no longer called for, they drop from his repertoire and eventually disappear. The genealogies of political winners are of course more likely to survive than those of losers. Henige (1980, p. 255), reporting on Ganda and Myoro kinglists, notes that the "oral mode . . . allows for inconvenient parts of the past to be forgotten" because of "the exigencies of the continuing present." Moreover, skilled oral narrators deliberately vary their traditional narratives because part of their skill is their ability to adjust to new audiences and new situations or simply to be coquettish. A West African griot employed by a princely family (Okpewho 1979, pp. 25–6, 247, n. 33; p. 248, n. 36) will adjust his recitation to compliment his employers. Oral cultures encourage triumphalism, which in modern times has regularly tended somewhat to disappear as once-oral societies become more and more literate.

(ix) Situational Rather Than Abstract

All conceptual thinking is to a degree abstract. So "concrete" a term as "tree" does not refer simply to a singular "concrete" tree but is an abstraction, drawn out of, away from, individual, sensible actuality; it refers to a concept which is neither this tree nor that tree but can apply to any tree. Each individual object that we style a tree is truly "concrete," simply itself, not "abstract" at all, but the term we apply to the individual object is in itself abstract. Nevertheless, if all conceptual thinking is thus to some degree abstract, some uses of concepts are more abstract than other uses.

Oral cultures tend to use concepts in situational, operational frames of reference that are minimally abstract in the sense that they remain close to the living human lifeworld. There is a considerable literature bearing on this phenomenon. Havelock (1978) has shown that pre-Socratic Greeks thought of justice in operational rather than formally conceptualized ways and the late Anne Amory Parry (1973) made much the same point about the epithet *amymōn* applied by Homer to Aegisthus: the epithet means not "blameless," a tidy abstraction with which literates have translated the term, but "beautiful-in-the-way-a-warrior-ready-to-fight-is-beautiful."

The Interiority of Sound

In treating some psychodynamics of orality, we have thus far attended chiefly to one characteristic of sound itself, its evanescence, its relationship to time. Sound exists only when it is going out of existence. Other characteristics of sound also determine or influence oral psychodynamics. The principal one of these other characteristics is the unique relationship of sound to interiority when sound is compared to the rest of the senses. This relationship is important because of the interiority of human consciousness and of human communication itself. It can be discussed only summarily here. I have treated the matter in greater fullness and depth in *The Presence of the Word*, to which the interested reader is referred (1967).

To test the physical interior of an object as interior, no sense works so directly as sound. The human sense of sight is adapted best to light diffusely reflected from surfaces. (Diffuse reflection, as from a printed page or a landscape, contrasts with specular reflection, as from a mirror.) A source of light, such as a fire, may be intriguing but it is optically baffling: the eye cannot get a "fix" on anything within the fire. Similarly, a translucent object, such as alabaster, is intriguing because, although it is not a source of light, the eye cannot get a "fix" on it either. Depth can be perceived by the eye, but most satisfactorily as a series of surfaces: the trunks of trees in a grove, for example, or chairs in an auditorium. The eye does not perceive an interior strictly as an interior: inside a room, the walls it perceives are still surfaces, outsides.

Taste and smell are not much help in registering interiority or exteriority. Touch is. But touch partially destroys interiority in the process of perceiving it. If I wish to discover by touch whether a box is empty or full, I have to make a hole in the box to insert a hand or finger: this means that the box is to that extent open, to that extent less an interior.

Hearing can register interiority without violating it. I can rap a box to find whether it is empty or full or a wall to find whether it is hollow or solid inside. Or I can ring a coin to learn whether it is silver or lead.

Sounds all register the interior structures of whatever it is that produces them. A violin filled with concrete will not sound like a normal violin. A saxophone sounds differently from a flute: it is structured differently inside. And above all, the human voice comes from inside the human organism which provides the voice's resonances.

Sight isolates, sound incorporates. Whereas sight situates the observer outside what he views, at a distance, sound pours into the hearer. Vision dissects, as Merleau-Ponty has observed (1961). Vision comes to a human being from one direction at a time: to look at a room or a landscape, I must move my eyes around from one part to another. When I hear, however, I gather sound simultaneously from every direction at once: I am at the center of my auditory world, which envelopes me, establishing me at a kind of core of sensation and existence. This centering effect of sound is what high-fidelity sound reproduction exploits with intense sophistication. You can immerse yourself in hearing, in sound. There is no way to immerse yourself similarly in sight.

By contrast with vision, the dissecting sense, sound is thus a unifying sense. A typical visual ideal is clarity and distinctness, a taking apart (Descartes' campaigning for clarity and distinctness registered an intensification of vision in the human sensorium—Ong 1967, pp. 63, 221). The auditory ideal, by contrast, is harmony, a putting together.

Interiority and harmony are characteristics of human consciousness. The consciousness of each human person is totally interiorized, known to the person from the inside and inaccessible to any other person directly from the inside. Everyone who says "I" means something different by it from what every other person means. What is "I" to me is only "you" to you. And this "I" incorporates experience into itself by "getting it all together." Knowledge is ultimately not a fractioning but a unifying phenomenon, a striving for harmony. Without harmony, an interior condition, the psyche is in bad health.

It should be noted that the concepts interior and exterior are not mathematical concepts and cannot be differentiated mathematically. They are existentially grounded concepts, based on experience of one's own body, which is both inside me (I do not ask you to stop kicking my body but to stop kicking *me*) and outside me (I feel myself as in some sense inside my body). The body is a frontier between myself and everything else. What we mean by "interior" and "exterior" can be conveyed only by reference to experience of bodiliness. Attempted definitions of "interior" and "exterior" are inevitably tautological: "interior" is defined by "in," which is defined by "between," which is defined by "inside," and so on round and round the tautological circle. The same is true with "exterior." When we speak of interior and exterior, even in the case of physical objects, we are referring to our own sense of ourselves: I am *inside* here and everything else is *outside*. By interior and exterior we point to our own experience of bodiliness (Ong 1967, pp. 117–22, 176–9, 228, 231) and analyze other objects by reference to this experience.

In a primary oral culture, where the word has its existence only in sound, with no reference whatsoever to any visually perceptible text, and no awareness of even the possibility of such a text, the phenomenology of sound enters deeply into human beings' feel for existence, as processed by the spoken word. For the way in which the word is experienced is always momentous in psychic life. The centering action of sound (the field of sound is not spread out before me but is all around me) affects man's sense of the cosmos. For oral cultures, the cosmos is an ongoing event with man at its center. Man is the *umbilicus mundi,* the navel of the world (Eliade 1958, pp. 231–5, etc.). Only after print and the extensive experience with maps that print implemented would human beings, when they thought about the cosmos or universe or "world," think primarily of something laid out before their eyes, as in a modern printed atlas, a vast surface or assemblage of surfaces (vision presents surfaces) ready to be "explored." The ancient oral world knew few "explorers," though it did know many itinerants, travelers, voyagers, adventurers, and pilgrims.

It will be seen that most of the characteristics of orally based thought and expression discussed earlier in this chapter relate intimately to the unifying, centralizing, interiorizing economy of sound as perceived by human beings. A sound-dominated verbal economy is consonant with aggregative (harmonizing) tendencies rather than with analytic, dissecting tendencies (which would come with the inscribed, visualized word: vision is a dissecting sense). It is consonant also with the conservative holism (the homeostatic present that must be kept intact, the formulary expressions that must be kept intact), with situational thinking (again holistic, with human action at the center) rather than abstract thinking, with a certain humanistic organization of knowledge around the actions of human and anthromorphic beings, interiorized persons, rather than around impersonal things.

The denominators used here to describe the primary oral world will be useful again later to describe what happened to human consciousness when writing and print reduced the oral–aural world to a world of visualized pages.

3.
Implications of Literacy in Traditional China and India

Kathleen Gough

In order to test and expand the hypotheses put forward by Goody and Watt it is necessary to have accounts of the uses of literacy in a wide range of societies. In what follows I shall discuss their suggestions at a very general level in the light of comparisons with India and China.

"Widespread" Literacy

An initial difficulty arises over the meaning of "widespread literacy." Was literacy more widespread in sixth-century Ionia or fifth-century Attica than, for example, in the heartlands of the Maurya or Gupta empires or in Han or Sung China? Granted that the majority of Greek citizens of the fifth century B.C. constituted a book-reading public, it is uncertain how widespread literacy was among non-citizens. McNeill, quoting Beloch and Gomme, concludes that "adult male citizens in Athens probably numbered between 35,000 and 50,000 on the eve of the Peloponnesian War, and the total population of Attica was probably between 250,000 and 350,000, of which somewhat less than half were slaves and disfranchised foreigners."[1] With a majority of women in classical Greece illiterate, it is possible that Gupta India of the fourth and fifth centuries A.D., or even the central region of the Maurya empire (fourth and third centuries B.C.), had almost as high a percentage of literate people, at least in the areas round their capitals.

In these empires, as in later, medieval India, literacy appears to have been universal among men of the two upper classes of society, the Brahmans (priests, lawgivers and scholars) and the Kshattriyas (rulers and military). Literacy was probably widespread, also, among the middle-ranking Vaishyas (traders, craftsmen and some of the peasantry), for early inscriptions record donations by wealthy merchants and craftsmen to religious causes. It was, moreover, the trading classes who favoured Buddhism and Jainism, with their rejection of Vēdic literature and rites and their promulgation of vernacular sacred writings. These three upper classes, the "twice-born," certainly had legal access to most of the writings of Hinduism, Jainism and Buddhism if they cared to make use of them.

The fourth class, of Sūdras or manual labourers, ranked much lower. They formed an "unclean," largely servile category, forbidden by law to amass wealth or to hear or recite the Sanskrit Vēdas. It seems probable that the Sūdras, together with the still lower-ranking Untouchables or exterior castes, were largely illiterate in ancient as in medieval north India. Even so, some Sūdras in ancient north India did acquire wealth and, although they were forbidden to study the Vēdas, there was no prohibition on their studying the later epics and *purānas* or reading the devotional vernacular literature of post-Mauryan times. In south India, again, the early Tamil kingdoms of the first to fourth centuries honoured poets from the Sūdra and even the Untouchable castes, as did the later Tamil kingdom of Chōla in the tenth to twelfth centuries (Basham 1954: 142–4; Sāstri 1955: 132).

While quantitative estimates are hazardous, it is possible that up to half of the men, and perhaps one-fifth or one-sixth of the women, were literate in the periods of greatest prosperity and brilliance of both the north and south Indian irrigation-based empires. The percentages may have been even higher in the small kingdoms of Kērala, based on rainfall agriculture and overseas commerce, in the sixteenth to eighteenth centuries.

As in Greece, writing in India was rapid and materials easily available, the most common being processed leaves of the talipot and palmyra palms. Birch-bark, sized cotton, silk, and thin slips of bamboo or wood were also used locally. Ink was applied with a reed pen in northern and central India. In the south, the letters were scratched with a stylus and the leaf then rubbed with powdered lamp-black (Basham 1954: 194, 198–9; Sāstri 1955: 132).

A similar level of literacy may have characterized the periods of high culture in China after the introduction of brush-writing and the standardization and simplification of letters in the Ch'in empire of the third century B.C. Needham notes that Han China of about 145 B.C. provided for the education of at least some peasants in local schools, to a level below that required of scholars intended for the bureaucracy. Hundreds of books written on wood, bamboo tablets, silk and paper were stored in libraries, and by 145 B.C. university chairs were established for each of the major divisions of learning. The peak of pre-modern Chinese learning was apparently reached in the Sung period of the tenth to thirteenth centuries A.D. Printing was widespread by A.D. 980, and a rapid form of cursive writing, comparable in speed to shorthand, was known by the tenth century and practised by Chinese scholars as far afield as Baghdad (Needham 1954: I, 101–2, 111, 219).

While the evidence of literacy rates is extremely unsatisfactory, we must, I think, place both the Indian and Chinese high civilizations, along with the Greek, in Parsons' category of "advanced intermediate" societies. As such, they contrast with Parsons' "archaic" societies, possessing an esoteric craft literacy confined to small, highly specialized groups, usually of religiosi or magical practitioners (Parsons 1966: 51).

Parsons defines advanced intermediate cultures as those having full literacy for adult males of an upper class. Such societies usually organize their cultures around a set of sacred writings, knowledge of which is expected of all educated men. He argues that only modern industrial societies institutionalize literacy for a majority of both men and women. It could perhaps be argued that fifth- and fourth-century Greece had a higher proportion of literacy than any other pre-modern society. Lacking adequate evidence, however, I am obliged to class the high cultures of India and China along with that of Greece on grounds of qualitative criteria such as the existence of universities, libraries, public inscriptions and village schools. More precise research may, however, reveal quantitative differences in literacy which are in fact crucial for some of the cultural differences to be discussed.

The Alphabet

Assuming that Greek, Indian and Chinese societies were all "advanced intermediate" with *relatively* widespread literacy, we come next to the question of the alphabet. The most salient fact is, of course, that although alphabetic writing has been known to the Chinese since the second century A.D., they have refused to accept it right up to the present time. The Chinese presumably rejected the alphabet because, by the time it was presented to them, their own more cumbersome script—a combination of ideographic and rebus symbols— had, over centuries, become the medium for a large body of literature, as well as being intertwined with religious institutions and accepted as the hallmark of the educated gentry.[2]

Chinese retention of predominantly ideographic writing seems to undercut some of the claims made for the alphabet by Goody and Watt. First, as I have argued, it is possible that literacy may have been almost as widespread in some periods of traditional China as was alphabetic writing in classical Greece. Second, this is certainly the case today. Universal literacy is an immediate goal in China, yet the Communist government, although it has devised a simplified script, has not instituted the alphabet. Widespread literacy does not, therefore, require the alphabet, although there can be little doubt that an alphabet, coupled with easily used writing instruments, greatly facilitates literacy. The fact that alphabetic writing, invented and permanently accepted only once in history, eventually spread from Phoenicia throughout the literate world with the exception of the extreme Far East, suggests that alphabetic writing has usually prevailed over ideographic because of its greater simplicity and analytic utility. The Chinese exception indicates, however, that ideographic writing *can* yield widespread literacy, and has done so where it was already deeply engrained before the advent of the alphabet.

It should perhaps be mentioned that the various Indian scripts are also not alphabetic in the strictest sense of the term, but semi-syllabic, a trait attributable to their direct Semitic origin (Kroeber 1948: 532). Only initial vowels have special characters, and the characters for consonants carry the vowel *a* unless a special diacritical sign is used to remove it. Where two consonants precede a vowel, they are condensed into a single character. Vowel sounds other than *a* are represented by a variety of diacritical marks attached to the character for the preceding consonant. Most Hindu scripts are distinguishable from Semitic in having twice as many letters, new symbols having been devised not only for compound consonants but for sounds which occur in Indian and not in Semitic languages. Thus Sanskrit has forty-eight letters; Malayālam, the Dravidian language of Kērala, fifty-three.

The letters of Indian scripts are arranged in a phonetic and logical order, in which groups of sounds formed against the back and front palates, gums, teeth and lips, follow each other in sequences. Kroeber regards this arrangement as evidence that phonetics and grammar had developed into sciences in India before writing was introduced (Kroeber 1948: 533). Apart from the early, undeciphered Indus script, it is true that no known Indian inscriptions date from before the mid-third century B.C. Basham, however, thinks it possible that writing was introduced from Mesopotamia by merchants in the Aryan period before 600 B.C. (Basham 1954: 43). Kosambi believes writing was introduced by 700 B.C. in view of the evidence of urban routines, trade, and accurately weighed silver coinage by that date (Kosambi 1966: 88). I am unable to judge whether or how the semi-syllabic character of Indian writing, or its probable introduction by merchants and early rejection by the priesthood, may have influenced Indian modes of thought. Certainly, the Brahmans, like Plato, have always regarded written transmission of knowledge as inferior to oral. The orthodox maintain this attitude to the present day. It is for this reason that, in spite of the vast bulk of Hindu religious literature, the Vēdas themselves are still transmitted and memorized orally in villages—often, it must be noted, with very little understanding of their meaning. Indeed, they are not known to have been regularly written down or systematically edited before the second half of the fourteenth century (Kosambi 1966: 78).

I turn now briefly to the implications of literacy for modes of thought, as discussed by Goody and Watt. The remarks that follow are tentative, both because of the imprecision of some of the concepts and, even more, my limited knowledge of Indian and Chinese literatures. A beginning may, however, be attempted.

The Distinction Between Myth and History

India is noted for its dearth of historical records. It can probably be said that myth and history scarcely diverged before the Muslim period. The reason most commonly given is the theocratic character of Hindu society in most periods and the supremacy of the Brahmans. In Buddhism and Jainism too, although Brahman supremacy and the belief in gods were rejected, the material world continued to be denigrated or even seen as unreal. The search for truth continued to mean primarily spiritual truth to be found through meditation and right living. In such a society, where the highest aim of the dominant literacy class was to lift its eyes from both the natural and social worlds towards other-worldly realities, it is perhaps not surprising that historiography failed to develop.

In China, by contrast, a this-worldly approach emphasizing profound interest in correct social relations was fostered by secular monarchs and bureaucracies of literati. Perhaps because of this, reliable historical research and exact chronological records appeared by the time of the first major empire (Han). According to McNeill, "the very bulk of surviving materials complicates the task of ascertaining the main lines of Chinese development, while giving (Chinese) political history an unrivalled precision" (1962: 304–5). Needham concludes that "the Chinese have one of the greatest historiographical traditions in the world" (1954: I, 74).

Lineal Conceptions of Time

Like all literate peoples, the Indians and Chinese had several conceptions of time, utilized in different intellectual contexts and by different social strata or occupational groups. In many contexts in both societies, especially among the common people, significant events were thought of as occurring cyclically, without precise measurement or chronology. This view of time applies of course to the succession of night and day, the light and dark halves of the moon, the annual seasons, the female menstrual cycle, and both the lunar and solar years. The Indians elaborated it to describe the four ages of human life and also the cycles of rebirth through which souls, both animal and human, were believed to pass.

Both Indians and Chinese thought of the universe, too, as existing in cyclical time, in contrast, for example, to the Hebrew view of time as a linear passage from the creation to the end of the world. The Hindus saw the universe as passing through cycles *(kalpas)*, each divided into fourteen secondary cycles *(manvantaras)* of 306,720,000 years. Each secondary cycle comprised seventy *mahāyugas* (aeons) and each *mahāyuga*, four *yugas*. Chaos supervened at the end of each *mahāyuga*, with the earth destroyed by flood or fire. The whole universe was thought to be eclipsed and recontained within the body of Brahma, the creator, at intervals within each *kalpa*. The Buddhists took a similar scheme of *kalpas* to China, together with a characteristically Indian view of the infinity of space and time, the plurality of worlds, and vast distances, comparable to light years, existing between the worlds. The Neo-Confucians of the Sung period also believed in time cycles, each terminated by chaos and each composed of a dozen ages.

As Leach points out (1958: I, 116), cyclical conceptions of time are in general characteristically primitive, since they do not require records or the notion of chronology. In the cycles of ages, however, the Indian and Chinese literati elaborated these primitive concepts through calculations of vast numbers. Since these numbers did not refer to empirical events they constituted a pseudo-scientific, "magical numerology." But they did set forth a view of the universe similar to the modern one in its stress on the magnitude of distances between planets and the infinity of time and space. Such conceptions of what Leach calls "magical time" are evidently widespread in early literate societies, the Babylonian and Mayan systems being comparable examples.

As might be expected from their greater concern with history, the Chinese had a stronger sense of chronology and thus of "linear time" than did the Indians. They were interested both in recording the correct chronological sequences of events, especially political events (what Leach calls "historical time") and also in accurately measuring the sequences in ten-year and sixty-year periods. Thus, although the Chinese, like the Indians, referred to events in terms of dynasties, their chronology of major events is judged accurate by modern historians back to 900 B.C., and is carried back with less certainty to 2,000 B.C., whereas Indian dynasties and major events can be dated only tentatively before the Muslim period. Both Indians and Chinese developed a number of calendars dating back to the beginning of particular dynasties, some of them of short duration. Both, of course, developed methods of measuring short divisions of the day through sundials, hour-glasses, etc., but the Chinese elaboration of water clocks and clockwork seems to show a greater concern with exact measurement of small units of time than was found in India.

In both countries, astronomy early became established as a science. Western classical astronomy influenced both countries, especially India, but both made advances on Greek astronomy as a result of their improvements in mathematics. The invention of the zero in India by the fifth or sixth century A.D., and its rapid transmission to China, was of course crucial in this respect and ideally requires a separate treatment in any discussion of the effects of systems of writing. It seems probable to me, indeed, that the presence or absence of the zero may be of greater significance for the development of several kinds of knowledge (astronomy, algebra, arithmetic and, ultimately, of course, the whole of modern experimental science) than is the distinction between ideographic and alphabetic writing. The subject is, however, too complex to be undertaken here.

As in ancient Greece, and in Europe generally until the seventeenth century, astronomy in both China and India remained bound up with astrology, as part of a belief in what Leach calls "magical time" (1958: I, 116). The movement of the heavenly bodies being believed to be co-ordinated with the fortunes of men, specialists made calculations from the planets to predict and guide actions both in the state and in the lives of individuals. Auspicious times had to be fixed for marriages, journeys, and other important undertakings, and portions of the day were regarded as favourable or unfavourable for particular activities.

Summing up, both India and China fit Goody and Watt's theories that societies with widespread literacy have some interest in exact time sequences and time-keeping devices, and some development of a linear concept of time. But cyclical and magical conceptions of time were also prominent in both countries, and in India, as contrasted with China, interest in the chronology of societal events was extraordinarily weakly developed.

Objective Descriptions of Space

Maps were prevalent in China from the third century B.C. Scientific cartography began with Phei Hsiu (A.D. 224–71), whose work has been compared with that of Ptolemy. The science developed in the Sung period, especially with the eleventh-century invention of the magnetic compass. By the fourteenth century Chinese maps were superior to European and comparable in accuracy to those of the Arabs (Needham 1954: III, 556). Chinese sailing charts were also highly developed, especially from the fifteenth century, with the scientific exploration of the South Seas and the Indian Ocean.

By contrast, Indian geography and cartography are poorly developed in the extant literature, although pilgrims, military conquerors, seamen and merchants must have had a sound practical knowledge of India and the neighbouring regions. Religious cosmography and geography dominated the scene, although a small élite of Indian scientists recognized that the earth was spherical, and Brahmagupta (seventh century A.D.) gave its circumference with fair accuracy (Basham 1954: 488). In China, religious cosmography seems to have been confined to Buddhism and Taoism and to have been overshadowed by scientific cosmography and geography from early times (Needham 1954: III, 566). Both civilizations developed exact land records, and Indian astronomers, like Chinese, had a fairly accurate knowledge of the longitudes of important places in their own country. The scientific exploration and recording of space, like that of time, was evidently more advanced in pre-modern China than in India.

The Sceptical Questioning of Traditions and the Conscious Search for Objective Truth

Forms of scepticism and of reverence for tradition vary, so that it is difficult to assess this criterion. I would judge India to have been more tradition-bound and less sceptical than China, but both civilizations incorporated both attitudes. Orthodox Brahmanical Hinduism placed the greatest possible emphasis on the sacredness of oral traditions, on other-worldly preoccupations and on the observance of traditional ritual and custom. Hence, probably, the weak development of geography, experimental physics and chemistry, as well as the comparative lack of interest in chronologies of social events. On the other hand, Indian medicine and surgery surpassed those of the Greeks in some respects, developing through the Hindu interest in yogic exercises and the Buddhist concern with charity hospitals. The science of bureaucratic politics also had at least one famous expression in the *Arthasāstra* of Kautilya, supposedly a Brahman adviser of Chandragupta, India's earliest great emperor, of the fourth century B.C. Indians also went far in mathematics, phonetics, grammar, astronomy and other knowledge concerned with non-textual experience. Some schools of philosophical sceptics, in both Hinduism and Buddhism, questioned the existence not only of God but of the material universe itself. Those who chose mysticism as the path to salvation have also usually denied the validity of ritual and myth. Indian science was not, however, systematically experimental until modern times.

With its emphasis on secular and social learning, Chinese scepticism entered more pervasively into scientific history and geography, attacks on myth and on traditional knowledge, and the recording and comparison of physical and social events. Wang Chhung, philosopher-scientist of the first century, systematically questioned much of the received knowledge of his time, including beliefs in ghosts and immortality, the anthropocentrism of nature, and the connection between ethical and cosmic irregularities. After Wang Chhung the sceptical rationalist tradition became incorporated into much of Confucian thought, and persistently combated both old superstitions and the new ones that appeared with the rise of Buddhism. Needham argues that traditional Chinese scepticism found its fullest development in humanistic studies, textual criticism and archaeology (1954: II, 390). China also outstripped other cultures at various periods in some branches of natural science, especially magnetic science, botany, zoology and pharmaceutics. Medieval Chinese science, in fact, contributed much that was essential to the groundwork of modern European science. Natural science in the Ming period was impeded from flowering to the extent that it did in Europe because of the Chinese failure to mathematize scientific hypotheses and to test them by experiment. Needham holds that the Chinese social structure, with its weaker development of overseas commercialism and its stricter separation of functions between mental and practical workers, was responsible for the failure to develop modern natural science. The same would be even truer of India, but there the scholarly élite was unconcerned not only with practical applications of most knowledge but also with the actual exploration of many facets of the material and social worlds.

Branches of Knowledge

The development of scientific logic came early in both India and China, supporting Goody and Watt's theory that writing (although not necessarily alphabetic writing) encourages sequential thought and the development of syllogisms. Both cultures divided knowledge into autonomous cognitive disciplines similar to those established by the Greeks, although, as we have seen, they emphasized and excelled in different fields. There was clear recognition of a world of knowledge transcending political units—especially in India, where empires were smaller and of shorter duration than in China. The question of the separation of natural and divine worlds, and of theology and science, is difficult in that early Buddhism, Confucianism and Taoism, as well as some schools of Hinduism, were in theory atheistic. If we shift the question to one of the extent of separation of the supernatural and the natural worlds, and of their study, this separation seems to have occurred, but to have been less complete in India and China than in modern Europe. Both in India and in China there were philosophers and scientists who disregarded or ridiculed the "knowledge" of religious specialists when it contradicted their own researches. On the other hand, such pseudo-sciences as alchemy, astrology and other forms of divination had an honourable place in the world of learning and appear to have been regarded by most scholars as inseparable from their cognate sciences such as chemistry and astronomy. I would question, in fact, whether the separation between supernatural and natural science has been as thoroughgoing anywhere in the past as it became in modern Europe with the application of mathematics to experimental science.

Social and Psychological Effects of Widespread Literacy

Substantially widespread literacy has not produced or been accompanied by "democracy as we know it" in either China or India, with the possible exception of India since 1947. The concept seems too vague to test in its present form, although it may eventually be possible to relate specific uses of literacy to specific forms of the state. It does seem improbable that centralized states containing more than about a million people can exist, or can hold together easily, without some use of writing for political administration. Beyond this it is hard to generalize directly from literacy to political structure. Pre-modern states with substantial literacy have included aristocratic, oligopolistic and democratic city-states, feudal regimes, and bureaucratic despotisms of the "Oriental" type. Modern mass society includes both fascism and parliamentary democracy, as well as military regimes with varying popularity, in the capitalist bloc, and both highly bureaucratic centralism and more decentralized forms of popular participation in the communist world. There is little doubt that both the Maurya and the Han empires offered less popular participation in government than did sixth- and early fifth-century Athens. It seems doubtful, however, whether this difference can be ascribed to differences in literacy rates, for Athens' overseas expansion from about the mid-fifth century was accompanied by the growth of marked wealth differences and a more authoritarian political system. As Kosambi points out, moreover, a simple contrast between the ideals of the *Arthasāstra* and Plato's *Republic* or Aristotle's *Politics* is "pretentious irrelevance," for "Aristotle's royal pupil Alexander did not put the learned Stagirite master's political ideas into action. Athenian democracy failed after a singularly brief span, for all the supposed practical wisdom of its constitution, precisely because of Plato's closest friends" (Kosambi 1966: 141). I am inclined to emphasize ecology and external political and economic relations as causal factors in the development of political systems rather than the spread of literacy. On the other hand, the distribution of literacy between social and occupational classes may well be, in large measure, a *result* of the political and economic systems. The society's values and idea system, which are themselves heavily conditioned (although not, I think, entirely determined) by its current technology and social structure, may also act back to some extent to shape political forms and the uses of literacy.

Thus, it can be argued that ancient Athens developed political democracy mainly because of its small size coupled with the industrial and commercial character of its economy—indeed, its incipient capitalism (Polanyi 1957: 64–96); whereas China and India developed their centralized bureaucratic empires on the basis of their agrarian irrigation economies. There was, however, in all these societies a particular kind of "set" to the idea system, which may itself have been determined in large measure both by past history and by the character of the political economy and of men's reactions to its strictures. Thus in India, from at least the sixth century B.C., a strong strain of other-worldly asceticism made for the formation of small communities of scholarly ascetics, who went to live separately in the forests under relatively democratic forms of self-government. Such men pursued their own research into the nature of the good life independently of the main political structure, and in a sense lived above it. Later, monasteries were built for such communities of both Hindu and Buddhist ascetics, and, in course of time, in both India and China, monastic communities often acquired wealth and developed their own hierarchical administrations. But in both Hinduism and Buddhism the ideal persisted of the small community of scholars living in voluntary poverty apart from the public domain. In ancient Greece, as in early China, by contrast, scholars who were out of power or alienated from the political scene, as were Socrates, Plato and Confucius, nevertheless studied politics and society rather than other-worldly salvation, for it was unthinkable in their societies that wise men would be unconcerned with public administration (McNeill 1962: 232–66).

A measure of democratic self-government also existed *within* some other occupational classes of traditional India and China, for example some merchant and peasant communities. But such institutions are probably not attributable to widespread literacy. Among south Indian Hindus, for example, the most egalitarian and democratic caste assemblies tend to be found among the lower castes of Harijans, almost all of whom were until recently illiterate. We cannot therefore simply attribute democracy to widespread literacy, although it is perhaps difficult for large-scale representative democracies—like large-scale dictatorships or bureaucracies—to function in the absence of substantial literacy.

Similarly, it does seem probable that widespread literacy tends to be accompanied by an interest in record-keeping. This interest was strongly developed in the political sphere in both India and China. Here again, however, I would argue that literacy in itself is a necessary but not a sufficient condition. Literacy, along with high economic productivity, makes possible complex political economies, which in turn require a more or less great emphasis on record-keeping.

Again, I would not precisely agree with Goody and Watt that widespread literacy of itself necessarily produced "a vast proliferation of more or less tangible distinctions based on what people had read" (see p. 58). Nor would I agree that the development of widespread literacy necessarily produces the psychological alienation of the modern specialist. I would argue that classes, whether modern or ancient, are based primarily on division of labour and relationships to the means of production, and that differences in levels of literacy and reading habits tend to spring from these arrangements rather than giving rise to them. Further, it does not seem to be true that literate society has no system of elimination and thus no structural amnesia, as Goody and Watt argue. Many books do, after all, go out of print, and it is possible for literate societies, like primitive ones, to ignore phases of their own histories or to reinterpret their histories in the light of current concerns. Similarly, the alienation of overspecialization may be, I suspect, a feature of highly bureaucratized modern industrial states (whether socialist or capitalist) rather than pre-eminently of an overaccumulation of literature. In future, with the development of cybernation and thus of prolonged leisure periods, it may be possible to overcome much modern alienation by broadening the interests of the highly literate, breaking down the separation between mental and manual work, and creating wider areas of self-government.

At all events, psychological alienation can certainly result from other causes than literate specialization. Confucius, Buddha and Plato apparently all experienced acute alienation, but in each case this seems to have stemmed mainly from political impotence and disapproval of the goals of their own societies, rather than from the overspecialization of the scholar. In short, alienation seems to stem from particular forms of complex political and economic structures rather than intrinsically from the spread of literacy.

The individualization of experience and the liking for privacy, again, do not seem to me necessarily to characterize literate society in general, although literacy may well be a necessary precondition for a high evaluation of privacy and individualism. In both China and India, the main body of literati evidently conformed rather strictly to the mores of their class and were discouraged from unwonted expressions of individual experience. Thus Granet writes of Chinese literate society in Han times:

> Civic morality, having gravitated towards an ideal of strained politeness, seems to tend solely to organizing among men a regulated system of relations, in which the actions befitting each age are fixed by edict, as are also those for each sex, each social condition and each actual situation. Finally, in political life, where the stage is reached of advocating the principle of government by history, it appears that it is claimed as sufficient for everything to follow solely the virtues of a traditionalist conformity. (Granet 1959: 427)

Compare Basham on the Sanskrit literati of classical Hindu society:

> The poets lived in a comparatively static society, and their lives were controlled in detail by a body of social custom which was already ancient and which had the sanction of religion behind it. They were never in revolt against the social system, and Indian Shelleys and Swinburnes were lacking. Most of this literature was written by men well integrated into their society and with few of the complex psychological difficulties of the modern literary man; hence the spiritual anguish of a Cowper, the heart-searchings of a Donne, and the social pessimism of a T. S. Eliot, are almost entirely absent. (1954: 415–16)

The main exceptions to these pictures of the conforming literati were, of course, the wandering mystics. Their devotional literature, tends, however, to deal with the relationship between devotee and supreme spirit rather than with unique or intimate interpersonal relations. Neither traditional Indian nor Chinese literature contains personal diaries, although Chinese has novels and numerous biographies, and some of the Indian dramas and narrative tales depict character with realism. The dialogue was also a preferred medium in the early philosophical literature of Hinduism, Buddhism, Taoism and Confucianism, as in ancient Greece. In all these cases the dialogue seems to me, however, the medium of a society where much learning is still transmitted orally, rather than necessarily an expression of the individualized experience of a highly complex literate society.[3]

In general I would suggest that the intense individualism of modern western society is chiefly (albeit indirectly) a product of capitalism rather than intrinsically of widespread literacy. To the extent that the Greeks anticipated it, this, too, may have resulted indirectly from the commercialism and incipient capitalism of their economy and the consequently high degree of individual action and experience enjoyed by the literate community.

Conclusions

Contemporary China indicates that, although advantageous, the alphabet is not essential for widespread literacy. We cannot say whether *alphabetic* writing has particular effects: China lacks the alphabet, and India has semi-syllabic scripts. The literacy rates for traditional China and India are unknown, but both, like Greece, had substantial if not widespread literacy and are classifiable as "advanced intermediate" literate civilizations.

Widespread writing does not necessitate a clear distinction between myth and history, as India shows. It may require some degree of "linear" codification of time and of reality generally, but this is variable: cyclical conceptions of time can co-exist with linear, or even remain dominant, in quite highly literate societies. The scientific exploration of space is also widely variable as between comparably literate civilizations. So, too, is the sceptical questioning of authority. Both China and India reveal a conscious striving for objective truth which seems to spring from literacy and from the consequent emergence of scientific logic; but in India the search took primarily "inner" and mystical forms, while in China it produced an extreme interest in societal verities and in history. In neither did it turn toward the application of mathematics to experimental science. China and India both suggest that widespread literacy may automatically produce distinctions between the main branches of knowledge similar to those found in the West. They also indicate, however, that these may be developed with widely varying emphases.

Apart from some concern with record-keeping and some tendency to develop large and complex political units, societies with substantial literacy do not appear necessarily to produce particular forms of political structure. Widespread literacy may be necessary for large scale representative democracy to function easily, but it certainly does not necessarily produce democracy. As literacy develops and the number of written words increases, social classes and occupational groups are necessarily divided from each other partly on the basis of reading habits. I would not, however, regard this as a primary *source* of division between social classes, and it can apparently occur with quite variable amounts of social mobility. Widespread literacy does not necessarily, so far as I can see, produce extreme individualization, a marked need for privacy, or alienation. It is suggested that, in their modern forms, these spring more from capitalism or (in the case of alienation) from the bureaucratization and personal impotence experienced in modern industrial society, rather than intrinsically from literacy.

Writing, like other communications media, is problematic because it forms part of both the technological and the ideological heritage of complex societies, as well as being intricately involved with their social structures. Difficulties arise because it is hard to disentangle the implications of literacy from those of other techniques (for example, plough agriculture, settled cultivation, rapid transport or power industries), or of other institutions (for example, specialized priesthoods or powerful governments) commonly found in advanced societies. Literacy appears to be, above all, an *enabling* factor, permitting large-scale organization, the critical accumulation, storage and retrieval of knowledge, the systematic use of logic, the pursuit of science and the elaboration of the arts. Whether, or with what emphases, these developments will occur seems to depend less on the intrinsic knowledge of writing than on the overall development of the society's technology and social structure, and perhaps, also, on the character of its relations with other societies. *If* they occur, however, there seems little doubt of Goody and Watt's contention that the use of writing as a dominant communications medium will impose certain broad forms on their emergence, of which syllogistic reasoning and linear codifications of reality may be examples. The partial supersession of writing by new communications media will no doubt throw into relief more and more of the specific implications of literacy.

4.
Unpackaging Literacy

Sylvia Scribner
Michael Cole

One of the important services anthropology has traditionally provided other social sciences is to challenge generalizations about human nature and the social order that are derived from studies of a single society. The comparative perspective is especially valuable when the topic of inquiry concerns psychological "consequences" of particular social practices, such as for example, different methods of child-rearing (permissive vs. restrictive) or schooling (formal vs. nonformal) or mass communication (oral vs. literate). It is a hazardous enterprise to attempt to establish causal relationships among selected aspects of social and individual function without taking into account the totality of social practice of which they are a part. How are we to determine whether effects on psychological functioning are attributable to the particular practices selected for study, or to other practices with which they covary, or to the unique patterning of practices in the given society? When we study seemingly "same" practices in different societal contexts, we can better tease apart the distinctive impact of such practices from other features of social life.

Here we apply one such comparative approach to questions about reading and writing practices and their intellectual impact. Our approach combines anthropological field work with experimental psychological methods in a study of "literacy without schooling" in a West African traditional society. We hope our findings will suggest a new perspective from which to examine propositions about the intellectual and social significance of literacy those uncertain status contributes to our educational dilemmas.

These dilemmas have been repeatedly stated. They revolve around implications for educational and social policy of reports that students' writing skills are deficient, and that there is a "writing crisis." Is this the case and if so, is it really a matter for national concern? Does it call for infusion of massive funds in new research studies and methods of instruction? Or is it merely a signal that we

From *Writing: The Nature, Development, and Teaching of Written Communication*, ed. Marcia Farr Whiteman, 1981, Hillsdale, New Jersey: Lawrence Erlbaum Associates, Inc. Copyright 1981 by Lawrence Erlbaum Associates, Inc. Reprinted by permission.

should adjust our educational goals to new "technologies of communication" which reduce the need for high levels of literacy skill? (See for example Macdonald, 1973.)

These questions call for judgments on the social importance of writing and thus raise an even more fundamental issue: on what grounds are such judgments to be made? Some advocate that pragmatic considerations should prevail and that instructional programs should concentrate on teaching only those specific writing skills that are required for the civic and occupational activities student groups may be expected to pursue. Many educators respond that such a position is too narrow and that it overlooks the most important function of writing, the impetus that writing gives to intellectual development. The argument for the general intellectual importance of writing is sometimes expressed as accepted wisdom and sometimes as knowledge revealed through psychological research. At one end of the spectrum there is the simple adage that "an individual who writes clearly thinks clearly," and at the other, conclusions purporting to rest on scientific analysis, such as the recent statement that "the cognitive restructurings caused by reading and writing develop the higher reasoning processes involved in extended abstract thinking" (Farrell, 1977, p. 451).

This is essentially a psychological proposition and one which is increasingly moving to the forefront of discussion of the "writing problem." Our research speaks to several serious limitations in developing this proposition as a ground for educational and social policy decisions. One of these is the frailty of the evidence for generalizations about the dependency of certain cognitive skills on writing, and the other is the restricted model of the writing process from which hypotheses about cognitive consequences tend to be generated. Before presenting our findings on Vai literacy, we shall briefly consider each of these in turn.

Speculations about Cognitive Consequences of Literacy

What are the sources of support for statements about intellectual consequences of literacy? In recent decades, scholars in such disciplines as philology, comparative literature and anthropology have advanced the thesis that over the course of history, literacy has produced a "great divide" in human modes of thinking. Havelock (1963) speculated that the advent of alphabetic writing systems and the spread of literacy in post-Homeric Greece changed the basic forms of human memory. Goody and Watt (1963) maintained that these same historic events laid the basis for the development of new categories of understanding and new logical operations, and in subsequent studies Goody (1977) has concluded that potentialities for graphic representation promote unique classificatory skills.

Ong's (1958) historical analyses of prose literary genres in the fifteenth century led him to conclude that the invention of the printing press gave rise to a new form of intellectual inquiry uniquely related to the printed text.

Intriguing as these speculations are, their significance for a theory of psychological consequences for *individuals* in *our* society is problematic on two counts. These scholars derive evidence for cognitive effects of literacy from historical studies of cultural and social changes associated with the advent of widespread literacy. Inferences about cognitive changes in *individuals* are shaky if they rest only on the analysis of *cultural* phenomena. The inconclusiveness of the great debate between Levy-Bruhl and Franz Boas (see Cole and Scribner, 1974) on the "logicality of primitive thought" reminds us of the limitations of reliance on cultural data as sole testimony to psychological processes. Secondly we need to distinguish between historical and contemporaneous causation (see Lewin, 1936). The development of writing systems and the production of particular kinds of text may, indeed, have laid the basis *historically* for the emergence of new modes of intellectual operation, but these over time, may have lost their connection with the written word. There is no necessary connection between the modality in which new operations come into being and the modality in which they are perpetuated and transmitted in later historical epochs. Forms of discourse initially confined to written text may subsequently come to be transmitted orally through teacher-pupil dialogue, for example, or through particular kinds of "talk" produced on television shows. One cannot leap to the conclusion that what was necessary historically is necessary in contemporaneous society. There is no basis for assuming, without further evidence, that the individual child, born into a society in which uses of literacy have been highly elaborated, must personally engage in writing operations in order to develop "literate modes of thought." That *may* be the case, but it requires proof, not simply extrapolation from cultural-historical studies.

While most psychologists have been interested in the psycholinguistic aspects of reading, some have concerned themselves with these theoretical conjectures on the cognitive consequences of writing. Vygotsky (1962) considered that writing involved a different set of psychological functions from oral speech. Greenfield (1968) has suggested that written language in the schools is the basis for the development of "context-independent abstract thought"—the distinguishing feature of school-related intellectual skills. Scribner (1968) speculated that mastery of a written language system might underlie formal scientific operations of the type Piaget has investigated. Olson (1975) argues that experience with written text may lead to a mode of thinking which derives generalizations about reality from purely linguistic, as contrasted to, empirical operations. In his view, schooling achieves importance precisely because it is an "instrument of literacy." "There is a form of human competence," he states, "uniquely associated with development of a high degree of literacy that takes years of schooling to develop" (p. 148).

These views, too, lack clear-cut empirical tests. Greenfield was extrapolating effects of written language from comparisons of schooled and unschooled child populations, but it is clear that such populations vary in many other ways besides knowledge of a written language system. Olson, to our knowledge, has developed his case from a theoretical analysis of the kind of inferential operations that the processing of written statements "necessarily" entails. Scribner employed the same method of procedure.

These are perfectly satisfactory *starting* points for a theory of the intellectual consequences of reading and writing but they do not warrant the status of conclusions. At a minimum, we would want evidence that the consequences claimed for literacy can be found in comparisons of literate and nonliterate adults living in the same social milieu whose material and social conditions of life do not differ in any systematic way.

We not only lack evidence for theoretical speculations about the relationship between writing and thinking, but in our opinion, the model of writing which underlies most psychological theorizing is too restricted to serve as a guide for the necessary research.

Some Dominant Conceptions of Writing

Although all disciplines connected with writing acknowledge that it has different "functions," these are often conceived as external to the writing act itself—that is the functions being served by writing are not seen as intrinsic to an analysis of component skills. In theory and in practice, writing is considered a unitary (although admittedly complex) phenomenon representing some given and fixed set of processes. These processes, it is assumed, can be ferretted out and analysed by the psychologist, linguist and educator without regard to their contexts of use. The call for the present conference suggests such a view. It urges that national attention, which for some years has been directed toward the "reading process," now be turned toward an investigation of the "writing process." Writing, together with reading, are described as "abilities" which it is the task of education to enhance.

The "writing process" is typically identified with the production of written discourse or text. Non-textual uses of writing, such as the notational systems employed in mathematics and the sciences which also require complex symbol manipulation, are excluded from the domain of writing, along with other types of graphic representation which use non-linguistic elements (diagrams, codes, maps, for example).

In practice, a prototypical form of text underlies most analyses of the writing process.[1] This is the expository text or what Britton and his colleagues (Britton et al., 1975) characterize as transactional writing. Transactional writing is described as writing in which it is taken for granted that the writer means what he says and can be challenged for its truthfulness and its logicality: ". . . it is the typical language of science and of intellectual inquiry . . . of planning, reporting, instructing, informing, advising, persuading, arguing and theorising" (Martin et al., 1976, p. 24, 25).

Models of the cognitive skills involved in writing are intimately tied up with this type of text. Thus in making the claim that certain analytic and inferential operations are only possible on the basis of written text, Olson (1975) selects the analytic essay to represent the "congealed mental labor" represented in writing. Nonliterate and literate modes of thought are basically distinguished by differential experience with the production and consumption of essayist text.

The development of writing skills is commonly pictured as a course of progression toward the production of expository text. Bereiter's (mimeo) suggested model of writing, for example, rests on the assumption that there is a lawful sequence in the growth of writing competence and that this sequence progresses toward the production of a well-crafted story or a logically coherent discussion of a proposition. At the apex of progressively more complex structures of writing skills is epistemic writing—writing that carries the function of intellectual inquiry. (Similar views are expressed by Moffett, 1968.)

What is apparent from this somewhat simplified sketch, is that most of our notions of what writing is about, the skills it entails and generates, are almost wholly tied up with school-based writing. Centrality of the expository text and well-crafted story in models of the writing process accurately reflects the emphasis in most school curricula. A recently completed study of secondary schools in England (Martin et al., 1976) found that writing classed as transactional (see definition above) constituted the bulk of written school work, increasing from 54 percent of children's writing in the first year to 84 percent in the last. Since such writing skills are both the aim of pedagogy and the enabling tools which sustain many of the educational tasks of the school, their preeminence in current research does not seem inappropriate. But we believe that near-exclusive preoccupation with school-based writing practices has some unfortunate consequences. The assumption that logicality is in the text and the text is in school can lead to a serious underestimation of the cognitive skills involved in non-school, non-essay writing, and, reciprocally, to an overestimation of the intellectual skills that the essayist test "necessarily" entails. This approach binds the intellectual and social significance of writing too closely to the image of the academic and the professional member of society, writ large. It tends to promote the notion that writing outside of the school is of little importance and has no significant consequences for the individual. The writing crisis presents itself as purely a pedagogical problem—a problem located in the schools to be solved in the schools through the application of research and instructional techniques. What is missing in this picture is any detailed knowledge of the role and functions of writing outside of school, the aspirations and values which sustain it, and the intellectual skills it demands and fosters. As our study of literacy among the Vai indicates, these facts are central to an evaluation of the intellectual and social significance of writing.

Three Literacies among the Vai

The Vai, a Mande-speaking people of northwestern Liberia, like their neighbors, practice slash-and-burn rice farming using simple iron tools, but they have attained a special place in world history as one of the few cultures to have independently invented a phonetic writing system (Dalby, 1967; Gelb, 1952; Koelle, 1854). Remarkably, this script, a syllabary of two hundred characters with a common core of twenty to forty, has remained in active use for a century and a half within the context of traditional rural life and in coexistence with two universalistic and institutionally powerful scripts—the Arabic and Roman alphabets. Widely available to all members of the society (though in practice confined to men), Vai script is transmitted outside of any institutional setting and without the formation of a professional teacher group.

The fact that literacy is acquired in this society without formal schooling and that literates and nonliterates share common material and social conditions allows for a more direct test of the relationship between literacy and thinking than is possible in our own society. Among the Vai we could make direct comparisons of the performance on cognitive tasks of reasonably well-matched groups of literate and nonliterate adults. To do so, however, required us from the outset to engage in an ethnographic enterprise not often undertaken with respect to literacy—the study of literacy as acquired and practiced in the society at large. Our effort to specify exactly what it is about reading and writing that might have intellectual consequences and to characterize these consequences in observable and measurable ways forced us away from reliance on vague generalizations. We found ourselves seeking more detailed and more concrete answers to questions about *how* Vai people acquire literacy skills, *what* these skills are, and *what* they do with them. Increasingly we found ourselves turning to the information we had obtained about actual literacy practices to generate hypotheses about cognitive consequences.

From this work has emerged a complex picture of the wide range of activities glossed by the term "writing," the varieties of skills these activities entail and the specificity of their cognitive consequences.

What Writing "Is" among the Vai

Our information about Vai literacy practices comes from a number of sources: interviews with some seven hundred adult men and women, in which anyone literate in one of the scripts was questioned extensively on how he had learned the script and what uses he made of it; ethnographic studies of literacy in two rural towns;[2] observations and records of Vai script teaching sessions and Qur'anic schools; analyses of Vai script and Arabic documents as they relate to Vai social institutions (see Goody, Cole, and Scribner, 1977).

We estimate that 28 percent of the adult male population is literate in one of the three scripts, the majority of these in the indigenous Vai script, the next largest group in Arabic and the smallest in English. There is a substantial number of literate men who read and write both Vai and Arabic and a small number of triliterates. Since each script involves a different orthography, completion of a different course of instruction and, in the cases of Arabic and English, use of a foreign language, multiliteracy is a significant accomplishment.[3]

As in other multiliterate societies, functions of literacy tend to be distributed in regularly patterned ways across the scripts, bringing more clearly into prominence their distinctive forms of social organization, and transmission and function. In a gross way, we can characterize the major divisions among the scripts in Vai life as follows: English is the official script of political and economic institutions operating on a national scale; Arabic is the script of religious practice and learning; Vai script serves the bulk of personal and public needs in the villages for information preservation and communication between individuals living in different locales.

In daily practice these distinctions are often blurred, raising a host of interesting questions about the personal and situational factors which may influence the allocation of literacy work to one or another script.

English script has least visibility and least impact in the countryside. It is learned exclusively in Western-type government and mission schools, located for the most part outside of Vai country. Students leave home to pursue their education and to win their place in the modern sector. Little is seen of English texts in the villages, but paramount chiefs and some clan chiefs retain clerks to record court matters in English, and to maintain official correspondence with administrative and political functionaries.

Arabic writing, on the other hand, is an organic part of village life. Almost every town of any size has a Qur'anic school conducted by a learned Muslim (often the chief or other leading citizen). These are usually "schools without walls"—groups of boys ranging in age from approximately four years to twenty-four, who meet around the fire twice a day for several hours of recitation and memorization of Qur'anic verses which are written on boards that each child holds. (Qur'anic teaching in West Africa is described in Wilks, 1968). In Islamic tradition, committing the Qur'an to memory (internalizing it in literal form)— is a holy act, and the student's progress through the text is marked at fixed intervals by religious observances and feasting. Initially, learning can only proceed by "rote memorization" since the students can neither decode the written passages nor understand the sounds they produce. But students who persevere, learn to read (that is, sing out) the text and to write out passages—still with no under-standing of the language. Some few who complete the Qur'an go on to advanced study under tutorship arrangements, learning Arabic as a language and studying Islamic religious, legal and other texts. In Vai country, there are a handful of outstanding scholars with extensive Arabic libraries who teach, study and engage in textual commentary, exegesis and disputation. Thus Arabic literacy can relate individuals to text on both the "lowest" (repetition without comprehension) and "highest" (analysis of textual meaning) levels. Arabic script is used in a variety of "magico-religious" practices; its secular uses include correspondence, personal journal notes and occasionally trade records. The overwhelming majority of individuals with Qur'anic training, however, do not achieve understanding of the language and their literacy activities are restricted to reading or writing out known passages of the Qur'an or frequently used prayers, a service performed for others as well as for oneself.

Approximately 90 percent of Vai are Muslim and, accordingly, Qur'anic knowledge qualifies an individual for varied roles in the community. Becoming literate in the Arabic language means becoming integrated into a close-knit but territorially extended social network, which fuses religious ideals, fraternal self-help, trade and economic relationships with opportunities for continuing educa-tion (see Wilks, 1968).

Knowledge of Vai script might be characterized as "literacy without education." It is typically learned within a two week to two month period with the help of a friend, relative or citizen who agrees to act as teacher. Learning consists of committing the characters to memory and practice in reading, first list of names, later personal letters written in the Vai script. Demonstration of the ability to write a letter without errors is a common terminating point for instruction. With rare exceptions, there are no teaching materials except such letters or other written material as the teacher may have in his personal possession. "Completion of lessons" is not the endpoint of learning: there are frequent consultations between ex-student and teacher. For practiced scribe as well as novice, literacy activities often take a cooperative form (e.g., A goes to B to ask about characters he can't make out) and sometimes a contentious one (e.g., A and B dispute whether a given character is correct or in error).

Vai script uses are overwhelmingly secular. It serves the two classical functions of writing: memory (preserving information over time) and communication (transmitting it over space) in both personal and public affairs, with a heavy emphasis on the personal.[4]

From an analytic point of view, focusing on component skills, it is useful to classify script functions according to whether or not writing involves the production of text or non-text materials. Non-textual uses range from very simple activities to complex record-keeping. Among the simple activities are the uses of individual written characters as labels or marking devices (e.g., marking chairs lent for a public meeting with the names of owners, identifying one's house, clarifying information displayed in technical plans and diagrams).[5] Record-keeping, most typically a list-making activity, fulfills both social cohesion and economic functions. Lists of dowry items and death feast contributions, family albums of births, deaths, marriages—all help to regulate the kinship system of reciprocal rights and obligations. Lists enlarge the scope and planful aspects of commercial transactions: these include records of yield and income from cash-crop farming, proceeds netted in marketing, artisan records of customer orders and payments received.

A mere "listing of lists," however, fails to convey the great variation in levels of systematicity, organization and completeness displayed in records. Some are barely decipherable series of names; others orderly columns and rows of several classes of information. Some genealogies consist of single-item entries scattered throughout copy books, others of sequential statements which shade off into narrative-like texts.

The more expert Vai literates keep public records from time to time when asked to do so. These are less likely to be continuing series than single list assignments: house tax payments for the current year, work contributions to an ongoing public project such as road or bridge-building, a population headcount and the like.

Personal correspondence is the principal textual use of the script. Letter-writing is a ubiquitous activity which has evolved certain distinctive stylistic devices, such as conventional forms of salutation and signature. It is not uncommon to see letters passed from hand to hand in one small town, and many people who are not personally literate participate in this form of exchange through the services of scribes. Since Vai society like other traditional cultures developed and still maintains an effective system of oral contact and communication by message and "grapevine," reasons for the popularity of letterwriting are not self-evident, especially since all letters must be personally sent and hand-delivered. Protection of secrets and guarantee of delivery are among the advantages most frequently advanced in favor of letters rather than word-of-mouth communication.

For all its popularity, letter-writing is circumscribed in ways which simplify its cognitive demands: majority of Vai literates correspond only with persons already known to them (78 percent of literates interviewed in our sample study reported they had never written to nor received a letter from a stranger). Many factors undoubtedly contribute to this phenomenon, among which the non-standardized and often idiosyncratic versions of script characters must figure prominently, but it is significant for hypotheses about intellectual skills that written communication among the Vai draws heavily upon shared background information against which the news is exchanged.

What about other texts? The first thing to note is that all textual material is held in private; texts are rarely circulated to be read, though on occasion and under special circumstances they might be made available for copying. Thus the relationship of Vai script literates to text is primarily as producer or writer, seldom as reader of another's work. This social arrangement has several important consequences. One is that reading is not an activity involving assimilation of novel knowledge or material; another is that existing texts reflect what people choose to write about, depending on their own interests and concepts of what writing is "for." Many texts are of a cumulative nature—that is, they are not set pieces, but rather comprise "journals" or "notebooks." Each such "book" might contain a variety of entries, some autobiographic (personal events, dreams), others impersonal and factual (facts of town history, for example). While not read as continuous texts, such materials are often used as important source books or data records and depending on their scope and age, may serve as archives.[6]

Some texts fit recognizable (in terms of Western literacy) genres. There are histories, for example, fables, books of maxims, parables, and advice. In at least one instance, we have been able to obtain a set of documents of a Muslim self-help organization which included a Vai-script written constitution and bylaws (see Goody, Cole, and Scribner 1977). As in the case of lists, the range of skills reflected in texts is broad. "Histories" may be a collection of what were originally notes on scattered sheets of paper, assembled under one cover with no apparent chronological or other ordering; at the other extreme they might be well-organized and fluent narrations of a clan history or ambitious accounts of the origin and migration of the Vai people as a whole. While we do not know the relationship between written and oral history and narrative, and thus cannot determine whether written works are continuous or discontinuous with respect to the oral tradition, there clearly are individual texts which bear the stamp of creative literary and intellectual work. But it must be added that texts of this nature are the exception; most histories are brief, often fragmentary and written stories rare discoveries.

There are two types of text rarely found thus far, Britton's (1975) two polar types—the poetic, concerned with exploring personal experiences and feelings, and the transactional or expository, basically concerned with examining ideas or presenting a persuasive argument.

Vai script literates are known in the community and admired for their knowledge of books. Motivations sustaining the script are not restricted to pragmatic ones; individuals will cite its utilitarian value for correspondence, records and "secrets" but will as often speak about the importance of the "book" for self-education and knowledge and for preserving the history and reputation of the Vai people. To be looked upon with respect and to be remembered in history are important incentives to many Vai journal-writers.

It is apparent from this quick review that Vai people have developed highly diversified uses for writing and that personal values, pride of culture, hopes of gain—a host of pragmatic, ideological and intellectual factors—sustain popular literacy. The level of literacy that obtains among the Vai must, however, on balance be considered severely restricted. Except for the few Arabic scholars or secondary school English students, literacy does not lead to learning of new knowledge nor involve individuals in new methods of inquiry. Traditional processes of production, trade and education are little affected by the written word.

Effects of Literacy

Should we conclude that these restrictions disqualify indigenous Vai literacy as "real literacy?" It clearly has social consequences for its practitioners and (we hypothesized) might have identifiable cognitive consequences as well. It seemed unlikely, however, that it would have the very general intellectual consequences which are presumed to be the result of high levels of school based literacy.

Nonetheless, this possibility was explored as part of our major survey of Vai adults at the outset of the project. In fact, we found no evidence of marked differences in performance on logical and classificatory tasks between non-schooled literates and nonliterates. Consequently, we adopted a strategy of making a functional analysis of literacy. We examined activities engaged in by those knowing each of the indigenous scripts to determine some of the component skills involved. On the basis of these analyses, we designed tasks with different content but with hypothetically similar skills to determine if prior practice in learning and use of the script enhanced performance.

Communication Skills

Since letter-writing is the most common use to which Vai script is put, it is reasonable to look here for specific intellectual consequences. In the psychological literature, written communication is considered to impose cognitive demands not encountered in face-to-face oral communication. In writing, meaning is carried entirely by the text. An effective written communication requires sensitivity to the informational needs of the reader and skill in use of elaborative linguistic techniques. We believed it reasonable to suppose that Vai literates' experience in writing and receiving letters should contribute to the development of these communicational skills. To test this proposition, we adapted a communication task used in developmental research (Flavell, 1968). With little verbal explanation, subjects were taught to play a simple board game and then were asked to explain the game without the board present to someone unfamiliar with it.

We compared a full range of literate and nonliterate groups, including junior high and high school students, under several conditions of play. Results were quite orderly. On several indices of amount of information provided in an explanation, groups consistently ranked as follows: high school students, Vai literates, Arabic literates, and nonliterates. Vai literates, more often than other non-student groups, provided a general characterization of the game before launching into a detailed account of rules of play. If there is anything to the notion that what is acquired in a particular literacy is closely related to practice of *that* literacy, the differential between Vai and Arabic literates is exactly what we would expect to find: on the average, Vai literates engage in letter-writing more frequently than Arabic literates. It is interesting, too, that both Vai and Arabic letter-writing groups were superior to all nonliterate groups.

Memory

We were also able to show specific consequences of Qur'anic learning. Regardless of what level of literacy they attain, all Arabic literates begin by learning to recite passages of the Qur'an by heart, and some spend many years in the process. Learning by memorization might promote efficient techniques for learning to memorize. To test this possibility, we employed a verbal learning task (Mandler and Dean, 1969) involving processes that our observations indicated matched those in Qur'anic memorization. In this task, a single item is presented on the first trial and a new item is added on each succeeding trial for a total of 16 trials and 16 items. The subject is required to recall the words in the order presented. Our comparison groups were the same as those used in the communication experiment. English students again ranked first, but in this task, Arabic literates were superior to Vai literates as well as to nonliterates in both amount recalled and in preservation of serial order. If this superiority were simply the manifestation of "better general memory abilities" on the part of Qur'anic scholars, we would expect Arabic literates to do better in *all* memory tasks, but this was not the case. When the requirement was to remember and repeat a story, Qur'anic students did no better, and no worse, than other groups. When the requirement was to remember a list of words under free recall conditions, there were no significant performance differentials. Superiority of Arabic literates was specific to the memory paradigm which shadowed the learning requirements of Qur'anic school.

Language Analysis

In a third domain, we were again able to demonstrate the superiority of Vai literates. Vai script is written without word division, so that reading a text requires as a first step the analysis of separate characters followed by their integration into meaningful linguistic units. Our observations of Vai literates "decoding" letters suggested that this process of constructing meaning was carried out by a reiterative routine of sounding out characters until they "clicked" into meaningful units. We supposed that this experience would foster skills in auditory perceptions of semantically meaningful but deformed (i.e., slowed down) utterances. Materials consisted of tape recordings in which a native speaker of Vai read meaningful Vai sentences syllable by syllable at a 2-second rate. The task was to listen and to repeat the sentence as well as to answer a comprehension question about it. Vai literates were better at comprehending and repeating the sentences than Arabic literates and nonliterates; and Vai literates with advanced skills performed at higher levels than Vai literates with beginning skills. Comparisons of performance on repetition of sentences in which words, not syllables, were the units showed no differences among literate groups but a sizeable one between all literate and nonliterate populations. The comparison of the two tasks isolates skill in syllable integration as a specific Vai script related skill.

Taken as a group, these three sets of studies provide the strongest experimental evidence to date that activities involved in reading and writing may in fact promote specific language-processing and cognitive skills.

Implications

Our research among the Vai indicates that, even in a society whose primary productive and cultural activities continue to be based on oral communication, writing serves a wide variety of social functions. Some of the pragmatic functions we have described are by no means trivial, either in indigenous terms or in terms of the concerns in economically developed countries for the promotion of "functional literacy" skills. Vai literates routinely carry out a variety of tasks using their script which are carried out no better (and perhaps worse) by their English-educated peers who have completed a costly twelve year course of school study. The record keeping activities which we described briefly in earlier sections of this paper provide the communities within which the literates live with an effective means of local administration. The fact that court cases were once recorded in the script and that religious texts are often translated into Vai as a means of religious indoctrination suggest that uses of writing for institutional purposes are fully within the grasp of uneducated, but literate, Vai people.

While the bulk of activities with the Vai script may be characterized in these pragmatic terms, evidence of scholarly and literary uses, even rudimentary ones, suggest that nonschooled literates are concerned with more than the "immediate personal gain" aspects of literacy. We could not understand in such narrowly pragmatic terms the effort of some Vai literates to write clan histories and record famous tales nor the ideological motivations and values sustaining long years of Qur'anic learning.

Of course we cannot extrapolate from Vai society to our own, but it is reasonable to suppose that there is at least as wide a range of individual aspirations and social practices capable of sustaining a variety of writing activities in our own society as among the Vai. Since our social order is so organized that access to better-paying jobs and leadership positions commonly requires writing skills, there are even more powerful economic and political incentives at work to encourage interest. It seems premature to conclude that only schools and teachers are concerned with writing and that writing would perish in this era of television if not artificially kept alive in academic settings.

An alternative possibility is that institutionalized learning programs have thus far failed to tap the wide range of "indigenous" interests and practices which confer significance on writing. Ethnographic studies of writing in different communities and social contexts—in religious, political and fraternal groups— might help broaden existing perspectives.

Our research also highlights the fact that the kind of writing that goes on in school has a very special status. It generates products that meet teacher demands and academic requirements but may not fulfill any other immediate instrumental ends. Is this an unavoidable feature of writing instruction?

When we look upon school-based writing within the context of popular uses of writing found among the Vai, we are also impressed by what appears to be the unique features of the expository or essay type text. In what nonschooled settings are such texts required and produced in our own society? Although developmental models of writing place such texts at the "highest stage" of writing ability, we find it difficult to order different types texts and writing functions to stages of development. Our evidence indicates that social organization creates the conditions for a variety of literacy activities, and that different types of text reflect different social practices. With respect to *adult* literacy, a functional approach appears more appropriate than a developmental one. The loose generalization of developmental models developed for work with children to instructional programs with adolescents and adults is certainly questionable.

With respect to intellectual consequences, we have been able to demonstrate that literacy-without-schooling is associated with improved performance on certain cognitive tasks. This is certainly important evidence that literacy does "count" in intellectual terms, and it is especially important in suggesting *how* it counts. The consequences of literacy that we identified are all highly specific and closely tied to actual practices with particular scripts; learning the Qur'an improved skills on a specific type of memory task, writing Vai script letters improved skills in a particular communication task. Vai literates and Arabic literates showed different patterns of skills, and neither duplicated the performance of those who had obtained literacy through attendance at Western-type English schools.

The consequences we were able to identify are constrained by the type of practices common in Vai society. We did not find, for example, that performance on classification tasks and logic problems was affected by nonschool literacy. This outcome suggests that speculations that such skills are the "inevitable outcome" of learning to use alphabetic scripts or write any kind of text are overstated. Our evidence leaves open the question of whether conceptual or logical skills are promoted by experience with expository text; in fact if our argument that specific uses promote specific skills is valid, we should expect to find certain skills related to practice in written exposition. The challenging question is how to identify these without reintroducing the confounding influence of schooling.

Perhaps the most challenging question of all is how to balance appreciation for the special skills involved in writing with an appreciation of the fact that there is no evidence that writing promotes "general mental abilities." We did not find superior "memory in general" among Qur'anic students nor better language integration skills "in general" among Vai literates. Moreover, improvements in performance that appear to be associated with literacy were thus far only observed in contrived experimental settings. Their applicability to other domains is uncertain. We do not know on the basis of any controlled observation whether more effective handling of an experimental communication task, for example, signifies greater communication skills in nonexperimental situations. Are Vai literates better than Arabic literates or nonliterates at communicating anything to anybody under any circumstances? We doubt that to be the case, just as we doubt that Qur'anic learning leads to superior memory of all kinds in all kinds of situations. There is nothing in our findings that would lead us to speak of cognitive consequences of literacy with the notion in mind that such consequences affect intellectual performance in all tasks to which the human mind is put. Nothing in our data would support the statement quoted earlier that reading and writing entail fundamental "cognitive restructurings" that control intellectual performance in all domains. Quite the contrary: the very specificity of the effects suggests that they may be closely tied to performance parameters of a limited set of tasks, although as of now we have no theoretical scheme for specifying such parameters. This outcome suggests that the metaphor of a "great divide" may not be appropriate for specifying differences among literates and nonliterates under contemporary conditions.

The monolithic model of what writing is and what it leads to, described at the beginning of this paper, appears in the light of comparative data to fail to give full justice to the multiplicity of values, uses and consequences which characterize writing as social practice.

5.
Literacy in Three Metaphors

Sylvia Scribner

Although literacy is a problem of pressing national concern, we have yet to discover or set its boundaries. This observation, made several years ago by a leading political spokesman (McGovern 1978), echoes a long-standing complaint of many policymakers and educators that what counts as literacy in our technological society is a matter "not very well understood" (Advisory Committee on National Illiteracy 1929).

A dominant response of scholars and researchers to this perceived ambiguity has been to pursue more rigorously the quest for definition and measurement of the concept. Many approaches have been taken (among them, Adult Performance Level Project 1975; Bormuth 1975; Hillerich 1976; Kirsch and Guthrie 1977–78; Miller 1973; Powell 1977), and at least one attempt (Hunter and Harman 1979) has been made to put forward an "umbrella definition." Each of these efforts has identified important parameters of literacy, but none has yet won consensual agreement (for a thoughtful historical and conceptual analysis of shifting literacy definitions, see Radwin [1978]).

The definitional controversy has more than academic significance. Each formulation of an answer to the question "What is literacy?" leads to a different evaluation of the scope of the problem (i.e., the extent of *il*literacy) and to different objectives for programs aimed at the formation of a literate citizenry. Definitions of literacy shape our perceptions of individuals who fall on either side of the standard (what a "literate" or "nonliterate" is like) and thus in a deep way affect both the substance and style of educational programs. A chorus of clashing answers also creates problems for literacy planners and educators. This is clearly evident in the somewhat acerbic comments of Dauzat and Dauzat (1977, p. 37), who are concerned with adult basic education: "In spite of all of the furor and the fervor for attaining literacy . . . few have undertaken to say what they or anyone else means by literacy. Those few professional organizations, bureaus and individuals who have attempted the task of explaining 'what is literacy?' generate definitions that conflict, contradict but rarely complement each other. . . . These 'champions of the cause of literacy' crusade for a national effort to make literacy a reality without establishing what that reality is."

What lies behind the definitional difficulties this statement decries? The authors themselves provide a clue. They suggest that literacy is a kind of reality that educators should be able to grasp and explain, or, expressed in more classical terms, that literacy has an "essence" that can be captured through some Aristotelian-like enterprise. By a rational process of discussion and analysis, the "true" criterial components of literacy will be identified, and these in turn can become the targets of education for literacy.

Many, although by no means all, of those grappling with the problems of definition and measurement appear to be guided by such a search for the "essence"—for the "one best" way of conceptualizing literacy. This enterprise is surely a useful one and a necessary component of educational planning. Without denigrating its contribution, I would like to suggest, however, that conflicts and contradictions are intrinsic to such an essentialist approach.

Consider the following. Most efforts at definitional determination are based on a conception of literacy as an attribute of *individuals;* they aim to describe constituents of literacy in terms of individual abilities. But the single most compelling fact about literacy is that it is a *social* achievement; individuals in societies without writing systems do not become literate. Literacy is an outcome of cultural transmission; the individual child or adult does not extract the meaning of written symbols through personal interaction with the physical objects that embody them. Literacy abilities are acquired by individuals only in the course of participation in socially organized activities with written language (for a theoretical analysis of literacy as a set of socially organized practices, see Scribner and Cole [1981]). It follows that individual literacy is relative to social literacy. Since social literacy practices vary in time (Resnick [1983] contains historical studies) and space (anthropological studies are in Goody [1968]), what qualifies as individual literacy varies with them. At one time, ability to write one's name was a hallmark of literacy; today in some parts of the world, the ability to memorize a sacred text remains the modal literacy act. Literacy has neither a static nor a universal essence.

The enterprise of defining literacy, therefore, becomes one of assessing what counts as literacy in the modern epoch in some given social context. If a nation-society is the context, this enterprise requires that consideration be given to the functions that the society in question has invented for literacy and their distribution throughout the populace. Grasping what literacy "is" inevitably involves social analysis: What activities are carried out with written symbols? What significance is attached to them, and what status is conferred on those who engage in them? Is literacy a social right or a private power? These questions are subject to empirical determination. But others are not: Does the prevailing distribution of literacy conform to standards of social justice and human progress? What social and educational policies might promote such standards? Here we are involved, not with fact but with considerations of value, philosophy, and ideology similar to those that figure prominently in debates about the purposes and goals of schooling. Points of view about literacy as a social good, as well as a social fact, form the ground of the definitional enterprise. We may lack consensus on how best to define literacy because we have differing views about literacy's social purposes and values.

These differing points of view about the central meaning of literacy warrant deeper examination. In this essay, I will examine some of them, organizing my discussion around three metaphors: literacy as adaptation, literacy as power, and literacy as a state of grace. Each of these metaphors is rooted in certain assumptions about the social motivations for literacy in this country, the nature of existing literacy practices, and judgments about which practices are critical for individual and social enhancement. Each has differing implications for educational policies and goals. I will be schematic in my discussion; my purpose is not to marshal supporting evidence for one or the other metaphor but to show the boundary problems of all. My argument is that any of the metaphors, taken by itself, gives us only a partial grasp of the many and varied utilities of literacy and of the complex social and psychological factors sustaining aspirations for and achievement of individual literacy. To illustrate this theme, I will draw on the literacy experiences of a Third World people who, although remaining at an Iron Age level of technology, have nevertheless evolved varied functions for written language; their experience demonstrates that, even in some traditional societies, literacy is a "many-meaninged thing."

Literacy as Adaptation

This metaphor is designed to capture concepts of literacy that emphasize its survival or pragmatic value. When the term "functional literacy" was originally introduced during World War I (Harman 1970), it specified the literacy skills required to meet the tasks of modern soldiering. Today, functional literacy is conceived broadly as the level of proficiency necessary for effective performance in a range of settings and customary activities.

This concept has a strong commonsense appeal. The necessity for literacy skills in daily life is obvious; on the job, riding around town, shopping for groceries, we all encounter situations requiring us to read or produce written symbols. No justification is needed to insist that schools are obligated to equip children with the literacy skills that will enable them to fulfill these mundane situational demands. And basic educational programs have a similar obligation to equip adults with the skills they must have to secure jobs or advance to better ones, receive the training and benefits to which they are entitled, and assume their civic and political responsibilities. Within the United States, as in other nations, literacy programs with these practical aims are considered efforts at human resource development and, as such, contributors to economic growth and stability.

In spite of their apparent commonsense grounding, functional literacy approaches are neither as straightforward nor as unproblematic as they first appear. Attempts to inventory "minimal functional competencies" have floundered on lack of information and divided perceptions of functionality. Is it realistic to try to specify some uniform set of skills as constituting functional literacy for all adults? Two subquestions are involved here. One concerns the choice of parameters for defining a "universe of functional competencies." Which literacy tasks (e.g., reading a newspaper, writing a check) are "necessary," and which are "optional"? The Adult Performance Level Project test (1975), one of the best conceptualized efforts to specify and measure competencies necessary for success in adult life, has been challenged on the grounds that it lacks content validity: "The APL test fails to meet this [validity] criterion . . . not necessarily because test development procedures were technically faulty, but because it is not logically possible to define this universe of behaviors [which compose functional competence] without respect to a value position which the test developers have chosen not to discuss" (Cervero 1980, p. 163).

An equally important question concerns the concept of uniformity. Do all communities and cultural groups in our class-based and heterogeneous society confront equivalent functional demands? If not, how do they differ? Some experts (e.g., Gray 1965; Hunter and Harman 1979) maintain that the concept of functional literacy makes sense only with respect to the proficiencies required for participation in the actual life conditions of particular groups or communities. But how does such a relativistic approach mesh with larger societal needs? If we were to consider the level of reading and writing activities carried out in small and isolated rural communities as the standard for functional literacy, educational objectives would be unduly restricted. At the other extreme, we might not want to use literacy activities of college teachers as the standard determining the functional competencies required for high school graduation. Only in recent years has research been undertaken on the range of literacy activities practiced in different communities or settings within the United States (e.g., Heath 1980, 1981; Scribner 1982a), and we still know little about how, and by whom, required literacy work gets done. Lacking such knowledge, public discussions fluctuate between narrow definitions of functional skills pegged to immediate vocational and personal needs, and sweeping definitions that virtually reinstate the ability to cope with college subject matter as the hallmark of literacy. On the other hand, adopting different criteria for different regions or communities would ensure the perpetuation of educational inequalities and the differential access to life opportunities with which these are associated.

Adapting literacy standards to today's needs, personal or social, would be shortsighted. The time-limited nature of what constitutes minimal skills is illustrated in the "sliding scale" used by the U.S. Bureau of Census to determine literacy. During World War I, a fourth-grade education was considered sufficient to render one literate; in 1947, a U.S. Census sample survey raised that figure to five years; and by 1952 six years of school was considered the minimal literacy threshold. Replacing the school-grade criterion with a functional approach to literacy does not eliminate the time problem. Today's standards for functional competency need to be considered in the light of tomorrow's requirements. But not all are agreed as to the nature or volume of literacy demands in the decades ahead. Some (e.g., Naisbitt 1982) argue that, as economic and other activities become increasingly subject to computerized techniques of production and information handling, even higher levels of literacy will be required of all. A contrary view, popularized by McLuhan (1962, 1964) is that new technologies and communication media are likely to reduce literacy requirements for all. A responding argument is that some of these technologies are, in effect, new systems of literacy. The ability to use minicomputers as information storage and retrieval devices requires mastery of symbol systems that build on natural language literacy; they are second-order literacies as it were. One possible scenario is that in coming decades literacy may be increased for some and reduced for others, accentuating the present uneven, primarily class-based distribution of literacy functions.

From the perspective of social needs, the seemingly well-defined concept of functional competency becomes fuzzy at the edges. Equally as many questions arise about functionality from the individual's point of view. Functional needs have not yet been assessed from the perspective of those who purportedly experience them. To what extent do adults whom tests assess as functionally illiterate perceive themselves as lacking the necessary skills to be adequate parents, neighbors, workers? Inner-city youngsters may have no desire to write letters to each other; raising one's reading level by a few grades may not be seen as a magic ticket to a job; not everyone has a bank account that requires the mastery of unusual forms (Heath 1980). Appeals to individuals to enhance their functional skills might founder on the different subjective utilities communities and groups attach to reading and writing activities.

The functional approach has been hailed as a major advance over more traditional concepts of reading and writing because it takes into account the goals and settings of people's activities with written language. Yet even tender probing reveals the many questions of fact, value, and purpose that complicate its application to educational curricula.

We now turn to the second metaphor.

Literacy as Power

While functional literacy stresses the importance of literacy to the adaptation of the individual, the literacy-as-power metaphor emphasizes a relationship between literacy and group or community advancement.

Historically, literacy has been a potent tool in maintaining the hegemony of elites and dominant classes in certain societies, while laying the basis for increased social and political participation in others (Resnick 1983; Goody 1968). In a contemporary framework, expansion of literary skills is often viewed as a means for poor and politically powerless groups to claim their place in the world. The International Symposium for Literacy, meeting in Persepolis, Iran (Bataille 1976), appealed to national governments to consider literacy as an instrument for human liberation and social change. Paulo Freire (1970) bases his influential theory of literacy education on the need to make literacy a resource for fundamental social transformation. Effective literacy education, in his view, creates a critical consciousness through which a community can analyze its conditions of social existence and engage in effective action for a just society. Not to be literate is a state of victimization.

Yet the capacity of literacy to confer power or to be the primary impetus for significant and lasting economic or social change has proved problematic in developing countries. Studies (Gayter, Hall, Kidd, and Shivasrava 1979; United Nations Development Program 1976) of UNESCO's experimental world literacy program have raised doubts about earlier notions that higher literacy rates automatically promote national development and improve the social and material conditions of the very poor. The relationship between social change and literacy education, it is now suggested (Harman 1977), may be stronger in the other direction. When masses of people have been mobilized for fundamental changes in social conditions—as in the USSR, China, Cuba, and Tanzania—rapid extensions of literacy have been accomplished (Gayter et al. 1979; Hammiche 1976; Scribner 1982b). Movements to transform social reality appear to have been effective in some parts of the world in bringing whole populations into participation in modern literacy activities. The validity of the converse proposition—that literacy per se mobilizes people for action to change their social reality—remains to be established

What does this mean for us? The one undisputed fact about illiteracy in America is its concentration among poor, black, elderly, and minority-language groups—groups without effective participation in our country's economic and educational institutions (Hunter and Harman 1979). Problems of poverty and political powerlessness are, as among some populations in developing nations, inseparably intertwined with problems of access to knowledge and levels of literacy skills. Some (e.g., Kozol 1980) suggest that a mass and politicized approach to literacy education such as that adopted by Cuba is demanded in these conditions. Others (e.g., Hunter and Harman 1979) advocate a more action-oriented approach that views community mobilization around practical, social, and political goals as a first step in creating the conditions for effective literacy instruction and for educational equity.

The possibilities and limits of the literacy-as-power metaphor within our present-day social and political structure are not at all clear. To what extent can instructional experiences and programs be lifted out of their social contexts in other countries and applied here? Do assumptions about the functionality and significance of literacy in poor communities in the United States warrant further consideration? Reder and Green's (1984) research and educational work among West Coast immigrant communities reveals that literacy has different meanings for members of different groups. How can these cultural variations be taken into account? How are communities best mobilized for literacy—around local needs and small-scale activism? or as part of broader political and social movements? If literacy has not emerged as a priority demand, should government and private agencies undertake to mobilize communities around this goal? And can such efforts be productive without the deep involvement of community leaders?

Literacy as a State of Grace

Now we come to the third metaphor. I have variously called it literacy as salvation and literacy as a state of grace. Both labels are unsatisfactory because they give a specific religious interpretation to the broader phenomenon I want to depict—that is, the tendency in many societies to endow the literate person with special virtues. A concern with preserving and understanding scripture is at the core of many religious traditions, Western and non-Western alike. As studies by Resnick and Resnick (1977) have shown, the literacy-as-salvation metaphor had an almost literal interpretation in the practice of post-Luther Protestant groups to require of the faithful the ability to read and remember the Bible and other religious material. Older religious traditions—Hebraic and Islamic—have also traditionally invested the written word with great power and respect. "This is a perfect book. There is no doubt in it," reads a passage from the Qur'an. Memorizing the Qur'an—literally taking its words into you and making them part of yourself—is simultaneously a process of becoming both literate and holy.

The attribution of special powers to those who are literate has its ancient secular roots as well. Plato and Aristotle strove to distinguish the man of letters from the poet of oral tradition. In the perspective of Western humanism, literateness has come to be considered synonymous with being "cultured," using the term in the old-fashioned sense to refer to a person who is knowledgeable about the content and techniques of the sciences, arts, and humanities as they have evolved historically. The term sounds elitist and archaic, but the notion that participation in a literate—that is, bookish—tradition enlarges and develops a person's essential self is pervasive and still undergirds the concept of a liberal education (Steiner 1973). In the literacy-as-a-state-of-grace concept, the power and functionality of literacy is not bounded by political or economic parameters but in a sense transcends them; the literate individual's life derives its meaning and significance from intellectual, aesthetic, and spiritual participation in the accumulated creations and knowledge of humankind, made available through the written word.

The self-enhancing aspects of literacy are often given a cognitive interpretation (Greenfield and Bruner 1969; Olson 1977). For centuries, and increasingly in this generation, appeals have been made for increased attention to literacy as a way of developing minds. An individual who is illiterate, a UNESCO (1972) publication states, is bound to concrete thinking and cannot learn new material. Some teachers of college English in the United States (e.g., Farrell 1977) urge greater prominence for writing in the curriculum as a way of promoting logical reasoning and critical thinking. Literate and nonliterate individuals presumably are not only in different states of grace but in different stages of intellectual development as well. Although evidence is accumulating (Scribner and Cole 1981) refuting this view, the notion that literacy per se creates a great divide in intellectual abilities between those who have and those who have not mastered written language is deeply entrenched in educational circles of industrialized countries.

The metaphor of literacy-as-grace, like the others, has boundary problems. For one thing, we need to know how widely dispersed this admiration of book knowledge is in our society. To what extent are beliefs about the value of literateness shared across social classes and ethnic and religious groups? How does book culture—more accurately, how do book cultures—articulate with the multiple and diverse oral cultures flourishing in the United States? Which people value literacy as a preserver of their history or endow their folk heroes with book learning? Are there broad cultural supports for book learning among wide sectors of the population? McLuhan and others have insisted that written literacy is a vestige of a disappearing "culture." Is this point of view defensible? And if so, what implications does it pose for our educational objectives?

I have described some current views of the meaning of literacy in terms of three metaphors. I have tried to indicate that each metaphor embraces a certain set of, sometimes unexamined, values; moreover, each makes assumptions about social facts in our society—the utilities of literacy and the conditions fostering individual attainment of literacy status. These metaphors are often urged on us as competitive; some choice of one or the other does in fact seem a necessary starting point for a definitional enterprise. But for purposes of social and educational planning, none need necessarily become paramount at the expense of the others; all may have validity. To illustrate this argument, I will briefly describe research on the social meaning of literacy among a West African people. Learning how literacy functions among a people far removed from us culturally and geographically may help us take a new look at its functions here at home.

Social Meaning of Literacy: A Case Study

My own consideration of the question "What is literacy?" was prompted by research experiences in a traditional West African society. Together with colleagues, I spent five years studying the social and intellectual consequences of literacy among the Vai people of West Africa (Scribner and Cole 1981). The material conditions of Vai life are harsh. Rural villages lack electricity and public water supplies; clinics and schools are scarce; dirt roads, often impassable in the rainy season, restrict social and economic exchanges. To the casual observer, Vai society is the very prototype of traditional nonliterate subsistence farming societies. Yet the Vai have practiced literacy for over 150 years, initially in a syllabic writing system of their own invention. The Vai script has been passed on from one generation to another in tutorial fashion without benefit of a formal institution such as a school and without the constitution of a professional teacher group. In addition to this indigenous script, literacy in the Arabic and Roman alphabets also flourishes in the countryside. The Vai are a Muslim people, and the Arabic script is the literacy for religious practice and theological learning. Missionaries and, more recently, the Liberian government have been disseminating English literacy, the official government literacy, through the establishment of Western-style schools. About one-third of the Vai male population is literate in one of these scripts, the majority in the Vai script. Many read and write both Vai and Arabic, and some outstanding scholars are literate in all three scripts. Since each writing system has a different orthography, represents a different language, and is learned in a different setting, becoming literate in two or more scripts is an impressive intellectual accomplishment. Why do people take the trouble to do it?

Certain obvious answers are ruled out. Literacy is not a necessity for personal survival. As far as we could determine, nonliteracy status does not exclude a person from full participation in economic activities or in town or society life. As we look around Vai country and see major activities and institutions continuing to function in the traditional oral mode, we are at a loss to define the literacy competencies that might be useful in everyday life. But Vai literates have not been at such a loss and have found no end of useful functions for writing. Commonly they engage in extensive personal correspondence, which for some involves the composition of thirty to forty letters per month. Since Vai society, like other traditional societies, maintains an effective oral grapevine system, reasons for the popularity of letter writing are not self-evident, especially since all letters must be personally sent and hand-delivered. Yet literates find the advantage of secrecy and guarantee of delivery more than compensation for the time and trouble spent in writing. Scholars (Hair 1963; Holsoe 1977) speculate that the usefulness of the Vai script in protecting secrets and allowing clandestine resistance to the central governing machinery of Liberia, whose official literacy was English, were important factors in its invention and longevity.

On closer study, we find that Vai script literacy also serves many personal and public record-keeping functions. Household heads keep albums for family births, deaths, and marriages; some maintain lists of dowry items and death feast contributions that help to regulate kinship exchanges. Records also enlarge the scope and planful aspects of commercial transactions. Artisans maintain lists of customers; farmers record the yield and income from cash-crop farming. The script also serves a variety of administrative purposes such as recording house tax payments and political contributions. Some fraternal and religious organizations maintain records in Vai script. All of these activities fit nicely into the metaphor of literacy as functional adaptation; the only surprising aspect is that so many varieties of pragmatic uses occur in an economic and social milieu in which modern institutions (schools, cash markets) still play a limited role.

Not all literacy uses are devoted to practical ends. Although the Vai script has not been used to produce public books or manuscripts, in the privacy of their homes, many Vai literates engage in creative acts of composition. Almost everyone keeps a diary; some write down maxims and traditional tales in copybooks; others maintain rudimentary town histories; some record their dreams and tales of advice to children; a few who might qualify as scholars produce extended family and clan histories. Townspeople, when questioned about the value of the script, will often cite its utilitarian functions, but will equally as often speak about its importance for self-education and knowledge. Vai script literates are known in the community, are accorded respect, and are sought out for their information and help as personal scribes or as town clerks. A Vai parable about the relative merits of money, power, and book learning for success in this world concludes with the judgment that the "man who knoweth book passeth all."

Why this excursion into a case of African literacy after our metaphoric discussion of the goals of literacy education in a technological society? Perhaps because Vai society, much simpler than ours in the range of literacy functions it calls for, nonetheless servies to highlight unnecessary simplicities in our attempts to define the one best set of organizing principles for literacy education. If we were called on as experts to devise literacy education programs for the Vai people, which metaphor would dominate our recommendations? Would we emphasize the spread of functional competencies, urging all farmers to keep crop records and all carpenters to list customers? This would be an effective approach for some, but it would neglect the interests and aspirations of others. Should we appeal to the cultural pride of the populace, suggesting Vai script literacy be extended as an instrument for group cohesion and social change? We might count on support for this appeal, but resistance as well; Qur'anic schools and the network of Muslim teachers and scholars are a powerful counterforce to the Vai script and a countervailing center for cultural cohesion. Moreover, families participating in the Vai script tradition do not necessarily repudiate participation in English literacy; some find it prudent to have one or more children in English school as well as Qur'anic school. As for literacy as a state of grace, aspirations for self-improvement and social status clearly sustain many aspects of Vai literacy both in the Arabic religious and Vai secular traditions. A diversity of pragmatic, ideological, and intellectual factors sustains popular literacy among the Vai.

The sociohistorical processes leading to multiple literacies among the Vai are not unique. In their research in Alaska, Reder and Green (1983) found community members practicing literacy in any one (or, occasionally, a combination) of three languages. Some used the Cyrillic script, introduced by the Russian Orthodox Church, for reading and writing Russian; others used that script for literacy activities in their native Eskimo language; and still others participated in English literacy. Each of these literacies, they report, occurred through distinct socialization processes and in well-defined, nonoverlapping domains of activity, and each had a distinctive social meaning. Wagner (in press) similarly documents the multiple meanings of literacy in contemporary Moroccan society, and other reports might be cited.

This is not to suggest, of course, that all cultural groups have elaborated rich functions for literacy, nor that all groups strive for participation in the official literacy of their state (as, for example, English in Alaska and throughout the United States). The value of the growing body of ethnographic studies for the "What is literacy?" question is twofold. First, it promotes skepticism of the "one best answer" approach to the improvement of literacy in our society. Second, it urges the need for understanding the great variety of beliefs and aspirations that various people have developed toward literacy in their particular historical and current life circumstances.

What implications does this analysis have for literacy policy and education? This is a question that calls for the continued, sustained, and thoughtful attention of educators and others in our society. One implication that I find compelling is the need to "disaggregate" various levels and kinds of literacy. If the search for an essence is futile, it might appropriately be replaced by serious attention to varieties of literacy and their place in social and educational programs. In this disentangling process, I would place priority on the need to extricate matters of value and policy from their hidden position in the definitional enterprise and to address them head on. The International Symposium for Literacy, closing UNESCO's Experimental World Literacy Program, declared that literacy is a fundamental human right (Bataille 1976). Literacy campaigns need no other justification. Setting long-range social and educational goals, however, pushes us farther toward an inquiry into the standard of literacy that is a desirable (valued) human right in our highly developed technological society, whose policies have such a powerful impact on the world's future. What is *ideal* literacy in our society? If the analysis by metaphor presented here contributes some approach to that question, it suggests that ideal literacy is simultaneously adaptive, socially empowering, and self-enhancing. Enabling youth and adults to progress toward that ideal would be a realization of the spirit of the symposium in Persepolis reflective of the resources and literacy achievements already available in our society. This suggests that long-term social and educational policies might be directed at maximal literacy objectives; minimal literacy standards would serve a useful function, not as goals but as indicators of our progress in equipping individuals and communities with the skills they need for "takeoff" in continuing literacy careers.

Recognition of the multiple meanings and varieties of literacy also argues for a diversity of educational approaches, informal and community-based as well as formal and school-based. As ethnographic research and practical experience demonstrate, effective literacy programs are those that are responsive to perceived needs, whether for functional skills, social power, or self-improvement. Individual objectives may be highly specific: to qualify for a promotion at work, to help children with their lessons, to record a family history. Anzalone and McLaughlin (1982) have coined the term "specific literacies" to designate such special-interest or special-purpose literacy skills. The road to maximal literacy may begin for some through the feeder routes of a wide variety of specific literacies.

These are speculative and personal views; others will have different conceptions. The notions offered here of ideal and specific literacies do not simplify the educational issues nor resolve the definitional dilemmas. I hope, however, that these concepts and the metaphoric analysis from which they flowed suggest the usefulness of "dissecting literacy" into its many forms and, in the process, clarifying the place of fact and value in discussions of the social meaning of literacy.

6.
The Legacies of Literacy

Harvey J. Graff

Until quite recently, scholarly and popular conceptions of the value of literacy have followed normative assumptions about the changes wrought by its *diffusion*. Furthermore, literacy has been intimately tied to post-Enlightenment, "liberal" social theories and expectations of the role of literacy and schooling in socioeconomic development, social order, and individual progress. This set of conjectures constitutes what I have come to call "the literacy myth." Along with other tenets of a worldview dominant in the West for the greatest part of the past two centuries, the "literacy myth" no longer suffices as a satisfactory explanation for the place of literacy in society, polity, culture, or economy.[1]

The past misconstrual of the meanings and contributions of literacy are rooted in the ideological origins of Western society. Expectations and assumptions of the primacy and priority of literacy and print for society and individual, the necessity of "functional" skills for survival (whatever they might be), or the mass condition of literacy as an index of the condition of civilization—all have been guiding assumptions that have obscured a deeper, more grounded understanding of the complexities of literacy.

A more adequate conceptualization of literacy must consider three things. First, a definition of literacy must be made explicit so that it can then be used comparatively over time and across space. If, for example, what is meant by literacy are the basic abilities to read and write, then the evidence of changes in such measures as Scholastic Aptitude Tests, undergraduate composition abilities, and Armed Forces Qualifying Tests as appropriate representations of literacy become problematic. The evidence of such measures should not be ignored but their application to understanding literacy should be made cautiously, if at all.

In my view, basic or primary levels of reading and writing constitute the only flexible and reasonable indications or signs that meet the essential criterion of comparability: a number of historical and contemporary sources, while not

From the *Journal of Communication*, 1982, 32(1): 12–26. © 1982 *Journal of Communication*. Reprinted by permission.

wholly satisfactory in themselves, may be employed (see table 6.1). Included here are measures ranging from the evidence of written documents, sources that reveal proportions of signatures and marks, the evidence of self-reporting (surprisingly reliable, in fact), responses to surveys and questionnaires, test results, and the like (see table 6.1).[2] Such basic but systematic and direct indications meet the canons of accuracy, utility, *and* comparability.

Some may question the quality of such data, or argue that tests of basic skills are too low a standard to employ. To account for such objections is a second component of a definition of literacy. Literacy, above all, is concerned with the human capability to use a set of techniques for decoding and reproducing written or printed materials. Writing and printing are separate, mechanical techniques. Neither writing nor printing per se are "agents of change"; their impacts are determined by the manner in which human beings exploit them. Literacy is a learned skill, usually acquired in a way in which oral ability or nonverbal, nonliterate communicative modes are not.[3]

Writings about the imputed "consequences," "implications," or "concomitants" of literacy have assigned to literacy's acquisition a truly daunting number of cognitive, affective, behavioral, and attitudinal effects. These characteristics usually include attitudes ranging from empathy, innovativeness, achievement-orientation, "cosmopoliteness," information- and media-awareness, national identification, technological acceptance, rationality, and commitment to democracy, to opportunism, linearity of thought and behavior, or urban residence. Literacy is sometimes conceived of as a skill, but more often as symbolic or representative of attitudes and mentalities. On other levels, literacy "thresholds" are seen as requirements for economic development, "take-offs," "modernization," political development and stability, standards of living, fertility control, and so on. But empirical investigations of these purported consequences and correlations are infrequent. Further, the results of macro-level, aggregative, or ecological studies are usually much less impressive either statistically or substantively than are the normative theories and assumptions.

Viewing literacy in the abstract as a foundation in skills that can be developed, lost, or stagnated is meaningless without connection to the possessors of those skills. Hence, understanding literacy requires a third specification—its use in and application to precise, historically specific material and cultural contexts. The major problem is that of reconstructing the contexts of reading and writing—how, when, where, why, and to whom literacy was transmitted, the meanings that were assigned to it, the uses to which it was put, the demands placed on literate abilities and the degrees to which they were met, the changing extent of social restrictedness in the distribution and diffusion of literacy, and the real and symbolic differences that emanated from the social condition of literacy among the population.

The meaning and contribution of literacy cannot be presumed but rather must be a distinct focus of research. The context in which literacy is taught or acquired is one significant area of research. The work of Cole and Scribner with the Vai people in Liberia and elsewhere suggests that the environment in which students acquire their literacy has a major impact on the cognitive consequences of their possession of the skill and the uses to which it can be put. Children who

Table 6.1
Sources for the Historical Study of Literacy in North America and Europe

Source	Measure of literacy	Population	Country of availability	Years of availability	Additional variables
Census	Questions: read and write, read/write Signature/mark (Canada 1851, 1861 only)	Entire "adult" population (in theory): ages variable; e.g., over 20 years, 15 years, 10 years	Canada, United States	Manuscripts: nineteenth century	Age, sex, occupation, birthplace, religion, marital status, family size and structure, residence, economic data
Wills	Signature/mark	20–50 percent of adult males dying; 2–5 percent of adult females dying	Canada, United States, England, France, etc.	Canada, eighteenth century on, U.S. 1660 on, others from sixteenth–seventeenth century on	Occupation, charity, family size, residence, estate, sex
Deeds	Signature/mark	5–85 percent of living landowning adult males; 1 percent or less of females	Canada, United States	Eighteenth century on	Occupation, residence, value of land, type of sale
Inventories	Book ownership	25–60 percent of adult males dying; 3–10 percent of adult females dying	Canada, United States, England, France, etc.	Seventeenth–eighteenth century on (quantity varies by country and date)	Same as wills
Depositions	Signature/mark	Uncertain: potentially more select than wills, potentially wider Women sometimes included	Canada, United States, England, Europe	Seventeenth–eighteenth century on (use and survival varies)	Potentially, age, occupation, sex, birthplace, residence
Marriage records	Signature/mark	Nearly all (80 percent +) young men and women marrying (in England)	England, France, North America	From 1754 in England; 1650 in France	Occupation, age, sex, parents' name and occupation, residence (religion—North America)

Table 6.1 (continued)

Source	Measure of literacy	Population	Country of availability	Years of availability	Additional variables
Catechetical examination records	Reading, memorization, comprehension, writing examinations	Unclear, but seems very wide	Sweden, Finland	After 1620	Occupation, age, tax status, residence, parents' name and status, family size, migration, periodic improvement
Petitions	Signature/mark	Uncertain, potentially very select, males only in most cases	Canada, United States, England, Europe	Eighteenth century on	Occupation or station, sex, residence, political or social views
Military recruit records	Signature/mark or question on reading and writing	Conscripts or recruits (males only)	Europe, esp. France	Nineteenth century	Occupation, health, age, residence, education
Criminal records	Questions: read, read well, etc.	All arrested	Canada, United States, England	Nineteenth century	Occupation, age, sex, religion, birthplace, residence, marital status, moral habits, criminal data
Business records	Signature/mark	1. All employees 2. Customers	Canada, United States, England, Europe	Nineteenth, twentieth century	1. Occupation, wages 2. Consumptions level, residence, credit
Library/mechanics institute records	Books borrowed	Members or borrowers	Canada, United States, England	Late eighteenth–early nineteenth century	Names of volumes borrowed, society membership
Applications (land, job, pension, etc.)	Signature/mark	All applicants	Canada, United States, England, Europe	Nineteenth–twentieth century	Occupation, residence, family, career history, etc.
Aggregate data sources[a]	Questions or direct tests	Varies greatly	Canada, United States, England, Europe	Nineteenth–twentieth century	Any or all of the above

[a]Censuses, educational surveys, statistical society reports, social surveys, government commissions, prison and jail records, etc. Source: Graff, *The Literacy Myth*, 325–27. This is a modified and greatly expanded version of table A in Lockridge, *Literacy in New England*.

were formally educated in schools designed for that purpose acquired a rather different set of skills as part of their training than those who learned more informally. Whereas previous empirical studies had confounded literacy with schooling, Scribner and Cole attempted to distinguish the roles and contributions of the two. In contrast with other researchers, they found that "the tendency of schooled populations to generalize across a wide range of problems occurred because schooling provides people with a great deal of practice in treating individual learning problems as instances of general classes of problems. Moreover, we did not assume that the skills promoted by schooling would necessarily be applied in contexts unrelated to school experience."[4] These findings of the restricted impacts of literacy have wide implications, especially regarding the time and place in which literacy is acquired and transmitted in circumstances outside the environment of the schoolroom and formal institutional settings.[5] Such research must also limit the assumptions and expectations that students carry to studies of literacy—such as presupposing literacy to be "liberating" or "revolutionary" in its consequences.

A second focus of research on literacy involves the tyranny of conceptual dichotomies in its study and interpretation. Consider the common phrases; literate and illiterate, written and oral, print and script, and so on. None of these polar opposites usefully describes actual circumstances; all of them, in fact, preclude contextual understanding.

The oral-literate dichotomy is the best example. The proclaimed decline in the pervasiveness and power of the "traditional" oral culture dating from the advent of moveable type obscures the persisting power of oral modes of communication. The work of Havelock on classical Greek literacy[6] or that of Clanchy on medieval English literacy[7] richly illustrates the concurrent and complementary oral and literate communicative processes. Clanchy reveals the struggle that writing and written documents waged for their acceptance from the eleventh through the thirteenth centuries—a time of rising lay literacy. Early written documents, impelled by the state and the interests of private property, faithfully reproduced the "words" of oral ceremonies and the rituals that traditionally had accompanied formal agreements; they were also adorned with the traditional badges of sealed bargains.[8] According to Havelock, Western literacy, from its "invention" in the Greek alphabet and first popular diffusion in the city-states of classical times, was formed, shaped, and conditioned by the oral world that it penetrated. Then literacy was highly restricted and a relatively unprestigious craft; it carried relatively little of the association with wealth, power, status, and knowledge that it would later acquire. Even with the encroachment of literacy, the ancient world remained an oral world, whether on street corners or in marketplaces, assemblies, theaters, villas, or intellectual gatherings. The word as spoken was most common and most powerful. This tradition continued from the classical era through the 1000 years of the Middle Ages and may well be reinforced today by the impact of the newer electronic media.

The oral and the literate thus complement and augment each other. The poetic and dramatic word of the ancients was supplanted, though not replaced, by a religion rooted in the Book, but propagated primarily by oral preaching and

Table 6.2
Key Points in the History of Literacy in the West

ca.3100 B.C.	Invention of writing
3100–1500 B.C.	Development of writing systems
650–550 B.C.	"Invention" of Greek alphabet
500–400 B.C.	First school developments, Greek city-states, tradition of literacy for civic purposes
200 B.C.–200 A.D.	Roman public schools
0–1200	Origin and spread of Christianity
800–900	Carolingian language, writing, and bureaucratic developments
1200 and onward	Commercial, urban "revolutions," expanded administration and other uses of literacy and especially writing, development of lay education, rise of vernaculars, "practical" literacy, Protestant heresies
1300 and onward	Rediscovery of classical legacies
1450s	Advent of printing, consolidation of states, Christian humanism
1500s	Reformation, spread of printing, growth of vernacular literatures, expanded schooling (mass literacy in radical Protestant areas)
1600s	Swedish literacy campaign
1700s	Enlightenment and its consolidation of traditions, "liberal" legacies
1800s	School developments, institutionalization, mass literacy, "mass" print media, education for social and economic development: public and compulsory
1900s	Nonprint, electronic media
late 1900s	Crisis of literacy

teaching. Classical and other forms of education long remained oral activities, with literacy by oral instruction. The written and then printed word were spread to many semiliterates and illiterates via oral processes; information, news, literature, and religion were thereby spread far more widely than purely literate means could have allowed. For many centuries, reading itself was an oral, often collective activity, not the private, silent one we now consider it to be.

The history of literacy has been biased toward explaining change, particularly as one of the key elements in the development of the "modern," industrialized West. Thus, it is not surprising that the history of literacy is also commonly a truncated one, ignoring, as irrelevant or inaccessible, the first 2000 years of Western literacy before the advent of moveable type. This linear perspective, with its emphasis on changes wrought by literacy, obscures the continuities and contradictions in the historical role of literacy. The role of tradition is a case in point. The use of elementary schooling and learning one's letters, for example, for political and civic functions such as moral conduct, respect for social order, and participant citizenship, was prominent in the Greek city-states during the fifth century before Christ. This use of literacy is a classical legacy that was regularly rediscovered by persons in the West during each age or reform movement (for a summary of key points in the history of literacy, see table 6.2). Recognizing this continuity or legacy of literacy allows us to consider the similarities and differences in rates of literacy, schooling configurations, practical and symbolic uses of literacy, and the like that accompany renewed recognition of the positive value of expanded popular literacy within the differing social or economic contexts.

Similarly, the strength of the ideal of the oral-literate dichotomy, as discussed earlier, also was due in part to the exaggerated emphasis on change and discontinuity. Finally, the primary users of literacy—the state, the church, and commerce—have remained in effect, regardless of the degree of social restrictiveness that regulated the supply curve of popular diffusion of literacy. Although the balance among these institutions has shifted, this triumvirate has retained its cultural and political hegemony over the social functions of literacy. The development of these three institutions and their uses of literacy illustrates the continuities and contradictions of literacy itself.

This significant link between literacy and religion is perhaps the best example. The sixteenth-century reformations, both Protestant and Catholic, are of course the most striking examples of this phenomenon. But the religious impulse to use reading for the propagation of piety and faith predates that time. Within the history of Western Christianity the dialectic between the oral and the written has resulted in different balances being struck in different periods, places, and sects. Literacy served to record for time immemorial the Word, but its influence and diffusion came, for centuries, overwhelmingly through oral means of teaching and preaching.

The Reformation constituted the first great literacy campaign in the history of the West, with its social legacies of individual literacy as a powerful social and moral force. One of the great innovations of the Reformation was the recognition that literacy, a potentially dangerous or subversive skill, could be employed (if controlled) as a medium for popular schooling and training on a truly unprecedented scale. The reform was hardly an unambiguous success in its time, but it may well have contributed more to the cause of popular literacy than to that of piety and religious practice.[9]

Literacy's relationship with the processes of economic development provides another striking example of the patterns of contradictions. In general, commerce and its social and geographical organization stimulated rising levels of literacy from the twelfth century onwards in advanced regions of the West.[10] However, major steps forward in trade, commerce, and even industry took place in some periods and places with remarkably low levels of literacy; conversely, higher levels of literacy have not been proved to be stimulants or springboards for "modern" economic developments. More important to economic development than high rates or "threshold levels" of literacy[11] have been the educational levels and power relations of key persons, rather than of the many. Major "take-offs," from the commercial revolution of the Middle Ages to eighteenth-century proto-industrialization in rural areas and even factory industry in towns and cities, owed relatively and perhaps surprisingly little to popular literacy abilities or schooling. In fact, industrialization often reduced opportunities for schooling and, consequently, rates of literacy fell as it took its toll on the "human capital" on which it fed. In much of Europe, and certainly in England—the paradigmatic case—industrial development (the "first industrial revolution") was neither built on the shoulders of a literate society nor served to increase popular levels of literacy, at least in the short run. In other places, typically later in time, however, the fact of higher levels of popular education *prior* to the advent of factory capitalism may well have made the process a different one, with different needs and results. Literacy, by the nineteenth century, became vital in the process of "training in being trained." It may also be the case that the "literacy" required for the technological inventiveness and innovations that made the process possible was not a literacy of the alphabetic sort at all, but rather a more visual, experimental one.[12]

The history of literacy shows clearly that there is no one route to universal literacy. In the history of the Western world, one may distinguish the roles of private and public schooling in the attainment of high rates of popular literacy, as well as the operation of informal and formal, voluntary and compulsory education. High rates of literacy have followed from all of these approaches in different cases and contexts. The developmental consequences are equally varied.

Historical experiences thus furnish a guide to such crucial questions as how and to what degree basic literacy contributes to the economic and individual well-being of persons in different socioeconomic contexts, and under what circumstances universal literacy can be achieved. History provides a basis for evaluating and formulating social policy. The costs and benefits of the alternative paths can be discerned too. Thus, the connections and disconnections between literacy and commercial development, a favorable relationship, and literacy and industrial development, often an unfavorable linkage at least in the short run of decades and half-centuries, offer important case studies and analogs for analysis. If nothing else, the data of the past strongly suggest that a simple, linear, modernization model of literacy as a prerequisite for development, and development as a stimulant to increased levels of schooling, will not suffice.

The example of Sweden is perhaps the most important in this respect. Near-universal levels of literacy were achieved rapidly and permanently in Sweden in the wake of the Reformation.[13] Under the joint efforts of the Lutheran church and the state, reading literacy was required for all persons under law, from the seventeenth century. Within a century, remarkably high levels of literacy among the population existed—without any concomitant development of formal schooling or economic or cultural development that demanded functional or practical employment of literacy, and in a manner that led to a literacy defined by reading and not writing. Urbanization, commercialization, and industrialization had nothing to do with the process of making the Swedish people perhaps the most literate in the West before the eighteenth century. Contrary to the paths of literacy taken elsewhere, this campaign, begun by King Charles XI, was sponsored by the state church. By legal requirement and vigilant supervision that included regular personal examination by parish clergy, the church stood above a system rooted in home education. The rationale of the literacy campaign, one of the most successful in Western history before the last two decades, was conservative; piety, civility, orderliness, and military preparedness were the major goals.[14]

The home and church education model fashioned by the Swedes not only succeeded in training a literate population, but it also placed a special priority on the literacy of women and mothers. This led to Sweden's anomalous achievement of female literacy rates as high or higher than male rates, a very rare result in the

Western transitions to mass literacy. Sweden also marched to its impressive levels of reading diffusion without writing; it was not until the mid-nineteenth century and the erection of a state-supported public school system that writing, in addition to reading, became a part of a popular literacy and a concern of teachers in this Scandinavian land. The only other areas that so fully and quickly achieved near-universal levels of literacy before the end of the eighteenth century were places of intensely pious religion, usually but not always Protestant: Scotland, New England, Huguenot French centers, and places within Germany and Switzerland.

The relation of literacy with social development points up the highly variable paths to societal change and maturity. From the classical period, leaders of polities and churches, reformers as well as conservers, have recognized the uses of literacy and schooling. Often they have perceived unbridled, untempered literacy as potentially dangerous, a threat to social order, political integration, economic productivity, and patterns of authority. But, increasingly, they also concluded that literacy, if provided in carefully controlled formal institutions created expressly for the purposes of education and supervised closely, could be a powerful and useful force in achieving a variety of important ends. Precedents long predated the first systematic efforts to put this conception of literacy into practice, in Rome, for example, and in the visionary proposals of the fifteenth- and sixteenth-century Christian humanists. With the Enlightenment and its heritage came the final ideological underpinnings for the "modern" and "liberal" reforms of popular schooling and institutional building that established the network of education-social-political-economic relationships central to the dominant ideologies and their social theoretical expressions for the past century and a half.

Although these crucial topics are not within my main focus here, the significance of literacy to individuals and groups throughout history is undoubted. There is already a large if uneven volume of studies with this emphasis, highlighting the value of literacy to individual success, the acquisition of opportunities and knowledge, and collective consciousness and action. The writings of Robert K. Webb, Richard Altick, Thomas Laqueur, and Michael Clanchy, among many others, make this case with force and evidence. The role of class- and group-specific demands for literacy's skills, the impact of motivation, and the growing perceptions of its values and benefits are among the major factors that explain the historical contours of changing rates of popular literacy. Any complete understanding and appreciation of literacy's history must incorporate the large, if sometimes exaggerated and decontextualized, role of demand (in dialectical relationship to supply) and the very real benefits that literacy may bring. Literacy's limits must also be appreciated, but cannot be if they are not specifically discussed.

It is important to stress the integrating and hegemony-creating functions of literacy provision through formal schooling. Especially with the transition from pre-industrial social orders based in rank and deference to the class societies of commercial and then factory capitalism, schooling became more and more a vital aspect of the maintenance of social stability, particularly during periods of massive, but often poorly understood, social and economic change.

Many persons, most prominently social and economic leaders and social reformers, grasped the uses of schooling and the vehicle of literacy for the promotion of the values, attitudes, and habits considered essential to the maintenance of social order and the persistence of integration and cohesion.[15]

Because of the nature of the evidence, virtually all historical studies have concentrated on the measurement of the extent and distributions of reading and writing; issues involving the level of the skills themselves and the abilities to use those skills have not attracted a great deal of attention. What research has been conducted, however, comes to the common conclusion that qualitative abilities cannot be deduced *simply* or *directly* from the quantitative levels of literacy's diffusion. Studies of early modern England, eighteenth- and nineteenth-century Sweden, and urban areas in the nineteenth century all suggest that there is a significant disparity between high levels of the possession of literacy and the usefulness of those skills. In Sweden, for example, where systematic evidence exists, a great many persons who had attained high levels of *oral* reading skill did not have comparable abilities in *comprehension* of what they read. This means that the measurement of the distribution of literacy in a population may in fact reveal relatively little about the uses to which such skills could be put and the degree to which different demands on personal literacy could be satisfied with the skills commonly held. Second, it is also possible that with increasing rates of popular literacy did not come ever-rising capabilities, or qualitative abilities—or, for that matter, declining capabilities.

Such evidence places the often-asserted contemporary decline of literacy in a new and distinctive context, leading to a fresher and historical perspective. Mass levels of ability to use literacy may have, over the long term, typically lagged behind the near universality of literacy rates. Perhaps we should pay more attention to longer term trends than a decade or two and to changes in popular communicative abilities and compositional effects among students, than to "competency examinations" and SAT test scores.[16] In the words of Galtung:

> What would happen if the whole world became literate? Answer: not so very much, for the world is by and large structured in such a way that it is capable of absorbing the impact. But if the world consisted of literate, autonomous, critical, constructive people, capable of translating ideas into action, individually or collectively—the world would change.[17]

Part Two

Historical Perspectives

7.
The History of Literacy and the History of Readers

Carl F. Kaestle

Literacy has profoundly affected the history of individuals and of nations, yet it received little attention from historians until about twenty-five years ago. Until then most historians were preoccupied with great men who were all literate. Literacy found only an incidental place in historians' work. There were, to be sure, studies of the readership of famous books, studies of printing and publishing, and references to expanding education; but in general historians did not give literacy a prominent place in their efforts to understand social relations or social change. In the past twenty-five years, however, many historians have become interested in studying mass behavior and belief—the everyday activities, ideology, and opportunities of ordinary people. These concerns define the field of social history today. The same concerns have influenced historians of politics, of culture, of ideas, of institutions, and of education. Along with other research topics fostered by the "new social history," the history of literacy has thrived. At the same time, literacy has become a prominent policy issue, within the United States and internationally. This attention has spurred historians further. The fact that our age is alert to the possible consequences of a communications revolution featuring television and computers has made us all the more interested in understanding earlier transformations. The fashionable formulations of Marshall McLuhan have become the subject of serious research. Presses have poured forth books and articles whose central purpose is to determine how many people were literate in past societies, how they acquired their literacy, and what difference it made.

Literacy can be a hot topic. As Furet and Ozouf (1982) explain, French historians on the left argue that the Revolution fostered literacy, while those on the right claim that the Revolution subverted educational progress made earlier by the Church. For Europe more generally, historians of literacy often note that Protestant areas have higher literacy rates than Catholic areas (Flora, 1973), but the correlation does not always hold (Cipolla, 1969; Maynes, 1984), and the importance of Protestant religion in fostering literacy has prompted much debate. Analysts of contemporary Third World countries look to the history of literacy in more developed countries to hypothesize threshold rates for economic and political development (Anderson, 1965). Lerner (1958) has linked literacy to urbanization, Rogers (1969) to political participation, Stone (1969) to revolutions, and Vinovskis (1981) to reduced fertility. All of these studies have a topical relevance to our own day. Thus the history of literacy is lively because of its many resonances with current affairs.

The history of literacy is also lively because it is full of surprises and reinterpretations. Even the issue of literacy in ancient history has prompted new ideas. Havelock (1976), for example, argued that in view of the artistic and political achievements of preliterate Greece, we should not equate cultural sophistication with literacy. For the modern West, revisionist historians have reconsidered the relationship of religion and literacy. Houston (1982) challenged the common generalization that Calvinist Protestantism gave Scotland a head start in literacy; he argued not only that literacy levels were lower than previously claimed but were more affected by demographic and regional differences within Scotland than by religion. In contrast, Lockridge (1974) identified Calvinism as the main driving force behind colonial New England literacy, but he disputed any connection between literacy and modernization, viewing Puritan educational activities instead as a conservative strategy.

Not only the explanations but even the basic facts about literacy trends are uncertain. Like many emerging social history topics, the history of literacy has displayed growing pains—inadequate data, fuzzy conceptualization, uncertain topic boundaries, and the intrusion of normative debates into the historical analysis. Although at first glance the term "literacy" seems straightforward, it proves very slippery. It can refer to a wide range of reading and writing skills, and historians' definitions vary. Also, because researchers generally lack direct evidence of reading ability, they often use evidence of writing ability as an estimate of reading ability. Even if we restrict our definition of literacy to reading alone, the term may imply a wide range of abilities.

In this essay "literacy" means the ability to decode and comprehend written language at a rudimentary level, that is, the ability to look at written words corresponding to ordinary oral discourse, to say them, and to understand them. Most historians of the subject seem to have this crude literacy skill in mind when they estimate literacy rates. Using this low-level reading skill as a definition may give a false sense of clarity to the research problem, however, for the very practice of using literacy as a dichotomous variable is an oversimplification. The categories "literate" and "illiterate" are neither precise nor mutually exclusive. Some individuals learned to read but then forgot how. Some were literate but rarely read. Some perceived themselves to be literate but were perceived by others as illiterate, or vice versa. Furthermore, individuals who were unable to read participated in literate culture by listening to those who could read. The worlds of literacy and oral communication are interpenetrating. As we shall see, this has been one of the important themes of recent research.

Nonetheless, there are good reasons to explore the expansion and consequences of crude literacy rates over time, as long as we remember that literate people have a wide range of abilities and that illiterate people are not wholly isolated from the influence of print. Historians began by counting people who signed their names on documents and comparing them to people who marked an "X." This was a crude beginning, but soon scholars were carrying on the necessary debates about the meaning of signing ability, the relationship of writing to reading, the relationship of literacy to schooling, the relationship of literacy to class, community, and religion at a given time, and the relationship of all of these to social changes like industrialization, migration, and political revolution.

In addition to these problems of interpretation, three background issues have shaped recent studies in the history of literacy. The first is about focus: whether historians should concentrate on the nominal possession of literacy, its expansion, and the social characteristics of literate people, or whether instead they should focus on the uses of literacy among those who are literate and how those uses change over time. Many recent essays, including the present review, urge the latter, broader view. The second background issue has to do with causation. Were changes in literacy principally causes or effects of other social changes? Eisenstein (1980) staked out a bold argument for the printing press as a neglected agent of cultural change, but she met much resistance from other scholars. Goody (1963, 1968) decided after some criticism that his earlier speculations about the "consequences" of literacy in traditional societies should be toned down and labelled "implications." Graff (1979) argued that literacy's efficacy in improving individual life chances was a "myth." The potency of literacy has been much debated. The third background issue is as fascinating as it is intractable: Does literacy have a liberating or constraining effect on individuals' lives? The answer, obviously, is a mixture, but the relative emphasis does much to define a historian's interpretation and is itself shaped by ideology as well as evidence. In Cremin's progressive view (1970, 1980), literacy is liberating and enlightening; similarly, modernization theorists have emphasized literacy's role in widening mental horizons and bolstering rationality. Meanwhile, Soltow and Stevens (1981), along with Graff (1979), have seen literacy as an ideology of middle-class schooling, in keeping with the trend in revisionist educational history to view schooling as an imposition.

Even though historians' serious attention to literacy is quite recent, there is already an immense literature on the subject. This review essay is restricted to works in English. The research may be summarized logically under three headings. First, there is a literature on the introduction of writing and its effects in early civilizations. Second, there is a literature on the history of literacy in the modern West, defined narrowly as trends in crude literacy rates, their causes, and their consequences. Third, and more broadly, there is a diffuse literature on the uses of print, encompassing such matters as the history of the book trade, of journalism, of literary tastes and reading interests, of libraries, and related subjects. This essay briefly reviews studies of literacy in traditional societies; it then presents the methodological problems and major substantive research results in the history of crude literacy rates. Finally, it surveys the world of scholarship about printed materials, and it advocates synthetic studies that integrate the histories of readers and texts. This essay does not review works on the history of instruction in reading, nor on the history of textbooks. The focus here is on the rates and uses of literacy among adults, with special reference to the United States. Other recent attempts to sum up the field, in different ways, include a detailed bibliography by Graff (1981); an anthology of excellent articles edited by Graff (1982b); as well as an article by Graff in which he previews his comprehensive history of literacy in progress (1982a). There is also an interesting, concise article by Resnick and Resnick (1977), in which they argue that for France and the United States literacy demands kept rising as literacy skill acquisition increased; an excellent review article by Houston (1983) that discusses the history of literacy in Europe from 1500 to 1850; and a suggestive essay by David B. Hall (1983) on the changing uses of literacy in New England from 1600 to 1850.

From Oral to Written Culture

The initial shift to written culture occurred in two ways. Some societies invented writing, others acquired it from abroad. The two historical processes raise different sorts of questions. The invention of writing was a long, slow process, and scholars have identified several stages, not only in the technical aspects of writing systems but also in the diffusion of literacy to different groups in society. Different periods are characterized by differences in the quality and functions of literacy among different groups, and changes in the relationship between literacy and oral communication. On the technical aspects of the history of writing, Gelb (1963) and Diringer (1968) are the standard authorities; on the intellectual and social consequences of the shift from oral to written culture, the most imaginative recent work is by Goody and Watt (1963), Havelock (1963), Goody (1968, 1971), Scribner and Cole (1981), Ong (1967, 1982), Clanchy (1979), and Stock (1983).

Writing began with pictures and then moved through various intermediate innovations, from direct representation to more mnemonic devices. Mnemonic symbols evolved into word-syllabic systems among the Sumerians, as well as the Aztecs and Mayans. Commerce prompted this break with representational writing, necessitating more abstract symbols that could record many different products and individuals. The Chinese, the Hittites, and the Egyptians also reached this stage of innovation. From Egyptian writing evolved various syllabic systems and ultimately the alphabetic writing of the Greeks. Beyond these technical stages of writing development, the early history of literacy may be roughly periodized by stages of diffusion. For some centuries after the introduction of alphabetic writing, literacy was restricted to a small elite and limited to a few functions, chiefly religion, accounting, genealogy, and, sometimes, political administration. Although literacy bestowed prestige and power on religious officials, lay leaders' power was not associated with literacy in this long period of "craft" or restricted literacy (Clanchy, 1979; Ong, 1982). Later, writing gained a foothold in more nonreligious spheres, prompting more general literacy among elites. Also, the diffusion of writing tended to consolidate and standardize vernacular language.

Some qualifications to the stage concept are in order. First, not all stages are necessary; for example, nonliterate societies can adopt alphabetic writing from abroad, skipping early picture and word-symbol stages. Second, although the stages of diffusion are generally sequential, they are sometimes reversible; for example, literacy narrowed in medieval Europe. Third, the stages are not mutually exclusive; they express gradual and overlapping developments.

Recent research has emphasized that these early developments took place in the context of mass illiteracy and pervasive oral culture. Oral culture did not atrophy in contact with written culture; rather, the written word modified and extended communication networks. Not only has the great majority of the earth's population been illiterate throughout history, but the great bulk of communication in literate societies is still oral. Nonetheless, writing allowed new modes of communication, administration, and record-keeping. Writing is a technology; it allowed innovations in economic, political, and cultural activities. Most profoundly, it allowed and encouraged new modes of thinking.

Did the introduction of writing create a great watershed in the history of culture and consciousness? For a long time, the shift to writing seemed to correspond with the shift from "traditional" to "modern" society or from "primitive" to "advanced" cultures, but these dichotomies no longer seem adequate. They are out of fashion among anthropologists and historians. Still, some fundamental changes can be associated with the advent of writing. Plato saw them coming and was ambivalent (Havelock, 1963). Later observers were a good deal more enthusiastic. Recently, however, anthropologists and historians of language have attempted a more balanced view. Goody (1971) criticized Lévi-Strauss's dichotomy between the "savage" and "domestic" mind, but argued that we still must be willing to chart the historical evolution of cognitive processes and acknowledge the central role of writing, because, as he had written earlier (1968), writing "changed the whole structure of the cultural tradition" (p. 67). Ong (1967, 1982) was careful to emphasize the overlap of oral and written cultures, and he expressed considerable admiration for oral traditions; nonetheless, he argued that "without writing, human consciousness cannot achieve its fuller potentials" (1982, p. 14). There is, then, a high degree of consensus about the technical capacities released by the invention of writing. The more difficult job of interpretation comes in the effort to determine the conditions under which these capacities are translated into fundamentally new forms of cultural enterprise and social organization. Both the timing and the inevitability are at issue when scholars assert the "consequences" of written culture.

Among the most important technological features of writing are these: it allows the replication, transportation, and preservation of messages, and it allows back-and-forth scanning, the study of sequence, deliberation about word choice, and the construction of lists, tables, recipes, and indexes. It fosters an objectified sense of time, and it separates the message from the author, thus "decontextualizing" language. It allows new forms of verbal analysis, like the syllogism, and numerical analysis, like the multiplication table. The long-range developments made possible by this technology have been profound, leading eventually to the replacement of myth by history and the replacement of magic by skepticism and science. Writing has allowed bureaucracy, accounting, and legal systems with universal rules. It has replaced face-to-face governance with depersonalized administration. On the other hand, it has allowed authorship to be recorded and recognized, thus contributing to the development of individualism in the world of ideas.

The initial assertion of these consequences by Goody and Watt, Havelock, Ong and others in the 1960s led to case studies to test whether they occurred regularly. Goody (1968) himself edited a sampling of such studies, the most interesting of which was reported in an article by Gough (1968) on literacy in traditional China and India. She qualified some aspects of the Goody and Watt (1963) formulation. For example, a clear distinction between the supernatural and the natural did not occur in China and India until long after the appearance of writing. Also, the emergence of history as distinct from myth was true for China but very weak in India. Skepticism was also stronger in China but was tempered in both countries by strong traditional forces. Although Gough noted that literate people in both countries evidenced some striving for objective, scientific truth, she doubted that the specialization of knowledge and consequent alienation Goody and Watt had hypothesized were a typical feature of preindustrial literate societies.

As a result of such modifications, literacy scholars began to emphasize various "brakes" on the expansion of literacy, and thus on the processes of objectification and bureaucratization in traditional societies. Writing materials were costly, and religious officials guarded their monopoly on literacy. Instead of wondering why literacy did not develop quickly, urged Clanchy (1983) "we should be asking 'Why did it develop at all considering the obstacles in its path?' " (p. 19). In his analysis of oral and written culture in England from 1066 to 1307, Clanchy (1979) portrayed a society that made a gradual but important transition from restricted clerical Latin literacy to more widespread secular, vernacular literacy, laying the groundwork for the print revolution of the sixteenth century, more than two thousand years after the invention of alphabetic writing. As a technology, writing had transforming potential, but its impact was neither automatic nor sudden.

When the question of literacy's initial impact is applied to a nonliterate society that adopts literacy from the outside, new questions arise. What is the impact of foreign language literacy upon indigenous oral culture? When a fully developed print culture meets a wholly oral culture, is the impact faster, slower, less complete, or just different than among the civilizations that invented writing? Because the group that brings literacy to a traditional society is often a colonizing power with a technological advantage, powerful changes often accompany the adoption of literacy; but it is very difficult to disentangle causes. One analysis that attributes central importance to literacy is Clammer's (1976) study of Fiji. Clammer claimed that literacy and Christianity were inseparable in the early missionary days and that Christian literacy lay at the heart of a rapid transformation of Fijian culture and administration. But Clammer elevated the causal potency of literacy beyond what he demonstrated. There is no doubt that Fijians saw literacy as part of Englishmen's superior magic and showed great enthusiasm for learning the alphabet. However, Parsonson (1967) had argued in an earlier study of Tahiti that natives enthusiastic for rudimentary education soon became disenchanted when they realized that literacy did not automatically bring with it the other powers of the whites and that disease was the main contribution of the English over the first several decades of contact. Was Parsonson wrong? Was Clammer wrong? Or was Fiji drastically different from Tahiti? Clammer's statement that their disagreement "merely depends on one's point of view" (p. 200) is insufficient to settle the debate. More detailed studies of other Pacific societies are required to assess the impact of writing on native culture and administration.

Literacy and Schooling

One of the best studies of the impact of outsiders' literacy on an indigenous culture is by Scribner and Cole (1981). Seeking to identify the psychological consequences of literacy, and in particular to distinguish between the effects of literacy and those of schooling, Scribner and Cole studied reading among the Vai tribe of Liberia, a small minority group prominent in commerce. The Vai made an exciting case study; they have their own script, taught informally at home. Many of them also acquire Arabic for religious purposes and English for business purposes. Subjects who had learned only Vai literacy showed few cognitive differences from nonliterates in categorization, logic, or explanation. Arabic literacy, although taught in more formal instructional settings, was traditional and sacred in its purposes and showed little of the cognitive impact of English literacy, which was taught in school and devoted to the kinds of activities often attributed to literacy in general. Vai and Arabic literates were not identical to nonliterates, however; the Scribner and Cole research results are more subtle than a brief summary can convey. Still, the main thrust of their work was to emphasize context and practice in the study of literacy's impact and to emphasize that some consequences attributed to literacy are actually consequences of schooling.

Recent studies of contemporary American literacy have reinforced the distinction between literacy and schooling. Olson (1977a, 1977b) has argued that literacy biases schooling toward certain cognitive tasks and styles. The dominance of written prose in schools insures emphasis on logical, abstract, universal knowledge, in contrast to the action-oriented, personal, common-sense knowledge of oral communication outside the school. Of course, the identity of schooling and literacy is not absolute, as Scribner and Cole pointed out. Among the Vai, vernacular literacy was family-oriented while English literacy was learned in schools and devoted to the mental processes that Olson associated with schools. Heath (1980, 1984) has also done interesting recent work on English literacy outside of schools. She found that working-class children in two communities in the American South learned and used literacy in different ways than the school expected—not as a hierarchical, sequential ability associated with analytic tools, but as a miscellaneous, situation-specific set of skills related to tasks like reading shopping lists, calendars, and advertisements.

What lessons can historians of literacy glean from these contemporary studies? Schooling and literacy are often linked, but not always and not necessarily. Some of the cognitive impact of literacy has been achieved chiefly through schools. The rise of formal schooling helped to shape and disseminate particular uses of literacy. Nonetheless, there can be worlds of literacy outside the school; and they are less structured and less abstract.

From Script to Print

Like the distinction between schooling and literacy, the distinction between script writing and print has prompted debate. Some of the most important alleged consequences of writing for science, secularization, and bureaucratization seem to have occurred substantially only after the spread of printing. Was printing, then, and not writing, the great turning point, technologically and psychologically? The issue is one of emphasis, but marvelously complex. Recent works of Eisenstein (1980) and Clanchy (1979, 1983) illustrate this dialogue. Clanchy, a medievalist, saw trends of secularization and the expansion of script literacy as necessary antecedents to print, while Eisenstein, an early modernist, saw a decisive turning point in print technology. Furthermore, Eisenstein was not interested in the role of printing in expanding literacy; she was interested in how printing transformed the modes of thinking and the uses of literacy among those already literate. In Eisenstein's judgment, scholars had underestimated the impact of the printing press as an agent of change; they had overlooked a communications revolution. Among the intellectual activities made possible by printing was the exact duplication of technical work, which allowed the expansion of data pools in astronomy, botany, and geography. Printing allowed the spread and preservation of Renaissance scholarship, so that it did not disappear like earlier revivals. Printing spawned cataloguing, indexing, cross-referencing, and other aids to analysis. Printing spread vernacular language and helped standardize language across dialects. Some of the consequences of print were contrasting or even paradoxical. Although standardized print made reading more impersonal, the development of authorship made individual celebrities possible. Print had a bridging, unifying effect in science, but it had a divisive, fragmenting effect in religion, making possible pamphlet wars and doctrinal polarization. Within religion print fostered both modern criticism and resistant fundamentalism.

Eisenstein rejected the view that printing only intensified previous trends. It set up wholly new opportunities and even reversed some trends, like the perpetual corruption of text in scribal culture. At times, Eisenstein seemed deliberately to overstate her case. The danger, she said, is not in exaggerating the importance of the advent of printing, but in "forcing an evolutionary model on a revolutionary situation" (p. 36). Critics reviewing the Eisenstein book argued in detail that developments were more gradual and that printing was less revolutionary (e.g., Grafton, 1980). Thus the book has been a prod to further debate. Taken with a grain of salt, it is also a lively starting point for the nonspecialist who wants to think about the consequences of the invention of the printing press.

Trends in Crude Literacy Rates

Printing launched us into the modern era of literacy. Although Eisenstein was principally interested in intellectual changes among literate people, most students of literacy after 1600 have been preoccupied with the expansion of literacy, its causes, and its consequences. Between 1600 and 1900 the countries of Western Europe moved from restricted literacy to mass literacy, with immense consequences for education, social relations, and communications. The exact trends, however, are difficult to trace. The evidence is skimpy and its validity suspect. National averages mask variation that could reveal causal possibilities, so the need for further studies is almost endless. Once the trends in crude literacy are estimated, it is difficult to get beyond them to the quality and meaning of literacy.

Signatures and Reading Ability

There is very little evidence about the extent of literacy before 1850 except that provided by people's ability to sign documents like marriage registers, army rolls, and wills. Because the relationship of signing ability to reading ability is uncertain, the validity of the measure is one of the most frequently discussed methodological problems in the history of crude literacy rates. The best discussions of this problem are in Schofield (1968), Lockridge (1974), Cressy (1980), and Gilmore (1982), but no one has a definitive answer. Schofield based his judgment on Webb's (1950) analysis of English surveys that compared the self-reported reading and writing abilities of some working class groups in the 1830s and 1840s. Schofield concluded that signing ability overestimates the number who could actually write but underestimates the number who could read at the most rudimentary level. On the basis of sketchy evidence, Schofield decided that signing ability conveniently approximated the proportion of people who could read "fluently." Lockridge, citing Schofield and others, stated confidently that "scholars agree" that signing ability corresponds to fluent reading ability (p. 7). Furet and Ozouf (1982) found a "spectacular proximity of the variables 'ability to sign the *acte de mariage*' and 'able to read and write' for both men and women" (p. 15) in nineteenth-century samples for whom both sorts of evidence were known. Cressy (1980) cited Schofield and Furet and Ozouf and concluded that "the statistical study of literacy over the last decade has been on the right track" (p. 55). Hamerow (1983), however, was more skeptical. Citing German data on reading and writing ability, he concluded that "the usual definition of literacy as the ability to sign one's name includes a large number, often half or more, of those whose mastery of the 3 R's was so inadequate that they should properly be classified as functional illiterates" (p. 182).

What can we say, then, about signature counting, the basis of most literacy studies for the period 1600 to 1850? Signing may correlate with fluent reading ability, but confidence on that score must be guarded. Whatever the absolute levels, trends in signing over time probably parallel trends in other literacy skills; but even this common-sense notion must be qualified. The relationship of signing and reading may vary by gender, by class, by place, and by period. For example, if schools taught reading earlier than writing, poorer children who had to work as they got older might have learned to read but not write (Spufford, 1979). On the other hand, in cases where the skills were taught together, the signing and reading abilities of adults would be more closely correlated. If elite providers of education promoted reading skill but feared writing instruction (Kaestle, 1976), many adult readers might have made X's on documents; but where reading and writing were equally encouraged, the two rates must have been closer. If historians of literacy explore such possibilities in their evidence, they can reasonably use signature counts as a rough indicator of the minimum number of people who were minimally literate. There may have been many who made an X and could nonetheless read; but the converse seems unlikely. Most who signed their names could probably read, even if some could only spell out letters and rarely used their literacy.

Crude Literacy Rates in Europe, 1600–1850

This section surveys some trends in crude literacy, explores their relationship to social changes, and makes some generalizations about the principal research findings. The starting point for a survey of European literacy rates is Cipolla (1969), still the only book-length survey of literacy in modern Europe and America. Although the book is brief and now dated, many of its generalizations are valid, and it provides many examples of changing crude literacy patterns. With the spread of vernacular print matter, crude literacy rose in Europe during the sixteenth century. In 1600 over 50% of town dwellers could read, Cipolla estimated, though in rural areas, where most people lived, less than half were literate. The combined total European rate was perhaps in the range of 35% to 40% literate. The progress of literacy was not linear. Wars, depressions, and disease disrupted much of seventeenth-century Europe, and in the nineteenth century the early stages of industrialization actually discouraged education because of the market for unskilled labor and the use of children in industry. Therefore, by 1850, Cipolla suspected, overall literacy in Europe was not much above 50%, though there was much variation.

In general the bias in literacy was toward the upper classes, toward males, and toward urban settings. Higher literacy was also associated with northern areas of Europe, Protestant areas and industrializing areas. How uniform were these biases and what caused them? About the first three factors there is little doubt. Literate people were disproportionately male, upper status, and urban, consistently and for fairly obvious reasons. Literacy was associated with power and was restricted by the powerful. Upper status and male occupations demanded literacy more than the jobs allowed to the poor and to women. Cities provided concentrations of population to support schools and printing presses, and they provided jobs requiring literacy.

The north-south bias, usually explained by Protestantism, industrialization, or both, is more complex. Research published since Cipolla's book sheds some light on these matters. There is no doubt that literacy rates in southern Europe were lower than in northern Europe and that this coincided generally with a Protestant-Catholic split. From Portugal and Spain, across southern Italy to Greece and the Balkans, literacy rose slowly in comparison to Prussia, the Lowlands, Scandinavia, and Britain. But the Southern tier was not just Catholic; it was also poorer and more rural than the North. Still, Catholics within a given country generally had lower literacy rates than Protestants. In 1871, 93% of Prussian Protestants were literate, while 85% of Prussian Catholics were. In the same year 90% of Irish Presbyterians could read, while 60% of Irish Catholics could (Cipolla, 1969). In nineteenth-century Quebec, communities that were predominately French Catholic had dramatically different literacy rates from those that were predominately English Protestant, even when controlling for rural-urban status. In 1844, for example, 12% in French-speaking communities and 60% in English-speaking communities in rural areas could read and write (Greer, 1978). Although the Counter-Reformation had placed Catholics in support of schooling and vernacular Bible reading, the effort lacked the intensity of Protestant concern for lay reading.

However, the religious factor could be outweighed by other factors. Bavaria and the Rhineland were highly literate Catholic areas (Cipolla, 1969), perhaps because of economic factors and generally high German school support. Northern France was more literate than southern France, though equally Catholic (Furet and Ozouf, 1982). In a fascinating regional comparison of schooling in the Vaucluse, in southern France, and northern Baden, in Germany, Maynes (1984) showed that the culture and customs of a region may affect people more than their own personal religion. Protestant communities in the Vaucluse, a predominantly Catholic region, had lower school enrollment rates than Catholic communities in Baden, a predominantly Protestant region, principally because traditional means of supporting schoolmasters were widespread and successful in Baden.

Two nations whose high literacy is often attributed to Protestantism are Sweden and Scotland. For Sweden there can be no doubt that the impetus was religious. The big surge in Swedish literacy occurred between 1660, when the national rate was about 35%, until 1720, when it reached a remarkable 90%. At this time Sweden was overwhelmingly agrarian. The literacy campaign was initiated by the Church and implemented with little emphasis on schools. Families were directed to instruct children or get them instructed. Ministers monitored progress closely, and church sanctions were levied against illiterates (Johansson, 1981). The Swedish campaign is unique and extremely well-documented: An activist Protestant church, prior to industrialization, effected a dramatic rise to nearly universal literacy in a span of about sixty years, mainly through family and clerical instruction.

The Scottish case is less clear. Historians have long cited Scotland as an example of high preindustrial literacy resulting from an interventionist Calvinist church. Recently, however, Houston (1982) has challenged this view, softening the contrast between Scotland and England and highlighting regional differences within Scotland. He found rural illiteracy to be very high in mid-seventeenth-century Scotland, and the national crude literacy average to be at least 5% behind England at that time. In the next 150 years of literacy trends, Houston concluded, "the role of education and religion was severely tempered by identifiable socio-economic constraints" (p. 89). Calvinist strongholds did not differ from otherwise similar areas in the spread of literacy. Houston was doubtful about the importance of state schools, because the northern counties of England, without state intervention and without intense Protestantism, achieved rates similar to the Scottish average. Houston reasserted the primary importance of socioeconomic factors, both for regions and individuals, in the acquisition of literacy, and he downgraded the importance of religion and schooling. In a rejoinder to Houston, Smout (1982) adduced evidence from the rural town of Cambuslang, the scene of a religious revival in the 1740s, to challenge the value of Houston's signature counting. Many of Cambuslang's 110 converts, chronicled in detailed interviews, could read well but not write, especially among the women. Reading, furthermore, was normally learned at school, though it could be acquired elsewhere. The convert's interviews depicted a society in which reading was expected and was widespread, even among those labelled as illiterate in Houston's figures. Thus literacy studies proceed: scholars conducting careful regional studies of signature rates revise national generalizations; then others use local studies to get beyond the mere signature rates, challenging the regional statistics with evidence about how individuals actually acquired and used literacy.

Just such a dialogue has been going on among scholars studying English literacy in the same period. In a detailed study using the traditional signature-counting methods, Cressy (1980) charted trends in English literacy during the Tudor and Stuart periods. Cressy doubted the importance of radical Protestantism because his literacy rates were so highly stratified by occupational group. He concluded that increases in literacy were driven by "pull" factors, that is, by demand, which differed by class. Cressy devoted his energies to mustering the complicated data and charting successive waves of expansion and recession in crude literacy rates. His book is an example of an approach now falling into disfavor among historians of literacy. In an important article criticizing Cressy's preliminary published studies, Spufford (1979) analyzed the spiritual autobiographies of 141 seventeenth-century men. Although these autobiographers were not typical of all Englishmen, their detailed accounts of education revealed that many of their contemporaries were literate nonwriters, and some of these were in the lower occupational groups whom Cressy thought were predominantly illiterate. Because reading was taught in families and in the earliest school years, it was socially more widespread than Cressy believed. Grammar schools and the universities were socially very restricted, but Spufford has revealed "a murky and ill-defined world in which grammar schooling was practically irrelevant," a world in which people nonetheless commonly acquired some reading ability and frequently came into contact with print.

The effort to trace crude literacy rates has become a minor industry among British historians. Much of the discussion has centered around the relationship of literacy and industrialization. Bowman and Anderson (1963) are often cited to the effect that a 40% crude literacy rate seems to be a prerequisite threshold for industrialization, but that is speculation from rough indicators. The actual process by which literacy might influence economic development, or vice versa, are uncertain. In his now-classic article on literacy in England from 1600 to 1900, Stone (1969) pointed out that the two great periods of expanding literacy, the seventeenth century and the later nineteenth century, coincided with cultural and political ferment while the industrial revolution of the late eighteenth and early nineteenth centuries began during a time of stagnant literacy rates. Schofield (1973), mustering a more thorough sample, found somewhat higher rates of literacy than Stone, but still agreed that economic growth did not depend on increased literacy. Not only did British factory manufacturing begin during a lull in literacy growth, but the immediate local impact of industrialization upon education and literacy was negative. This view has been pressed by Sanderson (1972), who discovered declining school enrollment and literacy rates in industrializing Lancashire. Early factory work did not require literacy for most workers, and child labor interfered with education. National rates showing increases during industrialization are misleading, argued Sanderson. When disaggregated, the data on the areas of industrial development show deteriorating literacy and schooling. Reanalyzing the same data, Laqueur (1974) showed that Sanderson's Lancashire decline started too early to be accounted for by industrialization and that an upturn had started by the early nineteenth century, when the full effects of industrialization should have been in force. Reversing Sanderson's argument, Laqueur attributed the eighteenth-century decline to massive population increase without adequate institutional apparatus for education, and he attributed the reversal of the downtrend to schooling efforts arising from industrialization and urbanization.

This debate has spawned many local case studies. In an interesting twist on Sanderson's theme, Stephens (1976) studied Devon, a county that thrived economically in the preindustrial cloth trade but declined economically when factory production began. Devon's male signature literacy rate increased from the 1640s to the 1750s while its economy thrived, but then declined until the 1790s, as had the rates in industrializing areas like Lancashire. This supports Sanderson's general point that the industrial revolution did not ride upon rising literacy rates, nor spur increased literacy in the immediate short run; but the Devon figures also support Laqueur's qualifications on Sanderson—the Devon decline is too early to attribute to factory industrialization, and the recovery is too early for any claim that industrialization depressed education beyond the earliest stages of factory development.

Furet and Ozouf's (1982) work explored in detail the relationship between literacy and industrializion in France. In early modern France, Protestantism and then the Counter-Reformation aimed to democratize literacy, and these impulses began the diffusion process. The long-run expansion of literacy, however, ran very much along socially stratified lines and corresponded with the growth of the market economy. For purposes of the history of literacy, therefore, France can be divided into two great regions—the north, which achieved mass literacy in the seventeenth and eighteenth centuries, and the south, where literacy was quite restricted until the nineteenth. Within these regions, of course, there was great variety. Towns in general had higher literacy, because they had concentrations of literate occupations and educating agencies. But in the nineteenth century, some towns failed to maintain their literacy advantage. Industrialization had depressing effects on literacy because of child labor, in-migration of uneducated workers, and rapid population expansion that outstripped the capacity of schools and other social agencies. Furet and Ozouf thus distinguished between the higher-literacy, old, commercial towns and the lower-literacy, new, industrial towns. They also distinguished between agricultural areas with new supplementary industries, which had the same inhibiting effect on literacy as in the cities, and old agricultural areas with seasonal labor patterns allowing more school and family education. Often such agricultural areas registered higher literacy rates than towns affected by industrialization.

The emerging picture, then, is one in which literacy is correlated with economic growth in a region but depressed temporarily by factory production. Commerce, the professions, schooling, and gradual population concentration were all associated with rising literacy. Child labor, rapid population growth, and the stress and insecurity of early industrialization inhibited the expansion of literacy. Works by Houston (1982), Furet and Ozouf (1982), Schofield (1973) and Stephens (1976) all support the generalization that literacy was boosted by the commercial aspects of urbanization, not the industrial aspects.

The Literacy Rise in Europe, 1850–1900

Literacy expanded rapidly in the last half of the nineteenth century, for both men and women. National consolidation, state intervention, and male suffrage added force to expanding capitalism to create school systems and encourage literacy. As Hamerow (1983) noted, in Hungary, Austria, England, France, and Prussia, school reform closely followed political independence or election reform. But these reforms only reinforced trends already in progress. England moved from about 69% male literacy in 1850 to 97% in 1900, and the national average for women rose from one-third in 1850, catching up to the male rate by 1900 (Schofield, 1973; Stone, 1969). In France the male rate moved from about 68% to 96%, while the female rate rose from 53% to 94% (Furet and Ozouf, 1976). In Belgium, the number of army recruits who could write increased from 56% to nearly 88% (Cipolla, 1969). Most major social changes in this period fostered increased literacy. Reformers had responded to the social disruptions of early industrialization by creating schools and other moral reform efforts; trade continually demanded more literate workers; women went to work outside the home and took on greater educational responsibilities for children in schools and at home; nation-states strove to instill loyalty and create national identity; rising productivity provided governments with resources for the development of institutions; and an expanding male franchise created pressures for education from above and below.

The Renaissance, the printing press, and the Reformation had planted seeds for the democratization of reading, but those impulses were not universally accepted and did not complete the process. In the nineteenth century, another watershed was passed: the governing classes began to encourage the universal spread of reading ability. The old conservative argument against popular literacy waned (Kaestle, 1976). In urban-industrial societies, states moved to shape and consolidate popular belief. At the same time that these forces for institutional provision grew, popular demand for practical, recreational, and devotional reading material increased also. About the motives and purposes of early school advocates there is much debate; the problem of causation still engages historians of nineteenth-century schooling. But there is no doubt about the rising rates of literacy and school enrollment in this period. In surveying the history of American literacy, we shall touch upon the question of whether all this literacy and schooling was a good thing, and, if so, for whom.

Literacy in America, 1600–1900

Literacy rates in colonial British America were quite high, and America's rise to universal white literacy was earlier than Europe's. But many of the same questions arise: the proper interpretation of signature rates, the causes of rising literacy, its content, and its value to individuals. Compared to English historians, students of American literacy from 1600 to 1900 are mere beginners. The literature consists of a book by Lockridge (1974) on colonial New England, a book by Soltow and Stevens (1981) on the nineteenth century to 1870, and a book by Graff (1979) on literacy in Ontario cities, plus about a dozen articles and some incidental references in educational histories.

Prior to Lockridge's study, some American cultural historians had dabbled in signature counting (e.g., Morison, 1935), establishing that American literacy measured in this way was high compared to that of Europe, and that a particularly large percentage of New England immigrants could sign their names. Lockridge made a careful study of signatures and marks on over three thousand New England wills from 1640 to 1800. He confirmed that British America had high signature literacy by European standards and that the rate in New England was higher than in the Southern or Middle Atlantic regions. Still, Lockridge found signature literacy to be lower in seventeenth-century New England than the more superficial previous studies had claimed. Beginning at about 60% in 1650 and rising slowly to 70% by about 1710, male signature literacy took off in the eighteenth century. By the time the Founding Fathers signed the Constitution, 90% of white males were signing documents. Female signature literacy paralleled male rates in the seventeenth century, rising slowly from 30% in 1650 to 40% around 1710, but then it tapered off, remaining below 50% through the late eighteenth century—"stagnant," to use Lockridge's phrase.

Lockridge's interpretations of these data have provoked both debate and further work on literacy in colonial America. He argued that Protestantism, and particularly the Puritan version of Calvinism, was the major driving force behind New England literacy, that it was accomplished chiefly through schools, and that its purpose was conservative. Although Calvinism may have "paved the way to modernity" (p. 45), it was intensely traditional in the seventeenth century. Because of their religious concerns, New England Puritans required towns to provide schools, but the laws did not work very well in the seventeenth century because of population dispersal. However, argued Lockridge, such laws worked to advance literacy in the eighteenth century. Lockridge distinguished his interpretation from three other recent versions. He contended that the reliance upon schooling was not a result of family breakdown in the face of the wilderness environment, as Bailyn (1960) had argued; that literacy in the eighteenth century was not "liberating" as Cremin (1970) had argued; and that it was not associated with modern attitudes, as Inkeles and Smith (1974) and other modernization theorists had argued.

As in the historiography of crude literacy in England, American historians have tested Lockridge's and Cremin's generalizations with local studies. Tully discovered nearly level male signature literacy for Chester County (around 72%) and Lancaster County (around 63%) in southeastern Pennsylvania during population, physical hardship, and contact with native Americans, but by selective migration, the shift to religious dominance, dissenters, new governing arrangements, and the separation from European institutions. The stresses of this situation, coupled with the Puritans' concern about religious decline, all combined to produce a focus on schooling in colonial New England. This focus was reinforced, as Cremin pointed out, by the colonists' traditional reliance on schools, which they brought from England. In any case, schooling did not have a very dramatic effect on expanding literacy in seventeenth-century New England. Although Cremin and Bailyn correctly emphasized the important educational roles of the family, the church, and the workplace, they both acknowledged a growing role for schools as the colonial period progressed. Whatever role an expanding press and a resurgent evangelical Protestantism may have played in the second half of the eighteenth century, the expansion of literacy also coincided with the establishment of more district schools, closer to the people.

As for Cremin's (1977) interpretation that eighteenth-century literacy was "liberating" rather than conservative, this reflects his optimistic general conviction that "on balance, the American educational system has contributed significantly to the advancement of liberty, equality and fraternity" (p. 127). There is, of course, evidence on both sides of the issue, which has animated historical debate about American education over the past fifteen years.

The enduring contribution of Lockridge's New England study, in addition to its careful mustering of the signature data and its detailed discussions of statistical techniques, is its warning against the automatic equation of literacy and a liberating modernity. Lockridge's conviction that Puritan literacy training was conservative is related to his conviction that British settlers in America were thoroughly European and premodern, indeed, even peasant-like. His emphasis on the conservative function of Puritan literacy may be exaggerated, but it serves a useful purpose; for too long historians' presumptions were the reverse. Literacy can serve many purposes, sometimes traditional and constraining, sometimes innovative and liberating.

As in the historiography of crude literacy in England, American historians have tested Lockridge's and Cremin's generalizations with local studies. Tully discovered nearly level male signature literacy for Chester County (around 72%) and Lancaster County (around 63%) in southeastern Pennsylvania during the eighteenth century, and he concluded that there had been no educational revolution nor expansion of "liberating" literacy in that rural setting. Beales (1978), testing Lockridge's generalization on rural Grafton, Massachusetts, in the midst of the 1748 religious revival, found levels slightly higher (98% males, 46% females), than Lockridge's figures would have led one to predict, and found no relationship between literacy and conversion among women. Attempting to reconcile the evidence from Lockridge, Cremin, and the minor modifications from the Tully and Beales single-site studies, we may speculate that crude literacy rates in eighteenth century America were perhaps lower in some places than Cremin's interpretation would suggest and higher, particularly for women, than in Lockridge's samples. Nor can the salient influence of revival religion or political ferment be predicted when one descends to the local level. But one should not expect such uniformity. Even if American researchers emulate their English colleagues and count many more signatures, generalizations about crude literacy rates in colonial America will remain tentative.

On the issue of female rates, however, evidence is mounting to suggest that the eighteenth and early nineteenth centuries were important years of increased crude literacy. Suspicions that some women who could not write could nonetheless read seem well-founded; furthermore, some fragmentary local evidence shows a more dynamic increase in women's signature-ability in the eighteenth century than Lockridge found. Tully (1972) found a sharp eighteenth-century rise in female signature literacy in his small Pennsylvania samples, and Auwers (1980) charted increasing female signature-writing in Windsor, an old Connecticut town, from 21% in the 1660s birth cohort to 94% in the 1740s birth cohort. In Auwers' late seventeenth-century data, female signing-ability correlated not with wealth but with parental literacy and parental church membership; in the eighteenth-century data, on the contrary, it correlated with wealth but not church membership, leading Auwers to remark that Windsor may have been enacting a cultural shift from "Puritan" to "Yankee." Windsor, Auwers admitted, was at the high-literacy end of the spectrum, but it foreshadowed more general developments. Kaestle (1983), in a general treatment of education after 1780, summarized the evidence for rising female literacy and increasing access to schooling for girls, during a period when republican ideology and preindustrial capitalism were spreading, and when females' role in educating children was receiving special emphasis.

In Auwers' Windsor study, a family's proximity to a school increased the chances of a daughter's acquiring literacy, reinforcing Lockridge's emphasis on schools. These data seem to support the commonsensical notion that increases in schools led to increases in learning. But not all literacy was acquired in schools. Moran and Vinovskis (1983) recently tried to redirect attention back to the family, arguing that the changing gender dynamics of instruction within the family generated pressure for more female education in the eighteenth century. In the late seventeenth century, they reasoned, church membership shifted strongly toward females. Thus, the catechizing role within the family fell increasingly to women; but they were at a relative disadvantage in literacy. The resolution of this tension was a rhetorical emphasis on pious, educated women in early eighteenth century New England and increased female access to school by the late eighteenth century. Gilmore (1982), studying over ten thousand signatures and marks on various documents in a Vermont county from 1760 to 1830, found almost universal male signature literacy throughout the countryside, but female rates, ranging from 60% to 90%, varying with the level of commercial involvement of the community.

By 1850, the crude literacy rates of white men and women, self-reported to U.S. Census marshalls, were nearly equal (Vinovskis and Bernard, 1978). The biggest gaps in literacy rates were between native whites, foreign-born whites, and nonwhites, but regional, income, and rural-urban disparities persisted. The most thorough investigation of these nineteenth-century developments was by Soltow and Stevens (1980). They began by considering whether male literacy was "nearly universal" by 1800. Some studies of signatures that report such high rates admit that a significant portion of the population never signed documents, like deeds or wills, and thus perhaps as much as one-fifth of the population is missing from the sample (e.g., Gilmore, p. 157). Soltow and Stevens surveyed petitions and army enlistment lists and concluded that male illiteracy as high as 25% was common in the early years of the republic. They also showed that the inability to sign remained widespread among certain groups of white males. Throughout the period 1800 to 1840, 30% of merchant seamen could not sign. Signature illiteracy among U.S. Army enlistees, at 42% in 1800 and still 35% in the 1840s, declined to 25% in the 1850s, to 17% in the 1870s, and to 7% in the 1880s.

In 1840 the United States Census began including a literacy question. Given all of the problems of interpreting signature rates, this might seem a great improvement in the evidence. However, the census marshalls never administered any test of literacy, so the results represent only the self-reported literacy or illiteracy of household residents. Furthermore, the questions differed from decade to decade, sometimes changing the age group, sometimes including separate questions on reading and writing, and, finally, adding a question on foreign-language literacy. At their worst, U.S. Census illiteracy statistics only measure people's willingness to admit illiteracy. At best, they can be taken to indicate a minimal estimate of crude illiteracy. While small changes over time may be due to changes in the phrasing or administration of the question, there is no reason to think that the major trends are artifacts.

Soltow and Stevens (1981) analyzed the aggregate rates in this Census data, but also, through samples of individual family schedules, they investigated the correlation of literacy with other factors. Their general theme is that nation-building, economic development, and population density all favored the provision of schools and fostered the development of an "ideology of literacy." The ideology concept was not very clear in their argument, but the data they mustered were clear. Literacy correlated most strongly with schooling, next with family wealth, and next with the population density of one's community. Not surprisingly, high literacy rates were biased toward the North and toward urban areas, but by 1870 the common school movement, the circulation of print matter, and improved transportation had reduced these biases.

Social class biases persisted. Like Cressy's work on seventeenth-century England, Graff's (1979) work on three Ontario cities in 1861 emphasized the correlation of literacy with one's place in the social structure. Graff concluded that literacy did not account for much in attaining income or occupational status, compared to ethnic group and family conditions. Stated as a causal speculation, it seemed that literacy helped a few people but not many. These results were not very surprising, but it is useful for Graff to have reminded us that illiteracy is more a symptom than a cause of disadvantage. The opposite view is what Graff called the "literacy myth." According to Graff, the belief that literacy by itself improved the careers of nineteenth-century urban dwellers is fallacious. This conclusion put him in the revisionist camp of educational historians but went beyond what is proved by the census literacy data. Ten percent or less were labelled illiterate in his three Ontario cities, and we know nothing of the relative reading abilities of the great majority of people, nor what impact literacy had on their lives.

Although Soltow and Stevens' (1981) work is the most detailed study of U.S. Census literacy information for the nineteenth century, the most convenient place to turn for a discussion of the trends in aggregate rates is Folger and Nam (1967). White illiteracy in the Census, male and female combined, declined from 10.7% in 1850 to 6.2% in 1900. While only 4.6% of the native-born whites admitted illiteracy in 1900, 12.9% of foreign-born whites did. Among nonwhites the reported illiteracy rate was 44.5%. At the turn of the century, concern about illiteracy was focused on black Americans and, to a lesser degree, upon recent European immigrants. The big story in nineteenth-century American literacy is the development of common school systems and the near elimination of self-reported outright illiteracy among whites.

Twentieth-Century Literacy: The American Case

The early twentieth century witnessed rapid urbanization, black migration northward, pressure for immigration restriction, and a resurgence of racist social theories. Given the white-black and native-foreign gaps in crude literacy, therefore, it is not surprising that Census monographs reflected anxieties about illiteracy among black people and European immigrants. Actually, immigrant illiteracy was concentrated in the recent arrivals and declined rapidly after the restriction of immigration in 1921; and black illiteracy decreased dramatically in the late nineteenth and early twentieth centuries, especially considering discrimination, hostility, poor resources, and fewer job incentives. Higher-order literacy skills are a different matter, of course, and these are not indicated in the Census. Even at the level of crude illiteracy, gaps remained between native and foreign-born, white and nonwhite, North and South, urban and rural; but the twentieth-century story is one of declining illiteracy and convergence of rates. Today, even though the percentages of outright illiterates are small, the absolute number of illiterates is still great. In 1979, only .6% of all persons fourteen years old and above were illiterate, but this equalled nearly a million people who had this significant social disadvantage.

As reported crude illiteracy rates declined among all groups, commentators and analysts turned their attention to higher-order skills. The term "functional literacy" gained popularity in the 1930s. At first it was applied simply to a level of schooling deemed sufficient to insure the ability to read most everyday print matter, usually the fourth or fifth grade. Later the term came to be associated with actual tests of practical reading tasks encountered outside of schools. In view of the pervasive achievement testing that existed in schools by the 1930s, and educators' growing concern about functional illiteracy, one would think that the history of higher-order literacy skills over the past fifty years would be familiar and precise. On the contrary, there is almost no historical work on the subject, and the sources are riddled with problems. Testing instruments have changed constantly, and it is difficult to control for the changing nature of the populations tested. There is a genre of "then-and-now" studies, in which a researcher deliberately administers an old test to an allegedly comparable group to measure change over long periods of time. Many such studies were done for various locations and groups in the United States, for points in time between 1900 and the early 1960s. These were reviewed by Farr, Tuinman, and Rowls (1974). Unfortunately, none of these studies completely escaped problems of changes in the test population. Because the trends in reading abilities were not very dramatic, the conclusions may be very much affected by changes in the average age of children in a given grade, or changes in urbanization or migration patterns in the test area. Almost all researchers who have conducted such then-and-now reading research have claimed an increasing level of reading abilities, but their data were inconclusive. Tests of functional illiteracy are not useful for historical purposes because they are all quite recent (with the interesting exception of Buswell, 1937); and they vary widely in content and the criteria they establish to label a person functionally illiterate.

For the recent past, we have better controlled measures of higher-order literacy abilities, from college entrance examination trends, from the National Assessment of Educational Progress results, and from re-norming exercises by the producers of standardized achievement tests. These data are the evidence in the tangled "test score decline" debate. They have their own deficiencies but are too complex to review here (see Stedman and Kaestle, 1985). A long-range perspective on measured literacy skills suggests, however, that there has been a great expansion of literacy skills in America during the twentieth century, evidenced by increasing educational attainment and increased circulation of print matter (Bormuth, 1978; Trow, 1961, 1962), and that the slight declines of recent years pale by comparison. The problems of today's illiterates, the dearth of writing practice in the schools, the absence of critical reading skills on the job, and the negative effect of the electronic media on reading activities are all matters of legitimate concern and have some basis in fact; but they should not lead us to invent a golden age of literacy in some earlier decade.

Trends in Crude Literacy: Conclusions

With a few important exceptions, historians of literacy have focused on the social differences between nominally literate and nominally illiterate people and on the relationship of literacy and schooling. They have done much detailed work; the most extensive studies of crude literacy available in English are for England, Scotland, France, Sweden, Canada, and New England. Nonetheless, reliable generalizations about the social concomitants of literacy are elusive, and historians have challenged many of the old, simple correlations. Writing about literacy in English communities, Stephens (1977) concluded, "We can discern no 'iron law,' no easy categorization, but only a tendency against which to set the unique history of each particular town" (p. 47).

Warnings about local variation are well taken. However, some tendencies have persisted in a variety of settings; thus, there are some generalizations left in the history of literacy. On the vexed and sometimes tautological question of whether literacy is necessarily correlated with modernization, however, caution is warranted. Although there is no doubt that literacy has generally proceeded along with other indices used by modernization theorists, literacy can also be used for culturally conservative purposes. Lockridge (1974) has argued that the Puritans used literacy in New England to maintain traditional religion, and Greer (1978) has argued that rising literacy facilitated a swing to conservative politics in eighteenth-century Quebec. The uses of literacy have not been the subject of much historical study, but obviously they are various. Princeton historian Lawrence Stone once remarked that if you teach a man to read the Bible, he may also read pornography or seditious literature; put another way, if you teach a woman to read so that she may know her place, she may learn that she deserves yours. These are the Janus faces of literacy.

There is only scant empirical evidence about the concrete consequences of literacy in the lives of individuals or groups. Educators have often associated literacy with economic advancement, but historians have done little to probe the connection. Some works on industrialization in nineteenth-century America touch upon the subject. Field (1980) argued that skill requirements declined rather than increased during the initial shift to factory labor in the United States, so there would be little real advantage to the educated industrial laborer sometimes hailed by manufacturers. Thernstrom (1964) documented the importance of child labor in the family economies of Newburyport shoe laborers and concluded that sending children to school would have been counterproductive for workers' families. Dublin (1979) found that literacy correlated with higher wages among Lowell's female textile workers, but not when controlling for ethnicity; he thus concluded that literacy was incidental to higher status in the mills. Graff (1979), relying on census data, also found that literacy had little weight in overcoming the ethnic bias of the social structure in Ontario cities. Vinovskis (1970), taking as his point of departure Horace Mann's claim that education contributed to greater industrial productivity, pointed out that Mann's evidence was biased, his motives political, and his estimates of the value of education greatly exaggerated. Nonetheless, as Vinovskis (1983) has recently reminded us, education was not worthless in nineteenth-century America. It was apparently more valuable economically to some groups than others. Kaestle (1983) summarized the sketchy evidence that high schools were of benefit to middling status white males (sons of both lower white collar workers and skilled craftsmen) in maintaining or improving intergenerational status. For women, education became an entree to teaching, and by the late nineteenth century female students predominated in America's public high schools.

In the present writer's judgment, the evidence on the issue of the returns to education may be summarized as follows. First, education paid off better for those in the middle reaches of society than for laborers. Second, there was a greater return for education in the twentieth century than in the nineteenth; skill levels were upgraded, education expanded, the clerical and service sectors burgeoned, and there was a tighter fit between schooling and one's occupational fate. Third, the benefits to literacy for members of oppressed groups are often more apparent collectively than individually, and in the long run rather than the short run. Thus, although the Irish shoe worker was probably correct in thinking that there would be little benefit in a high school education for his son in 1840, in the long run, Irish people as a group have benefitted from higher education levels. Similarly, higher education for blacks may have gained them little access to status in white society in the 1890s, but in the long run, education has helped to narrow racial inequalities. The same argument can be made for the history of women. What is implied, of course, is a history of frustration and bitterness for individuals facing a discriminatory world but realizing the necessity of acquiring literacy and then higher education as a resource in confronting economic and occupational inequality.

Literacy is discriminatory in two ways, with regard to access and with regard to content. Problems of discrimination are not over when access is gained; there is a cultural price-tag to literacy. Thus, the question of whether literacy is liberating or constraining also has to do with whether it is seen as an instrument of conformity or as an instrument of creativity. We need much more research on the functions of literacy for cultural consolidation and, in contrast, for the expression of alternatives.

If this is the state of our knowledge about the individual and group consequences of literacy in industrial society, what about its causes? The "causes" of literacy are generally inferred from correlations. Although recent scholars have emphasized regional rather than national averages, multiple factors instead of single, and some unexplained lags and incongruities, some correlations persist. Higher literacy rates generally correlate with higher social status, males, Protestants, industrializing regions, and dense population. These generalizations stand up fairly well for the modern West. The correlation of literacy with higher social status, a persistent theme, is hardly surprising, although as Auwers (1980) has demonstrated, the correlation can be stronger at some times than at others. The relationship between literacy and industrialization has occasioned a big debate, which can be resolved as follows: Defined as a long-term process in a region or nation, industrialization is reliably associated with rising literacy; in the short run, the onset of factory production may inhibit literacy training—and thus reduce literacy rates—locally because of child labor or immigration patterns. Among specific urban communities, rising literacy is more clearly correlated with commerce than with industry. Although it is difficult to disentangle religion from other factors, earlier rises in literacy also correlated with Protestantism. Male rates of estimated crude literacy are consistently higher than those of women until the twentieth century, if we accept signature-signing as a proxy for reading ability; but, as we have seen, there is reason to be skeptical about the illiteracy of those who mark with an "X." Finally, despite interesting short-run exceptions, rising literacy is associated with the expansion of schooling.

The most durable patterns, then, are the least surprising. Nonetheless, they are important features in the history of crude literacy rates. However, some historians of literacy have become increasingly skeptical of the validity of the literate-illiterate dichotomy and of the equation of signature ability or census responses with actual reading ability. The field is beginning to move away from studies with a central interest in crude literacy rates. The future will see more studies like those of Altick (1957), Laqueur (1976), Spufford (1981), or Moran and

Vinovskis (1983), that deal only incidentally with literacy rates but more centrally with the acquisition of literacy and its uses among adults.

The New History of Literacy

Introduction

There is no absolute dividing line between studies of crude literacy rates and studies of the uses of literacy. Soltow and Stevens' (1981) book, a study of literacy rates, included interesting material about the circulation of print matter, while Cremin's (1970, 1980) two volumes about educational history featured discussions about both the rates and functions of literacy. Still, little work has been done on the social history of different reading publics. A broad history of literacy must go beyond the labels of "illiterate" and "literate" to study the functions of reading in adults' lives, thus returning to the history of literacy the majority of the people who, in the modern West, have been able to read at some level. As we seek to understand the purposes and consequences of literacy, we must reach out into more general histories of education, culture, publication, and communication, and to contemporary theoretical works that might inform a synthesis of these materials. Scholars will need to take the best insights from fields like the sociology of literature and communications theory and apply them to topics ranging from the book trade, journalism, and library history, to education levels, reading activities, and the impact of the electronic media on reading.

Integration by Theory

Broadening the history of literacy to consider the uses of reading by adults may seem to make the subject hopelessly diffuse. One way to get control of the immensity of the subject is through theory. A successful theory about reading and social change could tell us which details are most important to understanding the whole subject. Through comparative work, we could develop generalizations that would fit a wide range of cases.

The word "theory" is sometimes used in an informal sense to mean a hypothesis about why a particular event happened. One may have a theory, for example, about why the Green Bay Packers lost their last football game against the Chicago Bears. In its formal sense, however, a theory in the social sciences attempts to explain many particular events and should strive for breadth, generality, and parsimony. For the subject under investigation, the theory should cover as many relevant aspects as possible; it should state general propositions that have as few exceptions as possible; and it should accommodate the greatest bulk of the evidence with the fewest propositions possible. Obviously, such theories are hard to construct, and many historians shy from the attempt. One cannot merely adopt a master view of how the world works and then apply it to historical situations like a cookbook. There must be a dialectic between central assumptions and concrete historical materials; the theory develops as the historical work proceeds.

Conceptual models stand in the mid-ground between systematic formal theories and explanations of single events. Models of explanation often help classify the phenomena under investigation, suggesting what to look at and how to structure the inquiry, without making causal generalizations. Three examples will illustrate the use of models by scholars interested in the history of print matter. Nord (1977) devised a model for studying press control. Research on freedom of the press had been dominated by the typology of Siebert, Petersen, and Schramm (1956), which specified four ideal types of control: authoritarian, libertarian, social responsibility, and soviet communist. Nord argued that these ideal types encompassed too many complex factors and did not specify continuous variables that could be investigated empirically. He proposed a model for research that assumed the following: mass media are controlled by the larger society, the control is complex and variable, and the two most salient sources of control are the government and the economic system. He then suggested some variables for measuring these two forms of control and ended with a spatial model that looked like a scatterplot, with one axis running from low to high governmental control and the other axis running from low to high economic constraints. This model for comparative research, he suggested, might be a step toward theory construction.

Darnton (1982) recently reviewed *l'histoire du livre*, an increasingly prominent subfield in cultural history. He suggested a model to bring more coherence to the sprawling interests of scholars pursuing the history of books. From their initial interests in bibliography, printing, and the publication history of great books, they have broadened their focus. In the 1950s, historians of the *Annales* school began inquiring into the circulation and uses of books among ordinary people. Ladurie (1974), for example, examined how people in some classes and areas of Languedoc province adopted the French language and Reformation texts more rapidly, while others clung to regional dialects, oral culture, and traditional religion. In a masterful chapter on the "paths of scripture," he argued the effects of Calvinism in eventually creating "a remodelled personality" (p. 171).

Darnton himself (1979) moved the field further by studying the dissemination of Enlightenment ideas. He dissected the publication, marketing, the distribution of the *Encyclopédie*. In the history of books, wrote Darnton, "the questions could be multiplied endlessly because books touched on such a vast range of human activity—everything from picking rags to transmitting the word of God. They were products of artisanal labor, objects of economic exchange, vehicles of ideas, and elements in political and religious conflict" (p. 1). In his review essay, Darnton (1982) proposed a model for relating the research on these diverse topics. The spatial model was based on the metaphor of a circuit. Beginning with a book's author, Darnton's model examined the connections between authors and publishers, then between publishers and printers, then on to printers, shippers, booksellers, and finally readers. He left the important but murky connection between readers and authors as a dotted line, not quite completing the circuit. As for readers themselves, he noted that historians cannot retrieve the inner meaning of reading for most people in the past, but that they can nonetheless do much valuable research on the reading activities, preferences, and apparent purposes of books among different groups. At each point in the circuit, Darnton argued, researchers must relate text transmission to the political, economic, and intellectual context of the period. As it stands, his circuit model is not a theory. It is a plan of research, ably illustrated by his earlier work. The model could lead to theory construction if researchers who adopted the model discovered recurring patterns of text dissemination in different areas and at different times.

Darnton focussed only on books, but the new history of literacy must consider all printed matter. The readers of books were until recently a small part of the reading public. Thus we must open our inquiry to newspapers, magazines, broadsides, and more fugitive publications. Even this expansion is not comprehensive, however. People's understanding of print were enmeshed in a thick web of oral communication. Historians of literacy must therefore try to relate changes in print functions to changes in oral traditions and, later, to the emerging electronic media. One model for thinking about communications in a comprehensive way was proposed by Lasswell (1948). He distinguished among control analysis (influences on the communicator), content analysis (what is being said), media analysis (means of communication), audience analysis (who is reached), and effect analysis (the impact of the communication on its audience). Such a model could be applied to a book, a radio program, a classroom or a peer group. One cannot, of course, do all of these things at once; it is necessary to work on manageable pieces. But models of communication remind historians of literacy about the relatively modest role of print in most people's daily experiences, human relationships, work life, and social beliefs.

The spatial models of Nord, Darnton, and Lasswell do not predict how communications will work in particular historical settings. A few researchers have gone further, attempting to deal with the history of print from the point of view of a more comprehensive theory of social structure and social change. One such scholar was Harold Innis (1964), who anchored social change in technological developments in communication. A student of Robert Park and a mentor to Marshall McLuhan, Innis saw communication as power and believed that technology expressed itself most saliently through communications media. When the adoption of writing transformed Greek city-states into the Alexandrian empire, for example, "the first great sledge-hammer blows of technology" had been delivered (p. 10). A technological determinist, Innis ranged over all of Western history to "show that sudden extensions of communication are reflected in cultural disturbances" (p. 31). Innis created a dichotomous scheme in which "time-biased" media like heavy clay tablets favored local government, oral tradition, and a monopoly of literacy, while "space-biased" media like papyrus or paper favored empire, innovation, and the expansion of literacy. Throughout history the two kinds of media have been in tension, each conferring power to different groups and structuring society and culture in different ways. Although modern history has favored space-biased media, Innis argued, any society that did not find a balance between the two communication worlds was unstable (see Carey, 1967). Innis's theory featured not only broad, predictive generalizations but also an element of nostalgia for the village, where oral communication, religion, and tradition were central.

For Innis the fulcrum of history was technology. For Raymond Williams (1961, 1977) it was the economy. Whereas Innis was a technological determinist, Williams worked out a theory of cultural materialism, more or less in a Marxist framework. In Williams' historical drama there have been three great revolutions in Western history— a democratic revolution, an industrial revolution, and an expansion of culture, which Williams called "the long revolution." The expansion of culture has been governed by the other two revolutions. The democratic revolution dictated continually widening audiences for culture, while the industrial revolution insured that the production of culture would take a commercial form. New forms of popular culture have often struck elite commentators as threats to the quality of print culture. Some of these, like the daily newspaper and the novel, seem in retrospect to have been cultural gains, Williams argued. Still, the most worrisome cultural problem of the twentieth century, according to Williams, is the expansion of the worst aspects of culture, due to the influence of the profit motive. The alternative to this historical tendency would be more governmental support and regulation of culture, with the particular pitfalls of that system. Williams urged new modes of analysis and creative thinking to move the long revolution into "a new and constructive stage" (1961, p. 354). Whether right or wrong on policy, Williams' succinct and forceful historical analysis is an excellent example of the use of theory to integrate different aspects of the history of literacy.

Some scholars use theory in less comprehensive ways, to inform research on some aspect of the history of literacy. Kelly (1974), pondering the value of imaginative literature as historical evidence, turned to anthropology for a definition of culture and to Berger and Luckmann (1966) for ideas about the sociology of knowledge. Armed with these theoretical perceptions, Kelly sorted out the possible cultural meanings of juvenile fiction. We cannot infer anything about readers' reaction to text solely from the text, he concluded, nor can we use the text itself as a description of actual social conditions. But we may treat the authors of such fiction as representing the values of a certain segment of society, expressing their goals and anxieties through didactic fiction. Other scholars in literary criticism and the field of American studies have worked on the relationship between fictional texts and their readers. Cawelti (1976), for example, in an excellent book about detective mysteries and Western adventures, defined and analyzed popular literary formulas as summations of cultural myths and called for more research on the audiences of popular fiction.

Displaying the interdisciplinary thrust of the new history of literacy, Heath (1978) explored the relationship between sociolinguistics and the social history of reading. She combined sociolinguists' theoretical propositions about politeness formulae with empirical work on 350 etiquette books of the nineteenth century. Contrary to what one might expect, etiquette books of the Jacksonian era laid great stress on class distinctions. This emphasis became muted later, an illustration of cultural lag in the dissemination of egalitarian ideals. The role of class was suggested by sociolinguistic theorists interested in etiquette; the historical data, Heath suggested tentatively, might in turn be used to test theories about how etiquette changed over time.

Bibliometrics, the application of mathematical techniques to the study of publication, has yielded some generalizations about authors' frequency of publication, their influence as measured by citations, differences in publication patterns among different disciplines, the growth of knowledge, and how knowledge becomes obsolete (Potter, 1981). Although scholars have derived certain "laws" on these matters, O'Connor and Voos (1981) question whether anything in bibliometrics yet qualifies as theory. The models yield predictive patterns but are unidimensional and lack causal explanations to match the patterns. By adopting multivariate models and pondering causal explanations, students of bibliometrics might provide some theoretical insights of interest to historians of literacy.

Integration by Collaboration

Theory construction is very demanding, and the interdisciplinary nature of theory construction in the history of literacy makes it particularly so. The attempt to discover general patterns and ponder their causes presses scholars to do comparative work. These interdisciplinary and comparative demands have fostered collaborative work on the history of literacy. Over 15 years ago an anthology of articles on literacy in several traditional societies helped Goody (1968) refine his ideas about the effects of literacy. Since that time, several conferences and other collaborative efforts have helped to move the field forward. In 1979 the Reimers-Stiftung Institute in Bad-Homburg, Germany, held an International Colloquium on Literacy, Economic Development, and Social Change. In 1980, at least four more conferences were held. Joan Simon brought together several of the leading historians of literacy from England, Sweden, Canada, and the United States at a seminar on Literacy, Education, and Society in Post-Reformation Europe, meeting at Leicester University (Simon, 1981). Later that year the Center for the Book at the Library of Congress held a conference on Literacy in Historical Perspective, which resulted in a book of essays edited by Resnick (1983). In Boston the Association of College and Research Libraries convened a conference on Books and Society in History to explore the connections between French-style *l'histoire du livre* and bibliographic studies in the Anglo-American tradition. Also, in the same year, the American Antiquarian Society in Worcester, Massachusetts, held a conference on Printing and Society in Early America, a meeting that resulted in an anthology of new research edited by Joyce, Hall, Brown, and Hench (1983). Collaboration is continuing at the American Antiquarian Society, where the Program in the History of the Book in American Culture funds research on the history of printed matter in the United States up to 1870. In 1981, David Olson gathered an interdisciplinary group together in Toronto to consider the nature and consequences of literacy for individuals and societies, resulting in a wide-ranging anthology (Olson, Torrence, and Hildyard, 1985). Conferences and anthologies do not result automatically in scholarly accomplishment, but these collaborative activities in the history of literacy have provided lively forums for mutual criticism, shared research, and discussing the conceptual problems associated with this broad topic.

Synthesis

Whether they collaborate or not, and whether they use theory or not, historians of literacy need to attempt more synthesis. A broader approach to the history of literacy in the United States could achieve two goals: first, to bring together into a more systematic analysis the existing secondary literature on the production and circulation of printed matter and, second, to move beyond the history of texts to the history of readers.

Once these goals are accepted, endless research gaps appear. We lack for American history even such an overview as Altick's *English Common Reader in the Nineteenth Century* (1957), a traditional but useful survey of the expansion of the English reading public and the consequent fears among elite English commentators about undesirable reading activities. Many more specialized studies are also needed: a new history of libraries and their use, a comprehensive history of consolidation in the publishing industry, a thorough review of the twentieth-century social science literature on the reading public, studies on the role of gender, race, and class in magazine marketing and consumption, and studies of diaries and autobiographies to determine the role of reading in ordinary people's lives.

The following discussion highlights some relevant secondary sources on the history of printed matter and then suggests some ways to get at the history of readers, a more difficult research topic. There are many works on best-selling books, ranging from Hackett's (1967) compendium of annual lists to Hart's delightful synthesis, *The Popular Book* (1950). There are works on the development of various genres of books such as dime novels (Curti, 1937), westerns (Cawelti, 1971), science fiction (Del Ray, 1979), and romances (McNall, 1981); and there are works on the technology, format, and marketing of books, ranging from Tebbel's (1975) encyclopedic history of book publishing in America to Davis's (1984) recent lively history of the paperback. The history of libraries has focussed more on internal professional development than on readers or the circulation of books. There are, however, some broad and imaginative individual studies of the expansion of libraries in the United States, attending to regional variation, private philanthropy, and the effects of government assistance (Campbell and Metzner, 1950; Daniel, 1961; Wilson, 1938).

Older works in the history of newspapers concentrated on the development of the industry and the biographies of the great publishers like Hearst and Pulitzer. Recently, revisionist historians of journalism have reexamined the values developed by journalists (Schiller, 1981; Schudson, 1978), but attention to the readers of newspapers has been slight. Histories of magazines also tend to fall into two categories: old-fashioned works about the industry in general, and newer works on the content of particular magazines or genres.

The development of national markets, brand names, and advertising added a new dimension to reading activities, particularly for women who ran households. Interest in the growth and functions of advertising has produced a trio of recent books, one by Ewen (1976) that overargued a Marxist analysis but presented much interesting material on the manipulative strategies of advertising theorists in the 1920s; one by Fox (1984) that concentrated on the internal history of industry; and one most recently by Schudson (1984), which challenged the Ewen thesis and downplayed the power of advertising. These books should cause historians of literacy to ponder the impact of advertising on households, on magazines and newspapers, and thus on the functions of reading over the past sixty years. Historians of recent trends in literacy will also have to consider the impact of radio and television on reading activities, a subject on which there are many discrete surveys but little synthesis across studies.

The effects of print technology, advertising, electronic media, literacy trends, and news production differ among different groups in United States history. There is not one reading public but several. Although there are some useful works on the black press (Daniel, 1982; Joyce, 1983), the immigrant press (Fishman, Nahirny, Hofman, and Hayden, 1966; Park, 1922), the religious press (Reilly, 1971), and the radical press (Kessler, 1984), we need more work on women as a category of readers, and we need more general analysis of the degree of segmentation and overlap of readership among different social groups.

There are several sources that will allow the historian of literacy to bring the readers into view along with the history of printed matter; these include circulation data, earlier social science research on readers, and individual life history materials that reveal the role of reading in everyday life in the past. Some imaginative things can be done with circulation and consumption data. Bormuth (1978), for example, charted the great expansion of printed matter produced and sold during recent decades as a counter-argument against claims about the "decline of literacy" and the "death of print." Earlier data on the volume of printed material is skimpier, with comparability and validity problems increasing as we reach back in time. Nonetheless, we need new attempts at time series for newspaper, magazine, and book circulation. For the most popular print form, newspapers, *Ayer's Directory* gives circulation figures beginning in 1880; the early figures are systematic but self-reported and therefore suspect. They are supplemented by other sources after 1900 and an expanding volume of specialized studies after 1940 (Ayer, 1880 et seq.; Bogart, 1981; Byerly, 1968; *Editor and Publisher* 1920 et seq.). Systematic figures for magazines published prior to World War I are not available. The Audit Bureau of Circulation, established in 1914, published reports on the circulation of magazines that carried advertising.

For books the record is also systematic for the twentieth century, but the validity of the measure is dubious. Alice Payne Hackett, a long-time editor of *Publishers' Weekly,* tabulated lists of best-selling books from bookstore surveys. For the period 1896 to 1965 she compiled lists of annual best-sellers and all-time best-sellers, both of which are important for students of the reading public (Hackett, 1967). Unfortunately the bookstore surveys are based on small samples, not controlled for store size, and not stratified for regional or other demographic factors. They do not capture books which garnered large sales across two calendar years. Best-seller lists give us a guess about some books that were very popular. There are no systematic figures for actual sales. Library circulation figures are even less systematic. There are some broad and imaginative individual studies (Campbell and Metzner, 1950; Daniel, 1961; Wilson, 1938) and progressively thorough statistics on the number of libraries, per capita library loans, and other matters, reported by the U.S. Office of Education and by the American Library Association (Schick, 1976).

Of course, even when we have circulation figures about particular books, magazines, or newspapers, they do not reveal the actual number of readers or who the readers were. Except through anecdotal evidence and occasional surveys, we cannot determine how many members of a family read newspapers, how many magazines were loaned to friends or were read in barbershops, and how many unopened books adorned coffee tables. Circulation figures give us an indication of the genres, subjects, authors, and forms popular at a given time. They provide an indirect window on the size of various reading publics.

In addition, there is a huge literature on the reading public, stretching back to the early twentieth century. There are literally thousands of studies, ranging from national surveys to research on particular areas or subgroups (see Purves and Beach, 1972). Most of these studies dealt only with respondents' stated reading preferences and they are of limited value. Even when people told the truth, their interests were only one factor determining what they actually read. The few studies that have examined the relationship between stated reading interests and actual reading have shown the important effects of readability, accessibility, and advertising in modifying a reader's stated interests (Carnovsky, 1934; Waples, 1932). Fortunately, there is a wide range of other studies that can take us beyond the conventional reader interest surveys. There are studies of book reading (Ennis, 1965; Link and Hopf, 1946), readership surveys of newspapers (Emig, 1928; Newsprint Information Committee, 1961; Sharon, 1973) and magazines (Faville, 1940; Murphy, 1962), in-depth community studies of reading activities (Hajda, 1963; Heath, 1980; Ormsbee, 1927), surveys of leisure-time activities (DeGrazia, 1962; Larrabee and Meyersohn, 1958; Reed, 1932; Robinson, 1977), and case study materials on individual readers (Gray and Monroe, 1929; Rasche, 1937; Smith and Tyler, 1942). Robinson (1980) surveyed studies from 1946 to 1977 that analyzed the amount of time people spent reading newspapers, magazines, and books. More work of this sort needs to be done, in order to synthesize this tradition of survey literature, work out problems of comparability where possible, and place the long-term trends in historical perspective.

These materials could be supplemented with autobiographical materials on the role of reading in individuals' lives, culled from memoirs and other life history materials. Much current research on reading emphasizes the interaction of text and reader. The reader's prior knowledge, motivation, and social situation are crucial to the meaning and success of reading activities (Amarel, 1982; Blachowitz, 1978). The best way a social historian can introduce this interaction into the history of literacy is through autobiographical materials that reveal how people learned to read and what it meant to them.

Conclusion

Historians of literacy have taught us a great deal in the past twenty years about the consequences of literacy and of print in the early modern West, and they have assiduously charted trends in signature writing and self-reported literacy for later centuries. Many generalizations have been tested and refined. We can say, indeed, that we know a lot about these matters. Although some historians have also done imaginative work on the uses of literacy in everyday life, we know much less about this important aspect of the subject. Consequently we need research on the functions of printed matter among different reading publics. If we aspire to discover the inner meanings of literacy for readers in the past, however, we may wish for the impossible. It is very difficult to trace printed works to their readers and still more difficult to trace meaning from the text to the reader. Even where we have some evidence about the uses of literacy, there is no way to summarize for a whole society the significance of so commonplace and pervasive an activity as reading. There will be, then, no comprehensive social history of the uses of literacy, and no comprehensive theory to explain the entire history of texts and readers. There is an open field, however, for new, detailed research on the individual items of an immense, exciting research agenda. There is also a need for broadly synthetic works that will relate different print genres to each other, to readers from different groups, to other forms of communication and to key developments in cultural and social history.

Collaboratively and individually, with or without theory, whether working on small pieces or large pieces of this research, historians of literacy will have to wrestle consciously with two problems that will shape their research: hypothesis formation and normative stance. It is not enough to open up the history of literacy to a broader definition, to focus on the uses of literacy and then to list all the topics begging to be researched. We must also try to formulate hypotheses about the functions of print and about the interaction of culture and technology in the development of print forms. Why does printed matter sometimes serve to consolidate and homogenize culture and sometimes serve to strengthen and perpetuate subcultures and alternative lifestyles? Is the process of cultural consolidation reversible? How do culture and social structure affect the timing and manner in which we adopt technological innovations in print production? How do technological changes in turn shape cultural forms and activities? These are some of the questions that will shape the new history of literacy.

Finally, studies of the uses of literacy inevitably face a normative question. The question of whether the reading public could be expanded without vulgarizing culture has worried elite commentators in the past as well as historians. In eighteenth-century China, as in England, the spread of popular reading materials gave rise to elite denunciations of the dire effects of novel-reading and other popular pleasures (Altick, 1957; Rawski, 1979). In the United States, debates about mass culture have become especially impassioned since the 1950s, when Dwight Macdonald (1957) argued that mass culture was "a parasitic, a cancerous growth on High Culture," which "mixes and scrambles everything together" and "destroys all values." Herbert Gans, (1974), rebutting similar arguments, argued that sociologists studying popular culture must proceed from the premise that people have a right to the culture they prefer and that more diversity in culture, rather than higher standards, was a positive good. A third perspective is exemplified by Richard Hoggart (1957), who argued that a genuine, self-consciously working-class culture in early twentieth-century England was gradually subverted by uncritical, materialistic, homogenizing culture. A fourth alternative is the outright admiration of modern mass print matter evidenced by some historians of popular culture (e.g., Blackbeard, 1981). One's normative judgments about past developments in popular print culture will affect one's historical account and one's predictions about the future. Whatever the future, it is clear that the reading public has expanded dramatically since the appearance of the printing press and especially during the past century. Mass education and cheap printed matter have affected every group. Historians of literacy are at a turning point. With the insights, methods, and concerns developed during recent years, they should soon be able to tell us much more about the meaning of these developments.

8.
The Coming of Literate Communication to Western Culture

Eric A. Havelock

During the centuries between 1100 and 600 B.C., when the civilization we know as classical Hellenism was born, the Greeks came to live as a dispersed people speaking various dialects of a common tongue, not only on the European peninsula we still call Greece, but in all the islands of the Aegean Sea, on the coasts of Anatolia, Thrace, and the Black Sea, and on the coasts of Sicily, South Italy, and North Africa. Essentially the Greeks were at this time a maritime people, clinging to the edges of the mainland rather than occupying and subduing it. Yet in thinking of the Greeks, it is always tempting to plant one's feet firmly on the Acropolis of Athens and survey the rest of the population from that vantage point. It is more correct in this instance, however, to regard the circumference as more significant than the center. And the circumference was the birthplace of the earliest Greek composition we have, known as the poems of Homer. The classical age becomes a matter of record at the moment when the Homeric poems were transcribed.

Possibly, as I have said elsewhere, the transcription was not a matter of a moment, but was a process spread over decades, not finalized in Athens until perhaps as late as the sixth century B.C. (There are scholars, including myself, who would accept such a conclusion, but it is controversial, and not crucial.) At some time—the year 1000 B.C. is often taken as a convenient starting point marking the inception of the manufacture of geometric pottery—the Greeks of the dispersion, as I have called it, began to develop the initial stages of what became the hallmarks of Greek classical culture: an architecture, a visual art, a poetry, and a political structure, the Greek *polis*. It seems indisputable that these were in position at a time when the people who placed them there could still neither read nor write.

From the *Journal of Communication*, 1980, 30(1): 90–98 by Eric A. Havelock. Reprinted by permission.

Therefore an understanding of literacy must begin with non-literacy.[1] Literacy when it came did not create a culture; it transmuted one which it inherited, and the process must have taken time. Non-literacy in Greece represented a cultural condition of immemorial antiquity during which evolutionary pressures molded the capacities of the human brain to the point where it could use language and form communities. Biologically we are all oralists, who have become literate only through cultural conditioning. Past and present intermingle in us, and it is possible that if literacy presents us with certain problems, these may not be soluble without reference to the habits of non-literacy.

Human culture is a creation of human communication; this I take to be a truism. My central concern is with language, both spoken and written. Borrowing a theoretic paradigm from social anthropology, the transmission of social culture can be described thus: as our genes hold in storage coded sets of information to guide the developing organism, from conception to death, a storage transferred from generation to generation, so at the level of social culture, societies in order to exist and enjoy their own forms of organic continuity have to place accumulated information in storage for re-use. The main method for doing this is linguistic. It is easy to see this in the case of documented information covering our law and literature, our science and technology, with which we educate ourselves and from which we absorb our values and attitudes, as we receive it and re-use it and make additions to it.

How does one get the same kind of results in a non-literate culture? In such a culture, storage and transmission between the generations can be carried on only in individual memories. Linguistic information can be incorporated in a transmissible memory, as against some one person's memory, only as it obeys two laws of composition: it must be rhythmic and it must be mythical, in the original Greek sense which the word "mythical" implies, meaning two things. Overall, it must be cast in the form of mythos as a tale; piecemeal, it must be cast in the form of mythos as a saying; the bits and pieces of cultural information must be governed by the syntax of the tale, one which describes an action performed by an agent rather than a law or principle or formula. The oral memory is unfriendly to such statements as "the angles of a triangle are equal to two right angles." But if you say "the triangle strode over the field of battle on its two straight legs defending its two right angles against the enemy," you are remodeling the equation retroactively to accord with the linguistic requirements of oral transmission. If you transfer the tense to the present or imperative and say "a triangle (always) protects its two right angles," or "it (is) better that it do so," or "it must do so," you have produced the equivalent of a saying, an oral maxim, apothegm, or aphorism—supposing strictly oral cultures were ever interested in triangles, which does not seem to be the case.

The felt need of the group for a sense of cultural identity and historical continuity cannot be satisfied by the mere transmission by word of mouth of a body of maxims and sayings or even by separate short stories, i.e., myths. It needs a great story within which these can be amalgamated in some way into that construct we call "national epic," essentially an oral form of composition. Such epics seem to have been recited and sung wherever oral cultures reached a given level of sophistication. They report and illustrate and recommend, indirectly through narrative, the mores and manners, law, religion, and government of the people concerned, who entrust the formation and recitation of such epics to professional singers and are continuously instructed by them as they listen to the recited poems and are encouraged to quote and repeat them. The mass of information is suspended like sediment in the great sweep of the tale.

Such is the theoretic or anthropological framework within which to place the two Homeric epic poems.[2] Seen in this light, they can be viewed as owing less to individual authorship—strictly a literate conception—than to a collegiate activity on the part of generations of composers, not excluding the possibility of individual genius among them. It is not appropriate to base critical judgments of such poetry on strictly literate standards of criticism, which means "literary" standards, provided, that is, that we possess the poetry in something like its original oral form, which for most national epics, for example the Icelandic Eddas or the Niebelungenlied, is not strictly the case. While both Homeric poems upon transcription entered the world of dawning literacy and became works of "literature" for us, they represent a condition of the strictly oral word as composed and sung in a non-literate society. The two Homeric poems left their oral source behind and became works of literature through the instrument we call the alphabet.

Textbooks and histories which deal in any way with these matters commonly use the word alphabet generically to cover a variety of early writing systems, the Greek one being only the latest in a series of such "alphabets." This failure of distinction is unfortunate, for it helps to obscure the fact that the adaptation when carried out amounted to a transformation of function and technological capability which was truly radical. The invention was revolutionary, even if like all inventions it arose through a fresh combination of previously experienced observations. The history of literacy would be served by restricting the term alphabet to the Greek system, as I propose to do.

The phonetic technology of the invention calls for brief exposition, since it was a technology with far reaching effects upon the history of Western culture. Not later than circa 700 B.C.,[3] plus or minus a few years, the invention was available to those who could use it. Its borrowing of written characters previously used by the Phoenicians illustrates the law that new invention is continuous with previous experience. The effort to symbolize the sounds of spoken speech, following upon the earlier and primitive uses of picture writing, had been going on in the Near East for centuries. The problem of these systems was that the sounds symbolized were the possible syllables of words, not the components of the syllables. The possible total of syllables in any tongue is too large, and their exhaustive definition too difficult, to be manageable except in some approximate and incomplete fashion. Systems of shorthand had to be devised to cut down the number and reduce the variety to be symbolized. The Phoenicians carried the shorthand principle to its ultimate by arranging a table of syllables in sets, according to their initial consonants, and then indexing the consonants, and then assigning a single character to each. The signs, the phonetic values, the names, and the memorized list the Greeks borrowed from the Phoenicians with some approximations to fit their own tongue. But they still did not have an instrument fit to translate the tongue fluently from sound to sight, from speech to sign, because the index supplied consonants but no vowels; in effect it applied a single label to a whole group of syllables.

It is usually said that the Greek contribution was to "invent" the five vowels *a, e, i, o, u,* and to assign "unwanted" signs of the Phoenician list to their signification. It is more to the point to say that by identifying all five vowels (some had been already identified in previous systems) in separation from the consonants, they isolated the consonants as separate components of language. Now, a consonantal sound by itself has a theoretic but not an actual existence in any tongue. It normally requires the addition of some vocalization to be pronounced. So what the Greeks really achieved in their act of "adaptation," as their borrowing of Phoenician is called, was an act of abstraction. They decided to use their ABC to symbolize sounds that existed analytically as mental objects but not empirically as spoken sounds. Once this happened, a language could be atomized exhaustively into less than thirty components, any two, three, or four of which could be combined to produce adequate symbolization for any required actual sound, i.e., syllable, with relative accuracy, as it was pronounced.

Recognition (the original Greek work for "reading") became automatic and swift. Ambiguity was banished, and fluency released. A universal instrument for recording the phonemes of any spoken tongue exhaustively and simply was now available, with the proviso that some residual approximation remained. The instrument devised proved to be precise enough for practical purposes.[4]

This invention, given the right social conditions for teaching it (a large order), could be learned by a majority of a given population, thus creating the possibility of a popular literacy. Yet at the time of the invention, and for some time after, the theoretic possibilities of literacy, either political or psychological, lay far in the future. The Greeks could not become literate overnight. Two things stood in the way. There was, obviously, as yet no ready supply of documented material which would make it worth one's while to learn to read it; and there was no technology for teaching it to preadolescent children, at an age when its use can be readily mastered: the institutional arrangements necessary for this purpose did not exist. A still more important factor which stood in the way was represented by the existing system of "musical" education[5] in the Greek sense. Any indoctrination in letters, i.e., reading or writing, was treated as strictly ancillary to oral competence. To preserve and transmit the traditions of Greek society remained the province of the poets for over two centuries after the documentation of poetry became possible. The poets[6] were essentially still oral poets, down to the time when a reading public came into existence, ready to comprehend new forms of written composition. The poets were called on to continue the didactic functions performed by Homer, most strikingly exemplified in the Athenian drama, in which traditional myths, i.e., orally remembered stories, are continually worked up in varying versions to entertain but also to instruct.

During this time the alphabet was becoming an instrument of some government and some law and some economic activity—but to a limited extent. It is only in the latter half of the fifth century that the evidences for its application begin to multiply. Thus in reconstructing an image of antique Greek history, one must imagine the beginning and slow increase of a cultural tension between the arts and ways of oral communication and those of the written, as the eye slowly invades the province of the ear, the reader the province of the listener. The character of classic Greek literature, during this period, is explicable by the fact that it is reproducing this unique tension in a form which could never recur except in a society starting from scratch, in which all knowledge of the alphabet had perished.

The initial use of the Greek alphabet therefore involves a paradox. Though its technology was such as to provide a capacity for designing and recording new forms of discourse, i.e., non-oral forms, for a long time it was used primarily for recording and perpetuating what had first been composed orally. This is strikingly evidenced even in the earliest inscriptions. If they attempt to say anything coherent, they do so in meter—sometimes of the roughest kind. The proper interpretation of this phenomenon is turned upside down by those whose notions of poetry and poetic function are derived from their own literate societies. The early appearance of inscribed verse is taken to indicate a sophistication on the part of ordinary people who must have already become highly literate in order to be able to use poetry for minor occasions. The reverse and correct judgment would estimate the practice of such verse making as a popular art widely and instinctively practiced in a society innocent of letters, and so unable to preserve a statement of some individual importance for even a generation unless it was first versified. The alphabet made possible not the creation but the transcription of the first European literate in the full sense of that word, and yet initially and for some time the original genius remained oral.

But the effects were to go deeper than that, affecting the structure of language and thought. It must be borne steadily in mind that in tracing what happened our concern is not with that ephemeral speech pronounced in conversation, but the speech preserved for re-use by a given culture, placed in storage to be repeated and added to, a repository of useful experience and necessary knowledge. It is the character of this kind of communication that controls the character of the culture. The range of experience and knowledge expressed in casual unrecorded speech never exceeds what is possible in preserved speech, and usually falls well below it.

Vocabulary and syntax had been controlled by the pressure to memorize. This limited anything that was said to what could be said rhythmically, and in narrativized form, meaning actions performed by agents, or events which happened to them. Even the wording of what is more easily recognizable as preserved wisdom—the maxims, aphorisms, parables, and proverbs—had to conform to these laws. Once the same speech is placed in documented form, the pressure to memorize is relieved, though not at first abolished. The document can lie around available for re-reading and re-consultation without prior necessity of oral recall. Therefore the pressures for poetry as a preservative, and for a restriction to narrative syntax, are relieved also. The twin possibilities exist of a preserved prose, and a prose which no longer tells a story. It can allow itself to express other types of discourse.

Of what precisely will these types consist? Let us begin with the subject of a sentence. Orally preserved speech requires this to be an agent doing something: the most readily available such is a human being, a hero let us say, but there are many varieties of non-human subjects which can be represented as functioning as agents. For example, the opening lines of the *Iliad* speak of a man's anger, to us a psychological phenomenon, which however behaves as a destroyer, that places afflictions upon people, and hurls their souls to Hades. This is the kind of standard idiom for describing in orally preserved speech what goes on in the world. We can reword by saying this is Homer's *description* of the *psychology* of the hero and its negative *effect* upon the *situation* of the Greek army, but in so doing, we are substituting our vocabulary of subjects and objects (which I have italicized) in place of his. This kind of vocabulary, conceptual and abstract, only became possible as an end product of the literate revolution. We speak as we think—speech indeed is the only perceptible evidence that thought exists. It is easy to fall into the supposition that though Homer spoke thus and so, he did so "poetically" as a "convention"; that if he had wanted to, he too could have described his story in terms of connections between abstractions like *description* and *situation* and *cause* and *effect;* in other words, that he could "think" as we do. But is this true? Could an oral culture "think" in this sense?

The premise that the technology of communication controls the content of what is communicated has been popularized in connection with modern radio, cinema, and television. I am applying it in a more radical fashion to a shift in the character of the human consciousness which occurred in ancient Greece, and which we inherit. Briefly I am arguing that the history of the human mind, as of the human language, falls into roughly two epochs, the pre-alphabetic and the post-alphabetic. The possibilities of the latter took time to realize themselves in Greece, and emerged in the writings of Plato and Aristotle. Even then they were not fully realized. The effects of the resolution accelerated after the European Renaissance and are still going on in our own day.

A linguistic statement requires verbs as well as subjects and objects. Orally preserved speech required these to be performative as when an agent, like Achilles' anger, does something—or else, situational, as when something happens or is present, or is born or dies. The oral syntax is unfriendly to that kind of statement which tries to place two subjects, or a subject and object, in a steady, unchanging relationship to each other, one fixed by their respective natures or essences, as we would say. Once this happens, the subject, or its "name," escapes from the narrative syntax. It tends to be connected by the verb *to be* used solely as a copula, as in the example cited earlier. The angles of a triangle *are* equal to two right angles. The removal of the memorization pressure, meaning the pressure to think of every phenomenon as an act or event, made it possible to document statements of this sort. An analytic syntax is slowly invented, and perfected in prose by Plato and Aristotle. As this happens, the symbols or names as the Greeks would say for subjects and predicates related to each other cease to symbolize agents and become symbolic of concepts, mental constructs which have been wrested and wrestled, so to speak, from the flux of the narrative.

One way of putting this is to say that alphabetic literacy substituted the abstract for the concrete, but we must be careful here to distinguish the abstractions represented in a mere word like Homeric anger and that which is expressed when anger becomes a phenomenon defined in analytic terms. The psychological and semantic revolution was one which involved changes in the syntax, by which terms are connected, not the terms by themselves as found in a dictionary.

In addition to the two advances registered in the alphabet—increased fluency of recognition and the removal of the pressure to memorize—is a third factor, the substitution of the eye for the ear in the reception of communication. The teaching and practice of literacy has thus involved some considerable manipulation in the use of the senses, and has done some violence to the way in which we have been programmed during our evolution as a species. Literacy is a late comer, a parvenu, in human history. For millennia we have been biologically conditioned to use and understand language only as it is spoken and heard, and in the interest of preserving some of the language for recall we have schooled ourselves as a species to develop a poetic language. Does one discard his inheritance overnight without some psychological damage to the organism— whether an individual or a society—which uses it? If it is desirable that a large majority of a modern population be literate, can this be accomplished without a prior linkage to the poetic and musical inheritance—in short, should children be rushed into reading before they have learned to speak fluently, to recite, to memorize, and to sing suitable verse available in their own tongue? Furthermore, can a society which values the abstract above the poetic ever understand societies which do not? I am thinking here in particular of what we call the Third World, on which we have occasionally made war, as in Vietnam, or occupied, as the European powers have done, or restructured with our technology, as in Iran, always it would appear to small purpose in the long run.

However, asking such questions is only a modern diversion. My tale is of that uniquely interesting people, the ancient Greeks. In their growing literature, aside from the slow emergence of abstract discourse, can be seen also a growing movement towards a more extended organization of what is said, and to a wider sweep of comprehension of what the content can be. In particular I am speaking of the birth of history and historical writing, which again emerged in the late fifth century in Athens. It is here, I think, that the evidence shows most clearly what the help of the eye was doing to recorded speech. It enables a composer to range over what he has said, and review it and rearrange it according to principles which I will call architectural rather than acoustic. The Homeric composer relied on an echo principle to produce his forms of unity and there is evidence in Greek drama of the persistence of the same technique. The complete writer may still use echo—he never forgets he is symbolizing a spoken tongue—but he also is guided by a vision which appreciates shape, and the arrangement of shapes.

This brings me to my last item among the effects of the alphabet, and not the least. Language increasingly available in visual documented form ceases to be an unseen impulse carried through the air—the winged word—and becomes an artifact, a thing in itself, an object of its own study. The evidence again is that this is exactly what occurred in Athens in the fifth century, as the sophists began to name the parts of speech and investigate their "grammar," which means the rules governing the written characters, the *grammata*.

As this happens to language, something happens to its users. In orality, the speaker and his speech remained one; what was spoken was his creation, in a sense it was himself, and it was difficult to think of this self apart from the words it spoke. As language assumed a new identity, so did the personality that spoke and used it. The composer began to separate himself from the written composition and believe in himself as an "authority," an "author." The separation attracted the attention of the philosophers, those first experimenters with a truly conceptual discourse. They began to propose the need for a vocabulary which would describe a man not just doing something, or saying something, but being himself and using language in order to think about himself. The twin concepts of the individual ego, the "soul," and the "intellect" which is part of the ego or soul, or which the ego employs to form concepts, were on their way to achievement when Plato was born. But would they have emerged into the discourse of Europe without the help of the alphabet?

9.
Hearing and Seeing *and* Trusting Writing

M. T. Clanchy

"Fundamentally letters are shapes indicating voices. hence they represent things which they bring to mind through the windows of the eyes. Frequently they speak voicelessly the utterances of the absent." In these antitheses John of Salisbury's *Metalogicon* grapples with the basic problems of the relationship between the spoken and the written word. The difference between sounds or voices *(voces)* and things or realities *(res)* was complicated for him, writing at the mid-twelfth century, by the controversy between Nominalists and Realists, between those who argued that universals were mere names and those who claimed they were real things. This philosophical controversy is not our concern here. John's remarks are relevant because, like much of *Metalogicon*, they seem to reflect his own experience as a secretary and drafter of letters as well as exemplifying current scholastic thought.

Numerous charters of the twelfth century are addressed to "all those seeing and hearing these letters, in the future as in the present" or to "all who shall hear and see this charter"; these two examples come from the charters of Roger de Mowbray who died in 1188. The grantor of another charter, Richard de Rollos, actually harangues his audience, "Oh! all ye who shall have heard this and have seen!" Early charters likewise quite often conclude with "Goodbye" *(Valete)*, as if the donor had just finished speaking with his audience. Documents made it possible for the grantor to address posterity ("all who shall hear and see") as well as his contemporaries. In the opening words of the Winchcombe abbey

EDITORS' NOTE: This essay is excerpted from M. T. Clanchy's *From Memory to Written Record: England, 1066–1307*, a historical study of the gradual and complex shift in England from oral to written modes of running government and doing business. The first half of the book traces the development of writing technology and the creation and proliferation of legal and commercial documents. The second half, from which our selection comes, discusses the changes in thought and attitude that accompanied the emergence of literacy. We have not reprinted Clanchy's copious footnotes; readers who wish to examine Clanchy's sources should consult his book.

cartulary, "when the voice has perished with the man, writing still enlightens posterity." Writing shifted the spotlight away from the transitory actors witnessing a conveyance and on to the perpetual parchment recording it. By the thirteenth century, when charters had become more familiar to landowners, donors cease addressing their readers, as Richard de Rollos did, and likewise they no longer conclude with *Valete*. Once it was understood that charters were directed to posterity, it must have seemed foolish to say "Goodbye" to people who had not yet been born. In place of such conversational expressions, thirteenth-century charters are more stereotyped; they are often impersonally addressed in some such form as "Let all persons, present and future, know that I, A of B, have given X with its appurtenances to C of D."

A comparable change occurs in wills. Until the thirteenth century the will was an essentially oral act, even when it was recorded in writing. The persons present witnessed the testator making his bequests "with his own mouth"; they "saw, were present, and heard" the transaction. By the end of the thirteenth century a man's final will no longer usually meant his wishes spoken on his deathbed, but a closed and sealed document. The witnesses no longer heard him; instead they saw his seal being placed on the document. When wills were first enrolled, as they were in London from 1258, the formula of probate still put emphasis on the witnesses who had seen and heard. But a generation later, by the 1290s, the London roll often omits the names of the witnesses, presumably because the written will was the preferred evidence. The validity of the will now depended primarily upon its being in a correct documentary form and not on the verbal assurances of the witnesses. This is another illustration of the shift from memory to written record between 1100 and 1300. Wills had been made in writing by the Anglo-Saxons; the novelty lay in their being closed and sealed documents.

Symbolic Objects and Documents

Before conveyances were made with documents, the witnesses "heard" the donor utter the words of the grant and "saw" him make the transfer by a symbolic object, such as a knife or a turf from the land. William the Conqueror went one better and jokingly threatened to make one donee "feel" the conveyance by dashing the symbolic knife through the recipient abbot's hand saying, "That's the way land ought to be given." Such a gesture was intended to impress the event on the memory of all those present. If there were dispute subsequently, resort was had to the recollection of the witnesses. Similar rules applied to the oral "records" of courts, which were retained (in theory at least) in the memory of those present. For example, if the record of the county court were disputed, the aggrieved litigant brought forward two witnesses who each gave evidence of what they had heard and seen. In such a case in 1212 the prior of Ware (in Hertfordshire) defended himself by "one hearing and one understanding," namely Jordan of Warew and Robert of Clopton; Robert also offered to prove the prior's allegation by battle, "as he was present and heard this." In this case some distinction is evidently being attempted between the knowledge of the two witnesses: Jordan had heard, or at least understood, less of the preceedings than

Robert. Likewise at Cheshunt (in Hertfordshire) in a seignorial court in 1220 a litigant challenged the record by "one person hearing and another seeing." Which testimony was thought preferable in this instance, that of the person who heard or of the other who saw, is unclear. These two exceptional cases suggest that the legal commonplace of making a record by "hearing and seeing" was not a mere formula made meaningless by repetition.

Documents changed the significance of bearing witness by hearing and seeing legal procedures, because written evidence could be heard by reading aloud or seen by inspecting the document. In John of Salisbury's definition, letters "indicate voices" and bring this to mind "through the windows of the eyes." Once charters were used for conveyances, "hearing" applied to anyone hearing the charter read out loud at any time, instead of referring only to the witnesses of the original conveyance. From there it was a short step to substitute "reading" for "seeing," as one of Roger de Mowbray's charters does, which is addressed to "all his own men and to the rest, *reading* or hearing these letters." This phrase plays also with the ambiguity of the word "letters," which in Latin (as in English) means both alphabetic symbols and missives.

A curiously worded grant for St Mary's priory at Monmouth is addressed to the donors, Richard de Cormeilles and Beatrice his wife, instead of to the recipients. The charter rewards Richard and Beatrice with divine bliss because they have given the tithes of Norton-Giffard to Mary the mother of God. She is the ostensible grantor of the charter, though the document itself was presumably written by a monk of St Mary's priory which was the terrestial beneficiary. The writer's Latin is eccentric—for example he spells *uxor* (for wife) as *hucxor*—but revealing in its phraseology. He includes the phrase *sicut presens breve loquitur* (as the present writing speaks), whereas ordinary usage would have *dicitur* (says) or *testatur* (attests) in place of *loquitur.* The writer also makes it clear that the named witnesses, who "saw and heard the gift solemnly exhibited by a book upon the altar," are "subsequent" and therefore secondary to the evidence of the writing itself. In making the writing "speak" and in putting the pre-literate witnessing ceremony of seeing and hearing into a subsidiary role, the naïve writer of this charter has exemplified John of Salisbury's scholastic definition (which is contemporary with the charter) that letters "speak voicelessly the utterances of the absent," the absent in this instance being the grantor, Mary the mother of God.

Once property was conveyed in writing, it would have seemed logical for the charter to supersede the symbolic object, such as the knife or turf, which had formerly been used in the witnessing ceremony. As the grant to Monmouth priory shows, that object had sometimes itself been a writing—a book solemnly exhibited upon an altar. Traditionally the book used for this purpose was the text of the Gospels. For example a gift of a saltpan was made to St Peter's priory at Sele in Sussex in 1153 "by the text of the Holy Gospel upon the altar of St Peter, many persons hearing and seeing." The Gospel book was used because it was customary to reinforce oaths with it (as is still the practice in law courts); thus in Edward I's wardrobe there was kept "a book, which is called *textus,* upon which the magnates were accustomed to swear." To replace a Gospel book by a charter in a conveyancing ceremony was a relatively small change in appearance (it was simply substituting one document for another), but a large one in substance. The charter in its text actually "represented" (in John of Salisbury's definition) in a durable record the terms of the conveyance, whereas the Gospel book merely symbolized the solemnity of the occasion for the witnesses. The Monmouth priory charter therefore distinguishes the written grant *(breve)*, which "speaks" to the hearers, from the symbolic book *(liber)* which is "exhibited" to the viewers.

Nevertheless, although it seemed logical to dispense with symbols and make full use of the potentialities of writing, contemporaries continued with their pre-literate habits long after charters had become common. In the rare instances where the conveyance appears to be made by the written document itself (as in the Monmouth priory charter), we should probably assume that the document is serving the ancient function of a symbolic object, rather than being considered primarily for its contents in a modern literate way. There are examples of the conveyancing document being presented on the altar like a Gospel book. In a charter of 1193 the abbot of Glastonbury states that "the present charter was placed on the altar of St Mary by me as an offering, the clergy and people of the same vill [of Street in Somerset] standing round." In the Guthlac roll (probably dating from the late twelfth century) King Ethelbald and twelve other benefactors of Crowland abbey in Lincolnshire are depicted pressing forward with opened scrolls to lay at the altar and shrine of St Guthlac. The writing on the scrolls is specific, giving in Latin the name of each donor and the property donated, such as "I, Alan de Croun give you, Father Guthlac, the priory of Freiston with appurtenances." One or two of the benefactors have their mouths open, as if voicing their gifts. As some of these charters cannot be traced and may well have been forged, the Guthlac roll could have been intended to provide a kind of documentary proof of the gifts in this peculiar form.

An explicit instance of a conveyance by the charter itself is a gift made by William of Astle in *c.* 1200 to the Knights Hospitaller. The last witness is Ivo clerk of Stafford, representing the Hospitallers, "in whose hand I, William, have made seisin with this charter in the church of Alderly." The usual rule was that a conveyance could not be made by a document alone, but depended on the recipient having "seisin" (meaning actual possession of the property). Nevertheless the exception to this rule in William of Astle's charter may merely prove it, as the charter, conveyed from hand to hand, is a substitute for the usual object symbolizing the transaction.

The unfamiliar idea of a writing being interpreted primarily as a symbolic object, rather than as a documentary proof, is most clearly evident when the object written upon is not a parchment, but something else. Thus an ivory whip-handle found at St Albans abbey had an inscription on it stating that "this is the gift of Gilbert de Novo Castello for four mares." The object, a whip, appropriately symbolized the gift of horses; the writing was ancillary. Similarly a knife is still preserved at Durham, which symbolized Stephen of Bulmer's agreement (perhaps made in the 1150s) with the monks of Holy Island at Lindisfarne about the chapelry of Lowick.

This knife is particularly interesting because its haft bears an inscription, which is comparable with the St Albans whip-handle and other inscribed knife hafts no longer extant. Whereas the hafts of these other knives were made of ivory, Stephen's is of hard horn (perhaps a deer's) and the inscriber has had difficulty making much impression on it. He was not perhaps an experienced carver but a scribe, possibly a monk of Lindisfarne, who only had a pen knife readily available. Although the lettering of the inscription is shaky and uneven, it is conceived in a bold monastic hand. Along one side of the knife's haft is written *Signum de capella de lowic* (the sign for the chapel of Lowick) and on the other side *de capella de lowic & de decimis de lowic totius curie & totius ville* (for the chapel of Lowick and for the tithes of Lowick from the whole court and the whole vill). As well as this inscription on the haft, a parchment label is attached (written in a comparable bold monastic hand), which gives fuller details of the agreement. This label cannot be described as a charter, as it is irregular in shape and is written on both sides. A statement on its dorse helps explain the purpose of the knife. It records that Stephen of Bulmer had not come in person to make the agreement at Holy Island, but sent Lady Cecily and Aschetin, the *dapifer* or steward, in his place. Probably Aschetin brought the knife with him as a symbol of Stephen's consent. It may well have been Stephen's own carving knife; the haft is heavy and shows signs of use and, although the blade is broken near the top, what remains of the knife still measures 13½ cm. It would thus have been an appropriate object for a steward, who probably carved at his lord's table, to bring as durable and substantial evidence that he truly represented his master.

Why go to the trouble of trying to write on a knife, when pen and parchment did the same job more efficiently? Ordinary writing materials were evidently available, as Stephen's knife has the parchment label on it as well as the inscription. The explanation may be that the parties to this agreement had more confidence in the evidence of the knife than in writing. Knives were traditional symbols for conveyances, whereas charters authenticated by seals were a relative novelty, though they should have been familiar to the monks of Lindisfarne if not to a northern knight like Stephen of Bulmer. Some contemporaries may also have thought that a knife was more durable than, and therefore preferable to, parchment and sealing wax. It was true that only the sparsest details of a conveyance could be engraved on the handle of a knife or a whip, but the tradition had been that the true facts of a transaction were engraved on the hearts and minds of the witnesses and could not be fully recorded in any form of writing however detailed. The symbolic knife would have been retained regardless of whether it had anything written on it, because it preserved the memory of the conveyance.

Only literates, who could interpret the "shapes indicating voices" (in John of Salisbury's definition of letters), were going to be convinced that the writing was superior to the symbolic object. Such objects, the records of the non-literate, were therefore preserved along with documents. Another example is the knife by which Thomas of Moulton gave the church of Weston in Lincolnshire to Spalding priory, which was deposited in its archive (*in secretario*) according to the charter confirming the gift. This latter knife is no longer preserved. To later archivists, knives and other archaic relics meant nothing unless they had inscriptions connected with them; such things were thrown away as medieval rubbish, because the language of memory which they expressed had no significance for literates.

It is possible that the seals, *signa* in Latin, attached to charters were seen by many contemporaries in a similar way as inscribed "signs." To students of diplomatic today seals are a method of authenticating documents which preceded the sign manual or written signature. To medieval people they may have appeared rather as visible and tangible objects symbolizing the wishes of the donor. The seal was significant even without the document. Early seals (that is, twelfth-century ones) tend to be disproportionately large—often 6 or 7 cm in diameter—compared with the writings to which they are attached. John of Salisbury, writing on behalf of Archbishop Theobald of Canterbury about the safekeeping of seals, says that "by the marks of a single impress the mouths of all the pontiffs may be opened or closed." Just as letters "speak voicelessly the utterances of the absent," seals regulate that speech. Emphasis on the spoken word remained.

The "signs" attached to documents, whether they took the form of inscribed knives or impressed wax or even ink crosses made by the witnesses, all helped to bridge the gulf between the traditional and the literate way of recording transactions. Pre-literate customs and ceremonies persisted despite the use of documents. The doctrine of livery of seisin—the rule that a recipient must have the property duly delivered to him and enter into possession (that is, seisin) of it, whether there was a document of conveyance or not—became a fundamental principle of the common law; but there are exceptions to it, like the charter of William of Astle to the Knights Hospitaller which has already been discussed. The treatise ascribed to Bracton insists (in the first half of the thirteenth century) that "a gift is not valid unless livery follows; for the thing given is transferred neither by homage, nor by the drawing up of charters and instruments, even though they be recited in public." Written words were thus entirely inadequate, and even spoken ones were insufficient, without physical symbols: "If livery is to be made of a house by itself, or of a messuage for any estate, it ought to be made by the door and its hasp or ring, by which is understood that the donee possess the whole to its boundaries." It followed also that a gift "may be valid though no charter has been made . . . and conversely the charter may be genuine and valid and the gift incomplete." The physical symbol, the door hasp or ring in Bracton's example, continued to epitomize the whole gift better than any document.

Likewise the drafting rule became general that the past tense should be used in charters for the art of giving: "Know that I, A of B, *have* given," not simply "I give." This emphasized that the ceremonial conveyance was the crucial transaction, whereas the charter was merely a subsequent confirmation of it. This rule only became firmly established in the thirteenth century. Numerous charters of the twelfth century depart from it, presumably because their more amateur draftsmen did not appreciate the relationship between written record and the passage of time. Similarly a generation or two after Bracton the need for the livery of seisin rule was not apparent to ordinary people. Some Derbyshire jurors, who had supposed in 1304 that a charter might suffice without it, were described by a second group of jurors as "simple persons who were not cognizant with English laws and customs." The doctrine of seisin, which had once been a self-evident and commonsense rule, had become with the spread of literacy one of those technical mysteries in which the common law abounded.

The Spoken versus the Written Word

The increasing use of documents created tension between the old methods and the new. Which was the better evidence, for example, seeing a parchment or hearing a man's word? How was the one to be evaluated it if conflicted with the other? A good illustration of this particular dilemma is Eadmer's account of the investiture controversy between St Anselm, archbishop of Canterbury, and Henry I. Both Anselm and the king had sent envoys to Pope Pashal II; Anselm sent two monks of Canterbury, while the king sent the archbishop of York and two other bishops. The envoys returned to England in September 1101 with papal letters addressed to the king and to Anselm prohibiting royal investiture of churches and exhorting resistance to them. When the pope's letter to Anselm had been publicly read out, Henry's envoys objected. They claimed that Paschal had given them a purely verbal message that he would treat the king leniently on the investiture question and would not excommunicate him; the pope had added that he did not wish this concession to be put in written form *(per carta inscriptionem)* because other rulers would use it as a precedent. Anselm's envoys replied that the pope had given no verbal message which conflicted in any way with his letters. To this Henry's bishops answered that Paschal had acted in one way in secret and another in public. Baldwin of Bec, Anselm's chief envoy, was outraged at this allegation and said that it was a calumny on the Holy See.

Dissension then arose in the audience. Those favouring Anselm maintained that credence should be given to "documents signed with the pope's seal" *(scriptis sigillo pape signatis)* and not to "the uncertainty of mere words." The king's side replied that they preferred to rely on the word of three bishops than on "the skins of wethers blackened with ink and weighted with a little lump of lead." They added further venom to the argument by alleging that monks were unreliable anyway, as they should not be engaged in worldly business. Eadmer puts the controversy into dialogue form:

> *Anselm's monks:* "But what about the evidence of the letters?"
>
> *Henry's bishops:* "As we don't accept the evidence of monks against bishops, why should we accept that of a sheepskin?"
>
> *Anselm's monks:* "Shame on you! Are not the Gospels written down on sheepskins?"

Obviously the conflict could not be quickly resolved. In Lent 1102 Anselm set out for Rome and opened on his way another letter from the pope, in which Paschal denied that he had ever given contradictory verbal instructions to the bishops or said that he was reluctant to set a precedent in writing. Who was telling the truth is of course impossible to resolve. Paschal was attempting to make peace and settle the investiture controversy by diplomacy. He may well therefore have said something off the record to the bishops which they had possibly exaggerated. Like all statesmen, the pope obviously had to make a formal denial of such secret negotiations once they became public.

The substance of the story is not our concern here, but the attitudes it reveals towards documentary evidence. Papal letters, sealed with the leaden bull and bearing the symbols and monograms of curial officials, were the most impressive documents produced in medieval Europe, their only rival being Byzantine imperial letters. Yet in Eadmer's story the papal bull is disparagingly described as a sheepskin blackened with ink with a bit of lead attached to it, an extreme example of a document being treated simply as a physical object rather than for its contents. Anselm's supporters were entitled to riposte that the Gospels too were written on parchment—in other words, that Christianity was essentially the religion of a book. At Orléans in 1022 a group of heretics had been burned for disparaging the book learning of the clergy cross-examining them, which they had called human fabrications "written on the skins of animals," whereas the heretics claimed to believe "in the law written in the inner man by the Holy Spirit." The heretics had therefore been arguing that the true written law *(lex scripta)* was not canon law nor Justinian's code, but inspiration retained in the mind alone; real writing was not man-made script on animal parchment. Such an idea may well have derived from the Scripture itself, most probably from St Paul's Second Epistle to the Corinthians, "written not with ink, but with the spirit of the living God . . . for the letter killeth, but the spirit giveth life." Early in the thirteenth century St Francis was to take up this theme as part of his revolt against the spiritually empty book learning of some monks: "Those religious have been killed by the letter who are not willing to follow the spirit of the divine letter, but only desire to know words and interpret them for other men." As so often in his work, Francis blended orthodox and heretical viewpoints in an insight of his own. Literacy was not a virtue in itself. Emphasis on the word inscribed spiritually on the minds of men, as contrasted with letters written on parchment, retained its strength in the Christian message as it did in secular conveyancing ceremonies.

The argument of Henry I's envoys, that their word was better evidence than a papal bull, would not in fact have appeared as outrageous or surprising to contemporaries as Eadmer suggests in his account of the controversy with Anselm. The principle that "oral witness deserves more credence than written evidence" was a legal commonplace. It was cited for example by Hubert Walter, archbishop of Canterbury, in a letter to Innocent III in 1200 controverting Gerald of Wales's well documented claim to be bishop-elect of St David's. Gerald conceded the point in his reply to the pope, but added that he had brought both documents and witnesses. Behind this principle lay the correct assumption that numerous documents used in legal claims, from the Donation of Constantine downwards, were forgeries. Not all those who relied on the traditional use of the spoken word, rather than parchments, were necessarily therefore obscurantist conservatives. The technology of written record was insufficiently advanced to be efficient or reliable. As a consequence, documents and the spoken word are frequently both used in a way which appears otiose to a modern literate. To make a record often meant to bear oral witness, not to produce a document. For example, in the civil war of Stephen's reign Robert earl of Gloucester and Miles earl of Hereford made a treaty of friendship in writing, in the form of a sealed letter; yet both parties in this document also name witnesses who are "to make legal record of this agreement in court if necessary."

The rule that oral witness is preferable to documents, like the rule that seisin is superior to a charter, shows how cautiously—and perhaps reluctantly—written evidence was accepted. Much important business continued to be done by word of mouth. Bearers of letters were often given instructions which were to be conveyed *viva voce*, either because that was convenient and traditional or because the information was too secret to write down. Twice, for instance, in March 1229 Henry III sent messengers to the count of Toulouse. In their mouths, the king wrote, he had put matters which they would disclose more fully to the count, since the business (presumably concerning a truce with Louis IX) could not be committed to writing because of the dangers of the roads. Similarly in the period of the baronial rebellion, when Henry was in France in 1260, he wrote to the earl of Gloucester instructing him to report on the state of the kingdom by Gilbert Fitz Hugh, the king's serjeant, who would tell the earl more fully *viva voce* about the king's situation. In such negotiations the letter itself did not convey essential information but, like a modern ambassador's letter of credence, was a symbolic object replacing the messenger's ring or other *signum* which had formerly identified him as a confidential agent of his master.

Oral messages were also used to give instructions which later generations would have put in writing. For example, in 1234 John le Franceis and John Mansel were authorized by royal letters of credence to conduct inquiries concerning Jews in certain counties and give instructions to sheriffs *viva voce*. An interesting but non-English case of oral delivery is the poem which the troubadour, Jaufre Rudel, lord of Blaye in the Gironde, sent to the Comte de Marche in *c*. 1150 "without a parchment document" *(senes breu de parguamina)* by the mouth of the jongleur, Filhol. The jongleur is thus being used as a kind of living letter. There is, however, a paradox in all such evidence, since historians can only know of the survival of oral ways of conveying information by extant written evidence. Jaufe Rudel's poem, once sent without a script, is written down nonetheless.

Much business was still done by word of mouth for the obvious reason that documents were bound to be relatively rare until printing made their automatic reproduction possible. The usual way of publishing new laws and regulations was by proclamation. The following instances from the Chancery records of Henry III for 1234 are typical. On 28 August the sheriff of Northumberland and some others were ordered to have it proclaimed *(clamari facias)* that pleas were to be adjourned until the coming of the eyre justices. On 29 August all sheriffs were to proclaim the regulations for supervising hundred courts in accordance with the revision of Magna Carta in 1234. On 1 September the sheriff of Norfolk and Suffolk was to proclaim throughout the two counties that no Jew was to lend money to any Christian in the king's demesne. Matthew Paris suggests that Henry III pursued a policy of legislating by proclamation: in 1248 the people were harassed by diverse precepts promulgated "by the voice of a crier" (*voce preconia*) throughout the cities of England; the king established a new fair at Westminster, for example, in this way. The proclamation to which Matthew gives most attention likewise occurred in 1248, when the king "ordered it to be proclaimed as law by the voice of a crier" that henceforward no man might castrate another for fornication except a husband in the case of his wife's adulterer. The reason for this was that John le Bretun had castrated the Norfolk knight, Godfrey de Millers, for lying with his daughter.

How extensively or frequently proclamations of this sort were made is not clear. Proclamations were a quick and effective way of conveying information in crowded cities like London, but were obviously less practical in the countryside. Most references to proclamations concern cities. For example, in 1252 Henry III had it proclaimed throughout London that no one should lend money to the abbot of Westminster; or in the preceding year a proclamation had been made against the royal judge, Henry of Bath, in London and in the king's court. One consequence for the historian of Henry III's government's use of the spoken word for legislation is that all trace of it is lost, unless a chronicler happened to record it or the Chancery rolls refer to it incidentally. Edward I is considered a great lawgiver partly because the legislation of his time is preserved in the statute rolls. In Henry III's reign less was written down, though a comparable amount of legislative activity probably took place.

Magna Carta became the great precedent for putting legislation into writing. Yet even it was not officially enrolled in the royal archives, although it was proclaimed extensively and repeatedly. Within a few days of King John's assent to it letters were sent to all his sheriffs, foresters, gamekeepers, watermen and other bailiffs informing them of the agreement between the king and the barons, "as you can hear and see by our charter which we have had made thereon," which they were ordered to have read publicly throughout their bailiwicks. As a result, in theory at least, everyone in England should have heard Magna Carta read out, although it is unlikely that a sufficient number of copies were available. Similarly when the barons again had the upper hand in 1265, they ordered the terms of Henry III's oath to keep peace with them to be published in the full county court at least twice every year, at Easter and Michaelmas. In 1300 transcripts of Magna Carta and the Charter of the Forest were delivered to every sheriff to read out "before the people" four times a year, at Christmas and Midsummer as well as at Easter and Michaelmas. Nevertheless by 1300 there had been a significant change, as considerable emphasis was now being put on seeing the document as well as hearing it. Sealed transcripts of Magna Carta were sent to all judges, sheriffs and civic officials and also to all cathedral churches. A precedent for the latter had been made in 1279 when Archbishop Pecham's council at Reading had ordered a copy of Magna Carta to be posted up in every cathedral and collegiate church in a public place "so that it can be clearly seen by the eyes of everyone entering"; in the spring of each year the old copy was to be taken down and a new fair copy substituted for it.

The clergy therefore assumed that the general public could read, or would at least be impressed by seeing the Latin text of Magna Carta. The royal government likewise was sufficiently alarmed to make Pecham have all these copies removed from church doors shortly afterwards. An even earlier precedent, though a fantastic one, occurs in Andrew the Chaplain's *Ars Amandi* of the later twelfth century. The king of love had written out the rules of love on a parchment for a British knight. His lady then called together a court of numerous knights and their ladies, each of whom was given a written copy of the rules to take home and issue to all lovers in all parts of the world. Like Archbishop Pecham, Andrew the Chaplain probably had higher expectations of the reading ability of the public than were justified.

Public readings of documents were done in the vernacular as well as in Latin and might reach a wider audience in that way. Thus in 1300, according to the chronicler Rishanger, Magna Carta was read out at Westminster "first in Latin [*litteraliter*] and then in the native tongue [*patria lingua*]." Similarly a year earlier letters of Pope Boniface VIII about the peace between England and France had been read out in Parliament "in Latin for the literate and in the native tongue for the illiterate." Also in 1299, according to the Worcester annals, royal letters concerning a new perambulation of the forests were "proclaimed in the city of Worcester in the mother tongue [*materna lingua*]." The "paternal" or "maternal" language might mean either English or French. Thus in 1254 the papal excommunication of infringers of Magna Carta was ordered to be published "in the English [*Anglicana*] and French [*Gallicana*] tongues" whenever and wherever appropriate. The use of English and French in this instance was probably a reiteration of existing practice, rather than an innovation, as it is likely that Magna Carta itself had been proclaimed throughout the land in both English and French in 1215.

The distinction the chroniclers wished to emphasize in the citations above was between the language of literacy (Latin) and spoken language; they were less concerned with which vernacular was used. To pedantic Latinists vernacular simply meant the spoken language. Gerald of Wales hoped that someone would translate his work into French and claimed that Walter Map used to tell him that he (Gerald) had written much, whereas Walter had said much. Although Gerald's writings (*scripta*) were more praiseworthy and durable than Walter's speeches (*dicta*), Walter had the greater profit because his *dicta* were accessible, since they were expressed in the common idiom, while Gerald's *scripta* were appreciated only by the declining few who knew Latin. In fact the distinction Gerald drew here between himself and Walter Map was misleading, as Walter also was a precocious Latinist. Possibly Gerald felt that Walter had been a more successful preacher and *raconteur* in the vernacular than he was. The point of the story from our angle, regardless of whether it is true or not, is that Gerald felt that the spoken vernacular brought greater prestige than written Latin.

Listening to the Word

Whatever the language, and whether the record was held solely in the bearer's memory or was committed to parchment, the medieval recipient prepared himself to listen to an utterance rather than to scrutinize a document visually as a modern literate would. This was due to a different habit of mind; it was not because the recipient was illiterate in any sense of that word. In his account of his claim to be bishop-elect of St David's Gerald of Wales describes a private audience in the pope's chamber with Innocent III in 1200, when the pope looked up a register listing all the metropolitan churches of Christendom and went through the rubrics until he found Wales. But when at a subsequent private audience Gerald showed the pope a transcript of a letter of Eugenius III which Gerald had found in another papal register, Innocent handed the transcript to Cardinal Ugolino and told him to read it; "and when it had been read and diligently heard, the pope replied that he was well pleased with it." Gerald's account of the earlier audience depicts the pope browsing through a reference book as a modern literate would do; but when at the subsequent audience the pope needs to absorb carefully the details of a letter, he has it read to him instead of scrutinizing it. Reading aloud in this case is not being done to enable everyone present to learn the contents of the letter, as the only persons at this private audience are Innocent, Gerald and Ugolino who is supporting him. Nor obviously was Innocent incapable of reading the script of papal registers. Yet he evidently found it easier to concentrate when he was listening than when he was looking; reading was still primarily oral rather than visual.

Indications of the same habit of mind appear in the "auditing" of monetary accounts. Abbot Samson of Bury St Edmunds "heard" the weekly account of his expenditure, yet he obviously could have consulted such a document (if the account were in documentary form at all), as his biographer Jocelin says that he inspected his *kalendarium* (his register of rents and so on) almost every day "as though he could see therein the image of his own efficiency as in a mirror." The modern word "audit" derives from a time when it was the habit to listen to, rather than to see, an account. Thomas of Eccleston in his description of the arrival of the Franciscan friars in England in 1224 records that when the superior heard the first annual account of the London friars and realized how little they had to show for such lavish expenditure, he threw down all the tallies and rolls and shouted "I'm caught" and "he never afterwards wanted to hear an account." In this instance accounts in writing existed, in the form of both wooden tallies and parchment rolls, yet the superior "heard" them nonetheless. H. J. Chaytor points out, however, that one must be careful of colloquial speech in such an instance as this. For example modern English uses the phrase "I have not heard from him for some time" to mean "I have had no letter."

Similarly in law courts "inspecting" a document might mean hearing it read aloud. Thus in 1219 in an action of warranty of charter in Lincolnshire William of Well, the defendant, is reported in the plea roll to "have come and claimed a hearing [*auditum*] of his father's charter" and it was duly heard. A generation later, in a similar action in Berkshire in 1248, the abbot of Beaulieu who was the defendant claimed that the plaintiff should "show" him the charter by which he should warrant her. The contrasting emphasis on hearing and seeing in these similar claims only thirty years apart may indicate a general change of attitude developing within this period, if only in the minds of the enrolling clerks; or more likely the two cases show the differing approach to documents of a knight, William of Well, and a monk, the abbot of Beaulieu.

Literary works, especially vernacular ones, were frequently explicitly addressed by the author to an audience, rather than to readers as such. Thus the nun of Barking in her French version of Ailred's life of Edward the Confessor in *c.* 1163 requests "all who hear, or will ever hear, this romance of hers" not to despise it because the translation is done by a woman. In the *Romance of Horn* by Master Thomas the author begins by addressing his audience: "Gentlemen, you have heard the lines of parchment" (*Seignurs, oi avez, le vers del parchemin*). The parchment is evidently thought of here as a direct substitute for a jongleur; it speaks and is heard, like the charter of Richard de Cormeilles for St Mary's priory at Monmouth. Likewise in the *Estoire de Waldef* (dating from *c.* 1190) the author refers to the *Brut* story:

> If anyone wants to know this history
> Let him read the *Brut,* he will hear it there
> [*Qui l'estoire savoir voldra*
> *Lise le Brut, illoc l'orra*].

A modern literate would not say "he will *hear* it there," but "he will *find* it" or "*see* it there." The emphasis in such works on hearing does not necessarily mean that their contents stem directly from oral tradition, but that reading continued to be conceived in terms of hearing rather than seeing. Until cheap printing supplied every "reader" with his own book, the emphasis on hearing was understandable.

Latin works too were generally intended to be read aloud—hence the speeches and frequent use of dramatic dialogue in monastic chronicles. Eadmer concludes the first book of his *Life of St Anselm* with an interval, as in a play: "But here, lest our unpolished speech [*oratio*] weary our readers or hearers by being too long drawn-out, we shall make our first halt in the work." Traditional monastic reading in particular bore little relation to a modern literate's approach to a book. *Lectio* was "more a process of rumination than reading, directed towards savouring the divine wisdom within a book rather than finding new ideas or novel information." The process is well illustrated by St Anselm's *Meditation on Human Redemption:* "Taste the goodness of your redeemer . . . chew the honeycomb of his words, suck their flavour which is sweeter than honey, swallow their wholsome sweetness. Chew by thinking, suck by understanding, swallow by loving and rejoining." Reading was a physical exertion, demanding the use not only of the eyes, but of tongue, mouth and throat. Writing was a similar act of endurance, requiring three fingers to hold the pen, two eyes to see the words, one tongue to speak them, and the whole body to labour. For these reasons some monks argued that work in the *scriptorium* was an adequate substitute for manual labour.

The system of punctuating and abbreviating words in Latin works was likewise intended primarily to assist someone reading aloud, rather than a person silently scrutinizing the page. N. R. Ker cites the case of a manuscript where the Latin word *neque* (neither), which is written out in full, has been amended throughout to *neq;* he suggests that writing *neque* out in full was likely to mislead an oral reader into stressing the second syllable; writing out the word in full was an error on the scribe's part which has been duly corrected. Some abbreviations were therefore intended to help pronunciation, rather than save the scribe's time when copying a book. Ideally a "reader" was expected to look at the text as well as listen to it, but that was the exception and not the rule. In the *Life of St Margaret* of Scotland the author considered it a point worth remarking that Margaret's daughter, Matilda (Henry I's queen) "desired not only to hear, but also to inspect continually the impress of the letters" of her mother's life. A school manual, not English unfortunately and later than our period, sums up in a dialogue the medieval meaning of "reading" *(lectio)*:

> "Are you a scholar, what do you read?"
> "I do not read, I listen."
> "What do you hear?"
> "Donatus or Alexander, or logic or music."

Donatus's *Ars Minor* and Alexander's *Doctrinale* were Latin textbooks. The term "reading" a subject has been preserved at Oxford and Cambridge; whereas some undergraduates think that "reading" implies studying books instead of hearing lectures, medieval students understood *lectio* primarily to mean that the master read while they listened.

Whole books were published by being read aloud. Gerald of Wales says that he published his *Topography of Ireland* in this way in *c.* 1188 by reading it at Oxford to different audiences on three successive days. But Gerald's action was not typical, as he boasts that "neither has the present age seen, nor does any past age bear record of, the like in England." The normal way of disseminating scholarly works, as distinct from popular romances, was by the modern method of circulating copies. For instance Herbert of Bosham assumed in his life of Becket that his readers will be able to study Becket's correspondence, which he omits for the sake of brevity, "because that book of letters is already in the possession of many persons and churches." If Becket is thought too exceptional an example because of his extraordinary popularity, Eadmer mentions in his appendix to St Anselm's *Life* that he intends to make a new start, because the *Life* has already "been transcribed by many and distributed to various churches." Distributing copies did not of course rule out public readings; on the contrary, as more books became available, the practice may have grown even more widespread.

Just as reading was linked in the medieval mind with hearing rather than seeing, writing (in its modern sense of composition) was associated with dictating rather than manipulating a pen. Reading and writing (in the sense of composition) were therefore both extensions of speaking and were not inseparably coupled with each other, as they are today. A person might be able to write, yet not be considered literate. As we have seen, Walter Map mentions a boy "who was not *litteratus,* although he knew how to transcribe any series of letters whatever." Literacy involved being learned in Latin, whereas writing was the process of making a fair copy on parchment, which was the art of the scribe. Some authors (notably the great monastic historians Orderic Vitalis, William of Malmesbury and Matthew Paris) did their own writing, but they are the exceptions and they distinguished that activity from composition.

Medieval distinctions are well illustrated by Eadmer. He explains that he had to conceal from St Anselm that he was "writing" his biography. When he had begun the work "and had had already transcribed on to parchment a great part of what I had composed [*dictaveram*] in wax," Anselm asked "what it was I was composing and copying" *(quid dictitarem, quid scriptitarem)*. The process of composing on wax tablets is thus described in Latin by the word *dictitare* (literally, "to dictate"), even though in Eadmer's case he was dictating to himself. The use of "writing" *(scriptitare)* is confined to making the fair copy on parchment. Similarly when Orderic Vitalis wishes to say that before the time of William the Conqueror the Normans had concentrated on war rather than reading and writing, the phrase he uses is *legere vel dictare*, not *legere vel scribere*. Numerous other examples of using "dictate" where a modern literate would use "write" could be given. Dictating was the usual form of literacy composition and the *ars dictaminis*, taught in the schools as part of rhetoric, was the skill governing it. Letter writing was thus an intellectual skill using the mouth rather than the hand. Peter of Blois, a busy secretary of state like John of Salisbury, boasted that the archbishop of Canterbury had seen him dictating to three different scribes on diverse subjects, while he dictated and wrote a fourth letter all at the one time.

Reading aloud and dictating permit the non-literate to participate in the use of documents, whereas reading and writing silently exclude the illiterate. When the voice is used, the clerk or scribe becomes no more than a medium between the speaker or hearer and the document. Neither the hearer of a book nor the *dictator* of a letter needs to be a master of every detail of the scribal technique himself, just as modern managers are not required to type or to programme computers. Obviously it is helpful if the manager understands how these things are done and has some experience of them, but this expertise is not indispensable. For these reasons medieval kings and their officials, such as sheriffs in the counties, did not need to be literate in the modern sense. Lack of literacy did not mean that they were ignorant or incapable of coping with business; they were as literate as the tasks required. As the number of documents increased and habits of silent visual reading became more common, levels of literacy (in the modern sense) presumably increased also; but there is no evidence of a crisis suddenly demanding numerous literates. Because the pre-literate emphasis on the spoken word persisted, the change from oral to literate modes could occur slowly and almost imperceptibly over many generations.

The text usually quoted to show that medieval attitudes towards literacy were similar to modern ones is John of Salisbury's quotation in *Policraticus* that "rex illitteratus est quasi asinus coronatus" (an illiterate king is like a crowned ass). In this passage John is primarily concerned that the prince should have wisdom, which is gained by reading the law of God daily. For that reason, and not for administrative requirements, the prince needs skill in letters. John concedes moreoever that it is not absolutely necessary for the prince to be *litteratus*, provided he takes advice from *litterati*, that is, from priests who like Old Testament prophets will remind the prince of the law of God. "Thus the mind of the prince may read in the tongue of the priest. For the life and tongue of priests are like the book of life before the face of the peoples." John is obviously thinking here of the spiritual, and not the worldly, value of reading, His discussion emphasizes that an illiterate prince can participate in wisdom through the medium of the priest's voice. The prince is not excluded by being illiterate: "nor is he altogether destitute of reading [*lectionis*] who, even though he does not read himself, hears faithfully what is read to him by others." John thus shows that in his day non-literates could participate in literate culture; he is not arguing for the absolute necessity of rulers being literate in either the medieval sense of being learned in Latin or the modern sense of having a minimal ability to read and write. Ironically the king of England at the time, Henry II, was literate in every sense of the word; yet he was not a good king by John's definition, as he refused to listen to the lectures of priests and was responsible for the murder of Becket.

From Chapter 9, "Trusting Writing"

Documents did not immediately inspire trust. As with other innovations in technology, there was a long and complex period of evolution, particularly in the twelfth century in England, before methods of production were developed which proved acceptable both to traditionalists and to experts in literacy. There was no straight and simple line of progress from memory to written record. People had to be persuaded—and it was difficult to do—that documentary proof was a sufficient improvement on existing methods to merit the extra expense and mastery of novel techniques which it demanded.

A modern literate tends to assume that statements in writing, especially if they are in print, are more reliable than spoken words. This assumption is the result of schooling in reading and writing from an early age and the constant use of documents, such as bills, for even the smallest transactions. The obvious advantage to a modern literate of documentary proof is that it cannot be as easily or as readily changed as a person's word. But this advantage of writing was less obvious in medieval England, since even literates did not use documents in ways which assured their effectiveness as proof. Most charters of the twelfth century were neither dated, nor autographed, nor were they copied into registers for future reference. In the earliest private charters draftsmen and scribes give the impression that, instead of sharing a common training in the drawing up of instruments, they are each making a personal and individual but necessarily amateur effort to master the complexities of documentary proof for the first time.

A charter whereby Ralf of St Audoen gave a salt-pan to Sele priory in Sussex illustrates the work of an amateur draftsman very well, even though it is dated (*Anno Domini* 1153) and autographed which is unusual. The draftsman or scribe, who was probably one of the monks of Sele, begins with a justification for written record: "Because it is appropriate that this should be brought to reach the notice of many, it is committed to the muniments of letters by provident deliberation, lest in the process of time it be destroyed by ruinous oblivion." The gift itself was publicly symbolized not by this charter, however, but by a more traditional form of writing—a Gospel book which was laid on the beneficiary's altar. The monks of Sele seem to have been determined to ratify the gift in as many ways as possible, both traditional and novel. Ralf's lord, William de Braose, made his autograph sign of the cross on the charter twice, once in the priory and again when the document was exhibited and ratified at his court in Bramber castle. Ralf also put his seal on the charter. Those who trusted the sign of the cross and those who favoured the more modern wax seal, which with its device of a knight on horseback was a symbol of feudal lordship, could therefore both be satisfied. For those who trusted neither, lists of witnesses were specified for both transactions. As F. M. Stenton commented of a Lincolnshire charter of similar date, "the transaction is unusually complicated, but it is probable that the expression of a grant in writing was often less important to the parties than the performance of ceremonial acts of which the charter itself makes no record." The writing was of secondary importance, and was hedged about with repetitious clauses, because less confidence was placed in it than in the oaths and public ceremonies which had traditionally sanctioned conveyances.

At first each charter tended to differ in its phraseology, because every document was felt to be an individual affirmation fixing human relationships at a certain point in time and space. Doubts about whether such stability was possible or appropriate may explain why early drafters of charters are often reluctant to state the time and place of writing and why they invoke the aid of God and his saints so frequently. The advantage to the historian today, though not to the property owner at the time, of this diversity of practice is that it provides a record, like an archaeological stratification, of how a literate mentality developed over generations. Information, which students of diplomatic have accumulated in order to date charters and identify forgeries, can be used to illustrate how attitudes to writing changed over the twelfth and thirteenth centuries. The evolution of common form is not commonplace, as it marks the stages in the gradual acceptance of literate ways of doing business.

Memory and Writing

Before documents were used, the truth of an event or transaction had been established by personal statements, often made on oath, by the principals or witnesses. If the event were too far in the past for that, the oldest and wisest men were asked what they could remember about it. Numerous examples could be cited of collective oral testimony being given from memory, particularly in cases involving the proof of age of feudal heirs. The example which follows illustrates the method in answer to a less routine question. In 1127 a writ of Henry I ordered a jury to be chosen of twelve men from Dover and twelve from Sandwich to settle a dispute between St Augustine's abbey at Canterbury and Christ Church about customs due at the port of Sandwich. The jurors were described as "twenty-four mature, wise seniors of many years, having good testimony." Each in turn then swore on a Gospel book in public that the tolls belonged to Christ Church, saying: this "I have received from my ancestors, and I have seen and heard from my youth up until now, so help me God and these Holy Gospels."

Whether in circumstances like these the jurors really told the historical truth is impossible to establish, since the past events in question were recorded only in peoples' living memories. As the jurors had publicly sworn on the Gospels that they were telling the truth, no more could be said, unless their Christian principles were to be impugned. Thus, without documents, the establishment of what passed for truth was simple and personal, since it depended on the good word of one's fellows. Remembered truth was also flexible and up to date, because no ancient custom could be proved to be older than the memory of the oldest living wise man. There was no conflict between past and present, between ancient precedents and present practice. Customary law "quietly passes over obsolete laws, which sink into oblivion, and die peacefully, but the law itself remains young, always in the belief that it is old." Written records, on the other hand, do not die peacefully, as they retain a half life in archives and can be resurrected to inform, impress or mystify future generations.

Those who objected in the Middle Ages to the literate preference for the artificial memory of written record, instead of the living memory voiced by wise men of age and experience, were in a long tradition—had they known it—which extended back to myths about the invention of writing. According to Socrates the god who invented writing had been rebuked by the king of Egypt, Thamus, who said:

> If men learn this, it will implant forgetfulness in their souls: they will cease to exercise memory because they rely on that which is written, calling things to remembrance no longer from within themselves, but by means of external marks; what you have discovered is a recipe not for memory, but for reminder.

Both to ignorant illiterates and to sophisticated Platonists written record was a dubious gift, because it seemed to kill living eloquence and trust and substitute for them a mummified semblance in the form of a piece of parchment. Henry I's partisans in the dispute with Anselm, who had called a papal bull a sheepskin "blackened with ink and weighted with a little lump of lead," were arguing for the priority of the personal testimony of the three bishops who exercised memory over the mere "external marks" of a writing. Those medieval Christians who recalled St Paul's warning, "the letter killeth, but the spirit giveth life," were in a similar long tradition. Likewise perhaps the Earl Warenne himself, when he allegedly produced before Edward I's judges the "ancient and rusty sword" of his ancestors, was appealing to a sign which was superior to any letters because it lived in people's memories.

Such objectors, moreover, had a case which was strong in substance as well as in sentiment, since numerous medieval charters were forged and the authenticity of the genuine ones was difficult to prove. Such a bewildering variety of "external marks: had been used in idiosyncratic attempts to demonstrate the authenticity of charters that written record was highly suspicious. There were thousands of authentic charters without dates or places of issue, some of them written by scribes who seem never to have wielded a pen before. Although most English charters had seals attached to them, a few were authenticated by inked crosses (some autographs and others not), or by other symbolic objects signifying the donor's wishes such as rings or knives. Nearly all charters listed witnesses to the transaction, ranging in numbers from the king's unique *Teste me ipso* (witness, myself) to the 123 individuals named in an agreement in Kent in 1176. It was common for a scribe to conclude his list of witnesses with some such phrase as "and many others who would take too long to enumerate," a description which was useless for future identification, although it recorded the impressiveness of the occasion at the time. Witnesses soon died anyway and some, like the saints who witness a Christ Church charter of *c.* 1200, may never have lived. Sometimes the scribe of the charter identifies himself as the last witness, offering a test of authenticity, but more often he does not.

In these circumstances, where practice was so varied, and even eccentric, both literate and illiterate were entitled to distrust charters. Authentic looking documents might well be forged, or conversely amateur scrawls might turn out to be genuine. In addition to inconsistencies and lack of uniform scribal training, the principal difficulty was that monks, who were the traditional experts in writing, were also the greatest forgers. The more powerful and ancient the house, the more likely it was that its documents would be forged in a professional manner. Of the seals used by Christ Church Canterbury, Archdeacon Simon Langton wrote to Gregory IX in 1238: "Holy Father, there is not a single sort of forgery that is not perpetrated in the church of Canterbury. For they have forged in gold, in lead, in wax, and in every kind of metal." Much the same, of course, could be said of the papal *curia* in an earlier period, when it had created the Donation of Constantine and other forged decretals.

Yet in theory at least it would have been relatively easy for English medieval writers to make documents whose authenticity could normally have been proved. Although no system of safeguards could cover all cases, the great majority could certainly be guaranteed. All that was required was to follow elementary principles were not followed in medieval England, nor elsewhere at century Italy and throughout the *pays du droit écrit* bordering on the Mediterranean, and ensure that each document was precisely dated and written by an authorized scribe or notary. Ideally, in addition, the notary needed to register a document in a record kept by a public authority. As is well known, these elementary principles were not followed in medieval England, no elsewhere at first in northern Europe. Although some notaries practised in England in the thirteenth century, their activities were normally restricted to a few types of ecclesiastical business. Similarly public registers of certain types of property transactions existed in England by 1200, in the Jewish *arche* and the royal feet of fines established by Hubert Walter, but there was no comprehensive system of registration. Sometimes the king's government could not trace its own documents, let alone other people's.

The reason why England did not develop a notarial system on the Roman model is generally thought to be simple and obvious: "customary law prevailed." Although correct, this explanation is inadequate, as customary law did not prevail in other areas of bureaucratic activity because twelfth-century England had been opened to Italian and other European influences, first by the Norman Conquest and then by the Angevins. Thus the accounting system of the Exchequer, which Richard Fitz Neal thought to be largely a product of immemorial custom when he wrote his *Dialogue of the Exchequer* around 1179, had in fact been created in Henry I's reign by French (and perhaps also Arabic) arithmetical expertise. The common law itself, as articulated by Henry II's writs, owed more to deliberate legislative thought than to custom. From the latter half of the twelfth century English royal officials were sufficiently influenced by the canon and civil law schools of Bologna to know that custom by itself was inadequate. Fitz Neal himself evoked Roman law, when he credited William the Conqueror with the intention of bringing "the conquered people under the rule of written law." Although Fitz Neal's remark has elements of anachronism when applied to William the Conqueror, it reflects the assumption of contemporary administrators in Henry II's reign that Roman *jus scriptum* could be applied to England.

Why England remained largely unaffected by the Roman notarial system, while being influenced by other continental bureaucratic procedures, is therefore a question worth pursuing further, as it goes to the roots of the non-literate's lack of understanding and consequent distrust of written modes of proof. Without documents memory had stemmed from the living wisdom of the local community whereas the dead hand of writing, the "mortmain" of the monks and clergy, defined and extended boundaries by its "external marks" across both time and space.

Dating Documents

The difficulties experienced by English writers of the twelfth century, when confronting problems they felt to be novel, are well illustrated by their variety of approaches to dating documents ranging from those who omit the date altogether to others who use more than one system of computation on the same document. To write out the date at the head of a letter is an elementary routine for a modern literate and was relatively simple likewise for a trained medieval notary. Thus an imperial notary, Henry of Asti, wrote the date as follows on an instrument drawn up in London: "Anno a nativitate Christi millesimo ducentesimo sexagesimo octavo, indictione undecima, die Mercurii xviii intrante mense Januraii, pontificatus domini Clementis papae iiii anno tercio." This date, Wednesday 18 January A.D. 1268, is expressed in a way which is familiar to a modern European, although the papal year (the third of Clement IV) and the reference to the eleventh indiction are Roman notarial refinements which now seem superfluous. For some transactions notaries were expected to record the hour as well as the day. Thus an episcopal notification from Lincoln in 1228 specifies times of dispatch and receipt of letters, as well as verifying the sender's seal. Even a common law judge, Roger of Seaton, followed notarial practice in 1279 when he acknowledged receipt of one letter from the Chancery "at about the ninth hour" and another "just a little after dark." These times are not more precise presumably because Seaton was estimating the hours by daylight and not by a clock.

The purpose of being precise about the year, month, day and even hour at which a document was issued or received was in order to settle subsequent disputes about its authenticity by checking the time. Thus Henry III assured Gregory X in 1272 that some royal letters patent, which were being exhibited at the papal *curia*, were forgeries because "we were not at Canterbury on that day and year"; in fact Henry was mistaken, but that is another story. Dates and places of issue had the added advantage of putting documents and their makers in a temporal and geographical perspective, which extended over centuries if the Christian system of years of grace *Anno Domini* was used.

Despite the advantages of stating when documents were issued, most twelfth-century charters do not do so. The eight extant bonds (the earliest of their kind) of the Flemish financier, William Cade, are significant in this respect, as it might be expected that records of debts would be drafted as precisely as possible. Yet none of the bonds bears a date of issue and three of them (nos. ii, v, viii) do not even specify the year in which the debt is to be paid, but only a day in relation to feast days of the church. Although the other five do specify the year, it is expressed in ways which are clumsy and could be ambiguous in the long term:

   i: After Henry, the king of England's son, espoused the daughter of the king of
      France [1160];
 iii: after the espousal of the king of England's son and the king's daughter;
  iv: after the king and Count Thierry of Flanders had talks together at Dover
      before the count went to set out for Jerusalem [1157];
  vi: after the king's great council at London [1163];
 vii: after Gilbert Foliot was received into the bishopric of London [1163].

Cade evidently did not expect his debts to be outstanding for long and so it was appropriate to date repayments in relation to current events.

More precise forms of dating begin in the last decade of the twelfth century. Royal letters are uniformly dated (by place of issue, day of the month and regnal year) from the accession of Richard I in 1189. Influenced by royal rather than papal practice, English bishops begin to date their solemn *acta* with regularity from the end of the twelfth century, although their secular enfeoffments and administrative precepts went on being undated until the end of the thirteenth century. Books and similar scribal work are likewise usually undated and unautographed, although there are notable exceptions like the chronicles of Matthew Paris or Domesday Book, one of whose volumes states that "this *descriptio*" was made in A.D. 1086. Other than Domesday, the earliest extant English book dated by its scribe is a text of St Augustine, which is stated to have been written at the Cistercian abbey of Buildwas in A.D. 1167; another book from Buildwas is similarly dated A.D. 1176.

Why not always give the date on a document in a precise and uniform way, if only as a routine precaution? Various explanations can be suggested for not doing so. One sometimes mentioned is that charters were seen as mere confirmations of transactions which had already taken place, and there was therefore no point in dating them. The difficulty with this explanation is that even when a charter was written after the event, it would still have been prudent, if the draftsman really had that regard for posterity which his preamble claimed, to specify in the text the date of the transaction itself and distinguish that from the date on which the charter was written. To specify both dates was good notarial practice. Another possible explanation for omitting dates is that they were difficult to compute without printed diaries. Gervase of Canterbury describes some of the problems: when exactly was the Crucifixion (in 32, 33 or 34 A.D.?) when should the year begin—at the Annunciation (25 March), the Passion (a moveable feast), Christmas, or the Circumcision (1 January)? Yet these difficulties were surmountable and since most early charters were written by monks, who were the experts in chronology, their lack of dates is still mysterious.

Other reasons for not dating documents are more profound. Until putting the date on a document became a mindless routine, dating required the scribe to express an opinion about his place in time. In relation to which persons, human or divine, and over what length of time was the date to be computed? A Jew might date his bond "from the Creation" and think of a continuum "from the beginning of time up to the end of the world," because the temporal order proceeded without intermission. For the pope, on the other hand, it was appropriate to begin a new era with the birth of Christ and to date letters *Anno Domini*, since the pope was Christ's vicar in unbroken succession from St Peter. A bishop or a monastic chronicler might likewise compute by years of grace, since bishops too were successors of the Apostles and monks had an accepted place in the Christian dispensation. Yet ecclesiastics did not date all their documents: enfeoffments and precepts were usually left undated, as has already been mentioned. In such instances omission of the date may not have been due to negligence, but to conscientiousness. Perhaps it was thought presumptuous or even blasphemous to associate worldly business with the time of Christ's incarnation. To record the year *Anno Domini* on a document was to give it a place in the chronology of Christian salvation in past, present and future time, as expounded by St Augustine in the *City of God*. Paradoxically, monks may have so rarely dated documents in the twelfth century or earlier because they were too conscious of the significance of time and of their place in posterity.

The non-religious, by contrast, had such a personal and short view of time that they too found it difficult at first to specify a numerical year on a document. Everyone knew which year was meant, the present one, and if there were doubt, some notable event could be referred to. Examples have already been given of William Cade dating his bonds in this frame of mind. The richest variety of memorable events in an early record appear in the guild rolls of Leicester (the earliest of their kind), which extend over the period 1196–1232. The first year is specified in relation to the release from captivity in France of the earl of Leicester (in 1196) and the second "after the death of the emperor of Germany" (Henry VI in 1197). Thereafter other events of national or international importance, such as the Interdict in John's reign or the death of William Marshal and the capture of Damietta by the crusaders (both in 1219), are interspersed with local events in Leicester, such as the dedication of St Nicholas's church (in ?1221) and the deaths or periods in office of town worthies like aldermen. Only three times are English regnal years referred to, and years *Anno Domini* are not used at all. Evidently the Leicester town clerks were uncertain of what standard to adopt for dating their rolls. By their variety of practices the rolls give an indication of how events, in Leicester and beyond, were viewed by the local community.

The earliest extant final concord made before royal justices is similarly dated not by a numerical year, but at the feast of Peter and Paul (29 June) "after the king took the allegiance of the barons of Scotland at York." This refers to the homage done to Henry II in York Minster in August 1175 after his defeat of King William the Lion. This concord, which concerns a lawsuit in Oxford between the canons of Osney and a widow and her daughters, has no direct concern with Anglo-Scottish politics. Nevertheless it was evidently assumed that the time when Henry II formally exhibited his superiority over the Scots would be remembered for at least as long as the settlement of this lawsuit at Oxford. Whether the drafters of this concord thought that their document would last only for a generation or so, or whether conversely they thought that Henry II's triumphant ceremony in York Minster would be remembered for centuries, is impossible to establish. Probably they had not given the matter much thought either way. They dated the concord not in relation to a documented time continuum stretching over centuries, but, as a non-literate might, in relation to a recent famous event. Despite their appeals to posterity, medieval writers seem to have found it difficult to imagine that their work might survive for centuries and that a time would come when only a professional historian knew when "the king took the allegiance of the barons of Scotland at York."

Even when a year is given *Anno Domini* on a document, a memorable event is sometimes specified as well, as if years of grace were too alien (except to the professionally religious) to inspire personal confidence. Thus a gift by the wife of Roger de Mowbray to Fountains abbey is dated A.D. 1176 "the year in which the fortresses of Thirsk and [Kirkby] Malzeard were razed." This event likewise concerns Henry II's defeat of William the Lion, as Roger de Mowbray had been among the rebels whose castles were demolished. The Mowbrays here recalled their personal humiliation by Henry II instead of the larger submission in York Minster. A concord made in the court of William de Ferrers is dated comparably by the fortunes of the local lord—"the year A.D. 1192, namely the year in which Earl William de Ferrers took to wife Anneis, sister of Ranulf, earl of Chester." Enough has been said to show that traditionally, before documentation was properly understood, the measurement of time was related to a variety of persons and events and not to an external standard.

The novelty of dating documents, and the variety of ways in which it might be done, is best summarized by the unnecessarily elaborate datary which Ralf de Diceto gave for his survey of the manors of St Paul's cathedral. His invention of distinctive *signa* for his chronicle and the St Paul's charters suggests that he was extraordinarily sensitive to modes of documentary proof. He therefore intended there to be no doubt about the year in which he made his survey. It was:

> The 1181st year AD, the 21st year of Pope Alexander III, the 27th regnal year of King Henry II of the English, the 11th regnal year of King Henry the son of the king, the 18th year that time had passed since the translation of Bishop Gilbert Foliot from Hereford to London, when this inquest was made by Ralf de Diceto, dean of London, in the first year of his deanship.

Ralf thus computes the year by six different systems which he arranges hierarchically, from years *Anno Domini* through the pope and the kings down to himself at the bottom in his first energetic year of office as dean of St Paul's.

In the thirteenth century, when charters were written in tens of thousands, methods of dating become less self-conscious and more uniform. A parody of datary in French, purporting to be written in a letter to the noble Lady Desire, sets out the commonest rules: "Given within the four seas of England, on the eve of St John the Baptist, in the 27th year of the reign of King Edward the son of King

Henry." The eve of St John the Baptist is 23 June (Midsummer's Eve) and the 27th year of Edward I's reign is 1299. Between the various possible ways of recording the year, month and day the commonest procedure adopted in England was to relate the day within each year to a feast of the church and to express the year in terms of regnal years. This compromise between church and state, which rejected years *Anno Domini* (as used in episcopal chanceries), and Roman calendar months (as used in the royal Chancery) probably seemed the most appropriate to knightly landowners. They trusted regnal years more than years *Anno Domini* because there was a more immediate point of reference in the king's coronation, which was a publicly remembered event. The growth of dating by regnal years, rather than by more personal events or by the regimes of lesser lords, also suggests that the king was becoming accepted as the head of the English community. Some knights were beginning, moreover, to learn the lengths of reigns of their kings from illustrated rolls which set them out in succession.

Although after 1300 many private charters still bear no date, forms of dating had become firmly established and commonplace. In general, after much preliminary hesitation, writers had got the measure of time. But because dating had evolved at the slow pace at which literate habits became acceptable, rather than being arbitrarily imposed by Roman law, English methods of dating documents remained complex and inconsistent. From a historical point of view, this variety of methods is a memorial to the formation of literate habits reflecting both feudal and Christian ways of thought. The evolution of the dating of documents is a measure of growing confidence in their usefulness as records.

10.
Defining "Literacy" in North American Schools

Social and Historical Conditions and Consequences

Suzanne de Castell
Allan Luke

Being "literate" has always referred to having mastery over the processes by means of which culturally significant information is coded. The criterion of significance has varied historically with changes in the kind of information from which power and authority could be derived. Educational attempts to redefine literacy, however, have not always faithfully reflected this fact. Studies of literacy in the more distant past (Havelock,[1] Hoggart[2] and Graff[3]), have emphasized relationships of literacy to evolving modes of social and political organization, yet contemporary educators and researchers have been reluctant to analyse literacy in terms of explicitly normative or ideological conditions. The redefinition of the processes of literacy instruction by educational psychologists in recent years has effectively concealed the necessity for addressing both the subjective and the social dimensions of literacy development. This encourages a view of literacy as a context-neutral, content-free, skill-specific competence which can be imparted to children with almost scientific precision. Literacy so seen bypasses controversial claims about what curriculum is worthwhile, what moral, social and personal principles should operate within the educational context. This, as we can see historically, has never been the case. And as we can come to see conceptually, it never will be the case.

Literacy instruction has always taken place within a substantive context of values.[4] In the European Protestant educational tradition on which the public schools of the New World were first based, commonality of religious belief was

From the *Journal of Curriculum Studies* 15(1983): 373–89. Copyright 1983 by Taylor & Francis, Ltd. Reprinted by permission of the publisher.

central to literacy instruction. The "criss-cross row"—the first line of the earliest 17th-century English reader, the Horn Book—was a graphic representation of the Cross, invoked to speed and guide the beginner's progress through the text. The expansion of literacy in Europe was initially inseparable from the rise of Protestantism, and the erosion of the Church's monopoly over the printed word (Eisenstein[5] and Chaytor[6]). The intent of the sixteenth- and seventeenth-century educational reformers was that "whosoever will" should have access to the word of God. It was believed that individual access to the word, even though it might involve uncomprehending repetition, would improve the soul of the reader *without* authoritative meditation by the cleric. This explains in part the importance ascribed in European schools to repetition and recitation of texts which children could not have been expected to "comprehend"—a religious and pedagogical tradition inherited by North American education in its earliest days. Aspects of that same tradition carried over into nineteenth-century 3Rs and classical literacy instruction, which augmented religious texts with venerable children's tales and literature. During the period of progressive reform, from 1900 to just after the Second World War, literacy instruction attempted to address the "practical" speech codes of everyday life. "Child-centred" curricula usurped the classics, and the normative stress moved from moral and cultural edification to socialization and civic ethics. After a neo-classical revival in the 1950s, the technocratic paradigm emerged, with a bias towards "functional skills" and the universal attainment of "minimum competence." As the touchstone of educational excellence moved from text to interaction to evaluation, what counted as literacy was systematically redefined (see table 10.1).

Classical and 3Rs Instruction

Long before the public schools movement in the 1860s, North American children received "3Rs" (reading, writing and arithmetic) in private and community schools. For the "common" child, literacy instruction took place in the home, at church, in the local shops, and in the few charity schools. Most communities had one-room schools where a teacher would provide the 3Rs, and moral and religious instruction to those children of various ages whose labour was not required by the family. In the élite private and preparatory schools of the mid-nineteenth century, like Boston's Roxbury Latin School (founded in 1645), children of the wealthy and influential studied "Latin for six years, French for five, German for four, and Greek for three."[7] Despite this differential provision of linguistic competence and cultural knowledge according to class status and geographic location, the blend of formal and informal schooling, family and religious education, and apprenticeship was nevertheless largely successful in creating a literate populus. In Upper Canada this loosely organized system "produced a basic literacy for a majority of students."[8] Of the mid-century US, Bowles and Gintis note that "it is particularly difficult to make the case that the objective of early school reform movements was mass literacy. In the U.S., literacy was already high (about 90 percent of adult whites) prior to the 'common school revival.' "[9] Whether there was a pressing economic need for a literate

Table 10.1

Theory into practice	Classical	Progressive	Technocratic
Philosophy	Cultivation of the 'civilized' person with the 'instinct' of a gentleman	Education as 'growth' the natural 'unfolding' of the child	Education as effective performance, behaviour modification
Psychology	*Plato:* Faculty psychology—reason, will, emotion. Learning by imitation. Reason must subdue the passions	*Dewey:* The mind as unfolding organism, social theory of mind (organism/environment)	*Thorndike:* Empiricism, testing *Skinner:* The mind as mechanism, learning through reinforcement (behaviour modification)
Sociology	Aristocracy	Democracy	Individualism/pluralism
Conception of literacy	Literacy as literature, detailed analysis of exemplary texts, specification or precise rules, principles, explicit attention to rhetorical appropriateness	Literacy as self-expression, communication as social interaction	Functional literacy 'survival skills,' minimum competence
Attitude to education	Intrinsic worth	Subjective/social significance	Instrumental value
Curriculum	Exemplary texts (1) the Bible, (2) the Classics, (3) the English literature greats', (4) North American 'classics,' grammar texts, handwriting, spelling, pronunciation	'Adventure' stories, civics, self-generated text, idiom of ordinary language	De-contextualized subskills of literate competence. Systematic programmed instruction guided by behavioural objectives Vocational education
Pedagogy	Rote-learning: oral recitation, copying, imitation of 'correct' speech and writing,' direct instruction	Projects: 'experiential' education, teacher/pupil interaction, teacher as 'guide,' 'discovery' method. Socialized instruction	Streaming or 'mastery learning' of common set of objectives. Learning 'packages,' with teacher as (preprogrammed) facilitator. Programmed instruction
Evaluation	Connoisseurship model; oration, oral reading, direct questioning	Local, classroom texts, written tests stressed over oration, products (or 'projects'), social skills stressed	Meeting behavioural objectives. Objective standardized testing (mass scale)
Outcome	Domestication	Socialization	Individuation/commoditization

populus at the time is problematic. Graff notes that most mid-nineteenth-century occupations required a minimal competence with print; far from requiring universal literacy, communities typically featured a division of literate labour.

Whatever the concrete practical demands for literacy, the popular association of illiteracy with crime, poverty, and immorality fuelled public enthusiasm for a universal free public education system. Ontario educator Archibald McCallum's comments reflected the popular conception of the consequences of illiteracy:

> Over seven percent of New England's population over ten years of age can neither read nor write; yet 80 percent of the crime in these states was committed by this small minority; in other words, an uneducated person commits fifty-six times as many crimes as one with education.[10]

The debate over illiteracy in nineteenth-century North America, then, was intimately connected with religious, ethical, and ultimately ideological questions. We find evidence of this in the theory and practice of 3Rs and classical instruction largely borrowed from existing European and British methods and texts. An overriding instructional emphasis on mental and physical discipline complemented perfectly mid-century educational goals: the domestication of a "barbarous" population, whose inclinations towards "materialism" and "ignorance" threatened cultural continuity, political order, and Protestant morality.

Universal free public school systems had been established in the majority of states and in Upper Canada by 1860. In the US over half of the nation's children were receiving formal education, and more students than ever before now had access to levels of schooling previously restricted to an élite few.[11] In Canada, under the direction of Egerton Ryerson, the Ontario Schools Act of 1841 had subsidized the existing common school system; by 1872 British Columbia had legislated a public school system modelled on that of Ontario.

Late nineteenth-century literacy instruction in Canada differed in one crucial respect from its American counterpart. For while Canadian schools imported curricula from England, teachers in America were provided with locally developed textbooks, in the tradition of the *McGuffey Readers*. Noah Webster's *American Spelling Book* (1873),[12] the most widely used textbook in US history, promoted not only American history, geography and morals, but was itself a model for an indigenous vocabulary and spelling. Textbooks and dictionaries of this period attempted to engender a national literacy and literature free, in Webster's words, of European "folly, corruption and tyranny." In Canada, by contrast, classrooms featured the icons of colonialism: British flags and pictures of royalty adorned the walls, younger students were initiated to print via the *Irish Readers*, and literature texts opened with Wordsworth's and Tennyson's panegyrics to the Crown. In Canada, the reduction of pauperism and crime associated with illiteracy was seen to require the preservation of British culture and a colonial sensibility; in the United States, "custodians of culture"[13] sought to assure economic independence and political participation. The match between these differing societal and educational ideologies, and the "civilizing" effects of traditional 3Rs and classical education was near perfect.

The model for this classical education was found in the philosophy, psychology, and social theory of Plato's educational treatise *The Republic*. Platonic faculty psychology subdivided the mind into three faculties: reason, will and emotion. The child, a "barbarian at the gates of civilization"[14] was regarded as a bundle of unruly impulses needing to be brought under the control of the faculty of "right reason," that is, morally informed rational judgement. Paraphrasing a speech of Ryerson's, the *Journal of Education* declared in 1860 that "a sensual man is a mere animal. Sensuality is the greatest enemy of all human progress" (in Prentice, p. 29). To that end, rigid discipline and rigorous mental training characterized classical instruction.

Adopting Plato's stress on mimesis and imitation as the basis for the development of mind, classical pedagogy stressed rote-learning, repetition, drill, copying, and memorization of lengthy passages of poetry and prose. Mental, moral and spiritual edification were to be had through exposure to, in the words of Matthew Arnold (1864), the "best that has been thought and said in the world." Accordingly, the intermediate and secondary grades adopted a "great books" literacy curriculum which featured the Bible, Greek and Roman classics and, after some debate, acknowledged works of English and American literature; "far more time [was] spent . . . on ancient history and dead languages than upon the affairs of the present or even recent past" (Joncich, p. 48). In the US, public high schools retained a modified classical curriculum, *sans* Greek, as a "uniform program." This universal implementation of a classical curriculum in secondary schools forced practical studies of law, book-keeping, and vocational skills outside the public system. In Canada, it was left to industry to initiate vocational education.[15]

Curricular material did not vary from grade to grade: the same literary texts, particularly the Bible, were studied in greater and greater detail and depth; underlying "truths" were explicated in terms of grammatical rules, rhetorical strategies, moral content, and aesthetic worth. In the elementary grades, students copied passages for "finger style" penmanship exercise, in preparation for advanced composition study. Thus, stylistic imitation and repetition, guided by explicit rules, dominated writing instruction; students at all levels undertook précis and recitation of exemplary texts.

Following the European model, reading took the form of oral performance to an audience. Individual reading time was limited and all students progressed at a fixed rate through the text. Both in graded and secondary schools, each student in turn would read passages aloud; those not reading were expected to listen attentively to the reader, since the intent of oral reading instruction was not merely to ascertain the reader's ability to decode the text, but to develop powers of effective public oration. Pronunciation, modulation, and clarity of diction were stressed. In the nineteenth-century classroom, reading was neither a private nor reflective act, but a rule-bound public performance.

While texts were meticulously dissected and analysed, and block parsing was a daily routine, the emphasis was not on mere grammatical correctness. In theory, analysis and repetition subserved the development of sensitivity to the aesthetic and didactic features of the text. Thus, the student's encounter with the text, from fairy-tales and Shakespeare, was to be both aesthetically pleasing and morally instructive—in accordance with the Horatian edict that literature should be *"dulce et utile."*

In the same way, vocabulary study subserved the ends of moral and literary education. Spelling lists often featured poetic language, Biblical and literary terminology. Precision of meaning and rhetorical effectiveness were to be achieved through the apt selection of words from this cultural lexicon: the range of vocabulary legitimated by "literati" as appropriate for each generic form of literate expression. The overriding sense of conformity and decorum was reflected in the rules which constrained classroom discourse and behaviour. Corresponding to each literate act was a correct bodily "habitus";[16] reading, writing and speaking were performed in prescribed physical postures. Moreover, "provincial" speech codes were frowned upon as evidence of rudeness or ignorance; textbooks of this period advised students to cultivate the friendship of children of higher station, so that they might assimilate more cultured and aristocratic speech habits.

At the secondary and college levels, unreflective and mechanical imitation was despised as the mark of an ill-bred social climber. Oration was the epitome of classical literate expression, for in the performance all of the diverse rules governing textual analysis and production could be organically unified. The truly successful high school student displayed not only a knowledge of rule-following, but of skilled and effective rule-breaking, which may have been, in the final analysis, what elevated performance from mere technique to the level of art. Implicit was an eighteenth-century ideal of "wit," following Addison (1714), that "there is sometimes a greater judgement shown in deviating from the rules of art than in adhering to them."

But if technical correctness was not a sufficient criterion of educational success beyond the grade school level, how could the attainment of classical literacy be evaluated? Evaluation in the 3Rs and classical classroom was carried out on a "connoisseurship" model. Under the oratorical model of formal examination, the examiner embodied, however tacitly, standards of cultural and disciplinary excellence and applied these unstated criteria to laud or correct the performance, often undertaken in the presence of trustees, clergy and parents. This system of assessment vested total control over evaluative criteria and procedures with the teacher or examiners, who retained the authoritative and final "word" in literacy instruction.

This view of knowledge was encouraged by an historically and critically specific ontology: the idealist conviction that knowledge was immutable, that forms of beauty, truth and morality were embodied, so far as they could be realized in the phenomenal world at all, in those authoritative texts passed down by each generation of élite literati. The experience of becoming literate was to be an initiation into a continuing cultural conversation with exemplary texts and human models.

The principal intent of nineteenth-century literacy instruction, then, was inextricably bound to the transmission of a national ideology and culture. In practice, this translated into a regimen of "benumbing"[17] drill, repetition, and physical constraint. This mode of literacy instruction meant to provide a universal sense of physical, legal, and moral discipline for a growing, diverse, and increasingly mobile populus while simultaneously ensuring that neo-British "high culture" would be preserved in North America well into the next century. For late nineteenth- and early twentieth-century students—even those 80 to 90 percent who left school by age 13—it would have been impossible to conceive of reading and writing as entities, or "skills," distinct from codes of conduct, social values and cultural knowledge.

Socializing the Recitation

Between 1900 and 1914, the number of public high schools in America doubled, and the student population increased by 150 percent. With increasing immigration and regional migration to urban centres, the provision and enforcement of compulsory education expanded; educational costs spiralled and per capita expenditure in the US rose from $24 in 1910 to $90 in 1930.[18] With the largest part of these costs shouldered by local taxpayers, the fact that in the early 1900s only about 15 percent of students continued beyond elementary school led to public complaints that schools were élitist, authoritarian, outmoded and inefficient. E. P. Cubberley, Stanford University's advocate of modern management, noted in 1913 that Portland schools had become a "rigidly" prescribed mechanical system, poorly adapted to the needs of the children of the community.[19]

Like their private school predecessors, late nineteenth- and early twentieth-century public high schools continued to exclude those students unwilling or unable to demonstrate excellence at the "civilizing" activities of recitation and literary study. And what *use* were these competencies anyway? The legitimation potential of classical literacy in a developing industrial democracy was rapidly eroded as the public was nurtured on scientific ideals and evolutionary theory by intellectuals of the day, and on scientific management and cost-accounting by its leading businessmen. And although these two influential groups expressed divergent views about what should be done, they were united in opposition to 3Rs and classical instruction.

The material stimulus for reform came from the application of business methods to schools. Educational administrators were called upon to produce results consistent in the public mind with the increasing tax burdens they were compelled to shoulder. The stage was set by the application of F. W. Taylor's,[20] and later J. F. Bobbitt's[21] work on "cost-eficient scientific management" to school administration, curriculum, and instruction. Accordingly, measures of costs per minute of instruction in each subject area were used to adjudicate educational value. Finding that 5.0 recitations in Greek were equivalent to 23.8 recitations in French, F. Spalding (1913) declared:

> Greater wisdom in these assignments will come, not by reference to any supposedly fixed and inherent values in these subjects, but from a study of local conditions and needs. I know of nothing about the absolute value of a recitation in Greek . . . the price must go down, or we shall invest in something else (Callahan).

Extensive building programmes were initiated, curricula were standardized, class size was increased, teaching hours were extended; testing of teacher, pupil, and administrator was introduced, and records and documents were collected to evaluate everything and anything pertaining to schools. With a supply-and-demand mentality, and a cost-benefit analysis, schools were seen as "factories in which raw materials are to be shaped and fashioned into products to meet the various demands of life" (Cubberley in Callahan).

But the fact that it was traditional pupil recitations that "educational experts" were quantifying illustrates the impoverishment of their ideas on instructional reform. Beyond the belief that schools were maintained by and for business and public interests, administrative efficiency experts had little of substance to offer teachers. With the failure of platoon schools in the late 1920s, unmanageably large classes, and organized teacher resistance to "industrialization," the stage was set for a new educational philosophy, one which would accommodate both scientific management and democratic individualism.

What Plato was for the classicists, John Dewey was for the progressives. Dewey articulated a philosophy of education which drew from experimental science, child psychology, evolutionary theory, and the moral aspects of American pragmatism. Adopting William James's[22] critique of innatism, and his call for early training in an optimal environment, Dewey saw educational reform as the principal means for American social evolution. Deweyan progressivism, therefore, originated as a self-conscious attempt to make schooling socially responsive: oriented towards a social future rather than a cultural past. Its goal was to provide the skills, knowledge, and social attitudes required for urbanized commercial and industrial society.

Progressives derived their definition of literacy from the social psychology of James and G. H. Mead.[23] Language, for Mead, was created and sustained by the pragmatics of intersubjective communication—communicative "acts" involving "symbolic interaction" with a "generalized social other." Within the pragmatists' expanded theory of communication, linguistic development and socialization were deemed inseparable. Hence, the classroom was to be a microcosm of the ideal social community, one which fostered the development of equality and social exchange, rather than authority and imitation. Teachers of the 1920s and 1930s were trained to view their classrooms as "learning environments"; within these democratic communities, children could "act out" the skills required for social and vocational life. Said Dewey:

> The key to the present educational situation lies in the gradual reconstruction of school materials and methods so as to utilize various forms of occupation typifying social callings, and to bring out their intellectual and moral content. This reconstruction must relegate purely literary methods—including textbooks—and dialectical methods to the position of necessary auxiliary tools in cumulative activities.[24]

The "integrated curriculum," "learning by discovery," and the "project method" were to enable the natural unfolding of the child in accordance with his/her developing interests.

Rote recitation of literature was replaced in this reconstructed environment. Dewey noted that conventional reading instruction "may develop book worms, children who read omnivorously, but at the expense of development of social and executive abilities and skills."[25] Thus, whereas classical literacy was grounded in the exemplary text, progressives focused on questions of instructional method and social use.

Nonetheless, the progressive mandate that education be socially useful, that training "transfer" across contexts,[26] made the content of literacy texts a crucial matter, albeit secondary to instructional concerns. Beginning in the 1910s and 1920s, American-prescribed and authorized readers, also used in Canada, reflected the dominant values and popular culture of commercial and industrial life. Stories of "adventure" and "friendship" featured vignettes of family life, work and play, and encouraged community service and individual achievement. Dick and Jane usurped Arthurian heroes; by the 1930s discussions of the latest "moving pictures" and radio programmes coexisted in secondary classrooms with the study of Shakespeare. Literacy texts portrayed a vision of a harmonious American social community, blessed with the gifts of technological advancement and material prosperity.

Progressive speaking and writing instruction placed an emphasis on practicality and expressiveness, rather than propriety. Students were encouraged to talk about their daily "experiences," to discuss emotional and contentious matters; colloquialism and regional dialects were more readily accepted, and practical "plain speaking" encouraged. In "creative writing" instruction students were expected to express their own ideas and experiences, rather than to reproduce literary style. Courses in "Business English" and journalism were introduced and grammar study became "functional" rather than "formal." Students learned library techniques and book reviewing, how to record the minutes of a meeting, and how to write laboratory reports.

This stress on the cultivation of practical linguistic expression was matched by a virtual reinvention of reading. Dewey's call for a more scientific method of instruction was answered by the developments in educational psychology. Influential studies by E. B. Huey,[27] E. L. Thorndike,[28] and W. S. Gray[29] indicated that oral reading instruction was inefficient and counterproductive. Thorndike proposed that:

> In school practice it appears likely that exercises in silent reading to find answers to given questions, or to give a summary of the matter read, or to list the questions which it answers, should in large measure replace oral reading (p. 324).

Reading, then, was a form of "reasoning"; the psychologists convincingly argued that oral decoding and memorization did not engender an understanding or "comprehension" of textual meaning.

Accordingly, classroom reading instruction was reformulated; students read silently and responded to "objective" comprehension questions. Within this new system, the teacher would be freer to attend to individual remediation, small-group projects, grading and classroom management, while each student progressed through the text at an "individualized" rate. However, many teachers were burdened with far larger classes as pedagogical reforms remained subservient to industrial reorganization. A "child-centred" instruction which attended to "individual differences" was more often a theoretical rationale than practical reality.

Throughout North America, school and public libraries flourished under both government and corporate financing; as a result, the classical school master's monopoly over the selection and use of the text was diminished. Students were encouraged to undertake popular and technical works "outside of what is conventionally termed good reading matter" (Dewey, p. 549): "dime-store" novels, magazines and newspapers, "how-to" books, and biographies of contemporary sports and political heroes. The curricular provision for "recreational" and "work reading" instruction was a sign of the attempt to integrate schooled literacy with all aspects of home and work life.

Oral examinations of reading were replaced with standardized and, hence, allegedly equitable, instruments of student assessment and teacher accountability. Standardized tests, like the *Thorndike-McCall Silent Reading Test*, were efficient and time-saving pedagogical devices and, moreover, provided valuable data which could be used to determine instructional efficiency and individual progress. It is significant that these first psychometric measures of literacy, early reading and language achievement tests, were welcomed by educators as objective and neutral devices which would end the nepotistic and arbitrary evaluative criteria of the connoisseurship model.[30]

Spelling instruction, as well, was modernized. Systematized pre- and post-test spelling instruction, for which students maintained their own progress charts, superseded the traditional "spelling bee." The lexicon of school literacy instruction changed noticeably; literary and religious terms were replaced by the language of democratic social life, names of institutions and occupations, and the terminology of business transactions and the industrial work-place.

Thus, evolutionary social reform and industrial development was the value framework pervading early and mid-twentieth-century literacy instruction. Literacy was seen as a vehicle for expression, social communication and vocational competence, rather than for the improvement of the soul. But its moral imperatives were no less strongly instilled. It was not until well after the Second World War that the neutrality of scientific pedagogy came to be seen as absolving teachers of their traditional moral and spiritual leadership roles. For the progressives, scientific intervention meant only the more equitable and efficient realization of stated normative and political goals, not their elimination from the educational field. In Dewey's words, education was both an art and a science; science enabled the optimal development of the art of education.

But the attempt to reconcile apparent contradictions and conflicts within social praxis, to totalize personal, social and empirical natures—Dewey's intellectual inheritance from Hegel—was, finally, the undoing of progressivism. For it was the very ambiguity of progressive rhetoric and sloganism in its attempt to dialectically resolve contradictions (between self and society, individual and institution, science and art, education and socialization) that led to the transformation of progressive ideals into industrial practices. The popular rhetoric of "individualization" of instruction, for example, was employed by both progressives and industrialists, but to very different ends. Throughout the progressive era, apparently harmonious, but actually divergent goals and practices caused education in general, and literacy instruction in particular, to vacillate between the extremes of a socialized education and an industrial socialization.

The Technology of Literacy Instruction

By the end of the Second World War, social and political conditions were set for a major shift in literacy instruction. Assessing the post-War era, historian H. Covell explained:

> The shocking discovery that many of the young men in military service could not read adequately, and the impetus given the study of science by the discovery of nuclear energy and the space race have combined to result in a greater emphasis on the need for continuing instruction . . . of the specific skills needed in reading.[31]

The term "functional literacy" was coined by the US Army to indicate "the capability to understand instructions necessary for conducting basic military functions and tasks . . . fifth grade reading level."[32] While our inheritance from the Army testing of the First World War was the concept of "IQ" as a measure of ability,[33] the educational legacy of the Second World War may have been "functional literacy" as a measure of vocational and social competence. Throughout the thirty-year development of the technocratic model, functional literacy remained a goal of North American schools, leading ultimately to the competency-based education movement of the 1970s.

After the Second World War, progressive education was besieged by public and media criticism. In his nefarious search for Communist influences, US Senator Joseph McCarthy singled out progressivism as overly permissive and anti-American. Scientists and industrialists indicted American schools for failing to keep pace with the Russians in the production of technical expertise. In *So Little for the Mind*, classicist educator Hilda Neatby argued that the "amorality" of progressive education had spawned "an age without standards."[34] Out of the by then unruly weave of "child-centred" instruction and industrial management, a "neutral" and efficient system of instruction emerged: the technocratic model was a refinement of the scientific strand of progressivism.

To educators of the "Atomic Age," then, it must have seemed eminently reasonable that schooling, along with other institutions, should become more scientific in order to promote universal literacy. Educational science would provide both the means and ends of education: a body of universally applicable skills of reading and writing, transferable to a variety of social and vocational contexts. The psychological research which had fitted so neatly with the industrial reforms of the progressive era, now established the direction of technological literacy instruction. Throughout the 1950s and 1960s, evaluation-oriented reading research stipulated to an ever-greater extent the instructional form and curricular content of North American literacy instruction. Following Thorndike, literacy was conceived of according to a behaviourist stimulus/response model.

The linguistic and ideational features of the text, the stimulus, could be structured and manipulated to evoke the desired skill-related responses, ranging from rudimentary "decoding" to more advanced skills of "comprehension." Student response could then be measured to determine the student's level of language development.

Literacy was thus scientifically dissected into individually teachable and testable subskill units. Educational publishers and, later, multinationals developed total packaged reading "systems," based as much on exacting marketing research, as on the insights of reading psychology. Beginning in the 1950s, teachers were introduced to the first in a series of "foolproof" methods for developing the "skills" of literacy (SRA, and later DISTAR, CRP). Among the inbuilt incentives of packaged programmes were promises of decreased planning and grading time, diagnostic tests, glossy audiovisual aids, precise directions for effective "teacher behaviour," and the assurance of scientific exactitude and modernity.

One widely used reading series, *Ginn 720*, a XEROX product revised for different countries to enable international distribution, defines its approach to literacy instruction:

> By using a management system the teacher can select specific objectives to be taught, monitor pupils' learning progress continuously, and diagnose the source of individual learning problems, prescribe additional instruction and meet pupils' needs and make sure the pupils have achieved proficiency in skills objectives (p. ii).

As a "professional," the technocratic teacher is encouraged to see the educational process in medical and managerial metaphors. Students are diagnosed, prescribed for, treated and checked before proceeding to the next level of instruction, which corresponds to a theoretical level of advanced literate competence. The *Ginn 720* student, for instance, is processed through fourteen such skill levels from ages six to fourteen.

A strong selling point of these programmes is their capacity to "individualize" instruction, based on the students' needs as assessed by accompanying diagnostic tests. Students with the same "needs" are grouped, and each reading group is assigned a basal reader, with adjunct worksheets and exercise books. Then, instructional "treatment" begins. Typically, teachers will monitor oral reading, review stories and conduct discussions with one group, while other groups work at their desks, completing worksheets of "fill in the blanks" and multiple-choice formats. Composition and literature study are not undertaken intensively until the secondary grades, when it is assumed that the student will have acquired the basic "skills" of literacy.

Because the dominant view since the Second World War has been to equate functional literacy with basic *reading* skills, it is only recently that a correlative systematization of writing instruction has begun. Elementary writing instruction remains a highly variable blend of progressive "creative writing" and "language experience" with skill-based exercises; most secondary writing instruction is undertaken in the context of literature study. This is partially the result of the continuing influence of university English literature departments on conventional approaches to writing and criticism. However, in light of increasing complaints about high school graduates' inability to write both essay and business formats, writing instruction is likely to follow a similar "research-and-development" process towards increased standardization.

How are speaking and listening skills defined within technocratic literacy instruction? The progressive acceptance of the child's own dialect and speech has carried over into today's schools, having been sustained by the progressive revival of the late 1960s. But relatively little attention is paid to oral language instruction in intermediate and secondary classrooms, apart from discussions of highly variable quality. As for listening skills, "management instructions" and "comprehension questions" delimit teachers' verbal behaviour. Student listening becomes first and foremost listening to instructions and questions, rather than to substantive explanations of curricular content.

Every attempt is made within technocratic literacy instruction to specify its "behavioural objectives" in value-neutral terminology. Consequently, explicit ideological content is absent, overridden by the instructional format and skills orientation of the literacy text. The "skills" to be taught are thus ideologically neutralized; lessons aim to improve students' ability to grasp "word meaning," "context clues," and "decoding skills." In the teacher's overview chart of the Ginn programme, literature study—the focal point of moral and social instruction in previous eras—is reduced to a body of neutral skills (for example "note the poet's use of animal symbolism," "use alliteration"). These guidelines clearly indicate to teachers that they need not consider literacy instruction a matter of moral or social edification, but should simply "facilitate" the programme as professionally as possible.

But such goals and practices are not value neutral. How is it possible to "infer character motivation," for instance, without calling into play personal and social values? Similarly, we must ask how a student can determine "structures of cause and effect" in a textual narrative without invoking normative rules of social context and action? As Wittgenstein[35] observed, every question and statement embodies a normative assumption; skills and concepts are not learned in isolation, but in the context of judgments.

The kind of research which focuses on the manner in which school readers inculcate social attitudes through the portrayal of particular roles, personality structures, and orientations to action,[36] yields little beyond a surface level of understanding of the cumulative effects of technocratic texts. Instructional systems—however non-sexist, non-racist and non-secular in *content*—communicate not only a synthetic world-view, but a particular attitude towards literacy: literacy is conceived of as a set of neutral behaviours within an attendant fabricated world-view, in which little of cultural or social significance ever occurs. What is conveyed to the teacher, correspondingly, is a reductive view of literacy instruction as the scientific management of skills transmission.

This claim to "neutrality" and cross-contextual validity places literacy instruction in line with the dominant belief that North American schools should assume no particular moral or political bias; there is an explicit avoidance of any story content or language that might appear to discriminate against, or exclude, any subcultural viewpoint. The result is an inherent blandness, superficiality and conservatism in the texts children read. What standardized readers communicate to children is "endlessly repeated words passed off as stories."[37] In order to capture the multinational market, publishers and editors must create a product which will pass as culturally significant knowledge in diverse social contexts, without offending the sensibilities of local parents, teachers, special-interest groups, politicians, and, of course, administrators who decide purchases. The result is a "watering down" of the content for marketing purposes. As Williams suggests, the larger the audience of a communications medium, the more homogeneous becomes the message and the experience for its consumers.[38] Technocratic literacy systems posit an imaginary "every-student" much as television networks seek to identify and communicate with "the average viewer."

Ironically, by attempting to address everyone, such literacy texts succeed in communicating with no-one. As a result, this literacy model actively militates against the development of full communicative competence. In the attempt to design behaviourally infallible instructional systems, curriculum developers exclude all but the most trivial levels of individual and cultural difference. As a result, the dramaturgical aspect of teaching, the moral convictions and cultural experience of students and teachers—key to both progressive and classical instruction—become "variables" which potentially interfere with the smooth operation of systematized pedagogy.

In secondary schools, the linear information processing model of technocratic instruction (stimulus/response, input/output), has led to an increase in "functional" exercises, such as reading classified advertisements, filling out job and credit applications, and so on. To enable ease and consistency of assessment, however, such tasks often encourage the learning of linear modes of functioning which exclude contextual factors. Several studies have questioned the validity of functional literacy assessment and the success of instruction in producing vocational competence.[39] Often, the pursuit of an explicitly "functional" literacy presents as legitimate educational knowledge information which is artificially simplified, linear, mechanistic, and essentially powerless.

Classicism was condemned for imposing a colonized aristocratic world view on every student. Progressivism was criticized for its subversive and "left-wing" ideology. But technocratic education imposes only the surface features, the "skills," of a world view, and a predominantly "middle class" one at that. We argue that where technocratic instruction dominates in classrooms and in teacher training institutions, the literacy of students will remain culturally and intellectually insignificant. And, given the informational content and cognitive simplicity of the texts and methods used, and the mechanistic character of the interactions prescribed, we have good reason for concern about the students who *succeed* in the programmes.

Literacy Instruction: Derived or Imposed?

By way of conclusion, we have little to offer beyond the observation that cries of falling standards and widespread "illiteracy" among today's graduates appear vacuous given the non-comparability of "literacy" as defined by the public education system since its inception. What we wish to consider in closing, however, are certain implications of this analysis for contemporary problems of pedagogy and research.

As the number and variety of students in public schools has increased, literacy curriculum, instruction and evaluation have become more and more standardized. With the relinquishing of family and community control over education to centralized government agencies came the expectation of universal mechanisms of accountability. The rise of standardized testing culminated in the recent move throughout North America towards universal functional literacy testing. The popular ethic of functional literacy, however, begs crucial questions: Functional at what? In what context? To what ends? And is it in the interests of the literate individual to become "functional" within any and every economic and political circumstance?

In liberal-democratic societies, participation in the political process implies not only the ability to operate effectively within existing social and economic systems, but also to make rational and informed judgements about the desirability of those systems themselves. Where the citizen has rights and duties with respect to political, social and economic orders, the literate exercise of such rights necessarily presupposed competences above and beyond those required to carry out limited interpersonal and occupational responsibilities. The glory of technocratic education—its neutralization of personal, social and political sanctions, indeed its independence from any substantive context and, therefore, content—produces students who follow instructions simply because they are there: the designated and assessed conditions of proceeding to the next level of instruction. In disregarding the social and ethical dimensions of communicative competence, technocratic education nurtures the literal, the superficial, and uncommitted, but "functionally" literate.

The tendency among both national and international development agencies has been to assume that increasing the percentage of a populus that can read and write—as measured by years of schooling or standardized tests—is essential to furthering a nation's political interests and social participation. The rush to modernize schooling in developing countries and to cut educational costs in developed countries serves to increase the appeal of cost-efficient and scientifically based "state-of-the-art" literacy programmes.

Yet models of literacy instruction have always been derived from concrete historical circumstances. Each has aimed to create a particular kind of individual, in a particular social order. In the US, the substance of literacy instruction was derived from distinctively American language, culture and economic life. In Canada, on the other hand, each era involved the importation of a model of literacy instruction, first from Britain, and subsequently from the US. School children recited "power should make from land to land, the name of Britain trebly great" (Tennyson 1883), evoking *en masse* God's salvation of their majesties in morning song, and learning to read and write, in the end, "for Queen and country." The question "Whose country?" was never asked. Later, in residential schools, Indian children were beaten for speaking their native tongue, and were taught to read "See, Jane, see! Jane helps mother in the kitchen." In effect, an imposed literacy model was reimposed to eradicate an indigenous native culture. As A. Wilden notes, the colonized sensibility is often convinced of the inauthenticity of its own cultural messages.[40] What are the social, cultural and political consequences of a national literacy which is based on imposed, rather than derived, culturally significant information?

Today, locally adapted literacy curricula are purchased from US-based multinational publishers. These corporations are able to absorb research and marketing costs, taking what are called "loss leaders" in the certainty of dominating the international educational market. Crucial in the success of this enterprise are two beliefs: first, that there is no necessary relationship between the processes of literacy acquisition and the literate product; and second, that it is possible to transmit literacy *per se,* as a value-free, context-neutral set of communicational skills. Both beliefs are false. Unless the instructional process itself is educational, the product cannot be an educated individual. The context within which we acquire language significantly mediates meaning and understanding in any subsequent context of use. Our analysis has indicated that the processes and materials of literacy instruction have been based historically on the ideological codes and material constraints of the society from which they are derived. We argue that the wholescale importation of a literacy model, imposed and not locally derived, into both developed and developing "colonies" counts as cultural imperialism. We cannot look at reading and writing *per se.* We have to ask instead what kind of child will take readily to and profit from a given model? What is the nature of motive formation that an instructional model depends on and develops? And, most importantly, what form of individual and social identity will the programme engender?

It is within this set of questions that educators have defined "what will count" as literacy in a given era. A literacy curriculum which is imposed, whether on individuals or entire cultures, cannot serve the same ends as one that is derived. We confront today two practical problems: solution of the alleged "literacy crisis" in developed countries, and the advancement of mass literacy in developing nations. The intention of this historical reconstruction has been to refocus debate on these questions, and to broaden the context of that debate beyond the disciplinary constraints of educational psychology and commerce, within which it has been largely confined for the last thirty years.

11.
From Utterance to Text

The Bias of Language in Speech and Writing

David R. Olson

The faculty of language stands at the center of our conception of mankind; speech makes us human and literacy makes us civilized. It is therefore both interesting and important to consider what, if anything, is distinctive about written language and to consider the consequences of literacy for the bias it may impart both to our culture and to people's psychological processes.

The framework for examining the consequences of literacy has already been laid out. Using cultural and historical evidence, Havelock (1973), Parry (1971), Goody and Watt (1968), Innis (1951), and McLuhan (1964) have argued that the invention of the alphabetic writing system altered the nature of the knowledge which is stored for reuse, the organization of that knowledge, and the cognitive processes of the people who use that written language. Some of the cognitive consequences of schooling and literacy in contemporary societies have been specified through anthropological and cross-cultural psychological research by Cole, Gay, Glick, and Sharp (1971), Scribner and Cole (1973), Greenfield (1972), Greenfield and Bruner (1969), Goodnow (1976), and others.

However, the more general consequences of the invention of writing systems for the structure of language, the concept of meaning, and the patterns of comprehension and reasoning processes remain largely unknown. The purpose of this paper is to examine the consequences of literacy, particularly those consequences associated with mastery of the "schooled" language of written texts.

In the course of the discussion, I shall repeatedly contrast explicit, written prose statements, which I shall call "texts," with more informal oral-language statements, which I shall call "utterances." Utterances and texts may be contrasted at any one of several levels: the linguistic modes themselves—written language versus oral language; their usual usages—conversation, story-telling, verse, and song for the oral mode versus statements, arguments, and essays for the written mode; their summarizing forms—proverbs and aphorisms for the oral mode versus premises for the written mode; and finally, the cultural traditions built around these modes—an oral tradition versus a literate tradition. My argument will be that there is a transition from utterance to text both culturally and developmentally and that this transition can be described as one of increasing explicitness, with language increasingly able to stand as an unambiguous or autonomous representation of meaning.

The Beginnings of a Literate Technology

Let us consider the origin of the assumption that the meaning is in the text and the implications of that assumption for language use. The assumption regarding the autonomy of texts is relatively recent and the language conforming to it is relatively specialized. Utterance, language that does not conform to this assumption, is best represented by children's early language, oral conversation, memorable oral sayings, and the like. Text, language that does conform to that assumption, is best represented by formal, written, expository prose statements. My central claim is that the evolution both culturally and developmentally is from utterance to text. While utterance is universal, text appears to have originated with Greek literacy and to have reached a most visible form with the British essayists. My argument, which rests heavily on the seminal works of Havelock (1963), McLuhan (1962), and Goody and Watt (1968), is that the invention of the alphabetic writing system gave to Western culture many of its predominant features including an altered conception of language and an altered conception of rational man. These effects came about, in part, from the creation of explicit, autonomous statements—statements dependent upon an explicit writing system, the alphabet, and an explicit form of argument, the essay. In a word, these effects resulted from putting the meaning into the text.

Meaning in an Oral Language Tradition

Luther's statement, that the meaning of Scripture depended not upon the dogmas of the church, but upon a deeper reading of the text, seems a simple claim. It indicates, however, the profound change that occurred early in the sixteenth century in regard to the presumed autonomy of texts. Prior to the time of Luther, who in this argument represents one turning point in a roughly continuous change in orientation, it was generally assumed that meaning could not be stated explicitly. Statements required interpretation by either scribes or clerics. Luther's claim and the assumption that guided it cut both ways: they were a milestone in the developing awareness that text could explicitly state its meaning—that it did not depend on dogma or interpretive context; more importantly, they also indicated a milestone in the attempt to shape language to more explicitly represent its meanings. This shift in orientation, which I shall elaborate later in terms of the "essayist technique," was one of the high points in the long history of the attempt to make meaning completely explicit. Yet it was, relatively speaking, a mere refinement of the process that had begun with the Greek invention of the alphabet.

Although the Greek alphabet and the growth of Greek literacy may be at the base of Western science and philosophy, it is not to be assumed that preliterate people were primitive in any sense. Modern anthropology has provided many examples of theoretical, mythical, and technological systems of impressive sophistication and appropriateness. It has been established that a complex and extensive literature could exist in the absence of a writing system. In 1928, Milman Parry (1971) demonstrated that the *Iliad* and the *Odyssey*, usually attributed to a literate Homer, were in fact examples of oral composition composed over centuries by preliterate bards for audiences who did not read. In turn, it was recognized that large sections of the Bible possessed a similar oral structure. The books of Moses and the Prophets, for example, are recorded versions of statements that were shaped through oral methods as part of an oral culture.

To preserve verbal statements in the absence of a writing system, such statements would have to be biased both in form and content towards oral mnemonic devices such as "formalized patterns of speech, recital under ritual conditions, the use of drums and other musical instruments, and the employment of professional remembrances" (Goody and Watt, 1968, p. 31). Language is thus shaped or biased to fit the requirements of oral communication and auditory memory (see, for example, Havelock, 1973, and Frye, 1971). A variety of oral statements such as proverbs, adages, aphorisms, riddles, and verse are distinctive not only in that they preserve important cultural information but also in that they are memorable. They tend, however, *not* to be explicit or to say exactly what they mean; they require context and prior knowledge and wisdom for their interpretation. Solomon, for example, introduced the *Book of Proverbs* by saying: "To understand a proverb and the interpretation; the words of the wise and their dark sayings," (1:6). Maimonides, the twelfth-century rabbi, pointed out in his *Guide of the Perplexed* that when one interprets parables "according to their external meanings, he too is overtaken by great perplexity!" (1963, p. 6).

The invention of writing did not end the oral tradition. Some aspects of that tradition merely coexist with the more dominant literate traditions. Lord (1960) in his *Singer of Tales* showed that a remnant of such an oral culture persists in Yugoslavia. Even in a predominantly literate culture, aspects of the oral tradition remain. Gray (1973) suggested that Bob Dylan represents the creative end of such an oral tradition in Anglo-American culture; the less creative aspects of that tradition show up in the stock phrases and proverbial sayings that play so large a part in everyday conversational language.

With the introduction of writing, important parts of the oral tradition were written down and preserved in the available literate forms. The important cultural information, the information worth writing down, consisted in large part of statements shaped to fit the requirements of oral memory such as the epics, verse, song, orations, and since readers already knew, through the oral tradition, much of the content, writing served primarily for the storage and retrieval of information that had already been committed to memory, not for the expression of original ideas.

Scripture, at the time of Luther, had just such a status. It consisted in part of statements shaped to the requirements of oral comprehension and oral memory. Scripture had authority, but since the written statements were shorn of their oral contexts, they were assumed to require interpretation. The dogma of the Church, the orally transmitted tradition, had the authority to say what the Scripture meant. In this context Luther's statement can be seen as profoundly radical. Luther claimed that the text supplied sufficient context internally to determine the meaning of the passage; the meaning was in the text. What would have led Luther to make such a radical claim? My suggestion is that his claim reflected a technological change—the invention of printing—one in a series of developments in the increasing explicitness of language, which we shall now examine.

Alphabetic Writing—Making Meanings Explicit

Significant oral-language statements, to be memorable, must be cast into some oral, poetic form. Consequently, as we have seen, these statements do not directly say what they mean. With the invention of writing, the limitations of oral memory became less critical. The written statement, constituting a more or less permanent artifact, no longer depended on its "poetized" form for its preservation.

However, whether or not a writing system can preserve the meaning of statements depends upon the characteristics of the system. An elliptical or nonexplicit writing system, like nonexplicit statements, tends to rely on prior knowledge and expectancies. An explicit writing system unambiguously represents meanings—the meaning is in the text. It has a minimum of homophones (seen/scene) and homographs (lead/lead) at the phonemic and graphemic levels, few ambiguities at the grammatical level, and few permissible interpretations at the semantic level.

The Greek alphabet was the first to approach such a degree of explicitness and yet to be simple enough to provide a base for mass literacy. Gelb (1952) differentiated four main stages in the development of writing systems. The first stage, which goes back to prehistory, involves the expression of ideas through pictures and pictographic writing. Such writing systems have been called ideographic in that they represent and communicate ideas directly without appeal to the structure of spoken language. While the signs are easily learned and recognized, there are problems associated with their use: any full system requires some four or five thousand characters for ordinary usage; their concreteness makes the representation of abstract terms difficult; they are difficult to arrange so as to produce statements (Gombrich, 1974); and they tend to limit the number of things that can be expressed.

The next stage was the invention of the principle of phonetization, the attempt to make writing reflect the sound structure of speech. In an attempt to capture the properties of speech, early phonetic systems—Sumerian, Egyptian, Hittite, and Chinese—all contained signs of three different types: word signs or logogens, syllabic signs, and auxiliary signs.

The third stage was the development of syllabaries which did away both with word signs and with signs representing sounds having more than one consonant. Whereas earlier syllabaries had separate signs for such syllables as *ta* and *tam*, the West Semitic syllabaries reduced the syllable to a single consonant-vowel sequence, thereby reducing the number of signs. However, since these Semitic syllabaries did not have explicit representations for vowels, the script frequently resulted in ambiguities in pronunciation, particularly in cases of writing proper names and other words which could not be retrieved from context. Semitic writing systems thus introduced phonetic indicators called Matres Lectionis (literally: "mothers of reading") to differentiate the vowel sounds (Gelb, 1952, p. 166).

The final stage in the invention of the alphabet, a step taken only by the Greeks, was the invention of a phonemic alphabet (Gelb, 1952; Goody and Watt, 1963). The Greeks did so, Gelb suggests, by using consistently the Matres Lectionis which the Semites had used sporadically. They discovered that these indicators were not syllables but rather vowels. Consequently the sign that preceded the indicator also must not be a syllable but rather a consonant. Havelock (1973) comments: "At a stroke, by this analysis, the Greeks provided a table of elements of linguistic sound not only manageable because of its economy, but for the first time in the history of *homo sapiens*, also accurate" (p. 11).

The faithful transcription of the sound patterns of speech by a fully developed alphabet has freed writing from some of the ambiguities of oral language. Many sentences that are ambiguous when spoken are unambiguous when written—for example, "il vient toujours a sept heures" ("he always comes at seven o'clock") versus "il vient toujours a cette heure" ("he always comes at this hour") (Lyons, 1969, p. 41). However, a fully developed alphabet does not exhaust the possibilities for explicitness of a writing system. According to Bloomfield (1939) and Kneale and Kneale (1962), the remaining lack of explicitness necessitated the invention of the formal languages of logic and mathematics.

To summarize, we have considered the extent to which meaning is explicitly represented in a statement. Oral language statements must be poetized to be remembered, but in the process they lose some of their explicitness; they require interpretation by a wise man, scribe, or cleric. Written statements bypass the limitations of memory, but the extent to which a writing system can explicitly represent meaning depends upon the nature of the system. Systems such as syllabaries that represent several meanings with the same visual sign are somewhat ambiguous or nonexplicit. As a consequence, they again require interpretation by some authority. Statements can become relatively free from judgment or interpretation only with a highly explicit writing system such as the alphabet. The Greek alphabet, through its ability to record exactly what is said, provided a tool for the formulation and criticism of explicit meanings and was therefore critical to the evolution of Greek literacy and Greek culture.

Written Text as an Exploratory Device

Writing systems with a relatively lower degree of explicitness, such as the syllabaries, tended to serve a somewhat limited purpose, primarily that of providing an aid to memory. Havelock (1973) states:

> When it came to transcribing discursive speech, difficulties of interpretation would discourage the practice of using the script for novel or freely-invented discourse. The practice that would be encouraged would be to use the system as a reminder of something already familiar, so that recollection of its familiarity would aid the reader in getting the right interpretation. . . . It would in short tend to be something—tale, proverb, parable, fable and the like—which already existed in oral form and had been composed according to oral rules. The syllabic system in short provided techniques for recall of what was already familiar, not instruments for formulating novel statements which could further the exploration of new experience. (p. 238)

The alphabet had no such limits of interpretation. The decrease in ambiguity of symbols—for example, the decrease in the number of homographs—would permit a reader to assign the appropriate interpretation to a written statement even without highly tuned expectations as to what the text was likely to say. The decreased reliance upon prior knowledge or expectancies was therefore a significant step towards making meaning explicit in the conventionalized linguistic system. The technology was sufficiently explicit to permit one to analyze the sentence meaning apart from the speaker's meaning. Simultaneously, written language became an instrument for the formulation and preservation of original statements that could violate readers' expectancies and commonsense knowledge. Written language had come free from its base in the mother tongue; it had begun the transformation from utterance to text.

The availability of an explicit writing system, however, does not assure that the statements recorded in that language will be semantically explicit. As previously mentioned, the first statements written down tended to be those that had already been shaped to the requirements of oral production and oral memory, the Greek epics being a case in point. Over time, however, the Greeks came to fully exploit the powers of their alphabetic writing system. In fact, Havelock (1973) has argued that the Greeks' use of this invention was responsible for the development of the intellectual qualities found in classical Greece:

> And so, as the fifth century passes into the fourth, the full effect upon Greece of the alphabetic revolution begins to assert itself. The governing word ceases to be a vibration heard by the ear and nourished in the memory. It becomes a visible artifact. Storage of information for reuse, as a formula designed to explain the dynamics of western culture, ceases to be a metaphor. The documented statement

persisting through time unchanged is to release the human brain from certain formidable burdens of memorization while increasing the energies available for conceptual thought. The results as they are to be observed in the intellectual history of Greece and Europe were profound. (p. 60).

Some of the effects of the Greeks' utilization of the alphabetic writing system are worth reviewing. First, as Goody and Watt (1968) and a number of other scholars have shown, it permitted a differentiation of myth and history with a new regard for literal truth. When the Homeric epics were written down, they could be subjected to critical analysis and their inconsistencies became apparent. Indeed, Hecataeus, faced with writing a history of Greece, said: "What I write is the account I believe to be true. For the stories the Greeks tell are many and in my opinion ridiculous" (cited in Goody and Watt, 1968, p. 45). Second, the use of the alphabetic system altered the relative regard for poetry and for prose. Prose statements were neither subtle nor devious; they tended to mean what they said. Havelock (1963) has demonstrated that Plato's *Republic* diverged from the tradition of the oral Homeric poets and represented a growing reliance on prose statements.

Third, the emphasis on writing prose, as in Aristotle's *Analytics* (see Goody and Watt, 1968, pp. 52–54), permitted the abstraction of logical procedures that could serve as the rules for thinking. Syllogisms could operate on prose premises but not on oral statements such as proverbs. Further, the use of written prose led to the development of abstract categories, the genus/species taxonomies so important not only to Greek science but also to the formation and division of various subject-matter areas. Much of Greek thought was concerned with satisfactorily explaining the meaning of terms. And formulating a definition is essentially a literate enterprise outside of the context of ongoing speech—an attempt to provide the explicit meaning of a word in terms of the other words in the system (see, for example, Bruner and Olson, in press; Goody and Watt, 1968; and Havelock, 1976).

The Greeks, thinking that they had discovered a method for determining objective truth, were in fact doing little more than detecting the properties implicit in their native tongue. Their rules for mind were not rules for thinking but rather rules for using language consistently; the abstract properties of their category system were not true or unbiased descriptions of reality but rather invariants in the structure of their language. Writing became an instrument for making explicit the knowledge that was already implicit in their habits of speech and, in the process, tidying up and ordering that knowledge. This important but clearly biased effort was the first dramatic impact of writing on knowledge.

The Greeks' concern with literacy was not without critics. Written statements could not be interrogated if a misunderstanding occurred, and they could not be altered to suit the requirements of listeners. Thus Socrates concluded in *Phaedrus:* "Anyone who leaves behind him a written manual, and likewise anyone who takes it over from him, on the supposition that such writing will provide something reliable and permanent, most be exceedingly simple minded" (*Phaedrus*, 277c, cited in Goody and Watt, 1968, p. 51). In the *Seventh Letter,* Plato says: "No intelligent man will ever be so bold as to put into language those things which his reason has contemplated, especially not into a form that is unalterable—which must be the case with what is expressed in written symbols" (*Seventh Letter,* 341 c-d, cited in Bluck, 1949, p. 176).

The Essayist Technique

Although the Greeks exploited the resources of written language, the invention of printing allowed an expanded and heterogeneous reading public to use those resources in a much more systematic way. The invention of printing prompted an intellectual revolution of similar magnitude to that of the Greek period (see McLuhan, 1962, and Ong, 1971, for fascinating accounts). However, the rise of print literacy did not merely preserve the analytic uses of writing developed by the Greeks; it involved as well, I suggest, further evolution in the explicitness of writing at the semantic level. That is, the increased explicitness of language was not so much a result of minimizing the ambiguity of words at the graphemic level but rather a result of minimizing the possible interpretations of statements. A sentence was written to have only one meaning. In addition, there was a further test of the adequacy of a statement's representation of presumed intention: the ability of that statement to stand up to analysis of its implications. To illustrate, if one assumes that statement X is true, then the implication Y should also be true. However, suppose that on further reflection Y is found to be indefensible. Then presumably statement X was not intended in the first place and would have to be revised.

This approach to texts as autonomous representations of meaning was reflected in the way texts were both read and written. A reader's task was to determine exactly what each sentence was asserting and to determine the presuppositions and implications of that statement. If one could assume that an author had actually intended what was written and that the statements were true, then the statements would stand up under scrutiny. Luther made just this assumption about Scripture early in the sixteenth century, shortly after the invention and wide utilization of printing. One of the more dramatic misapplications of the same assumption was Bishop Usher's inference from biblical genealogies that the world was created in 4004 B.C.

The more fundamental effect of this approach to text was on the writer, whose task now was to create autonomous text—to write in such a manner that the sentence was an adequate, explicit representation of the meaning, relying on no implicit premises or personal interpretations. Moreover, the sentence had to withstand analysis of its presuppositions and implications. This fostered the use of prose as a form of extended statements from which a series of necessary implications could be drawn.

The British essayists were among the first to exploit writing for the purpose of formulating original theoretical knowledge. John Locke's *An Essay Concerning Human Understanding* (1690/1961) well represents the intellectual bias that originated at that time and, to a large extent, characterizes our present use of language. Knowledge was taken to be the product of an extended logical essay—the output of the repeated application in a single coherent text of the technique of examining an assertion to determine all of its implications. It is interesting to note that when Locke began his criticism of human understanding he thought that he could write it on a sheet of paper in an evening. By the time he had exhausted the possibilities of both the subject and the new technology, the essay had taken twenty years and two volumes.

Locke's essayist technique differed notably from the predominant writing style of the time. Ellul (1964) says, "An uninitiated reader who opens a scientific treatise on law, economy, medicine or history published between the sixteenth and eighteenth centuries is struck most forcibly by the complete absence of logical order" (p. 39); and he notes, "It was more a question of personal exchange than of taking an objective position" (p. 41). In the "Introduction" to *Some Thoughts Concerning Education* (Locke, 1880), Quick reports that Locke himself made similar criticisms of the essays of Montaigne. For Locke and others writing as he did, the essay came to serve as an exploratory device for examining problems and in the course of that examination producing new knowledge. The essay could serve these functions, at least for the purposes of science and philosophy, only by adopting the language of explicit, written, logically connected prose.

This specialized form of language was adopted by the Royal Society of London which, according to its historian Sprat (1667/1966), was concerned "with the advancement of science and with the improvement of the English language as a medium of prose" (p. 56). The society demanded a mathematical plainness of language and rejected all amplifications, digressions, and swellings of style. This use of language made writing a powerful intellectual tool, I have suggested, by rendering the logical implications of statements more detectable and by altering the statements themselves to make their implications both clear and true.

The process of formulating statements, deriving their implications, testing the truth of those implications, and using the results to revise or generalize from the original statement characterized not only empiricist philosophy but also the development of deductive empirical science. The result was the same, namely the formulation of a small set of connected statements of great generality that may occur as topic sentences of paragraphs or as premises of extended scientific or philosophical treatise. Such statements were notable not only in their novelty and abstractness but also in that they related to prior knowledge in an entirely new way. No longer did general premises necessarily rest on the data of common experience, that is on commonsense intuition. Rather, as Bertrand Russell (1940) claimed for mathematics, a premise is believed because true implications follow from it, not because it is intuitively plausible. In fact, it is just this mode of using language—the deduction of counterintuitive models of reality—which distinguishes modern from ancient science (see Ong, 1958).

Moreover, not only did the language change, the picture of reality sustained by language changed as well; language and reality were reordered. Inhelder and Piaget (1958) describe this altered relationship between language and reality as a stage of mental development:

> The most distinctive property of formal thought is this reversal of direction between reality and possibility; instead of deriving a rudimentary theory from the empirical data as is done in concrete inferences, formal thought begins with a

theoretical synthesis implying that certain relations are necessary and thus proceeds in the opposite direction. (p. 251)

The ability to make this "theoretical synthesis," I suggest, is tied to the analysis of the implications of the explicit theoretical statements permitted by writing.

Others have made the same point. Ricoeur (1973) has argued that language is not simply a reflection of reality but rather a means of investigating and enlarging reality. Hence, the text does not merely reflect readers' expectations; instead the explicitness of text gives them a basis for constructing a meaning and then evaluating their own experiences in terms of it. Thus text *can* serve to realign language and reality. N. Goodman (1968), too, claims that "the world is as many ways as it can be truly described" (p. 6).

This property of language, according to Popper (1972), opens up the possibility of "objective knowledge." Popper claims that the acquisition of theoretical knowledge proceeds by offering an explicit theory (a statement), deriving and testing implications of the theory, and revising it in such a way that its implications are both productive and defensible. The result is a picture of the world derived from the repeated application of a particular literary technique: "science is a branch of literature" (Popper, 1972, p. 185).

Thus far I have summarized two of the major stages or steps in the creation of explicit, autonomous meanings. The first step toward making language explicit was at the graphemic level with the invention of an alphabetic writing system. Because it had a distinctive sign for each of the represented sounds and thereby reduced the ambiguity of the signs, an alphabetic system relied much less on readers' prior knowledge and expectancies than other writing systems. This explicitness permitted the preservation of meaning across space and time and the recovery of meaning by the more or less uninitiated. Even original ideas could be formulated in language and recovered by readers without recourse to some intermediary sage.

The second step involved the further development of explicitness at the semantic level by allowing a given sentence to have only one interpretation. Proverbial and poetic statements, for example, were not permissible because they admitted more than one interpretation, the appropriate one determined by the context of utterance. The attempt was to construct sentences for which the meaning was dictated by the lexical and syntactic features of the sentence itself. To this end, the meaning of terms had to be conventionalized by means of definitions, and the rules of implication had to be articulated and systematically applied.

The Greeks perfected the alphabetic system and began developing the writing style that, encouraged by the invention of printing and the form of extended texts it permitted, culminated in the essayist technique. The result was not an ordinary language, not a mother tongue, but rather a form of language specialized to serve the requirements of autonomous, written, formalized text. Indeed, children are progressively inducted into the use of this language during the school years. Thus formal schooling, in the process of teaching children to deal with prose texts, fosters the ability to "speak a written language" (Greenfield, 1972, p. 169).

The Effects of Considerations of Literacy on Issues of Language

On Comprehension

The comprehension of sentences involves several different processes. Ordinary conversational speech, especially children's speech, relies for its comprehension on a wide range of information beyond that explicitly marked in the language. To permit communication at all, there must be wide agreement among users of a language as to phonological, syntactic, and semantic conventions. A small set of language forms, however, maps onto an exceedingly wide range of referential events; hence, ambiguity is always possible if not inevitable. Speakers in face-to-face situations circumvent this ambiguity by means of such prosodic and paralinguistic cues as gestures, intonation, stress, quizzical looks, and restatement. Sentences in conversational contexts, then, are interpreted in terms of the following: agreed-upon lexical and syntactic conventions; a shared knowledge of events and a preferred way of interpreting them; a shared perceptual context; and agreed-upon prosodic features and paralinguistic conventions.

Written languages can have no recourse to shared context, prosodic features, or paralinguistic conventions since the preserved sentences have to be understood in contexts other than those in which they were written. The comprehension of such texts requires agreed-upon linguistic conventions, a shared knowledge of the world, and a preferred way of interpreting events. But Luther denied the dependence of text on a presupposed, commonsensical knowledge of the world, and I have tried to show that the linguistic style of the essayist has systematically attempted to minimize if not eliminate this dependence. This attempt has proceeded by assigning the information carried implicitly by nonlinguistic means into an enlarged set of explicit linguistic conventions. In this way written textual language can be richer and more explicit than its oral language counterpart. Within this genre of literature, if unconventionalized or nonlinguistic knowledge is permitted to intrude, we charge the writer with reasoning via unspecified inferences and assumptions or the reader with misreading the text.

Comprehension, therefore, may be represented by a set of procedures that involves selectively applying one's personal experiences or knowledge of the world to the surface structure of sentences to yield a meaning. In so doing, one elaborates, assimilates, or perhaps "imagines" the sentence. And these elaborative procedures are perfectly appropriate to the comprehension of ordinary conversational utterances. In turn, the sentence becomes more comprehensible and dramatically more memorable, as Anderson and Ortony (1975), Bransford and Johnson (1973), and Bransford, Barclay, and Franks (1972) have shown.

The price to be paid for such elaboration and assimilation is that the listener's or reader's meaning deviates to some degree from the meaning actually represented in the sentence. Such interpretation may alter the truth conditions specified by the statement. To illustrate, using Anderson and Ortony's sentence, if the statement "the apples are in the container" is interpreted as "the apples are in the basket," the interpretation specifies a different set of truth conditions than did the original statement. We could legitimately say that the statement had been misinterpreted. Yet that is what normally occurs in the process of understanding and remembering sentences; moreover, as we have shown in our laboratory, it is what preschool children regularly do (Olson and Nickerson, 1974; Pike and Olson, 1977; Hildyard and Olson). If young children are given the statements, "John hit Mary" or "John has more than Mary," unlike adults, they are incapable of determining the direct logical implications that "Mary was hit by John" or "Mary has less than John." If the sentence is given out of context, they may inquire, "Who is Mary?" Given an appropriate story or pictorial context, children can assimilate the first statement to that context and then give a new description of what they now know. If the sentence cannot be assimilated to their knowledge base, they are helpless to arrive at its implications; children are unable to apply interpretive procedures to the sentence meaning, the meaning in the text. They can, however, use sentences as a cue to speaker's meaning if these sentences occur in an appropriate context. Literate adults are quite capable of treating sentences in either way. What they do presumably depends on whether the sentence is too long to be remembered verbatim, whether it is written and remains available for repeated consultation, or, perhaps, whether the sentence is regarded as utterance or text.

On Learning a Language

The contrast between language as an autonomous system for representing meaning and language as a system dependent in every case upon nonlinguistic and paralinguistic cues for the sharing of intentions—the contrast between text and utterance—applies with equal force to the problem of language acquisition. A formal theory of sentence meaning, such as Chomsky's, provides a less appropriate description of early language than would a theory of intended meanings that admitted a variety of means for realizing those intentions. Such means include a shared view of reality, a shared perceptual context, and accompanying gestures, in addition to the speech signal. At early stages of language acquisition the meaning may be specified nonlinguistically, and this meaning may then be used to break the linguistic code (Macnamara, 1972; Nelson, 1974). Language acquisition, then, is primarily a matter of learning to conventionalize more and more of the meaning in the speech signal. This is not a sudden achievement. If an utterance specifies something different from what the child is entertaining, the sentence will often be misinterpreted (Clark, 1973; Donaldson and Lloyd, 1974). But language development is not simply a matter of progressively elaborating the oral mother tongue as a means of sharing intentions. The developmental hypothesis offered here is that the ability to assign a meaning to the sentence per se, independent of its nonlinguistic interpretive context, is achieved only well into the school years. It is a complex achievement to differentiate and operate upon either what is actually said, the sentence meaning, or what is meant, the speaker's meaning. Children are relatively quick to grasp a speaker's intentions but relatively slow, I suggest, to grasp the literal meaning of what is, in fact, said.

Several studies lend plausibility to these arguments. For example, Olson and Nickerson (1977) examined the role of story or pictorial context on the detection of sentence implications. Five-year-old children were given a statement and asked if a second statement, logically related to the first, was true. For instance, they were told, "John was hit by Mary," then asked, "Did Mary hit John?" The ability of these five-year-olds to answer such a question depended on how much they knew about the characters and context mentioned in the sentences. If they did not know who John and Mary were or why the experimenter was asking the question, they could not assign a full semantic interpretation to the sentence. This and other studies suggest that children, unlike adults, assign a speaker's meaning to a simple sentence if that sentence is contextually appropriate and directly assimilable to their prior knowledge, but they have difficulty assigning a meaning to the statement alone (Carpenter and Just, 1975; Clark, 1974; Olson and Filby, 1972; Hildyard and Olson). But by late childhood, at least among schooled children, meanings are assigned quite readily to the sentence per se. Children come to see that sentences have implications that are necessary by virtue of sentence meaning itself. They become progressively more able to exist in a purely linguistically specified, hypothetical world for both purposes of extracting logical implications of statements and of living in those worlds that, as Ricoeur (1973) notes, are opened up by texts. This, however, is the end point of development in a literate culture and not a description of how original meanings are acquired in early language learning.

On Reading

The relations between utterances and texts become acute when children are first confronted with printed books. As I have pointed out, children are familiar with using the spoken utterance as one cue among others. Children come to school with a level of oral competence in their mother-tongue only to be confronted with an exemplar of written text, the reader, which is an autonomous representation of meaning. Ideally, the printed reader depends on no cues other than linguistic cues; it represents no intentions other than those represented in the text; it is addressed to no one in particular; its author is essentially anonymous; and its meaning is precisely that represented by the sentence meaning. As a result, when children are taught to read, they are learning both to read and to treat language as text. Children familiar with the use of textlike language through hearing printed stories obviously confront less of a hurdle than those for whom both reading and that form of language are novel.

The decoding approach to reading exploits both the explicit nature of the alphabet and the explicit nature of written prose text. Ideally, since the meaning is in the text, the programmatic analysis of letters, sounds, words, and grammar would specify sentence meaning. But as I have indicated, it is precisely with sentence meaning that children have the most difficulty. Hence, the decoding of sentence meaning should be treated as the end point of development, not as the means of access to print as several writers have maintained (Reid, 1966; Richards, 1971).

The differences between utterances and texts may be summarized in terms of three underlying principles: the first pertains to meaning, the second to truth, and the third to function. First, in regard to meaning, utterance and text relate in different ways to background knowledge and to the criteria for successful performance. Conventional utterances appeal for their meaning to shared experiences and interpretations, that is, to a common intuition based on shared commonsense knowledge (Lonergan, 1957; Schutz and Luckman, 1973). Utterances take for content, to use Pope's words, "What oft was tho't but ne'er so well expressed" (cited in Ong, 1971, p. 256). In most speech, as in poetry and literature, the usual reaction is assent—"How true." Statements match, in an often tantalizing way, the expectancies and experiences of the listener. Because of this appeal to expectancies, the criterion for a successful utterance is understanding on the part of the listener. The sentence is not appropriate if the listener does not comprehend. A well-formed sentence fits the requirements of the listener and, as long as this criterion is met, it does not really matter what the speaker says—"A wink is as good as a nod."

Prose text, on the other hand, appeals to premises and rules of logic for deriving implications. Whether or not the premise corresponds to common sense is irrelevant. All that is critical is that the premises are explicit and the inferences correctly drawn. The appeal is formal rather than intuitive. As a consequence, the criterion for the success of a statement in explicit prose text is its formal structure; if the text is formally adequate and the reader fails to understand, that is the reader's problem. The meaning is in the text.

Second, utterance and text appeal to different conceptions of truth. Frye (1971) has termed these underlying assumptions "truth as wisdom" and "truth as correspondence." Truth in oral utterance has to do with truth as wisdom. A statement is true if it is reasonable, plausible, and, as we have seen, congruent with dogma or the wisdom of elders; truth is assimilability to common sense. Truth in prose text, however, has to do with the correspondence between statements and observations. Truth drops its ties to wisdom and to values, becoming the product of the disinterested search of the scientist. True statements in text may be counter to intuition, common sense, or authority. A statement is taken to be true not because the premises from which it follows are in agreement with common sense but rather because true implications follow from it, as Russell (1940) pointed out in regard to mathematics.

Third, conversational utterance and prose text involve different alignments of the functions of language. As Austin (1962) and Halliday (1970) argue, any utterance serves at least two functions simultaneously—the rhetorical or interpersonal function and the logical or ideational function. In oral speech, the interpersonal function is primary; if a sentence is inappropriate to a particular listener, the utterance is a failure. In written text, the logical or ideational functions become primary, presumably because of the indirect relation between writer and reader. The emphasis therefore, can shift from simple communication to truth, to "getting it right" (Olson, 1977b). It may be this realignment of functions in written language that brings about the greater demand for explicitness and the higher degree of conventionalization.

The bias of written language toward providing definitions, making all assumptions and premises explicit, and observing the formal rules of logic produces an instrument of considerable power for building an abstract and coherent theory of reality. The development of this explicit, formal system accounts, I have argued, for the predominant features of Western culture and for our distinctive ways of using language and our distinctive modes of thought. Yet the general theories of science and philosophy that are tied to the formal uses of text provide a poor fit to daily, ordinary, practical, and personally significant experience. Oral language with its depth of resources and its multitude of paths to the same goal, while an instrument of limited power for exploring abstract ideas, is a universal means of sharing our understanding of concrete situations and practical actions. Moreover, it is the language children bring to school. Schooling, particularly learning to read, is the critical process in the transformation of children's language from utterance to text.

12.
The Nature of Literacy

A Historical Exploration

Daniel P. Resnick
Lauren B. Resnick

Reports of low literacy achievement and widespread reading difficulties have lent strength to a still inchoate "back to basics" movement in education. The apparent suggestion is that methods of instruction that succeeded in the past can remedy many of our present problems. Looking backward for solutions, however, can succeed only when social conditions and educational goals remain relatively stable. Only by a serious examination of our history can we determine the extent to which older educational practices are likely to succeed in today's environment, for today's purposes. This paper begins such an examination by exploring selected European and American historical models of literacy standards and training in order to assess the degree to which the goals and practices of earlier times are relevant to our present needs.

Our research suggests that there has been a sharp shift over time in expectations concerning literacy. With changed standards come changed estimates of the adequacy of a population's literacy. To illustrate, if writing one's name were what was meant by literacy, we would not be worried that illiteracy was a national problem. Yet the signature was not always a demand easy to satisfy. Until well into the nineteenth century, the capacity to form the letters of one's signature was not a skill shared by the majority of the population, even in the more developed nations of Europe.[1] Even a somewhat more stringent literacy criterion would not force recognition of a major problem. If the ability to read aloud a simple and well-known passage were the measure, America would have a few "illiterates" but hardly a crisis. If we expected people to demonstrate after reading this simple passage, that they had registered its content at some low level, perhaps by saying who a story was about or what a named character did, we would probably find a low percentage of illiterates in our adult population.

But the number would start to rise, perhaps quite sharply, if unfamiliar texts were to be read and new information gleaned from them. And, if inferential rather than directly stated information were to be drawn from the text, we would probably announce a true crisis in literacy. If we used as a literacy criterion the ability to read a complex text with literary allusions and metaphoric expression and not only to interpret this text but to relate it sensibly to other texts, many would claim that only a tiny fraction of our population is "truly literate," a charge not infrequently made in discussions about standards of literacy at the university level.

We think that this nation perceives itself as having an unacceptable literacy level because it is applying a criterion that requires, at a minimum, the reading of new material and the gleaning of new information from that material. We shall argue in this paper that this high literacy standard is a relatively recent one as applied to the population at large and that much of our present difficulty in meeting the literacy standard we are setting for ourselves can be attributed to the relatively rapid extension to large populations of educational criteria that were once applied to only a limited elite. The result of this rapid extension is that instructional methods suitable to large and diverse populations rather than small and selected ones have not yet been fully developed or applied. Further, not all segments of our population have come to demand literacy skills of the kind that educators, members of Congress, and other government officials think necessary.

Our argument is that the standards currently applied to mass literacy have been with us for at most three generations. To examine the proposition that the current definition of literacy is a relatively new one, we have undertaken a selective review of published material on standards of literacy in various historical settings and on the social and political conditions under which these standards were applied. Some of the less commonly cited historical models seem especially instructive because of either the large size of the literate population, the high standards of literacy, or the democratic ideology. We will elaborate three major historical models for literacy development before the twentieth century: the Protestant-religious, the elite-technical, and the civic-national. To illustrate these models, we will describe literacy training and examinations in seventeenth-century Sweden, elite scientific and technical education in France since the eighteenth century, and schooling among the French peasants during the last century. In so doing, we shall try to relate particular kinds of literacy standards and instructional approaches to changing social needs and conditions. Finally, we will trace the changes in literacy standards that occurred in the first part of this century in the United States.

Having examined these historical cases, we will be in a position to consider the degree of fit between certain persisting traditions of education and present-day literacy standards. We shall also note a remarkable match between our conclusions and certain current theories of reading development that are based on observation of the stages through which individuals pass as they gain competence with the written word. In concluding we will consider various implications of our historical and theoretical analysis for current educational policy.

Models from the Historical Experience

Protestant-Religious Education

Historians have come to view the efforts of Protestant communities to bring their members into personal contact with biblical history and the Christian message as very important for the growth of literacy.[2] These efforts have also been recognized as significant in affecting social and economic development.[3] With respect to American development, Bernard Bailyn and Lawrence Cremin have described colonial literacy as so profoundly transforming that its development constituted a break with traditional attitudes.[4]

More recently, the connection between literacy and socioeconomic shifts has been called into question. Kenneth Lockridge has argued that literacy was of little significance for the shaping of modern social values in Protestant colonial New England.[5] The absence of such a relationship between schooling and economic development in Lancashire before the mid-nineteenth century has been one of the themes in the revisionist work of Michael Sanderson.[6] However, even for those who have been skeptical about its causal relationship to attitudes, the early modern Protestant experience with literacy has been seen as a watershed because of the great numbers of people who shared in that experience. In colonial New England, Lockridge estimates that male literacy, which was well above 60 percent for the generation born around 1700, became nearly universal by the end of the century;[7] in Scotland, Lawrence Stone found that the rate of literacy among adult males went from 33 percent around 1675 to almost 90 percent by 1800;[8] and in Sweden, Egil Johansson found that the number of males "able to read" in the parishes of Skelleftea went from half the population to 98 percent in the period from 1645 to 1714.[9]

The question of what kinds of knowledge defined literacy in these Protestant experiments has not been directly addressed by historians concerned with the relationship of literacy to economic and social development. We are able to respond to the question by considering the Swedish case, which represents the first instance of systematic record keeping relative to reading. To cite one example, the oldest extant registers of Möklinta parish in central Sweden, for the years from 1656 to 1669, offer columns to note whether or not minimum competency had been met in each of five areas.[10] The first involved the actual words to the text of the *Little Catechism;* the second, Luther's explanations of the words of the text; the third, the Confession of Sin; the fourth, morning and evening prayers; the fifth, prayers said at the table.[11] Questions on Lutheran creed and practice were apparently posed by the pastor on each of these topics. The examination assumed the availability of a printed catechism and prayer book in every home and prior discussion of these materials at catechetical meetings, attendance at which was to be checked off in a final column of the register.

No formal column for the capacity to read, as such, is to be found in this register (although one would be introduced in its successor), but all the questions assume the capacity to read, review, memorize, and recall familiar material. A second register, used during the period from 1686 to 1705, includes a corroborating column for "literacy," which was understood as the ability to read to the satisfaction of the examiner. An analysis of this material indicates that, while only one-fourth of the parish residents born in the early part of the seventeenth century were described as literate, the percentage grew to three-fourths for those born at the end of the century.

From the standpoint of current expectations, the literacy criterion that yielded these figures is a limited one. No unfamiliar material was given to the examinee. No writing was expected. No application of knowledge to new contexts was demanded. And no digressions from the text of the catechism and prayers were expected or permitted. The result was an exercise in the reading and memorizing of familiar material, to be recalled upon demand. Nevertheless, the Swedish experience, like the less controlled systems of early Protestant education in Scotland and the American colonies, represents more than simply a baseline of low literacy expectation. Instead, subsequent pedagogic efforts in literacy were heavily influenced by early religious activities.

The Elite-Technical Schools

A quite different tradition of literacy, one aimed at an elite, is represented by the growth of higher technical education in France. This system had its beginnings in the *collèges* and private academies of the Old Regime. The schools were run by such religious orders as the Oratorians and Jesuits, largely for sons of the aristocracy and bourgeoisie, although a few extremely able sons of the poor were accepted. Boys could enter at age seven and could stay until age seventeen or eighteen for an extended period of formal schooling. From these schools young men could enter a variety of state technical and professional schools that prepared their graduates for careers in civil and military public service.

By the eighteenth century, mathematics had become established as the touchstone of elite education. At all levels mathematics was stressed as the key to effective reasoning. For La Chalotais, in his *Plan d'éducation nationale* of 1763, it was "very possible and very common to reason badly in theology, or in politics; it is impossible in arithmetic and in geometry; if accuracy of mind is lacking, the rules will supply accuracy and intelligence for those who follow them." For Diderot, geometry was "the best and simplest of all logics, and it is the most suitable for fortifying the judgment and the reason."[12] But mathematics was deemed more than a better way to reason; it was central to the curriculum not only because of its alleged utility for developing young minds, but also because of its perceived usefulness to the state. It was essential for military purposes, civil engineering, and the monarchy's "civilizing" action in architecture, surveying, standard measures, and public finance.

In this context, literacy necessarily meant the acquisition of theoretical knowledge and the development of problem-solving capacities. But this criterion was thought to be applicable not to the whole population but only to a small elite. Competitive examinations restricted entry to the best state schools from the time of their establishment during the Old Regime; and the École Polytechnique, created during the Revolution, maintained the same standards of competitive entry.

The Revolution in no way challenged the definition or state support of this elite training at either the secondary or the graduate level. Established in 1795, the *écoles centrales* continued at the secondary level the scientific tradition of the *collèges* and academies of the Old Regime. The *écoles centrales* were succeeded by the *lycées,* which came to place greater emphasis on Latin than on mathematics. Despite this change in subject matter, a strong and visible place was maintained within secondary education for students who were preparing for the *grandes écoles.*[13]

Higher technical training was enshrined in the educational program of France and thus became—and continues to be—the distinguishing mark of the French graduate elite. Strong on theory and arrogant about their ability to apply knowledge to a variety of situations, these graduates have only recently found a world of technical literacy in which they feel comfortable despite the limits of their training. As Charles Kindleberger has argued, "Excessively deductive, Cartesian, geometric, mathematical, theoretical by nineteenth century standards, the system is coming into its own in a world of scientific sophistication."[14]

Civic-National Schooling

While elites continued to attend specialized academies, responsibility for mass education gradually shifted from religious communities to public bodies. We again consider France as an example. The French system of primary education has been credited with breaking new ground in secularizing education, universalizing schools, and fostering patriotism. From 1789 to 1914, this system of primary education increased the number of people with basic literacy from less than half to more than 90 percent of the French population.[15]

Primary education became a public commitment during the French Revolution. When the Revolutionary government introduced the first plan for national education in France in 1795, its major interest was military: the preservation of schools and training routes for those entering technical and military careers was considered essential. (Similarly, Napoleon's system of secondary education, the *lycée,* was focused on providing personnel for the nation's military and technical needs.) The 1795 plan contained only the outlines of a system for primary education. It neither provided funding for primary schools nor created a sufficient number to serve the predominantly rural public.[16]

Before legislation abolished the religious orders' endowments and their right to receive public and private contribution, these orders had played a major role in providing basic education. The restrictive measures of the Revolution, in combination with wartime activity, drove many of the clergy underground or abroad. This effectively dismantled the church system of primary education that had functioned at the village level.

However, even in those areas where public primary schools were established, it was difficult to separate primary education from religious instruction. The attempt to do so initially generated much hostility in conservative areas. For this and other reasons the separation between religion and public education was far from complete. Without public funding for school textbooks, religious materials continued to serve as beginning reading matter for children. The personnel of the old church primary schools also tended to reappear in the new secular ones.

Literacy levels appear to have remained fairly stable across the Revolutionary divide, despite the undermining of the church-run primary schools. There was no important growth in literacy, as measured by signatures on marriage contracts, in any department during the thirty years after the opening of the Revolution. Only one-quarter of the French departments had growth rates of more than one percent, in the male capacity to sign, and almost all of that growth was in the range of one to two percent. Twelve departments showed declines in the male capacity to sign during this period, but all were of less than one percent.[17]

The literacy expectations in the primary schools that did function before the 1830s remained modest. This is hardly surprising since primary education was largely a catch-as-catch-can affair for the first two post-Revolutionary generations in rural France. Children usually attended school for only the winter months, since the demands of family and farm had priority, and even then they did so irregularly. Those who attended generally left between the ages of ten and twelve after confirmation in the Church. Communions were held rather early, to coincide roughly with the end of the primary-school course.[18]

In addition to irregular school attendance, poorly prepared teachers may also have contributed to low levels of literacy. Teachers were not professionally trained before the 1830s, even though efforts to impose professional standards for their certification were first made in 1816.[19] The minimun standard was a demonstrated ability to read, write, and use simple figures, yet even this standard was not always met. For example, even after 1830, teachers who hired themselves out by the season at fairs in eastern France reportedly placed one, two, or three feathers in their caps to indicate what subject or subjects they knew how to teach: the first stood for reading, the second for arithmetic, and the third for Latin. In arithmetic, moreover, those who could only add and subtract far outnumbered those who could multiply and divide as well. One teacher, Sister Gandilhon, who ran a school at Selins (Cantal) in the 1840s, taught "prayers, the catechism and the first two rules of arithmetic." According to a contemporary, "she had heard of a third but never learned it."[20] The teaching of arithmetic was further complicated by the use of regional units for weights and measures, like the *pouce* and the *toise*, which had no relationship to the metric system introduced by the Revolution.[21]

The methods of reading instruction were equally primitive. Before the 1840s, the teaching of reading was characterized by instruction in the names of the letters ("ah, bay, say day . . . ."), independent of any relationiship to other vowels and consonants. From the pronunciation of letters, students moved directly to the pronunciation of words.[22] A study of a village in western France noted that one teacher, much respected, read aloud sentences from the children's readers and then had children repeat the sentences. According to a resident of the village:

> The children were not required to make any effort to understand the words or to attempt to associate the shapes with sounds and meanings. They merely repeated what had been said to them and gradually discovered . . . by the place on the page or the approximate shape of what they were being given to read the sounds they were required to emit to avoid being beaten.[23]

It is hardly surprising, given these methods, that many pupils did not learn how to read at all. Further, those who did manage to read generally worked only on religious books and simple readers.

Mastery may also have been rare because the language of instruction did not always match the vernacular of the region. Most of France was a nation of *patois*, and in many regions, Provençal, German, Italian, or Catalan was the major language. Since the language of instruction during most of the nineteenth century was almost universally French, the result was predictable. Even when students were able to read the written language fluently, inspectors in Britanny noted, "No child can give account of what he has read to translate it into Breton; hence there is no proof that anything is understood."[24]

Persisting Limits of the Civic-National Model

School attendance rose sharply throughout France as a result of two major reforms of the primary system of public education, the first in 1833 and the second in 1881–82.[25] Steps were taken under Ministers of Education Guizot and Ferry to democratize the system by increasing the number of primary schools, by reducing school fees, and by increasing the number of training colleges for teachers. These measures, in varying degrees, increased school attendance and contributed to the professionalization of teachers. However, despite these efforts toward democratization, primary schooling remained clearly distinct from the elite-secondary program.

Public schooling, moreover, did not for some time abandon its preoccupation with religious principles. Although in the field of education a civic religion of nationalism ultimately replaced traditional Catholic beliefs, schoolmasters remained dependent on local religious authorities for the nearly fifty years between the two reforms.[26] In 1833 the education minister attempted to make peace with the parish religious authorities in order to convince parents of the value of public primary schooling. "It is on the preponderant and united action of Church and State that I rely to establish primary instruction," Guizot told the legislature.[27] In practice this meant the responsibilities of the primary teacher included encouraging attendance at Mass, teaching prayers and biblical lore, and assisting the priest as needed. Reports from the 1840s and 1850s cite many examples of schools in which an alphabet book in Latin or a fifteenth-century *Life of Christ* served as the reading text.[28]

This educational alliance with the Church was broken by the Ferry reforms of 1881–82. The catechism was eliminated from the school reading program. Every *commune* was required to support a schoolmaster and a public school for girls as well as boys. A policy of free tuition, though not one of free books, replaced the earlier program of limited scholarships. For the first time school attendance was made compulsory, and the primary program was extended to age fourteen.[29] Finally, the national education ministry began a massive program of school construction.

Instruction was not designed to enlarge the skills of the literate or to encourage critical approaches to reading; rather, it was meant to cultivate a love of the familiar. History and geography texts were introduced to promote love of country.[30] The purpose of history instruction, for example, was unabashedly identified as patriotic. When questioned about the role of history in education, nearly 80 percent of the candidates for a *baccalauréat* in 1897 answered with statements about the "need to exalt patriotism."[31] Thus, despite the new curriculum, many of the criteria for literacy embedded in seventeenth- and eighteenth-century religious instruction were allowed to persist.

By the time of World War I, the successes of public primary schooling were clearly visible. Almost every child in the nation had relatively easy access to schools, and nearly all fourteen-year-olds by then had attended schools for seven years. Teachers were generally graduates of special training colleges located in each *département*. Attendance was increasingly regular for those enrolled in the schools, and students did not leave with the passing of winter. Inability to pay did not directly bar students' access to school. French was clearly the national language, and the metric system had triumphed over local measures. Statistics compiled by the Ministry of Education on years of schooling as well as the dramatic rise in the proportion of military recruits capable of signing their own names[32] are further evidence of these successes.

However, these facts do not inform us about the quality of education or the growth of individual capacity, and on these issues the evidence is mixed. Thabault observed that, while fewer than one-fifth of the inhabitants of his village knew how to form the letters of their names in 1833, more than half were able to do so thirty years later. Nevertheless, "the amount of knowledge that most of them had acquired did not make them very different from the completely illiterate."[33] By the eve of World War I, there had been considerable improvement in the knowledge of history, geography, and the French language. The inculcation of this knowledge took the form of a civic education, a new catechism based on patriotic devotion and civic duty. Eugen Weber has argued that this system, along with the army and improved transportation in the years from 1876 to 1914, contributed to the modernization of the attitudes and behavior of the French peasantry. But acculturation and adaptation do not necessarily produce generalized understanding, transferable learning, or reasoning skills.

Teaching Methods and Literacy Criteria in America

American methods of teaching reading were influenced initially by approaches developed in Europe. The classic method, as we have seen in the

French system, was alphabetic. Children were first drilled on the letter names and then on syllables. No attempt was made to select meaningful syllables or to emphasize comprehension; rather, accurate and fluent pronunciation was emphasized. The following description of reading instruction in the Sessional School in Edinburgh, Scotland, was reported to American educators in 1831. This account suggests the dominant goal of literacy instruction in the United States as well as in Scotland:

> English reading, according to the prevailing notion, consists of nothing more than the power of giving utterance to certain sounds, on the perception of certain figures; and the measure of progress and excellence is the facility and continuous fluency with which those sounds succeed each other from the mouth of the learner. If the child gather any knowledge from the book before him, beyond that of color, form and position of the letters, it is to his own sagacity he is indebted for it, and not to his teacher.[34]

Pedagogical reforms that had been introduced in Britain, Germany, and France during the eighteenth and nineteenth centuries later influenced instructional practice in the United States. The Prussian educator Friedrich Gedike[35] had introduced a "word method" of reading instruction which used words as the starting point for teaching the alphabet and spelling. Other reformers substituted the use of sounds, or "powers," of the letters for their names in the initial teaching of the alphabet. Although these reforms improved the teaching of fluent oral reading, they did not imply any new or greater concern for students' ability to understand what was read.

In the United States many forward-looking educators recognized that a greater emphasis on meaning would enliven instruction and make it more palatable to children. Putnam, in 1836, stressed the need for comprehension while criticizing the dominant instructional practice:

> A leading object of this work is to enable the scholar, while learning to *read*, to *understand*, at the same time, the *meaning* of the words he is reading. . . . if, for example, when the pupil is taught to read, he is enabled, at the same time, to discover the *meaning* of the words he repeats, he will readily make use of the proper inflections, and place the emphasis where the sense demands it. The monotonous sing-song mode of reading, which is common in schools and which is often retained in after life, is acquired from the exercise of reading what is not understood.[36]

Nearly fifty years later, Farnham voiced similar concern when proposing his sentence method of reading instruction:

> It is important that this two-fold function of reading should be fully recognized. The first, or silent reading, is the fundamental process. . . . The second, oral reading, or "reading aloud," is entirely subordinate to silent reading. While oral expression is subject to laws of its own, its excellence depends upon the success of the reader in comprehending the thought of the author.[37]

Although these educators laid the groundwork for new methods and standards in literacy, their ideas did not become common educational practice until much later. Fundamental change in the standards applied to reading instruction came early in the twentieth century with the advent of child-centered theories of pedagogy, which stressed the importance of intrinsic interest and meaningfulness in learning, and the introduction of standardized group testing during World War I.

The American entry into the war highlighted a national literacy problem. Under the leadership of Robert Yerkes, then president of the American Psychological Association, a group of psychologists prepared and validated group-administered forms of a general intelligence test.[38] This test had two forms—Army Alpha for literate recruits and Army Beta for recruits unable to take the Alpha form. The tests were administered in 1918 to 1.7 million men, and it was noted with dismay that nearly 30 percent could not understand the Alpha form because they could not read well enough. This discovery evoked the following comment by an American educator, May Ayres Burgess:

> . . . if those [men] examined were fairly representative of all, there must have been over one million of our soldiers and sailors who were not able to write a simple letter or read a newspaper with ease.
> . . . although one-fourth of the men could not read well enough to take tests based on reading, this deficiency was not caused by their never having learned to read. The fact is that an overwhelming majority of these soldiers had entered school, attended the primary grades where reading is taught, and had been taught to read. Yet, when as adults they were examined, they were unable to read readily such simple material as that of a daily newspaper.[39]

After army intelligence tests had alerted people to defects in reading instruction, the growth in the 1920s of graded and standardized achievement testing gave educators tools for evaluating their efforts. The development of testing was stimulated in part by the successes of the army testing program and by the growing receptivity of school administrators to what they regarded as scientific tools of management.[40] The army program had demonstrated the practicality and validity of group-administered psychological tests. Because group-administered reading tests required silent reading rather than oral, the ability to answer questions or follow directions based upon a simple text became the most typical test of reading competence. This focus on deriving the meaning of a text fit well with what the most forward-looking educators had already been advocating. The ability to understand an unfamiliar text, rather than simply declaim a familiar one, became the accepted goal of reading instruction and the new standard of literacy.

This newer standard, previously applied only to the programs of elite institutions, required the ability to gain information from reading and use that information in new contexts. The 1920s marked the first time in history that such a rigorous standard had been applied in the United States. This emphasis on deriving meaning from text bolstered the cause of those educators advocating changes in reading instruction. With this change in the criterion of literacy, national aspirations also rose for the portion of the population expected to meet this new standard.

Patterns of school attendance in this century best illustrate these radical changes. Reviewing data from several American cities, Leonard Ayres reported in 1909 that of one hundred children who were in school at age seven, ninety would still be there at age thirteen, fifty at age fourteen, and only thirteen of the original one hundred would remain in school at age sixteen.[41] Equally important were the large numbers of students not promoted; attendance at school for six or seven years by no means assured passage into the sixth or seventh grade. In general, Ayres found that, from any given grade level, 20 percent would not be promoted—if they returned to school at all.[42] Ayres's statistics clearly demonstrate that only a limited percentage of the population completed elementary school in the early part of this century. Whatever the eighth-grade level of reading competence may have been, only half of those attending school ever completed that grade. The literacy level that came closer to being universal was the fifth-grade level, which was comparable to that attained at the completion of primary schooling in nineteenth-century France. Although we cannot estimate exactly the functioning level of literacy at the beginning of the century, it seems fair to conclude that it did not approach present standards.

The Growth of Literacy Expectations

This article documents changes in literacy standards and teaching methods in the United States and some European countries, chiefly France, during the past several centuries. Our evidence suggests a rough progression in literacy expectation and performance. Expectations for popular literacy appeared after a long period in which the general population could not read. The earliest mass-literacy effort, Protestant-religious instruction, was intended to develop not a generalized capacity to read but only the mastery of a very limited set of prescribed texts. Although civic-national public schooling introduced a slightly broadened set of texts, students were not expected to use their reading skills to acquire new information but only to become fluent oral readers. Nonetheless, some individuals did learn to read for information and even to engage in critical and inferential reading similar to that demanded by elite schools.

It is only during the present century that the goal of reading for the purpose of gaining information has been applied in ordinary elementary schools to the entire population of students. Today, the term "functional literacy" has come to mean the ability to read common texts such as newspapers and manuals and to use the information gained, usually to secure employment.[43] The objectives of functional literacy may seem limited, yet this mass-literacy criterion is stronger than that of any earlier period of history. Achieving universal literacy as it is now defined poses a challenge not previously faced. We estimate that literacy standards in the United States in the 1990s will be both more demanding and more widely applied than any previous standard. The accompanying figure 12-1 permits a schematic comparison between the aspirations which we have projected for the United States and standards met by earlier literacy movements. Depending on how the figure is read we are either

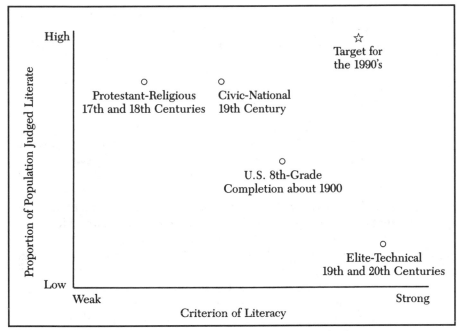

Figure 12.1. Schematic representation of shifts in literacy standards

attempting to increase by a significant degree the quality of literacy competence in our population, or to increase, also very significantly, the portion of our population to which an already established criterion is to apply.

The historical development of ever more demanding criteria for literacy mirrors to some extent a model for individual development of reading competence that has recently been proposed by Jeanne Chall.[44] In this sense, social phylogeny seems to reflect ontogeny. Chall points out that at successive stages in reading development, "the reader is doing essentially 'different' things in relation to printed matter, although the term reading is used to describe each of these stages." Further, "the successive stages are characterized by growth in the ability to read language of greater complexity, rarity, technicality, and abstractness, and with a change in how such materials are viewed and used."

Chall proposes five stages of reading. After a prereading period the first stage is initial reading or decoding. The essential aspect here "is the learning of the arbitrary set of letters and associating these with the corresponding parts of spoken words. . . ." The second stage is confirmation and fluency: "Essentially reading at this stage is a consolidation. . . . By reading familiar stories, smoothness and fluency are gained." Chall points out that at one time the Bible and religious tracts were familiar texts. The congruence between Chall's earlier stages and the literacy standards of the religious and civic-national periods is striking. During these periods reading instruction centered on mastering print, associating letters with words, and reading aloud. Chall's stage of confirmation and fluency seems parallel to the practice, highly valued in the nineteenth century, of public reading of texts. Chall's third stage, "reading for learning the new," is the first point at which mastering the ideas conveyed comes to be the dominant goal. For a long time reading for new information was not expected of many, and it is only now becoming a nearly universal standard.

Implications for Policy

Our review of the Protestant-religious, civic-national, and elite-technical educational efforts has been very selective, but it nonetheless suggests the novelty of our present situation. Educational leaders often argue as if "real literacy" is compromised by an acceptance of functional-literacy standards tied to very practical demands of work and citizenship such as filing tax returns and reading technical manuals. On the contrary, our findings suggest that the serious application to the entire population of the contemporary standard of functional literacy would represent a real and important increase in literacy. This is not to deny the ultimate possibility and desirability of seeking a still higher literacy criterion, but forms of pedagogy will almost surely have to change to accommodate the changes in both the literacy criterion and target population.

This discussion of changes in literacy standards has implications for the growing "back to basics" movement. Although the claim is frequently made that a return to basics would improve our educational system, the consequences of such a program are not clear. Presumably, proponents of basic education want schools to stress skills of literacy and mathematics more than certain recent additions to the curriculum. This much is reasonable. But, unless we intend to relinquish the criterion of comprehension as the goal of reading instruction, there is little to go *back* to in terms of pedagogical method, curriculum, or school organization. The old tried and true approaches, which nostalgia prompts us to believe might solve current problems, were designed neither to achieve the literacy standard sought today nor to assure successful literacy for everyone. Whatever the rhetoric of the common school, early dropping out and selective promotion were in fact used to escape problems that must now be addressed through a pedagogy adequate to today's aspirations. While we may be able to borrow important ideas and practices from earlier periods, there is no simple past to which we can return.

Part Three

Educational Perspectives

13.
School Literacy, Reasoning, and Civility

An Anthropologist's Perspective

Frederick Erickson

This paper takes a perspective on schools, teaching, and learning that places in the foreground the social organization and cultural patterning of people's work in everyday life. In that perspective the notion of literacy, as knowledge and skill taught and learned in school, is not separable from the concrete circumstances of its uses inside and outside school, nor is it easily separable from the situation of its acquisition in the school as a social form and as a way of life. The school can be seen as an arena of political negotiation that embodies individual and group interests and ideologies. It is reasonable to expect that various kinds of literacies might represent a variety of interests and be embedded in a variety of belief systems.

We can distinguish analytically between literacy and schooling, or between the arithmetical analog "numeracy," and schooling, or between the latest manifestation, "computer literacy," and schooling. In ordinary usage, however, the distinction between formal knowledge and school is blurred. This may be for good reasons, some of which I will explore in the discussion that follows. Literally, literacy refers to knowledge of letters and of their use in reading and writing, just as the ugly word numeracy refers to knowledge and use of numbers. But to be *lettered* means more than this, and has done so in the West since the establishment of European schools by the monastic chapters of cathedrals in the early Middle Ages.

Literacy, as *being lettered*, has to do with strategy and prestige. This prestige is partly due to the strategic power that comes from mastery of an information communication system. This prestige also is derived from values of aesthetics and moral virtue which mask the issue of power. Indeed, in 17th century English, to be *lewd* is not to be sexually unrestrained, but to be unlettered. It is only later in English usage that lewdness took on sexual connotations, which gradually became the main usage.

The prestigefulness of schooling also mixes power with the justification of power in morality. One is reminded that in the West, the institution of schooling began in the medieval Church, with literacy justified as a means to specialized knowledge that could be employed in maintaining the intellectual and social structure of the Church, which was seen as a means to collective and individual salvation. The same special knowledge of letters and numbers was also employed in maintaining the rule of secular landholders, whose growth and whose systems for distribution of food enabled the existence of feudal society itself. In colonial New England the institution of public schooling was also justified on moral grounds, with knowledge of letters being the route to individual salvation through reading the Bible, and the same specialized knowledge applying in the development of small freehold agriculture, commerce, and eventually industry. In the comments that follow I do not want to reduce schooling to a set of purely utilitarian functions, nor do I want to do so with literacy. But relationships between the various utilities and moralities of kinds of schooling, kinds of literacy, kinds of work, and kinds of power in society are central to the argument I will make. Let me begin with a few narrative vignettes.

Literacy in a Steel Plant

In 1965 I worked for a steel company in Chicago in helping to organize and conduct on a pilot basis a program of on-the-job training for high school dropouts. The company was a steel fabricating firm in which bars and sheets of steel were cut to ordered lengths and then shipped to buyers who used the steel in manufacturing. The program involved education in basic academic skills and work experience. The curricular emphasis of the program was the result of an informal analysis by company management of the reasons behind the high turnover of over 200 minority workers, largely black, who had been hired over a 2-year period. Most of these workers quit or were fired before having worked in an entry level job for 6 months. Absenteeism and lack of the elementary and reading computational skills necessary to read work orders and to measure and cut quantities of steel were reported by foremen and by plant managers as the major causes for the brevity of the careers of the new minority employees of the company. Accordingly, a program of training in basic skills was established, during which the trainees would be required to come to work every day, on time, and learn in the plant how to work the machines, and in the classroom how to read and compute.

As I worked with the trainees it became apparent that very few of the dozen trainees had much trouble with reading work orders, or with measuring lengths of steel. Three of the trainees did have difficulty with this that persisted. The others learned very quickly to measure and cut steel and to read the lengths and numbers of cut pieces that were written on the work orders. As the weeks progressed it also became apparent that the trainees experienced recurrent difficulties with their foremen and fellow workers, almost all of whom were Middle European immigrants or the children of immigrants. The trainees were criticized for talking unintelligibly and for standing in what looked to supervisors like lazy postures while working on their machines. Foremen would come by and say things like, "Get moving, you — — —. We're not paying you to — — —." After a few weeks most of the trainees became convinced that most of the white supervisors and workers were "racist." At the end of 12 weeks some of the trainees had quit, some had stayed. All but one, to my knowledge, were able by then to read work orders and cut steel. Most had been able to do this at the outset.

Literacy in a High School Night Program

Two of the steel company trainees decided that they would enroll in night school classes to begin again to work for their high school diplomas. I took one of them to registration one evening. He went through the registration procedure and signed up for an English course at the junior level, which was the level at which he had dropped out of school 2 years previously. The following week, on the morning after the young man had attended his first evening class I asked him what they were assigned to do. With despair in his eyes he said, "We're reading Beowulf."

Literacy on Ice

In the summer of 1981, while teaching at the University of Alaska, Fairbanks, I met an Eskimo in his mid-thirties who was now going to college and whose father had been a subsistence hunter. The son still hunted occasionally. He said that as a child he learned that "if you want to hunt seal you have to learn to think like a seal."

As an anthropologist my main questions about literacy and numeracy are these: Given that for approximately 5 million years human societies have managed to rear their young so that almost every one in the society was able to master the knowledge and skills necessary for survival, why does this not happen in modern societies with schools? Or does it happen—do schools teach what is necessary, but define and measure achievement in such ways that it looks as if large proportions of the school population fail? Why is it that when we know that the cognitive operations necessary to learn to speak a language are mastered by almost every child by age 5, many of those same children seem unable to learn to read in school, even though the cognitive complexity of learning to read, at least at the early stages, is so much less than that required to learn to speak? Why can a child make change successfully at the grocery store and fail to do those same arithmetic operations correctly when presented with a math worksheet in the classroom? In current public discourse about literacy, are we talking about knowledge and skill in decoding letters, or are we talking about being "lettered" as a marker of social class status and cultural capital? Do we see the school diploma mainly as evidence of mastery of knowledge and skill in literacy, in the literal and narrow sense of the term? I don't think so. I think that the high school diploma functions, for low SES students, primarily as a docility certificate. Were it otherwise, private industry could not be content to allow public schools to produce graduates—potential future employees—who cannot read, write, or do simple arithmetic. This would make especially good sense if ordinary work in most of the company's jobs does not really require literacy, as schools define it.

For those social sciences that take a societal and cultural perspective on the organization of human social life, a most fundamental concern about the relations between literacy and schooling is to question whether fostering literacy is in fact the central activity of public schooling as an institution of mass society. The school's other activities may play equally important roles, in contradiction to the role of the school in fostering literacy. These other activities include social sorting, the maintenance of prestige of the "high" forms of letteredness as items of cultural capital, child care for working parents, and keeping young people off the labor market.

The various activities of schools are organized so that class position is in most instances maintained from one generation to the next. One need not assume that school personnel do this deliberately. Yet survey data on school achievement consistently present us with an unavoidable social fact: Only in a minority of cases does the modern public school function for individuals or for society as Horace Mann envisioned that it would, as the "balance wheel of democracy." The issue can be investigated without deciding in advance whether one or another kind of activity (function) is predominant. A useful question is, "How do the various activities of schools work together—how are they organized in relationship—for students of varying class, racial, and ethnic backgrounds?" In short, the relations between the manifest curriculum of school subject matter—literacy and numeracy in the narrow sense—and the hidden curriculum of social sorting and ranking are an issue of central interest for the social sciences, as well as for educators and citizens.

Variation in Literacies and Intelligences

Cognitive Abilities as Domain-Specific

Recent work in cognitive anthropology and in cross-cultural psychology has investigated complex thought processes among nonliterate peoples as a topic of interest in its own right and as a baseline for comparison with the thought processes of literate people. It appears from this work that, contrary to an earlier view in anthropology and in lay opinion, nonliterate people are capable of systematic thinking that involves abstraction. Gladwin (1970), for example, investigated the reasoning that is involved in Polynesian navigation. Sailors from these islands are able to travel from one small atoll to another across hundreds of miles of open sea and arrive at their exact destination. They navigate using the stars and other orientation cues, but make use of the stars in ways very different from Western navigational reasoning. Their navigation system is thoroughly systematic, but its basic principles and categories differ fundamentally from the postulates and principles that form the foundation for Western navigation. The Polynesian system is taught by older navigators to neophytes without using writing.

Polynesian traditional navigation is an especially apt test case for the proposition that nonliterate thinking can be highly regular and abstract, since sailing provides a crucial test of the adequacy of the system of reasoning and of its teaching; if the system is flawed, or if the neophyte didn't learn it correctly, the boat and its crew are lost at sea. Interestingly, however, when given Western tests of mental ability, Gladwin's navigators scored very low. On the tests they seemed to lack the kinds of cognitive abilities they were able to demonstrate on the open sea.

Childs and Greenfield (1980) have done a series of investigations of the thinking underlying traditional weaving in Chiapas, Mexico, and of the ways that experienced weavers teach inexperienced ones. Lave (1977) has studied the arithmetic thinking of apprentice tailors in Liberia. Again, the weavers and tailors when working with thread and cloth can be seen to be capable of measurement operations and other kinds of reasoning that they are unable to display when given Western school-like intelligence and achievement tests.

In these and similar studies, people's abilities to reason appear to be domain-specific rather than generalizable across task domains that differ in surface form. This is a fundamental point.

Literacy and Schooling as Task Domains

A number of theorists have argued that even though nonliterate thinking can be shown to be systematic, there is still a qualitative difference between the thinking of nonliterate and literate people. Literacy, these scholars argue, enables one to escape the limitations placed on cognition by spoken discourse. Speaking occurs in real time, with an immediacy of presence between utterer and utterance. Written discourse steps outside real time. Once the writer has inscribed a text the writer is able to step back from it and take a distanced, critical view of its content. Reflective thinking and self-critical analysis is enabled by this, it is argued, by scholars such as Ong (1977), Goody (1977), Luria (1959), and Olson (1977).

Scribner and Cole (1981, p. 4) characterize these assertions as "Great Divide" theories. They maintain that to propose a vast qualitative gulf between literate and nonliterate reasoning is to repeat the more general presumption in cognitive and developmental psychology (e.g., both in classical learning theory and in Piagetian developmental theory) that reasoning abilities, once acquired, are relatively or absolutely context independent. Recent work by Cole and others is beginning to show us, in contrast to the conventional view of mental abilities as essentially fixed, that reasoning, literacy, and numeracy operations appear to be much more labile than was previously thought. Human reasoning seems to consist of skills that are reflexively constituted in the context of situation of use and purpose. This is a conception of thinking as sets of domain-specific and situation-specific operations rather than sets of general abilities.

Scribner and Cole (1981) speak of these cognitive operations as *practices:*

> By a practice we mean a recurrent, goal-directed sequence of activities using a particular technology and particular system of knowledge. We use the term "skills" to refer to the coordinated sets of actions involved in applying this knowledge in particular settings. A practice, then, consists of three components: technology, knowledge, and skills. . . . Literacy is not simply learning how to read and write a particular script but applying this knowledge for specific purposes in specific contexts of use. (p. 236)

Literacy, too, is seen as a practice: "Literacy is not simply learning how to read and write a particular script but applying this knowledge for specific purposes in specific contexts of use" (p. 236).

By extension, "numeracy," or the ability to navigate, or to run a micro-computer, or any other domain of knowledge and skill is seen as not just cognitive operation in isolation but as cognitive operation employing a specific technology toward specific ends. All "literacies," then, are radically constituted by their contexts of use. This is not the opposite of *context independence;* that is, it is not *context dependence* or *field dependence.* Rather, it is a fundamentally different notion of the relations between an individual's intellectual capabilities and the specific material and social situations in which those capabilities are employed. To call these capabilities *practices* is to say that an individual's ability to think is dialogically defined, that is, constituted by (a) other people in particular forms of social relationship, (b) the physical objects (utensils, tools) and symbols (words, numbers) with which the individual interacts, directly or vicariously, in doing the thinking. Change the physical form of the tools or symbols, or change the social forms of relations among the people with whom the individual is learning the practice (or is performing it once learned) and one has profoundly changed the nature of the interaction—the nature of the learning task. In doing so one has also changed what in ordinary parlance we call the *ability* of the individual.

From this point of view, it is not surprising that a child can display arithemetic competence while dealing with change at the grocery store and yet seem to lack that performance when doing what seems to be the "same" arith-metic problem on a worksheet or at the blackboard in the classroom, even if the problem were displayed using pictures of coins with which the child is familiar rather than using numerals with which the child might be less familiar. Still, a picture of a coin is not a coin, and relations with the teacher and fellow students are not the same as relations with a store clerk (when one has money) and one's little brother or friend (before whom one's display of appropriate performance carries no negative social and emotional consequences). The nature of the task in the store and in the classroom is very different and so is the nature of the abilities required to accomplish it.

Cursory reading in the current debates about excellence in education (e.g., National Commission on Excellence, 1983) and in standard textbooks in educational psychology used in undergraduate teacher education (e.g., Biehler,

1974, pp. 460–480, 571–576, 605–615; Good and Brophy, 1980, p. 487; Vander Zanden and Pace, 1984, pp. 99–120) shows that the unexamined presuppositions—the culturally learned ontological postulates—about the nature of individual ability that are current in policy decisionmaking and in teacher education are very different from the view just presented. This new view turns the notion of individual ability inside out by seeing it as socially constituted rather than as context independent and located inside the individual alone. This is so fundamental a critique of the conventional wisdom of educational practice in the United States that it bears further discussion.

We can ask what the evidence base is for the new perspective on ability, and on the nature of various literacies, broadly construed. The major study is that already cited: Scribner and Cole, 1981. In a set of related investigations they compared reasoning patterns of Liberians who were literate in Western script, in Arabic script, in a traditional Liberian script, with the reasoning patterns of Liberians who were nonliterate. Evidence for a subject's reasoning patterns was derived from analysis of that subject's behavior on standard tests and on specially designed tests. Data collection in some of the substudies included close observation and interviewing, so that those sources of information about the subject's reasoning processes were available in addition to the evidence of the outcomes of those processes that could be inferred from the content of the choices the subject made in completing the test items.

Scribner and Cole were also able to conduct a crucial comparison that had never been made before: that between literates and nonliterates, controlling for the influence of schooling independent of the influence of literacy itself on thought processes. This comparison was possible because of the traditional script found among the Vai, a Liberian tribal group. The Vai script is taught outside schools and is used for purposes such as letter writing and keeping farming lists and records. Vai script is not used in written interaction with Western or Muslim-schooled literates; that is, it is not used in interethnic commerce or in filling out governmental forms. Because among the Vai there were both unschooled and schooled persons who were literate in Vai script, Scribner and Cole were able to compare the performance of the two subgroups of Vai literates to see what effects schooling itself might have on the capacity of the Vai literates to demonstrate higher order cognitive skills in test situations. Scribner and Cole were also able to compare Vai literates and nonliterates, both sets of subjects not having attended either a Western European-derived school (British system) or a Muslim school.

The natural occurrence of these comparison groups in Liberia gave Scribner and Cole a natural experimental situation in which they could ask whether literacy per se influenced people to use so-called "higher order" thinking, or whether it appeared that those ways of thinking and the capacity to display them in Western test situations was a consequence of the experience of schooling rather than of literacy alone. This is a key issue in the debate over the "Great Divide" theories of the influence of literacy on thought. Proponents of the Great Divide theories have argued that literacy enables greater abstraction, decontextualized use of problem-solving skills, Western-style logical reasoning, and other aspects of what psychometricians consider to be higher order thinking.

Opponents of the Great Divide theories have argued that the capacity of literate people to display such skills in test situations is due not to the influence of literacy so much as it is to the influence of schooling. Students in school, it is argued, learn the point of test-like problem situations. They learn how to see in test items what the tester designed the item to test. Nonliterate people who are also nonschooled do not learn how to "read" the test items the way schooled people have learned to do. The ability to perform appropriately in school-like reasoning tasks, then, is seen not as evidence of inherent (culture-free) cognitive ability but as evidence of culture-specific learning. By going to school, children learn the cultural principles for acting in school-like ways when playing school-like reasoning games. Nonschooled (and nonliterate) people may possess the same reasoning abilities as do those who have been schooled; it is just that the nonschooled do not possess the cultural knowledge necessary to be able to play the school-like reasoning games that the test items present.

Scribner and Cole's results (1981, pp. 242ff) suggest that schooling by itself had much more influence on the capacity of the Vai to display ability with certain thought processes than did literacy by itself. Moreover, while attendance at English school did seem to influence students' thinking, that pattern of influence was not nearly so thoroughgoing, so absolute, as conventional wisdom would expect. The kinds of tasks at which the English-schooled Vai far outperformed their nonschooled fellows were tasks that entailed deliberate comment on the procedures that were being done: explanations of sorting patterns, of logic, of grammatical rules, of rules of games. Schooling showed some influence on some other tasks: story recall, abstraction, recall of lists of objects, logic problems. But on other tasks schooling showed no apparent influence: flexibility in sorting (number of dimensions used), word definitions, incremental recall. Urban experience, rather than schooling, seemed to influence a preference for grouping objects by class membership and the use of taxonomic clustering in free recall. These last findings, the authors note (1981, p. 243), run contrary to those from most other studies, as does the finding that urban experience rather than schooling influenced the subjects' performance in directions that other researchers would attribute to schooling.

In short, even schooling, which appeared to have stronger influence than literacy over subjects' ways of thinking, did not seem to stimulate what could be called overall cognitive competence. Rather, school seemed to stimulate a narrower set of abilities: the abilities involved in knowing how to comment to an observer and presumably to one's self, on what one has been doing in a task situation whose parameters are closed, in which algorithms for problem solution are predetermined, as part of the task structure itself.

The work of Scribner and Cole warns us against the fallacy of regarding school-like learning tasks as requiring greater capacity for higher order thinking than do everyday tasks in home, community, and work settings. Schools may foster students' abilities to recognize canonical forms of task solution and to communicate their insight about how to do such tasks in canonical forms of speaking, writing, and calculating with numbers. This point was underscored in the presidential address delivered by Richard Anderson at the 1984 annual meeting of the American Educational Research Association. In that talk Anderson identified features of lower order thinking in early grades reading instruction and achievement testing that mitigate against acquisition of more complex reading skills in the later grades. Lower order thinking and the ability to apply algorithms uncritically is what early grades achievement tests measure. Schools appear to be quite good at teaching those situation-specific canonical practices. But that is not reasoning, more broadly and more fundamentally construed.

Another fallacy this line of work warns us against is that of interpreting culturally patterned communicative performance uncritically, as evidence of the presence or absence of underlying cognitive competence (see the discussion of Cole and Bruner, 1971). An example of this is the fallacy of attributing *metacognitive ability* to students who have learned to talk in school-like ways about the reasons for their choices in experimental tasks and attributing lack of metacognitive ability to students who do not talk in school-like ways. This fallacy can be found in the work of current Piagetians (e.g., Flavell, 1977) and the students of referential communication in laboratory tasks (e.g., Asher, 1976; Glucksberg, Krauss, and Higgins, 1975; Markman, 1979). Sociolinguistic research on the cognitive complexity of Black English, for example, shows that nonstandard ways of speaking that on first glance may seem to indicate lower order thinking, especially the lack of capacity for abstraction and logical reasoning, are in fact ways of speaking that convey higher order thinking (see especially Erickson, 1984; Labov, 1972). The problem of cognitive competence—the ability to recognize and use higher order thinking—may lie more in the eye or ear and brain of the interpreter than in the mouth and brain of the speaker of a culturally nonstandard way of speaking. This is a problem of ethnocentric bias in the study of relations between language and thought, a problem of which much educational research on students' reasoning seems to be unaware.

Learning Tasks as Social Environments

Scribner and Cole's findings and Cole's earlier work (Cole, Gay, Glick, and Sharp, 1971) emphasize the culture-specific and situation-specific nature of learning tasks inside and outside school. Their work emphasizes as well the importance of the physical form of the objects or symbols by which the task is presented. This surface form provides cues to the schooled test subject about what responses to make and about what to comment on when explaining one's reasoning. Scribner and Cole's findings also point to the importance of another dimension of the learning task: that of social relations between the tester and the tested, or the teacher and the student. This is the other task dimension that was mentioned earlier in the example of making change at the grocery store.

Recent research on everyday thinking sheds further light on the importance of the dimension of social relations in learning tasks that ordinarily we think of as exclusively "cognitive" and abstracted from social context. Lave, Murtaugh, and de la Rocha (1984) have been investigating arithmetic reasoning of American adults while shopping in the supermarket. They find that the adults, from a wide range of schooling backgrounds, are able to make price comparisons that are virtually error-free when shopping, Given the same kinds of choice problems in a test situation, however, all their subjects made many errors. The more highly schooled made fewer errors than the less schooled, but all subjects made more errors of choice in the test than in the store. Does this suggest serious flaws in schooled Americans' capacities for abstract reasoning? Far from it, in the authors' interpretation.

Lave et al. (1984) see the crucial difference between the shopping task and the test task as lying not on the dimension of abstraction-concreteness but on the dimension of problem-definition by self or by other. This is a matter of social relations. In the grocery store price comparison occurs near the end of a long sequence of choice points that involve many factors besides price, for example, the size and shape of one's shelf space, taste preferences of family members, menu plans for the week. The nature of the price comparison problem—its definition, its relevance to the ultimate decision to buy—is in the hands of the shopper. Shoppers are very good at shaping the problems—the points of quantitative comparison—in ways that they can solve. In the test situation, however, the problem's quantitative parameters are established by the tester. According to Lave et al. it is not just that such a problem is "out of context"; it is that it is *in a context* in which the power relations are such that the subject has no influence on problem formulation.

The right to be proactive in shaping the cognitive task at hand appears to be important in reading as well as in arithmetic. In a participant observational study of reading practices of employees in a milk plant, for example, Scribner (1984) and Jacob (in press) found that workers who tested as very limited in reading ability developed effective means of reading work orders. They used noncanonical ways of redefining the reading tasks so that they could accomplish them successfully. If the workers had been forced to use canonical, school-like ways of deciphering written text they would have been unable to do their job in the plant, because they had not mastered the canonical form of the practice of reading. This is not to say that their noncanonical reading practices were less reasonable than those taught by schools. The workers' practices were reasonable—just according to a different system of reasons. Since the social organization of their work entailed the right to read the way they knew how, they were able to display competence that otherwise would not have been displayed.

Recent work by Rogoff and Gardner (1984) sheds further light on the issue of social relations as inherent in the constitution of learning tasks. They have been studying mothers teaching classification tasks to children in everyday teaching situations. One such task is arranging items purchased at the grocery store. Mothers and children were observed doing this task in a laboratory kitchen. The kind of instruction provided by the mothers is what Wertsch (1979) has characterized as *proleptic instruction;* the novice carries out simple aspects of a task under the guidance of an expert, who can demonstrate performance to the novice. The balance between observation and guided trial attempts on the part of the learner is established by mutual negotiation—learner seeking help and teacher providing it. This negotiation establishes the fluid, interactional system of social and cognitive support that Wood, Bruner, and Ross (1976) call *scaffolding*. The scaffolding is a matter of social relations as well as of subject matter content. In the everyday teaching scenes that Rogoff and Gardner have been observing, the scaffolding relationship between teacher and learner is jointly constructed. The child has rights to ask for a range of kinds of help. Like the grocery shopper, the child and the teacher have rights to redefine the task as part of the scaffolding negotiation. This social form of learning environment in everyday teaching situations is very different from that found in school learning environments. There, typically, the learner has much less right to help shape the task. In such a situation it may be that very often the teacher's one-sided attempts to construct a scaffold that reaches the learner don't work. The scaffold doesn't reach.

With the influence of various performance accountability systems, schools are increasingly places in which one individual (the teacher) sets absolute task parameters for others. Practice in such situations of performance no doubt improves student performance on standardized tests. It does not improve overall reasoning ability, if Cole is right about the domain-specific character of reasoning as sets of practices. Moreover, school-like task construction may do violence to civility, in the sense of a social contract that involves assent by the learner.

In the most extreme forms of school learning environments, not only does the learner have no rights to shape the learning task, but neither does the teacher. The test is the most extreme example of this. In observing experienced teachers administering standardized tests I have been repeatedly impressed by their frustration at not being able to explain simple confusions their students may have about particular items. The test as a social situation has removed the teacher's right to scaffold—to teach. Repeatedly teachers will attempt to break through this, not to cheat on behalf of the student, but to prevent the child from making what for that child is a nonvalid wrong answer—the child's reasoning is on the right track, it's just that the child is having trouble "reading" the task cues of the item. Children repeatedly seek such help. Again, it seems not simply to cheat but to do with the problem what they would do in ordinary problem solving at the grocery or in an everyday teaching situation, in which scaffolding is jointly constructed so that it fits both the task and the learner attempting the task; so that in Vygotsky's terms it bridges the *zone of proximal development* (Vygotsky, 1978, pp. 84–91). Mehan (1973) has shown professional test administrators and children jointly negotiate answers in individual test situations. This press toward scaffolding work by both teacher and student seems ubiquitous.

Another instance of a teaching situation in which the social rules prevent both teacher and student from scaffolding negotiation is the scripted lesson. The teacher's manual accompanying the basal reading book scripts the lesson partially. Some special remedial instruction for low performing students is entirely scripted, for example, the DISTAR curriculum developed for early grades students from impoverished families, often of racial or linguistic minority background. In these lessons the teacher's questions, and the student's choral responses, are mandated by a script. Neither the teacher nor the student has the right to reformulate the content of the questions and answers, or to reformulate the sequence in which they are asked, or the behavioral style of the question-answer routines (loud voice, hypercorrect pronunciation).

If social relations are an inherent dimension of learning tasks, and if the relationship of rights and obligations between teacher and learner does not include the right of both parties to engage in mutual scaffolding construction, we must ask what opportunities such school learning environments could provide as situations for the acquisition of reasoning skills. In addition, we must ask whether such environments can possibly be arenas for the enactment of civility, or whether civility—mutual commitment to participation in society, beyond the self—is impossible in such circumstances. It would seem that such environments are inimical to civility and that student disruption and resistance to learning and teacher frustration and "burnout" are reasonable responses to a work environment that is unreasonably controlled by external influences.

Ways of Speaking and Teacher-Student Interaction

Perspectives from Sociolinguistic Research

We have identified a factor that may limit students' acquisition of literacy and reasoning skills and that may vitiate civility in the school. This factor is not a fault of individual children or teachers. It is an aspect of social organization in schools—constraints on learner choice in task definition and on the ability of teachers and students to construct cognitive scaffolding together as they work on learning tasks. Some constraints come from outside the classroom: from administrative regulations and standard operating procedures and from the designers of curriculum materials. Other constraints come from within the room: from teachers' (and children's) culturally learned assumptions about the proper conduct of school teaching and learning.

Another factor has been identified by recent sociolinguistic research as a significant source of friction in classrooms and as an influence toward misjudgment of student performance and motivation by teachers. That factor is the attributions that are made about others on the basis of the language form they use in speaking. Interest in this issue has been central in sociolinguistics, an interdisciplinary field that links anthropology, sociology, social psychology, and linguistics. Sociolinguists have been concerned with what happens in social interaction and in perception when one or more persons use culturally patterned ways of speaking that do not match the cultural expectations of the others with whom they are interacting. This issue has been investigated in American classrooms in studies of cultural difference and cultural similarity between teachers and the students they teach.

Michaels and Collins (1984), for example, found that when working class American black children told narrative accounts in early grades classroom discussion the form the narratives took differed from the culturally standard narrative form used by middle class white children and white teachers. The standard form resembled written narrative, with an initial framing statement of the "point" to be made by the anecdote, followed by the story itself, which was thus framed as an instance of the more general point that was made. Within the narrative, key features of information were highlighted in culture-specific ways, grammatically and with voice tone.

When the working class black children told narratives they used culturally nonstandard narrative structure and nonstandard grammatical and intonational ways of marking emphasis at key points in the story. As they told stories in this way they were continually interrupted by the teachers. Close analysis of transcripts of the classroom dialogue revealed that the teachers interrupted the black children's stories precisely at those points at which the speech form differed from the culturally mainstream form of doing oral narration in ways similar to written narration. The teachers kept trying to repair points in the children's narratives, at which nothing had gone wrong, according to the cultural conventions of working class black oral discourse. The teachers apparently did not know how to "read" the children's talk as intelligible and coherent. This led to inappropriate attempts at scaffolding by the teacher, who apparently saw the child narrator as confused and/or inarticulate. The result repeatedly was frustration on the part of both teacher and child. A number of other researchers have found similar patterns of apparent cultural interference due to differences in ways of speaking and listening (e.g., DeStefano, Pepinsky, and Sanders, 1982; Eder, 1982; Erickson, 1979; see also the volume of relatively early work along these lines; Cazden, Hymes, and John, 1972).

Language form and discourse patterns are not the only aspects of speaking and listening that can lead to misperception of students by teachers. Cultural differences in assumptions of appropriateness in conversational turn-taking can also be a source of misperception that leads to trouble in the classroom. Gomes (1979), for example, reports that a kindergarten teacher misdiagosed a Cape Verdean child as potentially emotionally disturbed after three weeks of school, partly on the grounds that the child had been continually "interrupting" her and other children. Behaviorally, the child had been speaking before other persons' turns at speaking had been completed. That was what people did in the child's home. The teacher interpreted the child's culture-specific way of speaking as evidence of the child's emotional state. From the teacher's point of view that judgment made perfect sense. It was based, nonetheless, on misperception of the meaning of the child's actions, from the child's cultural point of view.

This line of work might seem to be claiming a simple, cultural determinist view of teacher-student conflict and of academic failure by cultural minority children. That is not the case. Cultural difference seems not only to be a source of conflict in social interaction; it can also be seen as a result of conflict. Social psychologists (e.g., Giles and Powesland, 1975) have found that in situations of experimentally induced conflict and negative affect, individuals who speak different dialects will speak progressively more broad forms of that dialect as interaction proceeds and conflict escalates. These experimental data trace a process of increased differentiation—what Bateson (1972, pp. 61–72) calls *schismogenesis*—across a short space of time. In a naturalistic study, Labov (1963–1972) has found a similar phenomenon occurring over a longer term. He finds that over a twenty-year period, features of the dialect spoken by natives of Martha's Vineyard have become increasingly different from the standard English spoken by upper middle class summer tourists. Labov interprets this as an instance of culture change as a symbol of political resistance in a situation of intergroup conflict. The islanders are dependent on the tourists as a source of income, but resent the situation of dependence, and manifest that by speaking in ways that are becoming more and more distinct from those of the tourists.

In an early grades classroom study, Piestrup (1973) found a similar phenomenon occurring in teacher-student interaction across a single school year. Working in recently desegregated schools, she audiotaped classroom dialogue between working class black students and their teachers. Some of the teachers were white; others were black. If over the course of the year the teacher reacted negatively to the child's nonstandard speech and continually attempted to get the child to speak more "correctly," the dialect features in the child's speech became broader as the year progressed. If the teacher did not react negatively to the child's speech at the beginning of the year, by the end of the year the dialect features in the child's speech had become less marked. The child was speaking more like standard English, apparently as a result of learning through the modeling of the teacher and the upper middle class white children in the room. This pattern held whether the teacher was white or black.

It seems that what Piestrup found was a process of cultural schismogenesis, or its absence, depending on the situation of micropolitics of cultural difference in the classroom. When the teacher made the child's way of speaking a grounds for conflict, the child joined in the conflict by becoming progressively more different from the teacher in interactional style. Apparently, in such a situation of conflict the child was refusing to learn from the modeling that was present in the scene and was also refusing to learn from direct instruction by the teacher. When the teacher did not make culture difference a ground for conflict, the child adapted in the direction of the normative style.

The classrooms Piestrup described can be seen as representing different civility conditions. In the former classrooms the children resisted commitment to a normative order and manifested that linguistically. In the latter classrooms the children manifested commitment to the normative order. Those were classrooms in which the teacher did not attempt to coerce commitment.

Cultural difference, then, seems to be entailed in the politics of intergroup contact and in the micropolitics of interaction in face-to-face encounters. In some situations culture difference can interfere with people's ability to work together. In other situations culture difference does not seem to interfere with successful cooperation, even though the interactional partners may have to work a bit harder at it than if they were not culturally different.

Piestrup's intriguing findings from classrooms are borne out in the experimental research of Giles and Powesland (1975) and in the naturalistic work reported in Erickson and Schultz (1982). In these studies of two-person conversations, cultural difference waxed and waned in its salience, depending on the micropolitics of the situation. Moreover, as cultural style difference became more marked, greater interactional difficulty occurred, and this covaried with negative person perception.

It would seem that culture difference plays a dual role in interactional trouble. Culture difference itself can lead to interactional trouble (lack of intelligibility, misunderstanding), which then may or may not become grounds for conflict that sustains and escalates. If the conflict is not sustained, even major interactional difficulties due to culture difference can be sidestepped, and cooperation can be maintained. However, if the conflict is sustained, the conflict itself apparently feeds back on the cultural difference, beginning a cycle of schismogenesis. On the other hand, in a situation in which conflicts exist at the outset, very small differences in cultural style (e.g., dialect, dress), which on the face of it should not prevent cooperation, can be used in interaction as *resources* for conflict. In other words, when people consciously or unconsciously go looking for trouble in interaction, they can find reasons for conflict in cultural difference.

Sociolinguistic research thus suggests that cultural difference in ways of speaking and listening is an important factor in the acquisition of literacy and reasoning in schools and in the creation and maintenance of conditions of civility in the school social system. Cultural difference does not simply cause conflict between teachers and students—interactional trouble that inhibits student learning. But cultural difference can contribute to already existing grounds for conflict. It can lead to momentary struggles that under some conditions can develop into sustained battles, and under other conditions can not only not make for further trouble, but can serve as a positive resource in teaching.

Literacy and the Politics of Social Identity: Achieving School Failure

In reviewing the possible roles of culture difference in classroom teaching and learning we discussed the micropolitics of face-to-face interaction. Social theory of macropolitical processes provides yet another perspective on the American pattern of low school achievement in the use of canonical literacy and reasoning practices by children of working class and minority background.

Resistance theory explains the puzzlingly low school performance of students who in the "literacies" of practical reasoning in everyday life display impressive competence. Resistance theory is a subset of reproduction theory, a critical perspective on the role of schools in society as perpetuating class distinctions from one generation to the next. Bourdieu and Passeron (1977), for example, argue that definition of public school learning tasks in the normative terms of upper middle class and upper class elite cultural knowledge (written literacy as essay-like prose, reasoning as academic-like logical rigor) serves to put students of non-elite family background at a disadvantage when competing with elite students. Elite cultural knowledge and elite social standing are thus *reproduced* from generation to generation by the unfair advantage that elite students bring to school: the possession of *cultural capital*.

Resistance theory points out that non-elite students cooperate in this situation of unfair competition by disadvantaging themselves still further by refusing to learn. Failure to learn simple tasks of literacy and numeracy, from this point of view, is seen not as evidence of innate disability in the student, but as political resistance. In self-defeating attempts to fight back the student resists being defined by the school as a person of less worth than others. The child's defiance provides a more acceptable self-image than does agreement with the school's definition. Whether covert or overt, witting or unwitting, this resistance is unsuccessful because it can be redefined by the school system either as evidence of stupidity and/or low motivation in the learner or as evidence of culpable recalcitrance—the mark of the unrepentent sinner who deserves severe punishment.

Reproduction theory and its constituent, resistance theory, view as a sham the ostensibly benign ideology of equality of educational opportunity, with the school as a rational, formal organization whose manifest aims are to deliver its services under conditions of maximum fairness. On the contrary, it is argued, the school sets up the non-elite child for failure by defining learning tasks in the way it does.

The argument of reproduction theory is persuasive but flawed. Reproduction theory explains the seeming contradiction that children who show abilities outside school that they don't inside school must not simply be stupid or lazy. But the argument is a bit too pat. It presumes mechanistic, "top-down" relations of cause and effect between the macro social order—social classes and their inherent conflict, institutions and their inherent contradictions between manifest and latent aims—and the micro social order of face-to-face relations in classrooms. It is an overdetermined social theory that denies any autonomous reality to social life and choice at the level of everyday conduct of life—in this case, the level of everyday life in classrooms. Ostensibly belonging to the stream of neo-Marxist critical theory, an overdrawn reproduction theory has all the weaknesses of vulgar Marxism. It denies any reality to social and cognitive choice at the level of the individual. We have seen empirical evidence of such choice in the current research in cognitive anthropology, cross-cultural psychology, and sociolinguistics that has been reviewed here, and we have seen the importance of such choice making by learners and by teachers in the interactional construction of learning environments that foster or inhibit student learning.

Resistance theory lacks some of the flaws of its parent, reproduction theory. It grants reality to social organization at the level of face-to-face relations and thus avoids the reductionism of reproduction theory. In a sympathetic yet critical review, Giroux (1983) takes resistance theory to task for fallacies of loose thinking, especially for the fallacy of overgeneralization. Every instance of student misbehavior—scrawled writing on an assignment, failure to complete an assignment, fighting, taking drugs, absenteeism—cannot be interpreted as evidence of resistance. The analysis of resistance as a phenomenon must be more judicious to be persuasive, Giroux argues. Still, resistance theory is attractive because it can account for linkages between macrosocial and microsocial processes without reducing either level to the other. Resistance theory, despite its limitations, is powerfully explanatory. It accounts more comprehensively and realistically for the phenomenon of massive school failure among the poor than does classical liberal social theory, whose naive view of schooling as an unmixed blessing for those deserving poor who are willing to take advantage of the opportunities given them ignores unpleasant facts of life in urban and rural schools with predominantly low SES student populations. Resistance theory, judiciously construed, also avoids the problem of crude determinism found in reproduction theory.

The point is not to assign blame for social pathology, identifying either the school and capitalist America as victimizer of innocent youth or the low achieving child as a defective incorrigible who deserves the judgment of failure that he or she receives. What is needed is a valid analysis of the pathology; moreover, we need an analysis of present conditions of illness that might point beyond itself to conditions of health. Resistance theory provides part of what is needed on the way to discovering some answers by allowing us to look at what is happening in schools without blaming a victim or castigating a victimizer.

The view is at once pessimistic and affirming. It proposes that children failing in school are working at achieving that failure. The view does not wash its hands of the problem at that point. It maintains, however, that intervention to break the cycle of school failure must start by locating the problem jointly in the processes of society at large and in the interactions of specific individuals. It is the frontline deliverers of educational services and their clients, that is, teachers (and other building-level staff) and students, who work together to achieve the school failure that is attributed to the student alone by the conventional wisdom of professional educators and of the lay public.

Student alienation from learning has been most obvious at the high school level, and a number of studies have documented it. In an interesting case study that was done before the advent of resistance theory, Cusick (1973) described student alienation from academic work in an urban high school. He traced the daily rounds of small sets of students who were friends. Cusick shows the students as remarkably adept at avoiding academic learning across the school day. They certainly seemed to be working actively at achieving school failure.

Student resistance has been described in high schools that differ considerably from the typical American ones. Willis (1977) has written a report of academic alienation among British working class high school youth. That study has become a modern classic. His research was done from the explicit perspective of resistance theory, which has developed mainly through the work of British scholars in the so-called "new sociology of education" (see Young and Whitty, 1977). Scollon and Scollon (1981) examine the issue of dramatic underachievement in written literacy by Alaskan natives in rural areas. The Scollons take a sociolinguistic and anthropological perspective. In their interpretation, Alaskan native teenagers come to see the acquisition of Western written literacy as a kind of metaphoric adoption of a new ethnic group identity. To become literate in school terms would be to disaffiliate symbolically from their parents and other members of the Alaskan native village, a few of whom are "literate" in traditional knowledge and skill, such as that involved in hunting, and many of whom are marginally literate in school-like practices of literacy. Caught in ambivalence between multiple cultural worlds, Alaskan native youth resist adopting the complete system of school-defined literacy, and then suffer the consequences of marginal acquisition. They do not belong fully to the old ways or to the new.

Resistance as an explanation for school failure has been most obvious and has seemed most plausible when applied to high school students. This may be partly due to the nature of the comprehensive high school curriculum, with explicit tracking and various options for student choice within tracks—options that students can take that disadvantage them further by the absence of challenge in the courses chosen. Current attention to student resistance in high school may also be due to the salience of adolescent acting out and authority testing, which is seen as part of a natural developmental process: identity formation on the way to adulthood.

Relatively little emphasis has been placed on resistance as an explanation for academic difficulties of children in the early grades. Children at that age, it is assumed, are not needing to distance themselves from adults the way teenagers do. Indeed, child development theory would suggest that the early grades student identifies with the teacher as a parent surrogate.

One notable exception to the lack of studies of student resistance at the grade school level is the work of McDermott (1974, 1977). In detailed micro-analysis of videotapes of instruction in reading groups, McDermott shows ways in which students in the "bottom" reading group work actively at not reading. The teacher, apparently unwittingly, cooperates with this. The analysis shows how, in the interactional tug of war that happens daily in the bottom reading group, the children in that group get much less reading instruction than do the children in the top group. But the children themselves help create that situation. It is not simply a matter of ethnic or racial bias on the teacher's part; the students are refusing to learn simple cognitive skills apparently as a form of micropolitical resistance.

This line of empirical and theoretical work suggests that we need to move beyond simple, single-factor explanations of school failure in literacy and reasoning and in the breakdown of the social contract of civility in schools. Explanations that locate the source of the problem in genetic deficits in learners, or in cultural deprivation, or even in cultural difference by itself, all seem inadequate. Reproduction theory, at least that which is crudely stated, also seems inadequate. We need theory and empirical work that accounts for and describes the macro- and micropolitical economy of the social and cultural organization of the teaching and learning of school literacy and reasoning practices. If we came to better understand the processes by which the unequal distribution of knowledge and skill in our society is produced (see Mehan, 1979) we would be doing more adequate social research. We would also be providing information on which to base policies that might transcend the partial attempts at amelioration of the recent past—efforts which were well intentioned but which in retrospect seem to have been misdirected. There seems at this point to be no quick fix, no single-factor amelioration for what appear to be mutually constituted sets of systemic problems across multiple levels of social structure.

Two Modest Success Stories and Some Questions about Them

It would be wrong to conclude with the previous paragraph. At best it ended on a bleak note. At worst, the previous discussion may have seemed to suggest that large-scale social change is the only way to better the educational chances of non-elite students. That may be true, but it is probably simplistic. In this final section we will consider two cases in which something less than societal transformation seemed to make a difference in the school performance of typically low-performing students. The cases involve changes in everyday practices at the levels of the school and classroom. While educational reform may well need to go beyond those levels, it may be instructive to consider some changes that principals and teachers could make within the existing school system.

A Case of Alaskan Native Children

Barnhardt (1982) reports a study of an Alaskan Athabaskan native village school in which the students did much better academically than did their typical native village school counterparts, as indicated by end of the year scores on standardized tests, which, in the present mood of concern for educational productivity are the basic currency of school administrators. (I do not mean to argue here for the validity of this ubiquitous criterion of productivity, but in this case and in the one that follows, the test scores do show clear differences from the usual pattern of low achievement by non-elite, cultural minority students.)

The village school had three classrooms, grades 1–2, 3–4, and 5–6. Each of the three teachers in the school was native Alaskan, and each was a lifelong resident of the village. The curriculum was in English. It was the standard curriculum mandated by the state.

Apparently, everything in the school was culturally mainstream except for the pattern of social relations the teachers used in delivering instruction. The teachers used means of exercising social control that were more indirect than those usually employed by nonnative teachers. These were patterns of indirection—ways of not putting individual children on the spot—that have been identified among various Native American groups in studies of child rearing and of home-school experience (see especially Erickson and Mohatt, 1982; Philips, 1972, 1982). In short, the content of instruction was standard, but the process of instruction was nonstandard in subtle ways. School instruction was congruent with patterns of social relationship found in home and community life in the village.

Indirect social control by the teachers provided opportunities for the children to make some choices that a more usual way of teaching might not have made available. There were opportunities to redefine learning tasks, as well as opportunities for self-pacing and for practice in private until mastery had been achieved. These opportunities for choice seem especially significant in light of our previous discussion of psychological research on the importance of a social relationship between teacher and student that allows each some leeway for negotiation—not too much, but not too little either. The leeway seems to have enabled the teachers and students to work out a form of proleptic instruction.

In these classrooms taught by unusually effective Native American teachers, students were held accountable for doing standard academic work. The social organizational means by which they accomplished that work differed slightly from the standard means more usually found in American classrooms.

That these differences were relatively small in amount does not mean that they were not significant in kind. Indeed, our earlier discussion of literacy activities as practices emphasized the importance of culture-specific patterns in the social relationships involved in tasks. According to that view, when one has changed slightly the nature of the social relationship between teacher and learner one has changed fundamentally the nature of the academic task.

Cultural congruence in school learning task definition is one explanation for the high achievement of the students in the Alaskan school. A competing interpretation is that since the teachers were lifelong members of the small village community they had much greater legitimacy than non-native teachers. They could hold students accountable for academic work under conditions of civility, given the legitimacy of their authority, from the point of view of the children and of their parents. Since I have already criticized cultural determinist arguments as inadequate, and since the competing interpretation is plausible, it may well be that both the cultural organization of instruction and the legitimacy of the instructor were working together. We still want from this case a clearer notion of what was going on. We want to know why fine tuning in social relationships, or legitimacy of the teacher, or both together might have influenced the Native American students to perform so well in this particular village school.

A Case of Hawaiian Native Children

Au and Mason (1981) report a study of culturally congruent reading instruction that begins to resolve some of the questions that remain from the Alaskan case. Here the cultural factor that seemed to make a difference was the turn-taking organization of first grade reading group conversations about stories in the basal reader.

Working class Hawaiian natives belong to a speech community in which it is customary to tell anecdotes and discuss them in small groups of speakers who talk while others are talking. Such simultaneous speaking is not seen as impolite interruption, but as comfortable engagement and as evidence of interest on the part of the participants in the conversation. The ubiquity of this pattern for the social organization of conversational participation was established by anthropological fieldwork (see Watson-Gegeo and Boggs, 1977). The name for such speech events in the community is *talk story*.

Au and Mason (1981) report that when reading story discussion was conducted with the overlapping turn-taking patterns characteristic of talk story, children spoke more coherently and learned more than they did when the lessons were conducted in a one-speaker-at-a-time pattern. The latter way of organizing group conversation is characteristic of school-like ways of speaking. The former way of organizing, allowing multiple speakers, is characteristic of community-like speech.

As in the Alaskan case, the teachers in Hawaii developed a mixed cultural form. Conversation in the reading lesson was not nearly so overlapping among speakers as it was in talk-story events in the community. But the teachers allowed children to move slightly in the direction of overlapping and co-narration. The teachers steered the discussion strongly, and in doing so gave higher order comprehension instruction. In exchange for that capacity to control topic, it seems, the teachers were allowing students to converse in ways that were familiar and comfortable to them. Au and Mason characterize this trade-off as a "balance of rights" between leadership and followership. It may be that this balance of rights provides the social organizational leeway for teacher and students to construct proleptic, mutually accommodating instruction, in which interaction could proceed by a mutually ratifiable social contract, and in consequence student resistance was not set off by the teacher's way of teaching.

Au and Mason's study is of special significance because it combined naturalistic observation and hypothesis generation with experimental hypothesis testing. The two treatment conditions (talk story-like, and non talk story-like conversation patterns) were varied across a series of lessons in which the reading difficulty was held constant. Tests administered immediately after the lessons, as well as error analysis and other proximal indicators of children's reading achievement within the lessons themselves, showed that the Hawaiian native children clearly read better when the social organization of lesson interaction was culturally congruent.

As in the Alaskan case, the social organization of lesson interaction by itself was probably not the only factor influencing the dramatically improved literacy acquisition of the children. The reading instruction received was only one part of a special program of curriculum and pedagogy developed by the Kamehameha Early Education Project in Honolulu. It seems significant, however, that when everything in the classroom stayed the same except the pattern of conversational turn-taking in the reading lesson, the reading achievement of the children was clearly higher than the culturally congruent form of social organization in instruction.

Why this was so is still not clear. We lack a theory of pedagogy that accounts for social cognition together with cognition about what we usually think of as the academic subject matter content (see Erickson, 1982, for elaboration on this point). It may be that culturally congruent instruction simplifies the task environment. In the Hawaiian case if familiar conversation patterns are used and the child does not have to attend to those as well as to the content discussed, perhaps the child is enabled to devote more attention to the content of reading instruction than the child could in a situation of unfamiliar conversational rules. But we can argue plausibly along other lines. It may be that culturally congruent instruction depoliticizes cultural difference in the classroom, and that such depoliticization has important positive influences on the teacher-student relationship. Such a situation in the classroom might prevent the emergence of student resistance and of intercultural schizmogenesis. In addition, macropolitical conflict may well bear on the micropolitics of classroom life in ways whose specifics we do not yet understand.

I have reviewed a number of new ways of thinking about academic learning tasks. The work raises more questions than it answers. At this point we still don't know what aspects of cultural patterning bear strongly on proleptic instruction and scaffolding. The notions of prolepsis, scaffolding, learning tasks as practices, culturally congruent instruction, resistance, and the micropolitics of classroom life are all emergent notions in developing theories. To continue new work along these new lines seems to be a good way to proceed in order to deepen our theoretical and practical understanding of schools as environments for learning literacy, reasoning, and civility.

To conclude, human learning as well as human teaching needs to be seen as a social transaction, a collective enterprise. Society, culture, teacher, and student interpenetrate in the definition and enactment of learning tasks. Much recent educational research on school and teacher effectiveness has taken an individualistic view of learning and teaching. The curricular reform attempts of the recent past attempted to change the academic content of instruction without institutionalizing the fundamental changes in social relations between teachers and students that would enable the kind of learning environment necessary for teaching higher order cognition in schools. The current public mood seems to be to constrain teacher-student interaction still further, to try to improve performance by getting tougher on teachers as well as on students. The lines of work reviewed here argue for a different approach and for a different definition of the problem. It may be that teachers need more control over their ways of teaching, not less. For classroom teachers to have more authority as well as more responsibility would be a change in the allocation of power—social change in schools as institutions and in the society that maintains those schools. From a sociocultural point of view, literacy, reasoning, and civility as daily school practices cannot be associated and reordered apart from the fabric of society in which those practices take place.

14.
Literacy and Schooling in Subordinate Cultures

The Case of Black Americans

John U. Ogbu

Literacy is currently receiving a good deal of attention from researchers, policy-makers, and professional educators. Common concerns are the development of literacy among children and the problem of literacy competence or functional literacy among adults. In industrialized nations like the United States these problems are regarded as particularly acute among the lower class and subordinate minorities.

The literacy problem of subordinate minorities, the focus of this paper, is threefold and relative, the latter because it derives partly from comparing minorities with the dominant group. One aspect of the problem is that a larger proportion of minorities has not successfully learned to read, write, and compute. Another is that a greater proportion of minorities is not functionally literate. That is, they are unable to demonstrate the ability to read, write, or compute in social and economic situations that require these skills; for example, they cannot fill out job applications and income-tax forms or read and comprehend instructional manuals and utilize the information. Third, school children among subordinate minorities lag behind their dominant-group peers in reading and computation as judged by classroom grades and scores on standardized tests.

Our research since the late 1960s has been on this lag in minority student's performance, and we have compared the situation in the United States with those in other countries like Britain, India, Israel, Japan, and New Zealand. For this paper, we will limit our discussion to black Americans, beginning with the current hypothesis that black children fail disproportionately in school because they come from a predominantly oral culture which engenders a discontinuity in

From *Literacy in Historical Perspective*, edited by Daniel Resnick. Washington, D.C.: Library of Congress, 1983.

their participation in the literate culture of the school. We will then suggest an alternative interpretation of the disproportionate school failure of black children in its historical and structural context.

Oral Culture, Literate Culture, and School Performance

Shifting Theories of Language Research

Over the past two decades, there has been a continuing shift in theories generated by language studies to explain the disproportionate failure among blacks to learn to read. A brief review of these theories, as provided by Simons (1976), will take us to the current hypothesis that school failure among blacks, especially in reading, is due to the fact that they come from an essentially oral culture.

Initially, the field of language studies was dominated by a deficit perspective, whose hypothesis (which still survives in some quarters) is that black dialect is inferior to standard English and constitutes a handicap in the thinking and learning of blacks. Ethnographic studies by Labov (1972) and others showed that this model was false, and it was replaced by the difference perspective, whose initial hypothesis asserted that black dialect is different from standard English but still constitutes a viable system of thinking and learning. Black children failed, especially in reading, because a "mismatch between children's language and the language used in school and in the reading texts interfered with black children's acquisition of reading skills" (Simons 1976:3). That is, schools did not use black dialect as a medium of teaching and learning.

Efforts to use black dialect in texts and in the classroom, while teaching standard English, did not, however, improve reading achievement among black children. Critics charged that the difference hypothesis focused too much on materials and teachers and failed to specify the mechanisms by which the interference or mismatch occurred. Critics proposed two types of interference, the first of which was phonological. It was thought that differences in pronunciation "might interfere with the acquisition of word recognition skills," but this was subsequently shown not to be a significant factor (Simons 1976:8; see also Rentel and Kennedy 1972). The second hypothesized interference was grammatical; that is, a "mismatch between black child's syntax and the standard English syntax of the texts used by the teacher" (Baratz 1969; Stewart 1969). But reading achievement among black children who read materials written in black dialect grammar did not significantly improve. It was concluded from these studies that black dialect was not the source of the failure of children to learn to read (Simons 1976:11).

In the early 1970s a new hypothesis moved beyond language *per se* to the broader area of communication strategies, speculating that school failure is caused by a mismatch between communicative etiquettes of teachers and students, especially during reading. The hypothesis holds that teachers and minority students who come from different cultures have different communicative strategies and interpretations of situated meanings that lead to miscommunication during reading activities. This interferes with children's acquisition of reading skills.

What is at issue is what is *communicated* by the classroom environment, not the differences in the cultural backgrounds or languages of the teacher and students. The goal of research is to isolate the processes that are meaningful to the participants in classroom communication. Philip's notion of participant structure (1972) provides the conceptual framework for this research. Basically, a participant structure is "a constellation of norms, mutual rights and obligations that shape social relationships, determine participants' perceptions about what is going on, and influence learning" (Simons 1976). Subordinate minority-group children have different participant structures at home than at school, and their generally poor school performance is attributed to this discontinuity.

I have criticized this mismatch hypothesis (Ogbu 1980a), on three grounds. First, it does not warrant generalization about minority school failure because it is based primarily on research into only one type of minority group, namely, castelike minorities. It does not explain why other minorities, who also have different participant structures at home than at school, learn to read in the same classrooms where blacks and similar groups fail. Second, the mismatch model ignores historical and societal forces which may actually generate the pattern of classroom processes. And third, although data and insights from studies based on the mismatch model can be used for remedial efforts (Simons 1976; Erickson 1978), they cannot lead to social change that would eventually eliminate the need for remedial efforts.

Oral Culture and Literacy

The most recent development in language studies focuses on literacy and attributes the disproportionate school failure of blacks and similar minorities to a discontinuity between their essentially oral cultures and the literate culture of the white middle-class represented by the public schools. This hypothesis is based on studies of literacy and its consequences in traditional or small-scale societies (Goody 1977; Luria 1976); on studies of language and communicative styles in minority communities (Labov 1969; Abrahams 1970; Kochman 1973); and on microethnographic studies of teacher-pupil interactions in classrooms (Erickson and Mohatt 1977, cited in Koehler 1978; Gumperz 1979; Philips 1972).

Reviewing studies of both nonliterate, small-scale societies and literate Western societies, Lewis (1979) argues that participants in oral cultures differ significantly from participants in literate cultures, whose sensory orientations are aural rather than oral. She cites a large body of evidence that these two sensory orientations generate contrasting notions of time, causality, space, and the self "which affect the way children are raised and interact with adults" (p. 2). Although the contrast is primarily between non-Western nonliterate populations and Western middle-class populations, she coins the term "residual oral cultures" or "residual oral peoples" to designate segments of Western societies (e.g., subordinate minorities and the lower class) in which many people have minimal knowledge of reading and writing, arguing that these populations resemble in many respects those of nonliterate small-scale societies. Lewis claims that the disproportionate school failure of minority and lower-class children in the United States is due to their participation in those essentially oral cultures. As she puts it,

> [In] our society, the schools as key institutions of literate culture tend to reject the oral tradition. As a result, the relatively illiterate find their assumptions about reality in conflict with school expectations. This conflict insures failure and exacerbates other experiences of race and class exclusion (p. 2).

One difficulty with Lewis's formulation is the questionable extent to which one can generalize from small-scale Asian and African societies to groups historically subordinated by their class, ethnic, and racial backgrounds in complex industrial societies. Furthermore, the introduction of literacy or schooling in the small-scale societies does not usually result in the same types of problems it often creates among subordinate minorities and the lower class in the United States (Heyneman 1979; van den Berghe 1979). To the contrary, the introduction of schooling in small-scale societies tends to increase cognitive and linguistic or communicative similarities to the pattern of middle-class populations of industrialized societies (Cole and Scribner 1973; Greenfield 1976; Luria 1976). Why, then, after generations of school attendance by blacks and centuries of interaction with whites, haven't their cognitive and communicative strategies changed to those of the white middle class?

Finally, we know that descendants of illiterate Asian and European immigrants (who might be regarded as "residual oral peoples") have achieved greater success in American public schools than subordinate minorities. For example, studies of Chinese peasant villages in the 1930s (Pepper 1971: 199; Snow 1961: 69) showed that illiteracy rates were often as high as 90 percent. But children of illiterate Chinese peasant immigrants have done quite well in American schools. Gumperz and Cook-Gumperz have proposed a sociolinguistic formulation of the problem (1979). Drawing from the work of Goody (1977) and Luria (1976), they contrast oral and literate cultures in terms of (1) storage and transmission of knowledge, (2) decontextualization of knowledge, and (3) cognitive strategies in communication and learning. They argue (1) that in oral cultures stored knowledge is static and its transmission inaccurate, whereas in literate cultures change is built into knowledge and its transmission is accurate; (2) that knowledge acquisition and transmission in literate cultures, unlike oral cultures, are decontextualized; and (3) that in literate cultures a distinctive mode of reasoning emerges that is separate from everyday activities. Using these three domains of change as criteria, the authors contend that the *home*, in contrast to *school*, is a place of oral culture, and they suggest the changes children must make in their cognitive and communicative strategies in order to learn and use written language effectively. They summarize the process involved in the transition from oral to written culture for all children as follows:

> Developmentally the transition from speaking to writing as a medium for learning about the world of others requires a change from the interpretative strategies of oral cultures in which children grow up, to the interpretative principles of discursive written language. The move into literacy requires children to

make some basic adjustments to the way they socially attribute meaning to events and the processes of every day world in order to be able to loosen their dependence upon contextually specific information and to adopt a decontextualized perspective. Among other things, they must learn to rely on an incrementally acquired knowledge rather than on what is said within any one context. In another dimension the move into literacy requires children linguistically to change their process of interpretation (p. 16).

Gumperz and Cook-Gumperz imply that literacy problems began in the present century with industrialization, bureaucratization, and other socioeconomic changes which have tended to (a) erase the boundaries between elite and popular education; (b) increase the dichotomy between speaking and writing; (c) make literacy prerequisite to economic survival; and (d) institute evaluation of literacy competence through methods which take no account of the socioeconomic changes (Gumperz and Cook-Gumperz 1979:11–12).

If this twentieth-century situation creates problems for all children, why do some children make the transition to literacy more easily than others? According to the authors, some oral cultures prepare children better than others: "The argument we have been developing," they state, "is that for all children the literacy experience requires essential changes in the processing of verbal information. For some children, however, the shift of understanding of written language is sometimes facilitated by early language experience; the child is able early in life to gain processing experience of the written word" (p. 27). Elsewhere, after reviewing several microethnographic studies of communicative interaction between teachers and children of subordinate groups (e.g., Native Americans, blacks, Native Hawaiians, rural Appalachians, and working-class British), Gumperz sums up the underlying cause of their disproportionate school failure as follows:

> This work highlights the point that children's responses to school tasks are directly influenced by values and presuppositions learned in the home. It demonstrates moreover that classroom equipments, spatial arrangements or social groupings of teachers and students are not the primary determinants of learning. What is important is what is *communicated* in the classroom as a result of complex processes of interaction between educational goals, background knowledge and what various participants perceive over time as taking place (1980:5).

The authors have certainly made an important contribution to our understanding of the cognitive and linguistic changes all children make in learning to use written language. But their implicit and explicit explanations of the special problem of minorities is essentially one of mismatch of communicative etiquettes which we previously criticized. Furthermore, in looking at the problem historically, we find that the educational experiences of blacks and other subordinate minorities in the United States (e.g., Chicanos, Indians) do not conform to the nineteenth century situation described by the authors (Ogbu 1978). Though many Americans idealize education for its own sake, for most Americans, and for blacks in particular, it has been aimed at developing marketable skills. We shall return to this point later.

The oral culture-literate culture discontinuity hypothesis seems inadequate to explain the disproportionate school failure of subordinate minority children. We shall suggest an adequate hypothesis which considers both historical and macro-structural forces that shape classroom processes under which children acquire their literacy. But first we wish to distinguish subordinate minorities from other minorities who do not necessarily share similar problems in school and from lower-class people for the same reason.

Stratification as a Context: Castelike and Class

We define a given population as a minority group if it is in a subordinate power relation to another population in the same society. A minority status is not determined by mere number because the subordinate group might outnumber the dominant group, as the Bantu in South Africa outnumber whites by more than 2 to 1. For some purposes, such as education, it is useful to distinguish different types of minorities, and in our work we have classified minorities into autonomous, castelike and immigrant types.

Autonomous minorities, which are represented in the United States by Jews and Mormons, are also found in most developing Asian and African nations. They are primarily numerical minorities who may be victims of prejudice but are not totally subordinated in systems of stratification, and their separateness is not based on specialized denigrated economic, political, or ritual roles. Moreover, they often have a cultural frame of reference which demonstrates and encourages success in education and other areas as defined by the larger society.

Castelike minorities—those we have referred to as subordinate minorities—are either incorporated into a society more or less involuntarily and permanently or are forced to seek incorporation and then relegated to inferior status. In America, for example, blacks were incorporated through slavery; Chicanos and Indians through conquest.

Castelike minorities are generally regarded as inherently inferior by the dominant group, who thus rationalize their relegation to inferior social, political, economic, and other roles. Until recently it was (and in many instances still is) more difficult for castelike minority-group members than for dominant-group members to advance on the basis of individual training and ability. The concept of a job ceiling (Ogbu 1978) at best describes the circumscribed occupational and economic opportunities historically faced by castelike minorities. A job ceiling is set by the pressures and obstacles that consign minorities to jobs at the lowest levels of status, power, dignity, and income and meanwhile allow the dominant group to acquire the jobs and rewards above those levels. As we shall argue, the access of castelike minorities to schooling and their perceptions of and responses to schooling have historically been shaped by the job ceiling and related barriers.

Immigrant minorities are those who have come more or less voluntarily (unless they are refugees) to their new society for economic, political, and social self-betterment. Immigrants may be subject to pillory and discrimination but have usually not internalized their effects. That is, at least in the first generation, they have not experienced such treatment as an ingrained part of their culture and thus have not been disillusioned to the same extent as castelike minorities. This is true even when the two minority types are faced with the same job ceiling and other barriers. Immigrants also tend to measure their success or failure against that of their peers in their homeland and not against the higher classes of their host society. (See Ogbu 1978, for further elaboration of these and other factors that differentiate immigrants from castelike minorities).

Minority groups do not usually accept subordination passively, though their responses vary. Some groups reduce or eliminate aspects of their subordination; others may actually reinforce some aspects of that subordination. Moreover, different types of minorities respond differently. Except for political emigres, the immigrants have the symbolic option of returning to their homeland or re-emigrating elsewhere. This option may, in fact, motivate the acquisition of education and literacy because immigrants can transfer these skills elsewhere for greater rewards. Because this option is usually not open to castelike minorities, they tend to develop various gross and subtle devices to raise, eliminate or circumvent the job ceiling and other barriers. We shall explore the important implications that these devices have for schooling and literacy.

Lower-Class and Castelike Minorities

Current discussion tends strongly to equate the education and literacy problems of castelike minorities with those of the lower class. But the differences between them appear in the attempt to distinguish castelike stratification from class stratification. "Caste" or "castelike" in this essay is a purely methodological reference to the structural form underlying the history of minority subordination in America and similar societies.

In a class stratification people are ranked by their education, their jobs, their behavior and how much money they make; that is, by achieved criteria. Lower-class individuals have difficulty advancing into higher classes by achieving more wealth and education or better jobs and social positions because they lack requisite training (education), ability, or proper connections. But class stratification, at least in the United States, has a built-in ideology which encourages lower-class people to strive for social and economic self-betterment that would put them and/or their children into higher classes. This social mobility occurs enough among white Americans that they view America as a land of great opportunity and success as a matter of ability, perseverance, and education (Berreman 1972; Warner *et al*. 1945).

In a castelike stratification people are, by contrast, assigned to their respective groups at birth or by ascribed criteria such as skin color, and they have few options to escape that designation. Each caste group (e.g., blacks in America) has its own class system but less opportunity for class differentiation and mobility than the dominant class system. For example, the job ceiling in the United States affects black-white racial stratification but not the stratification of social classes within the white group or within the black group. Caste thus gives class in the minority population added disadvantages: a white lower-class American is only lower class; a black lower-class American is also faced with a job ceiling and other caste barriers.

There is current debate over whether and to what extent class stratification has replaced racial or castelike stratification in America (Willie 1979; Wilson 1978). Since the 1960s, civil rights legislation and other efforts have raised the job ceiling and somewhat reduced other racial barriers, but they have not eliminated these barriers altogether. No one knows the extent to which blacks are now employed in more desirable jobs as a matter of compliance with the law. What is certain is that the number of blacks in top jobs more than doubled after affirmative action legislation went into effect in 1966 and 1972; that there is a strong white resistance to these laws; and that blacks are still underrepresented in desirable jobs and overqualified for the jobs that they do (Brimmer 1974; U.S. Commission on Civil Rights 1978).

Furthermore, the positive changes have not reached far enough to affect significantly the social and economic conditions of the black lower class; nor have they been consistent through the years because of economic recessions, white backlash, and changes in political climate. Statistics easily conceal the single most important indication that castelike stratification persists in America: the extraordinary supports (affirmative action, Equal Employment Opportunities Commission Appeals, Special Programs) that blacks need, but that whites do not, in order to move into the middle class. The pattern of change is significant for the problem of education and literacy in that black perceptions of American racial stratification and their opportunities within it have not grown to resemble the perceptions of the white population.

A Cultural Ecological Explanation of Black School Failure

The Framework

Cultural ecology provides a more adequate framework for understanding the literacy problems of black and similar minorities, whether we focus on school completion, functional literacy, or performance on classroom and standardized tests. This framework enables us to study the connections between the school or learning processes *and* societal forces (such as economic patterns and opportunities, intergroup relations, and status mobility in a given society) which affect school curricula, classroom attitudes and efforts, and various activities of school personnel and other members of the educational system.

Cultural ecology is the study of institutionalized and socially transmitted patterns of behavior interdependent with features of the environment (Netting 1968:11; see also Geertz 1962; Goldschmidt 1971; Bennett 1969). It does not deal with the over-all physical environment but with the effective environment, that is, those aspects that directly affect subsistence quest (techno-economic activities) and physical survival. In modern societies the effective environment is primarily the bureaucratized industrial economy. A given population's effective environment generally consists, however, of its resources, its ability to exploit these resources, and its level of technology. The principal economic activities or subsistence strategies depend upon the effective environment. And each mode of exploitation calls for specific skills, knowledge, and other attributes which facilitate subsistence and survival under the specific condition. Ecological adaptation for a given population consists of the congruence or fit between the population's strategies for subsistence, survival, and status and the instrumental competencies and related behaviors of its members. Adaptation for an individual consists of learning about resources and exploitative strategies and acquiring appropriate instrumental competencies and rules of behaviors for achievement as it is defined by for his or her social group.

Childrearing and formal education are culturally organized to insure that children in a given population meet these criteria for adaptation (Ogbu 1980). In modern societies the school is the principal institution adapting children to bureaucratized industrial economy in four ways: teaching them the basic practical skills of reading, writing, and computation essential for almost every subsistence activity in the economy; preparing them for more specialized job training when they later enter the labor force (Wilson 1973); socializing them by means of organizational features (teacher-pupil authority relations, the grading system, etc.) to develop social-emotional attributes essential for participation in the work force (Scrupski 1975; Wilcox 1978); and providing the credentials young adults need to enter the work force (Jencks 1972). In the latter role, schooling is more or less a culturally institutionalized device for allocating and rewarding individuals in society's status system, particularly in the economy (Ogbu 1979 a, b; 1980).

While ideologically most Americans do not see their schools this way, it is a reasonable analysis based on our own study of school and economic behaviors in Stockton, California. In our research, we asked people why they go to school; why they send their children to school; and why they pay taxes to support schools; we listened to public and private discussions and gossip about schooling, jobs, and related matters; we examined documents from local school systems and from city and county planning departments, as well as from employment and welfare agencies. These sources suggest that Stocktonians do not seek education for its own sake, to satisfy their curiosity, or for self-fulfillment, but in order to get jobs as adults and thereby achieve full adult status as defined by their community. Not only do Stocktonians believe that more and better schooling leads to more desirable jobs, higher income, and other social and economic benefits, but local statistics also tend to support their belief—for the majority whites: In Stockton, as elsewhere in the nation, whites with high school diplomas generally have a better chance at more desirable jobs and greater lifetime earning power than their peers with only elementary school diplomas; however they have less chance at desirable jobs and less earning power than their peers with college degrees.

The belief that economic opportunities are commensurate with educational achievement is a part of local white epistemology and is borne out historically by the actual experiences of most whites in the job market. The belief is communicated to local white children and reinforced in a variety of ways. These observations lead us to conclude that the school efforts of local whites are greatly influenced by their experiences in and perceptions of the connection between schooling and adult economic participation.

A major ecological consequence of castelike stratification and job ceiling is that blacks in Stockton and elsewhere in the United States have traditionally occupied economic positions characterized by scarce, dead-end, peripheral, or unstable jobs and by low wages, few chances for advancement on the job, and little social credit as measured by values of the larger society. Some ghetto blacks occupy economic positions that are almost devoid of any wage labor but that contain social resources such as other ghetto residents and caretaker institutions (Harrison 1972; Ross and Hill 1967). Equally important is the fact that the blacks' effective environment contains, in addition to these conventional resources, a subeconomy or "street economy" defined as "a market for the distribution of goods and services which are in demand but have been outlawed officially for social and moral reasons" (Bullock 1973: 100, see also Foster 1974; Heard 1968; Milner 1970; Wolfe 1970).

Educational Consequences

What are the educational consequences of the black effective environment? Because the traditional social and economic positions of blacks have not required much formal education or rewarded educational accomplishments highly, the pattern of schooling which has evolved for blacks generally prepares them for inferior roles. It does not qualify blacks for the more desirable social and economic positions open to whites, nor does it encourage blacks to achieve their maximum. These combined factors have traditionally affected black literacy as measured by school completion, functional literacy, and performance on classroom and standardized tests. We now want to suggest four specific ways in which these factors sustain the lag in black school performance by (a) promoting certain treatment or experiences of blacks in school and classroom and (b) fostering certain classroom attitudes, orientations, and behavior.

(1) White Perceptions of Blacks and Black Access to Education

Blacks have had some access to formal schooling ever since they were brought to America in the early seventeenth century. Although formal education was available to only a few in the South (where most blacks lived before emancipation), and although there was strong opposition to black education in both the South and the North, actual legal prohibitions against black education were instituted in the South only from 1832 to about 1861 after Nat Turner's Revolt (Bond 1966:21; Bullock 1970). Black access to the public schools increased after emancipation, and, as the following table shows, their illiteracy rates steadily declined.

However, factors important to understanding the present situation are concealed by the table. First, blacks have had to fight for almost every increase in their access to public schools; in neither the South nor the North have they been free as a matter of right to attend their community public schools (Bond 1966; Bullock 1970; Kluger 1977; Ogbu 1978). Second, black education in both the South and North has usually been inferior, often separate, and generally based on white perceptions and stereotypes of black status in society and especially in the economy. Third, because blacks do not share white perceptions of their status, they tend not to accept white standards of education for them. Consequently, since the second half of the nineteenth century, blacks have been fighting whites against both inferior and separate education (Kluger 1977).

Let us briefly summarize how white perceptions of black status have shaped black education historically and affected the quality of black literacy. (See table 14.1).

Before emancipation, blacks received occasional biblical education because their masters believed it would make them more obedient and faithful. After the Civil War, when blacks were relegated to peon-like status as sharecroppers or were limited to "Negro jobs" in domestic service and unskilled labor, education followed suit. The ruling white elites believed the tenant farming system would break down if black children received the same education as white children. They would, for example, learn to question the high rates of interest and the exploitative accounting methods the planters imposed on illiterate tenants. Thus, black education was starved of funds.

As the South urbanized, blacks at first received some "industrial" education, chiefly in cooking and low grade building skills. But when many desirable factory jobs began to require special training, black school curricula began, ironically, to emphasize classical and academic rather than industrial education, which was now offered in white schools (Bond 1966: 404, Myrdal 1944: 897–98; Ogbu 1978: 117).

We can conclude that, historically, if blacks did not qualify for desirable jobs it was because their education was designed to disqualify them, not because they were incompetent. Until perhaps the 1960s, American society never seriously intended blacks to achieve social and occupational equality with whites through education.

Even now, "subtle mechanisms" continue to adapt black and white graduates to different futures. One such mechanism for lowering the job ceiling is the disproportionate labeling of black children as educationally "handicapped." For example, in a recent court case brought by blacks against the San Francisco School District, evidence showed that blacks made up only 31.1 percent of the school enrollment in 1976–77, but constituted 53.8 percent of those categorized as educable mentally retarded and relegated to special classes. In the same year, in the twenty California school districts which enrolled 80 percent of black children, black students comprised about 27.5 percent of the school population but 62 percent of those labeled educable mentally retarded. In his decision favoring blacks the judge concluded that

> The statistical analyses of the statewide and district-by-district figures indicate the obvious. Their (i.e., black) apparent overenrollment could not be the result of chance. For example, there is less than one in a million chance that the overenrollment of black children and the underenrollment of non-black children in the E.M.R. classes in 1976–77 would have resulted under a color-blind system of placement (U.S. District Court for Northern California, 1979: 21–22).

The figures are similar to those of other large American cities, including Chicago and New York (see, for example, U.S. Commission on Civil Rights, 1974).

(2) Black Responses

We pointed out earlier that castelike minorities do not usually accept their

Table 14.1
Black and White Illiteracy, 14 Years Old and Over, by Region for Selected
Years, 1890–1969
(Numbers in thousands)

Area and year	Black			White		
	Illiterate			Illiterate		
	Total	Number	Percent	Total	Number	Percent
United States:						
1890	4259	2607	61	35818	2880	8
1910	823	91	11	43091	1944	5
1930	8027	1445	18	77357	2350	3
1947	10471	1152	11	95952	1919	2
1959	12210	910	7	109163	1709	2
1969	14280	509	4	127449	891	1
South:						
1890	3769	2462	65	7755	1170	15
1910	5308	1906	36	12790	1087	8
1930	6116	1351	22	18390	780	4
North and West:						
1890	631	208	33	28063	1710	6
1910	823	91	11	43091	1944	5
1930	1911	94	5	58967	1570	3

Source: U.S. Department of Commerce, Bureau of the Census. *Current Population Reports, Special Studies. Series P-23, No. 80, The Social and Economic Status of the Black Population in the United States: An Historical View, 1790–1978.* Table 68, p. 91.

subordination passively and that blacks have been fighting since emancipation for more and better schooling and against the job ceiling. Those responses, as they relate to schooling and jobs, may in fact contribute to the lag in the school performance, as we shall demonstrate.

A. Black School Conflict and Mistrust: History has left blacks with a feeling that whites and their institutions cannot be trusted to benefit blacks equitably. Public schools, particularly in the ghetto, are generally not trusted by blacks to provide black children with the "right education." This mistrust of schools arises partly from black perceptions of past and current discriminatory treatment by public schools. This treatment is fully documented in several studies (see Bond 1966, 1969; Kluger 1977; Weinberg 1977).

For over a century, having first "fought" against total exclusion from the public schools, blacks have been "fighting" against inferior education in both segregated and integrated schools. In the totally segregated Southern school systems, blacks of course identified strongly and therefore cooperated with "black schools." But their effectiveness was undermined by their simultaneous rejection of these same schools as inferior to white schools and thus their need to "fight" for school desegregation. Their attention, commitment, and efforts were diverted from maximizing achievement in black schools to the pursuit of equal resources and an ideal learning setting, namely, desegregated schools.

But in desegregated schools throughout the nation disaffection and mistrust also abound because blacks see inferior education perpetuated through many subtle devices they suspected the schools of using (e.g., biased testing, misclassification, tracking, biased textbooks, biased counseling, etc.), and because they doubt that these schools understand black children and their needs.

This doubt is particularly widespread at the moment: it was openly expressed by many blacks at public meetings and in ethnographic interviews during our fieldwork in Stockton. In a study of a desegregated high school, Slawski and Scherer (1977) also found that local blacks tended to attribute low school performance of black males to the school's inability to "relate to black males in ways that will help them learn." The point we would like to stress is that black mistrust and conflict with schools reduce the degree to which black parents and their children can accept as legitimate the schools' goals, standards, and instructional approaches. As a result they tend not to experience a need to cooperate with the schools or to follow their rules and requirements for achievement.

The same conflicts and mistrust also force the schools into defensive approaches to black education—control, paternalism, or actual "contests"—which divert the attention of both blacks and schools from the real task of educating black children. This contrasts sharply with the experience of white middle-class parents and their children, who tend to see the completion of school tasks and conformity with school standards as necessary, desirable, and compatible with their own goals. Ghetto blacks tend sometimes to interpret the same demands as deceptions or as unnecessary impositions incompatible with their "real educational goals." Perseverance at academic tasks thus becomes difficult for black children.

B. Disillusionment Over Job Ceiling and Academic Efforts: Throughout history a greater proportion of blacks than whites have been educationally better qualified or overqualified for their jobs yet underpaid for their educational achievements (Henderson 1967; Norgren and Hill 1964; Newman *et al.* 1978; Sharp 1970; U.S. Commission on Civil Rights 1978). Even in recent years their gradual penetration into more desirable jobs has been accomplished mainly through collective struggle for civil rights (Newman *et al.* 1978; Scott 1976; Ogbu 1978). Job opportunities remain the primary concern of black Americans today.

The job ceiling and related discriminatory practices shape black operations, which in turn influence their perceptions of and responses to schooling. Blacks are generally bitter, frustrated, and resentful at the job ceiling and other barriers to the full benefits of their education. The extent of this bitterness is evident in the time and resources they expend in efforts to break or circumvent the job ceiling (see Davis, Gardner and Gardner 1965; Dollard 1957; Drake and Cayton 1970; Ogbu 1974; Powdermaker 1968; Newman *et al.* 1978; Scott 1976) as are their strategies for achieving their objectives, such as "uncle tomming," boycotting white businesses, protesting, rioting, and appealing to the courts, to Fair Employment Practices Commissions, to the Equal Employment Opportunity Commission, and the like (see Drake and Cayton 1970:745; National Advisory Commission on Civil Disorders, *Report* 1968:61; Newman *et al.* 1978:10–26; Ogbu 1978; Powdermaker 1968:107, 100, 112; Schemer 1965:85).

When civil rights effectively expand black employment opportunities and other rewards for education, as they appeared to be doing in the 1960s, this encourages black students to work hard in school (Ginsberg *et al.* 1967). But a discouraging message is also communicated, namely, that without such a collective civil rights struggle, blacks automatically have fewer opportunities than whites to benefit from education.

Black children learn about the job ceiling and other barriers quite early in life, though not necessarily from explicit statements by their parents and other adults in their community. In our ethnographic research in Stockton, California, we have found, however, that black parents communicate contradictory attitudes toward schooling. They emphasize the need for their children to get more education than they did, and they insist that their children work hard to order to get good grades and to graduate from high school and college. However, the same parents, by being unemployed, underemployed, and discriminated against, and by gossiping about the similar experiences of relatives and other adults in the community, imply that even if the children succeed in school their chances at good jobs and other societal rewards are not as good as those of their white peers. It is also a part of local black epistemology that a black person must be "twice as good" or "twice as qualified" as the white in order to compete successfully in any situation where whites are judges. Thus the actual example of the lives of black parents can undercut their stated encouragements.

Black children also learn about the job ceiling from public demonstrations calling for more jobs and better wages and from mass media reports of these and related events. These sources convey to black children that the connection between school success and one's ability to get ahead is not as good for blacks as for whites. As black children get older and experience personal failures and frustrations in looking for part-time jobs and summer jobs, these negative messages are reinforced. Some perceptions of young blacks, such as their impression of unlimited employment opportunities for their white peers, may not be accurate (Ogbu 1974); they nonetheless lead to increasing disillusionment among blacks about their future and to doubts about the value of schooling (Ogbu 1974:100; see also Frazier 1940:134–47; Schulz 1969:159; Powdermaker 1968:321).

Not only do these perceptions discourage black children from developing serious attitudes toward school and from persevering in their schoolwork; they also teach them to "blame the system" rather than themselves for their failures. In our research in Stockton we have found that black children learn very early to blame the school system for their failures, just as their parents and black adults in general blame their failures on the larger "system." A resulting paradox is that black students may express high educational aspirations coupled with low academic effort and perseverance and thus low school performance.

C. Survival Strategies and Competencies Incongruent with Demands of Schooling: Another black response to the job ceiling is the evolution of "survival strategies." This effects even children much too young to understand the labor market and other barriers and has serious implications for school performance and classroom processes. There are two kinds of survival strategies. The purpose of the first kind is to increase conventional economic and social resources of the black community and to make available conventional jobs and other societal rewards. These strategies include collective struggles or civil rights activities (Newman et al. 1978; Scott 1976), clientship or uncle tomming (Dollard 1957; Myrdal 1944; Farmer 1968; Ogbu 1978). Civil rights strategy is well known to most people; but clientship also arises from the job ceiling and other barriers. Blacks learned long ago that one key to self-betterment within the caste system is through white patronage (i.e., favoritism, not merit alone), which can be solicited through some version of the old "Uncle Tom" role, that is, through compliance, dependence, and manipulation. More recently the reverse strategy of "shuckin' and jivin' " has been adopted, which is another defensive way to manipulate white patronage. The second kind of survival strategy, which includes hustling, pimping, and the like, exploits nonconventional economic and social resources or "the street economy" (Bullock 1973; Foster 1974; Heard 1968; Milner 1970; Wolfe 1970).

Thus within the black community success in terms of conventional jobs and resources often requires collective struggles and/or clientship *in addition to educational credentials*. Nonconventional forms of success and ways of making a living are also open to blacks. Thus "successful people" are not only those who succeed in conventional terms either with school credentials alone or with clientship and collective struggle as well, but also those who make it in the street through hustling and related strategies. They are admired, and they influence the efforts of others, including children, to succeed.

We have suggested that survival strategies may require knowledge, attitudes, and skills that are not wholly compatible with white middle-class teaching and learning behavior. We have also suggested that children learn the survival strategies during preschool years as a normal part of their cultural learning; consequently, the potential for learning difficulties may already exist when children enter school. Whether and to what extent those difficulties arise depends on the individual child's experience in school and the classroom. We suspect that insofar as children have become competent in these survival strategies they may lack serious attitudes toward schooling and toward academic tasks in general, including test taking.

Conclusion

In this paper we have argued that the disproportionate school failure of black children is not because they come from an oral culture, though we have not challenged the assertion that black culture is an oral culture. We have only noted that members of the so-called oral cultures of small-scale societies and immigrants into the United States from residual cultures of more complex societies do not manifest the same learning problems in school that are found among black and similar castelike minorities.

We have suggested an alternative view of the problem within an ecological framework in which school is a culturally organized means of preparing children for adult roles in the social and economic life of their society or social group. Within this framework the traditional social and economic positions of blacks have not required much education nor rewarded blacks highly for educational accomplishments. Black menial positions enforced by castelike or racial stratification has influenced how the dominant whites who control their schooling perceive them and define their educational needs. It has also influenced how blacks themselves perceive their opportunities and the importance of schooling.

The perceptions of whites have led them to provide blacks with inadequate schooling and to communicate attitudes in school settings that do not encourage blacks to maximum efforts. Black perceptions generate disillusionment about schooling and a lack of perseverance toward schoolwork; they lead to survival strategies that require knowledge, attitudes, and skills which may be incompatible with school requirements. Furthermore, it is likely that perennial conflict and mistrust between blacks and the schools interfere with the willingness of blacks to comply with school rules and standards and place the schools in a defensive posture toward blacks. Closer study is needed to determine how these factors contribute, singly and in combination, to the learning difficulties observed in classrooms.

Since the 1960s some efforts have been made to change black status and schooling, for example, through legislative and administrative channels noted earlier in the essay. The magnitude and quality of these changes, however, have not broken the job ceiling or significantly altered black expectations, especially among the lower segments of the black community.

During the same period, efforts have also been made to improve black schooling and raise academic achievement levels through school desegregation, compensatory education, pre-school (Headstart) educations, parent education and training, Follow-Through, special admissions, special scholarships, and many others (Ogbu 1978). These programs have helped many blacks to complete higher levels of schooling, to achieve greater functional literacy, and to improve their performance in classroom and on standardized tests. But the number benefiting from such programs remains small and many who do benefit probably do not come from the lower segments of the community. These programs remain ineffective for or unavailable to the majority. Moreover, they are essentially remedial and often based on misconceptions of the underlying causes of black school problems (Obgu 1978). Preventing learning problems before they develop will require a strategy that will simultaneously have to (a) consider the economic expectations of blacks as a root cause rather than a consequence of the school failure and literacy problem; (b) eliminate the gross and subtle mechanisms which differentiate black schooling from white schooling; and (c) examine black perceptions and "adaptive" responses, including the problem of mistrust and conflict in black relations with the schools.

15.
The Social Context of Literacy

Jay L. Robinson

This essay, like most in the genre, has its roots in experiences—past, past continuous, and even future since anticipation works on one's mind. Past are seven years as an English Department Chairman; past and continuing is my work with the English Composition Board at The University of Michigan helping to develop a writing program for undergraduates; and in my future is a chairmanship of a Ph.D. program in English and Education. All of these, lumped together with reading that a sabbatical has allowed me to do, have provoked me to think about the topics addressed in these pages: how literacy functions (and does not function) in our society; how society influences what we do as learners and teachers of literacy.

It is important to discuss the social context of literacy for several reasons, some of them perfectly obvious. It is obvious, for example, that teaching—any teaching—takes place only in some one or another social context: We teach something to somebody some place at some particular time in some particular society. What we do is influenced not only by the *what,* but also by the *where, when,* and *to whom.* It is also obvious, when we think about it, that the teaching of literacy is especially sensitive to the pressures of social context. Language in all of its uses is an intimate part of human experience: Language is expressive of identity and personality, but it is also socially binding and expressive of collective values. Written language is peculiarly public, more so than speech, and as a consequence its forms are carefully scrutinized; reading and writing are highly valued activities and society monitors their acquisition—as we know from myriad articles in the public media about Johnnies and Janes who can't read or write. We teachers of literacy meet students in a charged atmosphere. We need to be sensitive to the prevailing currents, if for no other purpose than to avoid electrocution.

A compelling reason for talking about the social context for literacy is that our profession has usually avoided the subject in spite of its importance, leaving it to sociologists, sociolinguists, and social historians. Let me cite just one example,

From *fforum: Essays on Theory and Practice in the Teaching of Writing,* ed. Patricia L. Stock. Copyright 1983 by Boynton/Cook Publishers. Inc. Reprinted by permission.

borrowed from an essay by Frank D'Angelo (*Literacy for Life*, 1983). Richard Ohmann, when he was Editor of *College English*, requested manuscripts for a special issue on the publicly proclaimed literacy crisis. This was his challenge to his colleagues:

> Is there a decline in literacy? in writing ability? If so, what are its causes? To what extent is it accountable to changes in schooling? To changes in American society? What can—or should—college English teachers be doing about it? Are there college programs that successfully make up deficits in verbal skills? Is "bonehead English" an idea whose time has come again? Do competency requirements for graduation help? Should this be a problem of the English department, or the whole college or university? Can we distinguish between the traditional basics— spelling, usage, etc.—and some others that have more to do with intellectual competence? Can English teachers usefully shape the national concern with verbal competence, rather than simply respond to needs expressed by pundits, legislators, regents, and businessmen?
>
> If, on the other hand, there has been no significant decline in reading or writing ability among college students, what explains the outcry? What can English teachers do to correct public misconceptions? Is our responsibility confined to the classroom, or does it include social and political action? (1976, p. 819).

Ohmann asked us to look at the social dimensions of the literacy crisis and at the social meaning of the public's concern; to decide whether or not a crisis existed and to discover its causes; and only then to reach decisions about how to deal with it. But when the special issue of *College English* appeared, Ohmann published his disappointment with the contributions:

> A large proportion merely reiterated the public concerns and in terms very similar to those employed by the media. Others devoted most of their energy to suggesting better ways to teach writing. We might infer from these facts that the profession accepts not only the public assessment of the literacy "crisis" but also the blame for it. Our original call queries whether in fact there has been a significant decline in reading and writing ability among students. Yet not one contribution reviewed and analyzed in any detail the assumptions, methods, and statistics of the testing on which so much of the public outcry seems to be based. Are these assumptions, methods, and statistics as invulnerable to criticism as our professional silence suggests? (1977, p. 44).

Nastier questions than Ohmann's last can be put: Does our profession's silence on such topics suggest that we are willing to let others tell us what to do and then develop methods for getting it done better or more efficiently? Does our silence imply contentment with the status quo? The world may well need a better rat trap, but does it really need a better sentence combiner?

A fact of life in our world is that the possession of literacy correlates almost perfectly with the possession of power and wealth. And in general, the more literacy one has or can control, the more power one can exercise—real power, not something metaphorical like the power of self-expression. Now I intend no causative implication in the statement; to achieve literacy does not necessarily earn one power, as we well know. But the powerful are usually themselves literate, or if not, they can purchase the services of those who are.

Another fact of life in our world is that the *profession* of literacy, as contrasted with its possession, correlates not with power and wealth but with relative powerlessness and relative poverty. English teachers do not exert much influence in the world of raw power, even though they live and work in it. The humanities, when compared with the sciences, the social sciences, or professional schools, are under-funded both within their own institutions and nationally, and humanists are under-represented both in academic governance and in government.

These facts of our own social existence are more than unpleasant, they are dangerous. The danger is not to our persons, yours and mine, nor even to our sense of personal worth. The danger is rather to our profession—to our collective sense of endeavor and to the ethics we apply in the teaching of literacy. We have or can claim to have two things useful to those who possess power—namely, the ability to make students literate and squatting rights in classrooms where literacy is assumed to be taught. But as poor cousins, we are particularly vulnerable both to the temptations of utility (we call it service), and to the temptations of the money that pays for our services. Methods can be endlessly adjusted to ends and aims, to the aims and ends of others as easily as to our own. And what if our academic discipline does not enjoy intellectual prestige? We can always try to achieve status by borrowing prestigious theory and adapting it to the demand for new methods. But when we do, does the right brain always know what the left brain is doing?

I am oversimplifying and being facetious, and with issues that are neither simple nor funny. We do have a responsibility to the society that sustains us, and at least equal responsibility to students whose pragmatic needs must be met. But we can meet these responsibilities only if we understand at least something of the social context in which literacy presently functions.

What kinds of things constitute the social context of literacy in our time? More than I can mention, of course, but I will touch on these four: First, on inherited conceptions of literacy and the values we attach to them; second, on real and socially perceived needs for literacy; third, on ideal and ethnically conceived needs for literacy; and fourth, on some few of our institutions for the fostering of literacy.

Inherited Concepts and Values

Practice is always rooted in concepts even when the concepts are unstated or even unstatable; and what we practice most energetically is that which we value most highly. The *concept* of literacy is highly valued in our own as in other Western and Westernized industrial societies. Historians, recognizing this special phenomenon, are now writing about a "literacy myth"—a configuration of generally held and privileged notions about literacy and its functions in modern society. Harvey J. Graff, for example:

> The rise of literacy and its dissemination to the popular classes is associated with the triumph of light over darkness, of liberalism, democracy, and of universal unbridled progress. In social thought, therefore, these elements relate to ideas of linear evolution and progression; literacy here takes its place among the other successes of modernity and rationality. In theory and in empirical investigation, literacy is conceptualized—often in stark and simple fashion—as an important part of the larger parcel of factors that account for the evolution of modern societies and states (p. xv).

With its wide acceptance, the literacy myth benefits us poor cousins, of course. Foundations fund our programs, deans find money for English departments, enlightened school boards reduce loads for writing teachers (though rarely), and in general our public and professional stock rises. In the short run, we prosper; but we might be better off in the longer run if we try to find out how much truth the myth contains and then act on that. What we inherit is not always to our good.

Robert Disch, in his introduction to *The Future of Literacy* writes that

> the twentieth century inherited a mystique of literacy born out of . . . two tendencies. One, essentially utilitarian, was committed to the functional uses of literacy as a medium for the spread of practical information that could lead to individual and social progress; the other, essentially aesthetic and spiritual, was committed to the uses of literacy for salvaging the drooping spirit of Western man from the death of religion and the ravages of progress (p. 3).

The utilitarian benefits of literacy, so goes the myth, are economic, social, and intellectual. Economic benefits include enhanced access to employment and to information leading to a better life (for example, information about birth control or about sanitation). Social benefits include a broadening of personal perspective beyond the tribal or local; acquisition of societal norms and values leading to public spiritedness; participation in democratic means of governance. Claims for the intellectual benefits of literacy have gone beyond the obvious ones of access to stored knowledge to stronger ones asserting a causal relation between literacy and general learning as well as between literacy and full cognitive development.[1] How many of these claims correspond to established fact?

In fact, we do not know, but in some few cases we are beginning to find out. And what we are discovering, when the myth is tested, is that it proves to be mythical. For only one example, consider the following results of historical research into the correlations of literacy with liberalized social attitudes and with expanded economic opportunity. In a study of literacy in Colonial New England, Kenneth A. Lockridge (1974) found that Protestantism was a stronger impetus to literacy than secular school laws; that schools were dominated by conservative, not progressive, educational impulses; and that when literacy became nearly universal in New England near the end of the 18th century, attitudes toward society and the larger world were not discernibly modified. In another study, treating some nineteenth-century Canadian cities, Harvey Graff found that:

> . . . literacy—a phenomenon suggestive of equality—contributed regularly as an element of the structure of inequality, reinforcing the steep ridges of stratifica-

tion, and also as a force for order and integration. It also served as a symbolic focus of other forces of inequality: ethnicity, class, sex, and age. Literacy, then, did not universally serve to benefit all who had attained it, but neither did it disadvantage all those who had not (p. 19).

Graff does not claim that literacy holds no potential for liberalization; rather he demonstrates that powerful, deeply embedded social forces can override its potential. Literacy can be an effective means of social control, when educational institutions use it for this purpose; or it can be a means of social liberation, when individuals are encouraged to think, read and write for themselves. Ohmann presses the pertinent question: Where do we stand as teachers when we emphasize means over ends or methods over purposes? In answering the question, we do well to be mindful that ours is a society that has sanctioned a back-to-basics movement, that is enamored with competency testing, and that presently values vocational over liberal education. Few vocations in our society encourage an exercise of literacy that is liberalizing and liberating.

Even if all of our students were to achieve literacy, not all would benefit unless allowed and encouraged by society to put their competencies to use. Our aims and especially our methods have to accommodate to this brute fact of social reality. We need to know much more than we now do about the forces and institutions in our society that constrain literacy, both those that inhibit its exercise and those that make it serve as an instrument of unconscious socialization to mores and values we would not endorse. Without such knowledge, we could well help create a reality more malignant than that figured in the literacy myth.

Real and Socially Perceived Needs for Literacy

So far I have been talking about literacy as a "buzz word"—as a concept or a symbol incorporating notions of aspiration and value. Now I want to define the term, or at least to limit its reference. Let *literacy* mean *functional literacy;* and let *functional literacy,* for the moment, mean only this: the ability to read and write well enough to compete for economic sufficiency. Such literacy is essential for all students and for all citizens, and insofar as we are able and insofar as social circumstances will allow, we must help provide it. I quote some experts on the demographics of literacy:

> *Ralph W. Tyler:* In 1800, the unskilled in all categories [of employment] comprised more than 80 percent of the labor force; in 1900 they made up 60 percent and in 1980, about 6 percent. The rapid development of employment in the various services . . . has largely taken place since 1948. Now, jobs requiring no schooling are few in number while tasks requiring at least a high school education make up nearly two thirds of employment opportunities (*Literacy for Life*, 1983).
>
> *Paul A. Stassman:* Since the 1950's our country has become predominantly occupied with the creation, distribution, and administration of information. By 1990 abut fifty percent of the workforce will not be producing food or manufacturing objects; instead the workforce will occupy most of its time just communicating (*Literacy for Life*, 1983).

Arthur M. Cohen and Florence B. Brawer: Literacy is certainly related to success in nearly all community college programs: transfer courses demand proficiency in reading, writing and/or mathematics, and licensure examinations admitting students to practice after completing a technological program are closed to students who cannot pass an entrance examination that is based on literacy (*Literacy for Life,* 1983).

Robben W. Fleming: Meanwhile, it is estimated that there may be as many as 57 million adult illiterates in the United States (*Literacy for Life,* 1983).

John Oxenham: In 1971, some 780 million people over the age of fifteen all over the world were classed as illiterate. . . . by 1980 they will total perhaps 820 million (p. 2).

Functional illiteracy does correlate with poverty and powerlessness; the problem of illiteracy is as urgent as any in our society.

But ironically, the needs of the poor could well be forgotten because recently we have discovered other needs among the better-off and the more influential. We have discovered that middle-class students don't write very well, not even those who enroll in prestigious schools; that businessmen don't write very well, or at least don't think that they do; that bureaucrats and lawyers write even worse; that the new information-society requires a new kind of literacy—in software, rather than in ordinary printed language. The *influential* public is now more often asking "Why can't Johnny write?" than it is "Why can't Johnny read?" Yet as Edward Corbett so accurately points out, reading is far more important for economic sufficiency (even for survival) than is writing:

> . . . writing will never be as crucial a skill for surviving or thriving in our society as reading is. Functional illiterates who cannot even write their names may suffer embarrassment because of their deficiency but they somehow manage to subsist in our technological society. But those functional illiterates who cannot even read street signs and simple directions are so severely handicapped that it is questionable whether they can survive, much less thrive, in our society. Thirdly, only a minuscule portion of the total population will regularly have to compose important, influential documents. The majority of literate people have to do some writing occasionally—letters, notes, fill-in-the-blanks forms—but only a minority have to write regularly and seriously in connection with their jobs (1981, p. 47).

The present emphasis upon writing over reading doubtless reflects a bias in favor of the upper of our social classes, where needs take precedence. If not restrained or balanced against the need for reading, the bias could well contribute to a widening of the gulf between rich and poor that now seems so permanent a feature of our national topography. As Richard Hendrix writes:

> The emphasis on writing clarifies the gap between a commitment in principle to universal opportunity and the fact of unequal opportunity. Writing ability is unevenly distributed in our society along class lines. Indeed, writing and access to writing improvement is as good an indicator of the difference between, say, white collar and blue collar career tracks as we are likely to find (p. 53).

Our problems are made more difficult to solve because just when we begin to recognize the number and complexity of them, the public develops an aversion to taxation and politicians a preference for bombs over books. How, then, are we to react to the perfectly legitimate demands placed upon us in our social role as teachers of literacy when we know that resources will be limited—perhaps severely?

We could, of course, take battlefield medicine as our model and practice triage on some principle of social utility, fitting our teaching to present social realities and comforting ourselves with some resigned but basically optimistic notion of social inevitability. Maybe only a minority do need to learn to write; maybe the masses need only to learn to read, and then only marginally; and maybe, because of technology, the masses don't even need to read. And maybe the socially disintegrating effects of such specialization could be avoided if some such vision of social interdependence as John Oxenham's is an accurate one:

> [F]or the masses to enjoy literature without literacy, a minority would need to be highly literate. The paradox evokes two reflections on technological change. One is that, as science and technology introduce new changes in production and services, a growing majority with decreasing skills seems to become increasingly dependent on a highly skilled but shrinking minority. The trend appears to lead to a dictatorship of technocrats. On the other hand, while a necessary consequence of the extension of specialization may well be the dependence of majorities upon minorities, oppressive technology is not the necessary end. The reason is simply that the proliferation of specializations generates a net of interdependence and a homeostatic distribution of power (p. 131).

Perhaps a stable and healthy interdependence can result from a planned distribution of the assets of literacy. Perhaps we can focus our attention and concentrate our resources upon training a fully literate elite without oppressing the masses. Perhaps that is what we are doing anyway, without much thought for the masses.

There is nothing of the conditional in these two assertions: Resources will be limited as we seek to meet needs for literacy; priorities will be set—either by us or by others, either by intention or through thoughtless inertia. Policy should be at least as well-planned as good writing. Right now we need good policy more than better lesson plans.

Ideals and Ethics

In June 1980 the English Composition Board of the University of Michigan sponsored a conference on "Literacy in the 1980's." Experts from various occupations and professions were invited to the conference and asked to respond to this question: "What will be the needs for literacy in your field as we look from now toward the end of the century?" As I review the conference, two presentations stand out: one by a lawyer and professor of law; another by a scientist who is also Manager of the Central Research Division of the Mobil Research and Development Corporation. These two impressed me because they called not for more emphasis upon utilitarian writing (and reading), but for a more expansive and humane literacy.

James White, Professor of Law at the University of Chicago and the author of a distinguished book on lawyers' use of language, described what he calls "the invisible discourse of the law": "unstated conventions by which the language [of law] operates . . . expectations that do not find explicit expression anywhere but are part of the legal culture that the surface language simply assumes" (pp. 48–49). But White did more than describe. First, he enriched existing definitions of (functional) literacy:

> I start with the idea that literacy is not merely the capacity to understand the conceptual content of writings and utterances, but the ability to participate fully in a set of social and intellectual practices. It is not passive but active; not imitative but creative, for participation in the speaking and writing of language includes participation in the activities it makes possible (p. 56).

Then he described a course in writing and reading that he teaches in The University of Chicago, which invites such participation. White helps his students to perceive how rule and procedure constitute social organization and govern social cooperation; how language is the means of such constitution; and how law is related to everyday social behavior. In so doing he demystifies the law, making it more subject both to lay understanding and to personal control. According to White:

> All this [can] be done with materials from the students' own life, without the use of legal terms or technicalities. It need not even be done in Standard English: the students' writing . . . should indeed reflect the way people actually speak in their own world. And one important lesson for us all might be the discovery that it is not only in the law, or only in the language of the white middle class, that community is constituted or that argument about justice proceeds (p. 58).

Paul Weisz, a scientist and businessman, called for clarity and broad comprehensibility in scientific language: for the development and use in science of a common language enabling more citizens "to benefit from the knowledge which abounds around us," a language that would also serve to combat the socially and intellectually fragmenting effects of specialization. He sees the need as essential:

> The relationship between division of knowledge in our society and presence of social tension is clear. As knowledge and activity become more sophisticated, the bridges of understanding and interaction grow weaker and weaker. Now, more than ever before, such bridges are needed for both social and psychological survival (*Literacy for Life*, 1983).

Weisz's concern echoes that expressed in the recent report of the Rockefeller Commission on the Humanities:

> Our citizens need to become literate in a multiple sense. We all need to understand the characteristics of scientific inquiry and the repercussions of scientific research. We must all learn something about the use of the media and of new technologies for storing, transmitting, and expanding knowledge. Without

this sort of literacy, our society as a whole will be less able to apply science and technology to humanistic needs, less able to measure the human effects of scientific achievements, less able to judge the information we produce and receive (*The Humanities*, 1980, pp. 18–19).

Our profession has begun to recognize that its own notions about needs for literacy do not always match day-to-day needs outside the classroom. But most who have argued for adjustment to the real world have addressed only economic needs. White and Weisz, both practitioners in the world of work, suggest other ways: White by linking language use with social behavior and to intellectual activity rooted in social practices; Weisz by linking the aims of writing with a democracy's needs for information and knowledge essential for the solution of human problems. Both programs are *ethical* in conception.

Caesar exacts his due, but we need not pay the tax-master so unthinkingly as to leave in his control all decisions about what social reality ought to be. Societies exist in the mind as well as in fact, in ethical standards for behavior as well as in behavior patterns. It is our particular obligation as teachers of literacy to recognize this, and with our students' help to frame ideals constructive of a world we would willingly inhabit. Ideals and ethics find their most permanent expression in public language.

Institutions: Who Teaches the What to Whom?

Existing institutions, like inherited concepts and values, are part of the social context for literacy. As things are now established, we English teachers are the ones customarily assumed to be responsible for teaching literacy (along with elementary school teachers, who can do anything). But given existing and shifting needs for literacy, it is not at all clear that we will continue to be held responsible or considered responsible enough to be so held.

In an article in a volume containing the proceedings of a conference sponsored by the National Institute of Education, Richard Hendrix—who is associated with the Fund for the Improvement of Postsecondary Education—asks this question: "Who is responsible for improving writing?" He says this about English departments:

> Writing instruction was for years a stepchild of English departments, who have always dominated it. As recently as fifteen years ago many colleges dropped composition altogether—partly on the basis that the high schools were handling the job, and mainly to give still greater emphasis to literary study. That development should make us hesitate about trusting that English departments, as they are presented constituted, will solve the problem.
>
> Now there has been a resurgence of active involvement by English faculty along with others. Writing instruction could be a boon for underemployed humanists, a large and influential group. But teachers trained in literature may not necessarily be well situated to work with beginning students, nor to prepare students for the kinds of writing tasks they will likely face after school. English

professors are not even necessarily good writers themselves, and their commitment to specialization has been at least as strong as any other discipline's (p. 56).

There are grounds for Hendrix's suspicion. They exist in the prevailing attitudes of most college and many high school English teachers toward the teaching of writing; in the way composition teachers are treated in their own departments; and in the way composition programs are funded, staffed, and managed. And in the meantime societal needs are not being met, neither by instructional programs that address vocational needs nor by research programs that address the need for better understanding of the relations of literacy to society, to learning, and to the determination of value. Can and will English departments change enough to meet such needs? My own experiences as a teacher of writing, as a program planner, and as an English department chairman, give me grounds for doubt at least as strong as that expressed by Hendrix.

The trouble with literacy is that it enters all aspects of human life in literate societies. The trouble with questions about literacy is that the important ones are general in their application to human discourse and its functions. The trouble with our answers, when we are English teachers, is that we are all specialists. And it is possible—at the least arguable—that a specialization in literature is less adaptable than many to a broad understanding of literacy.

Raymond Williams, in a challenging critique of dominant trends in literary study, reminds us that the term *literature* once applied more broadly than to imaginative works of a certain kind and quality. In one of its earlier usages, "it was often close to the sense of modern *literacy*"; its reference was to "a condition of reading: of being able to read and of having read" (pp. 45–54). Histories, biographies, works of philosophy, political and scientific treatises were once all works of literature. In his argument, Williams traces the specialization of the term to the domain of "creative" or "imaginative" works, and the development of literature departments in academies as units concerned exclusively with this narrowed domain and with the practice of criticism.

The problem arising from this development is that it invites us, as inheritors of the tradition, to equate "literacy" with knowledge of a special kind of literature, without recognizing that such an equation is a socially privileged and economically self-serving one: more a matter of status and value than of fact. The study of imaginative literature may well contribute to the complex of abilities, capacities, and attitudes that function in good reading and good writing; but to claim that it necessarily and sufficiently does is patently absurd.

If departments of English continue to define themselves as departments of literature and mean by that term imaginative works only, and if English teachers restrict themselves to reading only such works and commentaries on them, then there is need for new kinds of departments just as there is for differently prepared teachers. Harvey Graff gets to the heart of the problem:

> Discussions of literacy are confused and ambiguous—an ironic, and even startling, phenomenon, which contrasts sharply with the high value we assign to the skills of reading and writing. Vagueness pervades virtually all efforts to discern the meaning of literacy; moreover, there is surprisingly little agreement on or special

evidence for the benefits of literacy, whether socially or individually, economically or culturally. Rather, assumptions preempt criticism and investigation, and agencies and specialists whose business it is to promote literacy shrink from asking fundamental questions in their campaigns to disseminate skills (1979, p. 3).

Certain questions cannot be avoided any longer. Serious research is needed into literacy and its place in our present social context, and such research should take precedence over concern with method. There is little profit in trying to do better what cannot or should not be done.

- Reading v. writing re: priorities
- functional v. specialized literacy
- social dimensions of teaching, learning practice
- Place of English teachers

16.
Reading and Writing Requirements

Richard C. Richardson, Jr.
Elizabeth C. Fisk
Morris A. Okun

Extensive use of written language may be uncommon in most community college classrooms. A recent study of instructional practices (Cohen and Brawer, 1981) reported that while nearly all instructors used textbooks, they assigned an average of three to four hundred pages a semester (less than thirty pages a week). Fewer than a third required additional readings in outside reference materials, although a majority did provide a brief syllabus and some handout materials in class. Quick-score objective exams were the most common mode of student evaluation, along with in-class essay exams. Fewer than one third of the instructors required term papers or reports of any kind.

Secondary school classrooms have apparently also dropped or changed the requirements for reading and writing. The National Assessment of Educational Progress (1981) has found that students are seldom asked to interpret or summarize extended prose, that most tests ask only for literal recall. Not surprisingly, students' skills at the level of interpretation and synthesis are decreasing. In a study of recent high school graduates in Florida (McCabe and Skidmore, 1982), fewer than half the students reported using a library more than five times in high school or taking more than five essay tests. Fewer than one in six

From *Literacy in the Open-Access College*, by Richard C. Richardson, Jr., Elizabeth C. Fisk, and Morris A. Okun. Copyright 1983 by Jossey-Bass, Inc. Reprinted by permission of the publisher.

EDITORS' NOTE: Relying on an intensive case-study of the reading and writing behaviors at a community college, Richardson, Fisk, and Okun present a wide-ranging discussion of literacy in American open-access colleges. The authors situate their specific studies in broader political and economic contexts and offer a critical discussion of society's changing definitions of what it means to be literate. In the excerpt below, "Information-Transfer Courses" refer to traditional college courses (history, biology, economics) in which an instructor lectures—"disseminates information," as the authors say—and students take notes. "Basic Language Skills Courses" are best illustrated by remedial English and English-as-a-Second-Language classes. "Vocational Lab Courses" are "activity and equipment oriented" classes designed to impart an employable skill: word processing, cosmetology, automotive mechanics.

reported being required to read more than fifty pages a week. These students did not expect greater demands as they entered postsecondary education.

Our observations in Oakwood classrooms indicate a similar restriction in reading and writing. This chapter describes Oakwood students' use of written language and points out the characteristics that distinguish it from the type of reading and writing we advocate as necessary for the development of critical literacy.

Collecting data on classroom reading and writing was not an easy task. Because so much of the reading and writing was embedded integrally into ongoing activities, it was often overlooked by students and instructors alike. For example, when asked whether any in-class writing occurred, many students said no until directly questioned about taking notes. Then they would agree that they did in fact write in class. Similarly, at first students said they never read the textbook but then, on probing, described how they used the text in studying for tests. For our purposes, we explain this almost unconscious use of reading and writing by considering these uses of written language "operations," which occur in the service of goal-directed activity and are not themselves the subject of much attention (Leont'ev, 1974).

The operations we observed in Oakwood classrooms can be described along a number of simple dimensions borrowed and freely adapted from available sociolinguistic frameworks (Hymes, 1964). *Channel* refers to a medium of communication and is used to distinguish among operations involving written language (reading and writing), oral language (listening and speaking), and nonverbal communication (observing and manipulating). Operations can also be distinguished by whether they involve producing or receiving information. By cross-classifying these two dimensions, we catalogued as follows the communications we observed in Oakwood classrooms:

- *Productive written*—writing
- *Productive oral*—speaking
- *Productive nonverbal*—manipulating
- *Receptive written*—reading
- *Receptive oral*—listening
- *Receptive nonverbal*—observing

We used these categories to identify the classroom activities that involved the use of written language as an operation. Once identified, written language use could be further categorized using two other dimensions: the form in which language was presented, from discrete to continuous; and the degree of explicitness of the cues provided to meaning, from very specific to very general. Using these dimensions, two maximally contrasting categories of written language use could be described.

The first of these we termed *texting*. Texting involves the use of reading and writing to comprehend or compose connected language without the assistance of specific cues. Examples are reading a textbook chapter to gain an overview of the important events of the 1920s and writing an essay that argues for or against capital punishment. Texting represents a traditional (liberal arts) view of the type of written language use that colleges should promote and should expect their students to demonstrate. Consistent with this traditional view, the students we interviewed described themselves as "really reading" and "really writing" only when they were dealing independently with connected language.

In contrast to texting were operations we designated as _bitting_. Bitting was the use of reading or writing to understand or produce fragmented language when presented with specific external cues. Students were bitting when they read and copied from the blackboard a list of names that the instructor pointed to and identified as important and when they later recognized these names on a multiple-choice test. They were engaged in a somewhat more independent form of bitting when they skimmed a textbook to find answers to study-guide questions in preparation for a multiple-choice test. Bitting might involve either connected discourse (a textbook) or disconnected discourse (a list of names or definitions). In both instances, however, an information source was used to obtain fragments of meaning, and strong external cues were present.

The reading and writing observed at Oakwood approximated bitting closely enough to justify the generalization that bitting had become the norm for classroom written language. This was true in each of the three course types identified in Chapter Three, although there were unique characteristics of literacy in each setting.

Reading and Writing in Three Types of Classrooms

Information-Transfer Courses. In information-transfer courses, notegiving and notetaking were the characteristic reading/writing behaviors that facilitated one-way communication from instructor to students. Written language was a tool to help this interaction run more smoothly. Instructors used written language in class to make their presentation accessible to the whole group and to support their position as the single focus of attention. Students' use of written language in notetaking kept them in the role of receptive audience.

Students reported a number of reasons for notetaking. Some were making a record for use in studying for a test or as a guide to help in reading the text. Some were just using the notetaking activity to help themselves pay attention and to prevent boredom. Some simply said they took notes because the students around them did, and others admitted they had never thought about their reasons; notetaking was just what one did during a lecture.

Even the nature and arrangement of furniture and equipment facilitated the use of reading and writing in the dissemination of information. The instructor was encouraged to read from notes and write out key terms and concepts by the easy availability of a lectern and blackboard space. The writing armchairs facing the blackboard in evenly spaced columns emphasized the undifferentiated nature of the group and announced the student's role as notetaker.

Writing was not a factor, however, whenever storytelling, audiovisuals, or discussions became the focus of classroom activity. Perhaps the reason was that reading and writing were not considered appropriate for these supplementary activities or that these forms of interaction were thought of as peripheral to the main goal of the course, information transfer.

Outside class, students used written language only to prepare for in-class examinations, most of which were multiple-choice tests requiring literal recognition and recall of specific information. Though working independently, the students relied heavily on cues to importance given by instructors during lectures, as well as in written study guides. Students typically read their textbooks once through in a casual fashion to get an overall feel for the chapters or just to "get through" them. Then, when they studied for tests, they used notes, handouts, and textbooks in a skimming fashion in order to prepare to recognize specific information on multiple-choice tests. They could expect that few, if any, test items would require them to analyze, synthesize, or evaluate the information.

An analysis of the written materials used in information-transfer classes at Oakwood revealed the extent to which these materials were oriented toward bitting. In fact, many of them would have been difficult to "text." However, even in classes in which materials did seem suitable for texting, students read them in a texting manner only during the early part of a semester. As the semester progressed, interviews suggested a decreasing incidence of independent texting even by the most active participants in a course. Students soon discovered that tests could be passed with minimal reading. Thereafter, they did only the necessary bitting.

A small number of students did use reading and writing more elaborately in a "texting" fashion. When they took notes, they often tried to restructure and rewrite board notes in their own way. Because these few students read the relevant sections of the textbook before a lecture, they usually constituted the small responding audience in the classroom, prepared to answer and ask questions. The students in this responding audience used reading and writing to aid the acquisition of knowledge that they found interesting and valuable. Many of them enjoyed the process of learning itself and so gained satisfaction from carrying out reading and writing activities that they associated with a student role. However, because these students were in the minority, the literacy norms negotiated in Oakwood classrooms reflected not their style but the far more restricted "bitting" style of the majority in the attentive audience.

Basic Language Skills Courses. In basic language skills courses, reading and writing occurred within the social context of guided interaction. Instructors as socializers in a directive role did not want students to waste time on activities geared to information transfer, nor did they wish to require students to engage in much reading and writing outside a social context. The students, for their part, also preferred to do their writing and reading in the classroom under the instructor's direction, because they were unfamiliar with the content, form, and function of the reading and writing tasks in which they were engaged.

Typically, all course work was completed during class time. Reading and writing were used in completing workbook exercises and in drills conducted within a group setting under instructor or tutor guidance. Students were seldom asked to deal with more than a phrase or a brief sentence at a time, and their use of written language was constantly monitored. The student-centered arrangement of the classroom and the variable use of time facilitated this directed, social variety of literacy.

Vocational Lab Courses. In vocational lab courses, reading and writing were used whenever they contributed to the work being done. Students referred to manuals and written instructions as they tried to carry out tasks. Often, students shared their interpretations of the instructions and discussed the application to the current problem. The written word was a tool but seldom the final authority.

Vocational labs seem to operate largely according to an oral tradition — but an oral tradition supplemented by the selected use of written language. One researcher's description of the automotives class he observed illustrated this point:

> We followed the service manual and were able to do most of the adjustments. However, when troubles occurred, we fell back on more intuitive modes of work. Final adjustments were made by ear and feel rather than by what we had read in the manual. Taking this kind of written advice is all well and good, but the final verification or trust is ultimately put in how things sound or look. There is a whole set of criteria that will finally satisfy a good mechanic, but these things are not easily presented in written form.

To do well, a student in such a tradition has to be able to read, listen, observe, and share experiences with other students and the teacher. After a time, it becomes evident to learners that they will hear, see, or read important aspects of required knowledge a great number of times. With patience they will obtain the information as long as they are paying attention, without need for much use of written language.

"Bitting" in the Classroom

Although reading and writing were common activities in Oakwood classrooms, the use of written language was restricted in the way it was carried out and in the functions it seemed to serve. This minimal use may be typical of the extent to which written language use in open-access colleges is coming to resemble uses found among the general public, in contrast to the uses traditionally associated with higher learning.

First, the reading and writing that occurred were not of a type that could be used to communicate information by itself. Instead, reading and writing were used along with oral language and contextual cues and occurred as part of social interaction. This multimodal characteristic of literacy has been described as a primary aspect of modern society. Ong (1980) described the "secondarily oral tradition" we live with today. In a secondarily oral tradition, no single channel of communication is emphasized; people seek to transfer information by repetition and multiple modes. Dubois (1980) asserts that the greatest challenge for linguists today is to understand this current norm, the joint use of written and oral language.

Nor is the social-contextual integration of written language that we observed unusual. Heath (1982) found, in her study of literacy in home settings, that although the community was considered literate, most of the reading and writing occurred during social interactions. Reading and writing almost never stood alone. Individuals did virtually no solitary reading except when elderly men and women read their Bible alone. Heath also reported that families' literacy habits did not match those usually attributed to fully literate groups. Parents did not read to their children, encourage conversation about books, or write or read extended prose passages. Reading was not an individual pursuit, nor was it considered to have intellectual, esthetic, or critical rewards.

A third characteristic of the written language we observed was its disconnected form. Most of the writing produced by students and much of what they read was presented in discrete words and phrases. However, this characteristic in itself may not be alarming. Scribner and Jacob (1980), Mikulecky and Diehl (1979), and Jacob and Crandall (1979) all report the abbreviated nature of most writing used in job settings. As in the Oakwood research, these researchers found that people often failed to report much of the reading and writing they did because it had become so integrated into everyday tasks and also because its form did not fit their conception of "real" reading and writing:

> Literacy activities may involve reading and writing short-term notes and messages, filing and retrieving information from documents to answer a short question over the telephone. These would rarely be identified as literacy activities by people performing them, yet they require reading and writing, and, in fact, they occur frequently during the workday. It is these kinds of activities which people often discount as "not really reading" (Jacob and Crandall, p. 3, n. 3).

Of course, we were observing in an academic setting, not in the job environment, where the uses reported by these authors seem much more appropriate.

Bits of written language can be used as part of thoughtful, autonomous activity. Individuals often do use pieces of language as input as they go about creative problem solving, critical evaluation, and a search for holistic meanings. This realization, however, brings us closer to the source of our discontent with the reading and writing we observed at Oakwood and with much of what is reported in other educational settings.

The information communicated through written language remained as bits of isolated fact. It was not integrated or analyzed to achieve more holistic meaning. The college students we observed did not read textbooks to grasp both major themes and supportive detail, nor did they listen actively and critically to lectures and record comprehensive notes. Oakwood students were not required to synthesize, analyze, or evaluate information from texts and lectures. Instead, they learned discrete pieces of information in order to recognize or reproduce them intact on objective exams.

In addition, student reading and writing were highly dependent activities, shaped by the general nature of students' roles in the classroom. The most typical form of social interaction involved students serving as attentive audience, and in this situation students used reading and writing as part of passive, receptive activity. Concurrently, in the basic language skills courses, reading and writing became little more than procedures that students performed under the

Reading + Writing as procedural, not communicative

direction of watchful instructors. Only in the less numerous vocational lab courses did the use of written language acquire any degree of independence, although it was quite minimal and was integrated into the "job" activities of the "worker" students.

In many classrooms, written language was in danger of becoming merely procedural, losing its true communicative function. Bloome (1980) described this danger in a study of one student's reading behavior in a junior high school classroom, noting that the student had been learning "patterns of surface-level behavior that allowed her to participate in some written language events without necessarily having to use written language to effectively communicate over space and time . . . she has learned them procedurally and not substantively" (p. 18).

Summary Discussion

Community college classrooms like those at Oakwood might be praised for their movement toward a more modern, relevant use of written language as part of multimodal, contextually appropriate and socially integrated activity, as well as for their adoption of efficient and abbreviated forms of written communication. This praise must be qualified, however, when we recognize the lack of critical thinking required of students and the dependent role they assume as learners.

Texting forms of reading and writing are valuable precisely because they require analysis, synthesis, and evaluation, as well as providing the opportunity for students to express original opinions. It has been through written language that students performed much of their active learning. Now these forms of written language are being dropped, and no new forms of analytic and independent communication and information processing are being substituted. The result is a "silencing" of student expression and a lack of opportunity for students to engage in critical thinking. What is alarming is not simply the change in the form of written language or a diminution of the amount of reading and writing. Rather, it is the use of written language, and all language, in a noncritical and dependent manner.

Non-critical use of Language

17.
Toward a Composing
Model of Reading

Robert J. Tierney
P. David Pearson

We believe that at the heart of understanding reading and writing connections one must begin to view reading and writing as essentially similar processes of meaning construction. Both are acts of composing. From a reader's perspective, meaning is created as a reader uses his background of experience together with the author's cues to come to grips both with what the writer is getting him to do or think *and* what the reader decides and creates for himself. As a writer writes, she uses her own background of experience to generate ideas and, in order to produce a text which is considerate to her idealized reader, filters these drafts through her judgements about what her reader's background of experience will be, what she wants to say, and what she wants to get the reader to think or do. In a sense both reader and writer must *adapt* to their perceptions about their partner in negotiating what a text means.

Witness if you will the phenomenon which was apparent as both writers and readers were asked to think aloud during the generation of, and later response to, directions for putting together a water pump (Tierney et al., 1986; Tierney 1983). As Tierney (1983) reported:

> At points in the text, the mismatch between readers' think-alouds and writers' think-alouds was apparent: Writers suggested concerns which readers did not focus upon (e.g., I'm going to have to watch my pronouns here. . . . It's rather stubborn—so I better tell how to push it hard . . . he should see that it looks very much like a syringe), and readers expressed concerns which writers did not appear to consider (I'm wondering why I should do this . . . what function does it serve). As writers thought aloud, generated text, and moved to the next set of sub-assembly directions, they would often comment about the *writers' craft* as readers might (e.g., no confusion there. . . . That's a fairly clear descriptor . . . and

writer switching internal roles

↓

readers re-writing texts – against authors

we've already defined what that is). There was also a sense in which writers marked their compositions with an "okay" as if the "okay" marked a movement from a turn as reader to a turn as writer. Analyses of the readers' *think alouds* suggested that the readers often felt frustrated by the writers' failure to explain why they were doing what they were doing. Also the readers were often critical of *the writer's craft*, including writers' choice of words, clarity, and accuracy. There was a sense in which the readers' *think alouds* assumed a reflexive character as if the readers were rewriting the texts. If one perceived the readers as craftpersons, unwilling to blame their tools for an ineffective product, then one might view the readers as unwilling to let the text provided stand in the way of their successful achievement of their goals or pursuit of understanding. (p. 150)

These data and other descriptions of the reading act (e.g., Bruce 1981; Collins, Brown, and Larkin 1970; Rosenblatt 1976, 1980; Tompkins 1980) are consistent with the view that texts are written and read in a tug of war between authors and readers. These think-alouds highlight the kinds of internal struggles that we all face (whether consciously or unconsciously) as we compose the meaning of a text in front of us.

Few would disagree that writers compose meaning. In this paper we argue that readers also compose meaning (that there is no meaning on the page until a reader decides there is). We will develop this position by describing some aspects of the composing process held in parallel by reading and writing. In particular, we will address the essential characteristics of effective composing: planning, drafting, aligning, revising and monitoring.

Planning

Data?

As a writer initially plans her writing, so a reader plans his reading. Planning involves two complementary processes: goal-setting and knowledge mobilization. Taken together, they reflect some commonly accepted behaviors, such as setting purposes, evaluating one's current state of knowledge about a topic, focussing or narrowing topics and goals, and self-questioning.

use this in paper – content oriented authorship

Flower and Hayes (1981) have suggested that a writer's goals may be procedural (e.g., how do I approach this topic), substantive (e.g., I want to say something about how rockets work), or intentional (e.g., I want to convince people of the problem). So may a reader's goals be procedural (e.g., I want to get a sense of this topic overall), substantive (e.g., I need to find out about the relationship between England and France), or intentional (e.g., I wonder what this author is trying to say) or some combination of all three. These goals can be embedded in one another or addressed concurrently; they may be conflicting or complementary. As a reader reads (just as when a writer writes) goals may emerge, be discovered, or change. For example, a reader or writer may broaden, fine tune, redefine, delete, or replace goals. A fourth grade writer whom we interviewed about a project he had completed on American Indians illustrates these notions well: As he stated his changing goals, " . . . I began with the topic of Indians but that was too broad, I decided to narrow my focus on Hopis, but that was not what I was really interested in. Finally, I decided that what I really

[handwritten margin note: At what point in the process is he doing this?]

wanted to learn about was medicine men . . . I really found some interesting things to write about." In coming to grips with his goals our writer suggested both procedural and substantive goals. Note also that he refined his goals prior to drafting. In preparation for reading or writing a draft, goals usually change; mostly they become focussed at a level of specificity sufficient to allow the reading or writing to continue. Consider how a novel might be read. We begin reading a novel to discover the plot, yet find ourselves asking specific questions about events and attending to the author's craft—how she uses the language to create certain effects. *[handwritten: Inference the reader's function like "allowed".]*

[handwritten margin: "writers]

The goals that readers or writers set have a symbiotic relationship with the knowledge they mobilize, and together they influence what is produced or understood in a text (Anderson, Reynolds, Schallert, and Goetz 1977; Anderson, Pichert and Shirey 1979; Hays and Tierney 1981; Tierney and Mosenthal 1981). A writer plans what she wants to say with the knowledge resources at her disposal. Our fourth grade writer changed his goals as a function of the specificity of the knowledge domain to which he successively switched. Likewise readers, depending on their level of topic knowledge and what they want to learn from their reading, vary the goals they initiate and pursue. As an example of this symbiosis in a reader, consider the following statement from a reader of *Psychology Today*.

[handwritten margin: How are goals represented?]

> I picked up an issue of *Psychology Today*. One particular article dealing with women in movies caught my attention. I guess it was the photos of Streep, Fonda, Lange, that interested me. As I had seen most of their recent movies I felt as if I knew something about the topic. As I a started reading, the author had me recalling my reactions to these movies (Streep in "Sophie's Choice," Lange in "Tootsie," Fonda in "Julia"). At first I intended to glance at the article. But as I read on, recalling various scenes, I became more and more interested in the author's perspective. Now that my reactions were nicely mobilized, this author (definitely a feminist) was able to convince me of her case for stereotyping. I had not realized the extent to which women are either portrayed as the victim, cast with men, or not developed at all as a character in their own right. This author carried me back through these movies and revealed things I had not realized. It was as if I had my own purposes in mind but I saw things through her eyes. *[handwritten: Ideology and rhetoric]*

[handwritten margin: viz: Plato]

What is interesting in this example is how the reader's knowledge about films and feminism was mobilized at the same time as his purposes became gradually welded to those of the author's. The reader went *from* almost free association, *to* reflection, *to* directed study of what he knew. It is this directed study of what one knows that is so important in knowledge mobilization. A writer does not just throw out ideas randomly; she carefully plans the placement of ideas in text so that each idea acquires just the right degree of emphasis in text. A successful reader uses his knowledge just as carefully; at just the right moment he accesses just the right knowledge structures necessary to interpret the text at hand in a way consistent with his goals. Note also how the goals a reader sets can determine the knowledge he calls up; at the same time, that knowledge, especially as it is modified in conjunction with the reader's engagement of the text, causes him to alter his goals. Initially, a reader might "brainstorm" his store of knowledge and maybe organize some of it (e.g., clustering ideas using general questions such as who, what, when, where, or why *or* developing outlines). Some readers might make notes; others might merely think about what they know, how this information clusters, and what they want to pursue. Or, just as a writer sometimes uses a first draft to explore what she knows and what she wants to say, so a reader might scan the text as a way of fine tuning the range of knowledge and goals to engage, creating a kind of a "draft" reading of the text. It is to this topic of drafting that we now turn your attention.

Or "not thinking"

Drafting

We define drafting as the refinement of meaning which occurs as readers and writers deal directly with the print on the page. All of us who have had to write something (be it an article, a novel, a memo, a letter, or a theme), know just how difficult getting started can be. Many of us feel that if we could only get a draft on paper, we could rework and revise our way to completion. We want to argue that getting started is just as important a step in reading. What every reader needs, like every writer, is a first draft. And the first step in producing that draft is finding the right "lead." Murray (1982) describes the importance of finding the lead:

drafting and "the lead in"

> The lead is the beginning of the beginning, those few lines the reader may glance at in deciding to read or pass on. These few words—fifty, forty, thirty, twenty, ten—establish the tone, the point of view, the order, the dimensions of the article. In a sense, the entire article is coiled in the first few words waiting to be released.
>
> An article, perhaps even a book, can only say one thing and when the lead is found, the writer knows what is included in the article and what is left out, what must be left out. As one word is chosen for the lead another rejected, as a comma is put in and another taken away, the lead begins to feel right and the pressure builds up until it is almost impossible not to write. (p. 99)

From a reader's perspective, the key points to note from Murray's description are these: 1) "the entire article is coiled in these first few words waiting to be released," and 2) "the lead begins to feel right. . . ." The reader, as he reads, has that same feeling as he begins to draft his understanding of a text. The whole point of hypothesis testing models of reading like those of Goodman (1967) and Smith (1971) is that the current hypothesis one holds about what a text means creates strong expectations about what succeeding text ought to address. So strong are these hypotheses, these "coilings," these drafts of meaning a reader creates that incoming text failing to cohere with them may be ignored or rejected.

But these theories have been discredited...

Follow us as we describe a hypothetical reader and writer beginning their initial drafts.

A reader opens his or her textbook, magazine or novel; a writer reaches for his pen. The reader scans the pages for a place to begin; the writer holds the pen poised. The reader looks over the first few lines of the article or story in search of a sense of what the general scenario is. (This occurs whether the reader is reading a murder mystery, a newspaper account of unemployment, or a magazine article on underwater life.) Our writer searches for the lead statement or introduction to her text. For the reader, knowing the scenario may involve knowing that the story is about women engaged in career advancement from a feminist perspective, knowing the murder mystery involves the death of a wealthy husband vacationing abroad. For the writer, establishing the scenario involves prescribing those few ideas which introduce or define the topic. Once established, the reader proceeds through the text, refining and building upon his sense of what is going on; the writer does likewise. Once the writer has found the "right" lead, she proceeds to develop the plot, expositions, or descriptions. As the need to change scenarios occurs, so the process is repeated. From a schema-theoretic perspective, coming to grips with a lead statement or, if you are a reader, gleaning an initial scenario, can be viewed as schema selection (which is somewhat equivalent to choosing a script for a play); filling in the slots or refining the scenario is equivalent to schema instantiation.

As our descriptions of a hypothetical reader suggest, what drives reading and writing is this desire to make sense of what is happening—to make things cohere. A writer achieves that fit by deciding what information to include and what to withhold. The reader accomplishes that fit by filling in gaps (it must be early in the morning) or making uncued connections (he must have become angry because they lost the game). All readers, like all writers, ought to strive for this fit between the whole and the parts and among the parts. Unfortunately, some readers and writers are satisfied with a piecemeal experience (dealing with each part separately), or, alternatively, a sense of the whole without a sense of how the parts relate to it. Other readers and writers become "bogged down" in their desire to achieve a perfect text or "fit" on the first draft. For language educators our task is to help readers and writers to achieve the best fit among the whole and the parts. It is with this concern in mind that we now consider the role of alignment and then revision.

Aligning

In conjunction with the planning and drafting initiated, we believe that the alignment a reader or writer adopts can have an overriding influence on a composer's ability to achieve coherence. We see alignment as having two facets: stances a reader or writer assumes in collaboration with their author or audience, and roles within which the reader or writer immerse themselves as they proceed with the topic. In other words, as readers and writers approach a text they vary the nature of their stance or collaboration with their author (if they are a reader) or audience (if they are a writer) and, in conjunction with this collaboration, immerse themselves in a variety of roles. A writer's stance toward her readers might be intimate, challenging or quite neutral. And, within the contexts of these collaborations she might share what she wants to say through characters or as an observer of events. Likewise, a reader can adopt a stance toward the writer which is sympathetic, critical or passive. And, within the context of these collaborations, he can immerse himself in the text as an observer or eye witness, participant or character.

As we have suggested, alignment results in certain benefits. Indeed, direct and indirect support for the facilitative benefits of adopting alignments comes from research on a variety of fronts. For example, schema theoretic studies involving an analysis of the influence of a reader's perspective have shown that if readers are given different alignments prior to or after reading a selection, they will vary in what and how much they will recall (Pichert 1979; Spiro 1977). For example, readers told to read a description of a house from the perspective of a homebuyer or burglar tend to recall more information and are more apt to include in their recollections information consistent with their perspective. Furthermore, when asked to consider an alternative perspective these same readers were able to generate information which they previously had not retrieved and which was important to the new perspective. Researchers interested in the effects of imaging have examined the effects of visualizing—a form of alignment which we would argue is equivalent to eye witnessing. Across a number of studies it has been shown that readers who are encouraged to visualize usually perform better on comprehension tasks (e.g., Sodoski, in press). The work on children's development of the ability to recognize point of view (Hay and Brewer 1982; Applebee 1978) suggests that facility with alignment develops with comprehension maturity. From our own interviews with young readers and writers we have found that the identification with characters and immersion in a story reported by our interviewees accounts for much of the vibrancy, sense of control and fulfillment experienced during reading and writing. Likewise, some of the research analyzing proficient writing suggests that proficient writers are those writers who, when they read over what they have written, comment on the extent to which their story and characters are engaging (Birnbaum 1982). A number of studies in both psychotherapy and creativity provide support for the importance of alignment. For purposes of generating solutions to problems, psychotherapists have found it useful to encourage individuals to exchange roles (e.g., mother with daughter). In an attempt to generate discoveries, researchers have had experts identify with the experiences of inanimate objects (e.g., paint on metal) as a means of considering previously inaccessible solutions (e.g., a paint which does not peel).

Based upon these findings and our own observations, we hypothesize that adopting an alignment is akin to achieving a foothold from which meaning can be more readily negotiated. Just as a filmmaker can adopt and vary the angle from which a scene is depicted in order to maximize the richness of a filmgoer's experience, so too can a reader and writer adopt and vary the angle from which language meanings are negotiated. This suggests, for language educators, support for those questions or activities which help readers or writers take a stance on a topic and immerse themselves in the ideas or story. This might entail having students read or write with a definite point of view or attitude. It might suggest having students project themselves into a scene as a character, eye witness or object (imagine you are Churchill, a reporter, the sea). This might occur at the hands of questioning, dramatization, or simply role playing. In line with our hypothesis, we believe that in these contexts students almost spontaneously acquire a sense of the whole as well as the parts.

To illustrate how the notion of alignment might manifest itself for different readers, consider the following statement offered by a professor describing the stances he takes while reading an academic paper:

> When I read something for the first time, I read it argumentatively. I also find later that I made marginal notations that were quite nasty like, "You're crazy!" or "Why do you want to say that?" Sometimes they are not really fair and that's why I really think to read philosophy you have to read it twice. . . . The second time you read it over you should read it as sympathetically as possible. This time you read it trying to defend the person against the very criticisms that you made the first time through. You read every sentence and if there is an issue that bothers you, you say to yourself, "This guy who wrote this is really very smart. It sounds like what he is saying is wrong; I must be misunderstanding him. What could he really want to be saying?" (Freeman 1982, p. 11)

Also, consider Eleanor Gibson's description of how she approaches the work of Jane Austen:

> Her novels are not for airport reading. They are for reading over and over, savoring every phrase, memorizing the best of them, and getting an even deeper understanding of Jane's "sense of human comedy. . . ." As I read the book for perhaps the twenty-fifth time, I consider what point she is trying to make in the similarities and differences between the characters. . . . I want to discover for myself what this sensitive and perceptive individual is trying to tell me. Sometimes I only want to sink back and enjoy it and laugh myself. (Gibson and Levin, 1975, pp. 458–460)

Our professor adjusted his stance from critic to sympathetic coauthor across different readings. Our reader of Austen was, at times, a highly active and sympathetic collaborator and, at other times, more neutral and passive.

Obviously, the text itself prompts certain alignments. For example, consider how an author's choice of words, arguments, or selection of genre may invite a reader to assume different stances and, in the context of these collaborations, different roles. The opening paragraph of Wolfe's *Electric Kool-Aid Acid Test* (1977) illustrates how the use of first person along with the descriptive power of words (e.g., cramped . . . metal bottom . . . rising . . . rolling . . . bouncing) compels the reader to engage in a sympathetic collaboration with an author and be immersed as an active participant in a truck ride across the hills of San Francisco.

> That's good thinking there, Cool Breeze. Cool Breeze is a kid with 3 or 4 days' beard sitting next to me on the cramped metal bottom of the open back part of the pickup truck. Bouncing along. Dipping and rising and rolling on these rotten springs like a boat. Out the back of the truck the city of San Francisco is bouncing down the hill, all those endless staggers of bay windows, slums with a view, bouncing and streaming down the hill. One after another, electric signs with neon martini glasses lit up on them, the San Francisco symbol of "bar"—thousands of neon-magenta martini glasses bouncing and streaming down the hill, and beneath them thousands of people wheeling around to look at this freaking crazed truck we're in, their white faces erupting from their lapels like marshmallows—

streaming and bouncing down the hill—and God knows they've got plenty to look at. (p. 1)

Also, consider the differences in collaboration and role taking the following text segments invite. While both texts deal with the same information, in one text, the information is presented through a conversation between two children, and in the other text, the information is presented in a more "straight forward" expository style.

FLY

Lisa and Mike were bored. It was Saturday and they did not know what to do until Lisa had an idea. "I know a game we can play that they play in some countries . . .

Narrative

FLY

All over the world children like to play different games. In some countries, children enjoy playing a game called "Fly." *Exposition*

Code → message "tone"

We have found that readers of the first text usually assume a sympathetic collaboration with the writer and identify with the characters. They view the game through the eyes of the children and remain rather neutral with respect to the author. Our readers of the second text tend to have difficulty understanding the game at the same time as they are critical of the author. They adopt a role more akin to an observer who, lacking a specific angle, catches glimpses of the game without acquiring an overall understanding. Some of us have experienced a similar phenomenon as viewers of an overseas telecast of an unfamiliar sport (e.g., the game of cricket on British television). The camera angles provided by the British sportscasters are disorienting for the native viewer.

Clearly a number of factors may influence the nature of a reader's alignment and the extent to which his resulting interpretation is viable. A reader, as our last example illustrated, might adopt an alignment which interferes with how well he will be able to negotiate an understanding. Sometimes a reader might adopt an alignment which overindulges certain biases, predispositions, and personal experiences. Doris Lessing (1973) described this phenomenon in a discussion of readers' responses to her *The Golden Notebook:*

Ten years after I wrote [it], I can get, in one week, three letters about it. . . . One letter is entirely about the sex war, about man's inhumanity to woman, and woman's inhumanity to man, and the writer has produced pages and pages all about nothing else, for she—but not always a she—can't see anything else in the book.

The second is about politics, probably from an old Red like myself, and he or she writes many pages about politics. and never mentions any other theme.

These two letters used, when the book was—as it were—young, to be the most common.

The third letter, once rare but now catching up on the others, is written by a man or a woman who can see nothing in it but the theme of mental illness.

But it is the same book.

And naturally these incidents bring up again questions of what people see when they read a book, and why one person sees one pattern and nothing at all of another pattern, and how odd it is to have, as author, such a clear picture of a book, that is seen so very differently by its readers. (p. xi)

Such occurrences should not be regarded as novel. It is this phenomenon of reader-author engagement and idiosyncratic response which has been at the center of a debate among literary theorists, some of whom (e.g., Jakobson and Levi-Strauss 1962) would suggest that a "true" reading experience has been instantiated only when readers assume an alignment which involves close collaboration with authors. Others would argue that readers can assume a variety of alignments, whether these alignments are constrained by the author (Iser 1974) or initiated freely by the reader (Fish 1970). They would rarely go so far as to suggest the destruction of the text, but instead, as Tompkins (1980) suggested, they might begin to view reading and writing as joining hands, changing places, "and finally becoming distinguishable only as two names for the same activity" (p. ii). We do not wish to debate the distinctions represented by these and other theorists, but to suggest that there appears to be at least some consensus that effective reading involves a form of alignment which emerges in conjunction with a working relationship between readers and writers. In our opinion, this does not necessitate bridling readers and writers to one another. Indeed, we would hypothesize that new insights are more likely discovered and appreciations derived when readers and writers try out different alignments as they read and write their texts. This suggests spending time rethinking, reexamining, reviewing and rereading. For this type of experience does not occur on a single reading; rather it emerges only after several rereadings, reexaminations, and drafts. It is to this notion of reexamination and revision that we now turn. *Reader response theory reduced?* [handwritten]

Revising

While it is common to think of a writer as a reviser it is *not* common to think of a reader as someone who revises unless perhaps he has a job involving some editorial functions. We believe that this is unfortunate. We would like to suggest that revising should be considered as integral to reading as it is to writing. If readers are to develop some control over and a sense of discovery with the models of meaning they build, they must approach text with the same deliberation, time, and reflection that a writer employs as she revises a text. They must examine their developing interpretations and view the models they build as draft-like in quality—subject to revision. We would like to see students engage in behaviors such as rereading (especially with different alignments), annotating the text on the page with reactions, and questioning whether the model they have built is what they really want. With this in mind let us turn our attention to revising in writing.

We have emphasized that writing is not merely taking ideas from one's head and placing them onto the page. A writer must choose words which best represent these ideas; that is, she must choose words which have the desired impact. Sometimes this demands knowing what she wants to say and how to say

[handwritten margin note: Prescriptive! ↓ denaturalizing reading into forced multiple readings]

it. At other times, it warrants examining what is written or read to discover and clarify one's ideas. Thus a writer will repeatedly reread, reexamine, delete, shape, and correct what she is writing. She will consider whether and how her ideas fit together, how well her words represent the ideas to be shared and how her text can be fine tuned. For some writers this development and redevelopment will appear to be happening effortlessly. For others, revision demands hard labor and sometimes several painful drafts. Some rework the drafts in their head before they rewrite; others slowly rework pages as they go. From analyses of the revision strategies of experienced writers, it appears that the driving force behind revision is a sense of emphasis and proportion. As Sommers (1980) suggested, one of the questions most experienced writers ask themselves is "what does my essay as a *whole* need for form, balance, rhythm, and communication?" (p. 386). In trying to answer this question, writers proceed through revision cycles with sometimes overlapping and sometimes novel concerns. Initial revision cycles might be directed predominately at topical development; later cycles might be directed at stylistic concerns.

For most readers, revision is an unheard of experience. Observations of secondary students reveal that most readers view reading competency as the ability to read rapidly a single text once with maximum recall (Schallert and Tierney 1982). It seems that students rarely pause to reflect on their ideas or to judge the quality of their developing interpretations. Nor do they often reread a text either from the same or a different perspective. In fact, to suggest that a reader should approach text as a writer who crafts an understanding across several drafts—who pauses, rethinks, and revises—is almost contrary to some well established goals readers proclaim for themselves (e.g., that efficient reading is equivalent to maximum recall based upon a single fast reading).

Suppose we could convince students that they ought to revise their readings of a text; would they be able to do it? We should not assume that merely allowing time for pausing, reflecting, and reexamining will guarantee that students will revise their readings. Students need to be given support and feedback at so doing. Students need to be aware of strategies they can pursue to accomplish revisions, to get things restarted when they stall, and to compare one draft or reading with another. The pursuit of a second draft of a reading should have a purpose. Sometimes this purpose can emerge from discussing a text with the teacher and peers; sometimes it may come from within; sometimes it will not occur unless the student has a reason or functional context for revision as well as help from a thoughtful teacher.

Monitoring

Hand in hand with planning, aligning, drafting, and revising, readers and writers must be able to distance themselves from the texts they have created to evaluate what they have developed. We call this executive function monitoring. Monitoring usually occurs tacitly, but it can be under conscious control. The monitor in us keeps track of and control over our other functions. Our monitor decides whether we have planned, aligned, drafted, and/or revised properly. It decides when one activity should dominate over the others. Our monitor tells us when we have done a good job and when we have not. It tells us when to go back to the drawing board and when we can relax.

The complexity of the type of juggling which the monitor is capable of has been captured aptly in an analogy of a switchboard operator, used by Flower and Hayes (1980) to describe how writers juggle constraints:

> She has two important calls on hold. (Don't forget that idea.)
> Four lights just started flashing. (They demand immediate attention or they'll be lost.)
> A party of five wants to be hooked up together. (They need to be connected somehow.)
> A party of two thinks they've been incorrectly connected. (Where do they go?)
> And throughout this complicated process of remembering, retrieving, and connecting, the operator's voice must project calmness, confidence, and complete control. (p. 33)

The monitor has one final task—to engage in a dialogue with the inner reader.

When writers and readers compose text they negotiate its meaning with what Murray (1982) calls the other self—that inner reader (the author's first reader) who continually reacts to what the writer has written, is writing and will write or what the reader has read, is reading and will read. It is this other self which is the reader's or writer's counsel, and judge, and prompter. This other self oversees what the reader and writer is trying to do, defines the nature of collaboration between reader and author, and decides how well the reader as writer or writer as reader is achieving his or her goals.

Hermeneutic circle

A Summary and Discussion

To reiterate, we view both reading and writing as acts of composing. We see these acts of composing as involving continuous, recurring, and recursive transactions among readers and writers, their respective inner selves, and their perceptions of each other's goals and desires. Consider the reader's role as we envision it. At the same time as the reader considers what he perceives to be the author's intentions (or what the reader perceives to be what the author is trying to get the reader to do or think), he negotiates goals with his inner self (or what he would like to achieve). With these goals being continuously negotiated (sometimes embedded within each other) the reader proceeds to take different alignments (critic, co-athor, editor, character, reporter, eye witness, etc.) as he uses features from his own experiential arrays and what he perceives to be arrayed by the author in order to create a model of meaning for the text. These models of meaning must assume a coherent, holistic quality in which everything fits together. The development of these models of meaning occurs from the vantage point of different alignments which the reader adopts with respect to these arrays. It is from these vantage points that the various arrays are perceived, and their position adjusted such that the reader's goals and desire for a sense of

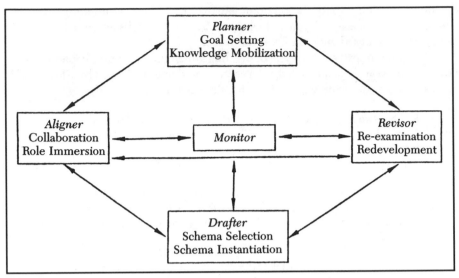

Figure 17.1. Some components of the composing model of reading

completeness are achieved. Our diagrammatic representation of the major components of these processes is given in figure 17-1.

Such an account of reading distinguishes itself from previous descriptions of reading and reading-writing relationships in several notable ways:

1. Most accounts of reading versus writing (as well as accounts of how readers develop a model of meaning) tend to emphasize reading as a receptive rather than productive activity. Some, in fact, regard reading as the mirror image of writing.
2. Most language accounts suggest that reading and writing are interrelated. They do not address the suggestion that reading and writing are multi-dimensional, multi-modal processes—both acts of composing.
3. The phenomenon of alignment as integral to composing has rarely been explored.
4. Most descriptions of how readers build models of meaning fail to consider how the processes of planning, drafting, aligning, and revising are manifested.
5. Previous interactional and transactional accounts of reading (Rosenblatt 1978; Rumelhart 1980) give little consideration to the transaction which occurs among the inner selves of the reader and writer.

What our account fails to do is thoroughly differentiate how these composing behaviors manifest themselves in the various contexts of reading and writing. Nor does it address the pattern of interactions among these behaviors across moments during any reading and writing experience. For example, we give the impression of sequential stages even though we believe in simultaneous processes. We hope to clarify and extend these notions in subsequent writings.

18.
Inventing the University

David Bartholomae[1]

Education may well be, as of right, the instrument whereby every individual, in a society like our own, can gain access to any kind of discourse. But we well know that in its distribution, in what it permits and in what it prevents, it follows the well-trodden battle-lines of social conflict. Every educational system is a political means of maintaining or of modifying the appropriation of discourse, with the knowledge and the powers it carries with it.

Foucault, "The Discourse on Language" (227)

Every time a student sits down to write for us, he has to invent the university for the occasion—invent the university, that is, or a branch of it, like History or Anthropology or Economics or English. He has to learn to speak our language, to speak as we do, to try on the peculiar ways of knowing, selecting, evaluating, reporting, concluding, and arguing that define the discourse of our community. Or perhaps I should say the *various* discourses of our community, since it is in the nature of a liberal arts education that a student, after the first year or two, must learn to try on a variety of voices and interpretive schemes—to write, for example, as a literary critic one day and an experimental psychologist the next, to work within fields where the rules governing the presentation of examples or the development of an argument are both distinct and, even to a professional, mysterious.

The students have to appropriate (or be appropriated by) a specialized discourse, and they have to do this as though they were easily and comfortably one with their audience, as though they were members of the academy, or historians or anthropologists or economists; they have to invent the university by assembling and mimicking its language, finding some compromise between idiosyncracy, a personal history, and the requirements of convention, the history of a discipline. They must learn to speak our language. Or they must dare to speak it, or to carry off the bluff, since speaking and writing will most certainly be required long before the skill is "learned." And this, understandably, causes problems.

Let me look quickly at an example. Here is an essay written by a college freshman, a basic writer:

From *When a Writer Can't Write: Studies in Writer's Block and Other Composing Problems*, ed. Mike Rose. Copyright 1985 by the Guilford Press. Reprinted by permission of the publisher.

In the past time I thought that an incident was creative was when I had to make a clay model of the earth, but not of the classical or your everyday model of the earth which consists of the two cores, the mantle and the crust. I thought of these things in a dimension of which it would be unique, but easy to comprehend. Of course, your materials to work with were basic and limited at the same time, but thought help to put this limit into a right attitude or frame of mind to work with the clay.

In the beginning of the clay model, I had to research and learn the different dimensions of the earth (in magnitude, quantity, state of matter, etc.) After this, I learned how to put this into the clay and come up with something different than any other person in my class at the time. In my opinion, color coordination and shape was the key to my creativity of the clay model of the earth.

Creativity is the venture of the mind at work with the mechanics relay to the limbs from the cranium, which stores and triggers this action. It can be a burst of energy released at a precise time a thought is being transmitted. This can cause a frenzy of the human body, but it depends of the characteristics of the individual and how they can relay the message clearly enough through mechanics of the body to us as an observer. Then we must determine if it is creative or a learned process varied by the individuals thought process. Creativity is indeed a tool which has to exist, or our world will not succeed into the future and progress like it should.

I am continually impressed by the patience and good will of our students. This student was writing a placement essay during freshman orientation. (The problem set to him was, "Describe a time when you did something you felt to be creative. Then, on the basis of the incident you have described, go on to draw some general conclusions about 'creativity'.") He knew that university faculty would be reading and evaluating his essay, and so he wrote for them.

In some ways it is a remarkable performance. He is trying on the discourse even though he doesn't have the knowledge that makes the discourse more than a routine, a set of conventional rituals and gestures. And he does this, I think, even though he *knows* he doesn't have the knowledge that makes the discourse more than a routine. He defines himself as a researcher, working systematically, and not as a kid in a high school class: "I thought of these things in a dimension of . . ."; "had to research and learn the different dimensions of the earth (in magnitude, quantity, state of matter, etc.)." He moves quickly into a specialized language (his approximation of our jargon) and draws both a general, textbook-like conclusion ("Creativity is the venture of the mind at work . . .") and a resounding peroration ("Creativity is indeed a tool which has to exist, or our world will not succeed into the future and progress like it should"). The writer has even, with that "indeed" and with the qualifications and the parenthetical expressions of the opening paragraphs, picked up the rhythm of our prose. And through it all he speaks with an impressive air of authority.

There is an elaborate but, I will argue, a necessary and enabling fiction at work here as the student dramatizes his experience in a "setting"—the setting required by the discourse—where he can speak to us as a companion, a fellow researcher. As I read the essay, there is only one moment when the fiction is broken, when we are addressed differently. The student says, "Of course, your materials to work with were basic and limited at the same time, but thought help to put this limit into a right attitude or frame of mind to work with the clay." At this point, I think, we become students and he the teacher, giving us a lesson (as in, "You take your pencil in your right hand and put your paper in front of you"). This is, however, one of the most characteristic slips of basic writers. It is very hard for them to take on the role—the voice, the person—of an authority whose authority is rooted in scholarship, analysis, or research. They slip, then, into the more immediately available and realizable voice of authority, the voice of a teacher giving a lesson or the voice of a parent lecturing at the dinner table. They offer advice or homilies rather than "academic" conclusions. There is a similar break in the final paragraph, where the conclusion that pushes for a definition ("Creativity is the venture of the mind at work with the mechanics relay to the limbs from the cranium . . .") is replaced by a conclusion which speaks in the voice of an Elder ("Creativity is indeed a tool which has to exist, or our world will not succeed into the future and progress like it should").

It is not uncommon, then, to find such breaks in the concluding sections of essays written by basic writers. Here is the concluding section of essay written by a student about his work as a mechanic. He had been asked to generalize about "work" after reviewing an on-the-job experience or incident that "stuck in his mind" as somehow significant: "How could two repairmen miss a leak? Lack of pride? No incentive? Lazy? I don't know." At this point the writer is in a perfect position to speculate, to move from the problem to an analysis of the problem. Here is how the paragraph continues however (and notice the change in pronoun reference):

> From this point on, I take my time, do it right, and don't let customers get under your skin. If they have a complaint, tell them to call your boss and he'll be more than glad to handle it. Most important, worry about yourself, and keep a clear eye on everyone, for there's always someone trying to take advantage of you, anytime and anyplace.

We get neither a technical discussion nor an "academic" discussion but a Lesson on Life.[2] This is the language he uses to address the general question, "How could two repairmen miss a leak?" The other brand of conclusion, the more academic one, would have required him to speak of his experience in our terms; it would, that is, have required a special vocabulary, a special system of presentation, and an interpretive scheme (or a set of commonplaces) he could use to identify and talk about the mystery of human error. The writer certainly had access to the range of acceptable commonplaces for such an explanation: "lack of pride," "no incentive," "lazy." Each would dictate its own set of phrases, examples, and conclusions, and we, his teachers, would know how to write out each argument, just as we would know how to write out more specialized arguments of our own. A "commonplace," then, is a culturally or institutionally authorized concept or statement that carries with it its own necessary elaboration. We all use commonplaces to orient ourselves in the world; they provide a point of reference and a set of "prearticulated" explanations that are readily available to organize and interpret experience. The phrase "lack of pride" carries with it its own account for the repairman's error just as, at another point in time, a reference to "original sin" would provide an explanation, or just as, in a certain university classroom, a reference to "alienation" would enable a writer to continue and complete the discussion. While there is a way in which these terms are interchangeable, they are not all permissible. A student in a composition class would most likely be turned away from a discussion of original sin. Commonplaces are the "controlling ideas" of our composition textbooks, textbooks that not only insist upon a set form for expository writing but a set view of public life.[3]

When the student above says, "I don't know," he is not saying, then, that he has nothing to say. He is saying that he is not in a position to carry on this discussion. And so we are addressed as apprentices rather than as teachers or scholars. To speak to us as a person of status or privilege, the writer can either speak to us in our terms—in the privileged language of university discourse—or, in default (or in defiance), he can speak to us as though we were children, offering us the wisdom of experience.

I think it is possible to say that the language of the "Clay Model" paper has come through the writer and not from the writer. The writer has located himself (he has located the self that is represented by the I on the page) in a context that is, finally, beyond him, not his own and not available to his immediate procedures for inventing and arranging text. I would not, that is, call this essay an example of "writer-based" prose. I would not say that it is egocentric or that it represents the "interior monologue of a writer thinking and talking to himself" (Flower 63). It is, rather, the record of a writer who has lost himself in the discourse of his readers. There is a context beyond the reader that is not the world but a way of talking about the world, a way of talking that determines the use of examples, the possible conclusions, the acceptable commonplaces, and the key words of an essay on the construction of a clay model of the earth. This writer has entered the discourse without successfully approximating it.

Linda Flower has argued that the difficulty inexperienced writers have with writing can be understood as a difficulty in negotiating the transition between writer-based and reader-based prose. Expert writers, in other words, can better imagine how a reader will respond to a text and can transform or restructure what they have to say around a goal shared with a reader. Teaching students to revise for readers, then, will better prepare them to write initially with a reader in mind. The success of this pedagogy depends upon the degree to which a writer can imagine and conform to a reader's goals. The difficulty of this act of imagination, and the burden of such conformity, are so much at the heart of the problem that a teacher must pause and take stock before offering revision as a solution. Students like the student who wrote the "Clay Model" paper are not so much trapped in a private language as they are shut out from one of the privileged languages of public life, a language they are aware of but cannot control.

Our students, I've said, have to appropriate (or be appropriated by) a specialized discourse, and they have to do this as though they were easily or comfortably one with their audience. If you look at the situation this way, suddenly the problem of audience awareness becomes enormously complicated. One of the common assumptions of both composition research and composition teaching is that at some "stage" in the process of composing an essay a writer's ideas or his motives must be tailored to the needs and expectations of his audience. A writer has to "build bridges" between his point of view and his readers. He has to anticipate and acknowledge his readers' assumptions and biases. He must begin with "common points of departure" before introducing new or controversial arguments. There is a version of the pastoral at work here. It is assumed that a person of low status (like a shepherd) can speak to a person of power (like a courtier), but only (at least so far as the language is concerned) if he is not a shepherd at all, but actually a member of the court out in the fields in disguise.

Writers who can successfully manipulate an audience (or, to use a less pointed language, writers who can accommodate their motives to their readers' expectations) are writers who can both imagine and write from a position of privilege. They must, that is, see themselves within a privileged discourse, one that already includes and excludes groups of readers. They must be either equal to or more powerful than those they would address. The writing, then, must somehow transform the political and social relationships between basic writing students and their teachers.

If my students are going to write for me by knowing who I am—and if this means more than knowing my prejudices, psyching me out—it means knowing what I know; it means having the knowledge of a professor of English. They have, then, to know what I know and how I know what I know (the interpretive schemes that define the way I would work out the problems I set for them); they have to learn to write what I would write, or to offer up some approximation of that discourse. The problem of audience awareness, then, is a problem of power and finesse. It cannot be addressed, as it is in most classroom exercises, by giving students privilege and denying the situation of the classroom, by having students write to an outsider, someone excluded from their privileged circle: "Write about 'To His Coy Mistress,' not for your teacher, but for the students in your class"; "Describe Pittsburgh to someone who has never been there"; "Explain to a high school senior how best to prepare for college"; "Describe baseball to a Martian."

Exercises such as these allow students to imagine the needs and goals of a reader and they bring those needs and goals forward as a dominant constraint in the construction of an essay. And they argue, implicitly, what is generally true about writing—that it is an act of aggression disguised as an act of charity. What they fail to address is the central problem of academic writing, where students must assume the right of speaking to someone who knows Pittsburgh or "To His Coy Mistress" better than they do, a reader for whom the general commonplaces and the readily available utterances about a subject are inadequate. It should be clear that when I say that I know Pittsburgh better than my basic writing students I am talking about a way of knowing that is also a way of writing. There may be much that they know that I don't know, but in the setting of the university classroom I have a way of talking about the town that is "better" (and for arbitrary reasons) than theirs.

I think that all writers, in order to write, must imagine for themselves the privilege of being "insiders"—that is, of being both inside an established and powerful discourse, and of being granted a special right to speak. And I think that right to speak is seldom conferred upon us—upon any of us, teachers or students—by virtue of the fact that we have invented or discovered an original idea. Leading students to believe that they are responsible for something new or original, unless they understand what those words mean with regard to writing, is a dangerous and counterproductive practice. We do have the right to expect students to be active and engaged, but that is more a matter of being continually and stylistically working against the inevitable presence of conventional language; it is not a matter of inventing a language that is new.

When students are writing for a teacher, writing becomes more problematic than it is for the students who are describing baseball to a Martian. The students, in effect, have to assume privilege without having any. And since students assume privilege by locating themselves within the discourse of a particular community—within a set of specifically acceptable gestures and commonplaces—learning, at least as it is defined in the liberal arts curriculum, becomes more a matter of imitation or parody than a matter of invention and discovery.

What our beginning students need to learn is to extend themselves into the commonplaces, set phrases, rituals, gestures, habits of mind, tricks of persuasion, obligatory conclusions, and necessary connections that determine the "what might be said" and constitute knowledge within the various branches of our academic community. The course of instruction that would make this possible would be based on a sequence of illustrated assignments and would allow for successive approximations of academic or "disciplinary" discourse. Students will not take on our peculiar ways of reading, writing, speaking, and thinking all at once. Nor will the command of a subject like sociology, at least as that command is represented by the successful completion of a multiple choice exam, enable students to write sociology. Our colleges and universities, by and large, have failed to involve basic writing students in scholarly projects, projects that would allow them to act as though they were colleagues in an academic enterprise. Much of the written work students do is test-taking, report or summary, work that places them outside the working discourse of the academic community, where they are expected to admire and report on what we do, rather than inside that discourse, where they can do its work and participate in a common enterprise.[4] This is a failure of teachers and curriculum designers who, even if they speak of writing as a mode of learning, all too often represent writing as a "tool" to be used by an (hopefully) educated mind.

Pat Bizzell is one of the most important scholars writing now on basic writers and on the special requirements of academic discourse.[5] In a recent essay, "Cognition, Convention, and Certainty: What We Need to Know About Writing," she argues that the problems of basic writers might be

> better understood in terms of their unfamiliarly with the academic discourse community, combined, perhaps, with such limited experience outside their native discourse communities that they are unaware that there is such a thing as a discourse community with conventions to be mastered. What is underdeveloped is their knowledge both of the ways experience is constituted and interpreted in the academic discourse community and of the fact that all discourse communities constitute and interpret experience. (230)

One response to the problems of basic writers, then, would be to determine just what the community's conventions are, so that those conventions can be written out, "demystified," and taught in our classrooms. Teachers, as a result, could be more precise and helpful when they ask students to "think," "argue," "describe," or "define." Another response would be to examine the essays written by basic writers—their approximations of academic discourse—to determine more clearly where the problems lie. If we look at their writing, and if we look at it in the context of other student writing, we can better see the points of discord when students try to write their way into the university.

The purpose of the remainder of this paper will be to examine some of the most striking and characteristic problems as they are presented in the expository essays of basic writers. I will be concerned, then, with university discourse in its most generalized form—that is, as represented by introductory courses—and not with the special conventions required by advanced work in the various disciplines. And I will be concerned with the difficult, and often violent, accommodations that occur when students locate themselves in a discourse that is not "naturally" or immediately theirs.

I have reviewed five hundred essays written in response to the "creativity" question used during one of our placement exams. (The essay cited at the opening of this paper was one of that group.) Some of the essays were written by basic writers (or, more properly, those essays led readers to identify the writers as "basic writers"); some were written by students who "passed" (who were granted immediate access to the community of writers at the university). As I read these essays, I was looking to determine the stylistic resources that enabled writers to locate themselves within an "academic" discourse. My bias as a reader should be clear by now. I was not looking to see how the writer might represent the skills demanded by a neutral language (a language whose key features were paragraphs, topic sentences, transitions, and the like—features of a clear and orderly mind). I was looking to see what happened when a writer entered into a language to locate himself (a textual self) and his subject, and I was looking to see how, once entered, that language made or unmade a writer.

Here is one essay. Its writer was classified as a basic writer. Since the essay is relatively free of sentence level errors, that decision must have been rooted in some perceived failure of the discourse itself.

> I am very interested in music, and I try to be creative in my interpretation of music. While in high school, I was a member of a jazz ensemble. The members of the ensemble were given chances to improvise and be creative in various songs. I feel that this was a great experience for me, as well as the other members. I was proud to know that I could use my imagination and feelings to create music other than what was written.
>
> Creativity to me, means being free to express yourself in a way that is unique to you, not having to conform to certain rules and guidelines. Music is only one of the many areas in which people are given opportunities to show their creativity. Sculpting, carving, building, art, and acting are just a few more areas where people can show their creativity.
>
> Through my music I conveyed feelings and thoughts which were impor-

tant to me. Music was my means of showing creativity. In whatever form creativity takes, whether it be music, art, or science, it is an important aspect of our lives because it enables us to be individuals.

Notice, in this essay, the key gesture, one that appears in all but a few of the essays I read. The student defines as his own that which is a commonplace. "Creativity, to *me*, means being free to express yourself in a way that is unique to you, not having to conform to certain rules and guidelines." This act of appropriation constitutes his authority; it constitutes his authority as a writer and not just as a musician (that is, as someone with a story to tell). There were many essays in the set that told only a story, where the writer's established presence was as a musician or a skier or someone who painted designs on a van, but not as a person removed from that experience interpreting it, treating it as a metaphor for something else (creativity). Unless those stories were long, detailed, and very well told (unless the writer was doing more than saying, "I am a skier or a musician or a van-painter"), those writers were all given low ratings.

Notice also that the writer of the jazz paper locates himself and his experience in relation to the commonplace (creativity is unique expression; it is not having to conform to rules or guidelines) regardless of whether it is true or not. Anyone who improvises "knows" that improvisation follows rules and guidelines. It is the power of the commonplace (its truth as a recognizable and, the writer believes, as a final statement) that justifies the example and completes the essay. The example, in other words, has value because it stands within the field of the commonplace. It is not the occasion for what one might call an "objective" analysis or a "close" reading. It could also be said that the essay stops with the articulation of the commonplace. The following sections speak only to the power of that statement. The reference to "sculpting, carving, building, art, and acting" attest to the universality of the commonplace (and it attests to the writer's nervousness with the status he has appropriated for himself—he is saying, "Now, I'm not the only one here who's done something unique"). The commonplace stands by itself. For this writer, it does not need to be elaborated. By virtue of having written it, he has completed the essay and established the contract by which we may be spoken to as equals: "In whatever form creativity takes, whether it be music, art, or science, it is an important aspect of *our* lives because it enables *us* to be individuals." (For me to break that contract, to argue that *my* life is not represented in that essay, is one way for me to begin as a teacher with that student in that essay.)

I said that the writer of the jazz paper offered up a commonplace regardless of whether it was "true" or not, and this, I said, was an example of the power of a commonplace to determine the meaning of an example. A commonplace determines a system of interpretation that can be used to "place" an example within a standard system of belief. You can see a similar process at work in this essay.

> During the football season, the team was supposed to wear the same type of cleats and the same type socks, I figured that I would change this a little by wearing my white shoes instead of black and to cover up the team socks with a pair of my own

white ones. I thought that this looked better than what we were wearing, and I told a few of the other people on the team to change too. They agreed that it did look better and they changed there combination to go along with mine. After the game people came up to us and said that it looked very good the way we wore our socks, and they wanted to know why we changed from the rest of the team.

I feel that creativity comes from when a person lets his imagination come up with ideas and he is not afraid to express them. Once you create something to do it will be original and unique because it came about from your own imagination and if any one else tries to copy it, it won't be the same because you thought of it first from your own ideas.

This is not an elegant paper, but it seems seamless, tidy. If the paper on the clay model of the earth showed an ill-fit between the writer and his project, here the discourse seems natural, smooth. You could reproduce this paper and hand it out to a class, and it would take a lot of prompting before the students sense something fishy and one of the more aggressive ones might say, "Sure he came up with the idea of wearing white shoes and white socks. Him and Billy White-shoes Johnson. Come on. He copied the very thing he said was his own idea, 'original and unique.' "

The "I" of this text, the "I" who "figured," "thought," and "felt" is located in a conventional rhetoric of the self that turns imagination into origination (I made it), that argues an ethic of production (I made it and it is mine), and that argues a tight scheme of intention (I made it because I decided to make it). The rhetoric seems invisible because it is so common. This "I" (the maker) is also located in a version of history that dominates classroom accounts of history. It is an example of the "Great Man" theory, where history is rolling along—the English novel is dominated by a central, intrusive narrative presence; America is in the throes of a great depression; during football season the team was supposed to wear the same kind of cleats and socks—until a figure appears, one who can shape history—Henry James, FDR, the writer of the football paper—and everything is changed. In the argument of the football paper, "I figured," "I thought," "I told," "they agreed," and, as a consequence, "I feel that creativity *comes from* when a person lets his imagination come up with ideas and he is not afraid to express them." The story of appropriation becomes a narrative of courage and conquest. The writer was able to write that story when he was able to imagine himself in that discourse. Getting him out of it will be difficult matter indeed.

There are ways, I think, that a writer can shape history in the very act of writing it. Some students are able to enter into a discourse, but, by stylistic maneuvers, to take possession of it at the same time. They don't originate a discourse, but they locate themselves within it aggressively, self-consciously.

Here is one particularly successful essay. Notice the specialized vocabulary, but also the way in which the text continually refers to its own language and to the language of others.

Throughout my life, I have been interested and intrigued by music. My mother has often told me of the times, before I went to school, when I would "conduct" the orchestra on her records. I continued to listen to music and eventually started to play the guitar and the clarinet. Finally, at about the age of twelve, I started to sit down and to try to write songs. Even though my instrumental skills were far from my own high standards, I would spend much of my spare time during the day with a guitar around my neck, trying to produce a piece of music.

Each of these sessions, as I remember them, had a rather set format. I would sit in my bedroom, strumming different combinations of the five or six chords I could play, until I heard a series which sounded particularly good to me. After this, I set the music to a suitable rhythm, (usually dependent on my mood at the time), and ran through the tune until I could play it fairly easily. Only after this section was complete did I go on to writing lyrics, which generally followed along the lines of the current popular songs on the radio.

At the time of the writing, I felt that my songs were, in themselves, an original creation of my own; that is, I, alone, made them. However, I now see that, in this sense of the word, I was not creative. The songs themselves seem to be an oversimplified form of the music I listened to at the time.

In a more fitting sense, however, I *was* being creative. Since I did not purposely copy my favorite songs, I was, effectively, originating my songs from my own "process of creativity." To achieve my goal, I needed what a composer would call "inspiration" for my piece. In this case the inspiration was the current hit on the radio. Perhaps with my present point of view, I feel that I used too much "inspiration" in my songs, but, at that time, I did not.

Creativity, therefore, is a process which, in my case, involved a certain series of "small creations" if you like. As well, it is something, the appreciation of which varies with one's point of view, that point of view being set by the person's experience, tastes, and his own personal view of creativity. The less experienced tend to allow for less originality, while the more experienced demand real originality to classify something a "creation." Either way, a term as abstract as this is perfectly correct, and open to interpretation.

This writer is consistently and dramatically conscious of herself forming something to say out of what has been said *and* out of what she has been saying in the act of writing this paper. "Creativity" begins, in this paper, as "original creation." What she thought was "creativity," however, she now calls "imitation" and, as she says, "in this sense of the word" she was not "creative." In another sense, however, she says that she *was* creative since she didn't purposefully copy the songs but used them as "inspiration."

The writing in this piece (that is, the work of the writer within the essay) goes on in spite of, or against, the language that keeps pressing to give another name to her experience as a song writer and to bring the discussion to closure. (Think of the quick closure of the football shoes paper in comparison). Its style is difficult, highly qualified. It relies on quotation marks and parody to set off the language and attitudes that belong to the discourse (or the discourses) it would reject, that it would not take as its own proper location.[6]

In the papers I've examined in this essay, the writers have shown a varied awareness of the codes—or the competing codes—that operate within a discourse. To speak with authority student writers have not only to speak in another's voice but through another's "code"; and they not only have to do this, they have to speak in the voice and through the codes of those of us with power and wisdom; and they not only have to do this, they have to do it before they know what they are doing, before they have a project to participate in and before, at least in terms of our disciplines, they have anything to say. Our students may be able to enter into a conventional discourse and speak, not as themselves, but through the voice of the community. The university, however, is the place where "common" wisdom is only of negative value; it is something to work against. The movement toward a more specialized discourse begins (or perhaps, best begins) when a student can both define a position of privilege, a position that sets him against a "common" discourse, and when he can work self-consciously, critically, against not only the "common" code but his own.

The stages of development that I've suggested are not necessarily marked by corresponding levels in the type or frequency of error, at least not by the type or frequency of sentence level errors. I am arguing, then, that a basic writer is not necessarily a writer who makes a lot of mistakes. In fact, one of the problems with curricula designed to aid basic writers is that they too often begin with the assumption that the key distinguishing feature of a basic writer is the presence of sentence level error. Students are placed in courses because their placement essays show a high frequency of such errors and those courses are designed with the goal of making those errors go away. This approach to the problems of the basic writer ignores the degree to which error is not a constant feature but a marker in the development of a writer. Students who can write reasonably correct narratives may fall to pieces when faced with more unfamiliar assignments. More importantly, however, such courses fail to serve the rest of the curriculum. On every campus there is a significant number of college freshmen who require a course to introduce them to the kinds of writing that are required for a university education. Some of these students can write correct sentences and some cannot, but as a group they lack the facility other freshmen possess when they are faced with an academic writing task.

The "White Shoes" essay, for example shows fewer sentence level errors than the "Clay Model" paper. This may well be due to the fact, however, that the writer of that paper stayed well within the safety of familiar territory. He kept himself out of trouble by doing what he could easily do. The tortuous syntax of the more advanced papers on my list is a syntax that represents a writer's struggle with a difficult and unfamiliar language, and it is a syntax that can quickly lead an inexperienced writer into trouble. The syntax and punctuation of the "Composing Songs" essay, for example, shows the effort that is required when a writer works against the pressure of conventional discourse. If the prose is inelegant (although I'll confess I admire those dense sentences), it is still correct. This writer has a command of the linguistic and stylistic resources (the highly embedded sentences, the use of parentheses and quotation marks) required to complete the act of writing. It is easy to imagine the possible pitfalls for a writer working without this facility.

There was no camera trained on the "Clay Model" writer while he was writing, and I have no protocol of what was going through his mind, but it is possible to speculate that the syntactic difficulties of sentences like the following are the result of an attempt to use an unusual vocabulary and to extend his sentences beyond the boundaries that would be "normal" in his speech or writing:

> In past time I thought that an incident was creative was when I had to make a clay model of the earth, but not of the classic or your everyday model of the earth which consists of the two cores, the mantle and the crust. I thought of these things in a dimension of which it would be unique, but easy to comprehend.

There is reason to believe, that is, that the problem is with this kind of sentence, in this context. If the problem of the last sentence is a problem of holding together these units—"I thought," "dimension," "unique," and "easy to comprehend"—then the linguistic problem is not a simple matter of sentence construction.

I am arguing, then, that such sentences fall apart not because the writer lacks the necessary syntax to glue the pieces together but because he lacks the full statement within which these key words are already operating. While writing, and in the thrust of his need to complete the sentence, he has the key words but not the utterance. (And to recover the utterance, I suspect, he will need to do more than revise the sentence.) The invisible conventions, the prepared phrases remain too distant for the statement to be completed. The writer must get inside of a discourse he can only partially imagine. The act of constructing a sentence, then, becomes something like an act of transcription, where the voice on the tape unexpectedly fades away and becomes inaudible.

Mina Shaughnessy speaks of the advanced writer as a writer with a more facile but still incomplete possession of this prior discourse. In the case of the advanced writer, the evidence of a problem is the presence of dissonant, redundant, or imprecise language, as in a sentence such as this: "No education can be *total*, it must be *continuous*. "Such a student Shaughnessy says, could be said to hear the "melody of formal English" while still unable to make precise or exact distinctions. And, she says, the pre-packaging feature of language, the possibility of taking over phrases and whole sentences without much thought about them, threatens the writer now as before. The writer, as we have said, inherits the language out of which he must fabricate his own messages. He is therefore in a constant tangle with the language, obliged to recognize its public, communal nature and yet driven to invent out of this language his own statements (19).

For the unskilled writer, the problem is different in degree and not in kind. The inexperienced writer is left with a more fragmentary record of the comings and goings of academic discourse. Or, as I said above, he often has the key words without the complete statements within which they are already operating.

It may very well be that some students will need to learn to crudely mimic the "distinctive register" of academic discourse before they are prepared to actually and legitimately do the work of the discourse, and before they are sophisticated enough with the refinements of tone and gesture to do it with grace or elegance. To say this, however, is to say that our students must be our students. Their initial progress will be marked by their abilities to take on the role of privilege, by their abilities to establish authority. From this point of view, the student who wrote about constructing the clay model of the earth is better prepared for his education than the student who wrote about playing football in white shoes, even though the "White Shoes" paper was relatively error-free and the "Clay Model" paper was not. It will be hard to pry the writer of the "White Shoes" paper loose from the tidy, pat discourse that allows him to dispose of the question of creativity in a such a quick and efficient manner. He will have to be convinced that it is better to write sentences he might not so easily control, and he will have to be convinced that it is better to write muddier and more confusing prose (in order that it may sound like ours), and this will be harder than convincing the "Clay Model" writer to continue what he has begun.[7]

19.
"Strangers No More"

A Liberatory Literacy Curriculum

Kyle Fiore
Nan Elsasser

College of the Bahamas
November 17, 1979

Dear Kyle, Pat and Larry,

I think our basic writing curriculum works! After ten weeks of discussing reading and writing about the generative theme of marriage, students have actually begun to use their newly won knowledge and skills for their own purposes. Last night we were reviewing for the final—a test designed, administered and graded by the College English Department—when Louise, one of my students, broke in to say that no test could measure what she had learned over the semester! Another student nodded in agreement. She said, "We've learned about marriage, men, and women. We've learned to write. We've learned about ourselves." Perfect Freirian synthesis! As if that weren't reward enough for one night, Eurena suggested that the class—all women—summarize and publish their knowledge. Then everyone jumped in. Our review of dashes and semicolons was forgotten as the class designed its first publication. It's hard to believe that in September these women had difficulty thinking in terms of a paragraph—now they want a manifesto! I'll keep you posted.

Love, Nan

Nan Elsasser's letter elated us. That semester she had been experimenting with a remedial English program we had designed[1] in the spring of 1978. We had first come together just after Christmas, drawn to each other by the desire to share our classroom frustrations, our successes, our gripes, over a common pitcher of beer. Trading stories with one another, we discovered we were four teachers in search of a curriculum. Standard English textbooks and

From Kyle Fiore and Nan Elsasser, " 'Strangers No More': A Liberatory Literacy Curriculum," *College English* 44(1982): 115–28. Copyright © 1982 by the National Council of Teachers of English. Reprinted by permission of the publisher and the authors.

traditional curricula did not fit our students at the University of Albuquerque and the University of New Mexico. Chicanos, Blacks, Anglos, and Native Americans, they had enrolled in our courses to gain writing skills which would help them succeed in college and carve a place for themselves in society. Once they arrived, however, our students found themselves strangers in a strange world. A wide gulf stretched between the classroom curriculum and their own knowledge gained in the barrios of Albuquerque and the rural towns and pueblos of New Mexico. Confronted by a course that negated their culture, many failed to master the skills they sought. Others succeeded by developing a second skin. Leaving their own customs, habits, and skills behind, they participated in school and in the world by adapting themselves to fit the existing order. Their acquisition of literacy left them not in control of their social context, but controlled by it.

We were troubled. We wanted our students to be able to bring their culture, their knowledge, into the classroom. We wanted them to understand and master the intricacies of the writing process. And we wanted them to be able to use writing as a means of intervening in their own social environment. Sparked by our common concerns, we decided to create a curriculum which would meet our goals. As we cast about for theories and pedagogies, we discovered the work of Lev Vygotsky and Paulo Freire. These scholars intrigued us because they believe writing involves both cognitive skills and social learnings. Their approaches parallel and complement each other. Vygotsky explores students' internal learning processes. Freire emphasizes the impact of external social reality.

Vygotsky's work clarifies the complex process of writing.[2] He postulates that learning to write involves the mastery of cognitive skills and the development of new social understandings. According to Vygotsky, we categorize and synthesize our lives through inner speech, the language of thought. In inner speech, a single word or phrase is embroidered with variegated threads of ideas, experiences, and emotions. The multileveled, personal nature of inner speech is illustrated by a woman student's response to a word association exercise: *sex:* home, time, never, rough, sleep.

Vygotsky explains that to transform the inner speech symbols to written text, this woman must consciously step outside the shorthand of her thoughts and mentally enter the social context she shares with her reader. Only from this common perspective can she begin to unfold the mystery of her thoughts to create written prose.

Focusing on the learner's environment, Freire discusses the social and political aspects of writing. A designer of liberatory or revolutionary literacy programs, Freire maintains that the goal of a literacy program is to help students become critically conscious of the connection between their own lives and the larger society and to empower them to use literacy as a means of changing their own environment. Like Vygotsky, Freire believes the transformation of thought to text requires the conscious consideration of one's social context. Often, Freire says, students unaware of the connections between their own lives and society personalize their problems. To encourage students to understand the impact of society on their lives, Freire proposes students and teachers talk about generative themes drawn from the students' everyday world. Investigating issues such as work or family life from an individual and a socio-historical perspective, students bring their own knowledge into the classroom and broaden their sense of social context.

For example, one woman beaten by her husband may think she has simply made a bad choice and must bear her lot with dignity. Another woman may think her husband would stop if she could live up to his expectations. When they talk with each other and other women, these two discover that brutality is a social phenomenon; it is widespread in the community. As they read, they learn that many aspects of their problem are rooted in the social realm and can best be attacked by pressing for legal changes, battered women's shelters, more responsive attitudes on the part of the police. Through continued discussion, these women realize how they can use literacy to win those changes by swearing out complaints in court, sending petitions to public officials, or writing newspaper articles and letters to the editor.

We decided to base our curriculum on Vygotsky's theory and Freire's pedagogy. Vygotsky's theory of inner speech would enable students to understand the writing process. Freire's pedagogy would encourage them to bring their culture and personal knowledge into the classroom, help them understand the connections between their own lives and society, and empower them to use writing to control their environment.

As advanced literacy teachers in traditional universities, we realized we could not use a pure Freirian approach. Designed for teachers in revolutionary settings, Freire's basic literacy programs do not consider the time constraint of semesters or the academic pressure of preparing students to meet English department standards. However, we thought it would be possible to combine Freire's goal of increasing students' critical consciousness with the teaching of advanced literacy skills. As Freire wrote in *Pedagogy in Process* (New York: Seabury, 1978), "The best way to accomplish those things that are impossible today is to do today whatever is possible" (p. 64).

That spring we met every Saturday at each other's houses. Spurred on by coffee and raised glazed doughnuts, we talked about the advanced literacy techniques we were using and explored ways to link those techniques with Vygotsky's and Freire's work. We designed word association exercises to Vygotsky's theory of inner speech. We charted ways to fit rhetorical forms in a Freirian investigation. We finished in May. That same month Nan Elsasser won a Fulbright to teach advanced literacy at the College of the Bahamas. She would be the first to try our curriculum. The next fall Elsasser kept us abreast of her experiment by mail. In the pages that follow we have summarized her letters and combined them with copies of student papers to create a first-person account of our curriculum in process.

The College of the Bahamas: An Experiment in Possibilities

Arriving in the Bahamas before the semester begins, I have a few days to learn about the college.

Located on the island of New Providence, the College of the Bahamas is a two-year community college offering daytime and evening classes. Over ninety percent of the students at the College are black Bahamians. Many work by day, attend school by night. Two-thirds of these students are women.

The language skills class I am to teach is the first in a series of four English courses offered by the college prep program. All of these courses are taught along traditional lines. To practice grammar students change tenses, add punctuation, or fill in blank spaces in assigned sentences. To demonstrate reading ability they answer multiple choice or true-false questions on short paragraphs. A colleague tells me the year before forty-five to sixty percent of the students failed to meet English department standards. She also shows me a College of the Bahamas study demonstrating no significant correlation between grades in English and grades in other academic subjects. Her revelations strengthen my determination to try out our curriculum.

I get to class early on the first night, worried my students' traditional expectations will make them leary of a new approach. Checking my roster, I discover all my students are women (later, I learn women make up two-thirds of the college's student body). I start class by introducing myself and describing the problems I've encountered teaching English traditionally. Telling the women we'll be using an experimental approach, I stress this experiment will succeed only if we can pick topics, discuss material, and evaluate results together. I admit class will lack coherency at times, and one student asks if they will be able to pass the standardized English exam given at the end of the semester. I say I think so, but that she is free to transfer if she wants a more traditional approach. She leaves; but the rest stay.

To establish a sense of common ground, I ask my students about their work and former schooling. Half of them clerk in banks. The others type or run computers. Collectively, these women represent the first generation of Bahamian women to enter the business world and go to college. They have an average of six years of education behind them. Recalling her early school days, one woman speaks of days spent copying poems from a colonial primer. Another recounts the times she stayed home to care for the younger ones while her mother went to sell her wares at the straw market. They all remember problems with writing.

So they can begin to understand the cause of their problems, we spend the next three weeks investigating the complexities of going from inner speech to finished written product. We begin with a series of word association exercises designed to illustrate Vygotsky's theory. Comparing their responses to trigger words such as *sex, home, work,* the women start to see that even at this most basic level they categorize and store information in various ways. Some students list contrasting affective responses. Others jot down visual images. One woman divides the inner speech word into subtopics, like an outline: "job: where you would like to work, type boss, what specific field." Contrasting their different ways of organizing and listing thoughts, students gain a strong sense of why they need to elaborate their thoughts in writing. To end the session, we each transform our private lists to public prose.

To continue our study of the transformations involved in writing clear, explicit prose, I look for a topic which will stress the value of personal knowledge, break down the dichotomy between personal and classroom knowledge, and require explicit elaboration. As a newcomer to the island, I ask them to advise me "What You Need to Know to Live in the Bahamas." I introduce this assignment by talking about writing as an interaction between process and product, personal and social points of view, concrete and abstract knowledge. A student writing a recipe for conch salad needs concrete knowledge about preparing conch combined with the abstract knowledge of an audience as people with some shared assumptions as well as some lack of common ground.

The women have a number of problems with this assignment, evidencing what Freire calls the inability to step outside immediate contextual realities and incorporate broader points of view. Some students write very brief suggestions. Others write in the first person or list topics of interest, but don't include concrete information. Still others complain they are stymied trying to figure out what I'd like to do. Though she knows I am a stranger to the island, the woman writing me a recipe for conch salad assumes conch is a familiar food. Yet another woman constructs an imaginary audience to help herself focus on the assignment: "What You Need to Know to Live in the Bahamas. A Young married couple on Vacation. Leisure Activities. Whatever your taste in holiday diversion you'll never be at a loss for something to do in the Bahamas. . . ."

This assignment extends over several sessions. Students write and rewrite their essays. During this time we develop the basic procedure we'll use to investigate a generative theme. First, we discuss the topic at hand (e.g., "What You Need to Know to Live in the Bahamas"). Then one student volunteers a thesis statement related to the topic. Other women help narrow and sharpen this statement and develop an essay outline. Students use these outlines as guidelines for their rough drafts. I reproduce the drafts, and we read and comment on them. After prolonged discussion, each woman rewrites her draft to meet the questions we've raised.

In moving from the discussion of inner speech to writing about the Bahamas, students take on more and more responsibility for the class. While in writing they are still trapped by their personal perspectives, in discussions they begin to critique and respond to one another's views. Gradually they start to investigate their environment. Before, they passively received knowledge. Now, they pursue it.

Freire states that students caught by their own subjectivity can break through personal walls and move to a collective social perspective through investigating generative themes. Such themes must be selected carefully so that they encourage students to write for a broader, more public audience and empower them to use writing to change their lives. Freire advises teachers searching for themes to involve themselves intimately in the students' culture and minutely observe all the facets of their daily lives, recording "the way people talk, their style of life, their behavior at church and work" (*Pedagogy of the Oppressed* [New York: Seabury, 1970], p. 103). Analyzing these observations with a team of other educators, the teacher will discern meaningful generative themes.

A stranger, unaccompanied by a "literacy team," I can't follow Freire's advice, and in my ignorance I turn to my students for help. We discuss generative themes, and they each select three issues from their daily lives that they would like to talk, read, and write about for the semester. When they bring in their suggestions, I list them on the board. We debate them briefly and they vote, picking marriage for their generative theme. This theme affects their lives economically, socially, and emotionally. Ninety percent of these women have been raised by two parents in traditional Bahamian homes. Seventy-five percent are now mothers. Two-thirds of these mothers are single parents totally responsible for their children's physical and emotional well-being.

Having chosen their theme, the women break into groups. They discuss the areas of marriage they want to investigate and construct an outline of subtopics, including *housework, divorce, sexuality,* and *domestic violence.* With these subtopics in hand, I start to hunt for reading materials. I look for articles which bridge the distance between students' lives and society. We'll use these articles as a basis for dialogues about individual problems, common experiences, and the larger social world.

My search of the college library yields nothing on contemporary Bahamian marriage. Writing back to the United States for articles, culling my old *Ms.* magazines, and hounding the local newsstand, I collect a packet which fits our course outline. Initial reading assignments come from popular magazines: an article on wife beating from *New Woman,* one entitled "Why Bad Marriages Endure" from *Ebony.* As students' reading skills and knowledge increase, we will use more advanced texts, such as *Our Bodies Ourselves* (2nd ed., New York: Simon and Schuster, 1976), and *The Longest War: Sex Differences in Perspective* by Carol Tavris and Carole Offir (New York: Harcourt Brace Jovanovich, 1977). At the end of the semester we will read *Nectar in a Sieve* (New York: New American Library, 1971), a novel by Kamala Markandaya about peasant marriage in India.

For the rest of the semester we spend about one week, co-investigating each subtopic of our marriage theme. I introduce each subject by handing out a related article. To help the women understand new information, I discuss the concepts I think unfamiliar, e.g., the historical concept of Victorian as a set of sexual attitudes. After reading and talking about the articles, we develop a thesis statement following the procedure we devised when writing essays on the Bahamas. When discussing articles and writing critiques students do not follow the traditional liberal arts criteria. Their criticism is not bound by the authors' intent or opinion, nor do they consider all articles equally valid. Rather, they judge the reading by whether or not it connects with their personal perspectives and tells them about marriage as a socioeconomic institution. They find much of value in *Our Bodies Ourselves.* They dismiss poet Judith Viorst as a spoiled middle-class housewife.

During our investigation students pass through three distinct phases as they hone their abilities to examine, critique, and write about marriage. They elaborate their own experience more skillfully, and they perceive stronger links between their own lives and the larger social context. They reach outside their own experience to seek new sources of knowledge. Finally, they become critically conscious of the way society affects their lives, and they begin to use writing as a means of intervening in their own social environment.

In the early weeks many women have trouble discerning the connections between their personal life and their social context. They analyze problems using concrete knowledge drawn from experience. They argue by anecdote. To encourage them to broaden their outlook, I ask for a definition of marriage as a social institution. In response, they describe what marriage should be ("communication," "love," "fidelity"), or they recite personal experiences ("men can come and go as they please, women cannot"; "men neglect their financial responsibilities"; "men have sweethearts"; "men are violent"). Posing questions targeting a social definition of marriage, I elicit broader, abstract responses: "legal procedure," "age requirements," "union between man and woman," "religious sanctioning of sex." Looking over this list, they ask me to throw out their earlier, more personal definitions.

Next, they construct lists of the positive and negative aspects of marriage as a social institution. These lists display a mixture of personal experiences, idealistic yearnings, and social traits:

Positive	Negative
Safe from rape and break-ins	Sex against our will
Not coming home to an empty house	Security sours relationships
Community approval of the relationship	Loss of freedom

Comparing these lists, the women start to talk about the social aspects of marriage. They conclude that the major benefit of marriage is security and social approval; its major shortcoming, a loss of freedom. Even after our extended dialogue, in their essays on "The Worst or Best Things about Marriage," women either write empty generalizations or briefly recount their own experience.

The Worst Thing About Marriage
By Rosetta Finlay

The worst thing about marriage is security, Whenever a couple is married they tend to become too sure of themselves. One would say, "All is well." I already have whom I want so I don't have to say I love you anymore; I don't have to show that I care as much. We don't have sex as often and you can go out with the boys while I go out with the girls.

This is where one would find time to go out of the home and look for the missing links in his marriage. That's when all the problem arises as soon as this happens, there's no end to problems.

The Best Thing About Marriage
By Eurena Clayton

I enjoyed being with my husband when we were dating and the things we did together drew us closer. After we got married my husband's business prevents us from doing as many things as we used to do together. Usually when we have a spare chance we take off on trips which we simply enjoy together. The feeling of not having to bother with the every day responsibilities is a great burden lifted for that period. We find ourselves taking in the movies, theatre, tennis, golfing or simply sightseeing.

There are special occasions such as anniversary or birthday which are always remembered. Sometimes for no reason you receive a beautiful gift which is always appreciated and thoughtful.

In order to achieve one's goal in life it is safe to pool both resources.

I suggest revisions for these essays, reproduce them, and pass them out. Students critique each other's papers, and each woman rewrites her piece. This time a number of students expand their essays through elaboration. However, at this stage no one goes beyond her own experience without writing platitudes, and few maintain a consistent focus throughout the entire paper. The woman writing this third draft has expanded and improved her mechanics and drawn clearer contrasts in her conclusion. She still reverts to an unrelated generality.

Draft III
By Rosetta Finlay

The worst thing about marriage is emotional security. When a couple is married, they tend to become too sure of themselves. One will say, "All is well I already have whom I want so I don't have to look nice anymore; I don't have to say I love you anymore; I don't have to show that I care as much; we don't have sex as often and you can go out with the boys while I go out with the girls."

Marriage shouldn't be taken so much for granted there's always improvement needed in every marriage. Marriage is like a job e.g.—one has a job everything is routine; you have a steady salary; steady hours nine o'clock in the morning to five o'clock in the evening; go to work every day and perform the duties your job position requires.

Marriage is very similar e.g.—one has a steady companion; cook every day; keep the house and laundry clean; have babies and bring them up. Apart from doing the house chores there's the chauffeuse part to be done and the office work.

I personally think that there is a lot more to be done if you want to have a successful marriage. Therefore if more interest is taken in these areas, marriage would be much better than what it is today.

In the sessions that follow, students evidence similar problems with the reading assignment. The article is about battered wives. Although they can read the words, the women have difficulty distinguishing major ideas from details. Where in writing they recounted personal experiences, now in reading they focus on anecdotes. They underline when, where, or how hard Frank hit Marlene, as opposed to the main concept this example illustrates.

To sharpen the contrast between a main idea and an illustration I ask them to list causes of domestic violence on the board. Then we start to talk about the difference between causes and anecdotes. It takes students several sessions to learn to select main points correctly on their own. During these sessions they also begin to gain a better grasp of the connections between their own lives and the forces of society.

I am reminded as I consider my students that teaching and learning are part of a single process. To present something in class is not to teach it. Learning happens when students make cognitive transformations, expanding and reorganizing the knowledge in their cerebral filing systems. Only then can they assimilate and act upon ideas.

By the end of Phase One the women have made several such transformations. They have an idea of their individual differences and a sense of the common ground they share. Although they still rely on personal experience as a source of knowledge, they are beginning to recognize how the outside society affects their lives. This awareness has improved their writing. They use more detail. They separate ideas and events into paragraphs. They sustain a third-person perspective with greater skill. They clarify generalizations with examples.

A "Typical" Bahamian Marriage
By Rosetta Finlay

"For richer, for poorer, for better, for worse, in sickness and in health, until death do us part." God has commanded his children to join in the holy matrimony and obey these rules. Unfortunately, the majority of the Bahamian marriages tend to focus more on the negative, than the positive aspects of marriage. A Typical Bahamian Marriage will begin with both, the male and female being in love with each other, so much in love that the husband will help with the house chores, such as washing the dishes, doing the laundry, taking out the garbage and making breakfast. It will even get to the point where the husband will stay up at night with their first child. Every Sunday the family will go to church and have dinner together. Later in the evening the husband and wife will go to the movies or a special function.

Week days, both the husband and wife will go out to work, usually they both work. After work the wife rushes home to prepare the dinner. The bills are paid by both the husband and wife's salary put together and if possible, a little is saved. For some period of time, the wife will satisfy her husband's need such as, sharing sex, understanding and the house chores. Then all of a sudden, for an unknown reason the husband changes.

He will start staying out X amount of hours and stop putting his share of monies towards the bills. Comes home and take out his frustration on his wife and children by, snapping at children and beating his wife. He does not even want to spend any time at home to help with the house chores or baby sit. He only comes home to change, if he is questioned about money it will end in a fight. Then he will leave home for another day or two.

The wife, is now in a situation where she does not have enough money to pay the bills and support the children, no husband to lean on and protect the family. She does not have any where to go, because he keeps telling her that she cannot go with out him. Getting a divorce in the Bahamas is completely out of the question. So she will have to, "grin and bear it" until death.

By mid-semester most women have entered Phase Two. We pause to take stock of our work. Looking back over their gains, women are sparked with pride. They begin seizing more control in class and start to generate their own theories on the writing mechanics. One night we tackle the problem of pronoun agreement. While aware they often switch back and forth in writing from *they* to *you, she/he,* and *I,* students have little success self-editing for pronouns because we don't know the cause of this problem. Then one woman comments she has no trouble writing general points in the third person. However, she says when she illustrates these points or gives advice, she starts mentally addressing a particular person and slips into a second-person referent. Examining several essays, classmates confirm her observation; as a result, they begin to catch and correct these errors.

Women also start to discover punctuation rules. Although I have not stressed punctuation as such, they observe patterns in the reading, and they hypothesize the rules themselves. While working on the use of logical connectors like *however* and *similarly*, a student asks if the first sentence always ends in a semicolon followed by the connector, a comma, and another sentence. After consulting with each other and essays, other students incorporate this rule in their writing.

During this phase students also break away from their total dependence on personal experience. They become more confident about gaining knowledge from class dialogues and reading. One night we debate whether or not women "ask for" rape. Remembering how reading about wife beating changed our stereotypes, one student asks for additional materials on rape. Others second her request. Spurred on by their own curiosity, they assail excerpts from Susan Brownmiller's *Against Our Will* and discuss how her theories and statistics destroy or reinforce their personal myths and beliefs.

Encouraged by their confidence and advancing skills, I begin to introduce the idea of rhetorical forms: cause and effect, definition, comparison and contrast. Rather than concentrating on these forms explicitly, we employ them as a means of pondering, exploring, and writing about various facets of marriage. When looking at the social forces that perpetuate wife beating, we cover cause and effect. To illustrate the relationships between wife beating and rape, we use comparison and contrast. The outline students construct for this topic clarifies the social similarities and differences between these two forms of violence.

Comparison and Contrast on Rape and Wife Beating

Comparison
      brutality to women
      –by men
      –at night
      –police take male side
      –society reluctant to believe women
      –female shame

Contrast
      –husband vs. stranger
      –predictability
      –sentence more severe for rape
      –provocation

In their essays comparing and contrasting rape and wife beating, the women bring together cognitive skills and social realizations. They now write from a unified perspective with more coherence, fewer sentence fragments, and more complex sentence structure. They combine information gained from discussions and reading with their personal knowledge to create a solid argument by crisp, focused examples.

Comparison and Contrast of Rape and Wife Beating
By Rosetta Finlay

In 1973 over half a million rapes were estimated by F.B.I. along with 14,000 wife abuse complaints in New York alone reached the family courts during a comparable period that same year. Rape and wife beating are common crimes done by men in our society.

Unfortunately, the women of our society have to turn to the law who are men for help. Very seldom a female will win a rape case to get protection from the law on a wife abuse complaint. Calling the police will not help, not when they ask you questions like, "Are there any witnesses to this assault?" "Look lady he pays the bills, doesn't he?" Only to conclude with "What he does in his house is his business." and "Why don't you two kiss and make up." They really don't act any different when called upon a rape assault not when they say things like, "well things certainly seem to be in order here now." "What was the problem?" "What were you wearing, were your pants tight?" On the other hand the female in wife abuse must think about her dependency upon her husband, when she thinks about taking her complaint to family court, eg:—who will pay the bills? In most cases the female doesn't work and what will she do without him, where will she turn after not working for years? This is where the female is trapped and cannot win.

Despite the trapping situation the women of our society have decided to fight against that to bring more rights and evidence for the female, for instance Judge Oneglia who as a lawyer specializes in marital problems, recommends that the female should get out of the house, go to a friend or neighbor, and cause as much disturbance as possible. The more witnesses the better. As in a rape case the victim must produce pictures or evidence of (bruises or semen) to corroborate the rape victim's testimony, another prohibits the introduction in court of evidence concerning a rape victim's previous sexual conduct.

The women in society have formed groups and organizations to fight and protect themselves from wife abuse and rape, for instance they have decided to get together with other women in their neighborhood or apartment building and establish a whistle signal. In cases where the female lives alone she should list only her first initial in the telephone directory and also keep all outside doors and windows dead bolt locked mostly used in a rape case. In a wife abuse case the women of our society have recommended to call a special meeting to discuss the problem inviting representatives from the police, clergy and social service agencies to participate. Hopefully, this would contribute to cut down on rape and wife abuse.

In Phase Three students begin to use writing as a means of intervening in their own social environment. A few weeks before the end of the semester the women decide to share the knowledge they have gained about marriage with the world outside classroom by publishing an open "Letter to Bahamian Men" in the island newspapers. Writing this manifesto takes four weeks. In addition to class time, we meet together on Sundays and put in hours of extra work. We start by writing individual letters. We discuss these letters in class, then outline a collective letter.

    A. Introduction
        1. Role of women in Bahamian society
        2. Oppression of women in marriage
    B. Women victims of men's inconsiderate actions
    C. Men's financial neglect of the family
    D. Men's lack of help at home
    E. Men's lack of responsibility for their children
    F. Men's failure to satisfy women sexually
    G. Conclusion: recommendations for Bahamian men

After considering the concerns each woman mentioned in her first letter, I assign each one a particular topic to develop. I organize the topics into a text, leaving gaps where I think there is a need for further work. From this point on my role is limited to copying, cutting and pasting. Equipped with her own copy, each women begins to edit her epistle. They go line by line, spending over an hour on each page. Students silent all semester defend their contributions vehemently. They argue over punctuation, style, and semantics. They debate whether to separate the list of men's inconsiderate actions with colons, semicolons, or full stops. One woman thinks a reference to *gambling* too colloquial. Another questions the use of *spend* vs. *squander.*

They consider the audience's viewpoint, calculating the effect of their words. They discuss whether to blame the issue of sweethearts on the men or the sweethearts themselves. One student observes that since the letter confronts the wrongs men perpetrate on women, it would be a tactical error to criticize other women. They finally compromise by using the term *extra-marital affairs.* Wanting to state their case clearly yet not run the risk of censorship, they rewrite the paragraph on sex several times. The final letter appears in both Nassau daily papers.

Dear Bahamian Men:

    The social, spiritual and economic growth of Bahamian society depends on men as well as women. For a very long time there has been a downward trend in male support of their wives and children. In the typical Bahamian marriage both the male and the female begin by thinking that they are in love, so much in love that the husband will help with the household chores. The husband will even stay up all night with their first child. Every Sunday the family will go to church and have dinner together. Later in the evening the husband and wife might go to a movie or a special function. Week days both the husband and wife will go to work. After work the wife rushes home to prepare dinner. The bills are paid by putting together both the husband and wife's salaries and if possible, a little is saved. For some time all will go very well in the home. Then all of a sudden, for some unknown reason, the husband begins to change.

    We are a group of women who have all been victims of men's inconsiderate actions. We would like to focus on the punishment, deprivation, discourtesy, mental anguish and death of the soul for which Bahamian men are responsible:

Punishment because some women are beaten by their husband; Deprivation because husbands give wives less and less to survive on each month; Discourtesy because extra-marital affairs disturb the home. Mental anguish is humiliation of the mind, for whose mind can be at ease in such a situation! Death of the soul deteriorates the whole body, for women are made to feel they serve no purpose.

These problems arise when the men begin to neglect their homes. The main problems between men and women in the Bahamas are: child raising, housekeeping, finances, and sex. Men are the root of most of these problems.

In most cases the male salary is more than the females. Despite this fact, the majority of Bahamian men neglect the financial upkeep of their families in some way or the other. Because of this, the greater part of the financial burden which includes savings, school fees, groceries, utilities, and even mortgages have been left to women. The male finds other things to do with his salary. Some men wait for the women to remind them about their bills. Others expect the women to pay all the bills. How can the female be expected to do all of this with a salary that is less than the males?

For centuries women have been solely responsible for housework. So men still think that a woman's place is in the home. Men expect women to work all day, come home and cook, wash dishes, clean house, wash clothes, prepare dinner and get the children ready for bed while they sit around and watch. It used to be that women did not work and were solely dependent on their husbands for support. Since women are now working and helping their husbands with most of the financial upkeep, there is no reason why the men can't be a part when it comes to housework. It is both the male's and the female's place to share the responsibilities of the home.

It takes two to produce a child and so it should be two to see to the upbringing of the child. Fathers do not spend sufficient time in the home. The most important stages in a child's life, the most cherished and once in a life time moments are when the child says his first words, makes his first step, and claps his hands for the first time. Fathers being around the home when moments like the above mentioned take place are important in children's lives. Here in the Bahamas fathers have failed to be real fathers, and children have been left totally dependent on their mothers. Having children and not supporting them is not a good way to prove one's manhood. A child should have both parents' care and attention. But before men see that their children are well taken care of they prefer to spend money on their own pleasure. Why be responsible for another life coming into the world if men don't care if the children are properly fed, have proper clothing to wear, and get a proper education?

Men tend not to realize the necessity in satisfying their partners when making love. Unfortunately, they are mainly concerned with the fulfillment of their desires. They come home at the most tiresome hours of the night, hop in bed and expect us to respond without any love or affection. Most Bahamian men don't take the time to caress women's bodies before have sex. Therefore, the instant they get into bed—if they're in the mood—women are expected to perform. However, when women are in the mood, they don't respond. This leaves women dissatisfied and angry.

Our recommendations to Bahamian men in relation to the above are as follows:

a) That men join in family worship at least twice a month.
b) That men stop putting most of the financial burden on women. 75% of the household responsibilities should be handled by men.

c) That men at least buy their children's groceries, pay school fees and buy clothes.

d) That men take their children out for recreation at least once a week.

e) That men do an equal share of the housework.

f) That men do not allow extra-marital affairs to damage or destroy their marriages.

g) That men make more effort to sexually satisfy their wives. Talk about the things that please them. Caress their women until they're ready for sex. Try not to climax until the women are ready.

Men, there is definitely room for improvement in love, affection and communication. Try it.

Sincerely,

English 016-06

Comparing this "Open Letter to Bahamian Men" with women's earlier essays on "Rape and Battered Wives," "The Worst Things in a Marriage," and life in the Bahamas demonstrates how, through the investigation of a generative theme, students can advance their reading and writing skills, recognize links between their own lives and the larger society, and develop ways of using their newfound writing skills to intervene in their own environment.

At the end of the semester all these women passed the College-administered English exam. Most received "B" grades on the essay component. Further, they decided to continue meeting throughout the next spring in order to read about women in other countries, broaden their understandings, and write a resource book for Bahamian women.

The success of this pedagogical experiment demonstrates that advanced literacy teachers can modify Freire's pedagogy to fit the needs of their students and the demands of the college. Through this approach students will achieve literacy in the truest, most profound sense: they will understand "their reality in such a way that they increase their power to transform it" (Darcy de Olivera and Rosiska de Olivera, *Guinea-Bissau Reinventing Education* [Geneva: Institute of Cultural Action, 1976], p. 48).

Part Four

Community Perspectives

20.
The Ethnography of Literacy

John F. Szwed

Literacy would appear to be one of the few elements of education that everyone agrees to be a necessity of modernity. The capacity to read and write is causally associated with earning a living, achieving expanded horizons of personal enlightenment and enjoyment, maintaining a stable and democratic society, and, historically, with the rise of civilization itself. "Underdeveloped" countries have had reading and writing touted to them as the means of a quantum leap into the future. And in the United States (especially since the 1960's) illiteracy has been singled out as a root cause of poverty.

Yet literacy as an ideal seems to be suffering a crisis. The wealthy nations of the world are now encountering rather massive failures in reading and writing among students at all levels; and it appears that despite universal schooling, a continuing percentage of the population of these nations has difficulties with these skills. In addition, there have developed "critics" of literacy, some of whom have questioned the feasibility of universal literacy as assumed in the West;[1] others now even raise questions about its ultimate relation to civilization.[2]

And behind all of this there are profound shifts appearing in the world's reading habits: in the U.S., for example, the reading (and publishing) of novels is in decline, while the reading of plays and poetry is at almost zero level. Instead, the amorphous area usually called non-fiction is on the ascendancy (though readers of an earlier generation might have difficulty in seeing the differences between the new techniques of non-fiction and fiction). The fact that many, perhaps most, English classes in the United States are geared toward fiction, drama and poetry makes this development all the more poignant.

Since professionals in the field of reading and writing instruction feel that there now exist sound, workable methods of teaching literacy, the responsibility for failure is assigned variously to poor teaching, overcrowded classes, family background (and the "culture of poverty"), the competition with the new media, or even to the directions of contemporary society itself.

From *Writing: The Nature, Development, and Teaching of Written Communication*, ed. Marcia Farr Whiteman, 1981, Hillsdale, New Jersey: Lawrence Erlbaum Associates, Inc. Copyright 1981 by Lawrence Erlbaum Associates, Inc. Reprinted by permission.

No agreement on definition

But the stunning fact is that we do not fully know what literacy is. The assumption that it is simply a matter of the skills of reading and writing does not even begin to approach the fundamental problem: What are reading and writing for? Is the nature of the ability to read and write something on which there is in fact near agreement? Can these skills be satisfactorily tested? Do writing and reading always accompany each other as learned skills? Should they? Even on questions of *functional* literacy, can we agree on what the necessary minimal functions are for everyday life? It is entirely possible that teachers are able to teach reading and writing as abstract skills, but do not know what reading and writing are for in the lives and futures of their students.

Focus on pragmatic meaningfull meaning of litracy

I propose that we step back from the question of instruction, back to an even more basic "basic," the *social meaning of literacy:* that is, the roles these abilities play in social life; the varieties of reading and writing available for choice; the contexts for their performance; and the manner in which they are interpreted and tested, not by experts, but by ordinary people in ordinary activities. In doing this, I am following a recent trend in language studies, one which recognizes that it is not enough to know what a language looks like and to be able to describe and measure it, but one must also know what it means to its users and how it is used by them.

Literacy has typically been viewed as a yes-and-no matter, easily determined: either one reads and writes or one doesn't. And put in such terms, the goal of education is to produce a society of people who are equally competent at these skills. But the fact that no society has yet reached this state should give us pause. Historically, we know that most societies have produced specialists who have handled many of the necessities of literacy: the priest-scribe relationship, for instance, is widely remarked upon in studies of the development of civilization. In contemporary complex societies we are well aware of the negative correlation of skills in literacy with lower socioeconomic standing. But a closer look suggests that even among those of privileged background, these abilities are complexly patterned, and not at all equally distributed—the range of what is or can be "read" or "written" among, say, doctors, lawyers and teachers is often surprising. And even among those of other socioeconomic classes there is a great variety of such skills, such as can be found spread among active church members, avid followers of sports, and committed members of political parties. Consider the case of ethnic or immigrant neighborhoods, where such a distribution of abilities has a considerable historical background—that is, where certain individuals have served (and continue to serve) as interpreters of the law, citizens' benefits and rights, and the like, as well as readers and writers of letters and public documents. The distribution of these skills in bilingual and immigrant neighborhoods and communities is a complex and unexplored area. And even though the range and the number of these communities is simply not known at present, their clustering in urban areas gives the matter some urgency.

Social distribution of litracy abilities

Beyond the question of who participates to what degree in reading and writing, there are even more vexing issues. Clearly, there are problems in defining the activities of reading and writing themselves. To take a simple case: what a school may define as reading may not take account of what students read in various contexts other than the classroom. A boy, otherwise labeled as retarded and unable to read assigned texts, may have considerable skill at reading and interpreting baseball record books. Or a student who shows little interest or aptitude for reading may read *Jaws* in study hall. The definitions of reading and writing, then, must include *social context* and *function* (use) as well as the reader and the text of what is being read and written.

The nexus at which reader, or writer, context, function and text join is sometimes glossed as reading *motivation.* Reading and writing skills may indeed vary according to motivation, with varying degrees of skill following different degrees of motivation. But all of these elements form a complex whole which should not be reduced to a simple diagnosis. A reader's motivation may also vary according to context, function and text. And even motivation itself is varied: one may be moved to read by nostalgia, ambition, boredom, fear, etc.

Throughout, what one might expect to discover is that absolutes are few in questions of literacy, and that the roles of individuals and their places within social groups are preeminent in determining both what is read and written and what is necessary to reading and writing.

It should not be surprising to see differences in literacy between members of different ethnic groups, age groups, sexes, socioeconomic classes, etc.[3] Indeed, one might hypothesize the existence of *literacy-cycles*, or individual variations in abilities and activities that are conditioned by one's stage and position in life. What I would expect to discover, then, is not a single-level of literacy, on a single continuum from reader to non-reader, but a variety of *configurations* of literacy, a *plurality of literacies*.

Even the everyday judgments of non-educators of what is or is not literate ability or activity is highly variable. Where for some, ability to spell is the primary marker, to others, choice of reading matter is foremost—the "classics" vs. gothic novels, the *New York Times* vs. tabloids, etc. To still others, success on standardized tests is everything. And such commonsense judgments, whether reasonable or not, help to shape the ultimate social definition of literacy.

Some words, then, about a few of these five elements of literacy—text, context, function, participants, and motivation.

Texts: What Is It That People Read and Write?

These are the primary questions, and on the surface they appear easily answered. Reading, for instance, would seem to be ascertainable by means of library circulation figures, publishers' sales figures, and questionnaires. But statistics are of limited use for a variety of reasons: first, because they have not been gathered for these purposes and thus give us only the grossest of information about texts (and none whatsoever about use). There is no agreement among publishers on what is a book, for instance. (Nor is there any among readers: magazines are often called "books" in much of the English-speaking world). What is literature? No agreement. Distinctions between genres and categories such as *functional literature* vs. *artistic literature* are of little use. Beyond the subjective judgments involved, it takes little imagination to think up artistic uses of functional literature or functional uses of artistic writing. (Can sports writing be

[handwritten: Difficulties defining text — and distribution of text]

artistic? Functional? Both?) And even seemingly well-established classes such as fiction vs. non-fiction are the basis of a very lively debate among scholars today.[4]

Circulation and sales figures tell us nothing about the informal circulation of literature, and at least among the working classes, borrowing and loaning of reading matter is common. One need only think of reading done in doctors' offices, the reading of newspapers and magazines found on public transportation, at work, etc., to sense the possibilities.

Consider also some of the reading matter that is not normally included under the category "literature": handbills, signs, graffiti, sheet music, junk mail, cereal boxes, captions on television, gambling slips and racing tip sheets, juke-box labels, and pornography. (In some small towns, "adult" bookstores are the only bookstores, and sometimes have holdings that rival, in number at least, the local library.) Victor-Levy Beaulieu, in *Manual de la petite littérature du Quebec* (1974), provides an anthology of the kind of literature which is produced and read within a rural parish in French Canada: it includes printed sermons, temperance tracts, stories of the lives of local saints and martyrs, parish monographs, and life stories used as models for improvement.

[handwritten: What texts are read where?]

In addition, there is the question of the relation of the form of the text to other aspects of reading or writing. Consider the need for short, broken passages (such as found in mysteries and *Reader's Digest* condensations) for brief commuter trips, as opposed to longer passages for longer trips (*War and Peace* for an ocean voyage, say) or the time needed to register "raw" meaning as well as rhymes, puns, and irony in public signs in shopping centers and along roads. (The eclipse of Burma Shave signs by increased speed limits is a case in point.)[5]

Nor, incidentally, does traditional concern with literacy take account of the influence of the character of typography on readers. One small but important example is the current debate over the widespread use of Helvetic type (as used by Amtrak, Arco, Mobil and numerous other business and governmental sign and logo uses). The issue turns on whether the type's nature (presumably depersonalized, authoritative, and straightforward) brings unfair and misleading pressure to bear on its readers, as it appears to be *the* face of the largest and most powerful forces in America. *[handwritten: Typeface and power]*

Function and Context: Why and Under What Circumstances is Reading and Writing Done?

Available statistics tell us nothing about the variety of functions that reading and writing can serve. To consider only the use of books, in addition to providing information and pleasure—they are bought as decorations, as status symbols, gifts, investments, and for other reasons yet to be discovered.

[handwritten: research question]

Similarly, virtually nothing is known about the social contexts of reading and writing and how these contexts affect these skills. A quick beginning inventory of reading contexts would include bedside reading, coffee-break and lunch-time reading, vacation reading, reading to children, Sunday reading (perhaps the day of most intense literary activity in the United States and

Europe), reading during illness, educational reading (both in institutions and informally), crisis reading (psychological, physical, spiritual), sexual reading, reading to memorize, commuter reading, reading to prevent interaction with others, etc. (In theory, at least, there is a form of reading specific to every room: books are sold for kitchens, coffeetables, desks, bedrooms *[The Bedside X]* or bathrooms. On the latter, see Alexander Kira, *The Bathroom.* N.Y.: Bantam, 1977, pp. 197–201, 287. There are also books designed for types of housing, as in English "country house" books, etc.)

Conventional thinking about reading and writing far too often uses a much out-dated model of literacy inherited from 19th century upper-class Europe. That "book culture" assumed many conventions which we can no longer assume: a small, well-educated elite; considerable spatial and temporal privacy (usually provided by large houses and the protection of wife and servants); a firm belief in the mimetic power and ultimate truthfulness of language; and possibly a belief in immortality and transcendance as mediated by books—that is, a sense that book life was somehow greater than real life.

We might here also postulate the possibility of a difference between public and private literacy, between what one reads and writes at work, at school and elsewhere. Susan U. Philips[6] has shown that at least in the case of one Native American group, there are substantial differences between these two domains, such that they may have direct and serious implications for education for literacy. For example, if children are not read to at home, and the school *assumes* that activity as part of its foundations for reading instruction, then such students are likely to encounter difficulties in learning to read. The important point to note here is not so much whether reading stories to children is or is not a proper or effective tool for preparing children to read, but the gaps between the two domains have serious consequences. And changes in home practices, even with the best intentions, are not easily accomplished and not necessarily desirable.

To cite yet another example: signs are written to be read but they are also located in certain locales and have specific designs and shapes. Thus the ability to read a public sign may take considerably more or less than the ability to read a book. For example, a sign on a building that marks a grocery store is on a building that looks like a grocery store and is located where a grocery store is likely to be. So the ability to read a sign (by definition a public event) involves at least a *different* set of skills than private reading.[7]

Something might also be said about differing *styles* of reading and writing. For example, beyond silent reading and reading aloud, there are speed reading (with all that it implies); active, engaged, critical reading vs. that which is detached and noncommittal; or the kind of reading Marcel Proust[8] was interested in: a comprehension of the text's contents, with the intention of setting off a variety of personal associations partly derived from the page and partly from the context within which it is read. Or to consider a more extreme example, Balinese Hindu priests orally read a text which, in addition to having certain standard word meanings, also has prescribed vocalizations of the words, body gestures to accompany them, and visual images to be kept in mind during the reading.[9]

I have kept most of the specifics of this discussion to reading, but the same questions can be applied to writing. We know very little about the range of uses to which writing is put, or rather, we know only just enough to put assumptions in doubt.

Educators often assume that reading and writing form a single standard set of skills to be acquired and used as a whole by individuals who acquire them in a progression of steps which cannot be varied or avoided in learning. But even preliminary thought on the problem indicates that these skills are distributed across a variety of people. For example, it is generally assumed that an author is the single master of his or her product, and that what was originally written emerges without interference as a book. But there are surely few authors who know all of the conventions and practices of editors and very few editors who know all of the practices of type setters, book designers and printers. The publication process, instead, often assumes the form of a kind of interpretation or translation of an author's original text.

The assumption of a single standard of writing is belied by even the writing habits that every one of us has. Most of us, when writing notes for ourselves, assume special conventions of spelling and even syntax and vocabulary that we would not use if we were writing for others. (Curiously, these private conventions seem to have a social character, in that we are usually able to interpret another's notes by analogy with our own procedures.)

Some variations in writing standards are even conditioned by our elaborate system of status communications. In most businesses, for example, it is a mark of success *not* to be directly responsible for one's own communications in written form—secretaries are employed to turn oral statements into acceptable written ones. (In this, the United States resembles other non-Western cultures of the world, some of which measure the importance of messages and their senders by the number of intermediaries involved in their transmission.)

Still another example of multiple standards in writing is offered by advertising, logos and store signs, where "non-standard" spellings often communicate quite specific meanings: "quik," "rite," "nite" and the like indicate inexpensiveness or relative quality and "kreem" and "tru-" ersatz products.

It is not only the assumption of a single standard that we must question, but also the assumption of a single, proper learning progression, such that one can only "violate" the rules when one has mastered them. Students quite properly often question this when learning the "rules" while at the same time reading works of literature which disregard them. Recently, some younger black poets (especially those published by the Broadside Press of Detroit) using unorthodox spellings and typography have been dismissed as simply semiliterate by critics not familiar with the special conventions developed to deal with black dialects and aesthetics.

Again, the point to be stressed overall is that assumptions are made in educational institutions about the literacy needs of individual students which seem not to be born out by the students' day-to-day lives. And it is this relationship between school and the outside world that I think must be observed, studied and highlighted.

One method of studying literacy—ethnography—represents a considerable break with most past research on the subject. I would contend that enthnographic methods, in fact, are the only means for finding out what literacy really is and what can be validly measured.

Questionnaires and social survey instruments on reading and writing habits do not escape the problems raised here in the study of literacy, and in fact they may compound them. An instrument sensitive enough to gather all of the needed information would have to contain all of the varieties of texts, contexts, and functions we are interested in to guide informants in properly answering them. In addition, written forms would not do if for only the simple reason that they assume a certain standard of literacy in order to be completed, and it is this very standard that we wish to investigate.

More to the point, any study which attempts to cut across American society—its socioeconomic classes, age groups, ethnic groups and the like— along the lines of a skill which characterizes one social group more than others and which has been assumed to be closely associated with success and achievement, must be tempered by a considerable relativism and by the suspension of premature judgments. There is in this sort of study a need to keep literacy within the logic of the everyday lives of people; to avoid cutting these skills off from the conditions which affect them in direct and indirect ways; to shun needless abstractions and reductionist models; in short, to stay as close as possible to real cases, individual examples, in order to gain the strength of evidence that comes with being able to examine specific cases in great depth and complexity.

Another factor which makes ethnography most relevant here is that we are currently inheritors—if unwilling inheritors—of another 19th century perspective, one of distrust of mass society and culture, if not simply of the "masses" themselves. Specifically, this is the notion that "mass education," "mass literacy," etc., necessarily involves a cheapening or a debasing of culture, language and literature.[10] And though we have in this country escaped many of the elitist consequences of this position, we nonetheless suffer from its general implications. We must come to terms with the lives of people without patronizing them or falling into what can become a sociology of pathos. We need to look at reading and writing as activities having consequences in (and being affected by) family life, work patterns, economic conditions, patterns of leisure, and a complex of other factors.[11] Unlike those who often attempt to understand a class of people by a content analysis of the literature written for them by outsiders, we must take account of the readers' activities in transvaluing and reinterpreting such material.[12]

Nor can we make the easy assumption that certain media are responsible for a reduction of use of another medium. We must first be sure of the social context, function, etc., of the competing media before we assume we understand their presumed appeal. As an example, we know little more than that television sets are switched on a great deal of the time in this country; but do we know how they are socially used? We must consider the possibilities of more than simple entertainment. For example, considering only context and participants, radio listening—now a solitary activity—would seem to be competing with books more than television, still largely a group activity.

Work in the ethnography of communication has been aided immensely in recent years by the considerable accomplishments of sociolinguistics. Students of this subject have contended that in addition to close descriptions of language codes themselves we need descriptions of rules of code usage, combined with a description of the social contexts within which the various uses are activated and found appropriate. Dell Hymes has provided a framework for such studies, by isolating types of communication acts and by analyzing them in terms of components which comprise each act, in the light of preliminary cross-cultural evidence and contrasts.[13] Such components include the participants in the act (as well as their status, role, class, etc.), the form of the message, its code, its channel of communication, its topic, its goal, its social and physical setting, and its social function. In fact, this entire preliminary discussion of questions of literacy derives from this perspective. It has put us in a position to pursue the following kinds of questions,[14] some of which were raised above.

- How is the ability to read and write distributed in a community?
- What is the relationship between the abilities to read and write?
- How do these abilities vary with factors such as age, sex, socioeconomic class and the like?
- With what kinds of activities are reading and writing associated, and in what types of settings do these activities take place?
- What kinds of information are considered appropriate for transmission through written channels, and how, if at all, does this information differ from that which is passed through alternative channels such as speech?
- Who sends written messages to whom, when, and for what reasons?
- Is the ability to read and write a prerequisite for achieving certain social statuses, and, if so, how are these statuses elevated by other members of the community?
- How do individuals acquire written codes and the ability to decode them—from whom, at what age, and under what circumstances, and for what reasons?
- What are the accepted methods of instruction and of learning both in and out of school?
- What kind of cognitive functions are involved?
- In summary, what positions do reading and writing hold in the entire communicative economy and what is the range of their social and cultural meanings?

Again, many of these questions may appear to have obvious answers, and some perhaps do, but until explored systematically, we must consider every element problematic. This must especially be the case in a large, multiparted, stratified society such as ours, a society continually reshaping itself through migration, immigration and the transformation of human resources.

Among the specific methods one would use for directly observing literacy in operation within a limited setting are (1) field observations of literacy analogous to those used by linguistics: i.e., observations of writing and reading activities in natural settings (subways, schools, libraries, offices, parks, liquor stores, etc.) and elicitation of these activities; (2) obtaining "reading" and "writing autobiographies"—that is, tape recorded personal statements on the use and meaning of specific activities and genres of reading and writing to individuals at various points in their lives; ascertaining writing activities in the form of letters to friends, for business purposes and the like, invitations, condolences, local sales and advertising activities, church readings, etc.; a reconnaissance of reading materials available within public view—signs, warnings, notices, etc.; and content analysis of reading materials ostensibly aimed at communities such as the one studied—e.g., "men's" and "women's" magazines, newspapers and the like—combined with readers' reactions and interpretations.

Throughout, the focus should be on the school and its relation to the community's needs and wishes, on the school's knowledge of these needs and wishes and on the community's resources. It is possible that this may involve bilingual or multidialectal speakers, and this puts a special burden on the study: we will need to pay special attention to reading and writing in several languages, (akin to the "code-switching" of multilingual speakers) and to the consequences to readers of not having available writing in their own languages or dialects. It may become necessary to separate reading and writing as such study progresses for a variety of reasons, but at the moment this separation would not be warranted, as it would prejudge the relationship between the two, something we simply are not able to do at this time. The end product, in addition to answering many of the questions posed here, should be an inventory of at least one American sub-community's literacy needs and resources, and should provide both the model for making other similar surveys elsewhere (perhaps more quickly) and for generalizing from this one.

Hymes taxonomy of communication:
- participants
- form of message
- code
- channel
- topic
- goal
- setting
- function

21.
The Development of
Initial Literacy

Yetta Goodman

When I first began to study how first graders learn to read, I discovered that even those children who had taken tests which predicted they were not good risks for learning to read provided evidence that they had all kinds of knowledge about written language. All were aware of the alphabetic nature of English print. They knew that the print in books and on other objects in the environment communicated written language messages. They knew how to handle books—which way was up, how and when to turn pages, and which aspects of the print were significant for reading and which were not. They knew that print was read from left to right most of the time. They were already predicting and confirming, using graphophonic, syntactic, and semantic cues with varying degrees of proficiency. They used pencils to write, observed the writing of others, and knew that what they had written could be read. It slowly became obvious to me that children's discoveries about literacy in a literate society such as ours must begin much earlier than at school age. Becoming increasingly aware of the significance of social context and with a developmental view of learning, I hypothesized that children develop notions about literacy in the same way that they develop other significant learnings: That is, children discover and invent literacy as they participate actively in a literate society. I believe that *all* children in our highly literate society become literate, even when they are part of a group within that society that values literacy in ways different from the majority.

In this chapter, I explore the kinds of learnings that all children develop as they become literate, the kinds of personal as well as environmental factors that play a role in literacy development, and the kinds of written language principles young children develop as they interact with their environment (Goodman, 1980; 1982). These explorations are based on research I have been doing with 2- to 6-year-olds since 1973 (Goodman and Altwerger, 1981) and on the research of

From *Awakening to Literacy*, ed. Hillel Goelman, Antoinette Oberg, and Frank Smith. Copyright 1984 by Heinemann Educational Books, Inc. Reprinted by permission of the publisher.

others who have greatly influenced my work (including many whose work appears in this book).

Generalizations about Literacy

Building on the work of Halliday (1975), K. Goodman and I extended to literacy learning the idea that learning language is learning <u>how to mean</u>. The child learns how to mean through written as well as spoken language. Initially, as children interact with the literacy events and implements in their culture, they grow curious and form hypotheses about their functions and purposes. They discover, as they are immersed in using written language and watching others use it, that *written language makes sense.* It communicates or says something. As this generalization begins to develop, children also become concerned with the organization of written language in terms of *how it makes sense*. They begin to find stability and order in the form of written language in the everyday context of its functional use. As these two generalizations are developing, children discover that *they can make sense through written language* as they use it themselves. They develop control or ownership of the strategies of comprehension and composition similar to those they have used in oral language, making allowances for the different constraints of written language forms and functions. They become more intuitively aware of the transactions among the reader, the writer, and the written text. These three overarching generalizations are driven by and, in turn, drive the development of the roots of literacy as children continue to experience written language.

The Roots of Literacy

Although it may seem obvious, it is important to remember that children's development of literacy <u>grows out of their experiences,</u> and the views and attitudes toward literacy that they encounter as they interact with social groups (the family, the local community, and other socio-economic classes, races, or ethnic groups). The soil in which the roots of literacy grows has significant impact on each child's development (Goodman, 1980). The ingredients in this soil include the amount of functional literacy that children encounter in the environment and the quality of those encounters; the attitudes and values about literacy expressed by other members in the social group; children's intuitive awareness of the symbolic nature of oral language, art, music, and dance; and children's own oral language.

Literacy can be said to have three major roots, each with smaller branches within it. These roots are:

1. The functions and forms that the literacy events serve,
2. The use of oral language about written language, which is part of the literacy event and reflects society's values and attitudes toward literacy,
3. Conscious awareness about literacy, including its functions, forms, and context.

Functions and Forms of Literacy

Children develop both reading and writing as they participate in meaningful literacy events. They develop control over functions and forms of reading. They respond to names, logotypes, and directions that usually occur as one- or two-word items embedded in conventional environmental settings. Their responses show understanding of the symbols' meanings even when the item is not read according to its conventional alphabetic form. For example, a stop sign may be referred to as "stop," "don't go," or "brake car" but, for the child, the meaning is the same. In learning to read environmental print, there seems to be little difference among social class groups.

The ability to read connected discourse, which includes books, newspapers, magazines, and letters, also develops through children's participation in literacy events. In this area, though, there are differences in responses among social classes. Although economically poor children develop ideas about connected discourse and know a good deal about how to handle books, middle-class children seem to develop greater flexibility and adult conventional knowledge about this type of reading. There are wide individual differences within all groups, but all the children who have been studied have some knowledge of book-handling before they come to school.

The functions and forms of productive writing also are developing in all the children we have studied before schooling. They know what purpose writing implements serve and, at a young age, they respond in different ways to "draw a boy" and "write boy." As with reading of connected discourse, productive writing varies a great deal from one household to another.

Using Oral Language about Written Language

Children and other members of society talk about the literacy events in which they participate. Words such as *read, write, pencil, story, letter,* and *book* all relate to concepts that are expressed orally during a literacy event. At 14 months of age, Alice brought her mother a book and said, "Read me, read me." Eduardo, aged 3½ years, pointed to a large *M* on a bulletin board and asked his dad, "Does that say McDonald's?" Children as young as 3 years begin to use *say* as a metaphor for *read.* "What does this say?" and "this says my name" are common expressions used by 3- and 4-year-old children in response to written language.

Children talk not only about written language that relates directly to the literacy event itself, but also about literacy experiences in relation to schooling, job hunting, books read, or bible use. These interactions all influence children's developing attitudes and values about literacy, including belief in their ability to learn to read and write. Some children as young as 3 years express the fear that learning to read or write will be very hard and can only be learned in school, whereas others are confident that they read already and that no one has to teach them because, as one youngster put it, "the words just fall into my mouth." These attitudes seem to be related to social class differences. Middle-class children tend to respond more confidently to learning to read than do lower-class children.

Conscious Knowledge about Literacy

At the same time that children use written language functionally to read and write and to talk about those experiences, they become aware of written language as <u>an object for study and discussion</u>. This conscious awareness—being analytic about the functions and forms of written language—develops in concert with the use of written language. It has been called, by some researchers, *linguistic* or *metalinguistic awareness*. Although I do not reject these labels, I believe it is important to distinguish a conscious or overt knowledge about language from intuitive awareness that children demonstrate when they use language. <u>Reading, writing, or using oral language in the context of reading and writing is not necessarily conscious knowledge. The child is using linguistic knowledge intuitively just as he or she does when speaking or listening.</u> Likewise, calling written forms by linguistic labels may not demonstrate conscious linguistic knowledge, since the child may at this point know the names of the forms and functions of literacy without consciously analyzing them. Children can appropriately call a dog by its name long before they can explain that it always has four legs and barks and why it is more like a cat than like an elephant or a fish.

There is evidence that children do begin early to develop conscious knowledge about the forms and functions of written language. Quincy, aged 4 years, says as he looks at the word *Ivory* on a card which has had its logotype retained: "It says soap, but you know if you put a dot up here (he points to the *i*) that's in my name, and if you put a line down here (he points to the *o*) that's in my name, and this . . . this . . . (he is pointing to the *y*) this is. (Then he points to each finger on his left hand with one of the fingers on this right hand as he continues his analysis.) This is a *q-u-i-n-c-y*. . . . That's a *y*." Quincy is an example of the many children who develop conscious knowledge about written language before they receive formal instruction in school.

Principles of Literacy Development

Thus children have many experiences with written language as they grow. For some children, these experiences begin when they are as young as 6 months old, as mothers and some fathers read to their children, enveloping the child and the book together into an emotionally satisfying literacy event. Other children generate written language in other kinds of literacy events (for example, looking for a particular gas station that sells at the lowest price; finding letters or words on highway signs during a family game in the car; or watching for a particular written symbol on television because, when that symbol appears, the child will be allowed to stay up late).

As children participate in literacy events, actively reading and writing, they develop three major principles about written language: The *relational* or *semiotic principles* are the understandings that children have about the ways that meaning is represented in written language, the ways that oral language is represented in written language, and the ways that both oral and written language interrelate to represent meaning. The *functional principles* are the understandings that children have about the reasons and purposes for written language. The *linguistic principles* are the understandings children have about how written language is organized and displayed so that communication can occur, considering the orthographic, graphophonic, syntactic, semantic, and pragmatic systems of language.

During early development, children may construct principles which they later have to discard. Some of these principles may actually interfere with the development of others for a period of time. The principles will overlap and interact, and the children will have to sort out which principles are most significant to meaning and which are not very useful; which operate differently given the constraints on each; and finally, which may be important in the understanding of other symbol systems the child is developing. These principles cannot be taught through traditional structured reading programs. They emerge for all children, but because of the idiosyncratic nature of the use of written language, the times and ways in which these principles emerge will vary extensively. *Emergent knowledge*

Relational Principles

Children learn to relate written language to meaning and, where necessary, to oral language. They develop the knowledge that some unit of written language represents some unit of meaning. Although this relationship may include words or letters, it also includes propositions, ideas, concepts, images, signs, symbols, and icons. Many children also know that their drawings represent ideas or things in the real world. They know the picture of a dog is not the dog itself but represents a dog. By the time most children enter school, they are aware that written language represents meaning. The developing writer and reader comes to know the relationships between writing, the object being represented, oral language, and the orthography.

These relational principles can be observed in a number of ways. Ferreiro and Teberosky (1982) suggest that children first believe that written language is a particular way of representing objects. It is not a drawing but acts like a drawing as the children respond to it. Children believe that print related to a picture says the name of the items represented in the picture, not that it is an oral language equivalent to the print. According to this theory, for children at a particular level of understanding, print that reads "the boy plays ball" says "boy" and "ball," although the children may interpret the picture as "the boy is playing ball." Children later develop the idea that there is an equivalence between oral and written language, first treating it as syllabic and finally as alphabetic.

My own research with children in English provides support for these conclusions drawn from research with children in Spanish and French. When told to write his name, 3-year-old Josh wrote what appeared to be a small— J As he did this he said, "This is a boy." Then, without any further probing, he wrote a much larger character— J —which resembled the first in form, and he said, "This is a dad." Finally, at the bottom of the paper, he made the same character even larger— J O —adding a second character which looked like an O superimposed over the first, and said, "This is the boy and the dad together."

Iconic use of written language

Josh's father's name is Joseph. Although the child was using characters that resembled the first two letters of both his and his father's names, these characters did not represent sounds for him; they represented "the boy" and "the dad." The child was able to represent his meanings in written language, and these meanings signified something in the child's personal experience. After a period of time of using size, shape, and number to invent written language forms, children develop alphabetic principles to relate oral and written language.

Children also show their developing awareness of the relationship between the length of the written string and the oral string. As they read or write, children will elongate their oral response to match their reading or writing. Eric, 4 years old, read "cee-ree-ull," stretching out the sound until he was finished pointing to the words *Kellogg's Raisin Bran*. As Mary wrote her name, she continued voicing the sounds of her name until she was finished writing it. Observation of children pointing with their fingers while an adult reads to them or of children's oral production as they watch an adult take dictation provides evidence of this developing principle.

Additional evidence of the development of the relational principle has been provided by researchers who have shown that children know written stories are represented in books following a particular story format (Doake, 1981; Haussler, 1982). They will repeat almost verbatim a whole story that has been read to them often, showing that they know how to represent the story form as well as its meaning.

Functional Principles

The degree to which literacy events are meaningful and purposeful to the child and the value those events have for the child will influence the development of functional principles. In homes where parents are college students, computer programmers, or authors, children will discover functional principles different from those developed by children whose parents read only the Bible daily or whose parents use writing selectively for shopping lists, filling out forms, and taking phone messages. Negative or positive statements made by adults about schooling and the ability to read and write, and the difficulty with or pleasure derived from reading and writing as shown by adults will also influence how children come to understand the functions of literacy.

Specific functional principles that children develop early include ownership and labeling, extension of memory, sharing information about self and others, invitations and expressions of gratitude, representation of real and imagined events (such as narratives), and control of behavior and information. For example, children will produce their own name as a label or recognize their name in appropriate settings. When children respond to printed items embedded in context, they tend to use nouns for naming items and imperative phrases for direction-giving signs in the environment. Stores and names of products and games usually are called by related names, whereas stop signs and school crossing signs elicit responses such as "don't go" or "watch out for kids." We have samples of children's notes, written a year or two before they enter school, which express a concern, a message, or an invitation for their parents or siblings. These are real uses of spontaneously produced written language.

In addition, the play in which children participate prior to schooling, both at home and in child care centers, demonstrates the development of functional principles. As children pretend to be mothers, gas station attendants, store clerks, doctors, or teachers, they use reading or writing appropriate to those occupations. The impact of home minicomputers and the new computer age in general on the functional principles of literacy that children develop can only be speculated about at this time, but that this understanding of literacy will appear in the play and real use of written language by children between the ages of 2 and 6 is unquestionable.

Linguistic Principles

Linguistic principles help young children solve the problems of (1) how the written language system is organized, (2) how the organization of written language changes, depending on its function and its relationship to other symbol systems, (3) what the units of written language are, depending on its functional and relational uses, (4) which features of written language are most significant in which settings, and (5) the stability of the organizational system (that is, which rules are most reliable and which are not very useful).

The evidence shows that children hypothesize about all the linguistic cueing systems needed for written language. The orthographic system, including directionality, spelling, punctuation, and form variations, as well as the graphophonic system, is new to children. The phonologic, syntactic, semantic, and pragmatic systems are developed through oral language use, and children exhibit a growing awareness of how these systems operate differently under the constraints of written language.

Children's early scribbling resembles the writing system used conventionally by adults in a society, but the writing of children in an Arabic literate culture will look different from the writing of children in an English literate culture. Samples of children's writing demonstrate that written language can be represented by single characters as well as in a scriptlike form. Punctuation, spacing, and directionality are used inventively at first and later, more conventionally.

Children seem to work through some of the same problems that the adult inventors of written language historically have had to solve, such as which way to display letters and how to organize the writing into units. Aesthetic issues are evident in children's work as they balance their art with their writing. Children explore these problems, discovering solutions that may be more appropriate for orthographic systems other than their own. For example, Roxanne, a 6-year-old, wrote a story with no spaces between her words, but she made the final letter in each word backwards when possible and underlined the last letter when it was not possible to reverse it. In Hebrew, some of the final letters of words are marked so that they look different from the same letter in medial or initial positions. When Roxanne was asked why she had done this, she said, "So you can read it better."

[Margin annotations: "Linkage of social/personal role develp. to type of literary level."; "personal to conventional"; "Ontogeny replicates phylogeny"]

The work of Charles Read (1975) and others has provided insights into the ways in which children invent a spelling system based on their knowledge of phonology. Their spelling becomes more and more conventionalized, regardless of instruction.

Punctuation is another convention that children begin to develop as they write. Bissex (1980) reports that her son used the exclamation mark before any other form of punctuation. Other children discover the use of the period, sometimes overgeneralizing its use as a word boundary marker before they control the use of space to separate words. At age 6 years, Jennifer used dialogue in her first-grade writing, but it was not until she was 7 years old that punctuation related to dialogue appeared in her stories:

January, Grade 1

. . . The mastr yald at hem you onle have two galns of hone he tot to the flor He sed tri to gev me som mor natr. [The master yelled at him, "You only have two gallons of honey." He talked to the flower. He said, "Try to give me some more nectar."]

March, Grade 2

. . . "So he said I will go to the camping stor, and I will ask what I need to go on my trip." . . . So he "said Im going camping"

Children provide evidence that they know about syntactic aspects of written language as well as the semantic and pragmatic aspects. For example, children develop control over the principle that some morphemic endings remain the same regardless of their phonologic composition. At age 4 to 6 years, children spell words such as *walked, jumped,* and *kissed* with the letter *t* at the end. (See Jennifer's spelling of *talked.*) Later, they realize that *ed* is the most common graphic representation of past tense in English. Some young readers overgeneralize this rule, reading or writing *walkted* for *walked.* Two first graders, in spontaneous writing, showed additional evidence of experimenting with morphemic issues. Carol, writing a letter to her grandparents, spelled the ordinal numbers as "firSt," "fourSt," "sixSt," as she was relating what grades she and her brothers were in. However, when she read the letter aloud, she produced the conventional oral English forms. Michael wrote to a friend about his "sidiren" and "bidren," but when he read his letter aloud, he read the words *sisters* and *brothers.* Could his morphemic endings have been overgeneralizations from the spelling of *children*?

Miscue analysis, which compares readers' observed oral responses to the listeners' expected responses, has provided evidence that children control syntax as they read. Miscues result in syntactically and semantically acceptable sentences, and substitution miscues are most often the same part of speech as the expected response. When children even as young as 3 years are reading or writing narrative stories, they usually begin with "once upon a time." We have never collected a child's letter that began with this traditional story starter. Rather, most letters open with "Dear _____," "how are you?" or the like.

There may be certain hierarchical sequences in the development of specific principles of language. For example, it seems that children develop a syllabic principle about written language before notions about alphabetic principles emerge. Also, children do not seem to represent the preconsonantal nasal when they begin to invent spelling in English, although it appears later in their development of literacy skills.

Learning to Become Literate

The development of written language is very complicated. The generalizations about and the roots and developing principles of literacy all interact as children develop control over making sense through written language. With this knowledge, children enter school where, too often, they are placed in a rigid instructional setting that ignores and is incompatible with what they already know. No published instructional program has ever provided the generalizations and concepts that people must develop to learn to read and write. A highly structured instructional system that focuses on mastery of one rule or skill before another loses sight of the complexity of learning written language. It oversimplifies what children really do learn and focuses some insecure children on insignificant and often erroneous principles about language.

In further research, each aspect of written language must be studied in greater depth and over longer periods of time. The focus should be on single subjects and on groups of children from widely different backgrounds who are reading and writing spontaneously. We must have more evidence of how capable the human toddler is of solving his or her personal needs for written language.

School is an important setting for literacy learning. There, the learning of literacy skills can be an exciting and stimulating experience; however, it can also be discouraging and inhibiting. Teaching children literacy through functional use has been advocated for more than eighty years (Iredell, 1898; Huey, 1908). Although there still is much that researchers and teachers must learn about literacy learning and teaching, we currently have the scientific foundation for helping teachers make learning to read and write an exciting literacy curriculum for all children.

22.
Rethinking Development *and* Organization

Jerome C. Harste
Virginia A. Woodward
Carolyn L. Burke

From Chapter 2, "Rethinking Development"

Researchers studying what young children know about print have found children in a state of "cognitive confusion." After many years of work in this area, however, we have yet to find a child who is "cognitively confused." In this chapter, we discuss three perspectives which we believe to be imperative in shaping a new theory of literacy learning. These three perspectives are: confusing product with process, confusing growth with experience, and confusing convention with language.

On Confusing Product with Process

Recently we asked a preschool teacher to have her 3-year-olds sign in each day to help her keep attendance and to help us trace written language growth and development. We made booklets for her so that the children could write their names on a clean page each day. When we offered her more booklets, she said, "This isn't working. The children aren't writing."

From *Language Stories and Literacy Lessons*, by Jerome C. Harste, Virginia A. Woodward, and Carolyn L. Burke. Copyright 1984 by Heinemann Educational Books, Inc. Reprinted by permission of the publisher.

EDITOR'S NOTE: "Children know much more than we or past researchers have ever dared to assume," assert Harste, Woodward, and Burke in the introduction to *Language Stories and Literacy Lessons*, and in the book they provide extensive illustration of the knowledge of literacy children acquire from their environment before they enter school. The existence of such knowledge challenges many theories about children, especially poor children, being deficient in their orientations toward written language and challenges, as well, the nature of much early-childhood language instruction.

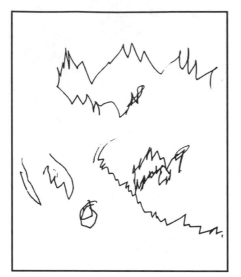 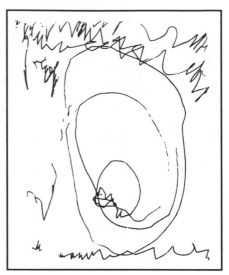

Figure 22.1. Uninterrupted writing and drawing samples (Marvin, age 3)

Figure 22.1 presents two typical products which this teacher was using in reaching her decision. In Uninterrupted Writing, Marvin was asked to write his name and anything else that he could write. In Uninterrupted Drawing, Marvin was asked to draw a picture of himself and to write his name. (Demographic information as well as a description of the tasks we used in this research study can be found in the Appendix to this volume; for more in-depth discussion, readers are referred to our original research reports.) Marvin's signature in Uninterrupted Writing closely resembles his signature at the bottom of Uninterrupted Drawing. When we contrast Marvin's writing with his art (top portion of Uninterrupted Drawing), we have to conclude, despite his teacher's evaluation, that not only is Marvin writing, but he has made important distinctions between art as a communication system and writing as a communication system.

Teachers and parents often view early drawing in much the same way that they view early writing, demeaning both by calling them "scribbles." When the product becomes representational or stereotypic, then, and only then, do they become excited. A typical example is Taisha (see figure 22.2).

Since Taisha's representation of her name as well as her representation of *people, houses, snow,* and *rain* coincide with adult notions of how these ought to be represented, these forms become valued. For many adults, literacy means "to represent the world on their terms, with their templates."

A first argument we wish to make is that the young child is a written language user long before his writing looks representational. We will argue that the decisions which the young child makes are, both in form and in kind, like those which we make as literate adults. When we confuse product with process we fail to note the onset of literacy and, in so doing, also fail to appreciate the real literacy achievement made by 3-year-olds.

To develop this point we will examine the products which Terry, another

Figure 22.2. Uninterrupted writing (Taisha, age 4)

3-year-old, produced in Uninterrupted Writing and Uninterrupted Drawing (see figure 22.3).

When we share these products without identifying which one is drawing and which one is writing, adults often initially find it difficult to say which is which. If, however, we examine the processes involved in producing these products (see figures 22.4 and 22.5), these confusions disappear.

The first four marks Terry made in Uninterrupted Writing form the letter *E*, which Terry says is his name. Note that at age 3, Terry has invented a mark which he takes to represent his name. Later, we will show that Terry consistently uses this mark to sign his name across written language encounters. Terry added a few more lines (Step 2). Significantly, these markings are linear, and, as is illustrated in figure 22.5, quite different from the lines he added during Uninterrupted Drawing. Terry wrote for twenty-five minutes in producing the product in figure 22.4. When asked to read what he had written (Step 3), Terry read, "A pig . . . King Kong . . . Monster . . . [and] Down," pointing to the places marked in figure 22.4.

Terry's Uninterrupted Drawing contrasts sharply with his writing. Art for Terry is global and circular and as such, contrasts with the linearity of what writing is for him. Terry began his self-portrait with the letter *E* (Step 1). Interestingly, Terry's art, like his writing, also evolved from the letter *E*, his name. Terry's subsequent decisions here, however, are quite different from those he made during writing, as is illustrated in his emerging product (Step 2).

Art is often thought to develop ahead of writing, and many even argue that children learn letter forms from their work in art. Tery's writing challenges that view. The decisions which Terry has made about writing facilitate his growth and development in art, and vice versa. The relationship here is a reciprocal one which becomes mutually supportive to written language literacy in the broadest sense.

We have found that by the age of 3 all children in our study could, under

Art and
writing

Uninterrupted Writing   Uninterrupted Drawing

Figure 22.3. Uninterrupted writing and uninterrupted drawing samples (Terry, age 3)

certain conditions, distinguish art from writing. Their decisions in writing, as in art, are systematic and organized. We found further that all 3-year-olds had developed a marking which to them symbolized their name. This marking acted as any symbol acts, serving to place-hold meaning during writing, and to reconstruct that meaning during reading.

Figure 22.6 shows the consistency of the markings of our 3-year-olds in representing their names from one writing to another. And, lest we forget, these are the writings of lower- and middle-class black and white children, not of upper-class children who supposedly have some school literacy advantage. We believe it is also important that we recognize these writings for what they are. They are not pseudo, preliterate marks or acts, but, both in form and in process, the stuff of real literacy, being invented from the inside out.

A second argument we wish to make is that in order to judge the quality of a literacy experience one must judge the quality of the mental trip taken, not the arrival point per se. To illustrate this argument we will use some of the selected examples collected from a story writing setting we used in our research (see figure 22.7). In this setting the child was given a paper and pen and told, "Today, you will write a story and I'll write a story. When we are done, we'll read our stories. You read your story to me and then I'll read my story to you."

In response to our request we received a variety of products. Jason drew a picture. Natasha also drew a picture, but not before she had written, "This is a puppy." Vincent wrote, "I like candy," using a rebuslike combination of writing and art.

If we, as adults, expect children to write when we ask them to write, then we would be more pleased with Natasha's and Vincent's work than with Jason's. What we wish to argue, however, is that to use such a criterion sells short both the child and the cognitive operations involved in real literacy.

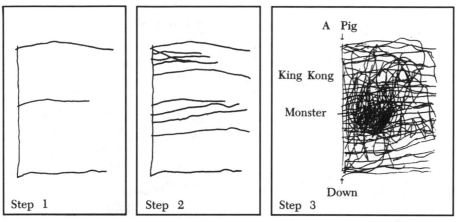

Figure 22.4. Steps in uninterrupted writing task (Terry, age 3)

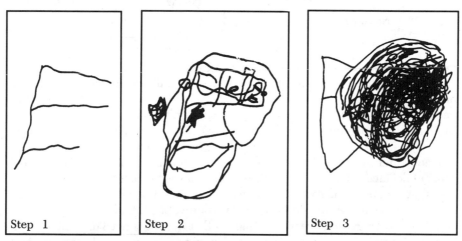

Figure 22.5. Steps in uninterrupted drawing (Terry, age 3)

Jason, when asked to read what he had written, read, "A ghost flying through the air. A dog barking. And when the ghost saw him, he came down and he bumped him on the nose!" In so doing, Jason demonstrates that he not only understands the rules governing what he is to do in this setting, but also the notion of storiness. What Jason has elected to do in this instance is simply to move to an alternate communication system to placehold his meaning. This option is one which we, as literate adults, can also make when writing.

Vincent, age 6, when asked to read what he had written, read the expected, "I like candy." Natasha, age 6, likewise read the expected, "This is a puppy." But it is important to understand that each child has communicated ideas in sentence form using graphics as symbols to placehold meaning. Vincent, like Jason, negotiated the contract on the floor from writing to drawing when he believed he could not spell candy. Importantly, neither Vincent's nor Natasha's products show knowledge of storiness, while Jason's product, despite its less conventional form, does. So from a process perspective, the products which we

Iconic writing

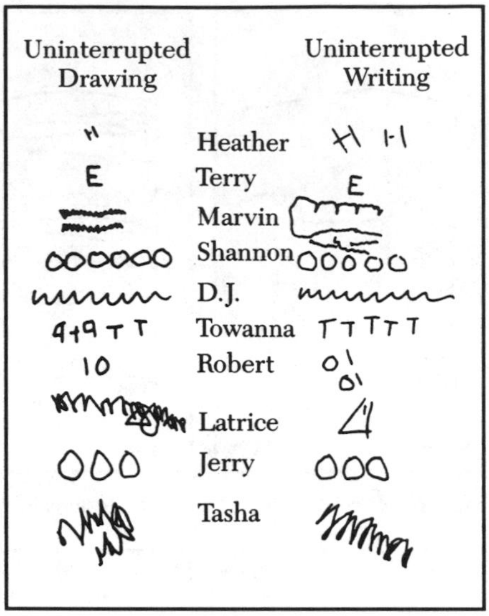

Figure 22.6. Name writing across tasks (3-year-olds)

might initially favor do not appear to be as good.

Given this single instance, we cannot realistically say if Vincent or Natasha have a notion of storiness or not. All we do know is that in this situation, they decided to respond in a particular way which didn't obviously show it, and that their way of responding differed from at least one other child, namely, Jason.

Results of correctness criteria

Trying to get ideas down on paper can be a constraining factor, especially if schools demand correctness of form. Our hunch is that both Natasha and Vincent decided to play it safe, so the product does not express all that they know, but is rather a function of their decision making given the constraints which they perceive to be operating in this particular context of situation.

A third argument we wish to make is that writing is not a monolithic skill. Language varies according to the circumstances of its use. Different settings mandate different products. Michelle at age 6, in what was our seventh session with her over the four-year period we studied her, was asked to write her name and anything else she could write. A transcript of her conversation with the researcher during the production of her product in figure 22.8 illustrates the key cognitive operations involved in her written language use and learning.

After initially writing *Where*, Michelle asked: "Did I write *where?*"

The researcher responded: "Yes."

Michelle: "I forgot how to write *tiger.*"

Researcher: "You write whatever you can."

Michelle: "It begins with *T* . . . [writes *t*] . . . but, I want to know how."

Researcher: "You write whatever you want to write."

Michelle: "I don't know how. . . . Is an *h* after this [pointing to the *t*]?"

Michelle writes *is*, squeezing it in between the *e* in *where* and the *t* in *this*.

Realizing she has a word card with *tiger* written on it, Michelle starts to leave the table, saying, "I'll be right back."

The researcher stops her, saying, "You write it how you think it is."

Jason, Age 5

Natasha, Age 6

Vincent, Age 6

Figure 22.7. Story writing (composite)

"I wish you'd tell me some words. I can't remember *tiger.*"

"You do the best you can. You'll remember it's *tiger,*" responds the researcher.

Michelle responds, "I don't know what to write. Can I write a picture? . . . Can I write a picture, if I don't know how to spell it?" *Eliciting expectations*

"You write whatever you like to write."

Michelle writes *This* and draws a flower. She then writes *It is in.* She reads to herself, "Where is this flower. It is in." She writes *the,* and draws some grass.

Again she reads the whole thing: "Where is this flower. It is in the grass." She writes her second *Where,* rereads all her writing, writes *is the,* and then draws another clump of grass. Without rereading she writes *It is,* saying the words to herself as she does so. After reading all she has written, Michelle writes *in herer.*

She then reads her completed text: "Where is this flower? It is in the grass. Where is the grass? It is in here."

Throughout this literacy event we can see Michelle clarifying for herself the expectations of writing under these conditions. She wants approval to get her word card so she can spell correctly and, later, to draw instead of write. Once she has made her decision to draw the words she cannot spell, she moves freely between writing and art to placehold meaning. By listening to Michelle we get a good picture of what constraints she sees operating in this setting. It is important to understand that this significant literacy event would have been lost if we had examined only product and not process. By watching Michelle write this product, however, which in itself means little, we can uncover the orchestrated literacy decision-making event which undergirds it. Strategies and constraints which are frozen in adult writing once again become visible. *re: Bartholomae*

The next day Michelle was asked to write a letter. Before this research session began, Michelle had shown the researcher the Sears catalogue and the doll she wanted for Christmas. The researcher used Santa as the person to whom Michelle should write her letter (see figure 22.9).

Michelle writes *DAE* and asks, "Does it spell *dolly?*"

The researcher responds, "You write it the best you can."

After writing *with,* Michelle reads, "Dolly with," and then writes *hr.* At

Figure 22.8. Uninterrupted writing (Michelle, age 6). Transcription (as read by child): "Michelle Morrison. Where is this (flower)? It is in the (grass). Where is the (grass). It is in here."

this point she asks, "Does this spell *her*?"

The researcher responds, "You're doing nicely writing this letter." Michelle sounds out *tr* and *ch*. She writes *ch* and crosses it out, saying, "Oh, is that right for *treasure*?"

The researcher says, "If you make a mistake you can cross it out." Michelle writes *thr chchrt*, and decides to cross out the final *rt*, as she asks, "Does that say *Treasure Chest*?"

The researcher responds, "You're doing well. You keep writing your letter."

After rereading, Michelle says, "I know how to spell *come*." Michelle reflects as much to herself as to the researcher, "You make funny *e*'s." As she makes another she says, "You make little circles and color it in," obviously loving not only the experience, but her new-found style.

Michelle writes *come with* and once more rereads her evolving text.

Michelle asks, "Does *cradle* start with *k* or *c*?" Michelle writes *KdL*, asking, "Does that say *cradle*?"

After writing *And*, Michelle once more rereads her text.

She writes *stLL* and asks, "Does that spell *stroller*?"

As she finished writing the letter, Michelle continued reading her text, making self-corrections and asking the researcher for reassurance that she was doing it right. When her message was complete, Michelle said that she was not going to use periods. She put her name at the top of the page, probably because of the first-grade practice of putting your name at the top of all papers (previously in the Letter-Writing task, Michelle had followed the convention of putting her name after the message). After finishing all her writing she was still not tired of the task, and she elected to draw a picture at the bottom of the letter.

In this letter-writing context as contrasted to the Uninterrupted Writing task, Michelle made several literacy decisions. From reading the catalogue she

Figure 22.9. Letter writing composites (Michelle, age 6). Transcription (as read by child): "Dolly with her treasure chest. Come with cradle and stroller and doll rocker, sleeper outfit, baby seat, little love panties and powder set."

was aware that the doll and all the things it came with were formatted graphically in a specific way. In writing letters over time, Michelle always used the graphic form for signing her message and had never negotiated a move to pictures. As she wrote this letter she was testing out her ideas about following the catalogue's graphic format. This forced her to test her ways of spelling to include both spelling as it sounds and spelling as it looks.

These examples show us that Michelle demonstrates good graphophonemic knowledge. As a writer, she is also actively engaged in the reading process. As a writer, Michelle herself is her own first reader. Attention span is not an issue when personal involvement and choice are an integral part of the process.

After writing her letter, Michelle paused, as if reflecting. Dejectedly she said, "Don't send it to Santa. I know it's not correct." Using the product, not the process, as the standard by which she judges her success in literacy, Michelle has all too willingly adopted the adult expectation that the product is the important indicator of "what I know." The adult focus on product in the environment in which Michelle is growing up begins to confuse her about what writing is. This focus seems to convince Michelle to value form over function and to reorder her literacy learning priorities accordingly. *[handwritten margin note: Compare to college literacy]*

But more positively, Michelle seems aware of different writing demands in different writing settings. Through working with us over the course of our research, Michelle learned that when she wrote with us, as opposed to when she wrote with her parents or in school, she could set aside certain concerns. She learned that she was allowed to and expected to experiment, to take risks, and to actively use all she knew about language. Under these conditions, Michelle came to understand and discover what real literacy was all about as we did. *[handwritten margin note: The Researcher as teacher]*

With a focus on product, we not only fail to see growth, but also to make and take the opportunities for literacy which abound around us. With a focus on product, we deny language users such as Michelle their most powerful language learning strategy: namely, active involvement—the kind of involvement which demands that they bring to bear all they currently know about language to test yet another new hypothesis. It is only when children are engaged in this way that both they and we can go about the business of understanding written language literacy. At bottom, written language literacy involves "the saga of learning how to mean" (Halliday, 1973) via markings which placehold and sign meaning. Understanding this process is as central to our growth as it is to that of the child's.

We began this section, "On Confusing Product with Process," with a language story telling about how a teacher, on the basis of surface feature form, rejected a sign-in activity as a valuable literacy learning experience. We close with the request: "Let them 'sign in,' please!"

On Confusing Growth with Experience

Most 5-year-olds can correctly identify the basic colors.
Most 6-year-olds can write their names.
Most 7-year-olds have a reading sight vocabulary of approximately 215 words.

Despite the fact that we seem to have no trouble responding to such statements, and despite the fact that such statements are capable of statistical verification (that is, we can test populations and come up with numerical counts and percentages), such statements, we would like to argue, are not useful predictors of accomplishment. The relationship which these statements feature, that between *age* and *accomplishment*, is based upon a loose correlation between *age* and *experience*.

The languaging of the children in our study demonstrates that experience is the operational factor in this pair. Experience makes the evolution of literacy predictable. This argument becomes clearer when we add a fourth statement:

Most adults can read.

While this statement is as verifiable as the first three, some of the pitfalls in its underlying reasoning are more easily visible. What does this "fact" lend to our assessment of any individual adult who does *not* demonstrate an ability to read? We cannot assume lack of age, but we should begin to ask questions about opportunities and experience.

Age pales into insignificance in the adult example. And it should also begin to pale when the language users we are interested in are children. Age has always been a convenience, an easier factor for language researchers and curriculum developers to manage than experience. But age is a dangerous criterion precisely because it does not consistently covary with the operational factor of experience.

Let us look at some responses which children gave when reading items common in their environment.

Reading responses have been ordered in figure 22.10 in relation to their approach to the conventional response to the item. For Dynamints, the trend is from a *functional* response, through a *categorical* response, to a *specified* response. When we examine the ages of the children who made these responses, we can see no clear age trends.

We will pay particular attention to Tyler and Michelle, the two youngest readers, as we look at their Jello, Crest, and Wendy's environmental print readings. In the readings of Jello we again find responses which range from functional, through categorical, to specified, with a dispersal of ages. Just as she does with Dynamints, Michelle seems to have the experiential edge on Tyler. An examination of the functional responses to this print environment is supportive of our age thesis. Both "We eat food" and "It should be a telephone number" are descriptors of selected past encounters which these readers feel should be related to this encounter.

Tyler is saying, "Hey, you're supposed to eat this." Daniel and Alison are saying, "This is crazy, they made the name look like a phone number." All three of their readings are the direct outcome of their personal functional knowledge of the world.

The Crest example is an instance in which Tyler seems to have a slight experiential edge on Michelle—Michelle's response is functional, while Tyler's is categorical. In reading this product label he is not in danger of being considered immature (as do all those studies which say that boys developmentally lag behind girls), as he was with his readings of Dynamints and Jello.

[margin annotation:] Functional
[margin annotation:] categorical

Now let's see if we can even the odds even more, not only between Tyler and Michelle, but between them and some of their older research mates. What happens when the children are asked to read an item which is brand new, where the experiential opportunities are severely restricted for everyone?

Wendy's as an item had only been physically available in the environment for about a month and television ads about it had been available for about a week before the readings. Tyler and Michelle are both successful at competing under these circumstances, despite the dispersed age ranges in this situation.

Now before we acquiesce to the danger of concluding that there might be a simple and direct relationship between an increase in experience and the production of a specified conventional response, we need to consider the reading which several of our language users gave to the graphic U.S. Mail logo.

As a response to the U.S. Mail logo (see figure 22.11) our informants read both *gas* and *gas station*. The fact that several of them concurred in their reading assured us that they had shared a focus on a common experiential background which we (older and wiser, as all researchers are) were unable to spot. We were forced to go out and reexperience gas stations, to confront them actively as our subjects obviously were doing, instead of simply encountering them, in order to perceive the significance of their outline configuration, limited text, style of lettering, geometric logo designs, and predominance of red, white, and blue coloring (see figure 22.12).

This experience was enough to make us think that we should be able to "fill up" at the post office. While the researchers' experience of both the U.S. Mail insignia and gas station logos was of longer duration than that of our informants, their present experiences were more acute. The currency, strength

Responses to Jello

*We eat Food	Tyler 3.3
*0–1–1	Daniel 4.2
*It should be a	
telephone #	Allison 4.1
pudding	Megan 4.2
Strawberries	Dawn 4.3
	Justin 6.4
	Jonathan 5.6
Jell-o	Michelle 3.4
	Charles 5.3
	Heather 6

Responses to Dynamints

Hot	Jonathan 5.6
vitamins/	
medicine	Tyler 3.3
mints	Daniel 4.2
Tic Tacs	Marc 5.5
	Heather 6.0
Dynamints	Michelle 3.4
	Allison 4.1
	Dawn 4.3

Responses to Wendy's

O.K., but I've	
seen her on T.V.	Megan 4.2
Water	Mara 5.5
Burger Queen	Dawn 4.3
Arby's	Jonathan 5.6
	Heather 6.0
Wendy's	Tyler 3.3
	Michelle 3.4
	Allison 4.1
	Dawn 5.1
	Justin 6.4

Responses to Crest

brush	Boyd 3.5
toothbrush	Michelle 3.4
toothpaste	Tyler 3.3
	Daniel 4.2
	Mara 5.3
toothpaste →	
CREST	Dawn 5.1
CREST	

Figure 22.10. Reading environmental print (composite)

Figure 22.11. U.S. Mail logo   Figure 22.12. Gas station logos

and commonality of their confrontations had led them to an agreed upon alternative response.

We encountered another mystery when our Bloomington and Indianapolis subjects were asked to read a highway sign displaying the name of their town (see figure 22.13). Some children in both cities gave the reading "book." While phonic analysis might seem to offer some explanation for the Bloomington sign, it loses all its promise in relation to the Indianapolis sign. In this instance, one of our informants filled in the experiential void of the researchers. By giving a reading of "Sesame Street" to the Indianapolis sign, this young person showed us that a number of our informants possessed experience which we simply lacked (see figure 22.14). In this instance, the researchers' ages worked as a clear obstacle to their experience. Our informants tended to display a greater facility in producing conventional adult responses in their readings of environmental print than they did for either their own written stories or for a published picture storybook.

It is quite easy to draw the assumption from these data that these two continuous texts are more complex than the environmental text and are therefore simply more difficult to read, an assumption which does not, however, hold up so well under continued examination. As the U.S. Mail logo example has already indicated, even the most spartan of environmental print settings is replete with graphics from alternative communication and signaling systems: container shapes, logos, color relationships, pictures, and print. These present a complex communication processing environment. Cue complexes are selectively per-

Not an age thing

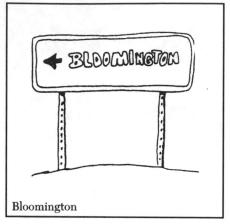

Figure 22.13. City marker signs

ceived as a function of their <u>transaction with the reader's experiential knowledge</u>. Even when, in our attempts to understand, we limit examination to the print environment alone, the linguistic complexities are greater, and the subjects' responses more varied, than common sense would predict. The U.S. Mail logo turned out to be the most lexically constrained text environment with which our readers were confronted, and even it was composed of something more extended than a single word. The other text environments were much more complex; they contained multiple syntactic and semantic units scattered over the item's surface. These <u>text environments</u> presented messages which included brand name, generic category, ingredients, amounts, and directions for use. All these messages were weighted for significance by their placement on the package, as well as by the size, shape and coloring of their letterings. Through this virtual forest of competing cues and messages (see figure 22.15), our subjects moved with credible composure, familiarity, and with a display of individual interest.

These young language users displayed the flexibility and confidence necessary to make individual decisions which can only come with the accumulating effect of personally significant experimental confrontations with environmental print; confrontations which were initiated on the day their mothers pulled their first diaper out of the Pamper's box, and which continued through feedings from the well-marked jars of Gerber's Baby Food right up to their first historic encounters with the Golden Arches of McDonald's. So, if they read boxes more conventionally than they read books, it just might be that it is not because environmental print is less complex than continuous text but because it is more familiar.

Why can most 5-year-olds identify colors and most 6-year-olds write their names? Because they live in environments which provide many meaningful and pleasant encounters with such processes.

What is one of the most valuable gifts we can give language users? We can litter their environment with enticing language opportunities and guarantee them the freedom to experiment with them.

Figure 22.14. Sesame Street sign on book cover

On Confusing Convention with Language

In first grade, Jason's teacher corrected his spellings of *heel, glass, broom, toys, car,* and *mitt* (see figure 22.16). She also corrected any faulty notions which Jason might have developed about the current practicality of authors who put together reading workbooks; we note particularly the teacher's correction of Jason's "cau" to "ox." In third grade, Jason's teacher corrected everything she knew how to correct, including his sentence structure and spelling (see figure 22.17). Her spelling corrections appear on almost everything except *ogre,* a word which she obviously didn't know to spell either.

From an instructional perspective, what all of Jason's experiences have in common in a concern for convention. This concern pervades written language instruction. It guides teachers in making decisions about "good handwriting," "correct spelling," "good grammar," and "well-formedness of stories."

Language conventions are defined as socially agreed upon rules of expression which have as their function the facilitation of communication. Notice that there is nothing in this definition which defines them as barriers to communication. We can communicate—and do so quite creatively—whether or not our speech or writing is conventional. Conventional control does not free creativity, and when overemphasized, it has quite the opposite effect. James Joyce broke the canons of convention with his stream of consciousness writing and in so doing, taught us a process by which to mean. So have Alison, Mike, and Charvin, all age 4.

Conventional control has been the bifocals through which we have viewed growth and development in language. This is more than just a poor prescription for eyeglasses; it also makes it appear as if growth to convention were the goal of the oral and written language curriculum. It causes us to see convention when we wish to see language, and in the process, to confuse not only ourselves but our students. When convention is the lens, we fail to see linguistic growth as continuous throughout the life of the language user and so, fail to appreciate linguistic achievement after convention has been reached.

Figure 22.15. Examples of complex test environments

A case in point is Alison's signature over a four-year period. Alison had written her name more or less conventionally since she was 3. Yet a far more interesting signature was the one she wrote at the age of 5 when she penned A-L-I-U-S-O-N. At 5, everything she knew about letter-sound correspondence compelled her to put a *u* in her name. She experimented with this form for a couple of weeks and then elected the optional spelling her parents had chosen.

At 7, however, she produced A-L-L-I-S-O-N as her signature. Since this signature was put on the flyleaf on a book being dedicated to the church library, Alison's mother was less than ecstatic with her decision to write her name with two l's. When she asked, in exasperation, "Alison! Why did you write two l's?" Alison replied, "You can, you know; some people write Alison that way."

Alison is an active language user; standard conventional form is for her one option among many. It is far more interesting to map the range of hypotheses which children like Alison test about language than it is to assume that convention is the sole option, and nonconvention either failure or carelessness. Convention and nonconvention are more a function of experience and perspective than of practice.

Probably no data better illustrate this point than do the cross-cultural data which we have collected. To observe that Alison does not control the conventions of her language is to focus on one act, but to miss the event.

Language, whether oral or written, is a social event of some complexity. Language did not develop because of the existence of one language user, but of

[margin note: Options w/ conventionality]

Figure 22.16. Corrected workbook page (Jason, age 6)

two. If we are to understand language, we must see it as an orchestrated transaction between two language users which has as its intent to convey meaning in a given context of situation. Pragmatics is the system of language which joins language users, not only through convention but through negotiation and discretion. This perspective is as important for our understanding of reading as it is for our understanding of writing. We have purposely selected a reading example to illustrate this point since convention is as big an issue in reading as it is in writing.

When we examine the set of responses we received after showing children a carton of Kroger's milk (see figure 22.18), we can readily agree that all the "milks" and "Krogers" are responses which answer the question we asked, namely, "What does that say?" while "Some milk goes in there," "A milk box," "Box that hold milk," and "A milk can," are better responses to questions such as, "What goes in there?" and "What is this?"

While clearly in these instances the children have not answered our question, what they have done is far more interesting. They have, like us on certain occasions, chosen to answer a question other than the one we posed. We do this all the time. In fact, it is a classic strategy used in passing doctoral qualifying examinations and essay tests more generally. The children here, like us, have exercised their options. That is, under certain conditions, <u>they either negotiate or reinterpret the communication contract put before them</u>. What at first then, may appear to be an unconventional response, from another perspective falls well within the range of conventional options, given the setting.

Convention has largely been viewed as relating to the graphophonemic and syntactic systems of language, but this is misguided. Oral and written language use involves the orchestration of not only graphophonemic and syntactic systems but of semantic and pragmatic systems. One cannot even begin to explore what hypotheses are being tested about convention at these levels until

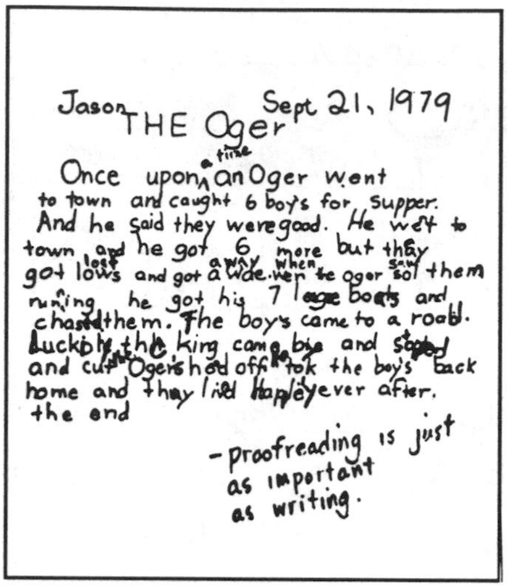

Jason THE Oger Sept 21, 1979

Once upon a time an Oger went
to town and caught 6 boys for supper.
And he said they were good. He went to
town and he got 6 more but they
got loos and got a wae.when te oger sol them
runing he got his 7 lage boats and
chast them. The boys came to a roobl.
Luckbly the King came bie and stoppd
and cut Ogers had off tok the boys back
home and thay lied Haployever after.
the end

— proofreading is just
as important
as writing.

Figure 22.17. The Oger (Jason, age 8)

one understands the nature of the communication contract which has been agreed upon. Convention is a function of context and involvement in the language process.

Engaging in the languaging event, that is, deciding to use paper and pencil or whatever, leads not only to the development of convention, but to the realization that one can build upon those conventions that others have used which have addressed similar issues. The relationship is one between personal convention and social convention. A personal convention is a decision reached because of a need experienced while participating in a language event.

It is Charvin's decision to placehold separate concepts with blobs using space and distance (see figure 22.19); this personal convention underpins his notion of wordiness and reflects his schematic readiness for understanding that concept as we know it.

It is Mike's decision to placehold meaning by using space, like Charvin, and by using a combination of letters and picturelike symbolic forms. This decision not only builds on Mike's knowledge of how to represent meaning through a series of pictures, but incorporates what he knows about both art and writing. It is these border scrimmages between systems (art and writing) which are often the most developmentally interesting. Mike's decisions, at 4 years of age, are a set of real writing decisions like those many of our ancestors came to make, which further reflect the literacy level they attained. Having come to his decision in a literate society, however, Mike is now ready to use the linguistic information which bombards him, not through wholesale adoption but rather, like us, through linguistic discretion.

It is important to understand in this regard that a very delicate balance exists in each of us between personal and social convention. Some of what is social convention will always elude us. We are always reminded of this fact whenever we send a final draft manuscript away to be published. We can never believe all

The mistaken notion that editors/teachers represent social convention, and not just a socially personally constructed personal convention

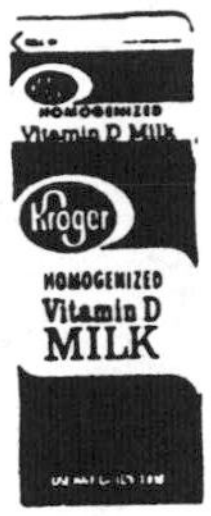

Print Setting: Kroger Milk

Some milk goes in there	(Nathan, Age 3)
Milk	(Tyler, Age 3)
Milk	(Michelle S., Age 3)
Milk	(Michelle M., Age 3)
Milk	(Boyd, Age 3)
Milk	(Daniel, Age 4)
Milk	(Dawn B., Age 4)
A Milk Box	(Jeremy, Age 4)
Box that holds milk in it.	(Megan, Age 4)
Milk	(Alison, Age 4)
Milk	(Jonathan, Age 5)
Milk	(Charles, Age 5)
Kroger	(Teddy, Age 5)
Milk	(Mara, Age 5)
Milk	(Dawn, Age 5)
A Milk Can	(Heather, Age 6)
Milk	(Leslie, Age 6)
Milk	(Emily, Age 6)
Milk	(Justin, Age 6)
Kroger's	(Denver, Age 6)

Figure 22.18. Reading response to Kroger's milk

the changes the publishers make—even with nonconvention aside! But it is personal convention which gives our language its style and makes it our own. Language convention, like language, is socially invented in a supportive environment which makes such discoveries available; it is not an heirloom like a grandfather's clock which is passed along from generation to generation, but rather, more like a civilization whose heritage is passed along by those immersed in it. And sometimes it is our personal convention, as in the case of James Joyce's stream of consciousness writing, which leads not only us, but others to new ways to mean.

ought not → is not? re: convention

Conventions are quite simply fringe benefits, artifacts of written language use in a community of written language users, not prerequisites to, nor criteria for, language use. If we can accept them for what they are, we will find that language conventions are interesting as fringe benefits of involvement in a literacy event.

This underrates the power of convention

Charvin, Age 4

Mike, Age 4

Figure 22.19. Uninterrupted writing (composite)

Conclusion

In this chapter, we have suggested that the most prevalent view of language development can be represented by a formula which states that: AGE in relationship to CONVENTION indicates GROWTH.

In contrast to this view of development, we would suggest a new formula in which EXPERIENCE is seen as TRANSACTING with PRINT SETTINGS, the results of which lead to new levels of PSYCHOLINGUISTIC AND SOCIOLINGUISTIC ACTIVITY. Because this process is cyclic and ongoing throughout life, the nature of literacy itself is forever changing, creating new personal and societal potentials for all of us.

From Chapter 7, "Organization"

Early Organizational Patterns

Although not as immediately evident in the surface structure texts as in those of more experienced written language users, the organizational decisions underlying the writing of children as young as 3 years old are discernible with study. Theoretically this discovery is important since it suggests that scribbling is not scribbling in the sense of being unorganized and random, but bears much similarity at a process level to the activity we have called writing.

Figure 22.20 presents DuJulian's (age 3) uninterrupted drawing and writing samples. Given the fact that DuJulian organizes his writing using a linear, up-down stroke (see Uninterrupted Writing Sample, figure 22.20), it is readily apparent which marks were made to placehold the picture of himself (see top section of Uninterrupted Drawing Sample, figure 22.20) and which were made to placehold his name (see bottom section of Uninterrupted Drawing Sample, figure 22.20). Art for DuJulian involves circular markings; writing involves linear strokes with up-down markings.

If the decisions which 3-year-olds make for art and for writing are indeed

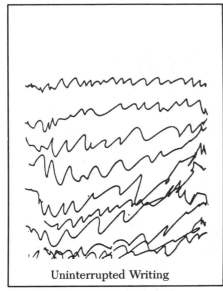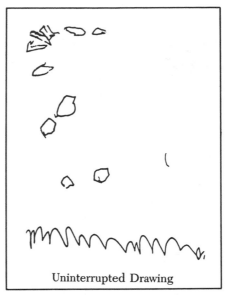

Uninterrupted Writing | Uninterrupted Drawing

Figure 22.20 Uninterrupted Writing and Uninterrupted Drawing Samples (DuJulian, Age 3).

different, then it follows that an examination of the sets of scribbles constituting the product of a task which asks them to draw a picture of themselves and sign their name should reflect these alternate decisions; in short, scribbling in art should look different from scribbling in writing. That this is, indeed, the case is readily apparent when we examine the samples in figure 22.21. Not only can scribble writing be differentiated from scribbles drawing, but we have found that adults have little difficulty, given the linearity of writing and the global cohesiveness of art, in differentiating which is which, even when the markings have not been labeled and categorized as in figure 22.21.

These data demonstrate the organization present in the products of art and writing scribbles. The unity of the child's decisions across art and writing, as well as the support such unity provides in motivating and driving literacy learning, needs further elaboration. In searching for the process principles underlying the decisions made for art as opposed to writing, one of the things to be noticed is that some children reserved up-down strokes for writing and circular markings for art; other children did just the opposite, i.e., used circular markings for writing and up-down strokes for art. For example, Robert (see figure 22.21) used an up-down stroke for writing and a circular stroke for art. Shannon, on the other hand (see figure 22.21), used a circular stroke for writing and an up-down stroke for art.

In studying this phenomenon we discovered that if the child's name begins with a letter which is made up of linear elements, such as the *L* in Latrice's name which is made up of two straight lines, the odds that the child's scribble writing is composed of up-down strokes is high. Similarly, if the child's name starts with a letter which is composed of curved elements, such as the *S* in Shannon, the odds are high that the child's scribble writing is circular. Among the

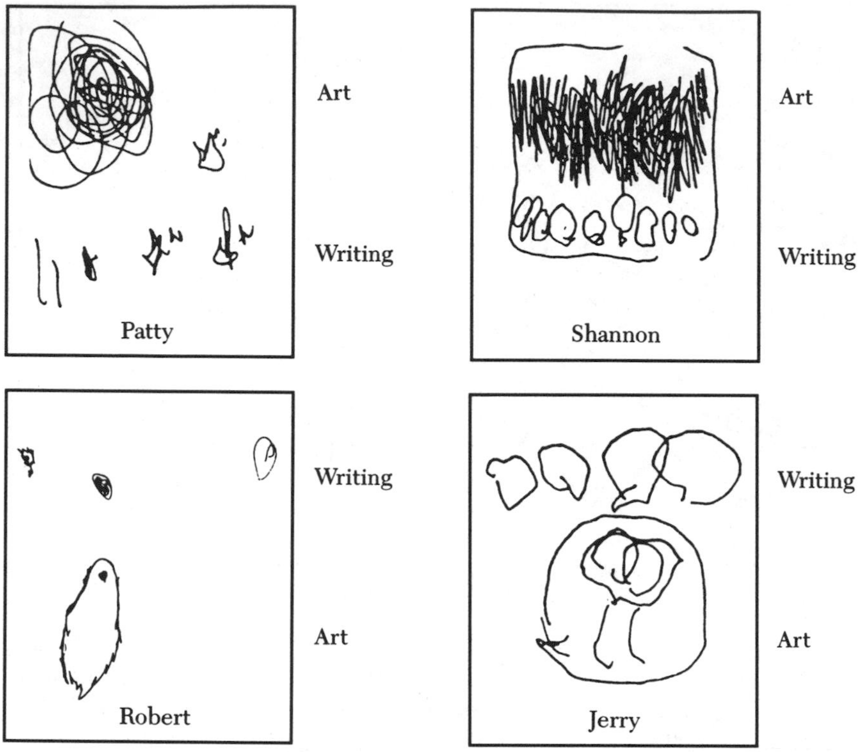

Figure 22.21. Uninterrupted drawing samples (self-portrait and name, age 3)

3-year-old sample, using this simple formulaic relationship, prediction as to the organization of writing and hence art for any individual child is 0.91. When all of the letters of the name are used and a proportion of linear letters to circular letters is calculated, the prediction made from the proportion which results rises to 0.93. While it appears to be largely irrelevant which organizational form is selected for art as opposed to writing for any given child regardless of the form of his or her name, the point is that a relationship exists between decisions made in writing and decisions made in art, and vice versa.

Later Organizational Patterns

Language is, of course, laced with organization. The reason age correlated with language is that three additional years allow the language learner twice the number of opportunities not only to encounter, but to discover more and more of these organizational features. In the sections that follow, two texts will be used for an extended discussion of some of the organizational features which are present in the written products of children two and three years older than those we have been examining.

Testing Your Child-As-Informant Skills

Because many adults assume children are in a state of "cognitive confusion"

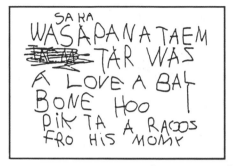 

Figure 22.22. Uninterrupted writing sample (Sara, age 5)

when, in fact, this label better describes their own present level of understanding, they miss much of the organization displayed by children. Before reading the translations for Sara's and Matt's texts (figures 22.22 and 22.23), one must assume, as we have trained ourselves to do in this project, that the decisions which these young writers have made are organized. (Readers can test their child-as-informant skills by attempting to read these children's written efforts). The pictures Sara and Matt include in their stories are an integral part of their texts. It should be kept in mind that children two and three years younger than Matt and Sara, when reading what they have written—long before their surface texts become as "conventional" as are Matt's and Sara's—demonstrate that their writing shares many of these same organizational features.

Surface Text Organization: A Pragmatic Perspective

A pragmatic perspective means asking what function the piece of writing was designed to serve. Knowing that Sara's surface text ("Once upon a time there was a loveable bunny who picked a rose for his mommy") was a Mother's Day card, we have to say that the product served as the expression of love, thoughtfulness, appreciation—in short, "mother's-dayness"—quite well.

This observation does not resolve all of the pragmatic issues surrounding Sara's text, however. While the surface text functions as a Mother's Day card, "Once upon a time" is more suggestive of a fairy tale than a greeting card. Sara's use of one genre in service of another adds to the intrigue of the piece and is a text strategy which will be discussed more fully later.

Pragmatically, Matt's surface text is easily recognized as having been produced after a trip to the zoo with his first-grade class. The fact that Matt's text is appropriate for this context would be evident if he asked adults to tell us where they might find such a piece of writing. In workshops we have conducted, almost without exception teachers can identify what events led up to the creation of Matt's text.

Pragmatically, it is also important to note that Matt's text has no title. Some educators and linguists would take this as evidence that the young child has not developed the ability to produce a "decontextualized" text. The context of situation, however, makes entitling this piece "My Trip to the Zoo" unnecessary,

Figure 22.23. Uninterrupted writing sample (Matt, age 6)

since this was an assumption which was shared by all of the language users in this setting.

Surface Text Organization: Graphophonemic Perspectives

Spelling the way it sounds. Much work has been done in this area (Marcel, 1980; Read, 1975; Baron, 1980; Marsh, Friedman, Welch and Desbery, 1980; Henderson and Beers, 1979, 1980; Zutell, 1978, 1979; Bissex, 1980; Chomsky, 1979). Our own analysis of the products which young children produce would suggest that there are essentially three sound-to-letter strategies employed: (1) spelling the way it sounds; (2) spelling the way it articulates; and (3) spelling the way it sounds out. Often more than one of these spelling strategies is involved in the single spelling of a word, i.e., JRESS for "dress" (Jeff, age 6) where the J is produced because *j*'s and *d*'s are formed at the same spot in the mouth (the point of articulation), and RES is produced on the basis of letter-sound correspondence. A fourth sound-to-print strategy is really a subtle instance of the first strategy, but has been termed "the letter-name strategy": the name of the letter coincides with a desired sound unit, as in R or "our," or in Sara's case, A as in "a loveable bunny." Sara's three uses of A's in "A LOVE A BAL BONE" demonstrate that the same marking can occur for entirely different sound-to-letter rules. Sara's first A is produced via a letter-name strategy; her second and third A's (LOVE A BAL) are produced via a letter-sound strategy.

Spelling the way it looks. Letter-sound observations are only a small portion of the spelling organizations and orchestrations which can be studied, and are probably the portion that has had the most intense observation by researchers to date. From the perspective of the young child as reader we might ask ourselves, "What evidence exists that past encounters with print have influenced the child's spellings?" We would then be looking for spelling which involves fine-tuning written language with written language itself, or which involves aspects of visual memory (Tenny, 1980). Since both of these surface texts are written using English letterlike forms, the thing we immediately know is that reading is involved in the spelling process and that no matter how phonetic a spelling may appear (R or "our"), just by virtue of the fact that it is placeheld with a recognizable letter of our alphabet, the spelling involves visual memory. Where else would these forms and this information come from? Those who suggest that children write first and read later and use "invented spelling" as their evidence, have failed to appreciate key transactions between reading and writing in literacy learning.

In Sara's text she writes FRO for "for." While we might wish to assume that the F and the R are produced on the basis of some sound-to-letter strategy, the very fact that these forms are recognizable as letters of our alphabet means that visual memory is inherently involved in what appears to be a phonetic act. Sara's inclusion of the O at the end of her FR is also motivated by visual memory. Having been a reader, Sara obviously recalls that there is an O in there somewhere and so tags it on at the end. Whether this piece of information was accessed because the FR didn't look long enough we don't know, though if this were the explanation offered, we might have a tendency to want to conclude that the child was spelling by using a phonetic strategy and confirming by using a visual memory strategy. The fact that both phonics and visual memory are involved in the production of even a single letter like the F just means that such efforts at bifurcation and order are misguided.

This point is important since many persons working in the area of "invented spelling" seem to believe that children initially spell using a phonetic strategy and that only later do they employ visual memory. We have shown that no such tidiness is possible, nor, we would argue, is it desired. The redundancy of cues across strategies sets up "tensions," permits reading experiences to transmit and support writing, and allows spelling systems to be mastered, if desired, via orchestration.

invented spellings

Spelling the way it means. In addition to looking at spelling organization in terms of sound and visual memory, we might also look at spelling organization based on meaning. In Sara's and Matt's surface texts we have several excellent examples. In these instances we would be looking for spellings which have morphemic and higher levels of semantic organization. LOVE A BAL ("loveable") in Sara's surface text is probably a spelling arrived at through a combination of syllabic and morphemic decisions. Sara's WASAPANATAEM ("Once upon a time") is an even better example, in which she demonstrates that for her, this spelling is one conceptual unit. Semantically, "once upon a time" is a unit which signals fairy tales. The meaning of each individual word adds up to be quite different from the meaning of the phrase itself. From a psychological processing perspective it makes more sense to write "once upon a time" as a single unit than to break it up into units unrelated to its meaning or psychological significance.

Sara's LOVE A BAL ("loveable") in contrast to her WASAPANATAEM ("Once upon a time") is a nice instance of how various ways to organize writing are not only conceptually possible, but are simultaneously being explored in a single setting by the young child. Think of how much less language confusion there might be in the profession of the originators of our language had decided to write in chunks of meaning (like Sara's WASAPANATAEM) rather than in words.

An interesting feature of Sara's surface text is the fact that she simultaneously tests at least three optional writing systems in a single setting: chunk writing by meaning (WASAPANATAEM); chunk writing by syllable (LOVE A BAL); chunk writing by words (BONE).

Matt's text has as many clear examples of his testing hypotheses relative to meaning in his spelling. Matt's refusal to divide the word LUNCH, which he squeezes on the line, suggests that for him LUNCH is a single conceptual unit and therefore not easily divided. Once children discover that in writing they can divide what previously had been a single conceptual unit by using a hyphen, they often divide everything and everywhere.

Alison, at 6.5 years of age, discovered the hyphen while reading a book. In this instance she asked what the "little mark" meant. For the next several weeks, hyphens appeared throughout her writing. In making her best friend Jennifer a birthday card, she began writing Jennifer's name on the left-hand side of the page, but then suddenly realized that if she continued in that fashion she wouldn't be able to apply her latest language discovery. She decided to erase and begin writing Jennifer well toward the right of the page, thereby running out of space and getting to use the hyphen.

The realization that concepts can be divided in writing when they are not able to be divided in real life comes late for most children—well after their early markings demonstrate application of a one-mark per one-concept rule. In fact this one-mark per one-concept notion is so natural that it is literally impossible to decide when children first develop a notion of "wordness." Our own frustrated attempts led us to conclude that when the child makes one blob for "a dog," another for "a tree," and a third for "a bear," the basic notion of "wordness" is evidenced. When one thinks about "wordness" from this perspective, the notion has so little power to explain growth in literacy that violations, "nonwordness" decisions like Sara's WASAPANATAEM, are more significant in understanding the evolution of literacy than are instances of the concept.

Other Spelling Strategies. There are, of course, other decisions which can be examined in spellings, even of those words which we have already looked at in Sara's and Matt's texts. In spelling "loveable" (LOVE A BAL) Sara, at least in part, may be resolving this spelling on the basis of how she has resolved similar spellings in the past. As reported in our earlier volume (Harste, Burke, Woodward, 1981), we have some evidence that children consciously spell by their own or someone else's rules, often adding silent *e*'s and the like after they have applied other initial strategies.

A final strategy which we have found enters into children's spelling decisions is one we entitle, "Knowing One Doesn't Know." Often in these instances language users select a different word, or put down some rendition of the word they want which placeholds the item until they have time to check on the spelling later. Which of these strategies they use—choosing another word or placeholding the word they want using the best spelling they can muster on the spot—is seemingly a function of present and past writing contexts and the child's sense of the risk involved. Nonetheless, "knowing one doesn't know" is a very complex strategy. The language user is saying that, after having tried all of the spelling rules which seem applicable, the only thing he knows is that application of known rules doesn't solve this spelling problem. Because realizing one doesn't know is a significant step in knowing, this is clearly a strategy worthy of further study.

23.
Protean Shapes in Literacy Events

Ever-Shifting Oral and Literate Traditions

Shirley Brice Heath

"the Proteus-nature . . . of ever-shifting language"
John Upton, *Critical Observations on Shakespeare*, 1747

Since the mid-1970s, anthropologists, linguists, historians, and psychologists have turned with new tools of analysis to the study of oral and literate societies. They have used discourse analysis, econometrics, theories of schemata and frames, and proposals of developmental performance to consider the possible links between oral and written language, and between literacy and its individual and societal consequences. Much of this research is predicated on a dichotomous view of oral and literate traditions, usually attributed to researchers active in the 1960s. Repeatedly, Goody and Watt (1963), Ong (1967), Goody (1968), and Havelock (1963) are cited as having suggested a dichotomous view of oral and literate societies and as having asserted certain cognitive, social, and linguistic effects of literacy on both the society and the individual. Survey research tracing the invention and diffusion of writing systems across numerous societies (Kroeber, 1948) and positing the effects of the spread of literacy on social and individual memory (Goody and Watt, 1963; Havelock, 1963, 1976) is cited as supporting a contrastive view of oral and literate social groups. Research which examined oral performance in particular groups is said to support the notion that as members of a society increasingly participate in literacy, they lose habits associated with the oral tradition (Lord, 1965).

The language of the oral tradition is held to suggest meaning without explicitly stating information (Lord, 1965). Certain discourse forms, such as the parable or proverb (Dodd, 1961), are formulaic uses of language which convey meanings without direct explication. Thus, truth lies in experience and is verified by the experience of listeners. Story plots are said to be interwoven with routine formulas, and fixed sayings to make up much of the content of the story (Rosenberg, 1970). In contrast, language associated with the literate tradition is portrayed as making meaning explicit in the text and as not relying on the experiences of readers for verification of truth value. The epitome of this type of language is said to be the formal expository essay (Olson, 1977). The setting for learning this language and associated literate habits is the school. Formal schooling at all levels is said to prescribe certain features of sentence structure, lexical choice, text cohesion, and topic organization for formal language—both spoken and written (Bourdieu, 1967). An array of abilities, ranging from metalinguistic awareness (Baron, 1979) to predictable critical skills (reported in Heath, 1980) are held to derive from cultural experiences with writing.

In short, existing scholarship makes it easy to interpret a picture which depicts societies existing along a continuum of development from an oral tradition to a literate one, with some societies having a restricted literacy, and others having reached a full development of literacy (Goody, 1968:11). One also finds in this research specific characterizations of oral and written language associated with these traditions.

But a close reading of these scholars, especially Goody (1968) and Goody and Watt (1963), leaves some room for questioning such a picture of consistent and universal processes or products—individual or societal—of literacy. Goody pointed out that in any traditional society, factors such as secrecy, religious ideology, limited social mobility, lack of access to writing materials and alphabetic scripts could lead to restricted literacy. Furthermore, Goody warned that the advent of a writing system did not amount to technological determinism or to sufficient cause of certain changes in either the individual or the society. Goody went on to propose exploring the concrete context of written communication (1968:4). to determine how the potentialities of literacy developed in traditional societies. He brought together a collection of essays based on the ethnography of literacy in traditional societies to illustrate the wide variety of ways in which *traditional,* i.e., pre-industrial but not necessarily pre-literate, societies played out their uses of oral and literate traditions.

Few researchers in the 1970's have, however, heeded Goody's warning about the possible wide-ranging effects of societal and cultural factors on literacy and its uses. In particular, little attention has been given in *modern* complex industrial societies to the social and cultural correlates of literacy or to the work experiences adults have which may affect the maintenance and retention of literacy skills acquired in formal schooling. The public media today give much attention to the decline of literacy skills as measured in school settings and to the failure of students to acquire certain levels of literacy. However, the media pay little attention to occasions for literacy retention—to the actual uses of literacy in work settings, daily interactions in religious, economic, and legal institutions, and family habits of socializing the young into uses of literacy. In the clamor over the need to increase the teaching of basic skills, there is much emphasis on the positive effects extensive and critical reading can have on improving oral language. Yet there are scarcely any data comparing the forms and functions of oral language with those of written language produced and used by members of social groups within a complex society. One of the most appropriate sources of data for informing discussions of these issues is that which Goody proposed for traditional societies: the concrete context of written communication. Where, when, how, for whom, and with what results are individuals in different social groups of today's highly industrialized society using reading and writing skills? How have the potentialities of the literacy skills learned in school developed in the lives of today's adults? Does modern society contain certain conditions which restrict literacy just as some traditional societies do? If so, what are these factors, and are groups with restricted literacy denied benefits widely attributed to full literacy, such as upward socioeconomic mobility, the development of logical reasoning, and access to the information necessary to make well-informed political judgments?

The Literacy Event

The *Literacy Event* is a conceptual tool useful in examining within particular communities of modern society the actual forms and functions of oral and literate traditions and co-existing relationships between spoken and written language. A literacy event is any occasion in which a piece of writing is integral to the nature of participants' interactions and their interpretive processes (Heath, 1978).

In studying the literacy environment, researchers describe: print materials available in the environment, the individuals and activities which surround print, and ways in which people include print in their ongoing activities. A literacy event can then be viewed as any action sequence, involving one or more persons, in which the production and/or comprehension of print plays a role (Anderson, Teale, and Estrada 1980:59). There are rules for the occurrence of literacy events, just as there are for speech events (Hymes, 1972). Characteristics of the structures and uses of literacy events vary from situation to situation. In addition to having an appropriate structure, a literacy event has certain interactional rules and demands particular interpretive competencies on the part of participants. Some aspects of reading and/or writing are required by at least one party and certain types of speech events are appropriate within certain literacy events. Speech events may describe, repeat, reinforce, expand, frame, or contradict written materials, and participants must learn whether the oral or written mode takes precedence in literacy events. For example, in filling out an application form, should applicants listen to oral instructions or complete the form? On many occasions, an interview consists of participating orally with someone who fills out a form based on the oral performance, and access to the written report is never available to the applicant in the course of the interview. Oral comments often contradict the usual assumption that written materials are to be read: You don't have to read this, but you should have it.

The having of something in writing is often a ritualistic practice, and more often than not, those who hold the written piece are not expected to read what they have. In other cases, the actual reading of the piece of written material may be possible, but not sufficient, because some oral attestation is necessary. A church congregational meeting may be an occasion in which all must read the regulations of applying for a loan or a grant for church support (this is usually done by having the minister read them aloud). But the entire congregation must orally attest that they have read and approved the regulations. On other occasions, the written material must be present, but the speech event takes precedence. A Girl Scout comes to sell cookies at the door; she passes out a folder asserting who she is, to which troop she belongs, and to which project her fund will go. After handing over this piece of paper, the Girl Scout talks about the cookies and the project which the sale will benefit. Few individuals read the folder instead of listening to the Girl Scout. Here, the speech event takes precedence at the critical moments of the interaction. It is important to know what the framing situations for literacy events are in a variety of contexts, for situations may differ markedly from each other and may, in fact, contradict such traditional expectations of literacy as those taught in school or in job training programs. For example, ways of asking clarification of the *uses* of written materials are often far more important in daily out-of-school life than are questions about the content. What will be done with forms submitted to the Department of Motor Vehicles after an accident is of as much consequence as, if not more consequence than, the actual content of the forms. Thus it may be hypothesized that examination of the contexts and uses of literacy in communities today may show that *there are more literacy events which call for appropriate knowledge of forms and uses of speech events than there are actual occasions for extended reading or writing.*

Furthermore, the traditional distinctions between the habits of those characterized as having either oral or literate traditions may not actually exist in many communities of the United States, which are neither non-literate nor fully literate. Their members can read and write at least at basic levels, but they have little occasion to use these skills as taught in school. Instead, much of their daily life is filled with literacy events in which they must know how to use and how to respond in the oral mode to written materials. In short, descriptions of the concrete context of written communication which give attention to social and cultural features of the community as well as to the oral language surrounding written communications may discredit any reliance on characterizing particular communities as having reached either restricted or full development of literacy or as having language forms and functions associated more with the literate tradition than with the oral, or vice versa.

The Community Context

Some testing of these ideas is possible from data collected in a Piedmont community of the Carolinas between 1969 and 1979. The community, Trackton, is a working-class all-Black community, whose adults work in the local textile mills and earn incomes which exceed those of many public school teachers in the state. All adults in this community can read and write, and all talk enthusiastically about the need for their children to do well in school. Ethnographic work in the primary networks within the community, the religious institutions, and work settings documented the forms and functions written and spoken language took for individual members of Trackton. The literacy event was the focus of descriptions of written language uses in these contexts.

At Home in Trackton

In the daily life of the neighborhood, there were numerous occasions when print from beyond the primary network intruded; there were fewer occasions when adults or children themselves produced written materials. Adults did not read to children, and there were few pieces of writing produced especially for children. Sunday School books, and single-page handouts from Sunday School which portrayed a Biblical scene with a brief caption, were the only exceptions. Adults, however, responded to children of all ages, if they inquired about messages provided in writing: they would read a house number, a stop sign, a name brand of a product, or a slogan on a T-shirt, if asked to do so by a child. In September, children preparing to go to school often preferred book bags, pencil boxes, and purses which bore labels or slogans. Adults did not consciously model, demonstrate, or tutor reading and writing behaviors for the young. Children, however, went to school with certain expectancies of print and a keen sense that reading is something one does to learn something one needs to know. In other words, before going to school, preschoolers were able to read many types of information available in their environment. They knew how to distinguish brand names from product descriptions on boxes or bags; they knew how to find the price on a label which contained numerous other pieces of written information. They knew how to recognize the names of cars, motorcycles, and bicycles not only on the products themselves, but also on brochures about these products. In these ways they read to learn information judged necessary in their daily lives, and they had grown accustomed to participating in literacy events in ways appropriate to their community's norms (see Heath, 1980, for a fuller description). They had frequently observed their community's social activities surrounding a piece of writing: negotiation over how to put a toy together, what a gas bill notice meant, how to fill out a voter registration form, and where to go to apply for entrance to daycare programs.

There were no bedtime stories, children's books, special times for reading, or routine sets of questions from adults to children in connection with reading.[1] Thus, Trackton children's early spontaneous stories were not molded on written materials. They were derived from oral models given by adults, and they developed in accordance with praise and varying degrees of enthusiasm for particular story styles from the audience. In these stories, children rendered a context, or set the stage for the story, and called on listeners to create jointly an imagined background for stories. In the later preschool years, the children, in a monologue-like fashion, told stories about things in their lives, events they saw and heard, and situations in which they had been involved. They produced these stories, many of which can be described as story-poems, during play with other children or in the presence of adults. Their stories contained emotional evaluation of others and their actions; dialogue was prevalent; style shifting in verbal and nonverbal means accompanied all stories.

All of these features of story-telling by children call attention to the story and distinguish it as a speech event which is an occasion for audience and storyteller to interact pleasantly to a creative tale, not simply a recounting of daily events. Story-telling is very competitive, especially as children get older, and new tricks must be devised if one is to remain a successful story-teller. Content ranges widely, and there is truth only in the universals of human experience which are found in every story. Fact as related to what really happened is often hard to find, though it may be the seed of the story. Trackton stories often have no obvious beginning in the form of a routine; similarly, there is no marked ending; they simply go on as long as the audience will tolerate the story (see Heath, 1980, and chapter 5 of Heath, 1984, for a fuller description).

In response to these stories, Trackton adults do not separate out bits and pieces of the story and question the children about them. Similarly, they do not pick out pieces of the daily environment and ask children to name these or describe their features. Children live in an on-going multiple-chaneled stream of stimuli, from which they select, practice, and determine the rules of speaking and interacting with written materials. Children have to learn at a very early age to perceive situations, determine how units of these situations are related to each other, recognize these relations in other situations, and reason through what it will take to show their correlation of one situation with another. The specifics of labels, features, and rules of behavior are not laid out for them by adults. The familiar routines described in the research literature on mainstream school-oriented parents are not heard in Trackton. They do not ask or tell their children: What is that? What color is it? Is that the way to listen? Turn the book this way. Let's listen and find out. Instead, parents talk about items and events of their environment. They detail the responses of personalities to event; they praise, deride, and question the reasons for events and compare new items and events to those with which they are familiar. They do not simplify their talk about the world for the benefit of their young. Preschoolers do not learn to name or list the features of items in either the daily environment or as depicted through illustration in printed materials. Questions addressed to them with the greatest frequency are of the type What's that like? Where'd that come from? What are you gonna do with that? They develop connections between situations or items not by specification of labels and features in these situations, but by configuration links.

Recognition of similar general shapes or patterns of links seen in one situation and connected to another pervade their stories and their conversations, as illustrated in the following story. Lem, playing off the edge of the porch, when he was about two and a half years of age, heard a bell in the distance. He stopped, looked at his older siblings nearby, and said:

> Way
> Far
> Now

It a church bell
Ringin'
Dey singin'
Ringin'
You hear it?
I hear it
Far
Now.

Lem here recalls being taken to church the previous Sunday and hearing a bell. His story is in response to the current stimulus of a distant bell. He recapitulates the sequence of events: at church, the bell rang while the people sang the opening hymn. He gives the story's topic in the line It a church bell, but he does not orient the listeners to the setting or the time of the story. He seems to try to recreate the situation both verbally and non-verbally so it will be recognized and responded to by listeners. Lem poetically balances the opening and closing in an *inclusio*, beginning Way, Far, Now, and ending Far, Now. The effect is one of closure, though he doesn't announce the ending of his story. He invites others to respond to his story: You hear it? I hear it. All of these methods call attention to the story, and distinguish it as a story. The children recall scenes and events through nonverbal and verbal manipulation. They use few formulaic invitations to recall, such as You know, You see, etc. Instead, they themselves try to give the setting and the mood as they weave the tale to keep the audience's attention. The recall of a setting may depend on asking the listener to remember a smell, a sound, a place, a feeling, and to associate these in the same way the storyteller does. A similar type of recall of relevant context or set of circumstances marks children's memories or reassociations with print. When they see a brandname, number, etc., they often recall where and with whom they first saw it, or call attention to parts now missing which were there previously. Slight shifts in print styles, decorations of mascots used to advertise cereals, or alteration of television advertising mottos are noticed by children.

Trackton children's preschool experiences with print, stories, and talk about the environment differ greatly from those usually depicted in the literature for children of mainstream school-oriented parents. Similarly, adults in Trackton used written materials in different ways and for different purposes than those represented in the traditional literature on adult reading habits and motivations (cf. Staiger, 1979; Hall and Carlton, 1977). Among Trackton adults, reading was a social activity which did not focus on a single individual. Solitary reading without oral explanation was viewed as unacceptable, strange, and indicative of a particular kind of failure, which kept individuals from being social. Narratives, jokes, sidetracking talk, and negotiation of the meaning of written texts kept social relations alive. When several members of the community jointly focused on and interpreted written materials, authority did not rest in the materials themselves, but in the meanings which would be negotiated by the participants.

New instructions on obtaining medical reports for children about to enter school provoked stories of what other individuals did when they were confronted with a similar task: all joined in talk of particular nurses or doctors who were helpful in the process. Some told of reactions to vaccinations and troubles they had had getting to and from the doctor's office. In the following conversation, several neighbors negotiate the meaning of a letter about a daycare program. Several neighbors were sitting on porches, working on cars nearby, or sweeping their front yards when a young mother of four children came out on her porch with a letter she had received that day.

> *Lillie Mae:* You hear this, it says Lem [her two-year-old son] might can get into Ridgeway [a local neighborhood center daycare program], but I hafta have the papers ready and apply by next Friday.
>
> *First female neighbor* (mother of three children who are already in school): You ever been to Kent to get his birth certificate?
>
> *Second female neighbor* (with preschool children): But what hours that program gonna be? You may not can get him there.
>
> *Lillie Mae:* They want the birth certificate? I got his vaccination papers.
>
> *Third female neighbor:* Sometimes they take that, 'cause they can 'bout tell the age from those early shots.
>
> *First female neighbor:* But you better get it, 'cause you gotta have it when he go to school anyway.
>
> *Lillie Mae:* But it says here they don't know what hours yet. How am I gonna get over to Kent? How much does it cost? Lemme see if the program costs anything [she reads aloud part of the letter].

Conversation on various parts of the letter continued for nearly an hour, while neighbors and Lillie Mae pooled their knowledge of the pros and cons of such programs. They discussed ways of getting rides to Kent, the county seat thirty miles away, to which all mothers had to go to get their children's birth certificates to prove their age at school entrance. The discussion covered the possibility of visiting Lillie Mae's doctor and getting papers from him to verify Lem's age, teachers now at the neighborhood center, and health benefits which came from the daycare programs' outreach work. A question What does this mean? asked of a piece of writing was addressed to any and all who would listen; specific attention to the text iself was at times minimal in the answers which followed.

Adults read and wrote for numerous purposes, almost all of them social. These were:

1) Instrumental—to provide information about practical problems of daily life (bills, checks, price tags, street signs, house numbers)
2) Interactional—to give information pertinent to social relations with individuals not in the primary group (cartoons, bumper stickers, letters, newspaper features, greeting cards)

3) News-related—to provide information about secondary contacts or distant events (newspaper items, political flyers, directives from city offices)
4) Confirmation—to provide support for attitudes or ideas already held (reference to the Bible, brochures advertising products, etc.)
5) Provision of permanent records—to record information required by external agencies (birth certificates, loan notes, tax forms). Trackton residents wrote most frequently for the following reasons:
6) Memory-supportive—to serve as a memory aid (addresses, telephone numbers, notes on calendars)
7) Substitutes for oral messages—to substitute for oral communication on those occasions when face-to-face or telephone contact was not possible or would prove embarrassing (thank-you letters to people in distant cities, notes about tardiness to school or absence at school or work, a request to local merchants for credit to be extended to a child needing to buy coal, milk or bread for the family).

On all of these occasions for reading and writing, individuals saw literacy as an occasion for social activities: women shopped together, discussed local credit opportunities and products, and sales; men negotiated the meaning of tax forms, brochures on new cars, and political flyers. The evening newspaper was read on the front porch, and talk about the news drifted from porch to porch. Inside, during the winter months, talk about news items interrupted on-going conversations on other topics or television viewing. The only occasions for solitary reading by individuals were those in which elderly men and women read their Bible or Sunday School materials alone, or school-age children sat alone to read a library book or a school assignment. In short, written information almost never stood alone in Trackton; it was reshaped and reworded into an oral mode. In so doing, adults and children incorporated chunks of the written text into their talk. They also sometimes reflected an awareness of a different type of organization of written materials from that of their usual oral productions. Yet their literacy habits do not fit those usually attributed to fully literate groups; they do not read to their children, encouraging conversational dialogue on books; they do not write or read extended prose passages; reading is not an individual pursuit nor is it considered to have intellectual, aesthetic, or critical rewards. But Trackton homes do not conform to habits associated with the oral tradition either. Literacy is a resource; stories do not fit the parable model; children develop very early wide-ranging language skills; and neither their language nor their parents' is marked by a preponderance of routine formulaic expressions.

At Church

Trackton is a literate community in the sense that its members read and write when occasions within their community demand such skiills. Outside the community, there are numerous occasions established by individuals and institutions in which Trackton residents must show their literacy skills. One of these situations is in the church life of the Trackton people. Most residents go to country churches for Sunday services, which are usually held twice a month. In these churches, the pastor serves not one, but several churches, and he also holds another job as well during the week. A pastor or reverend is always a man, usually a man who in his younger days was known as wild and had come to the Lord after recognizing the sins of his youth. Many pastors had been musicians entertaining in clubs before their conversion to religion. Few had formal theological training; instead they had gone to Black colleges in the South and majored in religion. Most had at least a four-year college education, and many had taken additional training at special summer programs, through correspondence courses, or in graduate programs at nearby integrated state schools. In their jobs outside the church, they were businessmen, school administrators, land-owning farmers, or city personnel.

The country churches brought together not only residents of Trackton, a majority of whom worked in textile mills, but also school-teachers, domestic workers, hospital staff, clerks in local retail businesses, and farmers. Levels of formal education were mixed in these churches, and ranged from the elderly men and women who had had only a few years of grammar school in their youth, to the minister and some school administrators who had graduate-level education. Yet, in the church, all these types and levels of literacy skills came together in a pattern which reflected a strong reliance on the written word in both substance and style. Everyone wanted others to know he could read the Bible and church materials (even if he did not do so regularly). Church was an occasion to announce knowledge of how to handle the style of written language as well as its substance. Numerous evidences of formal writing marked every church service, and on special occasions, such as celebration of the accomplishments of a church member, formal writing was very much in evidence. For these celebration services, there were brochures which contained a picture of the individual, an account of his or her life, lists of members of the family, and details of the order of service. Funeral services included similar brochures. All churches had hymn books, and a placard on either side of the front of the church announced the numbers of the hymns. Choir leaders invited the congregation to turn to the hymn and read the words with him; he announced the number of the verses of the hymn to be sung. The minister expected adults to bring their Bibles to church along with their Sunday School materials and to read along with him or the Sunday School director. Mimeographed church bulletins dictated the order of the service from the opening hymn to the benediction. The front and back covers of the bulletin contained drawings and scripture verses which illustrated either the sermon topic or the season of the year. Announcements of upcoming events in the recreational life of the church or political activities of the Black community filled one page of the bulletin. Reports of building funds and missionary funds were brief and were supplemented by the pastor's announcements in church service.

Yet many parts of the service move away from the formality of these written sources. The congregation often begins singing the hymn written in the book, but they quickly move away from the written form to 'raise' the hymn. In this performance, the choir leader begins the hymn with the written words and the congregation follows briefly; however, another song leader will break in with new words for a portion of the hymn; the audience waits to hear these, then picks up the words and follows. The hymn continues in this way, with different members of the congregation serving as song leader at various points. Some of the words may be those which are written in the hymnbook, others may not be. A member of the congregation may begin a prayer at a particular juncture of the hymn, and the congregation will hum until the prayer is completed. The ending of the hymn is to an outsider entirely unpredictable, yet all members of the congregation end at the same time. Hymns may be raised on the occasion of the announcement of a hymn by the choir leader, spontaneously during a story or testimonial by a church member, or near the end of a sermon. In the raising of a hymn, written formulas are the basis of the hymn, but these are subject to change, and it is indeed that change which makes the congregation at once creator and performer. The formulas are changed and new formulas produced to expand the theme, to illustrate points, or to pull back from a particular theme to pick up another which has been introduced in a prayer or in the sermon. Every performance of a particular hymn is different, and such performances bear the mark of the choir leader and his interactional style with the congregation.

A similar phenomenon is illustrated in oral prayers in church. These are often written out ahead of time by those who have been asked by the minister to offer a prayer at next Sunday's service. The prayer as follows was given orally by a 45-year-old female school teacher.

1   We thank thee for watchin' over us, kind heavenly Father
2   Through the night.
3   We thank thee, oh Lord.
4   For leadin' 'n guidin' us
5   We thank thee, kind heavenly Father
6   For your strong-arm protection around us.
7   Oh Lord, don't leave us alone.
8   We feel this evenin', kind heavenly Father, if you leave us
9   We are the least ones of all.
10 Now Lord, I ask thee, kind heavenly Father,
11 to go 'long with my family,
12 I ask thee, kind heavenly Father, to throw your strong-arm protectors around
13 Oh Lord, I ask thee, oh Lord,
14 to take care of my childrens, Lord, wherever they may be.
15 Oh Lord, don't leave us, Jesus.
16 I feel this morning, kind heavenly Father, if you leave me,
17 Oh, Lord, please, Lord, don't leave me
18 in the hands of the wicked man.
19 Oh Lord, I thank thee kind heavenly Father
20 for what you have done for me.
21 Oh Lord, I thank thee, kind heavenly Father
22 Where you have brought me from.
23 Oh Lord, I wonder sometime if I didn't have Jesus on my side,
24 Lord, have mercy now,
25 what would I do, oh Lord?
26 Have mercy, Jesus.
27 I can call on 'im in the midnight hour,
28 I can call on 'im, Lord, in the noontime, oh Lord,

29 I can call on 'im anytime o' day, oh Lord.
30 He'p me, Jesus,
31 Oh Lord, make me strong
32 Oh Lord, have mercy on us, Father
33 When we have done all that you have 'signed our hands to do, Lord,
34 Have mercy, Lord,
35 I want you to give me a home beyond the shinin' river, oh Lord,
36 Where won't be no sorrowness,
37 Won't be no shame and tears, oh Lord.
38 It won't be nothing, Lord, but glory, alleluia.
39 When we have done all that you 'signed our hands to do, kind heavenly Father,
40 And we cain't do no mo',
41 We want you to give us a home in thy kingdom, oh Lord.
42 For thy Christ's sake, Amen.

After the service, when I asked the schoolteacher about her prayer, she gave me the following text she had composed and written on a card she held in her hand during the prayer:

> Kind heavenly Father, we thank thee for watching over us through the night.
> We thank thee for thy guidance, kind heavenly Father, for your strong protection.
> We pray that you will be with us, Lord, be with our families, young and old, near and far.
> Lead us not into temptation, Lord. Make us strong and ever mindful of your gifts to us all. Amen.

A comparison of the oral and the written prayer indicates numerous differences, but the major ones are of four types.

Use of formulaic vocatives. *Oh Lord, kind heavenly Father,* and *Jesus* appear again and again in the prayer once the woman has left the printed text. In the written text, all but the final sentence contains such a vocative, but in the oral text, there are often two per sentence. In descriptions of folk sermons, such vocatives are said to be pauses in which the preacher collects his thoughts for the next passage (Rosenberg, 1970). Here, however, the thoughts have been collected, in that the entire text was written out before delivery, but the speaker continues to use these vocatives and to pause after these before moving on to another plea.

Expression of personal involvement. Throughout the written version, the woman uses *we*, but in the expanded oral version, she shifts from *we* to *I*, and uses *my* and *me* where the plural might have been used had she continued the pattern from the written version. She shifts in line 10 to a singular plea, speaking as the weak sinner, the easily tempted, and praying for continued strength and readiness to being helped by her Lord. The written prayer simply asks for guidance, (orally stated as *"leadin' "* and *"guidin' "*) strong protection ("strong-arm protection" and "protector" in the oral version). The plea that the sinner not be faced with temptation is expressed in the written version in a familiar phrase from the Lord's Prayer, and is followed by a formulaic expression often used in ministers' prayers,

"Make us ever mindful of . . ." At line 22, she stops using *thee, thy,* and *thou,* archaic personal pronouns; thereafter she uses second person singular *you.*

Expression in a wide variety of sentence structures. The written version uses simple sentences throughout, varying the style with insertion of vocatives, and repetitions of paired adjectives ("young and old," "near and far"). The spoken version includes compound-complex sentences with subordination, and repetition of simple sentences with variation (e.g., "I can call on 'im . . ."). There are several incomplete sentences in the spoken version (line 16–18), which if completed would have been complex in structure.

Use of informal style and Black English vernacular forms. The opening of the spoken version and the written version uses standard English forms, and the first suggestion of informality comes with the dropping of the *g* in line 4. As the prayer progresses, however, several informal forms and features associated with the Black English vernacular are used: *'long*(= along), childrens, *'im*(= him), anytime *o'day, he'p*(= help), *'signed*(= assigned), omission of *there* (in lines 36, 37) and use of *it* for standard English in line 38, double negative (lines 36, 37, 38, 40), *cain't*(= can't), and *mo'*(= more).

There is no way to render the shifts of prosody, the melodic strains, and the changes in pace which accompany the spoken version. The intonation pattern is highly marked, lilting, and the speaker breaks into actual melody at the end of line 10, and the remainder of the prayer is chanted. (Note that at this point she also shifted to the singular first person pronoun.) Sharp pitch modulations mark the prayer, and on one occasion (end of line 35), a member of the congregation broke in with a supporting bar of the melody, lasting only 3.5 seconds. All vocatives after line 6 are marked by a lilting high rise-mid fall contour.

It is possible to find in numerous studies of the religious life of Afro-Americans lengthy discussions of the historical role of the spoken word (see, for example, Levine, 1977:155ff, for a discussion of literacy and its effects on Black religion) Current research with preachers (e.g., Mitchell, 1970; Rosenberg, 1970) and gospel songwriters (e.g. Jackson, 1966; Heilbut, 1971) in Black communities underscore and pick up numerous themes from historical studies. Repeatedly these sources emphasize the power of words as action and the substantiating effect a dynamic creative oral rendering of a message has on an audience. Preachers and musicians claim they cannot stick to a stable rendering of written words; thoughts which were once shaped into words on paper become recomposed in each time and space; written words limit a performance which must be created anew with each audience and setting. Though some of the meaning in written words remains stable, bound in the text, the meaning of words people will carry with them depends on the integration of those words into personal experience. Thus the performance of words demands the calling in of the personal experience of each listener and the extension by that listener of the meanings of those words to achieve the ultimate possibility of any message.

In terms of the usual expectations of distinctions between the oral and literate mode, practices in the church life of Trackton residents provide evidence that neither mode is in control here. Members have access to both and use both. Oral spontaneous adjustments from the written material result in longer, more complex sentences, with some accompanying shifts in style from the formal to the more informal. Clearly in the oral mode, the highly personalized first person singular dominates over the more formal collective first person. Pacing, rate of speech, intonation, pitch, use of melodic phrases, and finally a chant, have much fluctuation and range from high to low when written materials are recomposed spontaneously. Spoken versions of hymns, prayers, and sermons show the speaker's attempt to identify with the audience, but this identification makes use of only some features usually associated with the oral tradition (e.g. high degree of involvement of speaker, extensive use of first person). Other features associated with oral performance (e.g. simple sentences linked together by simple compounds, and highly redundant formulaic passages which hold chunks of information together) are not found here. The use of literate sources, and even literate bases, for oral performances does not lead to a demise of many features traditionally associated with a pure oral tradition. In other words, the language forms and uses on such occasions bear the mark of both oral and literate traditions, not one or the other.

At Work

In their daily lives at home and in church, Trackton adults and children have worked out ways of integrating features of both oral and written language in their language uses. But what of work settings and contacts with banks, credit offices, and the employment office—institutions typical of modernized, industrial societies?

Most of the adults in Trackton worked in the local textile mills. To obtain these jobs, they went directly to the employment office of the individual mills. There, an employment officer read to them from an application form and wrote down their answers. They were not asked if they wanted to complete their own form. They were given no written information at the time of their application, but the windows and walls of the room in which they waited for personal interviews were plastered with posters about the credit union policy of the plant and the required information for filling out an application (names of previous employers, Social Security number, etc.). But all of this information was known to Trackton residents before they went to apply for a job. Such information and news about jobs usually passed by word of mouth. Some of the smaller mills put advertisements in the local paper and indicated they would accept applications during certain hours on particular days. Interviewers either told individuals at the time of application they had obtained jobs, or the employment officer agreed to telephone in a few days. If applicants did not have telephones, they gave a neighbor's number, or the mill sent a postcard.

Once accepted for the job, totally inexperienced workers would be put in the particular section of the mill in which they were to work, and were told to watch experienced workers. The foreman would occasionally check by to see if the observer had questions and understood what was going on. Usually before the end of the first few hours on the shift, the new worker was put under the guidance of certain other workers and told to share work on a particular machine. Thus in an apprentice-like way new workers came on for new jobs, and they worked in this way for only several days, since all parties were anxious for this arrangement to end as soon as possible. Mills paid in part on a piece-work basis, and each machine operator was anxious to be freed to work at his or her own rapid pace as soon as possible. Similarly, the new worker was anxious to begin to be able to work rapidly enough to qualify for extra pay.

Within each section of the mill, little written material was in evidence. Safety records, warnings, and, occasionally, reports about new products, or clippings from local newspapers about individual workers or events at the mill's recreational complex, would be put up on the bulletin board. Foremen and quality control personnel came through the mill on each shift, asking questions, noting output, checking machines, and recording this information. They often asked the workers questions, and the information would be recorded on a form carried by the foreman or quality control engineer. Paychecks were issued each Friday, and the stub carried information on Federal and state taxes withheld, as well as payments for health plans or automatic payments made for credit loans from the credit bureau. Millworkers generally kept these stubs in their wallets, or in a special box (often a shoe box, sometimes a small metal filebox) at home. They were rarely referred to at the time of issuance of the paycheck, unless a recent loan had been taken out or paid off at the credit bureau. Then workers would check the accuracy of the amounts withheld. In both the application stage and on the job, workers had to respond to a report or a form being filled out by someone else. This passive performance with respect to any actual reading or writing did not occur because the workers were unable to read and write. Instead, these procedures were the results of the mill's efforts to standardize the recording and processing of information. When asked why they did not let applicants fill out their own employment form, employment officers responded:

> It is easier if we do it. This way, we get to talk to the client, ask questions not on the form, clarify immediately any questions they have, and, for our purposes, the whole thing is just cleaner. When we used to have them fill out the forms, some did it in pencil, others had terrible handwriting, others gave us too much or too little information. This way, our records are neat, and we know what we've got when someone has finished an application form.

In the past, job training at some of the mills had not been done "on the floor," but through a short session with manuals, an instructor, and instruction "by the book." Executives of the mills found this process too costly and inefficient, and those who could do the best job of handling the written materials were not necessarily the best workers on the line.

Beyond the mill, Trackton adults found in banks, credit union offices, and loan offices the same type of literacy events. The oral performance surrounding a written piece of material to which they had little or no access was what counted or made a difference in a transaction. When individuals applied for credit at the credit union, the interviewer held the folder, asked questions derived from information within the folder, and offered little or no explanation of the information from which he derived questions. At the end of interviews, workers did not know whether or not they would receive the loan or what would be done with the information given to the person who interviewed them. In the following interview (see figure 23.1), the credit union official directs questions to the client

Total units of discourse: 16
4 elicitations directed to Cl, 4 responses by Cl
4 utterances directed to folder by Off
2 responses by Cl to folder information
2 announcements of exits by Off

A-CU5 Heath 1979
Cl: Client
Off: Credit Union Official
    (enters office where client is seated)

(1) Off: okay, hh, what kind of a loan do you ⌐hh wanna see about now?
                                                 (pause)
(2) Cl: ⌊well, hh, I wanna   wanted it for
        my hhh personal reserve.
        (exits)
(3) Off: let me get your folder. I'll be right back.
        (reenters)   (looking at folder)
(4)   and you want to increase it to seventeen.
        (looking toward client)
(5)   and your purpose?
                    (pause)
(6) Cl: I hhh need a personal   uh, I got some small bills.
                                        (looking at folder)
(7) Off: because when I did this, I, hhh, didn't know, but you were telling me both had to
      sign.
        (looking at client)
(8)   what kind of bills
(9) Cl: water, gas, clothes, hhh, water department.
                                (flips through folder, writing figures on pad)
(10) Off: okay, now you're paying fifty a month, and you want, you, hhh, ummmmm
      you want your payments to stay at that, okay, you live at 847 J. O. Connell,
                                  (pause)
      and you've been there three years, okay   um, let's see, we're gonna
      combine this, gross weekly salary is $146⌐46, forty-hour week
(11) Cl: ⌊no, about $170
      (looking at folder)   (pause)
(12) Off: you don't have a car and your rent is $120, and you still owe Sears, hhh   it's
      twenty =
(13) Cl: = no, it's more than that =
      (looking at client)
(14) Off: = what is it now?
(15) Cl: I think it's about $180 ⌐some
(16) Off: ⌊is that everything, yea, all we've got to do is apply to the
                          credit bureau,
      they decide, you can come back tomorrow.

Figure 23.1. Interview at credit union

primarily on the basis of what is in the written documents in the client's folder.[2] She attempts to reconcile the written information with the current oral request. However, the client is repeatedly asked to supply information as though she knows the contents of the written document. Referents for pronouns (*it* in 4, *this* in 7, *this* in 10, and *they* in 16) are not clearly identified, and the client must guess at their referents without any visual or verbal clues. Throughout this literacy event, only one person has access to the written information, but the entire oral exchange centers around that information. In (4) the credit union employee introduces new information: *it* refers to the amount of the current loan. The record now shows that the client has a loan which is being repaid by having a certain amount deducted from her weekly paycheck; for those in her salary range, there is an upper limit of $1700 for a loan.

But this information is not clear from the oral exchange, and it is known only to the credit union employee and indicated on documents in the client's folder. The calculation of a payment of $50 per month (10) is based on this information, and the way in which this figure was derived is never explained to the client. In (10) the official continues to read from the folder, but she does not ask for either confirmation or denial of this information. Her ambiguous statement, "We're gonna combine this," can only be assumed to mean the current amount of the load with the amount of the new loan, the two figures which will now equal the total of the new principal $1700. The statement of gross weekly salary as $146.66 is corrected by the client (11), but the official does not verbally acknowledge the correction; she continues writing. Whether she records the new figure and takes it into account in her calculations is not clear. The official continues reading (12) and is once again corrected by the client. She notes the new information and shortly closes off the interview.

In this literacy event, written materials have determined the outcome of the request, yet the client has not been able to see those documents or frame questions which would clarify their contents. This pattern occurred frequently for Trackton residents, who argued that neighborhood center programs and other adult education programs should be aimed not at teaching higher level reading skills or other subjects, but at ways of getting through such interviews or other situations (such as visits to dentists and doctors), when someone else held the information which they needed to know in order to ask questions about the contents of that written material in ways which would be acceptable to institution officials.

Conclusions

Trackton is a literate community in the sense that the residents are able to read printed and written materials in their daily lives, and on occasion they produce written messages as part of the total pattern of communication in the community. Residents turn from written to spoken uses of language and vice versa as the occasion demands, and the two modes of expression seem to supplement and reinforce each other in a unique pattern. However, the conventions appropriate for literacy events within the community, in their worship life, and in their workaday world call for different uses of speech to interpret written materials. In a majority of cases, Trackton adults show their knowledge of written materials only through oral means. On many occasions, they have no opportunity to attend directly to the written materials through any active use of their own literacy skills; instead, they must respond in appropriate speech events which are expected to surround interpretation of these written materials.

It is impossible to characterize Trackton through existing descriptions of either the oral or the literate traditions; seemingly, it is neither, and it is both. Literacy events which bring the written word into a central focus in interactions and interpretations have their rules of occurrence and appropriateness according to setting and participants. The joint social activity of reading the newspaper across porches, getting to the heart of meaning of a brochure on a new product, and negotiating rules for putting an antenna on a car produce more speaking than reading, more group than individual effort, repeated analogies and generalizations, and fast-paced, overlapping syntactically complex language. The spontaneous recomposing of written hymns, sermons, and prayers produces not parables, proverbs, and formulas, but re-creations of written texts which are more complex in syntactic structure, performance rules, and more demanding of close attention to lexical and semantic cues, than are their written counterparts. For these recomposing creations are, like community literacy events, group-focused, and members of the group show their understanding and acceptance of the meaning of the words by picking up phrases, single words, or meanings, and creating their own contribution to a raised hymn or a prayer.

In work settings, when others control access to and restrict types of written information, Trackton residents have to learn to respond to inadequate meaning clues, partial sentences, and pronouns without specified referents. In these latter situations, especially those in financial and legal institutions, Trackton residents recognize their deficiency of skills, but the skills which are missing are not literacy skills, but knowledge about oral language uses which would enable them to obtain information about the content and uses of written documents, and to ask questions to clarify their meanings. Learning how to do this appropriately, so as not to seem to challenge a person in power, is often critical to obtaining a desired outcome and maintaining a job or reputation as a "satisfactory" applicant, or worker.[3]

Descriptions of these literacy events and their patterns of uses in Trackton do not enable us to place the community somewhere on a continuum from full literacy to restricted literacy or non-literacy. Instead, it seems more appropriate to think of two continua, the oral and the written. Their points and extent of overlap, and similarities in structure and function, follow one pattern for Trackton, but follow others for communities with different cultural features. And it is perhaps disquieting to think that many of these cultural features seem totally unrelated to features usually thought to help account for the relative degree of literacy in any social group. For example, such seemingly unrelated phenomena as the use of space in the community and the ways in which adults relate to preschool children may be as important for instilling literacy habits as aspirations for upward mobility or curiosity about the world. In Trackton, given the uses of space and the ways in which adults interacted with preschool children, no amount of books suddenly poured into the community, or public service programs teaching parents how to help their children learn to read, would have made an appreciable difference. The linkage between houses by open porches, the preference of young and old to be outdoors rather than inside, the incorporation of all the community in the communication network of each household, and the negative value placed on individual reading, reinforced the social group's negotiation of written language. Formal writing always had to be renegotiated into an informal style, one which led to discussion and debate among several people. Written messages gave residents something to talk about; after they talked, they might or might not follow up on the message of the written information, but what they had come to know had come to them from the text through the joint oral negotiation of meaning.

Trackton children do not learn to talk by being introduced to labels for either everyday objects or pictures and words in books. Instead, without adjusted, simplified input from adults, they become early talkers, modeling their ways of entering discourse and creating story texts on the oral language they hear about them. They tell creative story-poems which attempt to recapture the settings of actions as well as the portrayal of actions. They achieve their meaning as communicators and their sense of their own worth as communicators through the responses they obtain to their oral language, not in terms of responses in a one-to-one situation of reading a book with an adult. Words indeed must be as "behavioral" as any other form of action (Carothers, 1959). They carry personal qualities, have a dynamic nature, and cannot become static things always retaining their same sense. As one mother said of her ways of teaching her two-year-old son to talk: "Ain't no use me tellin' 'im: learn this, learn that, what's this, what's that? He just gotta learn, gotta know; he see one thing one place one time, he know how it go, see sump'n like it again, maybe it be the same, maybe it won't." In each new situation, learning must be reevaluated, reassessed for both the essence of meaning that occurs across contexts and for the particular meaning obtained in each new and different context.

What does this mean for the individual readers in Trackton? How different is their way of comprehending literate materials from that more commonly ascribed to literate individuals? For example, current research in reading suggests three ways or levels of extracting meaning from print: attending to the text itself, bringing in experiences or knowledge related to the text, and interpreting beyond the text into a creative/imaginative realm or to achieve a new synthesis of information from the text and reader experience (see Rumelhart, 1976; Rumelhart and Ortony, 1977; Adams, 1980, for technical discussions of these processes). Trackton residents as a group do use these methods of getting information from print. One person, reading aloud, decodes the written text of the newspaper, brochure, set of instructions, etc. This level of extracting meaning from the text is taken as the basis for the move to the next level, that of relating the text's meaning to the experience of members of the group. The experience of any one individual has to become common to the group, however, and that is done through the recounting of members' experiences. Such recountings attempt to recreate the scenes, to establish the character of the individuals involved, and, to the greatest extent possible, to bring the audience into the experience itself. At the third level, there is an extension beyond the common experience to a reintegration. For example, what do both the text and the common relating of text's meaning to experience say to the mother trying to decide how best to register her child for a daycare program? Together again, the group negotiates this third level. The process is time-consuming, perhaps less efficient than one individual reading the information for himself and making an individual decision. But the end result has been the sharing of information (next year's mother receiving a similar form will hear this discussion re-created in part). Furthermore, the set of experiences related to the task at hand is greater than a single individual would have: the mother has been led to consider whether or not to enlist the doctor's help, which information to take for registration, and a host of other courses of action she might not have considered on her own. Thus Trackton residents in groups, young and old, are familiar with processes for comprehending text similar to those delineated for individual readers by reading teachers and researchers. Major differences between their experiences with literacy and those generally depicted in the mainstream literature are in the degree of focus on specific decoding skills (such as letter-sound relationships), the amount of practice at each level of extracting meaning available for each individual in the community, and the assignment of interpretive responsibility to the group rather than to any one individual.

There are still other questions which could be asked of the uses of oral and literate skills in Trackton. What of the social consequences of their uses of literacy? Because they do not frequently and intensively engage in reading and writing extended prose, is their literacy "restricted," and what has this meant for them in socioeconomic terms? Work in the textile mills provided an income equal to or better than that of several types of professionals in the region: schoolteachers, salesmen, and secretaries. Successful completion of composition and advanced grammar classes in high school would not have secured better paying jobs for Trackton residents, unless very exceptional circumstances had come into play in individual cases. Improved scores on tests of reading comprehension or the Scholastic Aptitude Tests would not necessarily have given them access to more information for political decision-making than they had through the oral medium of several evening and morning television and radio news broadcasts. They tended to make their political judgments for local elections on the basis of personal knowledge of candidates or the word of someone else who knew the candidates. In national and state elections, almost all voted the party, and they said no amount of information on the individual candidates would cause them to change that pattern.

These behaviors and responses to what Goody might term "restricted literacy" echo similar findings in the work of social historians asking hard questions about the impact of literacy on pre-industrial groups. For such diverse groups as the masses of seventeenth-century France (Davis, 1975), sixteenth and seventeenth-century England (Cressy, 1980), and colonial New England (Lockridge, 1974), social historians have examined the functions, uses, degrees, and effects of literacy. All agree that the contexts and uses of literacy in each society determined its values, forms, and functions. The societal changes which came with the advent of literacy across societies were neither consistent nor universal.

Cressy (1980) perhaps best summarizes the conclusions of social historians about the universal potentialities of literacy:

1) People could be rational, acquire and comprehend information, and make well-founded political, social, and religious decisions without being able to read or write.
2) Literate people were no wiser or better able to control their universe than were those who were illiterate.

In short, in a variety of times and places, "literacy unlocked a variety of doors, but it did not necessarily secure admission" (Cressy, 1980:189).

Cressy and other social historians underscore the fact that, in some societies, literacy did not have the beneficial effects often ascribed to it. Davis found that, for the unlettered masses of seventeenth-century France, printing made possible new kinds of control from the top segments of the society. Before the printing press, oral culture and popular community-based social organizations seemed strong enough to resist standardization and thrusts for uniformity. With literacy, however, people began to measure themselves against a widespread norm and to doubt their own worth. In some cases, this attitude made people less politically active than they had been without print or opportunities for literacy. Lockridge (1974), in his study of colonial New England, concluded that literacy did not bring new attitudes or move people away from the traditional views held in their illiterate days. Eisenstein (1979) suggested that shifts in religious traditions enabled print to contribute to the creation of new notions of a collective morality and to an increased reliance on rhetoric in the verbal discourse of sermons and homiletics.

But these are studies of pre-industrial societies; what of literacy in industrial societies? Stone (1969) proposed the need to examine in industrial groups the *functions* of literacy in a variety of senses ranging from the conferring of technical skills to an association with self-discipline. Stone further suggested that each society may well have its own weighted checklist of factors (e.g. social stratification, job opportunities, Protestantism, and sectarian competition) which causes literacy to serve one or another function. Sanderson (1972), building on Stone's work, showed that the economic development of the English industrial revolution made low literacy demands of the educational system. His argument points out the need to examine closely job demands for literacy; changes in mechanization may call for shifts of types of literacy skills. Indeed, in the English industrial revolution, the increased use of machinery enabled employers to hire workers who were less literate than were those who had previously done the hand work. Successful performance in cottage industries, for example, required a higher level of literacy for a larger proportion of workers than did mechanized textile work.

Research by economic and educational historians of the late nineteenth-century United States has examined the effects of literacy not only on the economic laws of supply and demand of job opportunities, but also on the values society placed on a correct oral reading style and acceptable performance on standardized tests. Reading for comprehension and an expansion of creative thinking were less frequently assessed in the late nineteenth century than they had been earlier (Calhoun, 1973). Soltow and Stevens (1977) point out the extent to which standardized measures of performance were lauded by parents, and they suggest that acceptable performance on these tests convinced parents their children would be able to achieve occupational and social mobility. Whether or not the schools taught children to read at skill levels that might make a real difference in their chances for upward occupational mobility is not at all clear. Nevertheless, if students acquired the social and moral values and generalized "rational" and "cultured" behaviors associated with literate citizens, occupational mobility often resulted.

This social historical research raises some critical questions for the study of communities in today's complex society. A majority of communities in the modern world are neither preliterate, i.e. without access to print or writing of some kind, nor fully literate (Goody, 1968). They are somewhere in between. Some individuals may have access to literacy and choose to use it for some purposes and not for others. Some communities may restrict access to literacy to some portions of the population (Walker, 1981); others may provide a climate in which individuals choose the extent to which they will adopt habits associated with literacy (Heath, 1980). As Resnick and Resnick (1977) have shown, the goal of a high level of literacy for a large proportion of the population is a relatively recent phenomenon, and new methods and materials in reading instruction, as well as particular societal and economic supports, may be needed to achieve such a goal.

Furthermore, in large complex societies such as the United States, the national state of technological development and the extent of intrusion of governmental agencies in the daily lives of citizens may have combined to set up conditions in which literacy no longer has many of the traditional uses associated with it. Understanding and responding to the myriad of applications, reporting forms, and accounting procedures which daily affect the lives of nearly every family in the United States bears little resemblance to the decoding of extended prose passages or production of expository writing, the two literacy achievements most associated with school success. Furthermore, television and other media have removed the need to rely on reading to learn the basics of news and sports events, how to dress properly for the weather, and what to buy and where to find it. Increasingly industry is turning to on-the-job training programs which depend on observation of tasks or audio-visual instruction rather than literate preparation for job performance; specialists handle reports related to production, quality control, inventory, and safety. In industry, the specialized demands of reporting forms, regulations and agency reports, and programming requirements call for a communications expert, not simply a "literate" manager. In a recent survey of employer attitudes toward potential employees, employers called not for the literacy skills generally associated with school tasks, but instead for an integration of mathematical and linguistic skills, and displays of the capability of learning "on one's own," and listening and speaking skills required to understand and give instructions and describe problems (Research for Better Schools, 1978).

These shifts in larger societal contexts for literacy are easily and frequently talked about, but their specific effects on communities such as Trackton, though occasionally inferred, are very rarely examined. It is clear that, in what may be referred to as the post-industrial age, members of each community have different and varying patterns of influence and control over forms and uses of literacy in their lives. They exercise considerable control within their own primary networks. In institutions, such as their churches, they may have some control. In other institutions, such as in their places of employment, banks, legal offices, etc., they may have no control over literacy demands. The shape of literacy events in each of these is different. The nature of oral and written language and the interplay between them is ever-shifting, and these changes both respond to and create shifts in the individual and societal meanings of literacy. The information to be gained from any prolonged look at oral and written uses of language through literacy events may enable us to accept the protean shapes of oral and literate traditions and language, and move us away from current tendencies to classify communities as being at one or another point along a hypothetical continuum which has no societal reality.

24.
The Nature of Reading at Work

William A. Diehl
Larry Mikulecky

One of the roles of reading instruction receiving increased attention is that of preparing individuals for the literacy demands of occupations. This role has been highlighted in recent years as part of the controversies surrounding functional literacy and minimum competency testing in the U.S. Recent research in functional literacy (Louis Harris and Associates, 1970; Northcutt, 1975; Murphy, 1975; Gadway and Wilson, 1975) has indicated that large numbers of Americans may not have sufficient reading skills to function in common (including occupational) situations. While other researchers (Fisher, 1978; Kirsch and Guthrie, 1977–1978; Mikulecky and Diehl, 1979) have raised important questions about the extent of these findings, the findings have been used as evidence that the American educational system has been grossly negligent in preparing students to "function" in society (Copperman, 1978). The demand that reading educators teach the minimum literacy competencies necessary to function in various settings, including occupational settings, gives rise to the question of what, in terms of literacy, is required.

Unfortunately, little research has been done to determine how literate a person should be to function in a particular adult situation. The nature of literacy demands in particular settings outside of schools has rarely been investigated. Instead, "representative" literacy tasks have traditionally been used in research as indicators of reading proficiency in various situations. Such tasks tend to be arbitrary, are not necessarily reflective of the real demands on individuals, and are completed in a testing situation that bears little resemblance to the setting in which the task is normally encountered. Since the settings differ, subjects do not have access to extralinguistic cues (e.g., machines, multiple materials, and advice of others) that they might normally use to help complete a functional reading task. In order to gain a more accurate picture of functional literacy demands and

From William A. Diehl and Larry Mikulecky, "The Nature of Reading at Work," *Journal of Reading* 24(1980): 221–28. Reprinted by permission of William A. Diehl and the International Reading Association.

the abilities needed by people facing the demands, it is necessary to research the pragmatic demands within the context of actual situations.

One purpose of the study reported here was to specify the literacy demands encountered in a broad range of occupations. One hundred seven subjects from one-hundred occupations and twenty-six workplaces were interviewed and tested at their work sites. The subjects ranged from a lawyer and a vice-president of a large corporation to assembly line workers and stone cutters. The subjects were selected from workplaces chosen randomly in a seventy-mile radius of Bloomington, Indiana (thus including Indianapolis). Subjects represented a full range of the occupations listed in the *Dictionary of Occupational Titles* (U.S. Employment Service, 1977) and appeared to be representative of the adult working population on such variables as sex, race, income earned and occupational category (Diehl, 1980). The subjects were administered the Diehl-Mikulecky Job Literacy Survey (1980), which includes items assessing the literacy demands encountered in occupations and the strategies employed by subjects in meeting the demands. The survey, which takes approximately an hour to complete, collects data on a number of variables hypothesized to affect functional literacy. In addition to information on literacy demands, it collects information on attitudinal factors, ability factors, and extralinguistic factors.

A portion of the survey asked subjects to show and describe the reading tasks they had completed on the job within the previous month. These tasks were rated according to type of display, frequency of use, and importance to the job. Additionally, where possible, the actual job reading materials used by individuals were collected and a readability level determined using the FORCAST formula, developed by Caylor and Sticht (1973) specifically for use with occupational material. Data were also collected on the amount of time spent per day on reading job materials. Based on responses to a series of questions, each piece of reading material cited by subjects was also categorized according to the type of strategy employed in completing the task. Four general categories were used, based on field-testing and on earlier work by Sticht (1977). The categories were:

- "Reading-to-learn" in which the subject reads with the intention of remembering text information and applies some learning strategy to do so;
- "Reading-to-do with no learning" in which the subject uses the material primarily as an aid to do something else (e.g., fix a machine) and later reports not remembering the information; these materials thus serve as "external memories" (Sticht, 1977);
- "Reading-to-do with incidental learning" in which the subject uses the material primarily as an aid to do something else, but in the process learns (remembers) the information;
- "Reading-to-access" in which the subject quickly reads or skims material to determine its usefulness for some later task or for some other person; the material is then filed or passed on.

These four general strategies (or purposes) were further divided into 16 specific strategies used with job materials. Diehl (1980) described these specific strategies.

Table 24.1
Descriptive Statistics on Reading Demands Reported

Reading tasks encountered on the job	Percent of total citations (339 tasks cited)
Type of display used	
Entire book	15%
Part of book: text	19
Part of book: chart, graph, etc.	12
1–3 page text	31
1–3 page chart	21
Other	2
Frequency of use	
Less than once a month	10%
Once a week to once a month	7
Two to four times a week	22
Daily	61
Importance to completing job task	
Not important	23%
Important, but not vital	56
Vital to job task completion	21
Type of general strategy employed	
Read-to-learn	11%
Read-to-do (no learning)	40 ⎱ 63% total.
Read-to-do (incidental learning)	23 ⎰ read-to-do
Read-to-assess	26
Readability of materials (measured by FORCAST, Caylor and Sticht, 1973)	
Mean grade equivalent for 106 pieces of material from 57 subjects = 10.9	
Standard deviation = 1.2 grade levels	
Range = level 8.4 to level 13.8	
Reported time spent per day reading job material	
Mean for 107 subjects = 112.5 minutes	
Standard deviation = 119 minutes	
Range = 0 minutes (10 subjects*) to 480 minutes (3 subjects)	
Median = 61 minutes	

*Although 10 subjects reported no reading, eight of them later in the interview cited reading materials they use "daily." Thus, only two subjects could be said to do no reading on the job.

Descriptive statistics on the "reading tasks" encountered on the jobs are presented in table 24.1.

Several striking results and conclusions can be drawn from the data reported in the table. First, reading at work appears to be a ubiquitous activity. Close to 99% of the subjects reported doing some reading each day at work. They reported an average of 113 minutes a day spent in job reading. Although this figure is higher than that reported in some other studies (Sharon, 1973–1974; Mikulecky, Shanklin, and Caverley, 1979), it may be because reading is so closely related to other job tasks that it often is overlooked by subjects reporting on time spent reading unless it is specifically probed. There are indications from other job research (Sticht, 1975) that the figure of 113 minutes (or close to two hours) accurately reflects job reading time.

While the 113 minute results should not be generalized to the total population, it does indicate that workers, overall, tend to read a great deal on the job, and probably read job materials more each day than any other type of material. This conclusion would suggest that job-related literacy is the most important type of functional literacy and should be stressed to a greater extent in functional literacy programs.

When the sample of subjects was divided into quartiles by variables that indicate job success, *t* tests revealed few significant differences (p<.01) between groups on job reading time. The variables were income earned, job prestige (Hodge, Siegel, and Rossi, 1966, p. 286–93), and job responsibilities (as rated by the Dictionary of Occupational Titles). Higher level occupations tended to involve more job reading, but not significantly more, indicating that time spent reading job materials is an important component of jobs at almost all levels.

Subjects reported that in most cases (56%) the reading tasks were "important, but not vital" to the completion of a job task. Information to be gained from the reading, in other words, was viewed as helpful (but not necessary) to completing a job task; either the same information could be gotten from another source (e.g., a co-worker) or the job could be completed (perhaps less efficiently) without the information. In 23% of the reading citations, subjects indicated the reading was "not necessary" and only in 21% of the citations were the reading tasks felt to be "vital" in completing a task. Overall, then, almost 80% of the reading tasks cited were felt not to be necessary to completing job tasks.

These results suggest that many of the literacy "demands" of a job are not really demands at all; rather, literacy materials are used, not so much out of necessity as because they make the job task easier or more efficient. It has been suggested that the literacy "demands" of the workplace are increasing with technological changes (Levin, 1975). It may be, instead, that demands are not increasing; it may be that the opportunities to use print to help carry out a job task are what is increasing. The distinction between "literacy demands" and "literacy availability" is an important one. It may be, as some researchers (Sticht, et al., 1972; Newman et al., 1978; Diehl, 1979) suggest, that some jobs are closed unnecessarily to people with little education or poor reading abilities, based on a false estimation of the "demands" of the job.

Results of this study indicate that reading tasks on the job tend to be highly repetitive and are completed in conjunction with specific job tasks. The majority (61%) of the 339 reading tasks cited by subjects were reported to be done "daily." An additional 22% of the reading tasks were performed at least once a week.

Most of these tasks (63%) were reading-to-do tasks. In such tasks, the material serves as a reference only—an external memory (Sticht, 1977)—and the information is applied directly, and usually immediately, to a job task. In some reading-to-do tasks (24% of the total), subjects learned the material—usually because of a repetition of the task or because the single trial was sufficient for learning. In most cases (40% of the total), subjects did not learn the material; they reported they would "read the material again tomorrow to do the same task."

These results suggest some important aspects of functional literacy tasks that may differ substantially from literacy tasks encountered in school and training settings. The job reading tasks appeared to be more integrated with other job tasks, more immediately applied to situations, and more repetitious than school reading tasks. These surface differences indicate the possibility that major differences in information processing demands exist between job (mainly reading-to-do) and school (mainly reading-to-learn) reading tasks. While the current study does not attempt to define or investigate such differences, some conjectures can be made based on the available evidence.

In reading-to-do tasks, the reader has access to extralinguistic cues that are usually directly related to the reading material; a one-to-one correspondence often exists between aspects of the job environment (e.g., the parts of a lathe sitting on a table in front of the worker) and the text (e.g., a diagram with lathe parts laid out; a written description of each part and how it fits with the other; a parts list with identification numbers). The main task for the worker, then, is to "crack the code" of the particular graphic display—to match the visual objects in the work environment to the particular form of representation of them in the text. Once the representation is understood, the worker can easily go from environment to text, checking each in a search for particular information.

The same type of process would occur when a worker used text to follow directions; the environment includes the machine (or form, or whatever) to which the directions are to be applied. The worker's main task is to understand the correspondence and use a combination of information from the text and from the environment to complete the task.

The existence of an information-rich environment should enable workers to gain information from the text they would not have gained if they read the information in isolation. By using both textual and environmental cues, workers should be able to gain more information than their simple "reading ability" would suggest they could. In fact, studies (Sacher and Duffy, 1978; Diehl, 1980) indicate that workers can successfully read and apply information from job materials up to two grade levels above their assessed reading levels. These studies support the idea that an information-rich environment may make a significant difference in how well information is processed.

It may be argued, then, that "cracking the code" is the primary task for the job reader—a task that will then enable the worker to select and use appropriate cues from the environment to help with reading the text. The fact that job reading tasks are done repetitively then becomes significant. The code need only be cracked once; once the correspondence between the print and the environment is understood, it becomes far easier to quickly get the necessary information from the text.

For example, the first time a salesperson encounters a specialized order form s/he must not only locate specific information (e.g., prices quoted) but, in the process, must learn how the graphic display corresponds to the job tasks (e.g., where and how products are listed; where and how estimates are quoted). Once this correspondence is understood, the salesperson can proceed more rapidly, and with less attention, through subsequent forms.

The locating and application of information involves less cognitive processing each time the information is used. In fact, the location and application of information becomes so easy that it is often done with a minimum of attention (which may explain why some workers forgot about reading tasks that they do daily, until probed, and which may explain why workers can use the same material daily for the same purpose).

Reading-to-learn tasks (which are probably most typical in school and training situations), on the other hand, are less related to an immediate context and require more attention than the reading-to-do tasks. Because the environment provides far fewer relevant cues or bits of information that correspond directly with the text, the reader probably must make many more inferences, must draw more extensively on cues from the text in developing a sense of meaning, must apply the information—if it is applied at all—in his/her own imagination, and must store the information in memory for later possible use or application. It would seem that the decontextualized nature of reading-to-learn tasks requires different cognitive processes than are required in reading-to-do tasks.

While the above discussion is conjecture, results from this study and others lend some support to the hypothesis that reading-to-do and reading-to-learn (or "functional" and "schooling") tasks differ from one another. Additional research, such as is currently being conducted by Mikulecky may indicate that, in fact, reading tasks as done in school are different from functional reading tasks. If this is true, it would question the premises on which "functional literacy" assessments are made (e.g., tests are given in a context different from that in which tasks are actually encountered). Further, if functional and schooling tasks are substantially different, and if functional tasks are indeed strongly influenced by context, the argument that schools do (or even should) prepare students to be functionally literate is questionable.

Conclusions

Five tentative conclusions about job literacy demands can be drawn from these data.

1. Reading on the job is a ubiquitous activity and may be the most prevalent type of reading done by employed adults. This makes job-related reading an important part of functional literacy.

2. Reading materials on the job tend to be viewed as external memories. Subjects tend not to learn the material, because they treat the material as information continually available to them.

3. Literacy tasks on the job are completed in an information-rich context. Because most of the tasks involve the application of information to a particular job task, the job task itself provides a number of extralinguistic cues that may help the reader gain information quickly with a minimum of attention.

4. Because the reading materials are used in an information-rich context, the main task of the job reader is to determine the relationship between the graphic display and objects in the environment. Use of the context and the repetitious nature of job tasks probably enable many workers to read material on the job that they would not be able to read in isolation.

5. Reading at work and reading in school settings may be quite different from each other, in terms of extralinguistic cues available, cognitive demands, and uses of information gained. Additional research in this area is needed; if research supports these indications, it would have important implications for the design of functional literacy tests and programs, as well as implications for schools and job-training programs.

25.
Who Are the Adult Illiterates?

Carman St. John Hunter
David Harman

The people we are looking at are variously described as illiterate, functionally illiterate, functionally incompetent, educationally disadvantaged, or undereducated. It is unlikely that any of them so describe themselves. They may feel only that they are powerless and at a disadvantage with respect to certain benefits of the society. They may also feel that their ability to achieve personal and work-related goals is limited or nonexistent.

How many such persons are there in the United States? One might assume that the answer to this question is readily available. However, external standards for quantifying literacy or classifying persons in relation to it do not exist. Some facts about conventional literacy are relatively easy to assemble. Persons who have difficulty with basic reading and writing skills are most apt to be found among those who have not completed elementary school. It is also possible to examine statistics about persons who do not have high school diplomas. While all who lack high school diplomas are not functionally illiterate by any means, the evidence is strong that the bulk of those who are functionally illiterate are found among persons who fail to graduate from high school (Fisher, 1978).

Furthermore, in our measurement-loving society, a number of tests have been devised to ascertain the ability of persons to perform a series of basic tasks. These provide rough indications of the number of persons who might fail in such tasks. Whether one can say dogmatically that those with any specific set of

From *Adult Illiteracy in the United States: A Report to the Ford Foundation*, by Carman St. John Hunter and David Harman. Copyright 1979 by McGraw-Hill. Reprinted by permission of the publisher.

EDITORS' NOTE: *Adult Illiteracy in the United States*, a report to the Ford Foundation by Carman St. John Hunter and David Harman, is the most complete survey of the topic available. They not only ask "who are the adult illiterates" but devote about two-thirds of their book to detailing what is being done about adult illiteracy: they offer specific recommendations, describe a wide variety of curricula and programs, and provide a lengthy annotated bibliography. Hunter and Harman's text is illuminated with statistical charts and tables which we did not have the space to reproduce; readers who wish to pursue the topic of adult literacy should consult the original.

difficulties are nonfunctional or functionally illiterate is doubtful. However, like the school-leaving statistics, they may be indicators of particular problems encountered by large numbers of adults in their daily lives.

In the Third World many persons who do not possess even basic literacy skills function effectively in their societies. In the United States and other industrialized nations this is also true for some individuals. Their number will be very small, however, because the demands of complex technological societies reach into every aspect of life.

In this chapter we seek to move closer to an understanding of the lives of the persons represented by the assembled data by relating educational attainment and, to a lesser degree, functional competency to other factors: regional location, urban and rural distribution; poverty, unemployment, and welfare; race, ethnic origin, sex, and age.

The available statistics—however inaccurate, distorted, culturally biased, and occasionally contradictory they may be—do have a kind of gross truth. We invite the reader, therefore, to ponder the figures and their relationships while bearing in mind that, like all numbers, they are single-minded abstractions from complex and changing realities, and thus to a degree inevitably misrepresent the situations they purport to describe.

Lies, Damned Lies, and Statistics

The educational planners who gather and publish data disagree not only about what constitutes conventional illiteracy and functional illiteracy but also about who is adult, that is, who should be included in the statistics. Some studies are based on persons over 14 years of age who are out of school; others use 15 as the starting point; still others 16; and some studies begin at age 25. These differences make it difficult to compare statistical reports and to reconcile their implications. Further compounding the confusion, in 1973 the U.S. Bureau of the Census discovered that it had underestimated the total population by about 5,300,000 persons when it counted in 1970. There are also an unknown number of illegal aliens (the Immigration Service puts the figure at a minimum of 850,000)[1] who are not included in the census figures, although they may turn up in some of the educational statistics.

Even if we agree on who and how many constitute the adult population, there are, as we noted earlier, no external criteria that definitely indicate conventional or functional literacy. The most widely available statistics come from the census, but the census-taker must rely on what people say about their educational attainment. Those who state that they have completed sixth grade are classified as literate. In the person-to-person sampling, individual census-takers may—or may not—ask those who have not completed sixth grade whether they can "read and write a simple message in any language." In both cases, however, the definitions are left to the census-taker and the respondent.

The available school-leaving statistics do not necessarily correlate with individuals' abilities to function or even to read. Indeed, they may reflect little more than increased age requirements for school attendance. Some cities, for instance, have placed the number of functional illiterates at half the number of their high school graduates. Thirty states have found it necessary to require that those seeking a high school diploma give evidence of being able to read and write at an *eighth grade* level.[2]

In addition to numbers, definitions, and standards of measurement, other confounding factors include bias—whether conscious or unconscious—not only among those who actually record the information, but also among survey-designers, questionnaire-writers, and the publishers of tests designed to measure reading levels or "competency" or coping skills; and the duplication of figures or double reporting that sometimes occurs.

The Numbers Game

Despite some discrepancies, two massive sets of data[3] at least suggest the dimensions of functional illiteracy in this country: one deals with "competency levels," the other with school completion.

Using Competency Critera

The Harris study commissioned by the National Reading Center in 1971 undertook to measure the ability of adult Americans to read and answer questions about a classified newspaper, a telephone directory, and a composite standard application form. From such data as the percentages of the sample unable to answer such questionnaire items as "What is the color of your eyes?" and "How long have you lived at your present address?" the study concluded that some 15 percent of adults have serious reading deficiencies (Harris et al., 1971).

It was, however, the 1975 report of the University of Texas at Austin setting forth the findings of its Adult Performance Level (APL) study that first caught the attention of the American media and thus of the public. That study, using sophisticated nationwide sampling techniques, also looked at the adult population from the point of view of individuals' ability to function regardless of their level of academic achievement. The report, citing specific examples and using language that was easily understandable, astonished many people. For example:

> When given a notice posted on a cashier's desk in a store describing the check cashing policy for that store, more than one out of five respondents did not draw the correct conclusion from the notice. . . .
> Fourteen percent of the sample, when asked to fill out a check in a simulated business transaction, made an error so serious that it was unlikely that the check would have cleared the bank (*Adult Functional Competency*, 1975, p. 21).
> Thirteen percent of the sample did not address an envelope well enough to insure that it would reach the desired destination, and 24 percent did not place a return address on the same envelope which would insure that it would be returned to the sender if delivery were not possible. These results indicate that an estimated 28 million adults would make a serious error in addressing an envelope (ibid., p. 28).

An official of the U.S. Office of Education, using the competency criteria of the APL study, infers that 57 million Americans do not have skills adequate to perform basic tasks. Almost 23 million Americans lacked the competencies necessary to function in the society (APL category 1). An additional 34 million Americans are able to function, but not proficiently (APL 2's) (Parker, 1976, p. 3). These and similar conclusions were widely reported amidst general cries of alarm.

Using Grade Completion Figures

In the United States, as noted above, completion of secondary school has become a kind of benchmark definition of functional literacy. Adults without high school diplomas are considered disadvantaged, and automatically form the "target population" for adult education activities. This view assumes that those with fewer than 12 years of schooling are less able than high school graduates to attain and sustain employment, earn and gain in earnings, and, in general, to participate fully in adult life. The Adult Education Act, passed by Congress in November 1966, states as its purpose

> the establishment of programs of adult public education that will enable all adults to continue their education *to at least the level of completion of secondary school* and make available to them the means to secure training that will enable them to become more employable, productive, and responsible citizens [emphasis added] (Adult Education Act, Section 302, PL 91–230).

It is not surprising, therefore, to discover that most American studies of educational attainment use graduation from twelfth grade as the critical point.

When we use the criterion of high school completion to help delineate the population that has not achieved functional literacy, we arrive at essentially the same figure as that arrived at by those who used competency levels: somewhere between 54 and 64 million. The total population of the United States in 1978 is estimated to be about 218 million. Of these, about 70 percent, 152.5 million, are "adult"; that is, 16 years or older. About 70 million of these adults have completed high school. Some 26 million are still in the educational system, in high schools, colleges and universities, or training schools of one kind or another. Those who most concern us are persons 16 and over who are not enrolled in school and have less than a high school education. The U.S. Bureau of Labor Statistics estimates their number at about 57,654,000, or 38 percent of the total population 16 and over (*Special Labor Force Report*, 1976). The figures were confirmed in a 1974 state-by-state analysis by the National Advisory Council on Adult Education (1974, pp. 101–151).[4]

We concentrate on those with less than a high school education primarily because more comparative figures are available. We do so, however, realizing that our focus on this group is arbitrary. It is clear that completion of high school is not a reliable indicator of functional literacy. It is equally clear that many persons who have not completed high school, or even grade school, are in fact functioning in ways that bring them personal satisfaction and contribute to their families' and society's well-being.

Three sets of data support this argument. Employment figures of March 1975 show, in general, that the higher rates of unemployment are among those with less than a high school education; the very highest rate of joblessness, however, is not among those with fewer than five years of school, as might be expected, but rather among high school drop-outs. Second, among men between the ages of 25 and 54 with fewer than five years of school, 89 percent were in the labor force. Finally, one researcher showed that although many recruits in low-level military occupations were unable to read the materials deemed necessary, they nevertheless performed their jobs adequately (Sticht, 1975). All these clues suggest that large numbers of persons who have less than a high school education are in fact functioning in this society. At what level, and with what degree of personal satisfaction, of course, the statistics do not tell us.

Where Are They?

Those persons in our society who lack sufficient reading and writing skills to function effectively are found in large numbers wherever there are poor people and wherever there are congregated racial and ethnic minority groups. They are found in city ghettos and doing hard physical labor on unmechanized farms. There are more of them, both in absolute numbers and in percentages, in the South than in the North, more in the East than in the West.

Nationwide, statistics are high even for those who have not completed grade school. The National Center for Educational Statistics (NCES) estimated that, in 1976, "the percentage of the adult population over 17 with an eighth grade education or less was 18.1 percent."[5]

In 1970 an estimated 16 million adults—11.3 percent of the adult population—had less than a fifth-grade education.
Two million adult Americans never attended any school at all[6] (*The Condition of Education*, 1976)

If we can trust the figures, it appears that in the South well over 20 percent of the adults have not completed the eighth grade.

In the South, 42 percent of the adults 25 and over who might be considered educationally disadvantaged (that is, who did not complete high school) have had fewer than eight years of schooling. Twenty-one of the fifty states have a million or more adults who have not completed high school and who are not currently enrolled in school. They are, by and large, those states with the largest total populations.

More undereducated adults live in urban than in rural areas—62 percent to 38 percent, respectively. Some 27 million are in cities, 17 million in "non-metropolitan areas." Over 15 percent of adults in rural areas have not even completed grade school. In general, those who live in the suburbs stay in school longer than those who live either in the inner city or in rural areas. In rural areas only about 46 percent complete high school, whereas in suburban areas the percentage is 70; in central cities, 61. Of the total suburban population, only about 7 percent have not completed grade school; in rural areas failure to finish grade school is more than double that percentage.

Who Are They?

In their valuable small volume *The Information Poor in America,* Childers and Post (1975, p. 11) report on the information and knowledge needs of "disadvantaged adults." They discuss the problems faced by the deaf and blind and list those other groups that "by virtue of their social, economic, cultural, educational, physical, or ethnic condition could be expected to suffer more deprivation than the rest of society." Their lists includes "the poor, the imprisoned, the elderly, the undereducated, the unemployed or those employed at a low level (unskilled and migrant workers, for example), and the racially . . . oppressed."

Our experience and reading confirm their findings. Both the available figures and descriptive and case-study materials suggest that there is no discrete "target population" on whom we can focus. Instead, there is great overlap. Those who are poor are likely not to have finished high school. Blacks and ethnic minorities make up a disproportionate number of the poor and the unemployed.

We have come to understand that the undereducated, with whom we are especially concerned, are also primarily the poor and racial and ethnic minorities. In the sections that follow we shall look at how the figures about educational achievement (primarily grade-completion statistics) relate to these two groups and to other socially disadvantaged groups.

The Poor

"Poverty," like "illiteracy," is not clearly defined. It, too, is relative and changes at different times and among different cultures. That poor people are unlikely to have high levels of formal schooling and that illiterate persons in our society are likely to be poor are relationships so well accepted as hardly to need verification. But perhaps other questions should be borne in mind. Which is the relevant fact: That good jobs and high pay are rewards for staying in school? Or that well-to-do families tend to keep their children in school longer? To what extent does school completion depend on economic factors?

Income

Of the 54.3 million persons 16 and over in 1970 who were not enrolled in school and who had less than a high school education, 75 percent earned less than $5,000 a year. Only 1 percent had incomes of $15,000 or more, compared to about 33 percent of all families in the United States (NACAE, 1974, p. 33). When average income is correlated with levels of schooling, we find significant differences between those with less formal education and those with more. Those who have completed high school have incomes about double those who have not completed grade school, and half again higher than those with eighth grade education. This situation prevails among all sectors of the population: men and women, white and black, and all age groups (ibid., p. 32). Those whose schooling stopped before the eighth grade have lifetime earnings about one-third of those with graduate study: in 1970, $250,000 contrasted to $800,000, a gap apparently widening (ibid.).

Employment

While it is true that the more education one has, the more likely one is to be an active member of the labor force, and while employment rates of adults who have graduated from high school are about double those who have not, the figures do not correlate directly to years of schooling completed. True, unemployment rates are lowest for college graduates, but they are not highest, as one might have expected, for those with almost no formal schooling, but for high school drop-outs. In March 1975, when the overall unemployment rate was 9.2 percent of the labor force, the unemployment rates of high school drop-outs were considerably higher than for those who had completed a lower grade. The latter, in turn, were also somewhat above the national level in unemployment.

There are a number of possible reasons why the unemployment rates tend to be higher for high school drop-outs than for those with less education. First, many of those with less than an eighth grade education are not in the labor force at all. Those who are tend to be older, more experienced workers whose lack of formal education may be offset by their on-the-job experience. Thus, those without jobs who have completed eighth grade or less tend to remain unemployed for longer periods than do high school drop-outs or the population at large.

Public Assistance

One other indicator often used to underline the problems faced by those in our society with less than a high school education is their appearance on the public welfare rolls. Although people go on welfare for a wide variety of reasons, across the board, for men and women, for blacks and whites, and for all age groups, a prime common denominator is the level of schooling attained. The proportion of persons with fewer than six grades of school on public assistance is more than double that among those with six to eight years and almost four times that among those with nine to eleven years of school (NACAE, 1974, p. 20).

Racial and Ethnic Minorities

The available statistics reveal additionally even more disturbing interrelationships among poverty, education, and racial/ethnic origin. Across all levels of education minority group members rank lower than majority group members.

In all parts of the country, but particularly in rural areas, the number of blacks and other minorities among the educationally disadvantaged is disproportionately high. Among rural blacks, for instance, 45 percent have not completed grade school; for the population as a whole the figure is about 15 percent. (The comparison figures for rural whites are not available.)

Blacks, of course, are by no means the only educationally disadvantaged racial or ethnic group. Hispanic groups, especially Hispanic women, have a noticeably lower level of educational attainment than either whites or blacks. All those for whom English is not the mother tongue—about 30 million Americans, or 13 percent—face special educational difficulties. This includes the large but unknown number of illegal aliens, mostly Spanish-speaking.[7] The 827,000 Native Americans also face special problems. Only 40 percent of adult urban Native Americans, and fewer than 25 percent of those who live in rural areas, have graduated from high school. Their representation in the work force is so low that they generally do not even appear on the charts. Even in such a central working age group as 35–44, the labor market participation rates for Native American males with fewer than 12 years of schooling is only 63 percent, compared with 86 percent for blacks and 93 percent for whites of the same age and similar schooling.[8] Among those for whom figures are available, Mexican Americans, many of whom are employed as migrant workers, leave school at the earliest ages.

The median family income for all Americans in 1970 was about $9,600, an increase of 70 percent in ten years. The median income for blacks during the decade rose at an even faster rate: from just over $3,000 in 1960 to about $6,000 in 1970. The median income of black families, however, still fell far short of the median of about $10,000 for white families.

The median level of school completion is also rising, and not only for whites.

For blacks, the rise in median level of school completion is dramatic—from 5 years and 8 months in 1940 to 11 years in 1975. Indeed, the gap has gradually narrowed so that only half a year's schooling now separates the medians of blacks and whites (12.1 as opposed to 12.5) (NACAE, 1974, p. 7).

As we have noted, hiring patterns seem to be related not to reading levels needed for job performance but, rather, to years of schooling completed. Although there are signs of a changing trend, whites still stay in school longer than blacks and other minorities. This and other social factors inevitably favor the dominant groups in our society. Simply put, poor parents are likely to have less schooling than well-to-do parents. Their children, in turn, have less schooling than the children of the middle and upper classes, and less potential for upward social and economic mobility. And they are more likely to be members of ethnic and racial minorities.

Other Groups

Within the three major overlapping groups of the educationally deprived—the poor, racial and ethnic minorities, and those with less than a high school education—are subgroups who suffer from more specific disadvantages. Primary among these are the young, the old, the imprisoned, and women. Statistical information about these groups is even more' elusive than data about the population as a whole. We strongly believe, however, that efforts must be made to understand their special situations as we attempt to address the needs of the educationally disadvantaged as a whole.

The Old and the Young

Among adults 16 years and over with less than a high school education and not enrolled in school, there is, as would be expected, a heavy concentration of older persons. About two out of three are 45 and over; one in four is 65 or older. Of those with less than a high school education, more than three-quarters of those 65 and over have not completed grade school.

Unemployment rates and public assistance rates are also disproportionately high among older Americans at every level of school completion.

Comprising only a quarter of the total labor force, young people in 1972 accounted for nearly half of the unemployed. The impact has been devastatingly disproportionate in black and other minority communities, where in some areas over half the young men have no jobs. The unemployment rate for older youths (20- to 24-year-olds) is also higher than it was a few years ago.

The U.S. Bureau of Labor Statistics reported figures for 1977 that showed unemployment rates even higher; 42.1 percent nationwide for young white people between the ages of 16 and 19, and 66.3 percent for minorities. New York City had the highest rate of youth unemployment among 11 major American cities, according to the study, which counted everyone of working age, not only those who were actively looking for jobs. In June 1977, 74 percent of New York City whites between the ages of 16 and 19 and 86 percent of blacks in the same age group did not have a full-time job (*New York Times,* Aug. 2, 1977b, p. 30).

Between 1965 and 1973, over 3.1 million young people between 16 and 21 years old dropped out of high school. In the period 1974 to 1975, 25.3 percent of all drop-outs between the ages of 16 and 24 were unemployed; 61.4 percent of those nonwhites who dropped out of school were unemployed.

Even completing high school does not adequately prepare young people for the job market or assure them of work for which they are prepared. One educator recommended strongly that blacks and other minority youngsters go to college. If they do not, he said, "they will never—or may never—get a job." He concluded:

> Trying to encourage minority youngsters to get an education, learn good work habits and seek employment that holds little for the future, while bombarding them every day with television and film images of success, mostly illegal, some legal, without telling them "how to" become legally successful, is [probably] impossible to do.
> . . . Soon the suffering youngsters of today will marry and have children who in a few years will inherit the problems of their parents, and the vicious circle will go on: poor education, lack of training, jobless youngsters, continuing welfare drain, chaos (Hodgkinson, 1977).

The Imprisoned

Persons who have been imprisoned have lower levels of educational achievement than the population at large. About 75 percent have not completed high school, as opposed to 38 percent of the total adult population. Some 35 to 42 percent have an eighth grade education or less. These figures are based on information from the 1970 census on educational levels for prisoners over 25. Because some 26 percent of all persons in prisons and jails are between the ages of 20 and 24, and because there is another large group of youthful offenders between 16 and 20 for whom figures were not available, these percentages may be somewhat skewed.

Women

Until recently, the median level of school completion was higher for women than men. This remains true for black and Hispanic women, but during the mid-1960s the pattern changed for whites. Between 1960 and 1970 (possibly to avoid or postpone being drafted) white young men began staying in school longer. The median level of school completion for white men jumped one-and-a-half grade levels in this decade, from 10.8 to 12.2. In 1970, the median school completion for white men and women was the same, 12.2. By 1978, men were staying in school longer. Of the population over 25 who have not completed high school, 20 million are men; 22 million are women. Of those who have an eighth grade education or less, more are men than women (6.7 million compared to 51.8 million). But of those who dropped out of high school, many more are women (10.3 million women to 7.9 million men).[9]

Despite their relatively higher level of schooling, women, as we know, have not participated in the labor force nor commanded salaries commensurate with their education. Women outnumbered men in participation in adult basic education (ABE) courses in 1970 by as much as 57 percent to 43 percent. As the National Advisory Council on Adult Education points out, "Certainly the economic benefits could not be that much of a lure." The 1970 census showed that white males with less than a grade school education earned a mean income of about $4,600; this rose to over $6,100 among those who completed eighth grade, an increase of about $1,500 a year. For women, however, the comparable figures are $2,000 and $2,400, an increase of $400 (NACAE, 1974, p. 73).

Despite the changes in federal legislation and policy prohibiting discrimination in hiring and wages, the earning gap between men and women has grown. Differences in pay based on sex are still larger than those based on race or national origin—particularly for working class women. As the environment changes and more support becomes available, however, they and their advocates will be able to press a large agenda of essential reforms at every level of American society. We know that early school tracking practices have negative effects on poor children (Persell, 1977). These are especially serious for lower-class girls who for years have been placed in courses in homemaking skills. For working women with little formal education engaged in service jobs, the difference between their salaries and those of men in the same work was 63 percent. For sales workers it was 57 percent and for assembly-line workers 41 percent. For women with five or more years of college the average gap between their salaries and men's (of equal education) was 35 percent. For women with four years of high school it was 42 percent and increased as the level of education attainment was lowered (Seifer, 1973).

Because few working women are members of unions (only one in seven)

388 • Carman St. John Hunter and David Harman

and because only one out of five union members is a woman, unions do not offer them much protection. Both external factors and internal psychological pressures keep women from challenging the status quo, although change may result from the current efforts of caucuses of women union members.

Working class women suffer disproportionately from economic marginality, unsatisfying jobs, poor working conditions, inadequate social and municipal services, deteriorating neighborhoods, and alienation from the American mainstream. Limited education and limited experience outside the home have held these women back. The situation is particularly difficult for those women who are the sole support for their families. Heretofore they have lacked any sense that the women's movement spoke for them. Although heightened consciousness from the largely middle-class women's movement has stimulated activity among women for whom new educational, job-training, and skill-development opportunities have long been available, the leadership potential of working class women has been systematically overlooked.

Beyond the Statistics

The statistical information, unreliable and limited though it is, bears out our basic thesis: People who lack basic or functional literacy skills are surprisingly large in number and also suffer from other major social and economic disadvantages.

Other information, perhaps more helpful, about the characteristics shared by most of the educationally impaired has appeared in sociological and anthropological studies, some in oral histories. These writings bring us closer to a gut understanding of what a low level of literacy may mean in people's lives.

The Information Poor in America gives us a portrait of the disadvantaged American "in his natural information habitat. . . . The prototypal disadvantaged American, . . . more than his average counterpart":

> Does not know which formal channels to tap in order to solve his problems, or what specific programs exist to respond to his needs;
> Watches many hours of television daily, seldom reads newspapers and magazine and never reads books;
> Does not see his problems as information needs;
> Is not a very active information seeker, even when he does undertake a search;
> May lean heavily on formal channels of information if it becomes apparent that the informal channels are inadequate and if his needs are strongly felt;
> Is locked into an informal information network that is deficient in the information that is ordinarily available to the rest of society. (Childers, 1975, pp. 42–43).

Jack Mezirow of Teachers College, Columbia University, has also added to our understanding of the multiple disadvantages of those who lack conventional or functional literacy skills. Mezirow speaks of "the future syndrome endemic to ghetto, barrio, and reservation—a continually reinforced conviction of failure and incompetence, bred by a grim history of frustrating school experiences and subsequent inability to support oneself and one's family, which becomes a self-fulfilling prophecy." His description of a 45-year-old black man evokes for us an image of what such a life is really like:

> eking out a living at an unstable succession of menial and arduous jobs, poor, haunted by failure, numbed with self-doubt, without study skills, and unable to read. Furthermore, going back to school seems an endless uphill struggle. Just learning the three R's means years of weary plugging, night after night, month after month. And then what? What will an eighth-grade education get you? Into the ninth grade is about all (Mezirow, et al., 1975, pp. 37–38).

One attempt to describe "the disadvantaged adult" that many educators found helpful in explaining their own experiences was the work of the Appalachian Adult Education Center (AAEC). After seven years of intensive work with disadvantaged adults, whom they define as "those over 16 years of age, who are (1) out of school, with less than a high school diploma, and/or (2) with a family income below a poverty index," George Eyster and his colleagues at the AAEC identified four groups, each with special needs and requiring different approaches and different services. The four groups are based on individual characteristics; indeed, members of different groups are often found in the same family. Individuals also fluctuate between groups at different times in their lives, or as their circumstances change.

Persons in the first two groups are the easiest to reach. Group 1 consists of "secure" and "self-directed" persons who respond well to group activities as well as to individualized instruction and are open to recruitment through the media. Group 2 consists of persons less economically and personally secure—those with large families and seasonal jobs, who must often work overtime. They have suffered some of the consequences of undereducation and underemployment and yet are eager learners capable of quickly achieving specific goals they set for themselves to improve their daily lives. The major difficulty in extending services to persons in this group is time; it is impractical to set rigid hours for class instruction for them because they do not know when they will have to work or tend to family responsibilities.

The third and fourth groups require more specialized instruction. Persons in Group 3 have been only sporadically employed in low-paying, short-term jobs. If they are to be reached, they need individualized recruitment contacts and one-to-one instruction. Group 4 consists of those most in need of, yet least accessible to service. The AAEC calls them "the stationary poor." They, too, require one-to-one instruction. Only by intensive attention will they be reached by any educational program.

Finally, we must add a note of caution. Those of us who prepare studies about disadvantaged people run the risk of perpetuating stereotypes. We tend to simplify complex lives into cases to be analyzed, or problems that need solutions, or statistics to be studied. This tendency, and our inability to interpret with understanding the first-hand information that people give us about their aspirations and their lives, are serious blind spots. It may well be that we can obtain a truer picture, or at least a fuller understanding, from reading Oscar Lewis's *La*

Vida (1968), Lillian Breslow Rubin's *Worlds of Pain* (1976), Elliot Liebow's *Tally's Corner* (1967), or Susan Sheehan's *A Welfare Mother* (1976) than from pondering accumulated masses of statistics.

Summary

One fact emerges clearly from all the statistical information available, whether the measure is competency or school completion. Despite the universal free education available in this country since early in the century, despite the fact that more and more young people of all races and ethnic groups are completing high school, and despite the recent evidence that those who do complete high school are achieving "acceptable" levels of literacy, a disproportionately large section of our adult population—well over a third—still suffers some educational disadvantage (Fisher, 1978). Among these millions of adults in our society are the functionally illiterate. Their exact number is not known.

We conclude that the aggregate message of all the statistics is more important than their specific accuracy. A much larger proportion of the U.S. population than had until recently been known or assumed suffers serious disadvantage because of limited educational attainment. In this country persons with limited education are often the same persons who suffer from one or more of the other major social disadvantages—poverty, unemployment, racial or ethnic discrimination, social isolation. Inadequate education will probably be only one manifestation of their deprivation. The greater the number of those disadvantages, the more serious the suffering for members of our society in which one's worth is judged by one's job, possessions, and credentials.

26.
Realities of Illiteracy

Anne Eberle
Sandra Robinson

It is not the myths alone that make life a steeple-chase for illiterate adults. The myths simply compound the impressive obstacles posed by the inability to read, write, and figure. The illiterate is surrounded with assumptions that reduce rather than increase her/his capacity to make choices that could result in changing the situation. The effects of illiteracy itself are impressive enough: the fear generated by the illiterate's continual vulnerability as (s)he moves through a world where others understand and act on the written word while (s)he cannot, and lack of control forced on anyone who must depend on others in every aspect of his or her life.

> *Lou:* It's a frightening feeling not to be able to . . . ah not to be able, well for example, if something is written on the screen, a movie screen or a television screen, and you can't read it, you don't know what's going on. You just never know what's going on unless someone tells you. It's a scary feeling, really. You just feel so backward, so out of place a lot of times. ("What If You Couldn't Read?," 1978, p. 1)

The fear is real. The consequences of the illiterate's helplessness can involve being and feeling lost, literally and perhaps otherwise.

> *Lem:* I never learned to read. The hardest thing about it is I've been places where I didn't know where I was. If you don't know where you are, and you can't read something, you're lost. It sure ain't fun to be lost. I never told anybody I couldn't read. They knew anyway. When I went to court or something and they asked me to fill something out, I'd have to tell them I can't do it. Have to tell them my story. (Cole, 1976, p. 246)

There is always the high potential for that gut-level loss of control which in some form haunts us all.

From *The Adult Illiterate Speaks Out: Personal Perspectives on Learning to Read and Write*. Washington, D.C.: U.S. Department of Education, 1980.

Annabelle: Once, I got stuck, and I had to fill out some papers, and nobody was with me. I was by myself and I just told the guy, "Gee, I can't do it," and he said, "I can't do it for you, you'll have to do it yourself," and I said, "I can't." Then I broke down, crying. Really, it bothered me, and I was so nervous over it. (Cole, 1976, p. 189)

The same student talks about dependence, here for transportation, but a heavier burden because it characterizes so many relationships for illiterate adults, so many situations in which they really have no options.

Annabelle: It makes it harder when you don't have a license. I could use it. There have been more times if I had a license, I could use it. You keep depending onto somebody to take you here or depend on somebody to go somewhere or something like that, and you feel like they could be doing something else. Or it ends up they feel sorry for you. Really, sometimes they want to do it, but not all the time. They got their own families, they have their own life to live. When you have to depend on somebody all the time, to doing something like that for you, it makes it harder for them, it makes it harder for you. I like to try to do things for myself if I can, and if I can't, why, I depend on somebody. (Cole, 1976, p. 191)

Lou talks about his feelings faced with this kind of dependence on others. His language reveals the fear of being "used" or manipulated that so many illiterates express in different ways. Some kinds of dependence can be healthy, others destructive. But the illiterate does not have a choice in the matter: if the landlord claims the lease says he can evict you if your baby cries, you have to believe him. Or the consequences of asserting some kind of choice may be too costly: if the landlord threatens to evict you under terms in your lease and you have to admit you cannot read in the course of maneuvering for time to get someone else to read the lease for you, your helplessness in that relationship is immediately projected into the indefinite future.

Lou: You know, when you depend on another person it's so . . . always find your whole life seems to depend on somebody else, what they do for you, what they . . . how they use it. And you don't feel like you accomplish anything for anybody, not even yourself. ("What If You Couldn't Read?," 1978, pp. 15–16)

For most illiterates, whatever their school experience was, they have a keen recollection of its particulars and a sense of its generic relationship to their situation as adults. Whatever did or did not happen in school has had a radical effect on the rest of their lives, and at some level they know it.

Rafer: I was a real terror when I started school. I went in there and had a hard time with it, and didn't really understand what was going on. All it seemed to me like was, you know, these people here were making me do something that I didn't want to do, and it seemed like a lot of work. I didn't want to do it, and I was having a hard time doing it when I did try doing it, so I just got mad and I didn't do anything. (Cole, 1976, p. 98)

The words "real terror," "hard time with it," "didn't want to," "just got mad" evoke the conflict between a kid and a system that so many illiterates remember in different ways. The system is designed for Most Children, but the Rafers and Annabelles and Ginnys who do not fit either have to be made to fit or find their own way of surviving until they are 16 and can legally abandon the conflict, often to the relief of school personnel who have found their presence "disruptive."

> *Angus:* I came out of school . . . when I was 16. I went to _____ to school, and the village of _____ said I was wasting their money to go to their school, so my ma says, "Okay," and she brought me out of school. They had their meetings, and everything . . . I can't think now what they call them, when the directors meet. They had a meeting about me! And they said I was wasting their school paper, and I was wasting their pencils. (Cole, 1976, p. 169)

Annabelle, even as a kid in primary school, sensed that the teacher, the school, wanted to work with winners.

> *Annabelle* (in school, where she had a speech impediment, after her palate was surgically removed): I was trying to talk all over and a lot words just bothered me to talk and it was hard and the teacher didn't want to take any attention. She didn't want to bother to find out what I'm saying. If she asked me something, and I tried to answer her the best way I could, she just didn't want to take any attention. She just didn't want to bother with me, and that was it. She says she got the rest, the other kids, to take care of, and she didn't want to take care of just one. She just wanted to work with the kids who can do things and that's it. And if anybody can't do it, well, that's too bad for them. (Cole, 1976, p. 193)

There is no particular need to flog the schools for these situations. In fact many schools, since the time of Annabelle's childhood, have vastly improved their capacity to respond effectively to the youngsters who do not fit an educational system designed for the majority. What is necessary is to perceive the attitudes, especially the self-image, engendered in adult illiterates by their school experiences. These enduring attitudes, almost more than the ability or inability to recognize the sound of "m," substantially define their ability *now*, at whatever age, to see themselves as potential learners again—not only as supplicants for education, but as capable of learning, of gaining skills, and of applying those skills in ways that will actually make a difference in their circumstances.

Angus was wasting the school's paper and pencils by his very presence. It may be that only one or two people felt this way and that others would have liked to help Angus more, but Angus's own certainty is that he was not worthy of the school's time, energy, and materials. Another nonreader, a woman in western Vermont, said that she had come to realize that she was doing wrong to take up the space in her small primary school and should leave so that someone better could have her place. She did leave.

She and Angus, in their separate places, go about trying to learn twenty and more years later what they were unworthy to learn as children because they did not grasp it quickly. It is as if a time machine spun them backwards until their present learning effort is but a day or two removed from that early failure. Despite all the skills they have gained since then for survival, parenting, and earning a living, as adult learners they step directly out of the school door through which they were briskly ushered and into the present struggle to learn. What they bring most instinctively to the present effort to gain literacy skills (and, eventually, literacy) is the feelings, the failures, and the inadequacy of those early losing battles. If they are to have access during this new learning process to the courage and confidence that all their gritty victories in the intervening years could provide for them, another person will be needed to continue to remind them of their competence.

The impact of illiteracy permeates the illiterate's present life in every aspect. Some come in the form of practical perplexities, frustrations, and anxiety about being "ripped off," shown up, made a fool of, and left helpless with no recourse.

> *Lou:* When I first started going out and meet people I had been to a place where I wanted to stop and I felt so tight and so worried about what was going to happen that I'd drive right by it and wouldn't stop, after driving fifteen or twenty miles to get there. Just wouldn't have the, uh, guts to stop. Afraid. Sometimes you just cannot face people. If you don't have the education that other people have you always, uh . . . well, feel like gettin' back somewhere and hidin'. ("What If You Couldn't Read?," 1978, p. 7)

The homely tasks that "everybody" who can read takes for granted become sources of frustration and perpetuate the feeling that one cannot do what "everybody" else can do. At first, that was essentially reading, but then it multiplied exponentially to encompass all the little activities that reading enables other people to do.

> *Freida:* I've never really read a book. Maybe someday I can. With recipes, I just look at them and I know what the words say. I wish sometimes I could understand them better. Like I had trouble canning this year. First time I've canned and I didn't understand it. But after awhile, I read it over and over, so I got it to come out right. Once in awhile, with recipes, I give up and get mad and put it to one side. Different things that I was trying to cook that didn't come out right, I'd throw them out. And I'd try them again. Mostly, I just remember how to cook things. But it would be nice to sit down and read a book. (Cole, 1976, pp. 120–21).

Being illiterate as a parent "matters," as Ginny says. It affects family relationships and respect. The effects of their parents' early failure to learn extends into the children's lifetime. This does not merely confine one's own life, but deprives the next generation of "something they should have."

> *Ginny:* The only real problem it brings up is reading to the boys. I can't read to them, and, of course, that's leaving them out of something they should have. It bothers you if you can't read, and if you can't read to your boys, it bothers you more. Oh, it matters, you believe it matters. I ordered all these books. The kids belong to a book club, they got them that way. They know I can't read because it

made me feel funny one day. Donny wanted me to read a book to him and Matthew, and I told Donny, I said, "I can't read." Well, he said, "Mommy, you sit down and I'll read it to you." Donny does fine on reading. I tried it one day reading from the pictures, and Donny looked at me and he said, "Mommy, that's not right." And he's only 5, so he knew I couldn't read from the pictures. (Cole, 1976, pp. 60–61)

It would be nice to think that a person could keep his or her illiteracy in one corner of life. That there would be some aspects of that life unaffected by it. But it does not work out.

Ernie: You know, it's funny, really. I've been married for 7 years. We got married in '68 and when I asked her to marry me. . . . It's hard, you know, you find somebody you love and you try, you know you got this problem with reading, and you know that you're going to have to provide for her, and how do you go about telling somebody that you want to marry that you can't read? Right? Man, it's like opening a bottle, putting a stick of dynamite in it, and hoping it don't go off. . . . Just the idear of telling somebody that I couldn't read. Hard to make it come out right. And then I found out she knew all about it. (Cole, 1976, pp. 45–46)

In one form or another, all illiterates live with that stick of dynamite in the bottle. For many, the most painful risk of explosion is in trying to get and keep a job. The illiterate who has developed skills that compensate for his/her inability to read and write well still has to endure the anguish connected with applying for the job. Some have stopped trying.

Lou: You find so many people who are out of work and don't go looking for a job. They seem to be able to work but never go. And everybody think, well, they're just lazy. They don't want to. They don't understand this fear that holds 'em back from being with the public, when they got a problem. ("What If You Couldn't Read?," 1978, p. 14)

Others, like Ernie, are prepared to take their self-respect in their hands and sweat it out with the application.

Ernie: As far as reading, I think the biggest hassle if you can't read is not working. If you're not working and you got to go out and try to find a job, well, what I do is go down and get an application. "Can I make these out later and drop them back?" And if they say, "No, you have to make them out here," well, I say, "I have a problem reading and I can't make it out." He says, "You can't make the application out?" I say, "No." "Well," he says, "well, we aren't hiring right now," or "I don't have time to make out the application with you," or something like this. And that was the story most of the time. It's a real hassle just going into a place and trying, just knowing that you are going to have to make out an application, hoping you can go in someplace and take it out and bring it back. (Cole, 1976, p. 46)

In many cases, the unwillingness of employers even to consider hiring anyone who does not read well (i.e., to help with the application in order to interview the applicant to determine whether (s)he has the skills needed for the job in question) seems related to the myth that those who cannot read well are probably incompetent in most other areas. In other cases, there will be reading and/or writing involved in a job that appears to require basically a manual skill, and the illiterate is left with the frustration of having a marketable skill rendered unmarketable because (s)he cannot handle the occasional need to deal with printed matter, requisition forms, supply catalogs, and the like.

> *Gordon:* I've lost a lot of jobs and I've been turned down for a lot of good jobs; jobs I could probably do as well as a college graduate, but I just didn't have the education. They're looking for education because for one reason, today, even if you're a janitor, there's still reading and writing involved. Like, if they leave a note saying, "Go to room so-and-so, this and that." You can't do it. You can't read it. You don't know. And they ain't going to hire somebody to run along and tell people what to do. (Cole, 1976, p. 123)

Gordon acknowledges that he misses out on some jobs that require him to be minimally literate. Eva has been caught in the whole credential circus. She has applied for work for which she believes she has the minimal skills required, but potential employers look only at how much time she served in school as an indicator of her potential as a productive employee. They ignore the fact that had she spent whatever number of years would make her worthy in their sight (8? 12?) she might never have been given an opportunity to learn the manual skills they expect on the job. From a radio interview with a woman student, in her early 30's, from Burlington, Vermont:

> *Interviewer:* So what do you do? Do you have a job besides just staying here?

> *Eva:* No, I don't work. What I do, I work around the home and that's all now. I tried jobs and all they see is—well, how far did you go in school? Sixth grade, fifth grade. Well, we'll get back to you. Never do hear from them. I don't know what you have to have any grades for to work, but the hell with it. ("Adult Literacy," 1979, p. 6)

"I don't know what you have to have any grades for to work," Eva declares. Indeed, at times it is difficult to perceive the relationship between the applicant's survival for a certain number of years of grade school and the skills actually required for a job being advertised. If there is no direct relationship, one may wonder whether the educational criterion is simply a convenient presorting device to narrow the field of applicants.

Illiterates rarely ask for special consideration; in fact, they tend, as Lou put it, to "feel like gettin' back to somewhere and hidin'." But they want to be considered for employment on the basis of their strengths, the skills they have, their willingness to work hard, their own integrity. As the job market tightens, Ph.D.'s apply for custodian's jobs, dozens or hundreds of applicants turn out for a routine, low-paying job simply because it's a job, and employers fall back on screening by educational credentials. Eva and many others finally drop out of the army of job seekers and say, "the hell with it."

Getting a chance to prove you can do the job is one major hurdle for many illiterates. Keeping the job, competing with literate co-workers, is another.

> *Gordon:* You have to work harder. Say like we was both hired to work on a job, and say like you had a nice education, and they see you doing things around, and right off you'd picked it up because you could read it, and somebody over there can't read it. But he's probably working three times harder to try and stay up with you, you know what I mean, not to have them say, "Well, that guy there is no good and you're all right." You have to prove everything you do. (Cole, 1976, p. 137)

> *Angus:* This is what was the difference between not knowing how to read and knowing how to read. I always put like that quite a bit extra into whatever I was doing. I always put extra effort into it because I figured, well, this guy beside of me, say he's got even a college degree, Like he was there for summer time help, and he walked around with his hands in his pockets, and didn't care. But to me, I had a family to support, and I had my future to look forward to. (Cole, 1976, pp. 160–61)

"You have to prove everything you do," Gordon says. You have to swim upstream against the myth that if you cannot read you probably are not as competent a worker as the college kid hired for the summer. You have to face your own apprehension that your literate co-workers know something that is going on that you do not know, and they will be in the right place at the right time for a promotion or even simply to avoid a personnel cut.

27.
The Adult Literacy Process as Cultural Action for Freedom *and* Education and Conscientização

Paulo Freire

"The Adult Literacy Process as Cultural Action for Freedom"

Every Educational Practice Implies a Concept of Man and the World

Experience teaches us not to assume that the obvious is clearly understood. So it is with the truism with which we begin: All educational practice implies a theoretical stance on the educator's part. This stance in turn implies—sometimes more, sometimes less explicitly—an interpretation of man and the world. It could not be otherwise. The process of men's orientation in the world involves not just the association of sense images, as for animals. It involves, above all, thought-language; that is, the possibility of the act of knowing through his praxis, by which man transforms reality. For man, this process of orientation in the world can be understood neither as a purely subjective event, not as an objective or mechanistic one, but only as an event in which subjectivity and objectivity are united. Orientation in the world, so understood, places the question of the purposes of action at the level of critical perception of reality.

From Freire, Paulo, "The Adult Literacy Process as Cultural Action for Freedom," *Harvard Educational Review*, 1970, 40, 205–12. Copyright © 1970 by the President and Fellows of Harvard College. All rights reserved.

From *Education: The Practice of Freedom*, by Paulo Freire. Copyright 1976 by Writers and Readers Publishing Cooperative.

EDITOR'S NOTE: Brazilian educator Paul Freire's work is as much a critique of traditional literacy instruction as it is an elaboration of a pedagogy that refuses to separate the acquisition of literacy from the acquisition of a critical perspective on culture. To introduce the reader to this work, therefore, we have provided two selections. The first outlines Freire's critical educational philosophy, while the second provides more specific details about his pedagogy. Readers interested in the latter topic may wish to examine the appendix to *Education: The Practice of Freedom*, where they will find a list of "generative words" and reproductions of the woodcut illustrations depicting Freire's ten "existential situations."

If, for animals, orientation in the world means adaptation to the world, for man it means humanizing the world by transforming it. For animals there is no historical sense, no options or values in their orientation in the world; for man there is both an historical and a value dimension. Men have the sense of "project," in contrast to the instinctive routines of animals.

The action of men without objectives, whether the objectives are right or wrong, mythical or demythologized, naive or critical, is not praxis, though it may be orientation in the world. And not being praxis, it is action ignorant both of its own process and of its aim. The interrelation of the awareness of aim and of process is the basis for planning action, which implies methods, objectives, and value options.

Teaching adults to read and write must be seen, analyzed, and understood in this way. The critical analyst will discover in the methods and texts used by educators and students practical value options which betray a philosophy of man, well or poorly outlined, coherent or incoherent. Only someone with a mechanistic mentality, which Marx would call "grossly materialistic," could reduce adult literacy learning to a purely technical action. Such a naive approach would be incapable of perceiving that technique itself as an instrument of men in their orientation in the world is not neutral.

We shall try, however, to prove by analysis the self-evidence of our statement. Let us consider the case of primers used as the basic texts for teaching adults to read and write. Let us further propose two distinct types: a poorly done primer and a good one, according to the genre's own criteria. Let us even suppose that the author of the good primer based the selection of its generative words[1] on a prior knowledge of which words have the greatest resonance for the learner (a practice not commonly found, though it does exist).

Doubtlessly, such an author is already far beyond the colleague who composes his primer with words he himself chooses in his own library. Both authors, however, are identical in a fundamental way. In each case they themselves decompose the given generative words and from the syllables create new words. With these words, in turn, the authors form simple sentences and, little by little, small stories, the so-called reading lessons.

Let us say that the author of the second primer, going one step further, suggests that the teachers who use it initiate discussions about one or another word, sentence, or text with their students.

Considering either of these hypothetical cases we may legitimately conclude that there is an implicit concept of man in the primer's method and content, whether it is recognized by the authors or not. This concept can be reconstructed from various angles. We begin with the fact, inherent in the idea and use of the primer, that it is the teacher who chooses the words and proposes them to the learner. Insofar as the primer is the mediating object between the teacher and students, and the students are to be "filled" with words the teachers have chosen, one can easily detect a first important dimension of the image of man which here begins to emerge. It is the profile of a man whose consciousness is "spatialized," and must be "filled" or "fed" in order to know. This same conception led Sartre, criticizing the notion that "to know is to eat," to exclaim: *"O philosophie alimentaire!"*[2]

This "digestive" concept of knowledge, so common in current educational practice, is found very clearly in the primer.[3] Illiterates are considered "undernourished," not in the literal sense in which many of them really are, but because they lack the "bread of the spirit." Consistent with the concept of knowledge as food, illiteracy is conceived of as a "poison herb," intoxicating and debilitating persons who cannot read or write. Thus, much is said about the "eradication" of illiteracy to cure the disease.[4] In this way, deprived of their character as linguistic signs constitutive of man's thought-language, words are transformed into mere "deposits of vocabulary"—the bread of the spirit which the illiterates are to "eat" and "digest."

This "nutritionist" view of knowledge perhaps also explains the humanitarian character of certain Latin American adult literacy campaigns. If millions of men are illiterate, "starving for letters," "thirsty for words," the word must be *brought* to them to save them from "hunger" and "thirst." The word, according to the naturalistic concept of consciousness implicit in the primer, must be "deposited," not born of the creative effort of the learners. As understood in this concept, man is a passive being, the object of the process of learning to read and write, and not its subject. As object his task is to "study" the so-called reading lessons, which in fact are almost completely alienating and alienated, having so little, if anything, to do with the student's socio-cultural reality.[5]

It would be a truly interesting study to analyze the reading texts being used in private or official adult literacy campaigns in rural and urban Latin America. It would not be unusual to find among such texts sentences and readings like the following random samples:[6]

> *A asa é da ave*—"The wing is of the bird."
> *Eva viu a uva*—"Eva saw the grape."
> *O galo canta*—"The cock crows."
> *O cachorro ladra*—"The dog barks."
> *Maria gosta dos animats*—"Mary likes animals."
> *João cuida das arvores*—"John takes care of the trees."
>
> *O pai de Carlinhos se chama Antonio. Carlinhos é um bom menino, bem comportado e estudioso*—"Charles's father's name is Antonio. Charles is a good, well-behaved, and studious boy."
>
> *Ada deu o dedo ao urubu? Duvido, Ada deu o dedo a arara. . . .*[7]
>
> *Se vocé trabalha com martelo e prego, tenha cuidado para nao furar o dedo.*—"If you hammer a nail, be careful not to smash your finger."[8]
>
> "Peter did not know how to read. Peter was ashamed. One day, Peter went to school and registered for a night course. Peter's teacher was very good. Peter knows how to read now. Look at Peter's face. [These lessons are generally illustrated.] Peter is smiling. He is a happy man. He already has a good job. Everyone ought to follow his example."

In saying that Peter is smiling because he knows how to read, that he is happy because he now has a good job, and that he is an example for all to to follow, the authors establish a relationship between knowing how to read and getting good jobs which, in fact, cannot be borne out. This naiveté reveals, at least, a failure to perceive the structure not only of illiteracy, but of social phenomena in general. Such an approach may admit that these phenomena exist, but it cannot perceive their relationship to the structure of the society in which they are found. It is as if these phenomena were mythical, above and beyond concrete situations, or the results of the intrinsic inferiority of a certain class of men. Unable to grasp contemporary illiteracy as a typical manifestation of the "culture of silence," directly related to underdeveloped structures, this approach cannot offer an objective, critical response to the challenge of illiteracy. Merely teaching men to read and write does not work miracles; if there are not enough jobs for men able to work, teaching more men to read and write will not create them.

One of these readers presents among its lessons the following two texts on consecutive pages without relating them. The first is about May 1st, the Labor Day holiday, on which workers commemorate their struggles. It does not say how or where these are commemorated, or what the nature of the historical conflict was. The main theme of the second lesson is *holidays*. It says that "on these days people ought to go to the beach to swim and sunbathe . . ." Therefore, if May 1st is a holiday, and if on holidays people should go to the beach, the conclusion is that the workers should go swimming on Labor Day, instead of meeting with their unions in the public squares to discuss their problems.

Analysis of these texts reveal, then, a simplistic vision of men, of their world, of the relationship between the two, and of the literacy process which unfolds in that world.

A asa é da ave, Eva viu a uva, o galo canta, and *o cachorro late,* are linguistic contexts which, when mechanically memorized and repeated, are deprived of their authentic dimension as thought-language in dynamic interplay with reality. Thus impoverished, they are not authentic expressions of the world.

Their authors do not recognize in the poor classes the ability to know and even create the texts which would express their own thought-language at the level of their perception of the world. The authors repeat with the texts what they do with the words, i.e., they introduce them into the learners' consciousness as if it were empty space—once more, the "digestive" concept of knowledge.

Still more, the a-structural perception of illiteracy revealed in these texts exposes the other false view of illiterates as marginal men.[9] Those who consider them marginal must, nevertheless, recognize the existence of a reality to which they are marginal—not only physical space, but historical, social, cultural, and economic realities—i.e., the structural dimension of reality. In this way, illiterates have to be recognized as beings "outside of," "marginal to" something, since it is impossible to be marginal to nothing. But being "outside of" or "marginal to" necessarily implies a movement of the one said to be marginal from the center, where he was, to the periphery. This movement, which is an action, presupposes in turn not only an agent but also his reasons. Admitting the existence of men "outside of" or "marginal to" structural reality, it seems legitimate to ask: Who is the author of this movement from the center of the structure to its margins? Do so-called marginal men, among them the illiterates, make the decision to move out to the periphery of society? If so, marginality is an option with all that it involves: hunger, sickness, rickets, pain, mental deficiencies, living death, crime, promiscuity, despair, the impossibility of being. In fact, however, it is difficult to accept that 40% of Brazil's population, almost 90% of Haiti's, 60% of Bolivia's, about 40% of Bolivia's, about 40% of Peru's, more than 30% of Mexico's and Venezuela's, and about 70% of Guatemala's would have made the tragic *choice* of their own marginality as illiterates.[10] If, then, marginality is not by choice, marginal man has been expelled from and kept outside of the social system and is therefore the object of violence.

In fact, however, the social structure as a whole does not "expel," nor is marginal man a "being outside of." He is, on the contrary, a "being inside of," within the social structure, and in a dependent relationship to those whom we call falsely autonomous beings, inauthentic beings-for-themselves.

A less rigorous approach, one more simplistic, less critical, more technicist, would say that it was unnecessary to reflect about what it would consider unimportant questions such as illiteracy and teaching adults to read and write. Such an approach might even add that the discussion of the concept of marginality is an unnecessary academic exercise. In fact, however, it is not so. In accepting the illiterate as a person who exists on the fringe of society, we are led to envision him as a sort of "sick man," for whom literacy would be the "medicine" to cure him, enabling him to "return" to the "healthy" structure from which he has become separated. Educators would be benevolent counsellors, scouring the outskirts of the city for the stubborn illiterates, runaways from the good life, to restore them to the forsaken bosom of happiness by giving them the gift of the word.

In the light of such a concept—unfortunately, all too widespread—literacy programs can never be efforts toward freedom; they will never question the very reality which deprives men of the right to speak up—not only illiterates, but all those who are treated as objects in a dependent relationship. These men, illiterate or not, are, in fact, not marginal. What we said before bears repeating: They are not "beings outside of"; they are "beings for another." Therefore the solution to their problem is not to become "beings inside of," but men freeing themselves; for, in reality, they are not marginal to the structure, but oppressed men within it. Alienated men, they cannot overcome their dependency by "incorporation" into the very structure responsible for their dependency. There is no other road to humanization—theirs as well as everyone else's—but authentic transformation of the dehumanizing structure.

From this last point of view, the illiterate is no longer a person living on the fringe of society, a marginal man, but rather a representative of the dominated strata of society, in conscious or unconscious opposition to those who, in the same structure, treat him as a thing. Thus, also, teaching men to read and write is no longer an inconsequential matter of *ba, be, bi, bo, bu,* or memorizing an alienated word, but a difficult apprenticeship in naming the world.

In the first hypothesis, interpreting illiterates as men marginal to society, the literacy process reinforces the mythification of reality by keeping it opaque and by dulling the "empty consciousness" of the learner with innumerable alienating words and phrases. By contrast, in the second hypothesis—interpreting illiterates as men oppressed within the system—the literacy process, as cultural action for freedom, is an act of knowing in which the learner assumes the role of knowing subject in dialogue with the educator. For this very reason, it is a courageous endeavor to demythologize reality, a process through which men who had previously been submerged in reality begin to emerge in order to re-insert themselves into it with critical awareness.

Therefore the educator must strive for an ever greater clarity as to what, at times without his conscious knowledge, illumines the path of his action. Only in this way will he truly be able to assume the role of one of the subjects of this action and remain consistent in the process.

From *Education and Conscientização*

Whoever enters into dialogue does so with someone about something; and that something ought to constitute the new content of our proposed education. We felt that even before teaching the illiterate to read, we could help him to overcome his magic or naïve understanding and to develop an increasingly critical understanding. Toward this end, the first dimension of our new program content would be the anthropological concept of culture—that is, the distinction between the world of nature and the world of culture; the active role of men *in* and *with* their reality; the role of mediation which nature plays in relationships and communication among men; culture as the addition made by men to a world they did not make; culture as the result of men's labor, of their efforts to create and re-create; the transcendental meaning of human relationships; the humanist dimension of culture; culture as a systematic acquisition of human experience (but as creative assimilation, not as information-storing); the democratization of culture; the learning of reading and writing as a key to the world of written communication. In short, the role of man as Subject in the world and with the world.

From that point of departure, the illiterate would begin to effect a change in his former attitudes, by discovering himself to be a maker of the world of culture, by discovering that he, as well as the literate person, has a creative and re-creative impulse. He would discover that culture is just as much a clay doll made by artists who are his peers as it is the work of a great sculptor, a great painter, a great mystic, or a great philosopher; that culture is the poetry of lettered poets and also the poetry of his own popular songs—that culture is all human creation.

To introduce the concept of culture, first we "broke down" this concept into its fundamental aspects. Then, on the basis of this breakdown, we "codified" (i.e., represented visually) ten existential situations. Each representation contained a number of elements to be "decoded" by the group participants, with the help of the coordinator. Francisco Brenand, one of the greatest contemporary Brazilian artists, painted these codifications, perfectly integrating education and art.

It is remarkable to see with what enthusiasm these illiterates engage in debate and with what curiosity they respond to questions implicit in the codifications. In the words of Odilon Ribeiro Coutinho, these "detemporalized men begin to integrate themselves in time." As the dialogue intensifies, a "current" is established among the participants, dynamic to the degree that the content of the codifications corresponds to the existential reality of the groups.

Many participants during these debates affirm happily and self-confidently that they are not being shown "anything new, just remembering." "I make shoes," said one, "and now I see that I am worth as much as the Ph.D. who writes books."

"Tomorrow," said a street-sweeper in Brasília, "I'm going to go to work with my head high." He had discovered the value of his person. "I know now that I am cultured," an elderly peasant said emphatically. And when he was asked how it was that now he knew himself to be cultured, he answered with the same emphasis, "Because I work, and working, I transform the world."[11]

Once the group has perceived the distinction between the two worlds—nature and culture—and recognized man's role in each, the coordinator presents situations focusing on or expanding other aspects of culture.

The participants go on to discuss culture as a systematic acquisition of human experience, and to discover that in a lettered culture this acquisition is not limited to oral transmission, as is the case in unlettered cultures which lack graphic signs. They conclude by debating the democratization of culture, which opens the perspective of acquiring literacy.

All these discussions are critical, stimulating, and highly motivating. The illiterate perceives critically that it is necessary to learn to read and write, and prepares himself to become the agent of this learning.

To acquire literacy is more than to psychologically and mechanically dominate reading and writing techniques. It is to dominate these techniques in terms of consciousness; to understand what one reads and to write what one understands; it is to *communicate* graphically. Acquiring literacy does not involve memorizing sentences, words, or syllables—lifeless objects unconnected to an existential universe—but rather an attitude of creation and re-creation, a self-transformation producing a stance of intervention in one's context.

Thus the educator's role is fundamentally to enter into dialogue with the illiterate about concrete situations and simply to offer him the instruments with which he can teach himself to read and write. This teaching cannot be done from the top down, but only from the inside out, by the illiterate himself, with the collaboration of the educator. That is why we searched for a method which would be the instrument of the learner as well as of the educator, and which, in the lucid observation of a young Brazilian sociologist,[12] "would identify learning *content* with the learning *process*."

Hence, our mistrust in primers,[13] which set up a certain group of graphic signs as a gift and cast the illiterate in the role of the *object* rather than the *Subject* of his learning. Primers, even when they try to avoid this pitfall, end by *donating* to the illiterate words and sentences which really should result from his own creative effort. We opted instead for the use of "generative words," those whose syllabic elements offer, through re-combination, the creation of new words. Teaching men how to read and write a syllabic language like Portuguese means showing them how to grasp critically the way its words are formed, so that they themselves can carry out the creative play of combinations. Fifteen or eighteen words seemed sufficient to present the basic phonemes of the Portuguese language. The seventeen generative words used in the State of Rio are presented in the Appendix.

The program is elaborated in several phases:

Phase 1. Researching the vocabulary of the groups with which one is working. This research is carried out during informal encounters with the inhabitants of the area. One selects not only the words most weighted with existential meaning (and thus the greatest emotional content), but also typical sayings, as well as words and expressions linked to the experience of the groups in which the researcher participates. These interviews reveal longings, frustrations, disbeliefs, hopes, and an impetus to participate. During this initial phase the team of educators form rewarding relationships and discover often unsuspected exuberance and beauty in the people's language.

The archives of the Service of Cultural Extension of the University of Recife contain vocabulary studies of rural and urban areas in the Northeast and in southern Brazil full of such examples as the following:

"The month of January in Angicos," said a man from the backlands of Rio Grande do Norte, "is a hard one to live through, because January is a tough guy who makes us suffer." (*Janeiro em Angicos é duro de se viver, porque janeiro é cabra danado para judiar de nós.*)

"I want to learn to read and write," said an illiterate from Recife, "so that I can stop being the shadow of other people."

A man from Florianópolis: "The people have an answer."

Another, in an injured tone: "I am not angry (*não tenho paixão*) at being poor, but at not knowing how to read."

"I have the school of the world," said an illiterate from the southern part of the country, which led Professor Jomard de Brito to ask in an essay, "What can one presume to 'teach' an adult who affirms 'I have the school of the world'?"[14]

"I want to learn to read and to write so I can change the world," said an illiterate from São Paulo, from whom *to know* quite correctly meant *to intervene* in his reality.

"The people put a screw in their heads," said another in somewhat esoteric language. And when he was asked what he meant, he replied in terms revealing the phenomenon of popular emergence: "That is what explains that you, Professor, have come to talk with me, the people."

Such affirmations merit interpretation by specialists, to produce a more efficient instrument for the educator's action.[15] The generative words to be used in the program should emerge from this field vocabulary research, not from the educator's personal inspiration, no matter how proficiently he might construct a list.

Phase 2. Selection of the generative words from the vocabulary which was studied. The following criteria should govern their selection:

a) phonemic richness;

b) phonetic difficulty (the words chosen should correspond to the phonetic difficulties of the language, placed in a sequence moving gradually from words to less of those of greater difficulty);

c) pragmatic tone, which implies a greater engagement of a word in a given social, cultural and political reality

Professor Jarbas Maciel has commented that "these criteria are contained in the semeiotic criterion: the best generative word is that which combines the greatest possible 'percentage' of the syntactic criteria (phonemic richness, degree of complex phonetic difficulty, 'manipulability' of the groups of signs, the syllables, etc.), the semantic criteria (greater or lesser 'intensity' of the link between the word and the thing it designates), the greater or lesser correspondence between the word and the pragmatic thing designated, the greater or lesser quality of *conscientização* which the word potentially carries, or the grouping of sociocultural reactions which the word generates in the person or group using it."[16]

Phase 3. The creation of the "codifications": the representation of typical existential situations of the group with which one is working. These representations function as challenges, as coded situation-problems containing elements to be decoded by the groups with the collaboration of the coordinator. Discussion of these codifications will lead the groups toward a more critical consciousness at the same time that they begin to learn to read and write. The codifications represent familiar local situations—which, however, open perspectives for the analysis of regional and national problems. The generative words are set into the codifications, graduated according to their phonetic difficulty. One generative word may embody the entire situation, or it may refer to only one of the elements of the situation.

Phase 4. The elaboration of agendas, which should serve as mere aids to the coordinators, never as rigid schedules to be obeyed.

Phase 5. The preparation of cards with the breakdown of the phonemic families which correspond to the generative words.

A major problem in setting up the program is instructing the teams of coordinators. Teaching the purely technical aspect of the procedure is not difficult; the difficulty lies rather in the creation of a new attitude—that of dialogue, so absent in our own upbringing and education. The coordinators must be converted to dialogue in order to carry out education rather than domestication. Dialogue is an I-Thou relationship, and thus necessarily a relationship between two Subjects. Each time the "thou" is changed into an object, an "it," dialogue is subverted and education is changed to deformation. The period of instruction must be followed by dialogical supervision, to avoid the temptation of anti-dialogue on the part of the coordinators.

Once the material has been prepared in the form of slides, filmstrips, or posters, once the teams of coordinators and supervisors have been instructed in all aspects of the method and have been given their agendas, the program itself can begin. It functions in the following manner:

The codified situation is projected, together with the first generative word, which graphically represents the oral expression of the object perceived. Debate about its implications follows.

Only after the group, with the collaboration of the coordinator, has exhausted the analysis (decoding) of the situation, does the coordinator call attention to the generative word, encouraging the participants to visualize (not memorize) it. Once the word has been visualized, and the semantic link established between the word and the object to which it refers, the word is presented alone on another slide (or poster or photogram) without the object it names. Then the same word is separated into syllables, which the illiterate usually identifies as "pieces." Once the "pieces" are recognized, the coordinator presents visually the phonemic families which compose the word, first in isolation and then together, to arrive at the recognition of the vowels. The card presenting the phonemic families has been called the "discovery card."[17] Using this card to reach a synthesis, men discover the mechanism of word formation through phonemic combinations in a syllabic language like Portuguese. By appropriating this mechanism critically (not learning it by rote), they themselves can begin to produce a system of graphic signs. They can begin, with surprising ease, to create words with the phonemic combinations offered by the breakdown of a trisyllabic word, on the first day of the program.[18]

For example, let us take the *tijolo* (brick) as the first generative word, placed in a "situation" of construction work. After discussing the situation in all its possible aspects, the semantic link between the word and the object it names is established. Once the word has been noted within the situation, it is presented without the object: *tijolo*.

Afterwards: *ti-jo-lo*. By moving immediately to present the "pieces" visually, we initiate the recognition of phonemic families. Beginning with the first syllable, *ti*, the group is motivated to learn the whole phonemic family resulting from the combination of the initial consonant with the other vowels. The group then learns the second family through the visual presentation of *jo*, and finally arrives at the third family.

When the phonemic family is projected, the group at first recognizes only the syllable of the word which has been shown:

(ta-te-*ti*-to-tu), (ja-je-ji-*jo*-ju), (la-le-li-*lo*-lu)

When the participants recognize *ti*, from the generative word *tijolo*, it is proposed that they compare it with the other syllables; whereupon they discover that while all the syllables begin the same, they end differently. Thus, they cannot all be called *ti*.

The same procedure is followed with the syllables *jo* and *lo* and their families. After learning each phonemic family, the group practices reading the new syllables.

The most important moment arises when the three families are presented together:

ta-te-ti-to-tu
ja-je-ji-jo-ju   THE DISCOVERY CARD
la-le-li-lo-lu

After one horizontal and one vertical reading to grasp the vocal sounds, the group (*not* the coordinator) begins to carry out oral synthesis. One by one, they all begin to "make" words with the combinations available:[19]

tatu (armadillo), *luta* (struggle), *lajota* (small flagstone), *loja* (store), *jato* (jet), *juta* (jute), *lote* (lot), *lula* (squid), *tela* (screen), etc. There are even some participants who take a vowel from one of the syllables, link it to another syllable, and add a third, thus forming a word. For example, they take the *i* from li, join it to *le* and add *te: leite* (milk).

There are others, like an illiterate from Brasília, who on the first night he began his literacy program said, *"tu já lê"* ("you already read").[20]

The oral exercises involve not only learning, but recognition (without which there is no true learning). Once these are completed, the participants begin—on that same first evening—to write. On the following day they bring from home as many words as they were able to make with the combinations of the phonemes they learned. It doesn't matter if they bring combinations which are not actual words—what does matter is the discovery of the mechanism of phonemic combinations.

The group itself, with the help of the educator (*not* the educator with the help of the group), should test the words thus created. A group in the state of Rio Grande do Norte called those combinations which were actual words "thinking words" and those which were not, "dead words."

Not infrequently, after assimilating the phonemic mechanism by using the "discovery card," participants would write words with complex phonemes (*tra, nha*, etc.), which had not yet been presented to them. In one of the Culture Circles in Angicos, Rio Grande do Norte, on the fifth day of discussion, in which simple phonemes were being shown, one of the participants went to the blackboard to write (as he said) "a thinking word." He wrote: *"a povo vai resouver os poblemas do Brasil votando conciente"*[21] ("the people will solve the problems of Brazil by informed voting"). In such cases, the group discussed the text, debating its significance in the context of their reality.

How can one explain the fact that a man who was illiterate several days earlier could write words with complex phonemes before he had even studied them? Once he had dominated the mechanism of phonemic combinations, he attempted—and managed—to express himself graphically, in the way he spoke.[22]

I wish to emphasize that in educating adults, to avoid a rote, mechanical process one must make it possible for them to achieve critical consciousness so that they can teach themselves to read and write.

As an active educational method helps a person to become consciously aware of his context and his condition as a human being as Subject, it will become an instrument of choice. At that point he will become politicized. When an ex-illiterate of Angicos, speaking before President João Goulart and the presidential staff,[23] declared that he was no longer part of the *mass*, but one of the *people*, he had done more than utter a mere phrase; he had made a conscious option. He had chosen decisional participation, which belongs to the people, and had renounced the emotional resignation of the masses. He had become political.

The National Literacy Program of the Ministry of Education and Culture, which I coordinated, planned to extend and strengthen this education work throughout Brazil. Obviously we could not confine that work to a literacy program, even one which was critical rather than mechanical. With the same spirit of a pedagogy of communication, we were therefore planning a post-literacy stage which would vary only as to curriculum. If the National Literacy Program had not been terminated by the military coup, in 1964 there would have been more than 20,000 culture circles functioning throughout the country. In these, we planned to investigate the themes of the Brazilian people. These themes would be analyzed by specialists and broken down into learning units, as we had done with the concept of culture and with the coded situations linked to the generative words. We would prepare filmstrips with these breakdowns as well as simplified texts with references to the original texts. By gathering this thematic material, we could have offered a substantial post-literacy program. Further, by making a catalog of thematic breakdowns and bibliographic references available to high schools and colleges, we could widen the sphere of the program and help identify our schools with our reality.

At the same time, we began to prepare material with which we could carry out concretely an education that would encourage what Aldous Huxley has called the "art of dissociating ideas"[24] as an antidote to the domesticating power of propaganda.[25] We planned filmstrips, for use in the literacy phase, presenting propaganda—from advertising commercials to ideological indoctrination—as a "problem-situation" for discussion.

For example, as men through discussion begin to perceive the deceit in a cigarette advertisement featuring a beautiful, smiling woman in a bikini (i.e., the fact that she, her smile, her beauty, and her bikini have nothing at all to do with the cigarette), they begin to discover the difference between education and propaganda. At the same time, they are preparing themselves to discuss and perceive the same deceit in ideological or political propaganda,[26] they are arming themselves to "dissociate ideas." In fact, this has always seemed to me to be the way to defend democracy, not a way to subvert it.

One subverts democracy (even though one does this in the name of democracy) by making it irrational; by making it rigid in order "to defend it against totalitarian rigidity"; by making it hateful, when it can only develop in a context of love and respect for persons; by closing it, when it only lives in openness; by nourishing it with fear when it must be courageous; by making it an instrument of the powerful in the oppression of the weak; by militarizing it against the people; by alienating a nation in the name of democracy.

One defends democracy by leading it to the state Mannheim calls "militant democracy"—a democracy which does not fear the people, which suppresses privilege, which can plan without becoming rigid, which defends itself without hate, which is nourished by a critical spirit rather than irrationality.

28.
The Nicaraguan National Literacy Crusade of 1980

Robert F. Arnove

Perhaps the single most impressive basic literacy campaign has been taking place in Nicaragua under the banner of the *Cruzada Nacional de Alfabetización* (CNA, Nicaraguan National Literacy Crusade of 1980). Mounted during the first year of a revolutionary regime, the campaign reduced the illiteracy rate from 50.2% of the population ten years of age and older to approximately 23% in five months and to 15% in nine months. This all-out attack on illiteracy occurred in a country devastated by a protracted civil war, with many of the youths killed or maimed, with a national economy in ruins, and with a per-capita foreign debt among the highest in the world.

The description of the Nicaraguan crusade that follows is based on my 16-day visit to that country during July and August of 1980, when the literacy campaign was in its final stages. I met with officials of the Ministry of Education and the CNA on several occasions, and I visited literacy projects, principally in Managua and the Department of Esteli. In addition, I visited education projects in and around Leon and Jinotepe. Although I have worked for some seven years as an educator and researcher in various Latin American nations (including a two-week tour of Cuba in 1977), I came away from my Nicaraguan visit surprised and impressed by the educational accomplishments of an impoverished country in the first years following a revolution.

Scope of the Campaign

The extent and rate of the mass mobilization were unprecedented. To reduce the illiteracy rate from 50% to 15% within a period of nine months meant that nearly every person who knew how to read and write had to teach those who did not; moreover, as adult learners gained minimal literacy skills, they too had to help those who lagged behind.

From *Phi Delta Kappan* 62(1980–81): 702–706. Copyright 1980 by Robert F. Arnove. Reprinted by permission of the author.

Wherever I went—the most remote rural areas, the low-income neighborhoods surrounding the cities, the suburbs, or the inner cities themselves—people were teaching and learning. They were learning in barns while chickens and pigs, chased by children, scurried about; on front porches; in the living rooms of adobe huts, while babies slept in mothers' arms; in the sitting rooms of luxurious houses; in the back sections of grocery stores; and in churches, schools, factories, and barber shops. In what was once downtown Managua, literacy classes were taking place in buildings first gutted by the 1972 earthquake and then again by the civil war. In the countryside classes were held nightly in rooms illuminated by gas lamps (some fifty-thousand donated by Swedish labor unions). Where electricity was available, the people studied by the light of solitary sixty-watt bulbs. In the urban and semi-urban areas, people who worked all day in offices, factories, and commercial centers taught in the early hours of the evening before returning home to eat. Many of these teachers were teenagers. In the rural areas, farmers who worked all day in the fields studied for hours in the evening; hands that had skillfully guided a plow now awkwardly guided a fragile pencil to write the first basic words of the primer. In the low-income neighborhoods of the towns and cities, virtually every second or third dwelling housed a literacy class in action. In the entire country there were some sixty-thousand Sandinista[1] Literacy Units (*Unidades Sandinista de Alfabetización*, or UAS); these literacy units often consisted of no more than a table, a few chairs or benches, an oilcloth on which to write with chalk, and, posted on walls, swatches of butcher paper showing letters of the alphabet and simple words.

With such mass mobilization—with everyone studying—adults were more willing to face the public embarrassment of attempting to write their names on a blackboard. The universal participation of people of all ages made it possible for adults more than sixty years of age to learn from youngsters twelve and thirteen years of age. And they did learn. Often middle-aged people, who read for their teenage literacy workers without hesitation, remained mute before an older teacher/supervisor visiting the literacy unit.

The imagery and vocabulary of struggle and a national war loomed large in the symbolism of the CNA. Just as six guerrilla armies victoriously converged in the wake of Somoza's flight from Nicaragua, so too, on 24 March 1980, six armies left Managua to wage war on illiteracy. The six national fronts of the People's Literacy Army were composed of some sixty-five thousand *brigadistas* (literacy workers), mostly high school students, who were to live in the rural areas of the country to work with, learn from, and teach the largely illiterate peasantry. The six fronts were divided into "brigades" at the municipal level, and the brigades in turn were divided into "columns" at the hamlet level. The columns were made up of four "squadrons" of thirty *brigadistas* each, and each squadron was age- and sex-grouped to insure homogeneity.

In the cities, approximately thirty-five thousand People's Literacy Teachers waged a parallel war effort. These teachers, drawn from the ranks of factory and office workers, professionals, housewives, and high school and university students, taught after work or during their spare time. The typical pattern was two to three hours of instruction a day, Monday through Saturday. Teachers and university-level education students were mobilized to supervise these literacy teachers, to provide inservice instruction, and to assist in developing educational materials.

Although no one was officially required or compelled to teach or become a *brigadista*, more than 225,000 literate adults volunteered to participate in the CNA. This figure represents more than 30% of the literate population aged ten and above.

A National Coordinating Commission was established under the auspices of the Ministry of Education to determine broad policy for deploying, supporting, and protecting the *brigadistas*. The commission consisted of twenty-four ministerial, political, military, educational, cultural, religious, and mass organizations. Parallel coordinating commissions for the CNA were established at departmental and municipal levels.

Literacy workers had to be transported to the remotest corners of Nicaragua, often inaccessible by road and even by four-wheel vehicles; they had to be housed, fed, and safeguarded. The dangers they were exposed to in the countryside reflected not only the ravages of underdevelopment—the scarcity of food and water and the scourge of diseases such as dysentery and malaria—but the imminent threat of attacks by ex-guardsmen who had fled to neighboring Honduras and sometimes slipped across the border to terrorize and murder *brigadistas*, who symbolized the revolutionary changes occurring in Nicaragua. In case of illness or injury, emergency medical services were available; and a permanent communications network was established to alert defense officials in the event of counterrevolutionary attacks.

Mass Organization

The Ministry of Education notes: A campaign of this nature "was not only a contradiction for the *somocista* dictatorship; it was impossible to accomplish, since the eradication of illiteracy in a country like Nicaragua can only be carried out through the organization and mobilization of the popular masses. This was not possible for *somocismo* and the dominant groups."[2]

The mass organizations that were instrumental in overthrowing the dictatorship were also crucial to the success of the Nicaraguan literacy campaign. The wide support for these organizations helps explain how Nicaragua, building on the Cuban model, was able to improve upon and exceed in scope and intensity the Cuban literacy campaign of 1961.[3] Organizations were formed in factories and neighborhoods by workers, women, and youths; they included tens of thousands of Nicaraguans who supplied the revolutionary army, established communications networks, administered first aid, obtained and distributed weapons, and erected barricades to do battle during the uprisings of 1978 and 1979.

Following the overthrow of the Somoza regime in July 1979, these mass organizations, in many cases renamed and reconstituted, took part in the battle against illiteracy. Thus it was that the Sandinista Workers Confederation assumed responsibility for literacy-related activities in the factories; the Association of

Rural Workers, for the rural areas; the Sandinista Defense Committees, for urban neighborhoods; the Sandinista Youth, for the participation of high school and university students in the People's Literacy Army; and the Association of Nicaraguan Women (AMNLAE), for mobilizing women as both students and teachers. Women were to play a key role in the CNA, for they saw it as an opportunity to rectify their previous exclusion from central roles in the society. Women were by far the least schooled and most illiterate group. But those who were literate seized the opportunity, and females represented a majority of the literacy workers. (In Cuba females had been 60% of the literacy educators and overall more successful than males, as measured by the number of learners who became literate.) Women also constituted the majority of technical advisors and teacher supervisors; and they assumed primary responsibility for the welfare of the *brigadistas* and for integrating them into homes and communities in rural areas.

Teachers were another group whose participation was essential to the success of the CNA. More than seven thousand teachers assisted in the preparation, supervision, and inservice training of the literacy workers. In addition, they helped maintain educational, cultural, and recreational activities for youths while schools were officially closed between March and September. Most of the teachers were involved in assisting the literacy workers, who generally received only minimal training of some seven days' duration.

Preparation and Pedagogy

The training program for literacy workers concentrated on showing them how to use the adult primer, *Dawn of the People (El Amanecer del Pueblo)*, a mathematics primer, and a teacher's guide. Rural literacy workers also received an introductory course in first aid and wilderness survival. As in Cuba, the most difficult aspect of the training was to prepare young workers—who were overwhelmingly from the urban middle class—to survive and succeed in the often squalid poverty of the countryside.

A pyramid of trainers was organized. Eighty trainees (half of them teachers, half students) were prepared in a fifteen-day course; these 80 trained 560. The multiplier effect proceeded in this fashion until more than 100,000 literacy workers were trained.

Some support was provided to literacy workers during their service in the field. In Saturday workshops, the literacy workers discussed with the supervisors problems ranging from pedagogical methods of motivating recalcitrant adults to technical problems of repairing the gas lamps that were indispensable to nighttime instruction in the parts of Nicaragua without electricity. Another principal component of the inservice training was the twice-daily radio broadcast of the program. *Puño el Alto* ("Fist in the Air"—the Sandinista salute). These broadcasts linked all national and local transmitters in the country. In addition, the Technical-Pedagogical Division of the CNA published a series of bulletins designed to inform literacy workers of the activities of the campaign in diverse parts of Nicaragua and to provide suggestions for instructional activities using local resources.

Learning activity centered on the primer, *Dawn of the People*. This reader, based in part on the pedagogical ideas of the Brazilian educator, Paulo Freire, contains twenty-three generative themes. Each theme, accompanied by a photograph, consists of generative polysyllabic words that can be broken down into minimal units of sound and meaning (phonemes and morphemes) and recombined by the learner to form new words. The initial themes pertain to the revolutionary heroes Augusto César Sandino and Carlos Forseca Amador. The later themes cover the wider topics of the struggle for national liberation, the end of exploitation by foreign and national elites, and the reforms and transformations occurring under the new Government of National Reconstruction. Each of these themes is built around emotionally charged generative words. Appropriately, the first such word is *revolución*. The words *La Revolución* contain all the vowels of the Spanish alphabet. Other generative words include *liberación, genocidio*, and *masas populares*. The sequence of pedagogical activity runs as follows: A group discussion, lasting approximately one hour, follows the presentation of each photograph. After this discussion comes one hour of practice related to reading the text—decoding and encoding the generative words.

Both in Cuba and Nicaragua, a primer was developed by a national team of educators in consultation with political leaders. To the credit of the Nicaraguan (as well as the Cuban) campaign, the literacy materials reflect careful pedagogical and linguistic planning in the selection and sequencing of content. The materials appear to be derived from solid scholarship, and they respect the experience and social world of the adult learner.

The most common criticisms of the literacy materials are not those of scholarship but of ideology. The most vocal opposition has been directed at the pro-FSLN (Sandinista National Liberation Front) content of the literacy crusade. Those who object to political propagandizing as part of the literacy process are apparently ignorant of the indoctrination that occurs in all education systems. What distinguishes one system from another is the subtlety of the indoctrination, the content of the message, and the sociopolitical purposes of instruction. To repeat the fundamental question posed by Freire, Is the object of a literacy campaign domestication or liberation?[4]

The Government of National Reconstruction posits that, under the successive regimes of the Somoza dynasty (1937–1979), education worked to legitimize an inequitable social order that prepared elite groups for leadership while denying fundamental knowledge and skills to the vast majoirty.[5] In contrast to the passivity and fatalism fostered in the masses by the previous regimes, the new Sandinista-led government proposes to instill a different set of values and a radically different ideology. The materials used in the literacy and postliteracy educational campaigns are designed to prepare people to play a more active role in creating a more prosperous and just society. In keeping with the philosophy of the present political leadership in Nicaragua, the values of nationalism, populism, and pluralism are stressed. But the campaign also emphasizes the values of a country attempting to create greater abundance through collective work efforts, personal sacrifice, and national austerity.

Outcomes

What impact has the literacy campaign had on the political life of Nicaragua? Despite the explicitly political message of the adult primer and the repetition of the same political message in a variety of media, the attempts of the Government of National Reconstruction to reshape popular values may not have been very successful. Certainly what is taught is not necessarily what is learned. Students may resist learning a particular message, the message may not be effectively communicated, and the most important lessons learned may derive more from the process, structure, and context of learning than from the explicit content.

In Nicaragua, opposition to the content of the literacy materials came not only from elite groups—including the middle class—but from destitute groups that viewed the new political system as a threat to their beliefs and values. Among the groups opposed to the ideology expressed in the literacy materials were indigenous and English-speaking populations of the Atlantic Coast, who for more than a century have been politically and commercially oriented toward England and the U.S. Historically, these people have seen the Spanish-speaking Pacific Coast region of Nicaragua as a source of repression. But opposition also came from conservative, devoutly Christian rural populations who thought that the political content of the Sandinista revolution was too closely associated with atheistic communism.[6]

Outright resistance to the political content of the readers clearly reduced the impact of the political message, and, in a number of communities, the reader was used but political themes were omitted. But these instances of deviation from the text are not the principal reasons that the political lessons of the literacy primer may not have been communicated as intended. Even where the literacy instructor used the lessons and faithfully followed the primer, many learners were grappling with letters, sounds, and parts of words—not with ideas. The most important task of the learners was to sound out and pronounce words correctly; the meaning of words and of sentences was secondary and may often have been lost. Moreover, as mid-August approached, the national goal of enabling so many learners to complete the course and pass the five-part literacy test[7] influenced the literacy workers to concentrate on rote drill at the expense of meaning.

Another reason for discussion of themes receiving short shrift was that, during the final stages of the CNA, younger people who had only recently undergone the literacy process themselves served as monitors, assisting those who had fallen behind. These young teachers and monitors lacked the experience and preparation to be able to lead extended discussions of the themes contained in the reader. A fourteen-year-old female instructor, coming to a topic such as the liberation of women, could briefly mention the theme of female exclusion from important jobs prior to the revolution, but she would probably be unable to delve into such complex issues as the nature of male/female relations before and after the 1979 revolution. It should not be surprising that the discussion of a number of themes was very brief, often limited to the literacy worker merely reading notes jotted down from the teacher's guide.

Other factors also inhibited free dialogue and critical consciousness-raising, especially in so short a time. Low-income and rural populations reached by the literacy campaign had traditionally been excluded from participating in decision making; they had been taught to defer to authority, to be mute and passive. When they spoke out and challenged authority, the response had always been punitive. Thus it was not uncommon to find that rural people felt uncomfortable discussing their opinions publicly or questioning authority—although that authority might be an adolescent teacher some twenty or thirty years their junior. Asking these learners to be active participants in their own education directly opposed ingrained traditions of subordination and self-deprecation. Perhaps for these reasons, the CNA moved in its final stages toward a traditional teacher-directed pedagogy and an almost mechanical approach to literacy instruction.

However, these aspects of the literacy process were the least crucial to the successful political results of the CNA. The most important lessons and examples of the crusade resided not in the literacy materials or the teacher/learner encounters but in the very existence of the campaign itself. The literacy crusade was a symbol of justice, of the concern of the new political regime for the most neglected areas of the country. The commitment of the revolutionary Sandinista regime to redress past wrongs was palpably present in the *brigadistas* who went to live with and assist impoverished rural families.

The literacy teachers themselves probably underwent the greatest transformation of values and behaviors. These largely middle-class youths experienced in an unforgettable way the poverty of rural Nicaragua. They toiled in the fields, shared the hardships and hunger of rural families, and fell victim to the same illnesses.[8] Many of the school dropouts and unemployed youths who worked with the literacy campaign in urban areas were, for the first time in their lives, fulfilling important societal roles. Such experiences could only improve their self-images and their views of the new society and their role in it.

Among other changes that were accelerated and magnified by the CNA was the liberation of women from their subordinate and marginal positions in Nicaraguan society. The literacy crusade undoubtedly contributed to different perceptions of women as political actors and social activists. If women could play key roles in the armed struggle against the previous regime and in the CNA, what roles were not open to them in post-Somoza Nicaragua?

Another significant outcome of the CNA was the strengthening of the mass organizations as effective means of popular participation in a postwar period of reconstruction. The continued democratization of post-Somoza Nicaragua depends on the vitality of these organizations. Furthermore, given the poverty of the country, these organizations must play a critical role in stimulating workers to higher levels of productivity and in mobilizing people to contribute voluntary labor to public works.

Thus the consequences of the CNA may be studied at various levels. The most obvious results are found in the number of adult learners who became at least minimally literate. At a deeper level, the outcomes of the CNA must be evaluated in relation to the transformation of political life, the integration of previously alienated groups into a collective effort, the winning of youths to the revolution, the changing of male and female roles, and the strengthening of mass organizations. The ultimate success of the campaign will be determined by the extent to which literacy skills are used in pursuit of the overriding goals of the national reconstruction—increased productivity, better health, adequate housing, improved family life, and effective communal action.

Notes
Notes on Contributors
Works Cited

Notes

1. The Consequences of Literacy

1. Some writers distinguish the field of social anthropology from that of sociology on the basis of its subject matter (i.e., the study of nonliterate or non-European peoples), others on the basis of its techniques (e.g., that of participant observation). For a discussion of these points, see Siegfried F. Nadel, *The Foundations of Social Anthropology* (London, 1951), 2.

2. Bronislaw Malinowski, "The Problem of Meaning in Primitive Languages," in C. K. Ogden and I. A. Richards, *The Meaning of Meaning* (London, 1936), 296–336, esp. 331. But see also the critical comments by Claude Lévi-Strauss, *La Pensée sauvage* (Paris, 1962), 6, 15–16.

3. *L'Année sociologique* 7 (1902–3): 1–72. See also S. Czarnowski, "Le Morcellement de l'étendue et sa limitation dans la religion et la magie," *Actes du congrès international d'histoire des religions* (Paris, 1925) 1: 339–59.

4. Jack Goody, unpublished field notes, 1950–52. See also E. E. Evans-Pritchard, *The Nuer* (Oxford, 1940), chap. 3, "Time and Space," and David Tait, *The Konkomba of Northern Ghana* (London, 1961), 17ff. For a general treatment of the subject, see A. Irving Hallowell, "Temporal Orientations in Western Civilisation and in a Preliterate Society," *American Anthropologist* 39 (1937): 647–70.

5. *Les Cadres sociaux de la memoire* (Paris, 1925); "Memoire et société," *L'Année sociologique*, 3rd series, 1 (1940–48): 11–177; *La Mémoire collective* (Paris, 1950). See also Frederic C. Bartlett on the tendency of oral discourse to become an expression of ideas and attitudes of the group rather than the individual speaker, in *Remembering* (Cambridge, 1932), 265–67, and *Psychology and Primitive Culture* (Cambridge, 1923), 42–43, 62–63, 256.

6. C. F. and F. M. Voegelin classify all these systems (Chinese, Egyptian, Hittite, Mayan, and Sumerian-Akkadian) as "alphabet included logographic systems"; because these make use of phonetic devices, they include, under the heading "self-sufficient alphabets," systems which have signs for consonant-vowel sequences (i.e., syllabaries), for independent consonants (IC)—e.g., Phoenician—or for independent consonants plus independent vowels (IC and IV), e.g., Greek. In this paper we employ "alphabet" in the narrower, more usual, sense of a phonemic system with independent signs for consonants and vowels (IC + IV).

7. *Protoliterate* is often employed in a rather different sense, as when S. N. Kramer ("New Light on the Early History of the Ancient Near East," *American Journal of Archaeology* 52 [1948]: 161) uses the term to designate the Sumerian phase in Lower Mesopotamia when writing was first invented. There seems to be no generally accepted usage for societies where there is a fully developed but socially restricted phonetic writing system. Sterling Dow ("Minoan Writing," *American Journal of Archaeology* 58 [1954]: 77–129) characterizes two stages of Minoan society: one of "stunted literacy," where little use was made of writing at all (Linear A); and one of "special literacy," where writing was used regularly but only for limited purposes (Linear B). Stuart Piggott refers to both of these under the name of "conditional literacy" (*Approach to Archaeology* [London, 1959], 104).

8. "Egyptian hieroglyphic writing remained fundamentally unchanged for a period of three thousand years," according to David Diringer (*Writing* [London, 1962], 48). He attributes the fact that it never lost its cumbrousness and elaboration to "its unique sacredness" (50).

9. Many authorities have commented upon the lack of development in Egypt after the initial achievements of the Old Kingdom; for a discussion (and a contrary view), see John A. Wilson in *Before Philosophy*, ed. H. Frankfort and others (London, 1949), 115–16 (pub. in U.S.A. as *The Intellectual Adventure of Ancient Man* [Chicago, 1946]).

10. "The world view of the Egyptians and Babylonians was conditioned by the teaching of sacred books; it thus constituted an orthodoxy, the maintenance of which was in the charge of colleges of priests" (Benjamin Farrington, *Science in Antiquity* [London, 1936], 37). See also Gordon Childe, *What Happened in History*, 121.

11. Gelb, *Study of Writing*, 196, maintains that all the main types of syllabary developed in just this way. Driver rejects the possibility that the Phoenician alphabet was invented on Egyptian soil, as it would have been "stifled at birth" by the "deadweight of Egyptian tradition, already of hoary antiquity and in the hands of a powerful priesthood" (*Semitic Writing*, 187).

12. "Immensely complicated," Driver calls the prealphabetic forms of written Semitic (*Semitic Writing*, p. 67).

13. For Hittite, see O. R. Gurney, *The Hittites* (London, 1952), 120–21. For Mycenaean, see John Chadwick, *The Decipherment of Linear B* (Cambridge, 1958).

14. *The Alphabet*, 214–18. On the "accidental" nature of this change, see C. F. and F. M. Voegelin, "Typological Classification," 63–64.

15. According to Ralph E. Turner, *The Great Cultural Traditions* (New York, 1941) 1: 346, 391, the Hebrews took over the Semitic system in the eleventh century B.C., and the Indians a good deal later, probably in the eighth century B.C.

16. E.g., Luke 20; Matthew, 23; in the seventh century B.C., even kings and prophets employed scribes, Jer. 26.4,18.

17. Driver, *Semitic Writing*, 87–90, where he instances the case of one scribe who, having no son, "taught his wisdom to his sister's son."

18. "If the alphabet is defined as a system of signs expressing single sounds of speech, then the first alphabet which can justifiably be so called is the Greek alphabet" (Gelb, *Study of Writing*, 166).

19. I Kings 17.4–6; see *A Dictionary of the Bible* . . . , ed. James Hastings (New York, 1898–1904), *s.v.* "Elijah."

20. 810a. From the age of ten to thirteen.

21. *L'Adoption universelle des caractères latins* (Paris, 1934); for more recent developments and documentation, see William S. Gray, *The Teaching of Reading and Writing: An International Survey, UNESCO Monographs on Fundamental Education* 10 (Paris, 1956), 31–60.

22. L. H. Jeffery, *The Local Scripts of Archaic Greece* (Oxford, 1961), 21; R. M. Cook and A. G. Woodhead, "The Diffusion of the Greek Alphabet," *American Journal of Archaeology* 53 (1959): 175–78. For north Syria, see Sir Leonard Woolley, *A Forgotten Kingdom* (London, 1953).

23. Chester Starr speaks of its use by "a relatively large aristocratic class" (171) and Miss Jeffery notes that "writing was never regarded as an esoteric craft in early Greece. Ordinary people could and did learn to write, for many of the earliest inscriptions which we possess are casual graffiti" (63).

24. 1.1114; in 414 B.C. See also Plato, *Apology*, 26d, and the general survey of Kenyon, *Books and Readers in Ancient Greece and Rome*.

25. *The Philosophy of Symbolic Forms* (New Haven, 1955) 2: xiii; and *An Essay on Man* (New York, 1953), esp. 106–30, 281–83. For Werner Jaeger, see esp. *The Theology of the Early Greek Philosophers* (Oxford, 1947).

26. "Magic, Science, and Religion" in *Science, Religion, and Reality*, ed. Joseph Needham (New York, 1925); rpt. *Magic, Science and Religion* (New York, 1954), 27. For an

appreciation of Lévy-Bruhl's positive achievement, see Evans-Pritchard, "Lévy-Bruhl's Theory of Primitive Mentality," *Bulletin of the Faculty of Arts, University of Egypt* 2 (1934): 1–36. In his later work, Lévy-Bruhl modified the rigidity of his earlier dichotomy.

27. See also Max Gluckman's essay "Social Beliefs and Individual Thinking in Primitive Society," *Memoirs and Proceedings of the Manchester Literary and Philosophical Society* 91 (1949–50): 73–98. From a rather different standpoint, Lévi-Strauss has analysed "the logic of totemic classifications" (*La Pensée Sauvage*, 48ff.) and speaks of two distinct modes of scientific thought; the first (or "primitive") variety consists in "the science of the concrete," the practical knowledge of the handy man (*bricoleur*), which is the technical counterpart of mythical thought (26).

28. "It was in Ionia that the first completely rationalistic attempts to describe the nature of the world took place" (G. S. Kirk and J. E. Raven, *The Presocratic Philosophers* [Cambridge, 1957], 73). The work of the Milesian philosophers Thales, Anaximander, and Anaximenes, is described by the authors as "clearly a development of the genetic or genealogical approach to nature exemplified by the Hesiodic *Theogony*" (73).

29. Hermann Diels, *Die Fragmente der Vorsokratiker* (Berlin, 1951), fr. 11, 23: see also John Burnet, *Early Greek Philosophy*, 2nd ed. (London, 1908), 131, 140–41, and Werner Jaeger, *The Theology of the Early Greek Philosophers* (Oxford, 1947), 42–47; Kirk and Raven, *The Presocratic Philosophers*, 163ff.

30. Diels, *Fragmente der Vorsokratiker*, fr. 40, 42, 56, 57, 106; see also Francis M. Cornford, *Principium Sapientiae: The Origins of Greek Philosophical Thought* (Cambridge, 1952), 112ff.; Kirk and Raven, *The Presocratic Philosophers*, 182ff.

31. For a picture of note taking (*hypomnemata*) among Athenians, see *Theaetetus*, 142c–43c.

32. Felix Jacoby notes that "fixation in writing, once achieved, primarily had a preserving effect upon the oral tradition, because it put an end to the involuntary shiftings of the *mnemai* (remembrances), and drew limits to the arbitrary creation of new *logoi* (stories)" (*Atthis* [1949], 217). He points out that this created difficulties for the early literate recorders of the past which the previous oral *mnemones* or professional "remembrancers" did not have to face; whatever his own personal view of the matter, "no true Atthidographer could remove Kekrops from his position as the first Attic king. . . . Nobody could take away from Solon the legislation which founded *in nuce* the first Attic constitution of historical times." Such things could no longer be silently forgotten, as in an oral tradition.

The general conclusion of Jacoby's polemic against Wilamowitz' hypothesis of a "pre-literary chronicle" is that "historical consciousness . . . is not older than historical literature" (201).

33. As writers on the indigenous political systems of Africa have insisted, changes generally take the form of rebellion rather than revolution; subjects reject the king, but not the kingship. See Evans-Pritchard, *The Divine Kingship of the Shilluk of the Nilotic Sudan* (The Frazer Lecture, Cambridge, 1948), 35ff.; Max Gluckman, *Rituals of Rebellion in South-East Africa* ([The Frazer Lecture, 1952], Manchester, 1954).

34. *Statesman*, 278. See also *Cratylus*, 424b–28c.

35. *Theaetetus*, 201–2. The analogy is continued to the end of the dialogue.

36. 184b. There were, of course, many precursors, not only Plato and his laws of the dialectic but the Sophists and grammarians with their semantic interests (see John Edwin Sandys, *A History of Classical Scholarship*, [Cambridge, 1921] 1: 27, 88ff.).

37. *Geography*, 608–9, cited in Sandys, *History of Classical Scholarship* 1: 86. See also ibid., 76–114, and James Westfall Thompson, *Ancient Libraries* (Berkeley, 1940), 18–21.

38. Cited in Harold A. Innis, "Minerva's Owl," *The Bias of Communication* (Toronto, 1951), 24. Innis was much occupied with the larger effects of modes of communication, as appears also in his *Empire and Communications* (Oxford, 1950). This direction of investigation has been taken up by the University of Toronto review *Explorations*; and the present authors are also indebted to the then-unpublished work of

Professor E. A. Havelock on the alphabetic revolution in Greece. Among the many previous writers who have been concerned with the Greek aspect of the problem, Nietzsche (*Beyond Good and Evil* [Edinburgh, 1909], 247), and José Ortéga y Gasset ("The Difficulty of Reading," *Diogenes* 28 [1959]: 1–17) may be mentioned. Among those who have treated the differences between oral and literate modes of communication in general, David Reisman ("The Oral and Written Traditions," *Explorations* 6 [1956]: 22–28, and *The Oral Tradition, the Written Word, and the Screen Image* [Yellow Springs, OH, 1956]) and Robert Park ("Reflections on Communication and Culture," *American Journal of Sociology* 44 [1938]: 187–205) are especially relevant here.

39. *Gulliver's Travels*, part 4, chap. 9, ed. Arthur E. Case (New York, 1938), 296.

40. *Chan Kom, a Maya Village* (Washington, DC, 1934); *The Folk Culture of Yucatan* (Chicago, 1941); *A Village That Chose Progress: Chan Kom Revisited* (Chicago, 1950); and for a more general treatment, *The Primitive World and its Transformations* (Ithaca, NY, 1953), 73, 108. See also Peter Worsley, *The Trumpet Shall Sound* (London, 1957). For the concept of *anomie*, see Emile Durkheim, *Le Suicide* (Paris, 1897), book 2, chap. 5.

41. Emile Durkheim, *The Division of Labor in Society*, trans. G. Simpson (New York, 1933), 130.

42. In the *Theaetetus*, for example, emphasis is placed on the inner dialogue of the soul in which it perceives ethical ideas "by comparing within herself things past and present with the future" (186b).

43. Jaeger, *Paiedeia* (Oxford, 1939) 2:18, speaks of the dialogues and the memoirs by many members of the circle of Socrates as "new literary forms invented by the Socratic circle . . . to re-create the incomparable personality of the master."

44. The authors are much indebted to John Beattie, Glyn Daniel, Lloyd Fallers, Moses Finley, Joseph Fontenrose, Harry Hoijer, the late Alfred Kroeber, Simon Pembroke, and Nur Yalman for reading and commenting upon earlier versions of this paper. They are also grateful to the Center for Advanced Studies in the Behavioral Sciences, California, for the opportunity of working together on the manuscript in the spring of 1960.

3. Implications of Literacy in Traditional China and India

1. William H. McNeill, *The Rise of the West* (Chicago: University of Chicago Press, 1962), 256 n.2. Parsons estimates that "the Athens of the Periclean Age had only about 30,000 citizens, including women and children, in a total population of about 150,000" (Talcott Parsons, *Societies: Evolutionary and Comparative Perspectives*, Foundations of Modern Sociology Series [New York: Prentice-Hall, 1966], 105).

2. Kroeber argues that it was the greater power and prestige of Chinese institutions, and thus of the Chinese script, that prevented the triumph of alphabetic writing in Korea as well, even though the Koreans twice developed a phonetic symbol-system—in the seventh century, in the form of a phonetic syllabary based on Chinese characters, and in 1446, of an alphabet derived, perhaps, from Pali (Alfred L. Kroeber, "The Story of the Alphabet," in *Anthropology* [New York: Harcourt, Brace, 1948], 495).

3. Goody and Watt argue for a particular affinity between the Platonic dialogues and the novel as a literary form, since both stress the need for personal selection, among conflicting ideas and attitudes, of an individual approach to one's culture. This may be true, but it is also true, as the authors point out, that Plato expressed disapproval of written as opposed to oral communication and that the Platonic dialogue, like the Upanishads and the Confucian and Taoist dialogues, issues from a society in which, in general, much learning was still transmitted orally.

4. Unpackaging Literacy

1. The narrative text is also a common prototype, but we are leaving aside for the

time being approaches to creative writing which have largely been initiated and developed outside the public school system.

2. These were carried out by Michael R. Smith, an anthropologist from Cambridge University.

3. Because this phenomenon is rarely encountered in our own culture, we tend to peg our "basic skills models" of writing very closely to the particular characteristics and structure of a single orthographic system and assumptions of prewriting fluency in the language represented. As Fishman (1975) suggests was the case with bilingualism, studies of multi-script-using communities might well enlarge the framework in which basic research on literacy is conducted. For accounts of other nonindustrialized societies with a number of simultaneously active scripts, see Gough, 1968; Tambiah, 1968; Wilder, 1972. Schofield (1968) reminds us that between the sixteenth and nineteenth centuries in England, early instruction in reading and writing was conducted with texts in English while higher education was conducted in classical Latin.

4. Public functions of Vai script appear to be declining as English becomes mandatory for administrative and judicial matters.

5. Gelb (1952) presents an interesting argument that social origins of nonpictorial writing systems are to be found in the use of individualized symbols as brands of ownership.

6. It is reported (Scribner, field notes) that an entire Vai community in Monrovia was able to retain its right to disputed land because an elderly kinsman had recorded in his book the names of the original deed-holders.

6. The Legacies of Literacy

1. See Bataille, *Turning Point*; Douglas, "Literacy"; Farr, Fay, and Negley, *Reading Achievement in Indiana*; Farr, Fay, and Negley, *Reading Achievement in the U.S.*; Goody, *Domestication*; Graff, *The Literacy Myth*; Graff, "Literacy Past and Present"; Johansson, "The Postliteracy Problem."

2. See table 6.1; see also Clanchy, *From Memory*; Cressy, *Social Order*; Furet and Ozouf, *Lire et écrire*; Graff, *The Literacy Myth* (introduction and appendixes); Johansson, *The History of Literacy*; Lockridge, *Literacy*; Schofield, "Measurement of Literacy."

3. For more on literacy as a learned skill, see Bantock, *Implications of Literacy*; Clanchy, *From Memory*; Cole, "How Education"; Cole et al., *Cultural Context*; Cremin, *American Education*; Cressy, *Social Order*; Eisenstein, *The Printing Press*; Furet and Ozouf, *Lire et écrire*; Goody, *Domestication*; Goody, *Literacy and Traditional Societies*; Goody, Cole, and Scribner, "Writing and Formal Operations"; Goody and Watt, "The Consequences of Literacy"; Graff, *Literacy in History*; Graff, *The Literacy Myth*; Graff, *The Legacies of Literacy*; Graff, ed., *Literacy and Social Development*; Lockridge, *Literacy*; Lockridge, "L'alphabétisation"; McLuhan, *The Gutenberg Galaxy*; McLuhan, *Understanding Media*; Olson, Review; Olson, "From Utterance to Text"; Ong, *Interfaces*; Ong, *Presence*; Ong, *Rhetoric*; Resnick and Resnick, "The Nature of Literacy"; Scribner and Cole, "Cognitive Consequences"; Scribner and Cole, "Literacy without Schooling"; Scribner and Cole, "Studying Cognitive Consequences."

4. Scribner and Cole, "Literacy without Schooling," 453; see also Goody, *Domestication*; Goody, *Literacy in Traditional Societies*; Goody, Cole, and Scribner, "Writing and Formal Operations"; Scribner and Cole "Cognitive Consequences"; Scribner and Cole, "Studying Cognitive Consequences."

5. Johansson, *The History of Literacy*; Laqueur, "Cultural Origins"; Laqueur, *Religion*; Laqueur, "Working-Class Demand"; Spufford, *Contrasting Communities*; Spufford, "First Steps"; Webb, *The British Working Class Reader*.

6. Havelock, *Preface*; Havelock, *Origins*; Havelock, "Preliteracy."

7. Clanchy, *From Memory*.

8. Aston, "Lollardy and Literacy"; Burke, *Popular Culture*; Clanchy, *From*

Memory; Davis, "Printing"; Finnegan, *Oral Literature*; Finnegan, *Oral Poetry*; Ganshof, *The Carolingians*; Gerhardsson, *Memory and Manuscript*; Graff, *The Literacy Myth*; Havelock, *Origins*; Havelock, "Preliteracy"; LeRoy, *Montaillou*; Martin, "Culture écrite."

9. Aston, "Lollardy and Literacy"; Cipolla, *Literacy and Development*; Gerhardsson, *Memory and Manuscript*; Graff, *The Literacy Myth*; Johansson, *The History of Literacy*; LeRoy, *Montaillou*; Lockridge, *Literacy*; Maynes, "Schooling the Masses"; Maynes, "The Virtues of Anachronism"; Strauss, *Luther's House*.

10. Bruneau, "Literacy"; Cipolla, *Literacy and Development*; Clanchy, *From Memory*; Goody, *Literacy in Traditional Societies*; Trigger, "Inequality and Communication."

11. Anderson, "Literacy and Schooling"; Bowman and Anderson, "Concerning the Role of Education"; Bowman and Anderson, "Education and Economic Modernization"; West, *Education and the Industrial Revolution*; West, "Literacy and the Industrial Revolution"; West, "The Role of Education."

12. Among a large literature on these issues, see Blaug, "Literacy and Economic Development"; Bowen, "Assessing"; Bowles and Gintis, *Schooling*; Dore, *Education*; Field, "Economic and Demographic Determinants"; Field, "Educational Expansion"; Field, "Educational Reform"; Field, "Occupational Structure"; Flora, "Historical Processes"; Furet and Ozouf, "Literacy and Industrialization"; Graff, *The Literacy Myth*; Gutman, "Work, Culture, and Society"; Johnson, "Notes"; Kaestle and Vinovskis, *Education and Social Change*; Katz, "The Origins of Public Education"; Katz, "Origins of the Institutional State"; Laqueur, Critique; Levine, "Education and Family Life"; Levine, *Family Formation*; McClelland, "Does Education"; Pollard, *The Genesis*; Sanderson, "Education and the Factory"; Sanderson, "Literacy and Social Mobility"; Sanderson, "Social Change"; Schofield, "The Dimensions of Illiteracy"; Stephens, "Illiteracy and Schooling"; Thompson, "Time"; Verne, "Literacy and Industrialization"; Vinovskis, "Horace Mann"; for an opposing view, see Anderson, "Literacy and Schooling"; Bowman and Anderson, "Concerning the Role of Education"; Bowman and Anderson, "Education and Economic Modernization"; Cole, *The Cultural Context*; Inkeles and Smith, *Becoming Modern*; West, "The Role of Education"; West, *Education and the Industrial Revolution*. On inventiveness, see Ferguson, "The Mind's Eye"; Ivins, *Prints*; Wallace, *Rockdale*.

13. Johansson, *The History of Literacy*; Johansson, "The Postliteracy Problem"; Leith, *Facets of Education*.

14. Winchester, "How Many Ways."

15. Appleby, "Modernization Theory"; Applewaite and Levy, "The Concept of Modernization"; Ballinger, "The Idea of Progress"; Commager, *The Empire of Reason*; Cremin, *American Education*; Furet and Ozouf, *Lire et écrire*; Gay, *The Enlightenment*; Graff, *The Legacies of Literacy*; Graff, *The Literacy Myth*; Johansson, *The History of Literacy*; Kaestle, " 'Between the Scylla' "; Kerber, "Daughters of Columbia"; Kuritz, "Benjamin Rush"; Leith, "Modernisation"; Leith, ed., *Facets*; Lockridge, *Literacy*; May, *The Enlightenment*; Maynes, "Schooling the Masses"; Meyer, *The Democratic Enlightenment*; Mortier, "The 'Philosophies' "; Nipperdey, "Mass Education"; Palmer, "The Old Regime Origins"; Schleunnes, "The French Revolution"; Vovelle, "Maggiolo en Provence"; Vovelle, "Y a-t-il une révolution?"

16. Bataille, *A Turning Point*; Cressy, *Literacy and the Social Order*; Douglas, "Literacy"; Farr, Fay, and Negley, *Reading Achievement in the U.S.*; Goody, *Domestication*; Graff, *The Literacy Myth*; Graff, "Literacy Past and Present"; Johansson, "The Postliteracy Problem."

17. Galtung, "Literacy," 93.

8. *The Coming of Literate Communication to Western Culture*

1. This is in marked difference from illiteracy, which describes a personal failure to become literate, an option which must be present in order for literacy to be possible.

2. In my *Preface to Plato*, and still more in my *Greek Concept of Justice*, I have offered analyses of extensive portions of both *Iliad* and *Odyssey* to demonstrate that these information materials do indeed inhere in the text.

3. The latest discussion, Coldstream's *Geometric Greece*, places the invention of the alphabet in the first half of the eighth century B.C. The dating problem would be only of marginal importance in the general context of the Greek literate revolution were it not for my conviction that the assignment of a date for the Greek alphabet to the first half of the eighth century owes as much to a preconceived bias in favor of literacy as it does to scholarship, a bias arising from a conviction conscious or otherwise that no culture worth the name could have been nonliterate, certainly not the Greek. I am tempted to repeat what I first wrote in 1963, speaking of "scholars of the written word," that when they "turn their attention to the problem of written documentation they betray a consistent tendency to press the positive evidence for it as far as they can and as far back as they can" *(Preface to Plato)*.

4. For a more extended explanation of alphabetic technology, see my *Origins of Western Literacy*.

5. *Mousike* refers to the joint arts of poetry, instrumentation, and dance as devised and produced in a partnership which is, I believe, typical of all oral culture in varying degree, and of a kind unique to them. This partnership is fundamentally a response to the need to memorize verbal statements already cast into rhythm by reinforcing this rhythm through the accompanying addition of the rhythms of melody and of bodily motion. As you recited you sang; as you sang you played an instrument; as you played you danced, these motions being performed collectively. Their unusually sophisticated partnership supplied mutual reinforcement. The tenacity with which Athens clung to this method of educating its youth is revealed by indirect reference to it as still a going concern as late as the last half of the fifth century. The schoolmaster was the *kitharistes*, the lyre player. His pupils, besides being taught deportment and discipline, along with the gymnastics practiced in the wrestling school, were trained in the memorization and recitation of the poets and in performance on musical instruments.

6. In viewing the orality of Greek civilization, we must not restrict our perspective to Homer and the Homeric age. What we call Greek literature, produced for 250 years after the alphabetic invention, remains overwhelmingly poetic, composed under audience control, published orally and preserved orally.

10. Defining "Literacy" in North American Schools

1. Eric Havelock, *Origins of Western Literacy* (Toronto: OISE Press, 1976).

2. Richard Hoggart, *The Uses of Literacy* (Harmondsworth: Pelican, 1958).

3. Harvey Graff, *The Literacy Myth: Literacy and Social Structure in the Nineteenth-Century City* (New York: Academic Press, 1979).

4. Harvey Graff, "The Legacies of Literacy," *Journal of Communications* 32 (1982): 12–26.

5. Elizabeth Eisenstein, *The Printing Press as an Agent of Change: Communications and Cultural Transformations in Early Modern Europe* 2 vols. (Cambridge: Cambridge University Press, 1979), 431.

6. H. J. Chaytor, *From Script to Print: An Introduction to Modern Vernacular Literature*, 2nd ed. (London: Sidwick and Jackson, 1966).

7. Geraldine Joncich, *The Sane Positivist: A Biography of Edward L. Thorndike* (Middletown, CT: Wesleyan University Press, 1968), 48.

8. Alison Prentice, *The School Promoters: Education and Social Class in Mid-Nineteenth-Century Upper Canada* (Toronto: McCelland and Stewart, 1977), 17.

9. Samuel Bowles and Herbert Gintis, "Capitalism and Education in the United States," *Society State and Schooling*, ed. M. F. D. Young and G. Whitt, (Brighton: Falmer Press, 1977), 192–227.

10. Archibald MacCallum, "Compulsory Education," *Family, School and Society in Nineteenth-Century Canada*, ed. A. Prentice and S. Houston (Oxford: Oxford University Press, 1975), 176–77.

11. Lawrence Cremin, *The Transformation of the School* (New York: Random House, 1961), 16.

12. Noah Webster, *American Spelling Book* (New York: Teachers College, 1962).

13. Henry F. May, *The End of American Innocence* (New York: Knopf, 1959), 30.

14. Richard S. Peters, "Education as Initiation," *Philosophical Analysis and Education,* ed. R. D. Archambault (London: Routledge and Kegan Paul, 1972), 197.

15. Henry Johnson, *A History of Public Education in British Columbia* (Vancouver: University of British Columbia Publications Centre, 1964), 65.

16. Pierre Bourdieu, "The Economics of Linguistic Exchange," *Social Science Information* 6 (1977): 645–68.

17. John Putman and George M. Weir, *Survey of the Schools* (Victoria: King's Printer, 1925).

18. Raymond E. Callahan, *Education and the Cult of Efficiency* (Chicago: University of Chicago Press, 1962).

19. David Tyack, "Bureaucracy and the Common School: The Example of Portland, Oregon, 1851–1913," *The American Quarterly* 19 (1967): pp. 475–98.

20. Frederick W. Taylor, *Principles of Scientific Management* (New York: Harper, 1911).

21. John F. Bobbitt, *The Curriculum* (Boston: Houghton Mifflin, 1918).

22. William James, *Talks to Teachers on Psychology* (New York: Henry Holt, 1899).

23. George H. Mead, *Mind, Self, and Society from the Standpoint of a Social Behaviorist* (Chicago: University of Chicago Press, 1934).

24. John Dewey, *Democracy and Education* (New York: Macmillan, 1915), 315.

25. John Dewey, *The Sources of a Science of Education* (New York: Liveright, 1929).

26. Edward L. Thorndike, *Principles of Teaching* (New York: A. G. Seiler, 1906).

27. Edmund B. Huey, *The Psychology and Pedagogy of Reading* (New York: Macmillan, 1909).

28. Edward L. Thorndyke, "Reading as Reasoning: A Study of Mistakes in Paragraph Reading," *Journal of Educational Psychology* 8 (1917): 323–32.

29. W. S. Gray, *The Twenty-fourth Yearbook of the National Society for the Study of Education* (Bloomington, IN: Public School Publishing Co., 1952).

30. Florence Goodenough, *Mental Testing: Its History, Principles, and Applications* (New York: Rinehart, 1949).

31. Harold M. Covell, "The Past in Reading: Prologue to the Future," *Journal of the Faculty of Education of the University of British Columbia* 1 (1961): 13–18.

32. Amiel T. Sharon, "What Do Adults Read?" *Reading Research Quarterly* 3 (1973): 148–69.

33. Stephen J. Gould, *The Mismeasure of Man* (New York: Norton, 1981).

34. Hilda Neatby, *So Little for the Mind* (Toronto: Clark, Irwin, 1953), 3.

35. Ludwig Wittgenstein, *Philosophical Investigations,* trans. G. E. M. Anscomb (Oxford: Blackwell and Mott, 1953).

36. David Pratt, "The Social Role of School Textbooks in Canada," *Socialization and Values in Canadian Society* ed. R. Pike and E. Zureik (McClelland and Stewart, Toronto, 1975), 2: 100–126; Satu Repo, "From Pilgrim's Progress to Sesame Street: 125 Years of Colonial Readers," *The Politics of the Canadian Public School,* ed. G. Martell (Toronto: James Lewis and Samuel, 1974), 118–33; Frances Fitzgerald, *America Revised: History Schoolbooks in the Twentieth Century* (New York: Vintage, 1980).

37. Bruno Bettelheim and Karen Zelan, "Why Children Don't Like to Read," *Atlantic Monthly* May 1981: 25–31.

38. Raymond Williams, *Communications* (London: Oxford University Press, 1976).

39. Irwin Kirsch and John Guthrie, "The Concept and Measurement of Functional Literacy," *Reading Research Quarterly* 4 (1977): 487–567; Suzanne de Castell, Allan Luke, and David MacLennan, "On Defining Literacy," *Canadian Journal of Education* 6 (1981): 7–18.

40. Antony Wilden, *The Imaginary Canadian* (Vancouver: Pulp Press, 1981).

11. From Utterance to Text

1. An early version of this paper was presented to the Epistemics meeting at Vanderbilt University, Nashville, Tenn., in February 1974 and was published in R. Diez-Guerrero and H. Fisher, eds., *Logic and Language in Personality and Society* (New York: Academic Press, in press).

I am extremely grateful to the Canada Council, the Spencer Foundation, and the Van Leer Jerusalem Foundation for their support at various stages of completing this paper. I am also indebted to the many colleagues who commented on the earlier draft, including Roy Pea, Nancy Nickerson, Angela Hildyard, Bob Bracewell, Edmund Sullivan, and Frank Smith. I would also like to thank Mary Macri, who assisted with the clerical aspects of the manuscript and Isobel Gibb, Reference Librarian at OISE, who assisted with the reference editing.

12. The Nature of Literacy

1. For the use of signatures in public oaths and as a source on literacy in seventeenth- and eighteenth-century England, see Roger S. Schofield, "The Measurement of Literacy in Pre-Industrial England," *Literacy in Traditional Societies*, ed. Jack R. Goody (Cambridge: Cambridge University Press, 1968), 311–25; and Richard T. Vann, "Literacy in Seventeenth-Century England: Some Hearth-Tax Evidence," *Journal of Interdisciplinary History* 5 (1974): 287–93. The uses of signatures for retrospective literacy assessment in France are discussed in Francois Furet and Vladimir Sachs, "La croissance de l'alphabétisation en France (XVIIIe–XIXe siècles)," *Annales: Economies, Sociétés, Civilisations* 29 (1974): 714–37.

2. Lawrence Stone, "Literacy and Education in England, 1640–1900," *Past and Present* 42 (1969): esp. 77–83, examines the relationship of Protestantism to the development of literacy.

3. For samples of current work exploring the effect of education on economic growth in different contexts, see Roger S. Schofield, "Dimensions of Illiteracy, 1750–1850," *Explorations in Economic History* 10 (1973): 437–54; and David McClelland, "Does Education Accelerate Economic Growth?" *Economic Development and Cultural Change* 14 (1966): 257–78. For the effect of education on personality change, see Howard Schuman, Alex Inkeles, and David Smith, "Some Social and Psychological Effects and Non-Effects of Literacy in a New Nation," *Economic Development and Cultural Change* 16 (1967): 1–14.

4. See Bernard Bailyn, *Education in the Forming of American Society: Needs and Opportunities for Study* (Chapel Hill: University of North Carolina Press, 1960), esp. 48–49; and Lawrence Cremin, *American Education: The Colonial Experience, 1607–1783* (New York: Harper & Row, 1970), 545–70. The counterargument by Kenneth Lockridge, *Literacy in Colonial New England: An Inquiry into the Social Context of Literacy in the Early Modern West* (New York: Norton, 1974), 28–29, overstates Cremin's position but not the thrust of his argument.

5. On the failure of colonial wills to offer evidence of nontraditional social behavior, see Lockridge, 33–35.

6. See Michael Sanderson, "Literacy and Social Mobility in the Industrial Revolution in England," *Past and Present* 56 (1972): esp. 89–95, and the later exchange with Thomas Laqueur in "Debate," *Past and Present* 64 (1974): 96–112.

7. Lockridge, *Literacy in Colonial New England*, 13, 87–88.

8. For Scotland, see Stone, "Literacy and Education in England," 79–80, 82–83, 123–24, 126–27, 135–36.

9. Egil Johansson, "Literacy Studies in Sweden: Some Examples," in *Literacy and Society in a Historical Perspective: A Conference Report*, ed. E. Johansson, Educational Reports Umeå (Umeå, Sweden: Umeå University and School of Education, 1973), 49. We would like to thank Professor Kjell Harnqvist for his assistance in pursuing this investigation.

10. This discussion is based on Johansson, "Literacy Studies in Sweden," 41–50, which includes reproductions of two pages from the registers.

11. The Little Catechism of Luther, translated into Swedish, with officially published "Explanations," functioned as did the Bible in Cromwellian England as a source of religious authority. One of the reasons for this was the failure of various projects to translate the Bible in its entirety into Swedish. The era of cheap Bibles opened in Sweden only at the beginning of the nineteenth century. See Michael Roberts, "The Swedish Church," *Sweden's Age of Greatness*, ed. M. Roberts (New York: St. Martin's Press, 1973), 138–40. Those who had not learned the Little Catechism were forbidden by law in 1686 to marry. See Claude Nordmann, *Grandeur at liberté de la Suède (1660–1792)* (Paris and Louvain: Béatrice-Nauwelaerts, 1971), 118.

12. See François de la Fontainerie, ed. and trans., *French Liberalism and Education in the Eighteenth Century: The Writings of La Chalotais, Turgot, Diderot and Condorcet on National Education* (New York and London: McGraw-Hill, 1932), 95, 230, quoted in Frederick B. Artz, *The Development of Technical Education in France, 1500–1850* (Cambridge: MIT Press, 1966), 68, 71. The centrality of mathematics is also discussed in Roger Hahn, *The Anatomy of a Scientific Institution: The Paris Academy of Sciences, 1666–1803* (Berkeley: University of California Press, 1971), esp. 95–97. For efforts to apply mathematics to social questions, see Keith Michael Baker, *Condorcet: From National Philosophy to Social Mathematics* (Chicago: University of Chicago Press, 1975), esp. 332–42.

13. For the struggle between humanist classicists and scientists for direction of the secondary-school program, see Antoine Prost, *Histoire de l'enseignement en France, 1800–1967* (Paris: A. Colin, 1968), 55–58.

14. Charles Kindleberger, "Technical Education and the French Entrepeneur," in *Enterprise and Entrepreneurs in Nineteenth- and Twentieth-Century France*, ed. Edward C. Carter II, Robert Forster, and Joseph N. Moody (Baltimore: Johns Hopkins University Press, 1976), 26–27.

15. For eighteenth-century growth rates in literacy, as estimated by marriage-contract signatures, see Furet and Sachs, "La croissance de l'alphabétisation," 726–27.

16. For primary and secondary schooling during the Revolutionary and Napoleonic years, see Maurice Gontard, *L'enseignement primaire en France de la Révolution à la loi Guizot (1789–1833)* (Paris: Belles Lettres, 1959); Louis Liard, *L'enseignement supérieur en France, 1789–1893*, 2 vols. (Paris: A. Colin, 1888–94); and Robert R. Palmer, ed. and trans., *The School of the French Revolution: A Documentary History of the College Louis-le-Grand . . . 1762–1814* (Princeton: Princeton University Press, 1975).

17. Furet and Sachs in "La croissance de l'alphabétisation," 722–37, argue that the Revolution accelerated trends in progress. The South continued to "catch up," the difference between male and female literacy rates narrowed, and the rate of literacy progress, within a narrow band, slowly moved forward. Evidence of some newly appreciated continuities in secondary education over the period from 1780 to 1836 are analyzed in the revisionist work of Dominique Julia and Paul Pressly, "La population scolaire en 1789," *Annales: Economies, Sociétés, Civilisations* 30 (1975): 1516–61.

18. See Eugen Weber, *Peasants into Frenchmen: The Modernization of Rural France, 1870–1914* (Stanford, CA: Stanford University Press, 1976), 319, for an example of this relationship as late as the 1860s.

19. For a discussion of these standards in the context of the 1816 rulings, see Gontard, *L'enseignement primaire*, 300–306.

20. For the contemporary sources, see Weber, *Peasants into Frenchmen*, 305–6.

21. On the metric system, made the only legal measure in 1840, see Weber, 30–35.

22. On the nineteenth-century pedagogy, see the observations of Prost, *Histoire de l'enseignement*, 119–24, 276–82.

23. Roger Thabault, *Education and Change in a Village Community: Mazières-en-Gâtine 1848–1914* (New York: Schocken Books, 1971), 61.

24. Cited in Weber, *Peasants into Frenchmen*, 306.

25. A table of legislation affecting French education at all levels, 1794–1967, may be found in Prost, *Histoire de l'enseignement*, 501–11.

26. For the preprofessional dependence of the French primary-school teacher on local religious authority during the early nineteenth century, see Peter V. Meyers, "Professionalization and Societal Change: Rural Teachers in Nineteenth-Century France," *Journal of Social History* 9 (1976): 542–46.

27. F. Guizot, *Memoires* 3: 69–70, cited in Gontard, *L'enseignement primaire*, 495–96.

28. See Weber, *Peasants into Frenchmen*, 305–6. In arguing the laicization of French education by the mid-nineteenth century, Michalina Clifford-Vaughn and Margaret Archer, *Social Conflict and Educational Change in England and France, 1789–1848* (Cambridge: Cambridge University Press, 1971), 202, have not presented a convincing argument.

29. Prost, *Histoire de l'enseignement*, 192–203. Legislation in 1886 was designed to eliminate the religious from a teaching role in public schools.

30. For an excellent discussion of the role of Ernest Lavisse in creating the "civic" and "national" history texts, see William R. Keylor, *Academy and Community: The Foundation of the French Historical Profession* (Cambridge: Harvard University Press, 1975), 92–100.

31. From Charles-Victor Langlois and Charles Seignobos, *Introduction aux études historiques* (Paris: Hachette et Compagnie, 1898), 288–89, cited in Keylor, 99, and Weber, *Peasants into Frenchmen*, 333. On the relationship of this kind of instruction to nation building, see Karl Deutsch, *Nationalism and Social Communication: An Inquiry into the Foundations of Nationality* (Cambridge: MIT Press; New York: Wiley, 1953), 92–99, 155.

32. A graph showing the rise in literacy measured by the capacity to sign in the years from 1830 to 1910 is offered in Prost, *Histoire de l'enseignement*, 96. Also given (98) is a graph showing the number and distribution of students in primary schooling from 1810 to 1890.

33. Thabault, *Education and Change*, 64. The relationship between the capacity to sign and the capacity to read is discussed by Schofield, "The Measurement of Literacy in Pre-Industrial England," 324; Furet and Sachs, "La croissance de l'alphabétisation," esp. 715–16, 720–21; and Stone, "Literacy and Education in England," 98–99.

34. From Mitford Mathews, *Teaching to Read: Historically Considered* (Chicago: University of Chicago Press, 1966), 55.

35. For an assessment of Gedike's work, see Mathews, 37–43.

36. Samuel Putnam, *The Analytical Reader* (Portland, ME: Wm. Hyde, 1836), cited in Charles C. Fries, *Linguistics and Reading* (New York: Holt, 1963), 10.

37. George Farnham, *The Sentence Method* (Syracuse, NY: C. W. Bardeen, 1881), cited in Fries, 11.

38. Clarence S. Yoakum and Robert M. Yerkes, *Army Mental Tests* (New York: Henry Holt, 1920), 2; and Lewis M. Terman, "Methods of Examining: History, Development, and Preliminary Results," *Psychological Examining in the United States Army*, ed. Robert M. Yerkes, Memoirs of the National Academy of Sciences, vol. 15, part 2 (Washington, DC: Government Printing Office, 1921): 299–546.

39. May Ayres Burgess, *The Measurement of Silent Reading* (New York: Russell Sage Foundation, 1921), 11–12.

40. See Raymond E. Callahan, *Education and the Cult of Efficiency* (Chicago: University of Chicago Press, 1962); and David B. Tyack, *The One Best System: A History of American Education* (Cambridge: Harvard University Press, 1974), 198–216.

41. Leonard P. Ayres, *Laggards in Our Schools: A Study of Elimination and Retardation in City School Systems* (New York: Russell Sage Foundation, 1909). This book was prompted by concern with the large number of school children who were older than they should have been for their assigned grade level.

42. Ayres, 20, 38, 66.

43. On functional illiteracy, see David Harman, "Illiteracy: An Overview," *Harvard Educational Review* 40 (1970): 226–30. The United States Census Bureau, however, uses the completion of six years of schooling as the standard for literacy. For a review of the relationship of six years of schooling to selected measures of reading ability, see John R. Bormuth, "Reading Literacy: Its Definition and Assessment," *Toward A Literate Society: The Report of the Committee on Reading of the National Academy of Education*, ed. John B. Carroll and Jeanne S. Chall (New York: McGraw-Hill, 1975), 62–63.

44. Jeanne S. Chall, "The Great Debate: Ten Years Later, with a Modest Proposal for Reading Stages," *Theory and Practice of Early Reading*, ed. Lauren B. Resnick and Phyllis Weaver (Hillsdale, NJ: Erlbaum, 1979).

15. The Social Context of Literacy

1. These last claims are now much in the literature, especially in literature justifying writing programs. Before believing them completely, teachers and administrators should read the very important book by Sylvia Scribner and Michael Cole, *The Psychology of Literacy* (Cambridge: Harvard University Press, 1981).

18. Inventing the University

1. This article represents an abridged version of a chapter in *When a Writer Can't Write: Studies in Writer's Block and Other Composing Problems*, ed. Mike Rose (New York: Guilford, 1985).

2. David Olson has made a similar observation about school-related problems of language learning in younger children. Here is his conclusion: "Depending upon whether children assumed language was primarily suitable for making assertions and conjectures or primarily for making direct or indirect commands, they will either find school texts easy or difficult" (107).

3. For Aristotle there were both general and specific commonplaces. A speaker, says Aristotle, has a "stock of arguments to which he may turn for a particular need."

> If he knows the *topic* (regions, places, lines of argument)—and a skilled speaker will know them—he will know where to find what he wants for a special case. The general topics, or *common*places, are regions containing arguments that are common to all branches of knowledge. . . . But there are also special topics (regions, places, *loci*) in which one looks for arguments appertaining to particular branches of knowledge, special sciences, such as ethics or politics. (154–55)

And, he says, "The topics or places, then, may be indifferently thought of as in the science that is concerned, or in the mind of the speaker." But the question of location is "indifferent" *only* if the mind of the speaker is in line with set opinion, general assumption. For the speaker (or writer) who is not situated so comfortably in the privileged public realm, this is indeed not an indifferent matter at all. If he does not have the commonplace at hand, he will not, in Aristotle's terms, know where to go at all.

4. See especially Bartholomae and Rose for articles on curricula designed to move students into university discourse. The movement to extend writing "across the curriculum" is evidence of a general concern for locating students within the work of the university: see especially Bizzell or Maimon et al. For longer works directed specifically at basic writing, see

Ponsot and Deen, and Shaughnessy. For a book describing a course for more advanced students, see Coles.

5. See especially Bizzell, and Bizzell and Herzberg. My debt to Bizzell's work should be evident everywhere in this essay.

6. In support of my argument that this is the kind of writing that does the work of the academy, let me offer the following excerpt from a recent essay by Wayne Booth ("The Company We Keep: Self-Making in Imaginative Art, Old and New"):

> I can remember making up songs of my own, no doubt borrowed from favorites like "Hello, Central, Give me Heaven," "You Can't Holler Down My Rain Barrel," and one about the ancient story of a sweet little "babe in the woods" who lay down and died, with her brother.
>
> I asked my mother, in a burst of creative egotism, why nobody ever learned to sing my songs, since after all I was more than willing to learn *theirs*. I can't remember her answer, and I can barely remember snatches of two of "my" songs. But I can remember dozens of theirs, and when I sing them, even now, I sometimes feel again the emotions, and see the images, that they aroused then. Thus who I am now—the very shape of my soul—was to a surprising degree molded by the works of "art" that came my way.
>
> I set "art" in quotation marks, because much that I experienced in those early books and songs would not be classed as art according to most definitions. But for the purposes of appraising the effects of "art" on "life" or "culture," and especially for the purposes of thinking about the effects of the "media," we surely must include every kind of artificial experience that we provide for one another. . . .
>
> In this sense of the word, all of us are from the earliest years fed a steady diet of art. . . . (58–59)

While there are similarities in the paraphrasable content of Booth's arguments and my student's, what I am interested in is each writer's method. Both appropriate terms from a common discourse (about *art* and *inspiration*) in order to push against an established way of talking (about tradition and the individual). This effort of opposition clears a space for each writer's argument and enables the writers to establish their own "sense" of the key words in the discourse.

7. Preparation of this manuscript was supported by the Learning Research and Development Center of the University of Pittsburgh, which is supported in part by the National Institute of Education. I am grateful also to Mike Rose, who pushed and pulled at this paper at a time when it needed it.

20. The Ethnography of Literacy

1. Cf. the many writings of Ivan Illich or Marshall McLuhan.

2. Cf. Lévi-Strauss' suggestion that far from being the mainspring of civilization—i.e., the invention that allowed the rise of city states, science, etc.—the initial function of literacy was state control of the masses, taxation, military conscription, slavery, etc. (Claude Lévi-Strauss, *Tristes Topiques* [London: Jonathan Cape, 1973], 298–300.

3. William Labov's work on this point is exemplary. See especially his "Relation of Reading Failure to Peergroup Status," *Language in the Inner City* (Philadelphia: University of Pennsylvania, 1972), 241–54.

4. Robert Escarpit, *The Book Revolution* (Paris and New York: UNESCO, 1966), and *The Sociology of Literature* (Painesville, OH: Lake Erie College Studies, 1965).

5. Frank Rowsome, Jr., *The Verse by the Side of the Road* (New York: E. P. Dutton, 1966). Other work on signs has been done by followers of Kevin Lynch, *The Image of the City* (Cambridge: MIT Press, 1960).

6. Susan U. Philips, "Literacy as a Mode of Communication on the Warm Springs Indian Reservation," *Foundations of Language Development: A Multidisciplinary Approach*, vol. 2, ed. Eric H. Lenneberg and Elizabeth Lenneberg (New York: Academic Press; Paris: UNESCO, 1975), 367–82.

7. *Signs of Life: Symbols in the American City*, program accompanying an exhibition at the Renwick Gallery, Washington, DC, Feb. 26–Sept. 30, 1976.

8. Marcel Proust, *On Reading* (New York: Macmillan, 1971).

9. C. Hooykaas, *Surya-Sevana, the Way to God of a Balinese Siva Priest* (Amsterdam: Noord-Hollandsche U. M., 1966). For this and the above example I am indebted to James Boon, "Further Operations of Culture in Anthropology," *The Idea of Culture in the Social Sciences*, ed. Louis Schneider and Charles Bonjean (Cambridge: Cambridge University Press, 1973), 1–32.

10. Raymond Williams, *Culture and Society* (London: Penguin, 1958).

11. A model of this sort is Richard Hoggart, *The Uses of Literacy* (London: Chatto and Windus, 1957). Unfortunately, there is less on the "uses" of literacy per se than one would wish.

12. For a sampling of work on writings for the working classes in Britain, see P. J. Keating, *The Working Classes in Victorian Fiction* (London: Routledge and Kegan Paul, 1971); Louis James, *Fiction for the Working Man* (London: Penguin, 1963).

13. See, for example, Dell Hymes, "The Ethnography of Speaking," *Anthropology and Human Behavior*, ed. Thomas Gladwin and William Sturtevant (Washington, DC: Anthropological Society of Washington, 1967); "The Anthropological Linguistic Theory," *American Anthropologist* 66 (1964): 6–56; "The Ethnography of Communication," *American Anthropologist* 66 (1964): 1–34; "Models of the Interaction of Language and Social Life," *Directions in Sociolinguistics*, ed. J. J. Gumperz and Dell Hymes, (New York: Holt, 1972), 35–71. My debt to Hymes in this paper should be obvious.

14. This list is adapted from Keith Basso, "The Ethnography of Writing," *Explorations in the Ethnography of Speaking*, ed. Richard Bauman and Joel Sherzer (Cambridge: Cambridge University Press, 1974), 425–32. Basso was in turn adapting his questions from the Hymes references in note 13.

23. *Protean Shapes in Literacy Events*

1. Preschool literacy socialization is a growing field of research heavily influenced by studies of social interactions surrounding language input to children learning to talk. For a review of this literature and especially its characterizations of how mainstream school-oriented families prepare their children for taking meaning from print, see Heath (1982). The most thorough study of literacy socialization in a comparative perspective is Scollon and Scollon (1981).

2. This transcript was first included in Heath (1979), a report on several types of literacy events in the work settings of Trackton residents. In these events, neither customarily expected literacy behaviors nor general conversational rules were followed.

3. Current work by linguists, sociologists, and anthropologists in medical, legal, and business settings repeatedly emphasizes the hazards of inappropriate behavior in these situations. See, for example, Cicourel (1981) for a survey of research in medical settings; O'Barr (1981) for a similar overview of legal studies. Gumperz (1976, 1977, and 1980) and Gumperz and Cook-Gumperz (1981) provide numerous theoretical and methodological perspectives on interethnic communication in professional contexts.

25. *Who Are the Adult Illiterates?*

1. Other estimates range from two million to twenty million. "Most prudent officials first settle on a figure of around 8 million, then qualify it by saying 'give or take 5 million.' There is only one solid indication that the population of illegal immigrants is

increasing: The sharp rise in the number of them found and expelled by agents of the Immigration and Naturalization Service. In 1966, the service expelled 133,000. Last year, it expelled 793,000" (*The New York Times*, 1 May 1977a).

2. In 1977 a high-ranking official of the New York City public schools defended the eighth-grade reading level as an adequate criterion for high-school graduation. He reminded those critical of the school system that most of the young people graduating from New York City high schools had reading levels superior to those of their parents, and pointed out that, by definition, approximately one-half of those graduating from high school will read below twelfth-grade level and one-half above.

3. This chapter draws on a great many statistical reports and studies. We relied most heavily on the *U.S. Census of the Population: 1970* and on the monthly updates to that census that are published as *Current Population Reports*; on publications of the National Center for Education Statistics (NCES), especially *The Condition of Education: 1976*; the National Advisory Council on Adult Education (NACAE), especially its report dated November 1974, *A Target Population in Adult Education*; the General Accounting Office; and the U.S. Bureau of Labor Statistics.

4. The U.S. Office of Education uses the figure fifty-four million. The most recent NACAE figures suggest that the numbers may be as high as sixty-five million.

5. In 1975, the U.S. Bureau of Labor Statistics, presumably working from more-or-less the same census data, arrived at 9 percent of the population over sixteen, or a total of 14,153,000.

6. Although this number probably includes immigrants, a large number of elderly people, and those with severe physical and mental handicaps, it is interesting to note that NCES reports that almost two million children between the ages of seven and seventeen were not enrolled in school in 1970 (*The Condition of Education*, 63).

7. The 130,000 refuges from Vietnam, Laos, and Cambodia have been targeted for special services through the Emergency Adult Education Program for Indo-Chinese Refugees.

8. Note that we do not equate successful functioning or leading creative and productive lives in their own communities or in the larger society with participation in the labor force by native Americans or by any other group. We are simply using the available statistical data for what they can tell us.

9. These figures can be explained only partly by the relative population numbers, that is, by the fact that, because women live longer than men, women outnumber men in the total population by about 100 to 94.8.

27. *The Adult Literacy Process as Cultural Action for Freedom and Education and Conscientização*

1. In languages like Portuguese or Spanish, words are composed syllabically. Thus, every nonmonosyllabic word is, technically, *generative*, in the sense that other words can be constructed from its decomposed syllables. For a word to be authentically generative, however, certain conditions must be present which will be discussed in a later section of this essay.

2. Jean Paul Sartre, *Situations I* (Paris: Librairie Gallimard, 1917), 31.

3. The digestive concept of knowledge is suggested by "controlled readings"; by classes which consist only of lectures; by the use of memorized dialogues in language learning; by bibliographical notes which indicate not only which chapter, but which lines and words are to be read; by the methods of evaluating the students' progress in learning.

4. See Paulo Freire, "La alfabetizacion de adultos, critica de su vision ingenua; compreension de su vision critica," in *Introducción a la acción cultural* (Santiago: ICIRA, 1969).

5. There are two noteworthy exceptions among these primers: (1) In Brazil, *Viver e lutar*, developed by a team of specialists of the Basic Education Movement, sponsored by the National Conference of Bishops. (This reader became the object of

controversy after it was banned as subversive by the then governor of Guanabara, Mr. Carlos Lacerda, in 1963.) (2) In Chile, the ESPIGA collection, despite some small defects. The collection was organized by Jefatura de Planes Extraordinarios de Educacion de Adultos, of the Public Education Ministry.

6. Since at the time this essay was written the writer did not have access to the primers, and was, therefore, vulnerable to recording phrases imprecisely or to confusing the author of one or another primer, it was thought best not to identify the authors or the titles of the books.

7. [The English here would be nonsensical, as is the Portuguese, the point being the emphasis on the consonant *d*. — EDITOR]

8. The author may even have added here, ". . . If, however, this should happen, put a little mercurochrome."

9. [The Portuguese word here translated as *marginal man* is *marginado*. This has a passive sense: he who has been made marginal, or sent outside society; as well as the sense of a state of existence on the fringe of society. — TRANSLATOR]

10. *La situacion educativa en America Latina*, Guadro no. 20 (Paris: UNESCO, 1960), 263.

11. Similar responses were evoked by the programs carried out in Chile.

12. Celso Beisegel, in an unpublished work.

13. I am not opposed to reading texts, which are in fact indispensable to developing the visual-graphic channel of communication and which in great part should be elaborated by the participants themselves. I should add that our experience is based on the use of multiple channels of communication.

14. "Educação de Adultos e Unificação do Culturea," *Revista de Cultura*, Estudos Universitários (Recife: Universidade do Recife, 1963), 2–4.

15. Luis Costa Lima, Professor of Literary Theory, has analyzed many of these texts by illiterate authors.

16. "A Fundamentação Teórica do Sistema Paulo Freire do Educação," *Revista de Cultura*, Estudos Universitários (Recife: Universidade do Recife, 1963).

17. Aurenice Cardoso, "Conscientização e Alfabetização-Visão Prática do Sistema Paulo Freire de Educação de Adultos," *Revista de Cultura*, Estudos Universitários (Recife: Universidade do Recife, 1963).

18. Generally, in a period of six weeks to two months, we could leave a group of twenty-five persons reading newspapers, writing notes and simple letters, and discussing problems of local and national interest.

Each culture circle was equipped with a Polish-made projector, imported at the cost of about $13.00. Since we had not yet set up our own laboratory, a filmstrip cost us about $7–$8. We also used an inexpensive blackboard. The slides were projected on the wall of the house where the culture circle met or, where this was difficult, on the reverse side (painted white) of the blackboard.

The Education Ministry imported 35,000 of the projectors, which after the military coup of 1964 were presented on television as "highly subversive."

19. In a television interview, Gilson Amado observed lucidly, "They can do this, because there is no such thing as oral illiteracy."

20. In correct Portuguese, *tu já lês*.

21. *Resouver* is a corruption of *resolver*; *poblemas* a corruption of *problemas*; the letter *s* is lacking from the syllable *cons*.

22. Interestingly enough, as a rule the illiterates wrote confidently and legibly, largely overcoming the neutral indecisiveness of beginners. Elza Freire thinks this may be due to the fact that these persons, beginning with the discussion of the anthropological concept of culture, discovered themselves to be more fully human, thereby acquiring an increasing emotional confidence in their learning which was reflected in their motor activity.

23. I wish to acknowledge the support given our efforts by President Goulart, by Ministers of Education Paulo de Tarso and Júlio Sambaquy, and by the Rector of the University of Recife, Professor João Alfredo da Costa Lima.

24. *Ends and Means* (New York and London, 1937), 252.

25. I have never forgotten the publicity (done cleverly, considering our acritical mental habits) for a certain Brazilian public figure. The bust of the candidate was displayed with arrows pointing to his head, his eyes, his mouth, and his hands. Next to the arrows appeared the legend:

You don't need to think, he thinks for you!
You don't need to see, he sees for you!
You don't need to talk, he talks for you!
You don't need to act, he acts for you!

26. In the campaigns carried out against me, I have been called "ignorant" and "illiterate," "the author of a method so innocuous that it did not even manage to teach him how to read and write." It was said that I was not "the inventor" of dialogue (as if I had ever made such an irresponsible affirmation). It was said that I had done "nothing original," and that I had "plagiarized European or North-American educators," as well as the author of a Brazilian primer. (On the subject of originality, I have always agreed with Dewey, for whom originality does not lie in the "extraordinary and fanciful," but "in putting everyday things to uses which had not occurred to others." *Democracy and Education* [New York, 1916], 187).

None of these accusations has ever wounded me. What does leave me perplexed is to hear or read that I intended to "Bolchevize the country" with my method. In fact, my actual crime was that I treated literacy as more than a mechanical problem, and linked it to *conscientização*, which was "dangerous." It was that I viewed education as an effort to liberate men, not as yet another instrument to dominate them.

28. The Nicaraguan National Literacy Crusade of 1980

1. *Sandinista* is the adjective derived from the name of the revolutionary hero Augusto Cesar Sandino, who fought against the U.S. Marine occupation of Nicaragua between 1927 and 1933. He advocated independence from foreign domination, education, land reform, and agricultural cooperatives.

2. "The Great National Literacy Campaign: Heroes and Martyrs for the Creation of Nicaragua," mimeographed report, trans. and ed. National Network in Solidarity with the Nicaraguan People (Managua: Nicaraguan Ministry of Education, 1980), 1. *Somocismo* refers to the corrupt social order that prevailed under the successive governments of the Somoza family between 1937 and 1979.

3. In Cuba, the struggle against Fulgencio Batista was waged, for the most part, from detachments or *focos* in the Sierra Maestra mountains involving fewer than five hundred guerillas. By contrast, the protracted struggle against Somoza took place for the most part in urban areas, in a country that was already 50 percent urban.

4. Paulo Freire, "The Adult Literacy Process as Cultural Action for Freedom," *Harvard Educational Review* 40 (1970): 205–23; and *Pedagogy of the Oppressed* (New York: Seabury Press, 1970). Also see Robert F. Arnove and Jairo Arboleda, "Literacy: Power or Mystification?" *Literacy Discussion* Dec. 1973: 389–414; and Jonathan Kozol, "A New Look at the Literacy Campaign in Cuba," *Harvard Educational Review* 38 (1978): 341–77.

5. Eighty percent of the children in rural areas were not in school, and 21 percent of the illiterates in the country were accounted for by youths in the 10–14 age group. Less than 25 percent of the appropriate age group (13–18) were enrolled in secondary schools.

6. While certain segments of the Catholic and Evangelical religions opposed the literacy campaign as "too political and too secular," these churches were principal agencies of support of the CNA. See Michael Dodson, "The Churches in the Nicaraguan Revolu-

tion," paper prepared for the ninth national meeting of the Latin American Studies Association, Bloomington, IN, 18 Oct. 1980: 25.

7. The final examination consisted of the learner writing his/her name, reading a paragraph containing vocabulary from the more advanced lessons (equivalent to a third- or fourth-grade primary education text), answering questions about the paragraph, taking dictation, and writing a brief essay on one of three themes.

8. Supplying food rations to the *brigadistas* used up a substantial proportion of the $25 million that the CNA cost; of this amount, $5 million was allocated for extra rations so that the *brigadistas* could help feed their poverty-stricken families.

Notes on Contributors

Robert F. Arnove is Professor of Comparative and International Education at Indiana University, Bloomington. He is the co-editor of *National Literacy Campaigns: Historical and Comparative Perspectives* and the author of *Education and Revolution in Nicaragua*. He has written extensively on education and social change.

David Bartholomae is Professor of English and Director of Composition at the University of Pittsburgh. He has written widely on composition theory and composition instruction, receiving the 1980 Braddock Award for his article, "The Study of Error." With Anthony Petrosky, he is co-author/editor of three books: *The Teaching of Writing; Facts, Artifacts and Counterfacts;* and *Ways of Reading.*

Carolyn L. Burke is Professor of Education at Indiana University, Bloomington. With Yetta Goodman she has written the *Reading Miscue Inventory Manual.* She has also edited *Reading Strategies: Focus on Comprehension* (with Yetta Goodman and Barry Sherman).

Michael T. Clanchy is Reader in Medieval History at the University of Glasgow and the General Editor of the series Foundations of Medieval History published by Holmes and Meier. He has written many articles, as well as *From Memory to Written Record: England 1066–1272* and *England and Its Rulers, 1066–1272.*

Michael Cole is currently Professor of Communication and Psychology at the University of California, San Diego, and Director of the Laboratory of Comparative Human Cognition. He was educated as an experimental psychologist, obtaining his degree from Indiana University in 1962. He has conducted research on human development in several cultural areas, focusing on the interrelationships among contexts, mediational means, and cultural context.

Suzanne de Castell is Associate Professor in the Faculty of Education at Simon Fraser University, British Columbia. She has published numerous essays on educational history, philosophy, and theory, and has co-edited *Literacy, Society and Schooling* and *Language, Authority and Criticism: Readings on the School Textbook* (forthcoming).

William A. Diehl taught in the Special Studies Division at the University of Georgia when he wrote (with Larry Mikulecky) "The Nature of Reading at Work."

Anne Eberle worked with the Vermont Adult Basic Education Program when *The Adult Illiterate Speaks Out: Personal Perspectives on Learning to*

Read and Write was published by the National Institute of Education in 1980.

Nan Elasser taught English composition at the College of the Virgin Islands when she wrote (with Kyle Fiore) " 'Strangers No More': A Liberatory Literacy Curriculum." She has also written (with Vera P. John-Steiner) "An Interactionist Approach to Advancing Literacy," *Harvard Educational Review*, 1977.

Frederick Erickson is chair of the Educational Leadership Division, Graduate School of Education, University of Pennsylvania. His research interests include topics in sociolinguistics, the anthropology of education, and ethnology, with a special focus on racial, cultural, and linguistic equity. Recent publications include a book (edited with Jeffrey J. Shultz) *The Counselor as Gatekeeper: Interaction in Counseling Education* and a chapter on "Qualitative Methods in Research on Teaching" in the third edition of *Handbook of Research in Teaching*.

Kyle Fiore taught American Studies and Women's Studies at the University of New Mexico when she wrote (with Nan Elsasser) " 'Strangers No More'; A Liberatory Literacy Curriculum." She is also the author (with Nan Elsasser and Yvonne Tixier y Vigil) of *Las Mujeres: Conversations from a Hispanic Community*.

Elizabeth C. Fisk (Skinner) is Faculty Research Associate for the National Center for Postsecondary Governance and Finance at Arizona State University. Her work has focused on the uses of written language in college settings and in the workplace. She recently contributed to an edited volume, *Integrating Work and Learning*.

Paolo Freire is a Professor of Education at the Catholic University of São Paulo. He was the general coordinator of Brazil's National Plan of Adult Literacy and has been a consultant for UNESCO's Institute of Research and Training in Agrarian Reform. His books include *Pedagogy of the Oppressed, Education for Critical Consciousness, Education: The Practice of Freedom, Pedagogy in Process*, and *The Politics of Education: Culture, Power, and Liberation*.

Yetta Goodman is Professor of Education at the University of Arizona. Her research focus over the years has been on reading and writing processes. She is especially interested in literacy development in young children.

Jack (John Rankin) Goody is William Wyse Professor of Anthropology at the University of Cambridge. He has written widely in anthropology; his books most relevant to the topic of literacy are *Literacy in Traditional Societies, The Domestication of the Savage Mind, The Interface Between the Written and the Oral*, and *The Logic of Writing and the Organization of Society*.

Kathleen Gough (Aberle) is Research Associate in Anthropology at the University of British Columbia. Among her books are *Matrilineal Kinships, Imperialism and Revolution in South Asia, Ten Times More Beautiful: The Rebuilding of Vietnam*, and *Rural Society in Southeast India*.

Harvey J. Graff is Professor of History and Humanities in the School of Arts and Humanities, University of Texas at Dallas. A specialist in comparative social and cultural history, he has published widely on historical and contemporary literacy, as well as on a variety of topics in history and the humanities. Recipient of fellowships from such agencies and institutions as NEH, ACLS, and the Newberry Library, he has written *The Literacy Myth, The Legacies of Literacy,* and *The Labyrinths of Literacy,* and has edited other volumes including *Growing Up in America,* the subject of his current work.

David Harman is Senior Lecturer in Education at Hebrew University, Jerusalem. He taught at Harvard University from 1971 to 1974, was chairman of Israel's national advisory council on youth from 1981 to 1983, and has served as a consultant to the World Bank, Thailand's Ministry of Education, and the Foundation for Child Development. His publications include *Learning to Be Parents* (with O. G. Brim) and a recent booklet from the Business Council for Effective Literacy, *Turning Illiteracy Around: An Agenda for National Action.*

Jerome C. Harste is Professor of Education at Indiana University. An author of children's books—*It Didn't Frighten Me, My Icky Picky Sister,* and others—Professor Harste's writings range widely. Together with Carolyn Burke and Virginia Woodward, he has recently completed a seven-year study of what preschool children know about reading and writing. Their book *Language Stories & Literacy Lessons* elaborates a new theoretical frame for rethinking the evolution of literacy. The recent videotape series *The Authoring Cycles: Read Better, Write Better, Reason Better* begins to explore the curricular potential of their findings.

Eric Alfred Havelock is Emeritus Professor of Classics at Yale University. He is the author of many books including *Preface to Plato, The Greek Concept of Justice: From Its Shadow in Homer to Its Substance in Plato, Origins of Western Literacy,* and *The Literate Revolution in Greece and Its Cultural Consequences.*

Shirley Brice Heath is Professor of English and Linguistics at Stanford University. She is interested in literacy and language change and has published a number of articles, chapters, and books on the subject, including *Ways with Words: Language, Life, and Work in Communities and Classrooms.*

Carman St. John Hunter worked with World Education—a nonprofit organization devoted to functional literacy in the third world—when she wrote *Adult Literacy in the United States* (with David Harman). More recently, she has edited a book for the International Council for Adult Education (with John Hunter and Martha McKee Keehn), *Adult Education in China.*

Carl F. Kaestle is Professor of Educational Policy Studies and History at the University of Wisconsin at Madison. He has written several books on the history of education, including *Pillars of the Republic: Common Schools and American Society 1780–1860.* His current research is on the history of the American reading public.

Allan Luke is Lecturer and Deputy Dean of Education at James Cook University of North Queensland. His current research centers on literacy, curriculum theory, and discourse analysis. He has published numerous articles and two anthologies: *Literacy, Society and Schooling,* coedited with S. de Castell and K. Egan; and *Language, Authority and Criticism,* coedited with C. Luke and S. de Castell. He is the author of *Literacy, Textbooks and Ideology: Postwar Literacy Instruction and the Mythology of Dick and Jane.*

Larry Mikulecky is Professor of Education and Director of the Learning Skills Center at Indiana University–Bloomington. He specializes in examining literacy demands and strategies of adolescents and adults in business, university, and secondary school settings. He has published extensively on the topic of adult literacy in the workplace.

John U. Ogbu, a native of Nigeria, is Professor of Anthropology at the University of California, Berkeley. He is the author of *The Next Generation: An Ethnography of Education in an Urban Neighborhood* and *Minority Education and Caste: The American System in Cross-Cultural Perspective*.

Morris A. Okun is Professor of Educational Psychology at Arizona State University. He specializes in stress and coping among college students and the elderly and has published a number of articles on this topic, including "Buffer and Booster Effects as Event-Support Transactions," *American Journal of Community Psychology*, forthcoming.

David R. Olson is Professor of Applied Psychology at the Ontario Institute for Studies in Education and Co-Director of the McLuhan Program in Culture and Technology at the University of Toronto. His major research is devoted to the analysis of the relation between the oral conversational language of preschool children and the formalized language of written texts. He is the editor of several works: *Literacy, Language and Learning: The Nature and Consequences of Reading and Writing* (with Nancy Torrance and Angela Hildyard); *Common Sense: The Foundations for Social Science* (with Frits van Holthoon); and *Developing Theories of Mind* (with Janet Astington and Paul Harris).

Walter Jackson Ong, S.J., is William E. Haren Professor of English and Professor of Humanities in Psychiatry at St. Louis University. He is the author of many books related to literacy, including *The Presence of the Word*, *Rhetoric, Romance, and Technology*, *Interfaces of the Word*, and *Orality and Literacy*.

P. David Pearson is Co-Director of the Center for the Study of Reading at the University of Illinois at Urbana-Champaign, where he also teaches undergraduate and graduate courses in literacy education. His research interests have recently focused upon validating cognitively based strategies of reading assessment.

Daniel P. Resnick is Professor of History at Carnegie Mellon University. His research interests are in literacy development, the comparative history of education, and the development of the professions. He has published a number of articles on the history of educational testing and is editor of *Literacy in Historical Perspective*.

Lauren B. Resnick is Professor of Psychology and Education and Director of the Learning Research and Development Center at the University of Pittsburgh. Her primary interest is the emerging field of the cognitive psychology of instruction, and her major current research focuses on the learning of mathematics and science. She has published widely on these and other topics and is the founder and editor of *Cognition and Instruction*, a major new journal in the field.

Richard C. Richardson, Jr., is Associate Director of the Center for Postsecondary Governance and Finance, and Professor of Educational Leadership and Policy Studies at Arizona State University. His current research focuses on access and achievement for minority students. His most recent book is *Fostering Minority Access and Achievement in Higher Education: The Role of Urban Community Colleges and Universities*.

Jay L. Robinson is Professor of English Language and Literature at the University of Michigan and Director of the Center for Educational Improvement through Collaboration. He specializes in English language with particular emphasis upon literacy and composition. He has published a number of books and essays in these areas and is presently preparing a collection of his own essays to be published under the title *Conversations on the Written Word* (forthcoming).

Sandra Robinson worked with the Vermont Adult Basic Education Program when she wrote (with Anne Eberle) *The Adult Illiterate Speaks Out: Personal Perspectives on Learning to Read and Write*.

Sylvia Scribner is Professor of Psychology at the Graduate Center, City University of New York. Her studies trace the influence of cultural systems such as literacy and technology on modes of thought. Her publications include *The Psychology of Literacy* (with Michael Cole) and numerous chapters on theoretical and practical intelligence.

John F. Szwed is Professor of Anthropology at Yale University. He has written on Afro-American anthropology and folk culture and has recently edited (with Roger D. Abraham) the book *After Africa: Extracts from British Travel Narratives and Journals of the Seventeenth, Eighteenth, and Nineteenth Centuries Concerning the Slaves, their Manners, and Customs in the British West Indies*.

Robert J. Tierney has taught at Harvard, has been affiliated with the Center for the Study of Reading at the University of Illinois, and is now Professor in the School of Education at Ohio State University. His current research focuses on the intersection of reading, writing, and learning.

Ian Pierre Watt is Professor of English and Director of the Humanities Center at Stanford University. His major interest has been English fiction, and he has written such books as *The Rise of the Novel; The English Novel, Scott to Hardy;* and *Conrad in the Nineteenth Century*.

Virginia A. Woodward is Associate Professor in Early Childhood Education at Indiana University in Bloomington. Her research interests include early literacy learning and collaborative learning, and she has published in each area. She and her colleagues Jerome Harste and Carolyn Burke conducted extensive research on young children's knowledge of written language, a study funded by NIE. The book *Language Stories and Literacy Lessons* resulted from this research on early literacy.

Works Cited

Abrahams, Rodger D. "Introductory Remarks to a Rhetorical Theory of Folklore." *Journal of American Folklore* 81 (1968): 143–58.

———. "The Training of the Man of Words in Talking Sweet." *Language in Society* 1 (1972): 15–29.

Achebe, Chinua. *No Longer at Ease*. New York: Ivan Obolensky, 1961.

Adams, M. J. "Failures to Comprehend and Levels of Processing in Reading." *Theoretical Issues in Reading Comprehension*. Ed. R. J. Spiro, B. C. Bruce, and W. F. Brewer. Hillsdale, NJ: Erlbaum, 1980.

Adult Education Act. Public Law 91–230, and all of its amendments through Oct. 1976.

Adult Functional Competency: A Summary. Austin Division of Extension, University of Texas, 1975. ED 114 609.

"Adult Illiteracy." *Options in Education*. Program nos. 148–49. Washington, DC: National Public Radio and the Institute for Educational Leadership of the George Washington University, 1979.

Advisory Committee on National Illiteracy. "Report." *School and Society* 30 (1929): 708.

Altick, R. D. *The English Common Reader: A Social History of the Mass Reading Public, 1800–1900*. Chicago: University of Chicago Press, 1957.

Amarel, M. "The Reader and the Text—Three Perspectives." *Reading Expository Materials*. Ed. W. Otto. New York: Academic Press, 1982.

Anderson, Alonzo B., William B. Teale, and Elette Estrada. "Low-Income Children's Preschool Literacy Experiences: Some Naturalistic Observations." *The Quarterly Newsletter of the Laboratory of Comparative Human Cognition* 2 (1980): 59–65.

Anderson, C. A. "Literacy and Schooling on the Development Threshold: Some Historical Cases." *Education and Economic Development*. Ed. C. A. Anderson and M. J. Bowman. Chicago: Aldine, 1965. 247–63.

Anderson, R. C., and A. Ortony. "On Putting Apples into Bottles: A Problem of Polysemy." *Cognitive Psychology* 7 (1975): 167–80.

Anderson, R. C., J. W. Pichert, and L. L. Shirey. *Effects of the Reader's Schema at Different Points in Time*. Technical Report No. 119. Urbana: Center for the Study of Reading, University of Illinois, 1979. ED 169 523.

Anderson, R. C., R. E. Reynolds, D. L. Schallert, and E. T. Goetz. "Frameworks for Comprehending Discourse." *American Educational Research Journal* 14 (1977): 367–82.

Anzalone, S., and S. McLaughlin. *Literacy for Specific Situations*. Amherst: Center for International Education, University of Massachusetts, 1982.

Appalachian Adult Education Center. *Community Education: Final Report*. Morehead, KY: Morehead University, 1975.

Applebee, A. N. *The Child's Concept of Story*. Chicago: University of Chicago Press, 1978.

Appleby, Joyce. "Modernization Theory and the Formation of Modern Social Theories in England and America." *Comparative Studies in Society and History* 20 (1978): 259–85.

Applewaite, H. B., and D. G. Levy. "The Concept of Modernization and the French

Enlightenment." *Studies on Voltaire and the Eighteenth Century* 84 (1971): 53–98.

Aristotle. *The Rhetoric of Aristotle*. Trans. L. Cooper. Englewood Cliffs, NJ: Prentice, 1932.

Arnove, Robert F., and Jairo Arboleda. "Literacy: Power or Mystification?" *Literacy Discussion* Dec. 1973: 389–414.

Artz, Frederick B. *The Development of Technical Education in France, 1500–1850*. Cambridge: MIT Press, 1966.

Asher, S. R. "Children's Ability to Appraise Their Own and Another Person's Communication Performance." *Developmental Psychology* 12 (1976): 24–32.

Aston, Margaret. "Lollardy and Literacy." *History* 62 (1977): 347–71.

Au, K. H., and J. Mason. "Social Organizational Factors in Learning to Read: The Balance of Rights Hypothesis." *Reading Research Quarterly* 17 (1981): 115–52.

Austin, J. L. *How to Do Things with Words*. Ed. J. O. Urmson. New York: Oxford University Press, 1962.

Auwers, L. "Reading the Marks of the Past: Exploring Female Literacy in Colonial Windsor, Connecticut." *Historical Methods* 13 (1980): 204–14.

Ayer, N. W. *American Newspaper Annual and Directory*. New York: Ayer, 1880–.

Ayres, Leonard P. *Laggards in Our Schools: A Study of Elimination and Retardation in City School Systems*. New York: Russell Sage Foundation, 1909.

Bailey, Richard W., and Robin Melanie Fosheim, eds. *Literacy for Life*. New York: Modern Language Association, 1983.

Bailyn, B. *Education in the Forming of American Society*. Chapel Hill: University of North Carolina Press, 1960.

Baker, Keith Michael. *Condorcet: From Natural Philosophy to Social Mathematics*. Chicago: University of Chicago Press, 1975.

Ballinger, Stanley E. "The Idea of Progress through Education in the French Enlightenment." *History of Education Journal* 10 (1959): 88–99.

Bantock, G. H. *The Implications of Literacy*. Leicester: Leicester University Press, 1966.

Baratz, Joan. "Teaching Reading in an Urban Negro School System." *Teaching Black Children to Read*. Ed. J Baratz and Roger Shuy. Washington, DC: Center for Applied Linguistics, 1969. 92–116.

Barclay, J. R. "The Role of Comprehension in Remembering Sentences." *Cognitive Psychology* 4 (1973): 229–54.

Barnhardt, C. "Tuning-In: Athabaskan Teachers and Athabaskan Students." *Cross-Cultural Issues in Alaskan Education*. Ed. R. Barnhardt. Vol. 2. Fairbanks: Center for Cross-Cultural Studies, University of Alaska, 1982.

Baron, Naomi. "Independence and Interdependence in Spoken and Written Language." *Visible Language* 1 (1979).

Baron, R. W. "Visual and Phonological Strategies in Reading and Spelling." *Cognitive Processes in Spelling*. Ed. U. Frith. London: Academic Press, 1980.

Bartholomae, David. "Teaching Basic Writing: An Alternative to Basic Skills." *Journal of Basic Writing* 2 (1979): 85–109.

———. "Writing Assignments: Where Writing Begins." *Fforum*. Ed. P. Stock. Montclair, NJ: Boynton/Cook, 1983. 300–312.

Bartholomae, David, and Anthony Petrosky. *Facts, Artifacts and Counterfacts: A Basic Reading and Writing Course for the College Curriculum*. Montclair, NJ: Boynton/Cook, 1986.

Bartlett, F. C. *Psychology and Primitive Culture*. Cambridge: Cambridge University Press, 1923.

———. *Remembering*. Cambridge: Cambridge University Press, 1932.

Basham, A. L. *The Wonder That Was India*. London: Sidgwick and Jackson, 1954.

Basso, Keith. "The Ethnography of Writing." *Explorations in the Ethnography of Speaking*. Ed. Richard Bauman and Joel Sherzer. Cambridge: Cambridge University Press, 1974. 425–32.

Bataille, L., ed. *Turning Point for Literacy: Proceedings of the International Symposium for Literacy, Persepolis, Iran, 1975*. Oxford: Pergamon Books, 1976.

Bateson, G. *Steps to an Ecology of Mind*. New York: Ballantine, 1972.

Beales, R. W. "Studying Literacy at the Community Level: A Research Note." *Journal of Interdisciplinary History* 9 (1978): 93–102.

Bennett, John W. *Northern Plainsmen: Adaptive Strategy and Agricultural Life*. Arlington Heights, IL: AHM Pub., 1969.

Bereiter, C. "Integration of Skill Systems in the Development of Textual Writing Competence." Unpublished mimeo, 1977.

Berger, P., and T. Luckmann. *The Social Construction of Reality*. Garden City, NY: Doubleday, 1966.

Berreman, Gerald D. "Race, Caste, and Other Invidious Distinctions in Social Stratification." *Race* 14 (1972): 383–91.

Bettelheim, Bruno, and Karen Zelan. "Why Children Don't Like to Read." *Atlantic Monthly* Nov. 1981: 25–31.

Biebuyck, Daniel, and Kahombo C. Mateene, eds. and trans. *The Mwindo Epic from the Banyanga*, as narrated by Candi Rureke. Berkeley and Los Angeles: University of California Press, 1971.

Biehler, R. F. *Psychology Applied to Teaching*. Boston: Houghton-Mifflin, 1974.

Birnbaum, J. C. "The Reading and Composing Behavior of Selected Fourth and Seventh Grade Students." *Research in the Teaching of English* 16 (1982): 241–60.

Bissex, G. *Gnys at Wrk: A Child Learns to Write and Read*. Cambridge: Harvard University Press, 1980.

Bizzell, Patricia. "Cognition, Convention, and Certainty: What We Need to Know about Writing." *Pre/Text* 3 (1982): 213–44.

―――――. "College Composition: Initiation into the Academic Discourse Communities." *Curriculum Inquiry* 12 (1982): 191–207.

―――――. "The Ethos of Academic Discourse." *College Composition and Communication* 29 (1978): 351–55.

Bizzell, Patricia, and Bruce Herzberg. " 'Inherent' Ideology, 'Universal' History, 'Empirical' Evidence, and 'Context-Free' Writing: Some Problems with E. D. Hirsch's *The Philosophy of Composition*." *Modern Language Notes* 95 (1980): 1181–1202.

Blachowitz, C. L. Z. "Semantic Constructivity in Children's Comprehension." *Reading Research Quarterly* 13 (1978): 188–99.

Blackbeard, B. "The Pulps." *Handbook of American Culture* 3 (1981): 195–223.

Blaug, Mark. "Literacy and Economic Development." *School Review* 74 (1966): 393–417.

Bloom, L. *Language Development: Form and Function in Emerging Grammars*. Cambridge: MIT Press, 1970.

Bloome, D. "Reading and Writing in a Classroom: A Sociolinguistic Ethnography." Paper presented at the meeting of the American Education Research Association. Los Angeles, Apr. 1981.

Bloomfield, L. *Linguistic Aspects of Science*. Chicago: University of Chicago Press, 1939.

Bluck, R. S. *Plato's Life and Thought*. London: Routledge and Kegan Paul, 1949.

Bobbitt, John F. *The Curriculum*. Boston: Houghton Mifflin, 1918.

Bogart, L. *Press and Public: Who Reads What, When, Where, and Why*. Hillsdale, NJ: Erlbaum, 1981.

Bond, Horace Mann. *Education of the Negro in the American Social Order*. New York: Octagon Books, 1966.

―――――. *Negro Education in Alabama: A Study in Cotton and Steel*. New York: Atheneum, 1969.

Boon, James. "Further Operations of Culture in Anthropology." *The Idea of Culture in the Social Sciences*. Ed. Louis Schneider and Charles Bonjean. Cambridge: Cambridge University Press, 1973. 1–32.

Booth, Wayne. "The Company We Keep: Self-Making in Imaginative Art, Old and New." *The Pushcart Prize, VIII: Best of the Small Presses*. Ed. Bill Henderson. Wainscott, NY: Pushcart, 1983. 57–95.

Bormuth, J. R. "Reading Literacy: Its Definition and Assessment." *Toward a Literate*

Society: The Report of the Committee on Reading of the National Academy of Education. Ed. J. B. Carroll and J. S. Chall. New York: McGraw-Hill, 1975.

―――――. "The Value and Volume of Literacy." *Visible Language* 12 (1978): 118–61.

Bourdieu, Pierre. "The Economics of Linguistic Exchange." *Social Science Information* 6 (1977): 645-68.

―――――. "Systems of Education and Systems of Thought." *International Social Science Journal* 19 (1967): 338–58.

Bourdieu, Pierre, and J. C. Passeron. *Reproduction: In Education, Society, and Culture*. Beverly Hills, CA: Sage, 1977.

Bowen, W. G. "Assessing the Economic Contribution of Education." *The Economics of Education*. Ed. Mark Blaug. Vol. 1. Harmondsworth: Penguin, 1968. 67–100.

Bowles, Samuel, and Herbert Gintis. "Capitalism and Education in the United States." *Society State and Schooling*. Ed. M. F. D. Young and G. Whitty. Brighton: Falmer Press, 1977. 192–227.

―――――. *Schooling in Capitalist America*. New York: Basic Books, 1976.

Bowman, M. J., and C. A. Anderson. "Concerning the Role of Education in Development." *Old Societies and New States*. Ed. C. Geertz. New York: Free Press, 1963. 247–79.

―――――. "Education and Economic Modernization in Historical Perspective." *Schooling and Society*. Ed. Lawrence Stone. Baltimore: Johns Hopkins University Press, 1976. 3–19.

Bracewell, R. J. "Interpretation Factors in the Four-Card Selection Task." Paper presented at the Selection Task Conference. Trento, Italy, Apr. 1974.

Bransford, J. D., and M. K. Johnson. "Consideration of Some Problems of Comprehension." *Visual Information Processing*. Ed. W. Chase. New York: Academic Press, 1973.

Bransford, J. D., J. R. Barclay, and J. J. Franks. "Sentence Memory: A Constructive versus Interpretive Approach." *Cognitive Psychology* 3 (1972): 193–209.

Brimmer, Andrew F. "Economic Development in the Black Community." *The Great Society: Lessons for the Future*. Ed. Eli Ginsberg and Robert M. Solow. New York: Basic Books, 1974. 146–63.

Britton, J., T. Burgess, N. Martin, A. McLeod, and H. Rosen. *The Development of Writing Abilities*. London: Macmillan, 1975.

Brown, R. *A First Language: The Early Stages*. Cambridge: Harvard University Press, 1973.

Bruce, B. "A Social Interaction Model of Reading." *Discourse Processes* 4 (1981): 273–311.

Bruneau, William A. "Literacy, Urbanization, and Education in Three Ancient Cultures." *Journal of Education* 19 (1973): 9–22.

Bruner, J. S. "From Communication to Language: A Psychological Perspective." *Cognition* 3 (1973): 255–87.

Bruner, J. S., and D. R. Olson. "Symbols and Texts as the Tools of Intellect." *Piaget's Developmental and Cognitive Psychology within an Extended Context*. Vol. 7 of *The Psychology of the 20th Century*. Zurich: Kindler.

Buhler, K. *Sprachtheorie*. Jena, Germany: Gustav Fischer, 1934.

Bullock, Henry Allen. *A History of Negro Education in the South: From 1619 to the Present*. New York: Praeger, 1970.

Bullock, Paul. *Aspiration vs. Opportunity: "Careers" in the Inner City*. Ann Arbor: University of Michigan Press, 1973.

Burgess, May Ayres. *The Measurement of Silent Reading*. New York: Russell Sage Foundation, 1962.

Burke, Peter. *Popular Culture in Early Modern Europe*. New York: Harper, 1978.

Burnet, J. *Early Greek Philosophy*. 2nd ed. London: A & C Black, 1908.

Buswell, G. T. *How Adults Read*. Supplementary Education Monograph 45. Chicago: University of Chicago, 1937.

Byerly, K. R. *Metropolitan and Community Daily Newspapers: A Comparison of Their*

Number, Circulation, and Trends for 1950, 1960, and 1968 in the Nation's 21 Most Populous Metropolitan Areas. Chapel Hill: University of North Carolina Press, 1968.

Calhoun, Daniel. *The Intelligence of a People*. Princeton: Princeton University Press, 1973.

Callahan, Raymond E. *Education and the Cult of Efficiency*. Chicago: University of Chicago Press, 1962.

Campbell, A., and C. Metzner. *Public Use of the Library and Other Sources of Information*. Ann Arbor: Institute for Social Research, University of Michigan, 1950.

Carcopino, J. *L'Ostracisme athénien*. Paris: F. Alcan, 1935.

Cardoso, Aurenice. "Conscientização e Alfabetização—Visão Prática do Sistema Paulo Freire de Educação de Adultos." Estudos Universitários. *Revista de Cultura*. Universidade do Recife, No. 2, 1963.

Carey, J. W. "Harold Adams Innis and Marshall McLuhan." *The Antioch Review* 27 (1967): 5–39.

Carnovsky, L. A. "A Study of the Relationship between Reading Interests and Actual Reading." *Library Quarterly* 4 (1934): 76–110.

Carothers, J. C. "Culture, Psychiatry, and the Written Word," *Psychiatry* 22 (1959): 307–20.

Carpenter, P., and M. Just. "Sentence Comprehension: A Psycholinguistic Processing Model of Verification." *Psychological Review* 82 (1975): 45–73.

Carrington, John F. *La Voix des tambours: comment comprendre le language tambouriné d'Afrique*. Kinshasa: Centre Protestant d'Editions et de Diffusion, 1974.

Carroll, J. B., and J. S. Chall, eds. *Toward a Literate Society*. New York: McGraw-Hill, 1975.

Cawelti, J. G. *Adventure, Mystery, and Romance*. Chicago: University of Chicago Press, 1976.

———. *The Six-Gun Mystique*. Bowling Green, OH: Bowling Green University Popular Press, 1971.

Caylor, John S., and Thomas G. Sticht. *Development of a Simple Readability Index for Job Reading Material*. Alexandria, VA: Human Resources Research Organization, 1973.

Cazden, C., D. Hymes, and V. John. *Functions of Language in the Classroom*. New York: Teachers College Press, 1972.

Cervero, R. M. "Does the Texas Adult Performance Level Test Measure Functional Competence?" *Adult Education* 30 (1980): 152–65.

Chadwick, J. *The Decipherment of Linear B*. Cambridge: Cambridge University Press, 1958.

———. "A Prehistoric Bureaucracy." *Diogenes* 26 (1959): 7–18.

Chafe, Wallace L. "Integration and Involvement in Speaking, Writing, and Oral Literature." *Spoken and Written Language: Exploring Orality and Literacy*. Ed. Deborah Tannen. Norwood, NJ: Ablex, 1982.

———. *Meaning and the Structure of Language*. Chicago: University of Chicago Press, 1970.

Chall, Jeanne S. "The Great Debate: Ten Years Later, with a Modest Proposal for Reading Stages." *Theory and Practice of Early Reading*. Ed. Lauren B. Resnick and Phyllis Weaver. Hillsdale, NJ: Erlbaum, 1979.

———. *Learning to Read: The Great Debate*. New York: McGraw-Hill, 1967.

Chase, S. *The Power of Words*. New York: Harcourt, 1954.

Chaytor, H. J. *From Script to Print: An Introduction to Modern Vernacular Literature*. 2nd ed. London: Sidgwick and Jackson, 1966.

Childe, V. G. *Man Makes Himself*. London: Watts, 1941.

———. *What Happened in History*. London: Penguin, 1942.

Childers, Thomas, and Joyce A. Post. *The Information-Poor in America*. Metuchen, NJ: Scarecrow Press, 1975.

Childs, C. P., and P. M. Greenfield. "Informal Modes of Learning and Teaching: The Case of Zinacanteco Weaving." *Studies in Cross-Cultural Psychology*. Ed. N. Warren, Vol. 2. London: Academic Press, 1980.

Chomsky, C. "Approaching Reading through Invented Spelling." *Theory and Practice of Early Reading*. Ed. Lauren B. Resnick and Phyllis Weaver. Vol. 2, Hillsdale, NJ: Erlbaum, 1979.

Chomsky, Noam. *Aspects of a Theory of Syntax*. Cambridge: MIT Press, 1965.

———. *Problems of Knowledge and Freedom*. London: Fontana, 1972.

———. *Syntactic Structures*. The Hague: Mouton, 1957.

Cicourel, Aaron V. "Language and Medicine." *Language in the USA*. Ed. Charles A. Ferguson and Shirley Brice Heath. Cambridge: Cambridge University Press, 1981.

Cipolla, C. *Literacy and Development in the West*. Harmondsworth: Penguin Books, 1969.

Clammer, J. R. *Literacy and Social Change: A Case Study of Fiji*. Leiden, Neth.: E. J. Brill, 1976.

Clanchy, M. T. *From Memory to Written Record: England, 1066–1307*. Cambridge: Harvard University Press, 1979.

———. "Looking Back from the Invention of Printing." *Literacy in Historical Perspective*. Ed. Daniel Resnick. Washington: Library of Congress, 1983.

Clark, E. "Non-Linguistic Strategies and the Acquisition of Word Meanings." *Cognition* 2 (1973): 161–82.

Clark, H. H. "Semantics and Comprehension." *Linguistic and Adjacent Arts and Sciences*. Vol. 12 of *Current Trends in Linguistics*. Ed. T. A. Sebeok. The Hague: Mouton, 1974.

Clifford-Vaughn, Michalina, and Margaret Archer. *Social Conflict and Educational Change in England and France, 1789–1848*. Cambridge: Cambridge University Press, 1971.

Cohen, A. M., and F. B. Brawer. "Instructional Practices in the Humanities and Sciences." Unpublished report. Center for the Study of Community Colleges, 1981.

Coldstream, John Nicholas. "The Recovery of Literacy." *Geometric Greece*. New York: St. Martin's, 1977.

Cole, Ellen. "The Experience of Illiteracy." Diss. Union Graduate School, Yellow Springs, OH, 1976.

Cole, Michael. "How Education Affects the Mind." *Human Nature* Apr. 1978: 51–58.

Cole, Michael, and J. S. Bruner. "Cultural Differences in Inferences about Psychological Processes." *American Psychologist* 26 (1971): 867–76.

Cole, Michael, J. Gay, J. Glick, and D. Sharp. *The Cultural Context of Learning and Thinking*. New York: Basic, 1971.

Cole, Michael, and Sylvia Scribner. "Cognitive Consequences of Formal and Informal Education." *Science* 182 (1973): 553–59.

———. *Culture and Thought*. New York: Wiley, 1974.

Coles, William E., Jr. *The Plural I*. New York: Holt, 1978.

Collins, A., J. S. Brown, and K. M. Larkin. "Inference in Text Understanding." *Theoretical Issues in Reading Comprehension*. Ed. R. J. Spiro, B. C. Bruce, and W. R. Brewer. Hillsdale, NJ: Erlbaum, 1980.

Commager, H. S. *The Empire of Reason*. Garden City, NY: Doubleday/Anchor, 1977.

The Condition of Education: A Statistical Report on the Condition of American Education together with a Description of the Activities of the National Center for Education Statistics. Washington, DC: National Center for Education Statistics, 1976.

Cook-Gumperz, Jenny, and John J. Gumperz. "From Oral to Written Culture: The Transition to Literacy." *Variation in Writing: Functional and Linguistic-Cultural Differences*. Vol. 1 of *Writing: The Nature, Development, and Teaching of Written Communication*. Ed. Marcia Farr Whiteman. Hillsdale, NJ: Erlbaum, 1981.

Copperman, Paul. *The Literacy Hoax: The Decline of Reading. Writing and Learning in the Public Schools and What We Can Do about It*. New York: Morrow, 1978.

Corbett, Edward P. J. "The Status of Writing in Our Society." *Variation in Writing:*

    Functional and Linguistic-Cultural Differences. Vol. 1 of *Writing: The Nature, Development, and Teaching of Written Communication.* Ed. Marcia Farr Whiteman. Hillsdale, NJ: Erlbaum, 1981.

Cornford, F. M. *Greek Religious Thought from Homer to the Age of Alexander.* London: Dutton, 1923.

Covell, Harold M. "The Past in Reading: Prologue to the Future." *Journal of the Faculty of Education of the University of British Columbia* 6 (1961): 13–18.

Cremin, Lawrence. *American Education: The Colonial Experience, 1607–1786.* New York: Harper & Row, 1970.

———. *American Education: The National Experience, 1783–1876.* New York: Harper & Row, 1980.

———. "Reading, Writing, and Literacy." *Review of Education* 1 (1975): 517–21.

———. *Traditions of American Education.* New York: Basic, 1977.

———. *The Transformation of the School.* New York: Random House, 1961.

Cressy, D. *Literacy and the Social Order: Reading and Writing in Tudor and Stuart England.* Cambridge: Cambridge University Press, 1980.

Current Population Reports. P-20, No. 295. Washington, DC: U.S. Bureau of the Census, 1976.

Curti, M. "Dime Novels and the American Tradition." *Yale Review* 27 (1937): 761–78.

Cusick, P. *Inside High School.* New York: Holt, 1973.

Dalby, D. "A Survey of the Indigenous Scripts of Liberia, and Sierra Leone." *African Language Studies* 8 (1967): 1–51.

D'Angelo, Frank. "Literacy and Cognition: A Developmental Perspective." *Literacy for Life.* Ed. Richard W. Bailey and Robin Melanie Fosheim. New York: MLA, 1983, 97–114.

Daniel, H. *Public Libraries for Everyone: Growth and Development of Library Services in the United States, Especially Since the Passage of the Library Services Act.* Garden City, NY: Doubleday, 1961.

Daniel, W. C. *Black Journals of the United States.* Westport, CT: Greenwood Press, 1982.

Darnton, R. *The Business of Enlightenment.* Cambridge: Harvard University Press, 1979.

———. "What Is the History of Books?" *Daedalus* 111 (1982): 65–83.

Dauzat, S. J., and J. Dauzat. "Literacy in Quest of a Definition." *Convergence* 10 (1977): 37–41.

Davis, Allison, B. Burleigh, and Mary R. Gardner. *Deep South: A Social Anthropological Study of Caste and Class.* Abridged ed. Chicago: University of Chicago Press, 1965.

Davis, K. C. *Two-Bit Culture: The Paperbacking of America.* Boston: Houghton-Mifflin, 1984.

Davis, Natalie. "Printing and the People." *Society and Culture in Early Modern France.* Stanford: Stanford University Press, 1975. 189–226.

de Brito, Jomard. "Educação de Adultos e Unificação de Cultura." *Revista de Cultura.* Estudos Universitários. Recife, Universidade do Recife, 1963.

de Castell, Suzanne, Allan Luke, and David MacLennan. "On Defining Literacy." *Canadian Journal of Education* 6 (1981): 7–18.

de Grazia, S. *Of Time, Work, and Leisure.* New York: Twentieth Century Fund, 1962.

de Laguna, G. *Speech: Its Function and Development.* 1927. College Park, MD: McGrath, 1970.

Del Rey, Lester. *The World of Science Fiction, 1926–1976: The History of a Subculture.* New York: Ballantine, 1979.

de Olivera, Carcy, and Roriska de Olivera. *Guinea-Bissau Reinventing Education.* Geneva: Institute of Cultural Action, 1976.

DeStefano, J. S., H. B. Pepinsky, and T. S. Sanders. *Communicating in the Classroom.* Ed. L. C. Wilkinson. New York: Academic Press, 1982.

Deutsch, Karl. *Nationalism and Social Communication: An Inquiry into the Foundations of Nationality.* Cambridge: MIT Press; New York: Wiley, 1953.

Dewey, John. *Democracy and Education*. New York: Macmillan, 1915.

——. *The Sources of a Science of Education*. New York: Liveright, 1929.

Diehl, William A. "Functional Literacy as a Variable Construct: An Examination of Attitudes, Behavior, and Strategies Related to Occupational Literacy." Diss. Indiana University, 1980.

——. "The Variable and Symbolic Natures of Functional Literacy: An Historical Review and Critique of Research." Master's thesis. Indiana University, 1979.

Diehl, William A., and Larry Mikulecky. "The Diehl-Mikulecky Job Literacy Survey." *Job Literacy*. Bloomington: Reading Research Center, School of Education, Indiana University, 1980. 65–78.

Diringer, D. *The Alphabet: A Key to the History of Mankind*. 3rd ed. New York: Funk and Wagnalls, 1948.

——. *Writing*. London: Thames and Hudson, 1962.

Disch, Robert. *The Future of Literacy*. Englewood Cliffs, NJ: Prentice-Hall, 1973.

Doake, D. "Book Experience and Emergent Reading in Preschool Children." Diss. University of Alberta, 1981.

Dodd, Ch. H. *The Parables of the Kingdom*. New York: Scribner's, 1961.

Dodson, Michael. "The Churches in the Nicaraguan Revolution." Paper prepared for the Ninth National Meeting of the Latin American Studies Association. Bloomington, IN, 18 Oct. 1980.

Dollard, John. *Caste and Class in a Southern Town*. 3rd ed. Garden City, NY: Doubleday/Anchor, 1957.

Donaldson, M., and P. Lloyd. "Sentences and Situations: Children's Judgments of Match and Mismatch." *Current Problems in Psycholinguistics*. Ed. F. Bresson. Paris: Editions du Centre National de la Recherche Scientifique, 1974.

Dore, Ronald. *Education in Tokugawa Japan*. London: Routledge and Kegan Paul, 1967.

Douglas, G. H. "Is Literacy Really Declining?" *Educational Records* 57 (1977): 140–48.

Drake, St. Claire, and Horace Cayton. *Black Metropolis: A Study of Negro Life in a Northern City*. 2 vols. New York: Harcourt, 1970.

Driver, G. R. *Semitic Writing from Pictograph to Alphabet*. London: Oxford University Press, 1954.

Dubin, T. *Women at Work: The Transformations of Work and Community in Lowell, Massachusetts, 1826–1860*. New York: Columbia University Press, 1979.

Dubois, B. L. Review of *The Language Makers*, by Roy Harris. *Language Learning* 30 (1980): 497–99.

Durkheim, E. *The Elementary Forms of the Religious Life*. Trans. J. W. Swain. London: Allen & Unwin, 1915.

Eder, D. "Differences in Communicative Styles across Ability Groups." *Communicating in the Classroom*. Ed. L. C. Wilkinson. New York: Academic Press, 1982.

Editor and Publisher. 1920–.

Eisenstein, E. *The Printing Press as an Agent of Change: Communications and Cultural Transformations in Early-Modern Europe*. Cambridge: Cambridge University Press, 1980.

Eliade, Mircea. *Patterns in Comparative Religion*. Trans. Willard R. Trask. New York: Sheed & Ward, 1958.

Ellul, Jacques. *The Technological Society*. New York: Vintage, 1964.

Emig, P. *Reading Habits of Newspaper Readers*. Gainesville: University of Florida, 1928.

Ennis, P. *Adult Book Reading in the United States: A Preliminary Report*. Chicago: National Opinion Research Center, 1965.

Erickson, Frederick. "Classroom Discourse as Improvisation: Relationships between Academic Task Structure and Social Participation Structure in Lessons." *Communicating in the Classroom*. Ed. L. C. Wilkinson. New York: Academic Press, 1982.

——. "Mere Ethnography: Some Problems in Its Use in Educational Practice." Past Presidential Address delivered at the Annual Meeting of the Council on Anthropology and Education. Los Angeles, Nov. 1978.

——————. "Talking Down: Some Cultural Sources of Miscommunication in Interracial Interviews." *Research in Nonverbal Communication*. Ed. A. Wolfgang. New York: Academic Press, 1979.

——————. Rhetoric, Anecdote, and Rhapsody: Coherence Strategies in a Conversation among Black American Adolescents." *Coherence in Spoken and Written Discourse*. Ed. D. Tannen. Norwood, NJ: Ablex, 1984. 81–154.

Erickson, Frederick, and G. Mohatt. "The Cultural Organization of Participation Structure in Two Classrooms of Indian Students." *Doing the Ethnography of School*. Ed. G. Spindler. New York: Holt, 1982.

Erickson, Frederick, and J. Shultz. *The Counselor as Gatekeeper: Social Interaction in Interviews*. New York: Academic Press, 1982.

Escarpit, Robert. *The Book Revolution*. Paris: UNESCO, 1966.

——————. *The Sociology of Literature*. Painesville, OH: Lake Erie College Studies, 1965.

Evans-Pritchard, E. E. "Lévy-Bruhl's Theory of Primitive Mentality." *Bulletin of the Faculty of Arts, University of Egypt* 2 (1934): 1–36.

——————. *Witchcraft, Oracles, and Magic among the Azande*. Oxford: Oxford University Press, 1937.

Ewen, S. *Captains of Consciousness: Advertising and the Roots of the Consumer Culture*. New York: McGraw-Hill, 1976.

Faik-Nzuji, Clémentine. *Enigmes Lubas-Nshinga: Etude structurale*. Kinshasa: Editions de l'Université Lovanium, 1970.

Farmer, James. "Stereotypes of the Negro and Their Relationship to Self-Image." *Urban Schooling*. Ed. Herbert C. Rudman and Richard L. Fetherstone. New York: Harcourt, 1968.

Farnham, George. *The Sentence Method*. Syracuse, NY: C. W. Bardeen, 1881.

Farr, R., J. Tuinman, and M. Rowis. *Reading Achievement in the United States: Then and Now*. Bloomington, IN: The Reading Program Center, 1974.

Farr, Roger, Leo Fay, and Harold H. Negley. *Then and Now: Reading Achievement in Indiana (1944–45 and 1976)*. Bloomington: Indiana University School of Education, 1978.

——————. *Then and Now: Reading Achievement in the U.S.* Bloomington: Indiana University School of Education, 1974.

Farrell, T. J. "Literacy, the Basics, and All That Jazz." *College English* 38 (1977): 443–59.

Faville, D. E. *How Sunset Magazine Subscribers Evaluate the Magazines They Read: A Study of Magazine Preferences*. Stanford, CA: Graduate School of Business, 1940.

Ferguson, Eugene. "The Mind's Eye: Nonverbal Thought in Technology." *Science* 197 (1977): 827–36.

Ferreiro, E., and A. Teberosky. *Literacy before Schooling*. Exeter, NH: Heinemann Educational Books, 1982.

Field, Alexander J. "Economic and Demographic Determinants of Educational Commitment: Massachusetts, 1855." *Journal of Economic History* 39 (1979): 439–59.

——————. "Educational Expansion in Mid-Nineteenth-Century Massachusetts." *Harvard Educational Review* 46 (1976): 521–52.

——————. "Educational Reform and Manufacturing Development in Mid-Nineteenth-Century Massachusetts." Diss. University of California, Berkeley, 1974.

——————. "Industrialization and Skill Intensity: The Case of Massachusetts." *Journal of Human Resources* 15 (1980): 149–75.

——————. "Occupational Structure, Dissent, and Educational Commitment: Lancashire, 1841." *Research in Economic History* 4 (1979): 235–87.

Finley, M. I. *The World of Odysseus*. New York: Viking, 1954.

Finley, M. I., ed. *The Greek Historians*. New York: Viking, 1959.

Finnegan, Ruth. *Oral Literature in Africa*. Oxford: Clarendon Press, 1970.

——————. *Oral Poetry*. Cambridge: Cambridge University Press, 1979.

Fish, S. "Literature in the Reader: Affective Stylistics." *New Literary History* 2 (1970): 123–62.

Fisher, Donald L. *Functional Literacy and the Schools*. Washington, DC: National Institute of Education, 1978.

Fisherman, J., V. C. Nahirny, J. E. Hofman, and R. G. Hayden. *Language Loyalty in the United States: The Maintenance and Perpetuation of Non-English Mother Tongues by American Ethnic and Religious Groups*. The Hague: Mouton, 1966.

Fishman, J. A. "The Description of Societal Bilingualism." *"Bilingualism in the Barrio*. Ed. J. A. Fishman, R. L. Cooper, and R. Ma. Bloomington, IN: Indiana University Publications, 1975. 605–11.

Fitzgerald, Frances. *America Revised: History of Schoolbooks in the Twentieth Century*. New York: Vintage, 1980.

Flavell, J. H. *Cognitive Development*. Englewood Cliffs, NJ: Prentice-Hall, 1977.

Flavell, J. H., P. J. Botkin, C. L. Fry, J. W. Wright, and P. E. Jarvis. *The Development of Role-Taking and Communication Skills in Children*. New York: Wiley, 1968.

Flesch, Rudolf. *Why Johnny Can't Read and What You Can Do about It*. New York: Harper & Row, 1955.

Flora, P. "Historical Processes of Social Mobilization: Urbanization and Literacy, 1850–1965." *Building States and Nations*. Ed. S. N. Eisenstadt and S. Rokkan. Beverly Hills, CA: Sage, 1973. 213–58.

Flower, Linda S. "Revising Writer-Based Prose." *Journal of Basic Writing* 3 (1981): 62–74.

Flower, L., and J. R. Hayes. "A Cognitive Process Theory of Writing." *College Composition and Communication* 32 (1981): 365–87.

Fodor, J. A., T. G. Bever, and M. F. Garrett. *The Psychology of Language*. Toronto: McGraw-Hill, 1974.

Foley, John Miles. "Oral Literature: Premises and Problems." *Choice* 18 (1980): 487–96.

Folger, J. K., and C. B. Nam. *Education of the American Population*. Washington, DC: GPO, 1967.

Fontainerie, François de la, ed. and trans. *French Liberalism and Education in the Eighteenth Century: The Writings of La Chalotais, Turgot, Diderot and Condorcet on National Education*. New York: McGraw-Hill, 1932.

Ford, W. G. "The Language of Disjunction." Diss. University of Toronto, 1976.

Foster, Herbert L. *Ribbin', Jivin', and Playin' the Dozens: The Unrecognized Dilemma of Inner City Schools*. Cambridge, MA: Ballinger, 1974.

Foucault, Michel. *The Archaeology of Knowledge*. Trans. A. M. Sheridan Smith. New York: Harper, 1972.

Fox, S. *The Mirror Makers: A History of American Advertising and Its Creators*. New York: William Morrow, 1984.

Frazier, E. Franklin. *Negro Youth at the Crossways: Their Personality Development in the Middle States*. Washington, DC: American Council on Education, 1940.

Freeman, M. "How to Read a Philosophical Text." Unpublished manuscript. Harvard University, 1982.

Freire, Paulo. "The Adult Literacy Process as Cultural Action for Freedom." *Harvard Educational Review* 40 (1970): 205–23.

———. "La alfabetizacion de adultos, critica de su vision ingenua; compreension de su vision critica." *Introducción a la acción cultural*. Santiago: ICIRA, 1969.

———. *Cultural Action for Freedom*. Monograph Series no. 1. Cambridge: Harvard Educational Review, 1970.

———. *Pedagogy in Process*. New York: Seabury, 1978.

———. *Pedagogy of the Oppressed*. New York: Seabury, 1970.

Fries, Charles C. *Linguistics and Reading*. New York: Holt, 1963.

Frye, Northrop. *The Critical Path*. Bloomington: Indiana University Press, 1971.

Furet, François, and Jacques Ozouf. *Lire et écrire*. Paris: Les Editions de Minuit, 1977.

———. "Literacy and Industrialization: The Case of the *Départment du Nord* in France." *Journal of European Economic History* 5 (1976): 5–44.

———. *Reading and Writing: Literacy in France from Calvin to Jules Ferry*. Cambridge: Cambridge University Press, 1982.

Furet, François, and Vladimir Sachs. "La croissance de l'alphabétisation en France (XVIIIe–XIXe siècles)." *Annales: Economies, Sociétés, Civilisations* 29 (1974): 714–37.

Gadamer, H. G. *Truth and Method*. New York: Seabury Press, 1975.

Gadway, Charles, and H. A. Wilson. *Functional Literacy: Basic Reading Performance*. Denver: National Assessment of Educational Progress, 1975.

Galtung, Johan. "Literacy, Education, and Schooling—For What?" *A Turning Point for Literacy*. Ed. Léon Bataille. New York: Pergamon Press, 1976. 93–105.

Gandz, S. "Oral Tradition in the Bible." *Jewish Studies in Memory of George A. Kohut*. Ed. Salo W. Baron and Alexander Marx. New York: Alexander Kohut Memorial Foundation, 1935.

Gans, H. *Popular Culture and High Culture*. New York: Basic Books, 1974.

Ganshof, F. L. *The Carolingians and the Frankish Monarchy*. Ithaca: Cornell University Press, 1971.

Gay, Peter. *The Enlightenment: The Science of Freedom*. New York: Knopf, 1969.

Gayter, M., B. Hall, J. R. Kidd, and V. Shivasrava. *The World of Literacy: Policy, Research, and Action*. Toronto: International Development Centre, 1979.

Geertz, Clifford. *Agricultural Involution: The Process of Ecological Change in Indonesia*. Berkeley and Los Angeles: University of California Press, 1962.

Geib, I. *A Study of Writing*. 1952. 2nd ed. Chicago: University of Chicago Press, 1963.

Gellner, E. Review of *Against Method*, by P. Feyerabend. *British Journal for the Philosophy of Science* 26 (1975): 331–42.

Gerhardsson, Birger. *Memory and Manuscript: Oral Tradition and Written Transmission in Rabbinic Judaism and Early Christianity*. Uppsala, Lund, and Copenhagen: Acta Seminarii Neotestamentici Upsaliensis, XII, 1961.

Gibson, E. J., and H. Levin. *The Psychology of Reading*. Cambridge: MIT Press, 1975.

Gibson, W. *Persona*. New York: Random House, 1969.

Giles, H., and P. F. Powesland. *Speech Style and Social Evaluation*. London: Academic Press, 1975.

Gilmore, W. J. "Elementary Literacy on the Eve of the Industrial Revolution: Trends in Rural New England, 1760–1830." *Proceedings of the American Antiquarian Society* 92 (1982): 87–178.

Ginzberg, Eli, et al. *The Middle-Class Negro in the White Man's World*. New York: Columbia University Press, 1967.

Giroux, H. "Theories of Reproduction and Resistance in the New Sociology of Education: A Critical Analysis." *Harvard Educational Review* 53 (1983): 257–93.

Givón, Talmy. "From Discourse to Syntax: Grammar as a Processing Strategy." *Syntax and Semantics* 12 (1979): 81–112.

Gladwin, T. *East Is a Big Bird*. Boston: Belknap Press, 1970.

Glucksberg, S., R. M. Krauss, and E. T. Higgins. "The Development of Referential Communication Skills." *Review of Child Development Research*. Ed. F. D. Horowitz. Vol. 4. Chicago: University of Chicago Press, 1975.

Goldschmidt, Walter. "Introduction: The Theory of Cultural Adaptation." *The Individual in Cultural Adaptation: A Study of Four East African Peoples*. By Robert B. Edgerton. Berkeley and Los Angeles: University of California Press, 1971. 1–22.

Gombrich, E. "The Visual Image." *Media and Symbols: The Forms of Expression, Communication, and Education*. The 73rd Yearbook of the National Society for the Study of Education. Ed. D. R. Olson. Chicago: University of Chicago Press, 1974.

Gomes, L. A. "Social Interaction and Social Identity: A Study of Two Kindergarten Children." Diss. Harvard Graduate School of Education, 1979.

Gontard, Maurice. *L'ènseignement primaire en France de la Révolution à la loi Guizot (1789–1833)*. Paris: Belles Lettres, 1959.

Good, T. L., and J. E. Brophy. *Looking in Classrooms*. 2nd ed. New York: Harper, 1980.

Goodenough, Florence. *Mental Testing: Its History, Principles, and Applications*. New York: Rinehart, 1949.

Goodman, K. S. "Reading: A Psycholinguistic Guessing Game." *Journal of the Reading Specialist* 6 (1967): 126–35.

Goodman, N. *Languages of Art: An Approach to a Theory of Symbols*. Indianapolis: Bobbs-Merrill, 1968.

Goodman, Y. "El desarrollo de la escritura en niños muy pequeños." *Nuevas Perspectivas Sobre los Piocesos de Lectura y-Escritura*. Ed. C. Ferreiro and M. Palacio. Mexico: Siglo Veintiuno, 1982.

――――. "The Roots of Literacy." *Claremont Reading Conference Forty-Fourth Yearbook*. Ed. Malcom P. Douglass. Claremont, CA: Claremont Graduate School, 1980.

Goodman, Y., and B. Altwerger. "Print Awareness in Preschool Children: A Study of the Development of Literacy in Preschool Children." Occasional Paper no. 4. Tucson: University of Arizona, College of Education, Program in Language and Literacy, 1981.

Goodnow, J. "The Nature of Intelligent Behavior: Questions Raised by Cross-Cultural Studies." *New Approaches to Intelligence*. Ed. L. Resnick. Potomac, MD: Erlbaum, 1976.

Goody, Jack. *The Domestication of the Savage Mind*. Cambridge: Cambridge University Press, 1971.

――――. "Literacy and Classification: On Turning the Tables." *Text and Context: The Social Anthropology of Tradition*. Ed. R. K. Jain. Philadelphia: Institute for the Study of Human Issues, 1977.

――――. "Religion and Ritual: The Definitional Problem." *British Journal of Sociology* 12 (1961): 142–64.

Goody, J., ed. *Literacy in Traditional Societies*. Cambridge: Cambridge University Press, 1968.

Goody, Jack, Michael Cole, and Sylvia Scribner. "Writing and Formal Operations: A Case Study among the Vai." *Africa* 47 (1977): 289–304.

Goody, Jack, and Ian Watt. "The Consequences of Literacy." *Comparative Studies in Society and History* 5 (1963): 304–45.

――――. "The Consequences of Literacy." *Literacy in Traditional Societies*. Ed. Jack Goody. Cambridge: Cambridge University Press, 1968.

Gough, K. "Implications of Literacy in Traditional China and India." *Literacy in Traditional Societies*. Ed. J. Goody. Cambridge: Cambridge University Press, 1968. 69–84.

Gould, Stephen J. *The Mismeasure of Man*. New York: Norton, 1981.

Graff, Harvey. "The Legacies of Literacy." *Journal of Communication* 32 (1982): 12–26.a.

――――. *Literacy in History: An Interdisciplinary Research Bibliography*. New York: Garland Press, 1981.

――――. *The Literacy Myth: Literacy and Social Structure in the Nineteenth-Century City*. New York: Academic Press, 1979.

――――. "Literacy Past and Present: Critical Approaches to the Literacy-Society Relationship." *Interchange* 9 (1978): 1–21.

Graff, H., ed. *Literacy and Social Development in the West*. Cambridge: Cambridge University Press, 1982.b.

Grafton, A. T. "The Importance of Being Printed." *Journal of Interdisciplinary History* 11 (1980): 265–86.

Granet, M. *Chinese Civilization*. New York: Barnes & Noble, 1959.

――――. *La Pensée chinoise*. Paris: La Renaissance du livre, 1934.

Gray, M. *Song and Dance Man: The Art of Bob Dylan*. London: Abacus, 1973.

Gray, W. S. *The Teaching of Reading and Writing: An International Survey*. Chicago: Scott, Foresman; UNESCO, 1965.

――――. *The Twenty-fourth Yearbook of the National Society for the Study of Education*. Bloomington, IN: Public School Publishing, 1952.

Gray, W. S., and R. Monroe. *The Reading Interests and Habits of Adults*. New York: MacMillan, 1929.

"The Great National Literacy Campaign: Heroes and Martyrs for the Creation of

Nicaragua." Mimeographed report. Trans. and ed. by National Network in Solidarity with the Nicaraguan People. Managua: Nicaraguan Ministry of Education, 1980.

Greenfield, P. "On Culture and Conservation." *Studies in Cognitive Growth*. Ed. Jerome S. Bruner, et al. New York: Wiley, 1966. 225–56.

———. "Oral and Written Language: The Consequences for Cognitive Development in Africa, the United States, and England." *Language and Speech* 15 (1972): 169–78.

———. "Oral or Written Language: The Consequences for Cognitive Development in Africa and the United States." Paper presented at the Symposium on Cross-Cultural Cognitive Studies. Chicago, 1968.

Greenfield, P. M., and J. S. Bruner. "Culture and Cognitive Growth." *Handbook of Socialization: Theory and Research*. Ed. D. A. Goslin. New York: Rand McNally, 1969.

Greer, A. "The Pattern of Literacy in Quebec, 1745–1899." *Histoire Sociale* 44 (1978): 293–335.

Grice, H. P. "Meaning." *Philosophical Review* 66 (1957): 377–88.

Gumperz, John J. "Conversational Inferences and Classroom Learning." *Ethnographic Approaches to Face-to-Face Interaction*. Ed. Judith Green and Cynthia Wallat. Norwood, NJ: Ablex, 1980.

———. "Language, Communication, and Public Negotiation." *Anthropology and the Public Interest: Fieldwork and Theory*. Ed. P. Sanday. New York: Academic Press, 1976.

———. "Sociocultural Knowledge in Conversational Inference." *Georgetown Round Table on Languages and Linguistics 1977*. Ed. M. Saville-Troike. Washington, DC: Georgetown University Press, 1977.

Gumperz, John J., and Jenny Cook-Gumperz. *Beyond Ethnography: Some Uses of Sociolinguistics for Understanding Classroom Environments*. Paper presented at the AERA Conference. San Francisco, April 1979.

———. "Ethnic Differences in Communicative Style." *Language in the USA*. Ed. Charles A. Ferguson and Shirley Brice Heath. Cambridge: Cambridge University Press, 1981.

Gurney, O. R. *The Hittites*. London: Penguin, 1952.

Gutman, Herbert. "Work, Culture, and Society in Industrializing America, 1815–1919." *American Historical Review* 78 (1973): 531–88.

Hackett, A. P. *70 Years of Best Sellers, 1895–1965*. New York: Bowker, 1967.

Hahn, Roger. *The Anatomy of a Scientific Institution: The Paris Academy of Sciences, 1666–1803*. Berkeley and Los Angeles: University of California Press, 1971.

Hair, P. E. H. "Notes on the Discovery of the Vai Script." *Sierra Leone Language Review* 2 (1963): 36–49.

Hajda, J. "An American Paradox: People and Books in a Metropolis." Diss. University of Chicago, 1963.

Hall, D. B. "The Uses of Literacy in New England, 1600–1850." *Printing and Society in Early America*. Ed. W. L. Joyce, E. Hall, R. D. Brown, and J. B. Hench. Worcester, MA: American Antiquarian Society, 1983.

Hall, Oswald, and Richard Carlton. *Basic Skills at School and Work: The Study of Albertown, an Ontario Community*. Toronto: Ontario Economic Council, 1977.

Halliday, M. A. K. *Explorations in the Functions of Language*. London: Edward Arnold, 1973.

———. "Language Structure and Language Function." *New Horizons in Linguistics*. Ed. J. Lyons. New York: Penguin, 1970.

———. *Learning How to Mean: Explorations in the Development of Language*. New York: Elsevier North-Holland, 1975.

Hamerow, T. *The Birth of a New Europe*. Chapel Hill: University of North Carolina Press, 1983.

Hammiche, B. "Functional Literacy and Educational Revolution." *A Turning Point for Literacy: Proceedings of the International Symposium for Literacy, Persepolis,*

Iran, 1975. Ed. L. Bataille. Oxford: Pergamon Press, 1976.

Harman, David. "Illiteracy: An Overview." *Harvard Educational Review* 40 (1970): 226–30.

———. Review of *The Experimental World Literacy Program. Harvard Educational Review* 47 (1977): 444–46.

Harman, G. "Deep Structure as Logical Form." *Semantics of Natural Language.* Ed. D. Davidson and G. Harman. Dordecht, Holland: Reidel, 1972.

Harms, Robert W. "Bobangi Oral Traditions: Indicators of Changing Perceptions." *The African Past Speaks.* Ed. Joseph C. Miller. London: Dawson; Hamden, CT: Archon, 1980. 178–200.

Harris, Louis, and Associates. *The 1971 National Reading Difficulty Index.* New York: 1971. ED 057 312.

———. *Survival Literacy: Conducted for the National Reading Council.* New York: Louis Harris and Associates, 1970.

Harrison, Bennett. *Education, Training, and the Urban Ghetto.* Baltimore: Johns Hopkins University Press, 1972.

Harste, Jerome, Carolyn Burke, and Virginia Woodward. "Children's Language and World: Initial Encounters with Print." *Bridging the Gap: Reader Meets Author.* Ed. J. Langer and M. Smith-Burke. Newark, DE: International Reading Association, 1981.

Hart, J. D. *The Popular Books: A History of America's Literary Taste.* New York: Oxford University Press, 1950.

Haussler, Myna. "A Psycholinguistic Description of Beginning Reading Development in Selected Kindergarten and First-Grade Children." University of Arizona, 1982.

Havelock, Eric. *The Greek Concept of Justice: From Its Shadow in Homer to Its Substance in Plato.* Cambridge: Harvard University Press, 1978.

———. *Origins of Western Literacy.* Toronto: Ontario Institute for Studies in Education, 1976.

———. *Preface to Plato.* Oxford: Basil Blackwell; Cambridge: Harvard University Press, 1963.

———. "The Preliteracy of the Greeks." *New Literary History* 8 (1977): 369–92.

———. "Prologue to Greek Literacy." *Lectures in Memory of Louise Tatt Semple, Second Series, 1966–1971.* Cincinnati: University of Oklahoma Press for the University of Cincinnati Press, 1973.

Hay, A., and W. F. Brewer. *Children's Understanding of the Narrator's Point of View in Prose.* Urbana: University of Illinois, Center for the Study of Reading, 1982.

Hayakawa, S. I. *Language in Thought and Action.* London: Allen and Unwin, 1952.

Hays, D., and R. Tierney. "Developing Readers' Knowledge through Analogy." *Reading Research Quarterly* 17 (1982): 256–80.

Heard, N. C. *Howard Street.* New York: Dial Press, 1968.

Heath, S. B. "The Functions and Uses of Literacy." *Journal of Communication* 30 (1980): 123–33.

———. "Language beyond the Classroom." Paper presented for the Delaware Symposium on Language Studies. University of Delaware, 1979.

———. *Outline Guide for the Ethnographic Study of Literacy and Oral Language from Schools to Communities.* Philadelphia: Graduate School of Education, 1978.

———. "Protean Shapes in Literacy Events: Ever-Shifting Oral and Literate Traditions." *Spoken and Written Language.* Ed. D. Tannen. Norwood, NJ: Ablex, 1982.

———. "Social History and Sociolinguists." *The American Sociologist* 13 (1978): 84–92.

———. "Toward an Ethnohistory of Writing in American Education." *Variation in Writing: Functional and Linguistic-Cultural Differences.* Vol. 1 of *Writing: The Nature, Development, and Teaching of Written Communication.* Ed. M. F. Whiteman. Hillsdale, NJ: Erlbaum, 1981.

———. *Ways with Words: Language, Life, and Work in Communities and Classrooms.* Cambridge: Cambridge University Press, 1984.

———. "What No Bedtime Story Means: Narrative Skills at Home and School."

Language in Society 11 (1982): 49–76.

Henderson, E., and J. W. Beers. "A Study of Developing Orthographic Concepts Among First Graders." Paper presented at the Annual Meeting of the International Reading Association. Atlanta, 1979.

Henderson, E., and J. W. Beers, eds. *Developmental and Cognitive Aspects of Learning to Spell*. Newark, DE: International Reading Association, 1980.

Henderson, Vivian W. "Regions, Race, and Jobs." *Employment, Race, and Poverty*. Ed. Arthur M. Ross and Herbert Hill. New York: Harcourt, 1967. 76–104.

Hendrix, Richard. "The Status and Politics of Writing Instruction." *Variation in Writing: Functional and Linguistic-Cultural Differences*. Vol. 1 of *Writing: The Nature, Development, and Teaching of Written Communication*. Ed. Marcia Farr Whiteman. Hillsdale, NJ: Erlbaum, 1981.

Heilbut, Tony. *The Gospel Sound: Good News and Bad Times*. New York: Simon and Shuster, 1971.

Henige, David. "'The Disease of Writing': Ganda and Nyoro Kinglists in a Newly Literate World." *The African Past Speaks*. Ed. Joseph C. Miller. London: Dawson; Hamden, CT: Archon, 1980. 240–61.

Henle, M. "On the Relation between Logic and Thinking." *Psychological Review* 63 (1962): 366–78.

Henle, P. *Language, Thought, and Culture*. Ann Arbor: University of Michigan Press, 1958.

Heyneman, Stephen P. "Why Impoverished Children Do Well in Ugandan Schools." *Comparative Education* 15 (1979): 175–85.

Hidi, S. "Effects of Temporal Considerations in Conditional Reasoning." Paper presented at the Selection Task Conference. Trento, Italy, Apr. 1974.

Hildyard A., and D. R. Olson. "On the Mental Representation and Matching Operation of Active and Passive Sentences by Children and Adults." Unpublished manuscript.

Hillerich, R. L. "Toward an Assessable Definition of Literacy." *English Journal* 65 (1976): 50–55.

Hodge, Robert W., Peter M. Siegel, and P. H. Rossi. "Occupational Prestige in the United States. 1925–63." *Class, Status, and Power*. Ed. Richard Bendix and Samuel Lipsett. 2nd ed. New York: Free Press, 1966. 286–93.

Hoggart, R. *The Uses of Literacy: Changing Patterns in English Mass Culture*. London: Chatto and Windus, 1957.

Holsoe, S. E. "Slavery and Economic Response among the Vai." *Slavery in Africa: Historical and Anthropological Perspectives*. Ed. S. Miers and I. Kopytoff. Madison: University of Wisconsin Press, 1977.

Hone, Joseph M. *W. B. Yeats*. London: Macmillan, 1942.

Hooykaas, C. *Surya-Sevana, the Way to God of a Balinese Silva Priest*. Amsterdam: Noord-Hollandsche U. M., 1966.

Houston, R. A. "Literacy and Society in the West, 1500–1850." *Social History* 8 (1983): 269–93.

———. "The Literacy Myth?: Illiteracy in Scotland, 1630–1760." *Past and Present* 96 (1982): 81–102.

Huey, Edmund B. *The Psychology and Pedagogy of Reading*. New York: Macmillan, 1908.

Hulme, T. E. *Reflections on Violence*. New York: P. Smith, 1941.

Hunter, C. S. J., and D. Harman. *Adult Illiteracy in the United States*. New York: McGraw-Hill, 1979.

Huxley, Aldous. *Ends and Means*. New York: Harper, 1937.

Hymes, Dell. "The Anthropological Linguistic Theory." *American Anthropologist* 66 (1964): 6–56.

———. "The Ethnography of Communication." *American Anthropologist* 66 (1964): 1–34.

———. "The Ethnography of Speaking." *Anthropology and Human Behavior*. Ed. Thomas Gladwin and William Sturtevant. Washington, DC: Anthropological Society of Washington, 1967.

————. "Introduction: Toward Ethnographics of Communication." *American Anthropologist* 66 no. 6, Part 2 (1964): 1–34.

————. "Models of the Interaction of Language and Social Life." *Directions in Sociolinguistics*. Ed. John J. Gumperz and Dell Hymes. New York: Holt, 1972. 35–71.

"Illegal Aliens." *New York Times* 1 May 1977, sec. 4: 3.

Inhelder, B., and J. Piaget. *The Growth of Logical Thinking*. New York: Basic Books, 1958.

Inkeles, A., and D. H. Smith. *Becoming Modern: Individual Changes in Six Developing Countries*. Cambridge: Harvard University Press, 1974.

Innis, H. A. *The Bias of Communication*. Toronto: University of Toronto Press, 1951. Rpt. 1964.

————. *Empire and Communications*. Oxford: Clarendon Press, 1950.

Iredell, H. "Eleanor Learns to Read." *Education* (1898): 233–38.

Iser, W. *The Implied Reader: Patterns in Communication in Prose Fiction from Bunyan to Beckett*. Baltimore: Johns Hopkins University Press, 1974.

Ivins, William M., Jr. *Prints and Visual Communications*. Cambridge: MIT Press, 1953.

Jackson, Mahalia. *Movin' On Up*. New York: Random House, 1966.

Jacob, E. "Literacy Tools: Reading and Writing of Entry-Level Production Workers." *Becoming a Worker*. Ed. C. Bosman and J. Reisman. Norwood, NJ: Ablex, 1986.

Jacob, E., and J. A. Crandall. "Job-Related Literacy: A Look at Current and Needed Research." Unpublished paper. Center for Applied Linguistics, Washington, D.C., 1979.

Jacoby, F. *Atthis*. Oxford: Oxford University Press, 1949.

————. *Die Fragmente der Griechischen Historiker*. Vol. 1. *Genealogie und Mythographie*. Berlin: Weidmann, 1923.

Jaeger, W. *Paideia*. Oxford: Oxford University Press, 1939.

————. *The Theology of the Early Greek Philosophers*. Oxford: Oxford University Press, 1947.

Jakobson, R., and C. Lévi-Strauss. "Les Chats de Charles Baudelaire." *L'Homme* 2 (1962): 5–21.

James, Louis. *Fiction for the Working Man*. London: Penguin, 1963.

James, William. *Talks to Teachers on Psychology*. New York: Henry Holt, 1899.

Jeffery, L. H. *The Local Scripts of Archaic Greece*. Oxford: 1961.

Jencks, Christopher. *Inequality*. New York: Basic Books, 1972.

Johansson, Egil. "The History of Literacy in Sweden." *Literacy and Social Development in the West: A Reader*. Ed. Harvey Graff. Cambridge: Cambridge University Press, 1981.

————. *The History of Literacy in Sweden, in Comparison with Some Other Countries*. *Educational Reports* no. 12. Umeå, Sweden: Umeå University and School of Education, 1977.

————. "Literacy Studies in Sweden: Some Examples." *Literacy and Society in a Historical Perspective: A Conference Report*. Ed. E. Johansson. Umeå, Sweden: Umeå University and School of Education, 1973.

————. "The Postliteracy Problem—Illusion or Reality in Modern Sweden?" *Time, Space, and Man*. Ed. Jan Sundin and Erik Söderlund. Stockholm: Almqvist and Wiksell, 1979. 199–212.

Johnson, Henry. *A History of Public Education in British Columbia*. Vancouver: University of British Columbia Publications Centre, 1964.

Johnson, Richard. "Notes on the Schooling of the English Working Class, 1780–1850." *Schooling and Capitalism*. Ed. R. Dale, G. Esland, and M. MacDonald. London: Routledge and Kegan Paul, 1976. 44–54.

Joncich, Geraldine. *The Sane Positivist: A Biography of Edward L. Thorndike*. Middletown, CT: Wesleyan University Press, 1968.

Jousse, Marcel. *Le parlant, la parole, et le souffle*. Paris: Gallimard, 1978.

Joyce, D. F. *Gatekeepers of Black Culture: Black-Owned Book Publishing in the United States, 1817–1981*. Westport, CT: Greenwood Press, 1983.

Joyce, W. L., B. Hall, R. D. Brown, and J. B. Hench, eds. *Printing and Society in Early*

America. Worcester, MA: American Antiquarian Society, 1983.

Julia, Dominique, and Paul Pressly. "La population scolaire en 1789." *Annales: Econo-mies, Sociétés, Civilisations* 30 (1975): 1516–61.

Kaestle, Carl F. "Literacy and Mainstream Culture in American History." *Language Arts* 58 (1981): 207–18.

———. *Pillars of the Republic: Common Schools and American Society, 1780–1860*. New York: Hill and Wang, 1983.

———. " 'Between the Scylla of Brutal Ignorance and the Charybdis of a Literary Education': Elite Attitudes toward Mass Education in Early Industrial England and America." *School and Society*. Ed. L. Stone. Baltimore: Johns Hopkins University Press, 1976. 177–91.

Kaestle, Carl, and Maris Vinovskis. *Education and Social Change in Nineteenth-Century Massachusetts*. Cambridge: Cambridge University Press, 1980.

Katz, Michael B. "The Origins of Public Education: A Reassessment." *History of Education Quarterly* 14 (1976): 381–407.

———. "Origins of the Institutional State." *Marxist Perspective* 1 (1978): 6–22.

Keating, P. J. *The Working Classes in Victorian Fiction*. London: Routledge and Kegan Paul, 1971.

Kelly, R. G. "Literature and the Historian." *American Quarterly* 26 (1974): 141–59.

Kenyon, F. G. *Books and Readers in Ancient Greece and Rome*. 2nd ed. Oxford: Clarendon Press, 1951.

Kerber, Linda K. "Daughters of Columbia: Educating Women for the Republic." *The Hofstadter Aegis*. Ed. Stanley M. Elkins and Eric L. McKitrick. New York: Knopf, 1974. 36–60.

Kessler, L. *The Dissident Press: Alternative Journalism in American History*. Beverly Hills, CA: Sage, 1984.

Keylor, William R. *Academy and Community: The Foundation of the French Historical Profession*. Cambridge: Harvard University Press, 1975.

Kindleberger, Charles. "Technical Education and the French Entrepreneur." *Enterprise and Entrepreneurs in Nineteenth- and Twentieth-Century France*. Ed. Edward C. Carter II, Robert Forster, and Joseph N. Moody. Baltimore: Johns Hopkins University Press, 1976.

Kirsch, I., and J. T. Guthrie. "The Concept and Measurement of Functional Literacy." *Reading Research Quarterly* 13 (1977–78): 485–507.

Kluger, Richard. *Simple Justice*. New York: Vintage, 1977.

Kneale, W., and M. Kneale. *The Development of Logic*. Oxford: Clarendon Press, 1962.

Kochman, Thomas. "Orality and Literacy as Factors in 'Black' and 'White' Communicative Behavior." *International Journal of the Sociology of Language* 3 (1974): 91–115.

Koehler, Virginia. "Classroom Process Research: Present and Future." *The Journal of Classroom Interaction* 13 (1978): 3–11.

Koelle, S. W. *Outlines of a Grammar of the Vai Language*. London: Church Missionary House, 1854.

Korzybski, A. *Science and Sanity: An Introduction to Non-Aristotelian Systems and General Semantics*. Lancaster, PA: Science Press, 1933.

Kosambi, D. D. *Ancient India*. New York: Pantheon, 1966.

Kozol, Jonathan. "A New Look at the Literacy Campaign in Cuba." *Harvard Educational Review* 48 (1978): 341–77.

———. *Prisoners of Silence: Breaking the Bonds of Adult Illiteracy in the United States*. New York: Continuum, 1980.

Kroeber, Alfred. *Anthropology*. New York: Harcourt, Brace, 1948.

Kuritz, Hyman. "Benjamin Rush: His Theory of Republican Education." *History of Education Quarterly* 7 (1967): 432–51.

Labov, W. *Language in the Inner City*. Philadelphia: University of Pennsylvania Press, 1972.

———. "The Logic of Nonstandard English." *Georgetown University Monographs in Language and Linguistics* 72 (1969): 1–31.

————. "The Logic of Nonstandard English." *Language in the Inner City: Studies in the Black English Vernacular*. Philadelphia: University of Pennsylvania Press, 1972.

————. "The Social Motivation of a Sound Change." *Word* 19 (1963): 273–309.

Lakoff, G. "Linguistics and Natural Logic." *Semantics of Natural Language*. Ed. D. Davidson and G. Harman. Dordrecht, Holland: Reidel, 1972.

Langlois, Charles-Victor, and Charles Seignobos. *Introduction aux études historiques*. Paris: Hachette et Compagnie, 1898.

Laqueur, Thomas. Critique of "Literacy and Social Mobility in the Industrial Revolution." *Past and Present* 64 (1974): 96–108.

————. "The Cultural Origins of Popular Literacy in England, 1500–1850." *Oxford Review of Education* 2 (1976): 255–75.

————. *Religion and Respectability*. New York: Yale University Press, 1976.

————. "Working-Class Demand and the Growth of English Elementary Education, 1750–1850." *Schooling and Society*. Ed. Lawrence Stone. Baltimore: Johns Hopkins University Press, 1976. 192–205.

Larrabee, E., and R. Meyersohn, eds. *Mass Leisure*. Glencoe, IL: Free Press, 1958.

Lasswell, H. D. "The Structure and Function of Communication in Society." *The Communication of Ideas*. Ed. L. Bryson. New York: Institute for Religious and Social Studies, 1948.

Lave, J. "Tailor-Made Experiments and Evaluating the Intellectual Consequences of Apprenticeship Training." *Quarterly Newsletter of the Institute for Comparative Human Development* 1 (1977): 1–5.

Lave, J., M. Murtaugh, and O. de la Rocha. "The Dialectic of Arithmetic in Grocery Shopping." *Everyday Cognition: Its Development in Social Context*. Ed. B. Rogoff and J. Lave. Cambridge: Harvard University Press, 1984. 67–94.

Leach, E. R. "Primitive Time-Reckoning." *A History of Technology*. Ed. C. Singer, E. S. Holmyard, and A. R. Hall. Oxford: Oxford University Press, 1958.

Leith, James A. "Modernisation, Mass Education, and Social Mobility in French Thought, 1750–1789." Vol. 2 of *Studies in the Eighteenth Century*. Ed. R. F. Brissenden. Canberra: Australian National University Press, 1973. 223–38.

Leith, James A., ed. *Facets of Education in the Eighteenth Century*. Vol. 167 of *Studies on Voltaire and the Eighteenth Century*. Oxford: Voltaire Foundation at the Taylor Institution, 1977.

Leont'ev, A. N. "The Problem of Activity in Soviet Psychology." *Soviet Psychology* 13 (1974): 4–33.

Lerner, D. *The Passing of Traditional Societies: Modernizing the Middle East*. New York: The Free Press, 1958.

LeRoy Ladurie, E. *Montaillou, The Peasants of Lanquedoc*. Urbana: University of Illinois Press, 1975.

————. *Montaillou: Promised Land of Error*. New York: Braziller, 1978.

————. *The Peasants of Languedoc*. 1966. Trans. J. Day. Urbana: University of Illinois Press, 1974.

Lessing, D. Introduction to *The Golden Notebook*. New York: Bantam, 1973.

Levin, Beatrice. "Reading Requirements for Satisfactory Careers." *Reading and Career Education*. Ed. Duane Nielsen and Howard Hjelm. Newark, DE: International Reading Association, 1975. 78–81.

Levin, Lawrence W. *Black Culture and Black Consciousness: Afro-American Folk Thought from Slavery to Freedom*. New York: Oxford University Press, 1977.

Levine, David. "Education and Family Life in Early Industrial England." *Journal of Family History* 4 (1979): 368–80.

————. *Family Formation in an Age of Nascent Capitalism*. New York: Academic Press, 1977.

Levine, Kenneth. *The Social Context of Literacy*. London: Routledge and Kegan Paul, 1986.

Lévi-Strauss, Claude. *The Savage Mind*. 1962. Chicago: University of Chicago Press, 1966.

————. *Tristes Topiques*. London: Jonathan Cape, 1973.

Lewin, K. *A Dynamic Theory of Personality*. New York: McGraw-Hill, 1936.

Lewis, Diane K. *Schooling, Literacy, and Sense Modality*. Unpublished manuscript. Santa Cruz, 1979.

Lewis, Oscar. *La Vida*. New York: Random House, 1968.

Liard, Louis. *L'enseignement supérieur en France, 1789–1893*. 2 vols. Paris: A. Colin, 1888–94.

Liebow, Elliot. *Tally's Corner: A Study of Negro Streetcorner Men*. Boston: Little Brown, 1967.

Link, H. C., and H. A. Hopf. *People and Books: A Study of Reading and Book-Buying Habits*. New York: Book Industry Committee, 1946.

Locke, John. *An Essay Concerning Human Understanding*. Ed. J. W. Yolton. London: Dent, 1961.

————. *Some Thoughts Concerning Education*. Cambridge: Cambridge University Press, 1880.

Lockridge, Kenneth A. *Literacy in Colonial New England: An Enquiry into the Social Context of Literacy in the Early Modern West*. New York: Norton, 1974.

————. "L'alphabétisation en Amérique." *Annales: Economies, Sociétés, Civilisations* 30 (1977): 503–18.

Lonergan, B. J. F. *Insight: A Study of Human Understanding*. New York: Philosophical Library, 1957.

Lord, Albert B. *The Singer of Tales*. Harvard Studies in Comparative Literature 24. Cambridge: Harvard University Press, 1965.

Luria, Aleksandr Romanovich. *Cognitive Development: Its Cultural and Social Foundations*. Trans. Martin Lopez-Morillas and Lynn Solotaroff. Ed. Michael Cole. Cambridge: Harvard University Press, 1976.

————. "The Directive Function of Speech." *Word* 15 (1959): 341–52.

Lynch, Kevin. *The Image of the City*. Cambridge: MIT Press, 1960.

Lyons, J. *Introduction to Theoretical Linguistics*. Cambridge: Cambridge University Press, 1969.

McCabe, H. B. *The Culture of a Community College*. New York: Praeger, 1978.

McCabe, R. H., and S. Skidmore. "The Literacy Crisis and American Education." *Junior College Resource Review* Spring 1982: 2–6.

MacCallum, Archibald. "Compulsory Education." *Family, School, and Society in Nineteenth-Century Canada*. Ed. A. Prentice and S. Houston. Oxford: Oxford University Press, 1975. 176–77.

McClelland, David C. "Does Education Accelerate Economic Growth?" *Economic Development and Cultural Change* 14 (1966): 257–78.

McDermott, R. P. "Achieving School Failure: An Anthropological Approach to Illiteracy and Social Stratification." *Education and Culture Process*. Ed. G. D. Spindler. New York: Holt, 1974.

————. "The Ethnography of Speaking and Reading." *Linguistics*. Ed. R. Shuy. Newark, DE: International Reading Association, 1977.

Macdonald, D. "A Theory of Mass Culture." *Mass Culture: The Popular Arts in America*. Ed. B. Rosenberg and D. M. White. New York: Free Press, 1957.

Macdonald, J. B. "Reading in an Electronic Media Age." *Social Perspectives on Reading*. Ed. J. B. Macdonald. Newark, DE: International Reading Association, 1973. 23–29.

McGovern, George. *Congressional Record* Sept. 1978: 14,834.

Maciel, Jarbas. "A Fundamentação Teórica do Sistema Paulo Freire de Educação." *Estudos Universitários. Revista de Cultura*. Universidade do Recife, No. 4, 1963.

McLuhan, Marshall. *The Gutenberg Galaxy*. Toronto: University of Toronto Press, 1962.

————. *Understanding Media: The Extensions of Man*. New York: McGraw-Hill, 1964.

McNall, S. A. *Who Is in the House? A Psychological Study of Two Centuries of Women's Fiction in America, 1975 to the Present*. New York: Elsevier North Holland, 1981.

Macnamara, J. "The Cognitive Basis of Language Learning in Infants." *Psychological Review* 79 (1972): 1–13.

McNeill, D. *The Acquisition of Language*. New York: Harper, 1970.

McNeill, W. H. *The Rise of the West*. Chicago: University of Chicago Press, 1962.

Maimon, Elaine P., G. L. Belcher, G. W. Hearn, B. F. Nodine, and F. X. O'Connor. *Writing in the Arts and Sciences*. Cambridge, MA: Winthrop, 1981.

Maimonides, M. *Guide of the Perplexed*. Trans. S. Pines, Chicago: University of Chicago Press, 1963.

Malinowski, Bronislaw. *Argonauts of the Western Pacific*. London: Routledge & Sons, 1922.

————. *Myth in Primitive Psychology*. London: Kegan Paul, Trench, Trubner, 1926.

————. "The Problem of Meaning in Primitive Languages." *The Meaning of Meaning: A Study of the Influence of Language upon Thought and of the Science of Symbolism*. Ed. C. K. Ogden and I. A. Richards. New York: Harcourt, Brace; London: Kegan Paul, Trench, Trubner, 1923. 451–510.

Mandler, G., and P. Dean. "Seriation: The Development of Serial Order in Free Recall." *Journal of Experimental Psychology* 81 (1969): 207–15.

Marcel, T. "Phonological Awareness and Phonological Representation." *Cognitive Processes in Spelling*. Ed. U. Frith. London: Academic Press, 1980.

Markandaya, Kamala. *Nectar in a Sieve*. New York: New American Library, 1971.

Markman, E. M. "Realizing That You Don't Understand: Elementary School Children's Awareness of Inconsistencies." *Child Development* 49 (1979): 168–77.

Marsh, G. M., V. Friedman, D. Welch, and P. Desberg. "The Development of Strategies in Spelling." *Cognitive Processes in Spelling*. Ed. U. Frith. London: Academic Press, 1980.

Martin, H.-J. "Culture écrite et culture orale, culture savante et culture populaire dans la France d'Ancien Régime." *Journale des Savants* n.v. (1975): 225–82.

Martin, N., P. D'Arcy, B. Newton, and R. Parker. *Writing and Learning across the Curriculum 11–16*. London: Ward Lock Educational, 1976.

Mathews, Mitford. *Teaching to Read: Historically Considered*. Chicago: University of Chicago Press, 1966.

May, Henry F. *The End of American Innocence*. New York: Knopf, 1959.

————. *The Enlightenment in America*. New York: Oxford University Press, 1976.

Maynes, Mary Jo. *Schooling for the People: Comparative Local Studies of Schooling History in France and Germany, 1750–1850*. London: Holmes and Meier, 1984.

————. "Schooling the Masses." Diss. University of Michigan, 1977.

————. "The Virtues of Anachronism: The Political Economy of Schooling in Europe, 1750–1850.: *Comparative Studies in Society and History* 21 (1979): 611–25.

Mead, George H. *Mind, Self, and Society from the Standpoint of a Social Behaviorist*. Chicago: University of Chicago Press, 1934.

Mead, Margaret. "Our Educational Emphases in Primitive Perspective." *American Journal of Sociology* 48 (1943): 633–39.

Mehan, H. "Assessing Children's School Performance." *Recent Sociology* 5 (1973): 240–64.

————. *Learning Lessons: Social Organization in the Classroom*. Cambridge: Harvard University Press, 1979.

Merleau-Ponty, Maurice. "L'oeil et l'esprit." *Les Temps modernes* 18 (1961): 184–85.

Meyer, Donald H. *The Democratic Enlightenment*. New York: Putnam's, 1976.

Meyers, Peter V. "Professionalization and Societal Change: Rural Teachers in Nineteenth-Century France." *Journal of Social History* 9 (1976): 542–46.

Mezirow, Jack, Gordon G. Darkenwald, and Alan B. Knox. *Last Gamble on Education*. Washington, DC: Adult Education Association, 1975.

Michaels, S., and J. Collins. "Oral Discourse Styles: Classroom Interaction and the Acquisition of Literacy." *Coherence in Spoken and Written Discourse*. Ed. D. Tannen. Norwood, NJ: Ablex, 1984. 219–44.

Mikulecky, Larry J., Nancy L. Shanklin, and David C. Caverly. *Adult Reading Habits, Attitudes, and Motivations: A Cross-Sectional Study*. Monograph in Language and Research Studies No. 2. Bloomington: Indiana University School of Education, 1979.

Mikulecky, Larry J., and William Diehl. "An Examination of Work-Related Literacy and Reading Attitudes." Paper presented at the Functional Literacy Conference. Bloomington, IN, June 1979.

————. *Job Literacy*. Reading Research Center Technical Report. Bloomington: Indiana University, 1979.

Miller, G. A., ed. *Linguistic Communication: Perspectives for Research*. Newark, DE: International Reading Association, 1973.

Milner, Christina Andrea. "Black Pimps and Their Prostitutes." Diss. University of California, Berkeley, 1970.

Mitchell, Henry H. *Black Preaching*. Philadelphia: Lippincott, 1970.

Moffett, J. *Teaching the Universe of Discourse*. Boston: Houghton-Mifflin, 1968.

Moorhouse, A. C. *The Triumph of the Alphabet*. New York: H. Schuman, 1953.

Moran, G. F., and M. M. Vinovskis. "The Great Care of Godly Parents: Early Childhood in Puritan New England." Paper presented at the Biennial Meeting of the Society for Research in Child Development. Detroit, Apr. 1983.

Morison, S. E. *The Puritan Pronaos*. New York: New York University Press, 1935. Reissued as *The Intellectual Life of Colonial New England*. New York: New York University Press, 1956.

Mortier, Roland. "The 'Philosophies' and Public Education." *Yale French Studies* 40 (1968): 62–76.

Murphy, D. R. *What Farmers Read and Like: A Record of Experiments with Readership on Wallace's Farmer and Wisconsin's Agriculturist, 1938–1961*. Ames: Iowa State University Press, 1962.

Murphy, Richard T. *Adult Functional Reading Study: Project 1: Targeted Research and Development Reading Program Objectives. Subparts 1, 2, 3*. Princeton: Educational Testing Service, 1975.

Murray, D. *Learning by Teaching*. Montclair, NJ: Boynton/Cook, 1982.

————. "Teaching the Other Self: The Writer's First Reader." *College Composition and Communication* 33 (1982): 140–47.

Myrdal, Gunnar. *An American Dilemma*. Vol. 2. New York: Harper, 1944.

Naisbitt, J. *Megatrends: Ten New Directions Transforming Our Lives*. New York: Warner, 1982.

National Advisory Commission on Civil Disorders. *Report*. Washington, DC: GPO, 1968.

National Advisory Council on Adult Education. *A Target Population in Adult Education*. Washington, DC: GPO, 1974.

National Assessment of Educational Progress. *Reading, Thinking, and Writing: Results from the 1979–80 National Assessment of Reading and Literature*. Denver: National Assessment of Educational Progress, 1981.

National Commission on Excellence in Education. *A Nation at Risk: The Imperative for Educational Reform*. Washington, DC: U.S. Department of Education, 1983.

Neatby, Hilda. *So Little for the Mind*. Toronto: Clark Irwin, 1953.

Needham, J. *Science and Civilization in China*. Cambridge: Cambridge University Press, 1954.

Neimark, E. D., and N. S. Slotnick. "Development of the Understanding of Logical Connectives." *Journal of Educational Psychology* 61 (1970): 451–60.

Nelson, K. "Concept, Word, and Sentence: Interrelations in Acquisition and Development." *Psychological Review* 81 (1974): 267–85.

Netting, Robert McG. *Hill Farmers of Nigeria*. Seattle: University of Washington Press, 1968.

Newman, Dorothy K., et al. "Learning without Earning." *Change* Mar. 1978: 38–43, 60.

Newman, Dorothy K., et al. *Protest, Politics, and Prosperity: Black Americans and White Institutions, 1940–1975*. New York: Pantheon Books, 1978.

Newsprint Information Committee. *A National Study of Newspaper Reading: Size and Characteristics of the Newspaper-Reading Public, March–April, 1961.* 2 vols. New York: Audits and Surveys Company, 1961.

"New York Is Lowest in Youth Employment." *New York Times* 2 Aug. 1977: 30.

Nietzsche, Friedrich. *Beyond Good and Evil.* Edinburgh: T. N. Foulis, 1909.

Nipperdey, Thomas. "Mass Education and Modernization—The Case of Germany." *Transactions of the Royal Historical Society* 27 (1977): 155–72.

Nord, D. P. "First Steps toward a Theory of Press Control." *Journalism History* 4 (1977): 8–13.

Nordmann, Claude. *Grandeur et liberté de la Suède (1660–1792).* Paris: Béatrice-Nauwelaerts, 1971.

Norgren, Paul H., and Samuel E. Hill. *Toward Fair Employment.* New York: Columbia University Press, 1964.

Northcutt, Norvell. "Functional Literacy for Adults." *Reading and Career Education.* Ed. Duane Nielsen and Howard Hjelm. Newark, DE: International Reading Association, 1975. 43–49.

Northcutt, Norvell, Nina Selz, E. Shelton Nyer, D. Hickok, and N. Humble. *Adult Functional Competency: A Summary.* Austin: Industrial and Business Training Bureau, University of Texas, 1975.

O'Barr, William M. "The Language of the Law." *Language in the USA.* Ed. Charles A. Ferguson and Shirley Brice Heath. Cambridge: Cambridge University Press, 1981.

Obiechina, Emmanuel. *Culture, Tradition, and Society in the West African Novel.* Cambridge: Cambridge University Press, 1975.

O'Connor, D. O., and H. Voss. "Empirical Laws, Theory Construction, and Bibliometrics." *Library Trends* 30 (1981): 9–20.

Ogbu, John U. "An Ecological Approach to Minority Education." Unpublished Manuscript. N.p., 1980a.

———. "Ethnoecology of Urban Schooling." Unpublished manuscript. N.p. 1980b.

———. *Minority Education and Caste: The American System in Crosscultural Perspective.* New York: Academic Press, 1978.

———. *The Next Generation: An Ethnography of Education in an Urban Neighborhood.* New York: Academic Press, 1974.

———. "Origins of Human Competence: A Cultural Ecological Perspective." Unpublished manuscript. N.p. 1979.

Ogden, C. K., and I. A. Richards, eds. *The Meaning of Meaning.* London: Kegan Paul, Trench, Trubner, 1923.

Ohmann, Richard. "The Decline in Literacy Is a Fiction, If Not a Hoax." *The Chronicle of Higher Education* 25 Oct. 1976: 32.

———. *English in America: A Radical View of the Profession.* New York: Oxford University Press, 1976.

Okpewho, Isidore. *The Epic in Africa: Toward a Poetics of the Oral Performance.* New York: Columbia University Press, 1979.

Olson, David R. "From Utterance to Text: The Bias of Language in Speech and Writing." *Harvard Educational Review* 47 (1977): 257–81.a.

———. "The Languages of Instruction: The Literate Bias of Schooling." *Schooling and the Acquisition of Knowledge.* Ed. R. C. Anderson, R. J. Spiro, and W. E. Montague. Hillsdale, NJ: Erlbaum, 1977.b.

———. Review of *Toward a Literate Society,* ed. John B. Carroll and Jeanne Chall. *Proceedings of the National Academy of Education* 2 (1975): 109–78.

———. "Writing: The Divorce of the Author from the Text." *Exploring Speaking-Writing Relationships: Connections and Contrasts.* Ed. B. Kroll and R. Vann. Urbana, IL: NCTE, 1981.

Olson, D. R., and N. Filby. "On the Comprehension of Active and Passive Sentences." *Cognitive Psychology* 3 (1972): 361–81.

Olson, D. R., and N. Nickerson. "The Contexts of Comprehension: Children's Inability to

Draw Implications from Active and Passive Sentences." *Journal of Experimental Child Psychology* 23 (1977): 402–14.

Olson, D. R., N. Torrence, and A. Hildyard, eds. *Literacy, Language, and Learning: The Nature and Consequences of Reading and Writing.* Cambridge: Cambridge University Press, 1985.

Ong, Walter J. *Interfaces of the Word.* Ithaca: Cornell University Press, 1977.

————. "Literacy and Orality in Our Times." *ADE Bulletin* 58 (1978): 1–7.

————. "Literacy and Orality in Our Times." *Journal of Communication* 30 (1980): 197–204.

————. *Orality and Literacy.* New York: Methuen, 1982.

————. *The Presence of the Word.* New Haven: Yale University Press, 1967; New York: Simon and Schuster, 1970.

————. *Ramus, Method, and the Decay of Dialogue.* Cambridge: Harvard University Press, 1958.

————. *Rhetoric, Romance, and Technology: Studies in the Interaction of Expression and Culture.* Ithaca: Cornell University Press, 1971.

Opie, Iona Archibald, and Peter Opie. *The Oxford Dictionary of Nursery Rhymes.* Oxford: Clarendon Press, 1952.

Opland, Jeff. "*Imbongi Nezibongo*: The Xhosa Tribal Poet and the Contemporary Poetic Tradition." *PMLA* 90 (1975): 185–208.

Oppenheim, A. Leo. *Ancient Mesopotamia.* Chicago: University of Chicago Press, 1964.

Ormsbee, H. G. *The Young Employed Girl.* New York: Women's Press, 1927.

Our Bodies, Ourselves. 2nd ed. New York: Simon and Schuster, 1976.

Oxenham, John. *Literacy: Writing, Reading, and Social Organization.* London: Routledge and Kegan Paul, 1980.

Packard, Randall M. "The Study of Historical Process in African Traditions of Genesis: The Bashu Myth of Muhiyi." *The African Past Speaks.* Ed. Joseph C. Miller. London: Dawson; Hamden, CT: Archon, 1980. 157–77.

Palmer, Robert R. "The Old Regime Origins of the Napoleonic Educational Structure." *De L'Ancien Régime à la Révolution Française.* Ed. Albert Crèmer. Göttingen: Vandenhoeck and Rupprecht, n.d. 318–33.

Palmer, Robert R., ed. and trans. *The School of the French Revolution: A Documentary History of the College Louis-le-Grand . . . 1762–1814.* Princeton: Princeton University Press, 1975.

Paris, S. G., and A. Carter. "Semantic and Constructive Aspects of Sentence Memory in Children." *Developmental Psychology* 9 (1973): 109–13.

Park, R. "Reflections on Communication and Culture." *American Journal of Sociology* 44 (1938): 187–205.

Park, R. E. *The Immigrant Press and Its Control.* New York: Harper and Brothers, 1922.

Parker, James. "Competency-Based Adult Education Profile and Related Resources." Draft manuscript. Washington, DC: U.S. Office of Education, Division of Adult Education, 1976.

Parry, Anne Amory. *Blameless Aegisthus: A Study of ἀμύμων and Other Homeric Epithets.* Mnemosyne: Bibliotheca Classica Batava, Supp. 26. Leyden: E. J. Brill, 1973.

Parry, Milman. "The Making of Homeric Verse." *The Collected Papers of Milman Parry.* Ed. A. Parry. Oxford: Clarendon Press, 1971.

Parsons, T. *Societies: Evolutionary and Comparative Perspectives.* New York: Prentice-Hall, 1966.

Parsonson, G. S. "The Literate Revolution in Polynesia." *Journal of Pacific History* 2 (1967): 39–57.

Pearson, L. *Early Ionian Historians.* Oxford: Clarendon Press, 1939.

Pepper, Suzanne. "Education and Political Development in Communist China." *Studies in Comparative Communism* 3 (1971): 132–57.

Persell, Caroline Hodges. *Education and Inequality.* New York: The Free Press, 1977.

Peters, Richard S. "Education as Initiation." *Philosophical Analysis and Education*. Ed. R. D. Archambault. London: Routledge and Kegan Paul, 1972.

Philips, S. *The Invisible Culture: Communication in Classroom and Community on the Warm Springs Indian Reservation*. New York: Longman Press, 1982.

———. "Literacy as a Mode of Communication on the Warm Springs Indian Reservation." *Foundations of Language Development: A Multidisciplinary Approach*. Ed. Eric H. Lenneberg and Elizabeth Lenneberg. Vol. 2. New York: Academic Press; Paris: UNESCO, 1975.

———. "Participant Structures and Communicative Competence: Warm Springs Children in Community and Classroom." *Functions of Language in the Classroom*. Ed. C. Cazden, V. John, and D. Hymes. New York: Teachers College Press, 1972.

Phillpotts, B. *Edda and Saga*. London: T. Butterworth, 1931.

Piaget, J. "Intellectual Evolution from Adolescence to Adulthood." *Human Development* 15 (1972): 1–12.

Pichert, J. W. *Sensitivity to What Is Important in Prose*. Technical Report No. 149. Urbana: University of Illinois, Center for the Study of Reading, 1979. ED 179 946.

Piestrup, A. *Black Dialect Interference and Accommodation of Reading Instruction in First Grade*. Monograph No. 4. Berkeley: Language-Behavior Research Laboratory, 1973.

Pike, R., and D. R. Olson. "A Question of *More* or *Less*." *Child Development* 48 (1977): 579–86.

Plato. *Phaedrus*. Trans. R. Hackforth. Cambridge: Cambridge University Press, 1952.

Polanyi, K. "Aristotle Discovers the Economy." *Trade and Market in the Early Empires*. Ed. K. Polanyi, C. M. Arensberg, and H. W. Pearson. Glencoe, IL: Free Press, 1957.

Pollard, Sidney. *The Genesis of Modern Management*. Harmondsworth: Penguin, 1968.

Ponsot, Marie, and Rosemary Deen. *Beat Not the Poor Desk*. Montclair, NJ: Boyton/Cook, 1982.

Popper, K. *Objective Knowledge: An Evolutionary Approach*. Oxford: Clarendon Press, 1972.

Potter, W. G., ed. *Bibliometrics*, a special issue of *Library Trends* 30 (1981): 1–172.

Powdermaker, Hortense. *After Freedom*. New York: Atheneum, 1968.

———. *Life in Lesu*. New York: Norton, 1933.

Powell, W. R. "Levels of Literacy." *Journal of Reading* 20 (1977): 488–92.

Pratt, David. "The Social Role of School Textbooks in Canada." *Socialization and Values in Canadian Society*. Ed. R. Pike and E. Zureik. Vol. 2. Toronto: McClelland and Stewart, 1975. 100–126.

Prentice, Alison. *The School Promoters: Education and Social Class in Mid-Nineteenth-Century Upper Canada*. Toronto: McClelland and Stewart, 1977.

Prost, Antoine. *Histoire de l'enseignment en France, 1800–1967*. Paris: A. Colin, 1968.

Proust, Marcel. *On Reading*. Trans. and ed. Jean Autretand and William Burford. New York: Macmillan, 1971.

Purves, A. C., and R. Beach. *Literature and the Reader: Research in Response to Literature, Reading Interests, and the Teaching of Literature*. Urbana: NCTE, 1972.

Putman, John, and George M. Weir. *Survey of the Schools*. Victoria: King's Printer, 1925.

Putnam, Samuel. *The Analytical Reader*. Portland, ME: Wm. Hyde, 1836.

Radin, P. *Crashing Thunder: The Autobiography of an American Indian*. New York: D. Appleton, 1926.

———. *Primitive Man as Philosopher*. New York: D. Appleton, 1927.

Radwin, E. "Literacy—What and Why." Unpublished manuscript. Harvard University, 1978.

Rasche, W. F. *The Reading Interests of Young Workers*. Chicago: University of Chicago Libraries, 1937.

Rawski, E. S. *Education and Popular Literacy in Ch'ing China*. Ann Arbor: University of

Michigan Press, 1979.

Read, C. *Children's Categorization of Speech Sounds in English*. Research Report No. 17. Urbana, IL: NCTE, 1975.

Reder, S., and K. R. Green. "Literacy as a Functional Component of Social Structure in an Alaska Fishing Village." *International Journal of the Sociology of Language* 42 (1983): 122–41.

Redfield, R. *The Primitive World and Its Transformations*. Ithaca: Cornell University Press, 1953.

Reed, D. *Leisure Time of Girls in "Little Italy": A Comparative Study of the Leisure Interests of Adolescent Girls of Foreign Parentage Living in a Metropolitan Community*. Portland, OR: privately printed, 1932.

Reid, J. F. "Learning to Think about Reading." *Educational Research* 9 (1966): 56–62.

Reilly, M. L. *A History of the Catholic Press Association, 1911–1968*. Metuchen, NJ: The Scarecrow Press, 1971.

Reisman, D. "The Oral and Written Traditions.: *Explorations* 6 (1956): 22–28.

———. *The Oral Tradition, the Written Word, and the Screen Image*. Yellow Springs, OH: Antioch Press, 1956.

Rentel, V., and J. Kennedy. "Effects of Pattern Drill on the Phonology, Syntax, and Reading Achievement of Rural Appalachian Children." *American Educational Research Journal* 9 (1972): 87–100.

Repo, Satu. "From Pilgrim's Progress to Sesame Street: 125 Years of Colonial Readers." *The Politics of the Canadian Public School*. Ed. G. Martell. Toronto: James Lewis and Samuel, 1974. 118–33.

Research for Better Schools. *Employer Attitudes toward the Preparation of Youth for Work*. Philadelphia: Research for Better Schools, 1978.

Resnick, D. P., ed. *Literacy in Historical Perspective*. Washington: Library of Congress, 1983.

Resnick, D. P., and L. B. Resnick. "The Nature of Literacy: An Historical Exploration." *Harvard Educational Review* 47 (1977): 370–85.

Richards, I. A. "Instructional Engineering." *The Written Word*. Ed. S. Baker, J. Barzun, and I. A. Richards. Rowley, MA: Newbury House, 1971.

———. *Mencius on the Mind*. London: Kegan Paul, Trench, Trubner, 1932.

Ricoeur, P. "Creativity in Language: Word, Polysemy, and Metaphor." *Philosophy Today* 17 (1973): 97–111.

Roberts, Michael. "The Swedish Church." *Sweden's Age of Greatness*. Ed. M. Roberts. New York: St. Martin's, 1973.

Robinson, J. P. "The Changing Reading Habits of the American People." *Journal of Communication* 30 (1980): 141–52.

———. *How Americans Use Time: A Social-Psychological Analysis of Everyday Behavior*. New York: Praeger, 1977.

Rockefeller Commission on the Humanities. *The Humanities in American Life*. Berkeley and Los Angeles: University of California Press, 1980.

Rogers, E. M. *Modernization among Peasants: The Impact of Communication*. New York: Holt, Rinehart and Winston, 1969.

Rogoff, B., and W. Gardner. "Adult Guidance of Cognitive Development." *Everyday Cognition: Its Development in Social Context*. Ed. B. Rogoff and J. Lave. Cambridge: Harvard University Press, 1984. 95–116.

Rose, Mike. "Remedial Writing Courses: A Critique and a Proposal." *College English* 45 (1983): 109–28.

———. *When a Writer Can't Write: Studies in Writer's Block and Other Composing Problems*. New York: Guilford, 1985.

Rosenberg, Bruce A. *The Art of the American Folk Preacher*. New York: Oxford University Press, 1970.

Rosenblatt, Louise M. *Literature as Exploration*. 3rd ed. New York: Noble and Noble, 1976.

————. *The Reader, the Text, the Poem: The Transactional Theory of the Literary Work*. Carbondale: Southern Illinois University Press, 1978.

Ross, Arthur M., and Herbert Hill, eds. *Employment, Race, and Poverty*. New York: Harcourt, 1967.

Rowsome, Frank, Jr. *The Verse by the Side of the Road*. New York: E. P. Dutton, 1966.

Rubin, Lillian Breslow. *Worlds of Pain*. New York: Basic Books, 1976.

Rumelhart, D. E. "Schemata: The Building Blocks of Cognition." *Theoretical Issues in Reading Comprehension*. Ed. R. J. Spiro, B. Bruce, and W. Brewer. Hillsdale, NJ: Erlbaum, 1980.

————. *Toward an Interactive Model of Reading*. Technical Report No. 56. Center of Human Information Processing. San Diego: University of California, 1976.

Rumelhart, D. E., and A. Ortony. "The Representation of Knowledge in Memory." *Schooling and the Acquisition of Knowledge*. Ed. R. C. Anderson, R. J. Spiro, and W. E. Montague. Hillsdale, NJ: Erlbaum, 1977.

Russell, Bertrand. *An Inquiry into Meaning and Truth*. London: Allen and Unwin, 1940.

Sacher, J., and Thomas Duffy. "Reading Skill and Military Effectiveness." Paper presented at the American Educational Research Association Conference. Toronto, Mar. 1978. ED 151 745.

Sadoski, M. "An Exploratory Study of the Relationships between Reported Imagery and the Comprehension and Recall of a Story." *Reading Research Quarterly* 19 (1983): 110–23.

Sampson, Geoffrey. *Schools of Linguists*. Stanford: Stanford University Press, 1980.

Sanderson, Michael. "Education and the Factory in Industrial Lancashire." *Economic History Review* 20 (1967): 266–79.

————. "Literacy and Social Mobility in the Industrial Revolution in England." *Past and Present* 56 (1972): 75–105.

————. "Social Change and Elementary Education in Industrial Lancashire." *Northern History* 3 (1968): 131–54.

Sandys, J. E. *A History of Classical Scholarship*. Cambridge: Cambridge University Press, 1921.

Sartre, Jean Paul. *Situations I*. Paris: Librairie Gallimard, 1947.

Sastri, Nilakanta K. A. *A History of South India from Prehistoric Times to the Fall of Vijayanagar*. Oxford: Oxford University Press, 1955.

Schallert, D., and R. J. Tierney. *Learning from Expository Text: The Interaction of Text Structure with Reader Characteristics*. Final Report. National Institute of Education, 1982.

Schemer, George. "Effectiveness of Equal Opportunity Legislation." *The Negro Employment Opportunity*. Ed. Herbert N. Northrup and Richard L. Rowan. Ann Arbor: University of Michigan Press, 1965. 67–107.

Schick, F. L. "Statistical Reporting of American Library Developments." *Library Trends* 25 (1976): 81–88.

Schiller, D. *Objectivity and the News: The Public and the Rise of Commercial Journalism*. Philadelphia: University of Pennsylvania Press, 1981.

Schleunnes, Karl A. "The French Revolution and the Schooling of European Society." *Proceedings of the Consortium on Revolutionary Europe*. Gainesville: University of Florida Press, 1977. 140–50.

Schofield, R. S. "Dimensions of Illiteracy in England, 1750–1850." *Explorations in Economic History* 10 (1973): 437–54.

————. "The Measurement of Literacy in Pre-Industrial England." *Literacy in Traditional Societies*. Ed. Jack Goody. Cambridge: Cambridge University Press, 1968. 311–25.

Schudson, M. *Advertising, the Uneasy Persuasion: Its Dubious Impact on American Society*. New York: Basic Books, 1984.

————. *Discovering the News: A Social History of American Newspapers*. New York: Basic Books, 1978.

Schulz, David A. *Coming Up Black*. Englewood Cliffs, NJ: Prentice-Hall, 1969.

Schuman, Howard, Alex Inkeles, and David Smith. "Some Social and Psychological Effects and Non-Effects of Literacy in a New Nation." *Economic Development and Cultural Change* 16 (1967): 1–14.

Schutz, A., and T. Luckmann. *The Structures of the Life World*. Trans. R. Zaner and H. Engelhardt. Evanston, IL: Northwestern University Press, 1973.

Scollon, R., and S. Scollon. *Narrative, Literacy, and Face in Interethnic Communication*. Norwood, NJ: Ablex, 1981.

Scott, Joseph W. *The Black Revolt*. Cambridge, MA: Schenkman, 1976.

Scribner, Sylvia. "Cognitive Consequences of Literacy." Mimeo. New York: Albert Einstein College of Medicine, 1968.

———. "Industrial Literacy." Final Report to the Ford Foundation. New York: CUNY, Graduate School and University Center, 1982. (a).

———. "Observations on Literacy Education in China." *Linguistic Reporter*. 25 (1982): 1–4. (b).

———. "Studying Working Intelligence." *Everyday Cognition: Its Development in Social Context*. Ed. B. Rogoff and J. Lave. Cambridge, MA: Harvard University Press, 1984.

Scribner, Sylvia, and Michael Cole. "Cognitive Consequences of Formal and Informal Education." *Science* 182 (1973): 553–59.

———. "Literacy without Schooling: Testing for Intellectual Effects." *Harvard Educational Review* 48 (1978): 448–61.

———. *The Psychology of Literacy*. Cambridge: Harvard University Press, 1981.

———. "Studying Cognitive Consequences of Literacy." Unpublished manuscript, 1976.

Scribner, Sylvia, and E. Jacob. *Industrial Literacy Project*. Progress Report. Washington, DC: Center for Applied Linguistics, 1980.

Scrupski, Adam. "The Social System of the School." *Social Forces and Schooling*. Ed. Kenneth Shimahara and Adam Scrupski. New York: McKay, 1975.

Seifer, Nancy. *Absent from the Majority: Working-Class Women in America*. New York: The American Jewish Committee, 1973.

Sharon, Amiel T. "Racial Differences in Newspaper Readership." *Public Opinion Quarterly* 37 (1973): 611–17.

———. "What Do Adults Read?" *Reading Research Quarterly* 9 (1973–1974): 148–69.

Sharp, Laure M. *Education and Employment*. Baltimore: Johns Hopkins University Press, 1970.

Shaughnessy, Mina. *Errors and Expectations*. New York: Oxford University Press, 1977.

Sheehan, Susan. *A Welfare Mother*. Boston: Houghton-Mifflin, 1976.

Sherzer, Joel. "*Namakke, Sunmakke, Kormakke*: Three Types of Cuna Speech Event." *Explorations in the Ethnography of Speaking*. Ed. Richard Bauman and Joel Sherzer. Cambridge: Cambridge University Press, 1974. 263–82, 462–64, 489.

Shih, Hu. *The Development of the Logical Method in Ancient China*. Shanghai: The Oriental Book Company, 1922.

Siebert, F. S., T. Peterson, and W. Schramm. *Four Theories of the Press*. Urbana: University of Illinois Press, 1956.

Signs of Life: Symbols in the American City. Program accompanying an exhibition at the Renwick Gallery, Washington, DC, 26 Feb.–30 Sept., 1976.

Simon, J. "Literacy and Popular Education in Post-Reformation Europe with Special Reference to Swedish Sources." *History of Education Society Bulletin* 27 (1981): 7–10.

Simons, Herbert D. *Black Dialect, Reading Interference, and Classroom Interaction*. Unpublished manuscript. University of California, Berkeley, 1976.

La situación educativa en América Latina. Cuadro no. 20. Paris: UNESCO, 1960.

Slawski, Edward J., and Jacqueline Scherer. "The Rhetoric of Concern—Trust and Control in an Urban Desegregated School." *Anthropology and Education Quarterly* 9 (1977): 258–71.

Smith, E., and R. Tyler. *Appraising and Recording Student Progress*. New York: Harper and Brothers, 1942.

Smith, F. *Comprehension and Learning*. Toronto: Holt, 1975.

———. *Understanding Reading*. New York: Holt, 1971.

Smith, M. F. *Baba of Karo, a Woman of the Muslim Hausa*. London: Praeger, 1954.

Smout, T. C. "Born again at Cambuslang: New Evidence on Popular Religion and Literacy in Eighteenth-Century Scotland." *Past and Present* 97 (1982): 114–27.

Snow, Edgar. *Red Star over China*. New York: Grove Press, 1961.

Soltow, Lee, and Edward Stevens. "Economic Aspects of School Participation in Mid-Nineteenth-Century United States." *Journal of Interdisciplinary History* 7 (1977): 221–43.

———. *The Rise of Literacy and the Common School in the United States: A Socio-economic Analysis to 1870*. Chicago: The University of Chicago Press, 1981.

Sommers, N. I. "Revision Strategies of Student Writers and Experienced Adult Writers." *College Composition and Communication* 31 (1980): 378–88.

Special Labor Force Report No. 186. Washington, DC: U.S. Bureau of Labor Statistics, 1976.

Spengler, Otto. *The Decline of the West*. Trans. C. F. Atkinson. New York: Knopf, 1934.

Spiro, R. J. "Remembering Information from Text: The 'State of Schema' Approach." *Schooling and the Acquisition of Knowledge*. Ed. R. C. Anderson, R. J. Spiro, and W. E. Montague. Hillsdale, NJ: Erlbaum, 1977.

Sprat, T. *History of the Royal Society of London for the Improving of Natural Knowledge*. Ed. J. I. Cope and H. W. Jones. St. Louis: Washington University Press, 1966.

Spufford, Margaret. *Constrasting Communities*. Cambridge: Cambridge University Press, 1974.

———. "First Steps in Literacy: The Reading and Writing Experiences of the Humblest Seventeenth-Century Spiritual Autobiogrphers." *Social History* 4 (1979): 407–35.

———. *Small Books and Pleasant Histories: Popular Fiction and Its Readership in Seventeenth-Century England*. London: Methuen, 1981.

Staiger, Ralph C. "Motivation for Reading: An International Bibliography." *Roads to Reading*. Ed. Ralph C. Staiger. Paris: UNESCO, 1979.

Starr, C. G. *The Origins of Greek Civilization*. New York: Knopf, 1961.

Staudenmayer, H. "Understanding Conditional Reasoning with Meaningful Propositions." *Reasoning, Representation, and Process*. Ed. R. J. Falmagne. Hillsdale, NJ: Erlbaum, 1975.

Stedman, L., and C. F. Kaestle. *One Hundred Years of Illiteracy: The Definition and Measurement of Reading Ability in America, 1880–1980*. Madison: Wisconsin Center for Education Research, 1985.

Steiner, G. "After the Book." *The Future of Literacy*. Ed. R. Disch. Englewood Cliffs, NJ: Prentice-Hall, 1973.

Stephens, W. B. "Illiteracy and Schooling in the Provincial Towns, 1640–1870." *Urban Education in the Nineteenth Century*. Ed. D. Reader. London: Taylor and Francis, 1977. 27–48.

———. "Illiteracy in Devon during the Industrial Revolution, 1754–1844." *Journal of Educational Administration and History* 8 (1976): 1–5.

Stewart, William A. "On the Use of Negro Dialect in the Teaching of Reading." *Teaching Black Children to Read*. Ed. Joan Baratz and Roger Shuy. Washington, DC: Center for Applied Linguistics, 1969. 156–219.

Sticht, Thomas G. "Comprehending Reading at Work." *Cognitive Processes in Comprehension*. Ed. M. A. Just and P. A. Carpenter. Hillsdale, NJ: Erlbaum, 1977.

——— *Literacy and Vocational Competence*. Occasional Paper No. 39. Columbus, OH: The National Center for Research in Vocational Education, 1978.

Sticht, Thomas G., ed. *Reading for Working: A Functional Literacy Anthology*. Alexandria, VA: Human Resources Research Organization, 1975. ED 102 532.

Sticht, Thomas G., John Caylor, Richard Kern, and Lynn Fox. "Project REALISTIC: Determination of Adult Functional Literacy Skill Levels." *Reading Research*

Quarterly 7 (1972): 424–65.

Stock, B. *The Implications of Literacy: Written Language and Models of Interpretation in the Eleventh and Twelfth Centuries.* Princeton: Princeton University Press, 1983.

Stone, L. "Literacy and Education in England, 1640–1900." *Past and Present* 42 (1969): 69–139.

Strauss, Gerald. *Luther's House of Learning.* Baltimore: Johns Hopkins University Press, 1975.

Strawson, P. R. *Meaning and Truth: An Inaugural Lecture Delivered before the University of Oxford.* Oxford: Clarendon Press, 1970.

Stubbs, Michael. *Language and Literacy: The Sociolinguistics of Reading and Writing.* London: Routledge & Kegan Paul, 1980.

Suppes, P., and S. Feldman. "Young Children's Comprehension of Logical Connectives." *Journal of Experimental Child Psychology* 12 (1971): 304–17.

Tambiah, S. J. "Literacy in a Buddhist Village in North-East Thailand." *Literacy in Traditional Societies.* Ed. Jack Goody. Cambridge: Cambridge University Press, 1968. 85–131.

Taplin, J. E., and H. Staudenmayer. "Interpretation of Abstract Conditional Sentences in Deductive Reasoning." *Journal of Verbal Learning and Verbal Behavior* 12 (1973): 530–42.

Tavris, Carol, and Carole Offir. *The Longest War: Sex Differences in Perspective.* New York: Harcourt, 1977.

Taylor, A. E. *Aristotle.* London: T. Nelson, 1943.

Taylor, Frederick W. *Principles of Scientific Management.* New York: Harper, 1911.

Tebbel, J. W. *A History of Book Publishing in America.* 3 vols. New York: Bowker, 1975.

Tenny, Y. J. "Visual Factors in Spelling." *Cognitive Processes in Spelling.* Ed. U. Frith. London: Academic Press, 1980.

Terman, Lewis M. "Methods of Examining: History, Development, and Preliminary Results." *Psychological Examining in the United States Army.* Ed. Robert M. Yerkes. Vol. 15. Washington, DC: GPO, 1921. 299–546.

Thabault, Roger. *Education and Change in a Village Community: Mazières-en-Gâtine 1848–1914.* New York: Schocken Books, 1971.

Thernstrom, S. *Poverty and Progress: Social Mobility in a Nineteenth-Century City.* Cambridge: Harvard University Press, 1964.

Thompson, E. P. "Time, Work-Discipline, and Industrial Capitalism." *Past and Present* 38 (1967): 56–97.

Thompson, J. W. *Ancient Libraries.* Berkeley and Los Angeles: University of California Press, 1940.

Thorndike, Edward L. *Principles of Teaching.* New York: A. G. Seiler, 1906.

———. "Reading as Reasoning: A Study of Mistakes in Paragraph Reading." *Journal of Educational Psychology* 8 (1917): 323–32.

Tierney, R. J. "Writer-Reader Transactions: Defining the Dimensions of Negotiation." *Fforum: Essays on Theory and Practice in the Teaching of Writing.* Ed. P. Stock. Montclair, NJ: Boyton/Cook, 1983.

Tierney, R. J., J. LaZansky, T. Raphael, and P. Cohen. "Author's Intentions and Reader's Interpretation." *Understanding Readers Understanding.* Ed. R. J. Tierney, P. Anders, and J. Mitchell. Hillsdale, NJ: Erlbaum, 1986.

Tierney, R. J., and J. Mosenthal. *The Cohesion Concept's Relationship to the Coherence of Text.* Technical Report No. 221. Urbana: Center for the Study of Reading, University of Illinois, 1981. ED 212 991.

Tompkins, J. P. *Reader-Response Criticism.* Baltimore: Johns Hopkins University Press, 1980.

Trigger, Bruce G. "Inequality and Communication in Early Civilizations." *Anthropologica* 18 (1976): 27–52.

Trow, M. "The Democratization of Higher Education in America." *Archives Européennes de Sociologie* 3 (1962): 231–62.

————. "The Second Transformation of American Secondary Education." *International Journal of Comparative Sociology* 2 (1961): 144–66.

Tully, A. "Literacy Levels and Education Development in Rural Pennsylvania, 1729–1775." *Pennsylvania History* 39 (1972): 301–12.

Tyack, David B. "Bureaucracy and the Common School: The Example of Portland, Oregon, 1851–1913." *The American Quarterly* 19 (1967): 475–98.

————. *The One Best System: A History of American Education.* Cambridge: Harvard University Press, 1974.

UNESCO. *Regional Report on Literacy.* Teheran: UNESCO, 1972.

United Nations Development Program. *The Experimental World Literacy Programme: A Critical Assessment.* Paris: UNESCO, 1972.

U.S. Commission on Civil Rights. *Bilingual/Bicultural Education: A Privilege or a Right?* Washington, DC: GPO, 1974.

————. *Social Indications of Equality for Minorities and Women.* Washington, DC: GPO, 1978.

U.S. Department of Commerce, Bureau of the Census. *The Social and Economic Status of the Black Population in the United States: An Historical View, 1790–1969.* Special Studies, Series P-23, No. 80. Washington, DC: GPO, 1979.

U.S. District Court for Northern California. *Larry P. v. Riles.* San Francisco, 1979.

U.S. Employment Service. *Dictionary of Occupational Titles.* 4th ed. Washington, DC: U.S. Employment Service, 1977.

van den Berghe, Pierre. Review of *Minority Education and Caste,* by John Ogbu. *Comparative Education Review* 24 (1980): 126–30.

Vander Zanden, J. W., and A. J. Pace. *Educational Psychology: In Theory and Practice.* New York: Random House, 1984.

Vann, Richard T. "Literacy in Seventeenth-Century England: Some Hearth-Tax Evidence." *Journal of Interdisciplinary History* 5 (1974): 287–93.

Verne, E. "Literacy and Industrialization—The Dispossession of Speech." *A Turning Point for Literacy.* Ed. Léon Bataille. New York: Pergamon Press, 1976. 211–28.

Vinovskis, M.A. *Fertility in Massachusetts from the Revolution to the Civil War.* New York: Academic Press, 1981.

————. "Horace Mann on the Economic Productivity of Education." *New England Quarterly* 43 (1970): 550–71.

————. "Quantification and the History of Education: Observations on Antebellum Education Expansion, School Attendance, and Educational Reform." *Journal of Interdisciplinary History* 14 (1983): 856–69.

Vinovskis, M. A., and R. Bernard. "Beyond Catharine Beecher: Female Education in the Antebellum Period." *Signs* 3 (1978): 856–69.

Voegelin, C. F., and F. M. Voegelin. "Typological Classification of Systems with Included, Excluded, and Self-Sufficient Alphabets." *Anthropological Linguistics* 3 (1961): 55–96.

Vovelle, Michel. "Maggiolo en Provence." Collogue sur le XVIII siècle et l'éducation. *Revue de Marseille* 88 (1972): 55–62.

————. "Y a-t-il une révolution culturelle au XVIIIe siècle?" *Revue d'histoire moderne et contemporaine* 22 (1975): 89–141.

Vygotsky, L. S. *Mind in Society: The Development of Higher Psychological Processes.* Ed. M. Cole, V. J. Steiner, S. Scribner, and E. Souberman. Cambridge: Harvard University Press, 1978.

————. *Thought and Language.* Trans. and ed. Eugenia Hanfmann and Gertrude Vakar. Cambridge: MIT Press, 1962.

Wagner, D. A., B. M. Messick, and J. Spratt. "Studying Literacy in Morocco." *The Acquisition of Literacy: Ethnographic Perspectives.* Ed. B. B. Schieffelin and P. Gilmore. Norwood, NJ: Ablex, 1986.

Walker, Willard. "Native Writing Systems." *Language in the USA.* Ed. C. A. Ferguson and Shirley Brice Heath. Cambridge: Cambridge University Press, 1981.

Wallace, A. F. C. *Rockdale*. New York: Knopf, 1978.

Waples, D. "Relation of Subject Interests to Actual Reading." *Library Quarterly* 2 (1932): 42–70.

Warmington, E. H. *Greek Geography*. London: J. M. Dent, 1934.

Warner, W. Lloyd, et al. *Who Shall Be Educated?* New York: Harper, 1945.

Wason, P. C., and P. N. Johnson-Laird. "A Conflict between Selecting and Evaluating Information in an Inferential Task." *British Journal of Psychology* 61 (1970): 509–15.

———. *The Psychology of Reasoning*. London: B. T. Batsford, 1972.

Watson-Gegeo, K. A., and S. T. Boggs. "From Verbal Play to Talk Story: The Role of Routine in Speech Events among Hawaiian Children." *Child Discourse*. Ed. S. Ervin-Tripp and C. Mitchell-Kernan. New York: Academic Press, 1977.

Webb, R. K. *The British Working-Class Reader*. London: Allen and Unwin, 1955.

———. "Working-Class Readers in Early Victorian England." *English Historical Review* 65 (1950): 333–51.

Weber, Eugen. *Peasants into Frenchmen: The Modernization of Rural France, 1870–1914*. Stanford: Stanford University Press, 1976.

Webster, Noah. *American Spelling Book*. 1873. New York: Teachers College, 1962.

Weiberg, Meyer. *A Chance to Learn: A History of Race and Education in the United States*. New York: Cambridge University Press, 1977.

Wersch, J. "From Social Interaction to Higher Psychological Processes." *Human Development* 22 (1979): 1–22.

West, E. G. *Education and the Industrial Revolution*. London: Batsford, 1975.

———. "Literacy and the Industrial Revolution." *Economic History Review* 31 (1977): 369–83.

———. "The Role of Education in 19th Century Doctrines of Political Economy." *British Journal of Educational Studies* 12 (1964): 161–74.

What If You Couldn't Read? Dorothy Tod Films. Montpelier, VT: 1978.

White, James B. "The Invisible Discourse of the Law: Reflections on Legal Literacy and General Education." *Fforum: Essays on Theory and Practice in the Teaching of Writing*. Ed. Patricia L. Stock. Upper Montclair, NJ: Boynton/Cook, 1983. 46–59.

Wilcox, Kathleen. "Schooling and Socialization for Work Roles." Diss. Harvard University, 1978.

Wilden, Antony. *The Imaginary Canadian*. Vancouver: Pulp Press, 1981.

Wilder, B. "An Examination of the Phenomenon of the Literacy Skills of Unschooled Males in Laos." Diss. Michigan State University, 1972.

Wilks, I. "The Transmission of Islamic Learning in the Western Sudan." *Literacy in Traditional Societies*. Ed. Jack Goody. Cambridge: Cambridge University Press, 1968. 161–97.

Williams, J. T. *Learning to Write or Writing to Learn?* London: The National Foundation for Educational Research, 1977.

Williams, R. *Communications*. London: Oxford University Press, 1976.

———. *Culture and Society*. London: Penguin, 1958.

———. *The Long Revolution*. London: Chatto & Windus, 1961.

———. *Marxism and Literature*. 1971. Oxford: Oxford University Press, 1977.

Willie, Charles Vert, ed. *Caste and Class Controversy*. New York: Green Hall, 1979.

Willis, P. E. *Learning to Labour*. Westmead, England: Saxon House, 1977.

Wilson, H. Clyde. "On the Evolution of Education." *Learning and Culture*. Ed. Solon T. Kimball and Jacquetta-Hill Burnett. Seattle: University of Washington Press, 1973. 211–41.

Wilson, L. R. *The Geography of Reading*. Chicago: University of Chicago Press, 1938.

Wilson, William Julius. *The Declining Significance of Race*. Chicago: University of Chicago Press, 1978.

Winchester, Ian. "How Many Ways to Universal Literacy?" Paper presented to the Ninth World Congress of Sociology. Uppsala, 1978; and to the University of Leicester Seminar on the History of Literacy in Post-Reformation Europe, 1980.

Wittgenstein, Ludwig. *Philosophical Investigations*. Trans. G. E. M. Anscomb. Oxford: Blackwell and Mott, 1953.

Wolfe, Tom. *Electric Kool-Aid Acid Test*. New York: Bantam, 1977.

————. *Radical Chic and Mau-Mauing the Flack Catchers*. New York: Strauss and Giroux, 1970.

Wood, B., J. S. Bruner, and G. Ross. "The Role of Tutoring in Problem Solving." *Journal of Child Psychology and Psychiatry* 17 (1976): 89–100.

Yeats, W. B. *Autobiographies*. London: Macmillan, 1955.

Yoakum, Clarence S., and Robert M. Yerkes. *Army Mental Tests*. New York: Henry Holt, 1920.

Young, M., and G. Whitty, eds. *Society, State, and Schooling*. Rimger, England: Falmer Press, 1977.

Zutell, J. *Linguistic and Psycholinguistic Perspectives on Brain Mechanisms and Language*. Columbus: Early and Middle Childhood Education, Ohio State University, 1979.

————. "Some Psycholinguistic Perspectives on Children's Spelling." *Language Arts* 55 (1978): 844–50.

Eugene R. Kintgen is Professor of English, Chair of the Literacy Commitee, and Associate Dean of the Graduate School at Indiana University. He is the author of *The Perception of Poetry* and co-author (with Owen Thomas) of *Transformational Grammar and the Teacher of English: Theory and Practice*, as well as numerous articles on Old English literature, stylistics, and reader-centered approaches to the perception of poetic language. His current research interest is the history of reading, more specifically, the conventions of reading in Elizabethan England.

Barry M. Kroll is Associate Professor of English at Indiana University, where he teaches writing and the teaching of composition. In addition to essays on the theory and practice of composition, he has published research on children's informative and persuasive writing skills and has edited two collections of articles. Curently his research focuses on college students' orientations to knowledge and authority, and the ramifications of these orientations for reading, writing, and critical thinking.

Mike Rose holds masters degrees in education and in English and a doctorate in educational psychology from UCLA. He has taught in and administered a number of preparatory and develomental writing programs and is currently Associate Director of the UCLA Writing Program. He has written on the cognition of composing, pedagogy, curriculum development, and policy. His published works include *Writer's Block: The Cognitive Dimension* (SIU Press, 1984) and numerous articles.